BORLAND®

C++BUILDER™

HOW-TO

THE DEFINITIVE C++BUILDER PROBLEM-SOLVER

John Miano, Thomas Cabanski, Harold Howe

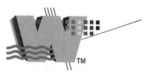

Waite Group Press™
A Division of
Sams Publishing
Corte Madera, CA

Publisher: Mitchell Waite
Associate Publisher: Charles Drucker

Acquisitions Manager: Susan Walton

Editorial Director: John Crudo
Project Editor: Stephanie Wall
Developmental Editor: Harry Henderson
Technical Editor: Michael Radtke

Production Manager: Cecile Kaufman
Senior Designer: Karen Johnston
Production Editors: Cameron Carey, Kate Talbot
Copy Editor: Ann Longknife
Illustrations: Sadie Crawford, Wil Cruz, Tammy Graham, Oliver Jackson
Production: Carol Bowers, Jeanne Clark, Elizabeth Deeter, Lisa Pletka, Shawn Ring

© 1997 by The Waite Group®, Inc.
Published by Waite Group Press™, 200 Tamal Plaza, Corte Madera, CA 94925.

Waite Group Press™ is a division of Sams Publishing.

Printed in the United States of America
99 98 97 • 10 9 8 7 6 5 4 3

*Library of Congress Cataloging-in-Publication Data
Miano, John, 1961-
    C++builder how-to / John Miano, Thomas Cabanski, Harold Howe.
        p.   cm.
    Includes index.
    ISBN 1-57169-109-X
    1. C++ (Computer program language)   I. Cabanski, Thomas, 1965-
    II. Howe, Harold, 1971-   . III. Title.
QA76.73.C153M497   1997
005.13'3--dc21   97-13749
                                                                         CIP

DEDICATION

To Drs. Ralph and Margaret Miano
—John Miano

To my wife Julie, for understanding the long hours, and to my parents, for giving me a love of reading, writing, and education
—Tom Cabanski

To my Dad, for teaching me what hard work means
—Harold Howe

A B O U T   T H E   A U T H O R S

John Miano is the chief Engineer of Colosseum Builders, Inc., where he specializes in developing systems for the broadcast and entertainment industries. He graduated from The College of Wooster with a B.A. in mathematics. For the past eleven years he has worked in the software consulting industry, developing UNIX and Windows-based systems. John lives in Summit, New Jersey, with his cats, Mycroft and Irene. He can be reached at `miano@worldnet.att.net`.

Tom Cabanski owns and operates Common Sense Consulting, which specializes in multi-tier client/server and Internet/intranet application development. He started his career as a mainframe COBOL programmer and has since developed systems using everything from APL to Z (a proprietary printer programming language). He currently lives in Kingwood, Texas, and can be reached at `tomc@vonl.com`.

Harold Howe works as a design engineer and computer programmer for Technology Resource Group, a Des Moines–based engineering and consulting firm. He earned a B.S. in electrical engineering from Iowa State University. Harold started programming in high school, using BASIC and Pascal, and later moved up to C and C++ programming for embedded systems. Since then, he has been programming in Windows and has written shareware programs using C++ and Borland's OWL class library. Harold can be reached at `hhowe@trgnet.com`.

TABLE OF CONTENTS

CONTENTS

ACKNOWLEDGMENTS

Creating a book is a complex task. Until you write one, it is impossible to appreciate the amount of work and the number of people involved. Considering this complexity, it was a surprise to the authors how smoothly things went. For this, we credit Stephanie Wall at the Waite Group Press for guiding us through the process.

Many other people at the Waite Group made major contributions. Lisa Goldstein, Susan Walton, and Joanne Miller got the project started. Rebekah Darksmith helped us throughout. Kate Talbot led the production effort, and Dan Scherf created the CD-ROM. Harry Henderson and Michael Radtke reviewed the book and made invaluable suggestions.

We received a tremendous amount of support from Borland as well. Nan Borreson's help was considerable, as was technical assistance from Todd Howitt, Steve Barnett, and Robert West.

This project started out as a revision of *Borland Delphi How-To*. We would like to acknowledge Gary Frerking, Nathan Wallace, and Wayne Niddery, the authors of that book. Though almost all the material in *Borland C++Builder How-To* is new, their work gave us many ideas for this one.

John Miano would like to thank Galina Norkin and John Missale for their assistance in scheduling work. He would also like to thank Anne, Stephen, and Paul Miano and Safi Bajwa for their encouragement and assistance.

Tom Cabanski would like to thank Stephanie Wall at Waite Group Press for her gentle prodding through this project. In addition, he would like to thank the many people who helped him along in his career: Kent Monroe, who gave him his first job as a programmer; Edward James Konecki, the best MIS manager on the planet, who never missed an opportunity to remind him that he had a brain; Pete Postlewaite, who started him thinking about independent consulting; and Bob Koseck, who helped him advance his career and introduced him to his wife.

Harold Howe would like to thank his wife Andrea and his son Nate for their patience during the writing of this book. He would also like to thank Steve Barnett and Robert West of Borland for the technical assistance they provided via the Borland Web forums. Lucian Wischik provided crucial help for the screen saver section. Finally, the participants of the CompuServe Borland forums and the Borland Web forums provided much needed help at critical times.

INTRODUCTION

"What took so long?" That is the reaction most C++ developers have when they try C++Builder for the first time. Until now, creating Windows applications in C++ has been a nightmare. Application developers had the choice of using the Windows API with its baroque programming interface or using class libraries that are known more for their complexity than for their ease of use. Writing Windows applications was such a difficult task that even experienced C++ developers would resort to using tools such as Visual Basic and PowerBuilder, in spite of their unsuitability for large applications. As the years passed and the use of Windows steadily grew, C++ development tools still remained in the dark ages. Finally, with C++Builder there is a C++ development environment that makes Windows programming enjoyable. Development shops should no longer have second thoughts about using C++ to develop Windows applications.

The purpose of *Borland® C++Builder™ How-To* is to help you solve problems that are frequently encountered when developing Windows applications. This book is not a replacement for manuals or help files but rather a supplement to them. As you read through this book, you may want to refer to these other materials from time to time. Neither is this book an introduction to programming. It is assumed that the reader already knows C++ and has a basic knowledge of C++Builder.

This book is organized into a series of problems, or How-To's, in a question-and-answer format. Each How-To has a problem description, the technique for solving the problem, a step-by-step solution, and an explanation of how the solution works. The level of complexity of the How-To's ranges from very easy to quite difficult (beginning to advanced). For the convenience of the reader, the source code for all the How-To programs is included on the accompanying CD-ROM. The CD-ROM also includes some expanded examples and all the additional tools required by the How-To's.

There are a couple of conventions that you should be aware of before you begin this book. In the source listings, the code entered by the programmer is shown in boldface to differentiate it from code that is automatically generated by C++Builder. Most of the How-To's have one or more tables that tell how to set property values for the controls used in the example. These tables list only the properties whose value you need to change from the default. Due to differences in video displays, you may

need to adjust some position and size properties to make the applications appear the same on your system as they do in the figures.

Chapter 1, "Forms," describes how to solve commonly encountered problems when working with C++Builder forms. Working with forms is the most basic task of visual development in C++Builder. Unlike most visual development tools, C++Builder allows you to create forms and components at runtime. Learn how to draw a background on an MDI form and drag a window without a title bar.

Chapter 2, "Standard Components and Classes," shows how to use many of the fundamental classes in the VCL library. Overcome some of the limitations in the standard components, and learn how to use the sophisticated features of the VCL library to create slick, professional-looking applications.

Chapter 3, "Text Controls," covers controls that handle keyboard input. Use of the Rich Edit control is covered in detail.

Chapter 4, "Mouse and Menu," contains How-To's that show how to create menus that go beyond the ordinary. Build menus that use different fonts or use graphics. Even create a menu at runtime.

Chapter 5, "Graphics," shows you how to use advanced graphics features in your application. Learn how to draw animation, fade pictures in and out, and use advanced capabilities of the Canvas.

Chapter 6, "Environment and System," shows how to interact with the operating system. All but the simplest programs need to get information about the environment they are running on. Learn how to determine the amount of disk space and memory that is available, how to place an icon in the "tray" on the task bar, and how to drag and drop files.

Chapter 7, "Peripherals," describes how to control and get information about common peripherals. Learn how to determine whether there is a disk in a floppy drive and how to use a modem from an application.

Chapter 8, "Internet," shows how to use the Internet controls that come with C++Builder. You can easily create applications in C++Builder that incorporate Web browsing or FTP.

Chapter 9, "Multimedia," covers audio, video, and graphics in C++Builder applications. As computers have become more powerful, users have come to expect sophisticated features like these. In C++Builder, creating multimedia applications is a breeze.

Chapter 10, "Printing," contains How-To's that show how to use the printer in C++Builder. Almost every application needs to be able to print data, and the How-To's in this chapter show various ways to do this, including using the Canvas, printing lines of text, and using Quick Reports.

Chapter 11, "Database," shows how to use the database controls in C++Builder to create data-aware applications. Most visual development tools allow developers to easily create front-ends for databases, and C++Builder is no exception. Learn how to view and edit data in a database and how to create a BDE alias at runtime.

Chapter 12, "Threads," contains How-To's that show how to use multiple threads in an application. Both Windows 95 and Windows NT allow you to create

multiple threads of execution within a process. Learn how to create C++Builder applications that use threads to perform multiple tasks simultaneously.

Chapter 13, "OLE," describes how you can use OLE in your applications. Use OLE to allow multiple applications to communicate with each other, to create C++Builder applications that incorporate other applications, and to create an OLE server application that can be used by another application.

Chapter 14, "Exceptions," shows how to use exception handling in your applications. In order to write robust applications, you must expect the unexpected. Exception handlers allow your application to recover from errors.

Chapter 15, "Custom Components," is an introduction to creating custom components. The ability to easily add new components to the Component Palette is one of C++Builder's most powerful features. Create your own components and use them at design time.

Chapter 16, "The Polished Application," shows how to implement features commonly found in professional applications. Learn how to create a professional-looking About screen, or a splash screen that is displayed when your application starts.

Chapter 17, "Tips and Tricks," contains How-To's that show you how to do things that are a little unusual. How can you recover from a corrupted form file? How can you incorporate parsing in your application? Find out how to do this and more.

INSTALLATION

The CD-ROM that accompanies this book contains the source code and utilities used to create the applications in *Borland® C++Builder™ How-To*. You will find some expanded sample programs and shareware tools that work with C++Builder. In addition, we are providing you with a trial version of C++ Builder.

The CD-ROM contains a compiled version of the application in each How-To, which you can run directly from the CD-ROM. However, to run the applications from within the C++Builder IDE, you must first install them on your hard drive.

To install the contents of the CD-ROM to your hard drive, run the WSETUP program located in the root directory of the CD-ROM. The WSETUP program will ask you what files you wish to install and where you want to install them.

Installing FLEX and BISON

Use the following steps to install the GNU FLEX and BISON programs used in How-To 17.1:

1. Create a directory called C:\BISON or another name of your choosing.

2. Copy the contents of the \3RDPARTY\BISON directory on the CD-ROM to the C:\BISON or the directory you created in the previous step.

3. Create a directory called C:\FLEX or another name of your choosing.

4. Copy the contents of the \3RDPARTY\FLEX directory on the CD-ROM to the C:\FLEX or the directory you created in the previous step.

5. Edit your AUTOEXEC.BAT file and add the following line to the end of the file:

```
PATH=C:\FLEX;C:\BISON;%PATH%
```

You should be able to run BISON and FLEX by opening an MS-DOS prompt window and typing BISON or FLEX on the command line.

CD-ROM Map

The source code files for the How-To's are stored uncompressed on the CD-ROM, so you can browse the files or copy them without running the WSETUP program. The organization of the CD-ROM is shown in Figure I-1.

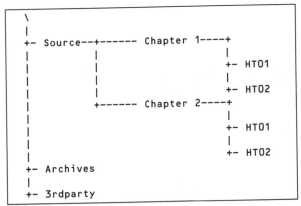

```
\
|
+- Source--+------ Chapter 1----+
|          |                    |
|          |                    +- HT01
|          |                    |
|          |                    +- HT02
|          +------ Chapter 2----+
|                               |
|                               +- HT01
|                               |
|                               +- HT02
|
+- Archives
|
+- 3rdparty
```

Figure I-1 Map of the CD-ROM

CHAPTER 1

FORMS

1

FORMS

How do I...

C++Builder™ applications are form based. Every window and every dialog is a form. Forms allow you to visually design the user interface for your programs. You can create applications, such as console mode programs and DLLs, without using forms, but for most GUI designs you will want to utilize the visual power contained in the C++Builder form.

3

Forms act as containers that organize controls in a logical manner, a benefit for both the programmer and the user. The tricks and techniques in this chapter show you how to maximize the benefits of using forms in application design. You'll learn how to position forms, modify the default behavior of a form, customize the appearance of a form, and much more.

The concept of using forms might be foreign to you if you're more familiar with traditional C++ compilers such as Borland C++, Microsoft Visual C++, or Watcom C++. Delphi and Visual Basic programmers should already be acquainted with form-based, visual program design. For you, the greatest challenge of C++Builder may be learning the C++ language itself. This chapter introduces both programming backgrounds to the form-based approach of C++Builder.

1.1 Automatically Center a Form in My Application

Forms have a property called `Position` that allows you to control where the form will be displayed. Setting `Position` to `poScreenCenter` puts a form in the center of the screen, a handy option for forms that act as modal dialog boxes. However, sometimes you might want to place a dialog box in the center of the main form instead of centering it in the screen. This How-To shows how you can center a second form within the application's main form regardless of the main form's position on the screen.

1.2 Create a Form on the Fly at Runtime

Occasionally you may need to create and display a form entirely from scratch at runtime. Creating a form at runtime takes a little work, but the reward can be worth the effort. This How-To constructs a form at runtime and then adds controls to the form based on user input.

1.3 Drag a Captionless Window

Sometimes you may have a small form that functions as a system utility, such as a clock, a desktop calculator, or a resource monitor. You might want to remove the form's caption bar to minimize the amount of space consumed by the application. However, removing a form's caption bar prevents the user from dragging the form to a new location on the desktop. This How-To demonstrates how you can allow the user to drag a captionless form.

1.4 Set Minimum and Maximum Sizes for My Forms

Users appreciate having the ability to resize forms, but sometimes you may want to put a restriction on the size of a form to prevent it from becoming downright ugly. If a form becomes too small, it could conceal important information. This How-To demonstrates how you can team up with Windows to restrict the minimum and maximum sizes of your forms.

1.5 Make ENTER Act Like TAB in My Forms

It's natural for some computer users to finish an Edit box entry by pressing ENTER. Normally Windows will simply beep right back in their face if they do this. This How-To illustrates how you can accommodate users who want to use ENTER to finish one Edit box entry and move on to the next.

1.6   Paint an Interesting Background on an MDI Parent Form

C++Builder allows you to change the background color of all forms, including forms that have the `FormStyle` property set to `fsMDIForm`. However, painting a custom picture in the MDI background can be difficult because the MDI client window can thwart your drawing efforts. This How-To shows how to combat the MDI client and draw your own graphical MDI background.

1.7   Customize a Window's Title Bar with Graphics

Normally your application cannot have graphics in its non-client areas. But Microsoft Office applications have decorated title bars, so there must be a way for you to achieve the same thing. This How-To describes how you can achieve the same professional look as the big boys by adding custom graphics to the title bar of your main form.

1.8   Ask Whether the User Really Wants to Close a Form

The conspicuous location of a form's close button (X) makes it easy for users to accidentally close a form. This How-To shows you how to prompt users for confirmation before they inadvertently close a form and possibly lose changes to a document.

1.9   Show a Splash Screen When the Program Starts

All windows and dialog boxes are forms in C++Builder, and a splash screen is no exception. This How-To guides you through the process of adding a professional looking splash screen to your program.

1.10   Display My Own Modal Dialog Box

You might be taken aback by all this form business if you're moving up to C++Builder from another C++ development environment. If you're trying to create a dialog box, you may be wondering what happened to the RC files. In C++Builder you create dialog boxes using forms instead of RC files. This How-To demonstrates how to design a simple modal dialog box using the form-based approach of C++Builder.

COMPLEXITY
BEGINNING

1.1   How do I...
Automatically center a form in my application?

Problem

`TForm` contains a property called `Position` that I can set to `poScreenCenter` to center a form in the middle of the screen. Sometimes I would rather center a form

within the bounds of my application. How can I center my form in the application's main form instead of the centering it in the screen?

Technique

The `TForm` class contains two properties, `Top` and `Left`, that determine the position of the upper left corner of a form. You can center a second form within the application's main form by calculating new values for the `Top` and `Left` data members of the second form before you display it.

Steps

Run the `CENTER.EXE` example found on the CD-ROM. Size and position the main form anywhere on the screen. Select Form|Show and notice that the child form appears centered within the bounds of the main form as shown in Figure 1-1. Close the child form, resize the main form, and then open the child form again. Notice that it still pops up in the center of the main form.

1. Create a new project by selecting File|New Application. Select File|Save Project As to save the project. Name the unit `MAINFORM.CPP` and name the project `CENTER.MAK`.

2. Add a second form to the project using File|New Form. Select File|Save As and name the new form `CENTFORM.CPP`. You won't work with `Form2` until step 8, so you can minimize it for now.

3. Size `Form1` so it resembles the picture in Figure 1-1.

4. Place a menu on `Form1` using the `MainMenu` control from the Standard tab of the Component Palette. Double-click on the `MainMenu` component to bring up the Menu Designer. Create a `File` menu item and add two subitems called `Show` and `Exit`.

5. Create an `OnClick` event handler for the `Exit` menu item. Add the following code to the event-handler function.

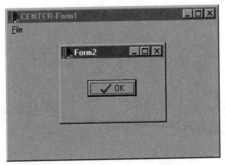

Figure 1-1 CENTER at runtime

TIP

You can create an `OnClick` handler for a menu item by double-clicking the item from the Menu Designer, by selecting the menu item from the form viewer, or by double-clicking next to `OnClick` in the Object Inspector. C++Builder will choose a function name for you, but you can change the name using the Object Inspector.

```
void __fastcall TForm1::Exit1Click(TObject *Sender)
{
   Close();
}
```

NOTE

`TForm::Close` closes a form. This terminates the program if the form is also the main application form.

6. Create an `OnClick` event handler for the **Show** menu item of **Form1**. Add code that centers **Form2** before displaying it.

```
void __fastcall TForm1::Show1Click(TObject *Sender)
{
   // Determine the size of the application frame.
   TRect Rect = Application->MainForm->BoundsRect;

   // Calculate the top and left edges of Form2.
   Form2->Left =((Rect.Right - Rect.Left)-Form2->Width)/2 + Rect.Left ;
   Form2->Top = ((Rect.Bottom - Rect.Top)-Form2->Height)/2 + Rect.Top ;
   Form2->ShowModal();
}
```

NOTE

`Form2->ShowModal` launches `Form2` modally. The `ShowModal` function does not return until the user closes `Form2`. You could launch `Form2` nonmodally by using the `Show` function instead of `ShowModal`.

7. The code in step 6 accesses a pointer to **Form2**, the child form. At this point, **Form1** has no idea who **Form2** is. Stay in the Code Editor and move up to the top of **MAINFORM.CPP**. Add this `#include` statement:

```
#include <vcl\vcl.h>
#pragma hdrstop

#include "MAINFORM.h"
#include "CENTFORM.h"    // Add include for Form2.
```

> **NOTE**
>
> The CENTFORM.H header file contains an extern prototype for the Form2 pointer.

8. You're done working with **Form1**. Bring up **Form2** and place a **BitBtn** component from the Additional tab of the Component Palette. Change **BitBtn1**'s **Kind** property to **bkOK** using the Object Inspector. Size **Form2** so it matches the child form in Figure 1-1.

9. Double-click on **BitBtn1** to create an **OnClick** event handler. Add code to close the child form when the user presses the button.

```
void __fastcall TForm2::BitBtn1Click(TObject *Sender)
{
   Close();
}
```

10. Compile and test the program.

How It Works

In step 6 you created a function called **TForm1::Show1Click**. This function displays **Form2** when the user selects Form|Show from the main menu. **Show1Click** starts by calculating the coordinates of the main form using the **BoundsRect** property. It then calculates the **Top** and **Left** edges of **Form2** using the coordinates of the main form and the **Height** and **Width** properties of **Form2**.

> **NOTE**
>
> **Application->MainForm** points to the main form of the application. In this example, **Form1** is the main form, so you could have used **BoundsRect** instead of **Application->MainForm->BoundsRect**. Adding **Application->Mainform** ensures that the code works from any class.

Comments

TForm1::Show1Click assumes that the **Form2** pointer already points to a valid object. By default, C++Builder applications automatically create their forms when the program starts. You can see the form creation code inside the **WinMain** function of **CENTER.CPP**. You will need to add code to create the **Form2** pointer if you remove **Form2** from the list of automatically created forms.

What if the main form is partially off the screen? Run the program again and move the main window down towards the bottom of the screen so the menu is barely visible. Select File|Show and note what happens. **Form2** pops up off-screen and now

the application is effectively frozen. You could prevent this by using `GetSystemMetrics` to ensure that `Form2` stays on the screen.

COMPLEXITY
ADVANCED

1.2 How do I...
Create a form on the fly at runtime?

Problem

I would like to write an application that can create a form based on run-time information. Can I create a form from scratch at runtime using C++Builder?

Technique

The Visual Component Library (VCL) provides all the tools needed to accomplish this task. You will need to work with `TForm` and the classes that encapsulate the VCL components. Creating a form from scratch involves instantiating a form pointer, creating and positioning the controls, and calling `Show` or `ShowModal` to display the form.

NOTE

This How-To creates a form in code completely from scratch. You may prefer to dynamically create and destroy an IDE-designed form. Refer to How-To's 1.9 and 1.10 to see how to implement this technique.

Steps

Run `RUNTIME.EXE`. Select a value from the Combo box and click the push button to create a form from scratch. The new form dynamically creates a set of Check boxes such that the number of Check boxes matches the number selected into the Combo box. Figure 1-2 shows `RUNTIME` during execution. Try opening the dynamic form again using a different number in the main form's Combo box.

1. Create a new project. Save the unit as `MAINFORM.CPP`; save the project as `RUNTIME.MAK`.

2. Add a unit to the project using File|New Unit. Choose File|Save As, and name the unit `DYNAFORM.CPP`.

3. Add a Combo box, a Label, and a push button to `Form1` so it resembles Figure 1-2. Size the form accordingly. Set properties to match Table 1-1.

Table 1-1 Components, properties, and settings for `Form1` in the RUNTIME project

COMPONENT	PROPERTY	SETTING
Form1		
Label1	Caption	Number of controls in the new form:
Button1	Caption	&Create dynamic form
ComboBox1	Items	0,1,2,3,4, & 5
	Style	csDropDownList

NOTE

You add strings to the Combo box by clicking on the ellipsis button (...) in the `Items` property of the Object Inspector. This launches the String List Editor. Type each Combo box entry on its own line followed by a carriage return.

4. Double-click `Button1` and add this `OnClick` event-handling code:

```
void __fastcall TForm1::Button1Click(TObject *Sender)
{
  TNewForm *NewForm = new TNewForm(Application,ComboBox1->ItemIndex);
  NewForm->ShowModal();
  delete NewForm;
}
```

5. The `OnClick` handler in step 4 needs to know about the `TNewForm` class. Add this `#include` statement to `MAINFORM.CPP`:

```
#include <vcl\vcl.h>
#pragma hdrstop

#include "MAINFORM.h"
#include "DYNAFORM.h"
```

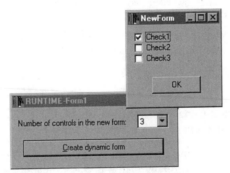

Figure 1-2 RUNTIME at runtime

6. Open DYNAFORM.H and type in the class declaration and #includes for TNewForm.

```
#ifndef DynaFormH
#define DynaFormH
//--------------------------------
#include <vcl\Classes.hpp>
#include <vcl\Controls.hpp>
#include <vcl\StdCtrls.hpp>
#include <vcl\Forms.hpp>
#include <vcl\ComCtrls.hpp>

class TNewForm : public TForm
{
private:  // User declarations
  TCheckBox *CheckBoxes[5];
  TButton    *OKButton;
  void __fastcall OKButtonClick(TObject *Sender);
public:  // User declarations
  virtual __fastcall TNewForm(TComponent* Owner, int Count);
};
#endif
```

7. DYNAFORM.CPP will contain the code for TNewForm. Open DYNAFORM.CPP and add the TNewForm constructor.

```
#include <vcl\vcl.h>
#pragma hdrstop

#include "DYNAFORM.h"
//----------------------------------------------

__fastcall TNewForm::TNewForm(TComponent* Owner, int Count)
  : TForm(Owner,0)
{
  // Set properties for the form.
  Height = Count * 16 + 100;
  Width  = 150;
  Position = poScreenCenter;
  Caption="NewForm";

  // Create an array of Check boxes based on the Count value.
  if ( (Count > 0) && (Count <=5))
  {
    for (int j=0; j < Count;j++)
    {
      CheckBoxes[j] = new TCheckBox(this);
      CheckBoxes[j]->Parent = this;
      CheckBoxes[j]->Top = 10 + 16*j;
      CheckBoxes[j]->Left= 10;
      CheckBoxes[j]->Caption= "Check" + AnsiString(j+1);
    }
  }

  // Create a push button that will close the form.
```

continued on next page

continued from previous page

```
OKButton = new TButton(this);
OKButton->Parent = this;
OKButton->Top=Count*16 + 30;
OKButton->Left=(Width-OKButton->Width)/2;
OKButton->OnClick = OKButtonClick;
OKButton->Caption = "OK";
}
```

8. Now add the code for the OKButtonClick function. Type this function into DYNAFORM.CPP just below the constructor code:

```
void __fastcall TNewForm::OKButtonClick(TObject *Sender)
{
  Close();
}
```

9. Compile and test the program.

> **NOTE**
>
> You may receive warning messages for hiding a virtual TForm constructor. The compiler is warning you that the two-argument constructor for TNewForm conceals the one-argument virtual constructor of the TForm base class. You must use the two-argument constructor for dynamically created forms, so you can safely disregard the warning.

How It Works

In step 4 you coded an OnClick handler for Form1 that constructs, displays, and deletes an instance of TNewForm. The TNewForm class encapsulates the dynamic form and its controls. The constructor for TNewForm (step 7) takes a Count argument that determines how many Check boxes should be displayed. The dynamic form sizes itself based on Count so it can accommodate the Check boxes and a push button.

Constructing a Dynamic Form

The TForm VCL class contains two constructors: a virtual, one-argument constructor, and a two-argument constructor. C++Builder uses the one-argument constructor for visually created, design-time forms. For example, the constructor for TForm1 in MAINFORM.CPP calls the one-argument base constructor because you created Form1 visually using the IDE. The two-argument constructor exists for one reason only: constructing dynamic forms. The two-argument constructor creates forms that do not have an associated DFM file.

C++Builder uses a DFM file to store resources and property settings for forms that you create at design time. Design-time forms have both a DFM file and an associated CPP unit. Dynamic forms, such as TNewForm, have a CPP unit but no DFM file. C++ constructs dynamic forms using a set of default properties.

In step 7 you coded the TNewForm constructor like this:

```
__fastcall TNewForm::TNewForm(TComponent* Owner, int Count)
  : TForm(Owner,0)
{
...
```

The zero argument to the base class invokes the alternative constructor for dynamic forms. The VCL doesn't care what value you pass as the second argument to the base constructor. In fact, the VCL header files call this variable **Dummy** to indicate that its value means nothing. Nonetheless, you must construct dynamic forms using the alternative, two-argument, constructor. Otherwise, you will encounter run-time errors.

In Delphi (Pascal), the TForm constructors have different names, Create and CreateNew, and both functions take a single argument. In C++, constructors must have the same name as the class. The only way to provide two constructors in C++ is to use functions with different argument patterns. The two-argument TForm constructor works as a C++ version of the Delphi CreateNew function.

Adding Controls to a Dynamic Form

Because dynamic forms don't use DFM files, you must construct controls, assign event handlers, and set properties for TNewForm at runtime. You must construct a control before you can assign its properties. The constructor code from step 7 creates the controls for TNewForm and then assigns properties for each control.

You should always set the **Left** and **Top** properties for dynamically created controls. Otherwise, the components will appear in the corner of the form. You should also set the **Caption** property for buttons, Check boxes, and other controls where Caption plays a necessary role.

Dynamically created controls will not appear if you forget to set their Parent property.

In this How-To, the dynamic form should close when the user clicks the OKButton. You coded a function called OKButtonClick in step 8 that closes the dynamic form. However, simply coding this function does not associate it with a control. You must assign OKButtonClick to a component's event handler. In step 7 you added this line to the TNewForm constructor.

```
OKButton->OnClick = OKButtonClick;
```

This statement attaches the OKButtonClick function to the OnClick event for OKButton. As a result of this assignment, OKButtonClick will execute when the user clicks the OKButton.

Deleting a Dynamic Form

The code from step 4 constructed a TNewForm pointer and then displayed the form using ShowModal. ShowModal returns when the user closes the dynamic form. After the form closes, you must delete the NewForm pointer to de-allocate memory consumed by the form.

Notice that you did not code a destructor for TNewForm. So who deletes the TCheckBox and TButton pointers of TNewForm? It turns out that the VCL automatically deletes controls for you when you delete their Owner. You would need to add a destructor to TNewForm if it contained pointers to nonvisual objects.

Comments

You may have noticed that positioning dynamic controls can be a tedious chore. You can cheat by using the C++Builder IDE to simplify this task. Place a component on a form. Press CTRL-C to copy it, move to the code editor, and then press CTRL-V to paste. C++Builder automatically inserts code for a component that matches the one you placed on the form.

Many opportunities exist for creating forms at runtime from scratch. In this How-To, the number of Check boxes varies based on user input. You could easily extend this to include different components and different component properties. The components could be chosen based on a text file, a remote network, or the format of a database table. As you build on this example, you may need to design a way to move data to and from the controls in a dynamic form. You could make the controls publicly accessible or provide public Get and Set access functions.

COMPLEXITY
BEGINNING

1.3 How do I...
Drag a captionless window?

Problem

I'd like to make a small application—such as a clock, a media player, or a resource monitor—that takes up as little space as possible. I want the user to be able to move

the application's window, but I don't want to waste space by adding a caption bar. How can I create a captionless main window that the user can drag using the mouse?

Technique

Windows issues hit testing events to determine the cursor position during mouse activity. You can make Windows think that the client area of your program is a caption bar by responding to hit testing events. Users will be able to drag your application by clicking on the client area just as they would drag it using a caption bar.

Steps

Run DRAGCAPTION.EXE. The application doesn't actually do anything, but note that the caption bar has been removed from the main window. Click on the client area of the program and drag the window to a new location. Figure 1-3 shows the program in action.

1. Create a new project using File|New Application. Name the unit MAINFORM.CPP and name the project DRAGCAPTION.MAK.

2. Add a PopupMenu component to Form1. You can find the PopupMenu control on the Standard tab of the Component Palette. Double-click on PopupMenu1 and add two menu items: Stay On Top and Exit.

3. Create an OnClick event handler for the Exit menu item. Place a call to Close in the handler function.

```
void __fastcall TForm1::Exit1Click(TObject *Sender)
{
  Close();
}
```

4. Create an OnClick handler for the Stay On Top menu item. This code checks or unchecks the menu item and then alters the FormStyle property to match the new setting.

```
void __fastcall TForm1::StayOnTop1Click(TObject *Sender)
{
  StayOnTop1->Checked = !StayOnTop1->Checked;   // Toggle check in menu
  if(StayOnTop1->Checked == true)
    FormStyle = fsStayOnTop;
  else
    FormStyle = fsNormal;
}
```

Drag Me!

Figure 1-3
DRAGCAPTION at runtime

5. Add a **Label** component to **Form1** so its appearance matches Figure 1-3. Set the form's properties to match Table 1-2.

Table 1-2 Components, properties, and settings for **Form1** in the DRAGCAPTION project

COMPONENT	PROPERTY	SETTING
Form1	BorderIcons	[] (all false)
	BorderStyle	bsDialog
	PopupMenu	PopupMenu1
Label1	Caption	Drag Me
PopupMenu1	MenuItem	Stay On Top
	MenuItem	Exit

6. All C++Builder forms have a caption bar at design time. You must override the **CreateParams** method in your **TForm** derived class to remove the caption at runtime. Open **MAINFORM.H** and add a prototype for **CreateParams** to the **TForm1** class.

```
private:  // User declarations
  void __fastcall CreateParams(TCreateParams &Params);
```

7. The VCL passes a **TCreateParams** structure as the only argument to **CreateParams**. This structure contains a **WndClass** structure, dimension information, a bitwise **Style** member, and other data. Open **MAINFORM.CPP** and type the function body for **CreateParams**. This code clears the **WS_CAPTION** style bits from the **TCreateParams** structure:

```
void __fastcall TForm1::CreateParams(TCreateParams &Params)
{
  TForm::CreateParams(Params);  // Call base class first;
  Params.Style &= ~WS_CAPTION;  // then clear caption bits.
}
```

8. **Form1** can respond to **WM_NCHITTEST** messages and make Windows think the client area is a caption bar. Go back to **MAINFORM.H** and insert a function prototype and a message map for the hit testing function. The class declaration for **TForm1** should look like this when you're done:

```
class TForm1 : public TForm
{
__published:  // IDE-managed Components
  TLabel *Label1;
  TPopupMenu *PopupMenu1;
  TMenuItem *StayOnTop1;
  TMenuItem *Exit1;
  void __fastcall Exit1Click(TObject *Sender);
  void __fastcall StayOnTop1Click(TObject *Sender);
```

```
private:  // User declarations
   void __fastcall CreateParams(TCreateParams &Params);
   void __fastcall WMNCHitTest(TMessage &Msg);
public:  // User declarations
   virtual __fastcall TForm1(TComponent* Owner);
BEGIN_MESSAGE_MAP
   MESSAGE_HANDLER(WM_NCHITTEST,TMessage,WMNCHitTest)
END_MESSAGE_MAP(TForm)
};
```

9. Add the code for the WMNCHitTest function to MAINFORM.CPP:

```
void __fastcall TForm1::WMNCHitTest(TMessage &Msg)
{
   if (GetAsyncKeyState(VK_LBUTTON)<0) // Is left button down, if so
     Msg.Result = HTCAPTION;          // report caption area hit
   else
     Msg.Result = HTCLIENT;           // Otherwise, report a client area⇐
hit.
}
```

> **NOTE**
>
> GetAsynchKeyState is a Windows API function that determines whether a key or a mouse button is pressed.

10. Compile and test the program.

How It Works

Windows sends the form a **WM_NCHITTEST** message whenever the mouse cursor moves over the form and whenever the user clicks a mouse button. These messages launch the **WMNCHitTest** function that you coded in step 9. The form must respond by telling Windows whether the mouse cursor is over a client or non-client area (such as the menu, caption bar, or window frame).

The form reports that the mouse is over the client area of the form for all **WM_NCHITTEST** messages that arrive while the left mouse button is up. If the left mouse button is down, **Form1** tells Windows that the mouse is over the caption bar. Windows decodes this as a request by the user to drag the form. Windows then pipes out a series of **WM_SYSCOMMAND** messages to drag the frame.

Comments

This How-To utilizes two functions that alter the default behavior of the program. The **CreateParams** function allows you to customize the appearance of the main form by removing the caption bar. The **WMNCHitTest** function demonstrates how you can respond to Windows messages directly. These two functions point out how versatile C++Builder can be. C++Builder thoroughly encapsulates the intricacies of the Windows operating system, but it does not prevent you from interacting with the OS directly when the need arises.

1.4 How do I...
Set minimum and maximum sizes for my forms?

Problem

Users want me to make my forms sizable so the program can adapt to different screen sizes. This is okay, but if a form becomes too large or too small the results can get pretty ugly. How can I impose a minimum or maximum size to a resizable form?

Technique

You can set minimum and maximum size limits for a form by responding to the Windows **WM_GETMINMAXINFO** message. Windows handles the chore of enforcing the size limits once you set values in response to this message. You have the ability to control the minimum and maximum tracking sizes, the maximized window size, and the maximized window position.

Steps

Run **MINMAX.EXE**. Figure 1-4 shows the program at runtime. Size and position the main form. Notice how Windows prevents you from enlarging or reducing the frame too much. Click on the maximize icon and observe that the maximized frame does not fill the entire screen.

1. Create a new project and save the unit as **MAINFORM.CPP** and save the project as **MINMAX.MAK**.

2. Place a **Label** on **Form1** using Figure 1-4 as a guideline. The **Label** control will display the **Width** and **Height** of the form when the program runs.

3. Size the main form so its **Height** and **Width** are both between 100 and 250. This ensures that the design time sizes match the limits that will be imposed by the code.

4. Open **MAINFORM.H**. Add a function prototype and a message map for the **WM_GETMINMAXINFO** event. The **TForm1** class should look like this when you finish:

```
class TForm1 : public TForm
{
__published: // IDE-managed Components
  TLabel *Label1;
private:        // User declarations
  void __fastcall WMGetMinMaxInfo(TWMGetMinMaxInfo &Msg);  //Prototype for⇐
msg handler
```

```
public:    // User declarations
    virtual __fastcall TForm1(TComponent* Owner);

BEGIN_MESSAGE_MAP
    MESSAGE_HANDLER(WM_GETMINMAXINFO,TWMGetMinMaxInfo,WMGetMinMaxInfo)
END_MESSAGE_MAP(TForm)
};
```

5. Open `MAINFORM.CPP` and add the function body for the
`WMGetMinMaxInfo` function.

```
void __fastcall TForm1::WMGetMinMaxInfo(TWMGetMinMaxInfo &Msg)
{
    Msg.MinMaxInfo->ptMaxSize.x=300; //ptMaxSize is the size of the window
    Msg.MinMaxInfo->ptMaxSize.y=250; //when the window is fully maximized.

    // ptMaxPosition is the coordinate of the form s upper left
    // corner when it s maximized.
    Msg.MinMaxInfo->ptMaxPosition.x=GetSystemMetrics(SM_CXSCREEN)-300;
    Msg.MinMaxInfo->ptMaxPosition.y=0;

    Msg.MinMaxInfo->ptMaxTrackSize.x=300; //ptMaxTrackSize = max size allowed
    Msg.MinMaxInfo->ptMaxTrackSize.y=250; //by dragging with the mouse.

    Msg.MinMaxInfo->ptMinTrackSize.x=170; //ptMinTrackSize = min size allowed
    Msg.MinMaxInfo->ptMinTrackSize.y=150; //by dragging with the mouse.
}
```

6. Create an `OnResize` handler for `Form1` and insert code that updates
`Label1` every time the form resizes.

```
void __fastcall TForm1::FormResize(TObject *Sender)
{
    Label1->Caption = "Width = "      + AnsiString(Width) +
                      "  Height = " + AnsiString(Height);
}
```

7. That's it. Compile and test the program.

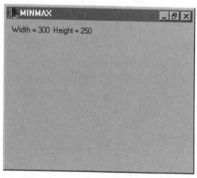

Figure 1-4 MINMAX at runtime

How It Works

As you can see, this example won't win you any code writing awards for program length, but it accomplishes exactly what you set out to do. Windows sends your application a `WM_GETMINMAXINFO` message every time the user tries to size the main form. The message map in `MAINFORM.H` tells C++Builder that you want your `WMGetMinMaxInfo` function to handle these messages. The argument to `WMGetMinMaxInfo` contains a Windows `MINMAXINFO` structure. This structure contains several `POINT` items for returning the size constraints of the form. Your job is to place your constraints in the message's `MINMAXINFO` structure.

The `MINMAXINFO` structure allows you to control four parameters: the minimum size of the form, the maximum size of the form, the maximized position of the form, and the maximized size of the form. This How-To specifies values for all four parameters. If you don't want to alter a parameter, then simply leave that portion of `Msg.MinMaxInfo` alone.

> **TIP**
>
> `TWMGetMinMaxInfo` is declared in `INCLUDE\VCL\MESSAGES.HPP` and the `MINMAXINFO` structure is listed in `INCLUDE\WIN32\WINUSER.H`.

> **NOTE**
>
> The `ptMinTrackSize` and `ptMaxTrackSize` members of `MINMAX-INFO` restrict how small or large the user can size a form by dragging the form's window frame. `ptMaxSize` controls the size of the window when it's maximized. Due to a limitation in Windows, you cannot effectively set `ptMaxTrackSize` less than `ptMaxSize`. If you do, Windows will use the smaller `ptMaxTrackSize` as a substitute for `ptMaxSize`. You can set `ptMaxTrackSize` larger than `ptMaxSize`, but this has little use.

Comments

Experiment with the values in `WMGetMinMaxInfo` to get a feel for how the `MINMAXINFO` parameters affect your program. This How-To exemplifies how C++Builder lets you get down and dirty with the Windows API when you need to.

1.5 How do I...
Make [ENTER] act like [TAB] in my forms?

Problem

I have written a program that requires the user to fill in many Edit boxes. It would be nice if [ENTER] could advance the input focus to the next Edit box. This is more intuitive than using [TAB]. How do I make [ENTER] act like [TAB] in my forms?

Technique

The boolean **KeyPreview** property of **TForm** allows a form to preview keyboard messages before they reach the form's controls. This gives the form a chance to detect and intercept [ENTER] presses. To mimic [TAB], the form can swallow [ENTER] events and reissue a Windows message that focuses the next control in the tab sequence.

Steps

Run **ENTER2TAB.EXE**. Figure 1-5 shows the program in action. Check the Check box and then type a string into the first Edit box. Use [ENTER] to finish the entry and advance the input focus to the next Edit box. Keep entering data like this until you reach the Next button. Observe that even if the Check box is checked, pressing [ENTER] on the focused Next button launches an **OnClick** handler instead of advancing the input focus. Now uncheck the Check box and verify that you can no longer use [ENTER] to advance the input focus.

1. Create a new project and save the unit as **MAINFORM.CPP**. Save the project as **ENTER2TAB.MAK**.

2. Table 1-3 lists the components and properties for **Form1**. Add these controls to **Form1** using Figure 1-5 as a guideline for layout. **Edit1** is the top Edit box.

Table 1-3 Components, properties, and settings for **Form1** in the ENTER2TAB project

COMPONENT	PROPERTY	SETTING
Form1	KeyPreview	true
CheckBox1	TabOrder	0
	Caption	Use [ENTER] key to tab.
Edit1	TabOrder	1
Edit2	TabOrder	2

continued on next page

continued from previous page

COMPONENT	PROPERTY	SETTING
Edit3	TabOrder	3
Edit4	TabOrder	4
Button1	TabOrder	5
	Caption	&Next
Label1	Caption	Name:
Label2	Caption	SSN:
Label3	Caption	Birth Date:
Label4	Caption	Occupation:

3. Select Form1 using the Combo box in the Object Inspector. Create an OnKeyPress event handler for Form1. The OnKeyPress handler watches for ENTER presses and takes action when it detects one. Add this code to the event handler:

```
void __fastcall TForm1::FormKeyPress(TObject *Sender, char &Key)
{
  if( (Key == VK_RETURN) && (CheckBox1->Checked == true))
  {
    Key=0;                          // Swallow the key here.
    Perform(WM_NEXTDLGCTL,0,0);  // Focus next control.
  }
}
```

4. Create an OnClick handler for the Next button. Type in this code to clear out the Edit boxes whenever Button1 is pushed:

```
void __fastcall TForm1::Button1Click(TObject *Sender)
{
  Edit1->Text = "";
  Edit2->Text = "";
  Edit3->Text = "";
  Edit4->Text = "";
}
```

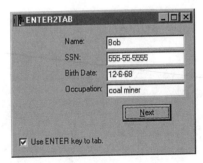

Figure 1-5 ENTER2TAB at runtime

5. Compile and test the program.

How It Works

Windows normally sends keyboard events directly to the focused control in a form. Most controls simply ignore ENTER. In fact, a single-line Edit box will beep at the user if it receives an ENTER press. If a form wants to act on ENTER, it must intercept the key press before the focused control receives it. `TForm::KeyPreview` allows a form to inspect keyboard events before they reach the focused control. In step 2, you set `Form1`'s `KeyPreview` property to `true`, which gives the `OnKeyPress` handler of `Form1` first crack at detecting keyboard activity.

With `KeyPreview` set to `true`, the `OnKeyPress` handler of `Form1` executes once every time the user presses a nonsystem key. You coded the `OnKeyPress` handler in step 3. The `Key` argument to `FormKeyPress` contains the Windows key code for the character that was pressed. If the Check box is checked, `FormKeyPress` must do two things when `Key` equals `VK_RETURN`:

1. Prevent normal processing of ENTER.

2. Mimic TAB by focusing the next control.

> **NOTE**
> `VK_RETURN` is the Windows key code for ENTER. Consult the Win32 reference for a list of possible VK codes.

The code for executing these two tasks looks like this:

```
Key=0;                          // Swallow the key here.
Perform(WM_NEXTDLGCTL,0,0);     // Focus next control.
```

Zeroing the `Key` argument prevents normal processing of ENTER. The `Perform` function call handles the focus change. Calling `Perform` is equivalent to sending a message, except that the VCL processes the event directly instead of routing it through the normal Windows event chain.

> **NOTE**
> `WM_NEXTDLGCTL` is a Windows message that advances the input focus to the next control in a form.

Comments

In most cases, this technique works well. The code in this How-To modifies the normal behavior of Windows, so you should let users disable this feature. Also, you will have to add smarter code if your form contains Memos, Rich text controls, String grids, or other controls that use ENTER as part of their normal behavior.

The tactics described in this How-To can be used to detect other key presses as well. For example, you could add a simple hotkey system to your program using the same technique presented here. It's important to know which event handler will be called for a particular key. Table 1-4 helps clarify which events you should look for.

Table 1-4 The Windows keyboard messages

FORM HANDLER	WINDOWS MESSAGE	KEYS
OnKeyPress	WM_CHAR	alpha-numeric, space bar, ENTER, backspace, number pad keys, ESC, CTRL+key, SHIFT+key
OnKeyDown	WM_KEYDOWN	all WM_CHAR keys + INS, DEL, HOME, END, PGUP, PGDN, function keys, CTRL, SHIFT, arrow keys
	WM_SYSCHAR	ALT + key combinations
	WM_SYSKEYDOWN	ALT + key combinations

NOTE

You will not receive certain key events if the key means something to Windows. For example, you won't get key events for ENTER if a button has the input focus and you will never get TAB events if a form contains controls that can be focused.

You may be wondering why the Key value cannot be changed to **VK_TAB** in step 3 to simulate a press of TAB. This would not work, and it's important to understand why. Somebody has to send a **WM_NEXTDLGCTL** message to your program in order for a focus change to occur. Windows performs this task by detecting the TAB key press. When Windows detects a TAB press, it sends **WM_NEXTDLGCTL** to your form, but it does not send **WM_KEYDOWN** or **WM_CHAR** events because the TAB press has already been handled. By the time you detect an ENTER press, Windows has already looked for TAB and will not detect your change in the **Key** value. This explains why you must explicitly send the **WM_NEXTDLGCTL** message yourself.

COMPLEXITY
ADVANCED

1.6 How do I...
Paint an interesting background on an MDI parent form?

Problem

Normally I can use a form's canvas to draw its background, but when I have an MDI form, the only thing I seem to be able to change is its background color. Nothing

happens when I draw on the canvas of an MDI parent form. I would like to add a more interesting background to my MDI program. How do I paint my own MDI background using C++Builder?

Technique

The MDI background region is actually a separate window called the MDI client window. The MDI client window manages MDI child forms and is present in all Windows MDI programs. Unfortunately, the VCL does not encapsulate the MDI client window, which means that you don't have a **TCanvas** object that can draw the MDI background. To successfully paint a custom MDI background, you must subclass the MDI client window using the Windows API. Subclassing allows you to receive messages intended for the MDI client window. You can safely paint your own background by intercepting the **WM_ERASEBKGND** message.

Steps

Run **MDIBACK.EXE**. Figure 1-6 shows the program during execution. You should immediately notice the blue to black gradient present in the background of the program. Create a few child forms using the menu and observe that the background pattern does not interfere with the appearance of the child forms. Try sizing the main window of the program. Notice how the background realigns itself whenever you change the size of the main form.

1. Before you can draw on an MDI background, you need to get a simple MDI program up and running. Select File|New Application to make a new project. Choose File|Save Project As and name the unit **PARENT.CPP** and name the project **MDIBACK.MAK**. Change the **Name** property of the main form to **MDIParent**.

Figure 1-6 MDIBACK at runtime

2. Choose File|New Form to add a second form to the project. Select File|Save As and name the new unit `CHILD.CPP`. Change the `Name` property of the new form to `MDIChild.`

3. Set properties for the two forms to match the values in Table 1-5.

NOTE

The menu items in Table 1-5 will be created in step 4.

Table 1-5 Components, properties, and settings for the `MDIBACK` project

COMPONENT	PROPERTY	SETTING
Form	Name	MDIParent
	FormStyle	fsMDIForm
MainMenu	Name	MainMenu1
	MenuItem	&File
	MenuItem	&New MDI Child
	MenuItem	E&xit
Form	Name	MDIChild
	FormStyle	fsMDIChild

4. Place a `MainMenu` component on `MDIParent`. Double-click `MainMenu1` and add a `File` menu item and two subitems called `New MDI Child` and `Exit`. Create an `OnClick` handler for the `Exit` menu item and insert a call to `Close` to shut down the program.

```
void __fastcall TMDIParent::Exit1Click(TObject *Sender)
{
  Close();  // Close program when the user clicks Exit.
}
```

5. `MDIParent` will be responsible for creating child MDI forms. For this reason, the application should not auto-create an instance of `TMDIChild`. Choose Options|Project, click the Forms tab, and remove `MDIChild` from the list of automatically created forms. Additionally, you don't need the global `TMDIChild` pointer located in `CHILD.CPP` and `CHILD.H`. Delete these two lines (you don't have to delete them, but it does clean up your files a bit).

```
extern TMDIChild *MDIChild;    (delete from CHILD.H)
TMDIChild *MDIChild;           (delete from CHILD.CPP)
```

6. In order to create MDI child forms, `MDIParent` will need to know about the `TMDIChild` class. Open `PARENT.CPP` and type a `#include` statement for the `TMDIChild` header file.

```
#include <vcl\vcl.h>
#pragma hdrstop

#include "PARENT.h"
#include "CHILD.h"
```

7. Clicking the **New MDI Child** menu item will create a new child form.
Create an **OnClick** handler for the **New MDI Child** menu item, and insert
this code:

```
void __fastcall TMDIParent::New1Click(TObject *Sender)
{
    // Create a new MDI child. Use the application as the owner for the form.
    // This insures that the application object will delete all the TMDIChild
    // pointers when the program closes.
    new TMDIChild(Application);
}
```

8. Specifying **Application** as the owner of the MDI child forms ensures that
the application object will delete each **TMDIChild** pointer when the program closes. However, it's wise to de-allocate resources as soon as the user
closes an MDI child form. Create an **OnClose** handler for **MDIChild** and
insert code that tells the application to free memory as soon as the user
closes a child form.

TIP

Make sure you create an **OnClose** handler for **MDIChild** and not
MDIParent.

```
void __fastcall TMDIChild::FormClose(TObject *Sender, TCloseAction &Action)
{
    // Request that our pointer gets deleted after
    // we finish closing.
    Action = caFree;
}
```

TIP

Steps 1-8 show how to create a simple MDI program. If you're new
to MDI programming with C++Builder, you may want to compile
and test the program now before moving on. Make sure you can
create new MDI forms using the program's menu.

---

9. Open **PARENT.H** and add functions, variables, and a message map to the
TMDIParent class declaration.

```
class TMDIParent : public TForm
{
__published:    // IDE-managed Components
```

continued on next page

continued from previous page

```
    TMainMenu *MainMenu1;
    TMenuItem *File1;
    TMenuItem *NewMDIChild1;
    TMenuItem *Exit1;
    void __fastcall Exit1Click(TObject *Sender);
    void __fastcall NewMDIChild1Click(TObject *Sender);
private:  // User declarations
    Pointer OriginalClientProc;
    Pointer ClientObjectInstance;
    virtual void __fastcall CreateWnd();
    virtual void __fastcall DestroyWnd();
    virtual void __fastcall ClientProc(TMessage &Msg);
    virtual void __fastcall DrawClientWindow (HDC &Hdc) ;
    void __fastcall WMEraseBkgnd(TWMEraseBkgnd &Msg);
public:  // User declarations
    __fastcall TMDIParent(TComponent* Owner);
BEGIN_MESSAGE_MAP
    MESSAGE_HANDLER(WM_ERASEBKGND,TWMEraseBkgnd,WMEraseBkgnd)
END_MESSAGE_MAP(TForm)
};
```

10. Open **PARENT.CPP**, and type in the body for the **CreateWnd** function. This function subclasses the MDI client window using the API **SetWindowLong** function.

```
void __fastcall TMDIParent::CreateWnd(void)
{
    // Let the base class CreateWnd do what it needs to do to.
    // Create a main window for the program.
    TForm::CreateWnd();

    // Subclass the MDI client window so we can replace its default
    // message handler with our own. MakeObjectInstance transposes
    // the ClientProc function into a form that the API likes.
    // SetWindowLong then subclasses the MDI client (ClientHandle)
    // using the return value from MakeObjectInstance.
    ClientObjectInstance = MakeObjectInstance (ClientProc) ;
    OriginalClientProc = (Pointer) SetWindowLong (ClientHandle,
                                                  GWL_WNDPROC,
                                                  (long)⇐
ClientObjectInstance);
}
```

11. Stay in **PARENT.CPP** and type the body for the **ClientProc** function. **ClientProc** uses **DrawClientWindow** to draw a custom MDI background whenever it receives a **WM_ERASEBKGND** message. **ClientProc** uses **CallWindowProc** to pass all other messages on to the original window procedure.

```
void __fastcall TMDIParent::ClientProc (TMessage &Msg)
{
    switch (Msg.Msg)
    {
      case WM_ERASEBKGND:
```

```
      // Intercept the message for painting the background and
      // draw the background ourself.
      DrawClientWindow ((HDC) Msg.WParam) ;
      Msg.Result = true;
      return;
   case WM_HSCROLL:
   case WM_VSCROLL:
      // Scrolling the client area can goof up our drawing. If the user⇐
scrolls
      // the client area, pass the message on to the original procedure⇐
and
      // then request a complete repaint of the background.
      Msg.Result = CallWindowProc ((FARPROC)OriginalClientProc,⇐
ClientHandle,
                                Msg.Msg, Msg.WParam, Msg.LParam);
      InvalidateRect (ClientHandle, 0, true) ;
      break;
   default:
      // Pass all other messages on to the original window procedure
      // stored in OriginalClientProc.
      Msg.Result = CallWindowProc ((FARPROC)OriginalClientProc,⇐
ClientHandle,
                                Msg.Msg, Msg.WParam, Msg.LParam);
      break;
   }
}
```

12. Stay in PARENT.CPP, and code the DrawClientWindow function. ClientProc passes DrawClientWindow a device context on which to draw. DrawClientWindow uses that device context to paint a gradient background.

NOTE

DrawClientWindow utilizes the graphics features of C++Builder. Chapter 5, "Graphics," covers graphics in greater detail.

TIP

You could replace the code in DrawClientWindow with your own code that draws bitmaps or paints a different background pattern.

```
void __fastcall TMDIParent::DrawClientWindow (HDC &Hdc)
{
   // This routine paints a gradient background that slowly
   // changes from StartColor at the top to black at the bottom.
   const int    NumGradients = 64;   // Number of shading levels
   const TColor StartColor = clBlue; // Initial color

   TRect rect ;                          // Calculate size of backgnd.
   ::GetClientRect (ClientHandle, (RECT *) &rect) ;
```

continued on next page

continued from previous page

```
// Painting a shaded gradient is slow and can cause flickering.
// Eliminate flicker by using memory bitmaps and BitBlt.
Graphics::TBitmap *MemBitmap = new Graphics::TBitmap;
MemBitmap->Width = rect.Right - rect.Left;
MemBitmap->Height= rect.Bottom- rect.Top;
MemBitmap->Canvas->Brush->Style = bsSolid;
MemBitmap->Canvas->Brush->Color = clBlack;
MemBitmap->Canvas->FillRect(Rect(0,0,
                                    MemBitmap->Width,
                                    MemBitmap->Height));
// Calculate the height of each little gradient section.
int GradientHeight = MemBitmap->Height / NumGradients;

// Calculate individual RGB intensities of the starting color.
int InitialRed    = GetRValue(StartColor);
int InitialGreen = GetGValue(StartColor);
int InitialBlue  = GetBValue(StartColor);
int RedIncrement  = (InitialRed + 1)  / NumGradients; // Calculate
int GreenIncrement= (InitialGreen + 1)/ NumGradients; // increment of
int BlueIncrement = (InitialBlue + 1) / NumGradients; // each gradient

TColor FillColor;
// The for loop draws each gradient section. The loop stops one pass
// away from black because black was drawn by FillRect above.
for (int j=0;j< NumGradients;j++)
{
   rect.Bottom = rect.Top + GradientHeight;
   FillColor = (TColor) RGB( InitialRed   -(RedIncrement * j),
                             InitialGreen -(GreenIncrement* j),
                             InitialBlue  -(BlueIncrement * j));
   MemBitmap->Canvas->Brush->Color = FillColor;
   MemBitmap->Canvas->FillRect(rect);
   rect.Top += GradientHeight;
}

// Use API BitBlt to copy pixels to the screen.
::BitBlt(Hdc,0,0,MemBitmap->Width, MemBitmap->Height,
         MemBitmap->Canvas->Handle,0,0,SRCCOPY);
delete MemBitmap; // Delete the temporary bitmap.
}
```

13. Type the function body for `DestroyWnd` into `PARENT.CPP`. `DestroyWnd` cleans up resources that were consumed by `CreateWnd`.

```
void __fastcall TMDIParent::DestroyWnd ()
{
  SetWindowLong (ClientHandle, GWL_WNDPROC, (long) OriginalClientProc) ;
  FreeObjectInstance (ClientObjectInstance) ;
  TForm::DestroyWnd();
}
```

14. Windows sends `WM_ERASEBKGND` messages to `MDIParent` whenever the user resizes the main form. This causes an unwanted flicker because `MDIParent` draws its background just before the MDI client window

draws the gradient background. You can prevent flicker by intercepting `WM_ERASEBKND` messages that reach `MDIParent`. Stay in `PARENT.CPP` and type the function body for `WMEraseBkgnd`.

```
void __fastcall TMDIParent::WMEraseBkgnd(TWMEraseBkgnd &Msg)
{                        // Tell Windows to forget about the
  Msg.Result = false;    // background. MDI client will draw
}                        // it later.
```

NOTE

Don't confuse this `WM_ERASEBKGND` handler with the subclassed handler in `ClientProc`. `WMEraseBkgnd` blocks events that reach the parent form. These messages are unwanted, whereas the `WM_ERASEBKGND` events that reach `ClientProc` are critical to making the program work.

15. Compile and test the program.

How It Works

You may have thought that drawing your own MDI background would have been as simple as drawing on the MDI parent form. Unfortunately, this is not the case. The MDI background is a separate window, called the MDI client window, that appears behind the MDI child forms. Drawing your own MDI background involves four steps:

1. Create an MDI application.

2. Subclass the MDI client's normal window procedure.

3. Intercept `WM_ERASEBKGND` messages in your custom window procedure.

4. Draw your own background.

Creating an MDI Application

Before you can draw on an MDI background you need an MDI program to work with. Steps 1 through 8 guide you through the process of creating a simple MDI application. MDI programs use two different types of forms: MDI parent forms and MDI child forms.

The `FormStyle` property (step 3) of `TForm` determines whether a form acts as an MDI parent, an MDI child, or neither. Setting `FormStyle` to `fsMDIForm` converts the form into an MDI parent. Likewise, you create MDI children by setting `FormStyle` to `fsMDIChild`. You can then display an MDI child by simply creating an instance of the child form (step 7).

The Object Repository contains an MDI application template that can help you create an MDI project. The template handles steps 1-8 for you, plus it adds some additional functionality. To use this template: choose File|New, click the Projects tab, and select MDI application.

TForm contains a host of MDI helper functions. You might want to investigate the following functions in the VCL help file: `ArrangeIcons`, `Cascade`, `Next`, `Previous`, and `Tile`.

Subclassing a Custom Window Procedure

The Win32 interface operates by sending messages to windows. Each window has a function called a window procedure (sometimes called `WndProc`) that runs when a message needs to be processed. You can handle messages yourself by replacing the default window procedure with your own function. Subclassing refers to the process of replacing a default window procedure with your own custom procedure.

In step 10, you use the API `SetWindowLong` function to replace the MDI client's window procedure with the `ClientProc` function of `TMDIParent`. `SetWindowLong` returns the address of the default window procedure already in place. You store this address in `OriginalClientProc`, which allows you to call the old function when you don't want to alter the default processing of a message.

The third argument to `SetWindowLong` must be the address to a function that looks like:

```
LRESULT CALLBACK MyFunction(HWND hWnd, UINT message, WPARAM wParam, LPARAM⇐
lParam)
```

This is quite ugly. Fortunately, C++Builder provides a function called `MakeObjectInstance` that allows you to use a cleaner looking method as your sub-classed window procedure. `MakeObjectInstance` creates an `LRESULT CALLBACK` function. This new function calls the function that was passed as a parameter to `MakeObjectInstance`. In step 10, `MakeObjectInstance` creates a `CALLBACK` function that filters messages to the `ClientProc` method. `MakeObjectInstance` returns the address for this new function, which is stored in `ClientObjectInstance` and subsequently passed as an argument to `SetWindowLong`.

Handling Subclassed Messages

`ClientProc` (step 11) responds to messages that Windows tries to send to the MDI client window. `ClientProc`'s primary job is to detect the `WM_ERASEBKGND` message.

Windows sends the MDI client window a `WM_ERASEBKGND` message when it wants the MDI client to redraw its background. `ClientProc` intercepts these requests and then calls `DrawClientBackground` to paint the custom MDI background.

`ClientProc` uses the API function `CallWindowProc` to pass all other messages to the MDI client's original window procedure. Recall that the subclassing code in step 10 saved the address of the original window procedure in `OriginalClientProc`.

In the case of scroll messages (`WM_VSCROLL` and `WM_HSCROLL`), `ClientProc` executes a call to `InvalidateRect` after calling the default window procedure. To understand why this is necessary, comment out the `InvalidateRect` call and run the program again. Create an MDI child and move it down past the edge of the main window. This should cause a vertical scroll bar to appear on the MDI client. Click on the vertical scroll bar to bring the child form back into view. The gradient background becomes distorted because portions of the MDI client scroll instead of repainting. `InvalidateRect` fixes the gradient by requesting that the MDI background be completely repainted.

Drawing the MDI Background

When Windows sends a `WM_ERASEBKGND` message, it embeds a handle to a device context in the `WParam` argument. `ClientProc` passes this device context to `DrawClientBackground`. The `DrawClientBackground` function uses the device context to fill the MDI background with a gradient pattern.

Comments

Subclassing should be your last resort for enhancing a VCL component. Overriding virtual methods and message handlers is a better solution, provided they have the firepower to get the job done. Drawing a custom MDI background requires that you take the subclassing approach. Even though subclassing is a low-level technique, this How-To forces you to work with only a handful of API functions.

There are two main reasons why you may need to use the API to subclass a window directly. First, some VCL objects, such as MDI forms and Combo boxes, have special child windows that cannot be controlled through the VCL. You must use subclassing to access these child windows. Second, you must employ subclassing if you want to create a Custom control that modifies the behavior of an existing Windows control.

This example serves as a template for drawing other types of backgrounds on an MDI form. You could draw a company logo in the center of the background, or you could tile a bitmap across the background to create a watermark. All you have to do is replace the code in the `DrawClientWindow` function with code that suits your needs.

1.7 How do I...
Customize a window's title bar with graphics?

Problem

I would like to add custom graphics to the title bar of my forms. I have seen Microsoft applications that do this. How can I?

Technique

Windows sends your application **WM_NCPAINT** and **WM_NCACTIVATE** messages that signal when it's time to draw the non-client areas of the form. Normally your application passes these messages on to **DefWindowProc**, but you can intercept them and draw the title bar yourself. The technique involves letting **DefWindowProc** draw some of the non-client areas and then drawing your own title bar after it returns.

> **NOTE**
> The terms title bar and caption bar mean the same thing.

Steps

Run **TITLEBAR.EXE**. Figure 1-7 shows the program in action. Notice the heart-beat light flashing in the right portion of the title bar. Depending on your system settings, you may also see a gradual shade from black to the active caption color.

1. Create a new project. Name the unit **MAINFORM.CPP**, and name the project **TITLEBAR.MAK**.

2. Place a **MainMenu** component on the form. Add a **File** menu item and an **Exit** subitem. Create an **OnClick** handler for the **Exit** menu item, and insert this code:

```
void __fastcall TForm1::Exit1Click(TObject *Sender)
{
  Close();
}
```

3. Add these private data members and functions to the **TForm1** class in **MAINFORM.H**:

```
private: // User declarations
  TCanvas *WindowCanvas;
  TRect CaptionRect;
```

```
AnsiString CustomCaption;
TColor FinalCaptionColor;
int     FinalBlueIntensity;
int     FinalGreenIntensity;
int     FinalRedIntensity;
bool    IsNT35;
bool    HeartBeat;
bool CanDrawMyCustomCaption(void);
void CalculateCaptionRect(void);
void DrawGradient(void);
void DrawIcon(void);
void DrawCaptionString(void);
void DrawHeartBeatLight(void);
```

4. Just below the declarations you added in step 3, type in prototypes and a message map for the **WM_NCPAINT** and **WM_NCACTIVATE** handler functions. **TForm1** will also need a destructor, so place this prototype in the public section.

```
  void DrawCaptionString(void);
  void DrawHeartBeatLight(void)
  void __fastcall WMNCPaint(TMessage &Msg);
  void __fastcall WMNCActivate(TWMNCActivate &Msg);
public:  // User declarations
  virtual __fastcall TForm1(TComponent* Owner);
  __fastcall ~TForm1(void);
BEGIN_MESSAGE_MAP
  MESSAGE_HANDLER(WM_NCPAINT,TMessage,WMNCPaint)
  MESSAGE_HANDLER(WM_NCACTIVATE,TWMNCActivate,WMNCActivate)
END_MESSAGE_MAP(TForm)
};
```

5. Open up **MAINFORM.CPP** and add the function body for **WMNCActivate**. This function will run once every time the application activates or deactivates.

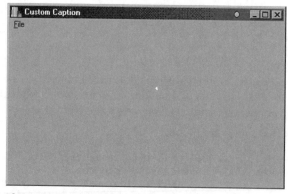

Figure 1-7 TITLEBAR at runtime

```
void __fastcall TForm1::WMNCActivate(TWMNCActivate &Msg)
{
  Msg.Result = true;                 // Always handle this message.
  if ((bool)Msg.Active == false)   // If non-active draw default
  {                                  // non-active title bar.
    DefWindowProc( Handle, Msg.Msg, Msg.Active, 0 );
    // Add code here to draw caption when window is inactive.
    // In this example, we leave the inactive caption alone.
    return;
  }
  TMessage PaintMsg;                  // If active, do same thing as WMNCPaint.
  PaintMsg.Msg     = Msg.Msg;        // Create a MSG to pass to WMNCPaint, and
  PaintMsg.WParam = Msg.Active;      // call the function directly so painting
  WMNCPaint(PaintMsg);                // happens now.
}
```

6. Stay in `MAINFORM.CPP` and type in the function body for the `WM_NCPAINT` handler.

```
void __fastcall TForm1::WMNCPaint(TMessage &Msg)
{
  // Use default processing to draw min/max/close buttons, menu, and the
  // frame. The caption bar is drawn too, but we paint over that later.
  DefWindowProc(Handle, Msg.Msg,Msg.WParam,Msg.LParam);

  // Check for any reason not to draw the custom caption.
  if(CanDrawMyCustomCaption() == false)
    return;

  // Create a DC for the entire window, then assign
  // the handle to the window canvas.
  HDC WindowDC = GetWindowDC(Handle);
  WindowCanvas->Handle  = WindowDC;

  CalculateCaptionRect(); // Calculate size of caption bar.
  DrawGradient();            // Draw the shaded gradient.
  DrawIcon();              // Patch the icon.
  DrawCaptionString();
  DrawHeartBeatLight();     // Draw the LED heartbeat.

  ReleaseDC(Handle, WindowDC); // Free resources.
  WindowCanvas->Handle = 0;
}
```

7. Now add the code for the `CanDrawMyCustomCaption` function to `MAINFORM.CPP`. This function prevents custom drawing when things might get goofed up by the shading.

```
bool TForm1::CanDrawMyCustomCaption(void)
{
  // Under certain conditions we don't want to shade the custom caption.
  // This function bundles all of the reasons into one.
  if (WindowCanvas == 0)           // WMNCPaint can execute after
    return false;                   // destructor has been called.
  if(Application->Active == false)  // Can get WM_NCPAINT messages
```

```
      return false;              // when inactive.
   if(Width < 150)               // Shading looks poor at very small
      return false;              // widths.
   if(IsNT35 == true)            // NT 3.5 has win3 style system menu
      return false;              // and centered caption text, so⇐
forget it.

   // Shading looks poor if it s from black to a very light color. Word⇐
actually
   // shades from white instead of black for light caption colors. We will⇐
just not
   // shade for light colored captions. Light colors have high RGB values.
   FinalCaptionColor = TColor(GetSysColor(COLOR_ACTIVECAPTION));
   FinalBlueIntensity = GetBValue(FinalCaptionColor);
   FinalGreenIntensity= GetGValue(FinalCaptionColor);
   FinalRedIntensity  = GetRValue(FinalCaptionColor);
   // Is at least one of the RGB values dark, if not, don't draw the⇐
shading
   if ((FinalBlueIntensity < 128) || (FinalGreenIntensity < 128) ||⇐
(FinalRedIntensity < 128) )
      return true;
   else
      return false;
}
```

8. The `WMNCPaint` function from step 6 uses five functions to draw the custom caption bar. Type these functions into `MAINFORM.CPP`:

```
void TForm1::CalculateCaptionRect(void)
{
   // Determine the coordinates of the custom area of the caption. The⇐
left, top,
   // and bottom must be calculated precisely. The right value is an⇐
arbitrary
   // value that keeps us away from the min/max buttons.
   CaptionRect.Left = GetSystemMetrics(SM_CXFRAME);
   CaptionRect.Right= Width- 4*GetSystemMetrics(SM_CXSIZE); //Stay away⇐
from btns.
   CaptionRect.Top  = GetSystemMetrics(SM_CYFRAME);
   CaptionRect.Bottom=CaptionRect.Top + GetSystemMetrics(SM_CYCAPTION)-1;
}


void TForm1::DrawGradient(void)
{
   // Shading involves gradually increasing RGB color values from 0 (black)
   // to the final RGB value of the caption color. The Increment values
   // will be multiplied by 0,1..31 to create 32 shades. The FinalXXX
   // values are calculated inside of CanDrawMyCustomGraphics
   int    BlueIncrement = (FinalBlueIntensity+1) / 32; // Max intensity is⇐
255,
   int    GreenIncrement= (FinalGreenIntensity+1)/32;  // adding 1 makes⇐
number
   int    RedIncrement  = (FinalRedIntensity+1)/32;    // evenly divisible⇐
by 32.
```

continued on next page

continued from previous page

```
    TRect Section = CaptionRect;
    // SectionWidth represents the width of each gradient section. Caption
    // bar will contain 36 gradient sections, 5 sections will be black, the
    // remaining 31 sections will be between black and the caption color.
    int    SectionWidth = (CaptionRect.Right - CaptionRect.Left)/36;
    TColor FillColor(clBlack);
    Section.Right = Section.Left + 5*SectionWidth; //Draw 5 sections of⇐
black.
    WindowCanvas->Brush->Color = FillColor;         //Configure the brush.
    WindowCanvas->Brush->Style = bsSolid;
    WindowCanvas->FillRect(Section);                //Fill in black sections.
    Section.Left+=5*SectionWidth;                   //Move section over.

    for (int j=1;j<=31;j++)                // Loop through the shades of color
    {                                      // from black to the caption⇐
color.
        Section.Right = Section.Left + SectionWidth; // Size the section.
        FillColor = (TColor) RGB((RedIncrement*j),   // Create dithered color
                              (GreenIncrement*j), // based on loop index.
                              (BlueIncrement*j));
        WindowCanvas->Brush->Color = FillColor;      // Set brush to new⇐
color.
        WindowCanvas->FillRect(Section);             // Brush fill the⇐
section.
        Section.Left += SectionWidth;                // Move section over.
    }
}


void TForm1::DrawIcon(void)
{
    // Need to redraw the system icon because DrawGradient just painted
    // over it with black.  DrawGradient painted over it because the icon
    // had the caption color surrounding it.
    int IconWidth = GetSystemMetrics(SM_CXSMICON); // Calculate width and
    int IconHeight= GetSystemMetrics(SM_CYSMICON); // height of icon.
    TRect Section;
    Section.Left=CaptionRect.Left+2;   // Determine where the icon belongs.
    Section.Top =CaptionRect.Top +1;
    Section.Right=Section.Left + IconWidth; // Size the rect to hold the⇐
icon.
    Section.Bottom=Section.Top + IconHeight;

    // Paint the application icon; could avoid stretching by
    // supplying a 16 by 16 icon.
    DrawIconEx(WindowCanvas->Handle, Section.Left, Section.Top,  // API call.
               Application->Icon-⇐
>Handle,IconWidth,IconHeight,0,NULL,DI_NORMAL);
}


void TForm1::DrawCaptionString(void)
{
    // Need to draw our own caption string. Must avoid using the Caption
    // form member to avoid flicker.
```

```
    RECT r;                                    // Need an API style rect.
    r.left=CaptionRect.Left + 2 + 16 + 4; // Size the rect.
    r.right=CaptionRect.Right-20;
    r.top = CaptionRect.Top;
    r.bottom = CaptionRect.Bottom;
    SetBkMode(WindowCanvas->Handle,TRANSPARENT); // Transparent mode so text
    WindowCanvas->Font->Color=clWhite;           // does not wipe out⇐
shading.
    WindowCanvas->Font->Style = WindowCanvas->Font->Style << fsBold;
    DrawText(WindowCanvas-⇐
>Handle,CustomCaption.c_str(),CustomCaption.Length(),
              &r,DT_SINGLELINE|DT_VCENTER);       // Draw with vert⇐
centered text.
}


void TForm1::DrawHeartBeatLight(void)
{
    // Draw a little LED style heartbeat indicator. This is just an
    // ellipse with varying fill color.
    TRect Section = CaptionRect;
    int cYCaption = GetSystemMetrics(SM_CYCAPTION);
    if(HeartBeat == true)
      WindowCanvas->Brush->Color = (TColor) RGB(0,255,0); // Bright green
    else
      WindowCanvas->Brush->Color = clBlack;
    WindowCanvas->Pen->Color=clBlack;
    WindowCanvas->Ellipse(Section.Right-cYCaption/2,
                          Section.Top  +cYCaption/4,
                          Section.Right,
                          Section.Bottom-cYCaption/4);
}
```

9. Add this code to the constructor for Form1 in MAINFORM.CPP:

```
__fastcall TForm1::TForm1(TComponent* Owner)
  : TForm(Owner)
{
  CustomCaption = "Custom Caption";
  Caption = "";
  WindowCanvas = new TCanvas;
  // This code determines if we are running on NT3.X.
  TOSVersionInfo ver;
  ver.dwOSVersionInfoSize = sizeof(TOSVersionInfo);
  GetVersionEx( &ver);
  if(ver.dwMajorVersion < 4)
  {
    // If the OS is NT 3.5, the custom caption won't be drawn.
    // Use the Caption property as usual, since the custom
    // caption won't be able to draw the string.
    IsNT35 = true;
    Caption = CustomCaption;
  }
  else
    IsNT35 = false;
}
```

10. The constructor from step 9 creates a **TCanvas** pointer. Stay in **MAINFORM.CPP** and type a destructor for **Form1** that deletes this pointer when the program terminates.

```
__fastcall TForm1::~TForm1(void)
{
  delete WindowCanvas;
  WindowCanvas = 0;  // Zero canvas so CanDrawMyCustomCaption can
                     // block use of an invalid pointer.
}
```

11. Place a **Timer** component on **Form1**. You can find the **Timer** control on the Standard tab of the Component Palette. Set the timer's **Interval** property to 500. Create an **OnTimer** event for the timer component and type in this code to toggle the heart beat and redraw the caption:

```
void __fastcall TForm1::Timer1Timer(TObject *Sender)
{
  HeartBeat = !HeartBeat;
  Perform(WM_NCPAINT,1,0);
}
```

12. The shaded title bar needs to be redrawn when the user sizes the application. Create an **OnResize** handler for **Form1,** and add this code:

```
void __fastcall TForm1::FormResize(TObject *Sender)
{
  Perform(WM_NCPAINT,1,0);
}
```

13. Well, you're done. Compile and test the program.

How It Works

The heart of this example consists of two message-handling functions called **WMNCActivate** and **WMNCPaint**. **WMNCActivate** is smaller, so let's tackle it first.

How **WMNCActivate** Works

Windows sends your application a single **WM_NCACTIVATE** message every time the program activates or de-activates. You receive an activate message when the program starts, when you [Alt]-[Tab] to the program, when you maximize the application by clicking the taskbar icon, or when you click on the window when it's inactive. Likewise, the deactivate message streams in when you [Alt]-[Tab] away from the program, minimize the program, or click on another program on the desktop.

WMNCActivate (step 5) handles **WM_NCACTIVATE** messages for your program. The VCL passes a **TWMNCActivate** structure to the **WMNCActivate** function. The **Active** member of this structure indicates whether the program has been activated or deactivated. If **Active** is **false**, **WMNCActivate** uses **DefWindowProc** to paint

the inactive title bar. When `Active` is `true`, the custom title bar must be painted from scratch. In this case, `WMNCActivate` can let `WMNCPaint` do the work. The code formulates a message and then calls `WMNCPaint` to paint the title bar. `WMNCActivate` calls `WMNCPaint` directly rather than queuing up a message.

NOTE

Windows may ask your application to redraw an inactive caption. For this reason, `WMNCPaint` cannot assume the title bar is an active title bar.

How `WMNCPaint` Works

`WMNCPaint` (step 6) has a handful of work to do. It must draw the menu, the window frame, the border icons, the system menu, the title bar, and the title bar text. This is too much work to go through just to obtain a title bar with custom graphics. For this reason, `WMNCPaint` always calls `DefWindowProc` to handle most of these chores. You can draw your graphics on top of what `DefWindowProc` has done.

The first statement in `WMNCPaint` calls `DefWindowProc`. Next, the code asks the `CanDrawMyCustomCaption` function for permission to draw the custom title bar. `CanDrawMyCustomCaption` (step 7) checks that the application is active, that the window is not too narrow, and a few other things. If any bad conditions exist, the paint function returns, leaving the user with a default caption.

Once `WMNCPaint` decides it is safe to do some drawing, the next step is to obtain a device context (DC) and a canvas to draw on. The `GetWindowDC` API function (step 6) retrieves a DC for the entire window. This code obtains a DC and then assigns that DC to the `WindowCanvas` data member:

```
HDC WindowDC = GetWindowDC(Handle);
WindowCanvas->Handle  = WindowDC;
```

After configuring a canvas to draw on, `WMNCPaint` calls five helper functions to draw the custom title bar. As you can see, the five helper functions (step 8) utilize `GetSystemMetrics` to position the graphics. It's important to use `GetSystemMetrics` rather than hard coded values.

Other Functions

The remaining functions in this How-To aid `WMNCPaint` in some way. The `TForm1` constructor (step 9) creates the `WindowCanvas` pointer, checks for Windows NT 3.5, and wipes out the `Caption` string of the form to prevent flickering during the calls to `DefWindowProc`. The `OnResize` handler (step 12) posts a `WMNCPAINT` message to update the caption after the frame is resized. This ensures that the shading and the heart-beat indicator will realign themselves if the user sizes the form. The `Timer` control and its `OnTimer` handler (step 11) provide a way to toggle the heart-beat light.

Comments

You may notice a slight flicker in the title bar when the heart-beat light toggles. This happens because of the **DefWindowProc** call. **DefWindowProc** completely redraws the caption bar and the system menu. The shading code repaints these regions a second time. The flicker is caused by the default Windows caption appearing on the screen before the shaded black is drawn on top of it. For this reason, you should only draw animated title bar graphics on top of a default title bar instead of a custom shaded bar.

> **TIP**
>
> You may want to investigate the Windows concept of regions if you must draw animated graphics on top of a shaded caption bar without the annoying flicker. Regions would allow you to tell **DefWindowProc** not to paint the shaded portion of the caption bar. The Win32 help contains a section devoted to regions.

This How-To works pretty well, but a few details were left out. First, the title bar should never be without its caption text. Code should be added to draw the caption text under all conditions (inactive caption and narrow window). You can weasel out of this by drawing all of your graphics to the right of the caption text. This would allow you to use the **TForm** caption as you normally do. Second, the title bar's icon is redrawn using a copy of the application's icon. This results in scaling that could be avoided by supplying the application with a 16x16 icon. Lastly, Windows 95 allows users to change the font of the caption bar text. The code in this How-To ignores these settings.

> **TIP**
>
> This How-To painted graphics in the title bar. What if you also wanted to put a control in the title bar? Unfortunately, Windows will not let you place regular controls in the title bar of your program. However, you can create your own control by responding to certain non-client messages. The **WMNCPaint** and **WMNCActivate** functions would paint the control. You would bring the control to life by responding to non-client mouse and hit testing events. To make life easy, the CD-ROM contains a Delphi control that lets you add buttons to the caption bar.

COMPLEXITY
BEGINNING

1.8 How do I...
Ask whether the user really wants to close a form?

Problem

In order to avoid data loss, I want to prompt users for confirmation when they try to exit my application. I want users to have a chance to cancel the action and return to the program. How do I add this simple feature to my C++Builder program?

Technique

OnCloseQuery is the beast you seek. The Object Inspector lists OnCloseQuery as one of the available events for a form. You can create an OnCloseQuery handler function that determines whether or not a form can close. This handler function can prevent a form from closing by setting one of its arguments to false.

Steps

Run CANCLOSE.EXE. A simple editor should appear as shown in Figure 1-8. Try to close the program. A message box should pop up and ask you whether you want to save your changes or not.

> **NOTE**
>
> This How-To only describes how to use OnCloseQuery to ask your users if they want to save their data. The editor does not actually save any files. Check out Chapter 3, "Text Controls," for a demonstration of how to make a fully functional editor.

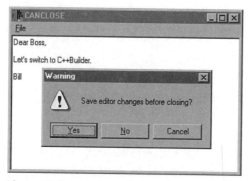

Figure 1-8 CANCLOSE at runtime

1. Create a new project using File|New Application. Click File|Save Project As. Name the unit **MAINFORM.CPP** and name the project **CANCLOSE.MAK**.

2. Place a **RichEdit** control on the form and set its **Align** property to **alClient**. The **RichEdit** control is located on the Win95 tab of the Component Palette.

3. Plop a **MainMenu** component onto the form. Double-click the menu component to launch the Menu Designer. Add a **File** menu item and an **Exit** subitem. Create an **OnClick** handler for the **Exit** menu item, and add this code:

```
void __fastcall TForm1::Exit1Click(TObject *Sender)
{
  Close();
}
```

4. Close the Menu Designer. Select **Form1** into the Object Inspector. Click on the Object Inspector's Events tab. Locate the **OnCloseQuery** item, and double-click next to it. Type this code into the **FormCloseQuery** function that C++Builder constructs for you:

```
void __fastcall TForm1::FormCloseQuery(TObject *Sender, bool &CanClose)
{
  // Add code to determine if editor changes were made.
  // If no changes, set CanClose to true and return.

  int ExitCode = Application->MessageBox("Save editor changes before⇐
closing?",
                                                    "Warning",
MB_YESNOCANCEL|MB_ICONWARNING);
  switch(ExitCode)
  {
    case IDCANCEL:
      CanClose = false; // Don't save and don't exit.
      break;
    case IDYES:
      CanClose = true;   //Add code for saving.
      break;
    case IDNO:
      CanClose = true;   // Skip the saving and just close.
      break;
  }
}
```

5. Compile and test the program.

How It Works

The **OnClick** handler for the **Exit** menu item (step 3) calls the VCL function **TForm::Close**. **Close** doesn't just close the form on its own. It asks the **OnCloseQuery** handler for permission first. The **OnCloseQuery** handler function

(step 4) must approve before the program can exit. `FormCloseQuery` executes when you choose File|Exit or when you click on the close icon in the program's title bar. The form will not close if `FormCloseQuery` sets `CanClose` to `false`. Setting `CanClose` to `true` allows the program to close, but it's up to you to save changes before `FormCloseQuery` returns.

> **NOTE**
>
> See what happens when you change the `Close` call in step 3 to `Application->Terminate()`. `Terminate` provides a suicidal way to close a program.

Comments

This How-To demonstrates a simple task that many Windows programs utilize. The `OnCloseQuery` handler will probably find its way into many of your programs.

COMPLEXITY
BEGINNING

1.9 How do I...
Show a splash screen when the program starts?

Problem

Professional-looking applications display a cool splash screen when they start. These splash screens often display company logos, copyright notices, program information, and registration terms. How can I add a splash screen to my C++Builder application?

Technique

Splash screens are nothing more than decorated forms that respond to timer events. The `WinMain` function can launch the splash screen when the program starts. The splash screen closes itself after a timer expires.

Steps

Execute `SPLASH.EXE`. A splash screen should appear that contains a picture. Figure 1-9 shows the program during start up. The splash screen should close after a couple of seconds.

1. Create a new project. Save the unit as `MAINFORM.CPP` and save the project as `SPLASH.MAK`.

Figure 1-9 SPLASH at startup

2. Add a menu to **Form1** using the **MainMenu** tool. Double-click the menu component and use the Menu Designer to create a **File** menu item and an **Exit** subitem. Create an **OnClick** event handler for the **Exit** subitem. Insert a call to **Close** in the new handler function. Close the Menu Designer when you're finished.

```
void __fastcall TForm1::Exit1Click(TObject *Sender)
{
   Close();
}
```

3. Add a second form to the project using File|New Form and save it as **SPLASHFORM.CPP**. This form, **Form2**, will be the splash screen.

4. By default, C++Builder programs automatically create their forms during start up. These form objects exist for the duration of the program. This process is called auto-creation. It is wasteful to auto-create the splash form because it will only be displayed for an instant. Choose Options|Project and remove **Form2** from the auto-creation list.

5. Place an Image control and a Timer control on **Form2**. The Image control resides on the Additional tab of the Component Palette. The Timer control can be found on the System tab. Set properties to match Table 1-6.

NOTE

The **Interval** value of **Timer1** sets the splash time in milliseconds. Vary this value to suit your needs.

Table 1-6 Components, properties, and settings for `Form2` in the SPLASH project

COMPONENT	PROPERTY	SETTING
Form2	BorderIcons	(all false)
	BorderStyle	bsDialog
	FormStyle	fsStayOnTop
	Position	poScreenCenter
Image1	Align	alClient
	Stretch	true
Timer1	Interval	4000

6. Double-click on the image component to activate the Picture Editor. The Picture Editor allows you to load a picture into the image. Click the Load button and locate a bitmap file. This How-To uses the **CHEMCIAL.BMP** picture provided with C++Builder. Select this file or a bitmap file of your choice.

TIP

C++Builder provides a handful of cool bitmaps. You can find these in the IMAGES\SPLASH subdirectory of C++Builder.

7. Create an `OnTimer` handler for the Timer control on `Form2`. This handler closes the splash screen when the timer expires.

```
void __fastcall TForm2::Timer1Timer(TObject *Sender)
{
  Close();
}
```

8. Open **SPLASHFORM.H** and add a `CreateParams` function prototype to the `TForm2` class.

```
private:   // User declarations
  void __fastcall CreateParams(TCreateParams &Params);
```

9. Most splash screens do not contain a caption bar. The `CreateParams` function allows you to remove the caption at runtime by modifying the window's style of the form. Use the Code Editor to enter the `CreateParams` function into **SPLASHFORM.CPP**.

```
void __fastcall TForm2::CreateParams(TCreateParams &Params)
{
  TForm::CreateParams(Params);  // Call base class first,
  Params.Style &= ~WS_CAPTION;  // then remove the caption.
}
```

> **NOTE**
>
> Steps 8 and 9 remove the caption bar from the splash screen. You could also remove the caption bar by setting the splash form's BorderStyle property to bsNone, but this would also remove the form's border. Many splash screens, including the C++Builder splash screen, use this borderless approach.

10. The splash screen can now be activated by the application. Open SPLASH.CPP, and modify the WinMain function to display the splash screen when the program starts.

> **TIP**
>
> You can quickly access the WinMain function by selecting View|Project Source from the C++Builder menu.

```
WINAPI WinMain(HINSTANCE, HINSTANCE, LPSTR, int)
{
  try
  {
    Application->Initialize();
    Form2=new TForm2(Application);
    Form2->Show();              // Show splash screen now.
    Form2->Update();            // Paint splash screen now.
    Application->CreateForm(__classid(TForm1), &Form1);
    Application->Run();
  }
  catch (Exception &exception)
  {
    Application->ShowException(&exception);
  }
  return 0;
}
```

11. The WinMain function cannot call Form2->Show without seeing the class declaration for TForm2. Stay in SPLASH.CPP, and add a #include for the TForm2 header file.

```
#include <vcl\vcl.h>
#pragma hdrstop
#include "SPLASHFORM.H"
```

12. Somebody needs to delete the Form2 pointer after the splash screen closes. The easiest way to do this is by using the Action argument of the form's OnClose handler. The VCL will automatically delete a form object if the OnClose handler sets Action to caFree. Create an OnClose handler for Form2, and insert this code:

> **TIP**
>
> Make sure the OnClose handler is for Form2, the splash screen form.

```
void __fastcall TForm2::FormClose(TObject *Sender, TCloseAction &Action)
{
  Action = caFree;
};
```

13. Compile and test the program.

How It Works

C++Builder generates a WinMain function that contains code for constructing a program's forms. WinMain normally calls Application->Run after the forms have been created. Run displays the main form in addition to doing tons of other stuff.

The splash screen can be displayed by creating the Form2 pointer and calling Form2->Show just before Form1 is created (step 10). Show displays the splash screen nonmodally, which allows the main application form to appear behind the splash screen. Form2->Update paints the splash screen immediately before the next statement executes. The main form will appear while the splash screen is displayed. The splash screen stays on top because you set its FormStyle property to fsStayOnTop (step 5).

The splash screen must decide when to close itself. It handles this task by looking for the timer to expire. Form2 calls Close as soon as a timer event occurs (step 7).

Comments

You can add static text components to the splash screen that display the program's name, version number, copyright date, and of course, the program's author. Because splash screens are just forms, you can utilize any C++Builder component that suits your needs.

Sometimes you might not want the splash screen to close so easily. For example, you might want to display a shareware notice that requires the user to click an Accept button. To add this nagging feature:

✔ Remove the timer component and its event handler function from Form2.

✔ Place a push button on Form2 and add the Close function to its OnClick handler.

Additionally, you could replace the Show and Update calls in step 10 with a single ShowModal call. This would force the user to acknowledge the splash screen before your main form appears.

1.10 How do I...
Display my own modal dialog box?

Problem

Standard C++ compilers use resource files (*.RC) to hold the resource script of a dialog box. I don't see any mention of RC files in C++Builder. How do I create a dialog box for my application?

Technique

Every window is a form in C++Builder. You create a dialog box just as you create any other form. You simply change a few properties of the form to get the appearance of a dialog box. You invoke the dialog using **TForm::ShowModal**. **ShowModal** returns an integer value that describes how the dialog form was closed.

> **NOTE**
>
> You don't use RC files to create dialog boxes in C++Builder because forms offer a much simpler approach. This does not mean that you can't use resource files in your projects. Chapter 4, "Mouse and Menu," and Chapter 5, "Graphics," contain How-To's that use compiled resource files to store bitmaps, icons, and cursors.

Steps

Run **MODAL.EXE**. Push the Options button to show a modal dialog for manipulating program settings. Figure 1-10 shows the dialog box. Note that the dialog acts like a standard windows dialog. Modify some of the controls and click the OK button. The data in the main form updates when the dialog closes. Repeat this step again, but this time, use the Cancel button to close the dialog. Observe that the data in the main form remains unchanged.

1. Create a new project by selecting File|New Application. Name the unit **MAINFORM.CPP** and name the project **MODAL.MAK**.

2. Add a second form to the project and name its unit **DIALOGFORM.CPP**. Change the **Name** property of the new form to **DLGForm**.

3. Place controls on **DLGForm** using the dialog box in Figure 1-10 as a layout guideline. Allow C++Builder to automatically name the controls. Change properties to match Table 1-7.

Table 1-7 Components, properties, and settings for **DLGForm** in the **MODAL** project

COMPONENT	PROPERTY	SETTING
DLGForm	BorderIcons	[] (all false)
	BorderStyle	bsDialog
Edit1	Text	""
CheckBox1	Caption	Standard Checkbox
RadioGroup1	Caption	Radio Group
	Items (strings)	Radio 0, Radio 1, Radio 2
ListBox1	Items (strings)	item 0, item 1,...,item 9
ComboBox1	Items (strings)	cb item 0,...,cb item 4
	Style	csDropDownList
BitBtn1	Kind	bkOK
	ModalResult	mrOk
BitBtn2	Kind	bkCancel
	ModalResult	mrCancel

NOTE

When you enter the strings for ListBox1, place each item on its own line. The String List Editor should contain 10 entries when you're done. Similarly, enter the 5 items for ComboBox1 on separate lines too.

4. Add **Label** controls and a **Button** control to **Form1** so it matches Figure 1-11 at design time. The labels along the left half of the form will not change as the program runs, so they use the names that C++Builder gives them (**Label2**, **Label3**, etc). The labels along the right half of the form will change according to the dialog settings. Change the **Name** property of these labels to match the names shown in Figure 1-11 (**EditValue**, **CheckValue**, etc). Table 1-8 lists the controls for **Form1**.

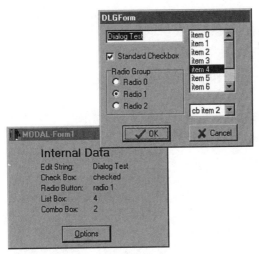

Figure 1-10 MODAL at runtime

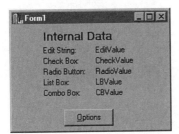

Figure 1-11 Form1 at design
time

Table 1-8 Components, properties, and settings for Form1 in the MODAL
project

COMPONENT	PROPERTY	SETTING
Form1		
Label1	Caption	Internal Date:
Label2	Caption	Edit String:
Label3	Caption	Check Box:
Label4	Caption	Radio Button:
Label5	Caption	List Box:
Label6	Caption	Combo Box:
EditValue (Label)		
CheckValue (Label)		
RadioValue (Label)		

COMPONENT	PROPERTY	SETTING
LBValue (Label)		
CBValue (Label)		
Button1	Caption	Options

5. You may want to save memory resources by dynamically creating and destroying the dialog box as you need it. If so, choose Options|Projects and remove **DLGForm** from the project's auto-creation list. Skip this step if you would rather have your dialog box created automatically by **WinMain** when the program starts.

6. Double-click on the push button in **Form1** and add this **OnClick** event handler. You should call **new** and **delete** only if you removed **DLGForm** from the project's auto-creation list in step 5.

```
void __fastcall TForm1::Button1Click(TObject *Sender)
{
   // New DLGForm only if you removed it from the auto-creation list.
   DLGForm = new TDLGForm(Application);

   InitializeDialogValues();
   int ReturnCode = DLGForm->ShowModal();

   if (ReturnCode == mrOk)
     CopyDialogValues();

   // Delete DLGForm only if you removed it from the auto-creation list.
   delete DLGForm;
}
```

7. Form1 needs to see the class prototype for **DLGForm**. Type this **#include** in **MAINFORM.CPP**:

```
#include <vcl\vcl.h>
#pragma hdrstop

#include "MAINFORM.h"
#include "DIALOGFORM.H"
```

8. The main form needs some type of data that the dialog box can modify. Add these declarations to the **TForm1** class in **MAINFORM.H**. **TForm1** also needs prototypes for the two helper functions used in step 6. The **TForm1** class should look like this when you finish this step:

```
class TForm1 : public TForm
{
__published: // IDE-managed Components
   TLabel *Label1;
   TLabel *Label2;
   TLabel *Label3;
```

continued on next page

continued from previous page

```
  TLabel *Label4;
  TLabel *Label5;
  TLabel *Label6;
  TLabel *EditValue;
  TLabel *CheckValue;
  TLabel *RadioValue;
  TLabel *LBValue;
  TLabel *CBValue;
  TButton *Button1;
  void __fastcall Button1Click(TObject *Sender);
private:  // User declarations
  bool CheckState;          // Bool data
  int  RadioSelection;      // Radio type data
  int  LBIndex;              // Two index forms of data.
  int  CBIndex;
  void InitializeDialogValues(void);  // 2 pvt: functions for
  void CopyDialogValues(void);          // manipulating dlg form.
public:  // User declarations
  virtual __fastcall TForm1(TComponent* Owner);
};
```

9. Now add the function bodies for the two helper functions to
MAINFORM.CPP. InitializeDialogValues copies data from the private
data members of TForm1 to the dialog controls in DLGForm.
CopyDialogValues moves data in the opposite direction and updates the
value labels.

```
void TForm1::InitializeDialogValues(void)
{
  DLGForm->Edit1->Text           = EditValue->Caption;
  DLGForm->CheckBox1->Checked    = CheckState;
  DLGForm->RadioGroup1->ItemIndex = RadioSelection;
  DLGForm->ListBox1->ItemIndex   = LBIndex;
  DLGForm->ComboBox1->ItemIndex  = CBIndex;
}


void TForm1::CopyDialogValues(void)
{
  EditValue->Caption = DLGForm->Edit1->Text;
  CheckState         = DLGForm->CheckBox1->Checked;
  RadioSelection     = DLGForm->RadioGroup1->ItemIndex;
  LBIndex            = DLGForm->ListBox1->ItemIndex;
  CBIndex            = DLGForm->ComboBox1->ItemIndex;

  if (CheckState == true)
    CheckValue->Caption = "checked";
  else
    CheckValue->Caption = "unchecked";

  RadioValue->Caption = AnsiString("radio ") + AnsiString(RadioSelection);
  LBValue->Caption    = AnsiString(LBIndex);
  CBValue->Caption    = AnsiString(CBIndex);
}
```

10. The data members and the captions for the value labels need to be initialized. Change the `TForm1` constructor in `MAINFORM.CPP` to initialize these variables.

```
__fastcall TForm1::TForm1(TComponent* Owner)
    : TForm(Owner),
      CheckState(false),
      RadioSelection(0),
      LBIndex(0),
      CBIndex(0)
{
  EditValue ->Caption = "";
  CheckValue->Caption = "unchecked";
  RadioValue->Caption = "radio 0";
  LBValue    ->Caption = "0";
  CBValue    ->Caption = "0";
}
```

11. Compile and test the program.

How It Works

The heart of this How-To lies within the `Button1Click` handler function of `TForm1` (step 6). The call to `InitializeDialogValues` copies data from the private data variables into the controls of `DLGForm`. `Form1` can access `DLGForm`'s controls because IDE-managed controls use the `published` scope, which is similar to `public`. `ShowModal` displays the dialog after `DLGForm`'s controls have been configured.

`DLGForm`'s OK and Cancel buttons each have a `ModalResult` property, which can be set using the Object Inspector. `ShowModal` returns the `ModalResult` of the button that is pressed. The `ShowModal` result can be decoded to see if the user wants to save any changes that were made. If the result was `mrOk`, `Form1` calls `CopyDialogValues` to retrieve the new settings.

Comments

The `ModalResult` property of a component determines the return value of `ShowModal`. Set a button's `ModalResult` to `mrNone` if the dialog should remain open when the button is pressed.

Many Windows 95 applications combine separate dialogs into one multipaged dialog using a tab control. C++Builder encapsulates multipage dialogs using the `TabControl` and `PageControl` components. Chapter 2, "Standard Components and Classes," contains a How-To that describes how you can use a multipage form in your application.

STANDARD COMPONENTS AND CLASSES

2

STANDARD
COMPONENTS AND
CLASSES

How do I...

The How-To's in this chapter demonstrate how to use some of the basic VCL classes and controls and how to overcome some of their limitations. Some of these control classes will be used on other How-To's. In fact, the `AnsiString` class, described in 2.1, is used in every How-To.

2.1 Use the `String` Class

Most applications need to manipulate strings. VCL uses a `String` class rather than a null-terminated `char` array to represent strings. This How-To demonstrates the most important features of the `String` class.

2.2 Use Properties with `Set` Values

Many components in VCL have properties with values that are Sets. Sets are implemented as template classes in VCL. This How-To shows how to use `Set` properties in an application.

2.3 Create a Combo Box That Best Matches User Input

Applications such as Quicken use Combo boxes that search for the drop-down list item that best matches the input as the types in keystrokes. This How-To shows how you can implement this behavior using a TComboBox control.

2.4 Use Drag-and-Drop to Move Items from One List Box to Another

For many types of applications, dragging and dropping elements is a way to build an intuitive user interface. Most VCL controls have support for drag-and-drop built into them. This application demonstrates how to use VCL controls to implement drag-and-drop.

2.5 Add a Horizontal Scroll Bar to a List Box

The TListBox control does not automatically create a horizontal scroll bar when the text in the list is too wide to be displayed, nor does it have a property to allow your application to specify when a scroll bar is to be displayed. This How-To shows how to use the Windows API to make the scroll bar display a horizontal scroll bar.

2.6 Add Images to a List Box

Some applications display graphics as well as text within a list box. The standard font dialog box uses a list box graphic to mark TrueType fonts. This How-To uses the built-in capabilities of the TListBox control to draw graphics and text.

2.7 Create a Windows 95–Style Scroll Bar

Windows 95 introduced a variable sized scroll box to the scroll bar control. The size of the scroll box gives the user a visual clue as to the amount of data that is hidden. The VCL TScrollBar control only displays a fixed sized scroll box. This How-To uses the Windows API to change the size of the scroll box in a TScrollBar control.

2.8 Create a Multipage Dialog Box

When an application requires a user to enter data into a dialog box in a particular order, it is a good idea to create a multipage dialog. This How-To shows how to use the `TPageControl` class to create a multipage dialog.

2.9 Create a Multipanel Status Bar

Applications such as Microsoft Word use a status bar with multiple panels to display the state of the application. This How-To uses the TPanel control to create a similar status bar.

2.1 How do I...
Use the String **class?**

COMPLEXITY
BEGINNING

Problem

I have programmed in C for many years but one of the things causing me to have a hard time making the transition to C++Builder™ is figuring out how to use the String class that all the VCL controls use. How do I use a String variable and how do I translate it to a traditional C string?

Technique

For this How-To you will create a simple application that uses many of the features of the AnsiString class.

Steps

Run the **ANSISTRING.EXE** program shown in Figure 2-1. Each tab on the main form demonstrates one or more of the major functions of the String class. Try the functions on each tab and then look at the code to see how each feature is implemented.

1. Select File|New Application from the main menu to create a new blank project. Select File|Save Project As and save the project as AnsiString.

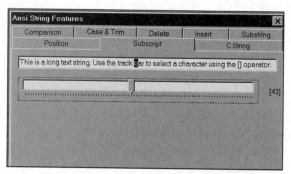

Figure 2-1 AnsiString **program**

2. Place a Page control on the main form. Click with the right mouse button over the page control to display the context menu and select New Page. Repeat this process to create eight Tab pages.

3. Add the properties and settings as shown in Table 2-1. The controls follow the Tab page they are to be placed on.

Table 2-1 Components, properties, and settings for `AnsiString`

COMPONENT	PROPERTY	SETTING
Form1	BorderStyle	bsDialog
	Caption	Ansi String Features
	Height	300
	Position	poDefaultPosOnly
	Width	540
PageControl1	Align	alClient
	MultiLine	True
TabSheet1	Caption	Comparison
Label1	Caption	A
	Left	10
	Top	14
Label2	Caption	B
	Left	10
	Top	44
Label3	Caption	Enter text and click Compare.
	Left	340
	Top	10
Edit1	Height	24
	Left	30
	Text	
	Top	10
	Width	200
Edit2	Height	24
	Left	30
	Text	
	Top	40
	Width	200
Button1	Caption	Compare
	Height	25
	Left	440

COMPONENT	PROPERTY	SETTING
	Top	184
	Width	75
Panel1	BevelOuter	bvLowered
	Caption	
	Height	130
	Left	30
	Top	70
	Width	130
Label4 (On Panel1)	Caption	
	Left	8
	Top	8
TabSheet2	Caption	Case && Trim
Label5	Caption	Enter text and click Format.
	Left	360
	Top	10
Edit3	Height	24
	Left	10
	Text	
	Top	10
	Width	300
Button2	Caption	Format
	Height	25
	Left	440
	Top	184
	Width	75
Panel2	BevelOuter	bvLowered
	Caption	
	Height	100
	Left	10
	Top	40
	Width	300
Label6 (On Panel2)	Caption	
	Left	2
	Top	2
TabSheet3	Caption	Delete
Label7	Caption	Text

continued on next page

continued from previous page

COMPONENT	PROPERTY	SETTING
	Left	10
	Top	16
Label8	Caption	1. Enter some text.
	Left	300
	Top	10
Label9	Caption	2. Select the text you want to delete.
	Left	300
	Top	30
Label10	Caption	3. Click on the Delete button.
	Left	300
	Top	50
Edit4	Height	24
	Left	50
	Text	
	Top	10
	Width	225
Button3	Caption	Delete
	Height	25
	Left	440
	Top	184
	Width	75
TabSheet4	Caption	Insert
Label11	Caption	Text
	Left	10
	Top	10
Label12	Caption	String To Insert
	Left	10
	Top	40
Label13	Caption	1. Enter text into both edit boxes.
	Left	10
	Top	145
Label14	Caption	2. Use the mouse to select the insert point in the first edit box.
	Left	10

COMPONENT	PROPERTY	SETTING
	Top	165
Label15	Caption	3. Click on the Insert button.
	Left	10
	Top	185
Edit5	Height	24
	HideSelection	False
	Left	105
	Text	
	Top	10
	Width	265Edit6
	Height	24
	Left	105
	Text	
	Top	40
	Width	265
Button4	Caption	Insert
	Height	25
	Left	440
	Top	184
	Width	75
TabSheet5	Caption	Substring
Label16	Caption	1. Enter some text in the edit box.
	Left	260
	Top	10
Label17	Caption	2. Select the substring to extract with the mouse.
	Left	240
	Top	30
Label18	Caption	3. Click on the Extract button.
	Left	240
	Top	50
Edit7	Height	24
	HideSelection	False
	Left	10

continued on next page

continued from previous page

COMPONENT	PROPERTY	SETTING
	Text	
	Top	10
	Width	190
Button5	Caption	Extract
	Height	25
	Left	440
	Top	184
	Width	75
Panel3	BevelOuter	bvLowered
	Caption	
	Height	25
	Left	10
	Top	10
	Width	190
TabSheet6	Caption	Position
Label19	Caption	Text
	Left	10
	Top	14
Label20	Caption	Search String
	Left	10
	Top	44
Label21	Caption	1. Enter a text string and the string to search for.
	Left	250
	Top	10
Label22	Caption	2. Click on the Position button.
	Left	250
	Top	30
Button6	Caption	Position
	Height	25
	Left	440
	Top	184
	Width	75
Panel4	BevelOuter	bvLowered
	Caption	

COMPONENT	PROPERTY	SETTING
	Height	40
	Left	10
	Top	90
	Width	215
Edit8	AutoSelect	False
	Height	24
	HideSelection	False
	Left	105
	Text	
	Top	10
	Width	120
Edit9	Height	24
	Left	105
	Text	
	Top	40
	Width	120
TabSheet7	Caption	Subscript
Label23	Caption	---
	Left	500
	Top	64
Edit10	AutoSelect	False
	Height	24
	HideSelection	False
	Left	10
	ReadOnly	True
	Text	This is a long text string. Use the track bar to select a character using the [] operator.
	Top	10
	Width	505
TrackBar1	Height	45
	Left	10
	Min	1
	Top	50
	Width	470

continued on next page

continued from previous page

COMPONENT	PROPERTY	SETTING
TabSheet8	Caption	C String
Label24	Caption	A
	Left	10
	Top	14
Label25	Caption	B
	Left	10
	Top	44
Label26	Caption	Enter two strings; then click on Format.
	Height	16
	Left	290
	Top	10
	Width	225
Panel5	BevelOuter	bvLowered
	Caption	
	Height	40
	Left	30
	Top	72
	Width	250
Label27(On Panel5)	Caption	
	Left	8
	Top	8
Edit11	Height	24
	Left	30
	Text	
	Top	10
	Width	120
Edit12	Height	24
	Left	30
	Top	40
	Width	120
Button7	Caption	Format
	Height	25
	Left	440
	Top	184
	Width	75

4. Go to the application's main form and double-click on the Compare button on the "Compare" Tab Sheet to create an `OnClick` event handler for it. Add the following code to the handler in the Code Editor:

```
void __fastcall TForm1::Button1Click(TObject *Sender)
{
  // Demonstration of String Comparison Operators
  String logical [2] = { "False", "True" } ;
  String A = Edit1->Text, B = Edit2->Text ;

  Label4->Caption = "A == B " + logical [A == B] + "\n"
              + "A != B " + logical [A != B] + "\n"
              + "A > B " + logical [A > B] + "\n"
              + "A >= B " + logical [A >= B] + "\n"
              + "A < B " + logical [A < B] + "\n"
              + "A <= B " + logical [A <= B] + "\n"
              ;
}
```

5. Go to the Case & Trim Tab Sheet on the main form and double-click on the Format button. Add the following code to the `OnClick` event handler in the Code Editor:

```
void __fastcall TForm1::Button2Click(TObject *Sender)
{
  // Demonstration of String Case Conversion and Trim Functions.
  String text = Edit3->Text ;
  Label6->Caption = "Uppercase\t= '" + text.UpperCase () + "'" + "\n"
              + "Lowercase\t= '" + text.LowerCase () + "'" + "\n"
              + "Trim    \t\t= '" + text.Trim () + "'" + "\n"
              + "TrimLeft\t\t= '" + text.TrimLeft () + "'" + "\n"
              + "TrimRight\t= '" + text.TrimRight () + "'" + "\n"
              ;
}
```

6. Select the Delete Tab Sheet and double-click on the Delete button. Modify the `OnClick` handler for the button so that it looks like this:

```
void __fastcall TForm1::Button3Click(TObject *Sender)
{
  // Delete Substring
  String text = Edit4->Text ;
  text.Delete (Edit4->SelStart + 1, Edit4->SelLength) ;
  Edit4->Text = text ;
}
```

7. On the Insert Tab Sheet double-click on the Insert button and add the following in the Code Editor:

```
void __fastcall TForm1::Button4Click(TObject *Sender)
{
  // Insert Substring
  String text = Edit5->Text ;
  String inserttext = Edit6->Text ;
  text.Insert (inserttext, Edit5->SelStart + 1) ;
  Edit5->Text = text ;
}
```

8. On the Substring Tab Sheet double-click on the Extract button and modify the OnClick event to look like this:

```
void __fastcall TForm1::Button5Click(TObject *Sender)
{
  // Substring Function
  String text = Edit7->Text ;
  Panel3->Caption = text.SubString (Edit7->SelStart + 1, Edit7->SelLength)⇐
;
}
```

9. Switch to the Substring Tab Sheet, double-click on the Position button, and add the following code to the OnClick event handler:

```
void __fastcall TForm1::Button6Click(TObject *Sender)
{
  // Pos (Search for Substring) String function
  String text = Edit8->Text ;
  int position = text.Pos (Edit9->Text) ;
  if (position != 0)
  {
    Edit8->SelStart = position - 1 ;
    Edit8->SelLength = Edit9->Text.Length () ;
    Panel4->Caption = "Position " + String (position) ;
  }
  else
  {
    Edit8->SelLength = 0 ;
    Panel4->Caption = "Not Found" ;
  }
}
```

10. Click on the Subscript Tab Sheet; then double-click on the Track Bar. In the Code Editor add this code to the OnChange event:

```
void __fastcall TForm1::TrackBar1Change(TObject *Sender)
{
  // [] String operator
  String text = Edit10->Text ;
  if (text != "")
  {
    TrackBar1->Max = Edit10->Text.Length () ;
    TrackBar1->Enabled = true ;
    Label23->Caption = "[" + String (TrackBar1->Position) + "] = '"
                     + String (text [TrackBar1->Position]) + "'" ;
    Edit10->SelStart = TrackBar1->Position - 1 ;
    Edit10->SelLength = 1 ;
  }
  else
  {
    TrackBar1->Enabled = false ;
    Label23->Caption = "(Null)" ;
    Edit10->SelLength = 0 ;
  }
}
```

11. Go to the C String Tab Sheet, double-click on the Format button, and add
the following to the OnClick event handler:

```
void __fastcall TForm1::Button7Click(TObject *Sender)
{
  // Using Ansi Strings as C Strings
  String buffer ;
  buffer.SetLength (512) ;
  int length = sprintf (buffer.c_str (), "'%s' + '%s' = '%s'",
                        Edit11->Text.c_str (),
                        Edit12->Text.c_str (),
                        (Edit11->Text + Edit12->Text).c_str ()) ;
  buffer.SetLength (length) ;
  Label27->Caption = buffer ;
}
```

12. Select the Page Control with the mouse by clicking on any of the tabs.
Press F11 to display the Object Inspector. Go to the Events page and
double-click on the OnEnter event. Add the following to the event handler
in the Code Editor:

```
void __fastcall TForm1::PageControl1Enter(TObject *Sender)
{
  TrackBar1Change (Sender) ;
}
```

13. Compile and test the project.

How It Works

Unlike most other programming languages in widespread use, C and C++ do not
have a string data type. In C, character strings are simply arrays of bytes and there
are no string operators such as concatenation and substring extraction. In C, string
manipulations have to be implemented in library functions. Using them is error-prone
and handling dynamic strings is difficult. Though the C++ language has no built-
in string support, it is possible to create string classes that are defined so that they
behave in a manner similar to strings in other programming languages. The VCL library
defines an AnsiString class that makes it simple to manipulate dynamic strings.
In the file SYSDEFS.H, String is typedef'ed as AnsiString. Defining the String
type this way makes it easier to switch to multibyte character sets. For this discus-
sion the two will be considered as one and the same.

The representation of a string in the AnsiString class is considerably different
from that of a C/C++ string. A native C/C++ string is represented simply as a byte
array of characters with a null byte marking the end of the string. There is no built-
in way for the string to grow once it is created and the standard library functions
are unable to manipulate a string that contains embedded null characters.

The `AnsiString` class contains a pointer to a record that holds the actual string. The main components of this record are the text of the string, the length of the string, and a reference count for the record. By using a pointer to the string data, it is possible for more than one `AnsiString` object to reference the exact same string. A comparison of the two string representations is shown in Figure 2-2.

So why would you want to have more than one `string` variable reference the same string record? The answer is that each string that gets created requires memory to be allocated from the heap. When you assign one `AnsiString` variable to another, all that happens is the string record's reference count gets incremented and the destination variable gets a pointer to the record. No additional memory needs to be allocated for an additional copy of the string.

Several constructors are used for the `AnsiString` class. The most useful `AnsiString` constructors are shown in Table 2-2. The constructors with `int` and `double` arguments are useful for converting these types in string expressions.

Table 2-2 Important `AnsiString` constructors

CONSTRUCTOR	FUNCTION
`AnsiString(const char* src);`	Converts a C string to an `AnsiString`
`AnsiString(char src);`	Creates a one character string
`AnsiString(int src);`	Converts an integer to a string
`AnsiString(double src);`	Converts a double to a string

The `AnsiString` class defines a number of operators and number functions to make manipulating a string simple. Table 2-3 lists the important operators and functions of the `AnsiString` class along with the corresponding standard C library function. Most of these functions are used in the `AnsiString` application.

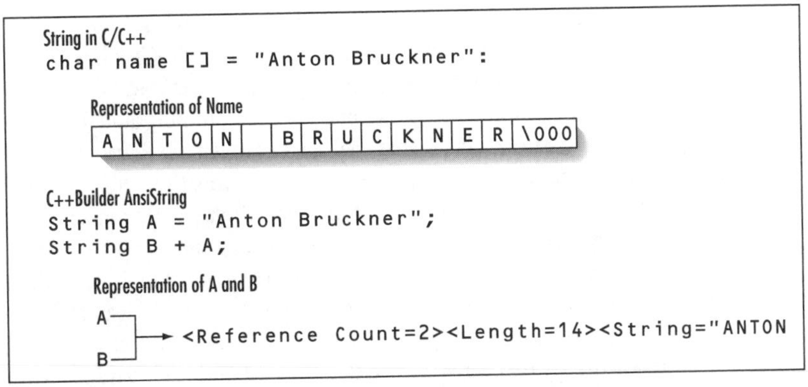

Figure 2-2 `AnsiString` and C string representations

Table 2-3 Common AnsiString member functions and operators

FUNCTION	DESCRIPTION	C LIBRARY EQUIVALENT
=	Assignment	strcpy
+=	Concatenation	strcat
+	Concatenation	None
==, !=, <, <=, >, >=	Comparison	strcmp
[]	Character reference	[] operator
c_str	Conversion to C-style string	None
Delete	Remove a substring	None
Insert	Insert a substring	None
Length	String length	strlen
LowerCase	Convert to all lowercase	strlwr
Pos	Search for a substring	strstr
SetLength	Set string length	None
SubString	Extract a substring	None
ToInt	Convert to integer	sprintf
ToDouble	Convert to double	sprintf
Unique	Make string unique	None
UpperCase	Convert to all uppercase	strupr

The Comparison Tab Sheet of the AnsiString application demonstrates how to compare AnsiString objects to one another. The AnsiString class defines the same six comparison operators (==, !=, <, <=, > and >=) that are defined for numeric expressions, and their behavior is equivalent to the standard strcmp function.

On the Case & Trim Tab Sheet, the OnClick event handler for the button uses some of the basic edit functions defined in the AnsiString class. The UpperCase and LowerCase member functions return a case-converted copy of the string. The TrimLeft and TrimRight member functions return a string, with leading or trailing spaces and characters removed respectively, while the Trim member removes spaces from both ends of the string. Keep in mind that these functions return a copy of the object's string. This statement:

```
MyString.UpperCase () ;
```

does not change the value of the object MyString. To convert a string to uppercase, you would have to use

```
MyString = MyString.UpperCase () ;
```

The Delete, Insert, Substring, and Position Tab Sheets demonstrate substring features of the AnsiString object. There are a couple of things to keep in mind when working with substrings of the AnsiString class. First, the AnsiString class considers the start of the string to be at position one in contrast to a C/C++ string where

the first position is zero. The other thing to be aware of is that, unlike the behavior of strings in some other C++ class libraries, you cannot update a string by assigning a value to a substring. The C++Builder compiler will accept an expression like this:

```
MyString.SubString (2, 4) = "Fred" ;
```

However, the value of **MyString** will not be changed. The value of the temporary substring gets updated, then discarded.

The "Subscript" Tab page has an example using the **[]** operator. The **[]** operator is used to access individual characters within a string. Unlike **char** arrays, the index of the first character position with the **[]** operator is one, just like all the other **AnsiString** operators.

Watch out for possible unexpected side effects of the **[]** operator. Remember that when you assign the value of one string to another, only one copy of the string is kept and both strings reference the same string. If **A** and **B** are string variables and you have a code sequence like

```
A = "1YZ ;
B = A ;
B [1] = 'X' ;
```

then not only does **B** == "XYZ" but **A** == "XYZ" as well. The substring member functions (such as **Delete** and **Insert**) make a new copy of the string value but the **[]** does not. The solution to this problem is to call the **Unique** member function before using the **[]** operator to assign a value to a character in a string. The **Unique** function ensures that a **String** variable is the only reference to a particular string record. If you do this instead

```
A = "1YZ ;
B = A ;
B.Unique () ;
B [1] = 'X' ;
```

then **B** == "XYZ" and **A** is still "1YX".

The **OnClick** handler for the button on the last tab sheet demonstrates how you can use an **AnsiString** with functions that expect a C-style string. The **c_str** member function returns a pointer to the actual string data referenced by a String expression. This data has an extra null terminator so you can use it anywhere you would use a C-style string, such as in a call to a C library or Win32 API function.

When you call the **c_str** function to use an **AnsiString** variable in a call to a standard library function, the length of the string does not change. You have to use the **SetLength** member function to adjust the length of the string. Otherwise, whatever characters happen to be in the string's buffer following the null character are still part of the string. In this example, the return value from **sprintf**, the number of bytes stored in the string, is used in a second call to **SetLength**. Without the call to **SetLength**, the length of the string in the variable **buffer** will remain at **512** with the characters at the end of the string having unpredictable values.

When you use the `c_str` function, you need to use the same precautions as when using the `[]` operator. Whenever you call `c_str`, you should ensure that a call to the `Unique` function is not needed first.

Comments

You have probably noticed that in this application temporary variables are used frequently rather than updating string property values directly. When you use a property in an expression, you are actually using a copy of the property's value, which can produce unexpected results. An expression like

```
Edit1->Text += "suffix" ;
```

appears to append the string `"suffix"` to the value of `Edit1`'s text property value. In actuality, this expression fetches the value of the `Text` property into a temporary, appends `"suffix"` to it, and then discards the value.

Though it is easy to change string values from `AnsiString` to C string format, it is a good practice to stick with one style or another. For user interface code that uses VCL objects, use the `AnsiString` type consistently and avoid using C-style strings and standard library functions. If you have other code modules that use C-style strings, do not mix in `AnsiStrings` as well. Only convert between string formats to have one part of the code call another.

COMPLEXITY
BEGINNING

2.2 How do I...
Use properties with Set values?

Problem

Many VCL objects have properties whose values are `Set`s. These are easy to use in design mode but when I update a set property value at runtime, I get unpredictable results.

Technique

In this How-To you will create a simple application that updates the `Options` property of a String Grid. This property is implemented as a `Set` and is typical of `Set` properties throughout VCL.

Steps

Run the program `SETS.EXE`. The `TStringGrid` class defines a `Set` property called `Options` that changes the appearance of the grid. Below each of the first two grids on this application is a pair of check boxes that update the `Options` property with values that control whether the grid displays horizontal or vertical lines. See what

happens when the values in these check boxes are changed. Under the third string grid there are buttons labeled Or and And. Clicking on one of these buttons updates the Options property of the third grid using the logical operation on the button on the Options properties of the two other grids. Figure 2-3 shows the effect of clicking the Or button.

1. Select File|New Application from the main menu to create a new blank project. Select File|Save Project As and save the project as Sets.

2. Add the properties and settings as shown in Table 2-4.

Table 2-4 Components, properties, and settings for Sets

COMPONENT	PROPERTY	SETTING
Form1	BorderStyle	bsDialog
	Caption	Set Properties
	Height	250
	Position	poDefaultPosOnly
	Width	600
CheckBox1	Caption	Vertical Lines
	Left	25
	State	cbChecked
	Top	160
CheckBox2	Caption	Horizontal Lines
	Left	25
	State	cbChecked
	Top	190
CheckBox3	Caption	Vertical Lines
	Left	240
	State	cbChecked
	Top	160
CheckBox4	Caption	Horizontal Lines
	Left	240
	State	cbChecked
	Top	190
Button1	Caption	Or
	Height	25
	Left	460

COMPONENT	PROPERTY	SETTING
	Top	150
	Width	75
Button2	Caption	And
	Height	25
	Left	460
	Top	190
	Width	75
Panel1	Align	alTop
	Height	145
StringGrid1 (On Panel1)	Align	alLeft
	Width	200
StringGrid2 (On Panel1)	Align	alClient
StringGrid3 (On Panel1)	Align	alRight
	Width	200

3. Double-click on `CheckBox1` and add the following code to the `OnClick` event handler in the Code Editor:

```
void __fastcall TForm1::CheckBox1Click(TObject *Sender)
{
  TGridOptions options = StringGrid1->Options ;
  if (CheckBox1->Checked)
    options << goVertLine ;
  else
    options >> goVertLine ;
  StringGrid1->Options = options ;
}
```

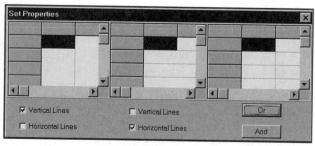

Figure 2-3 Sets program

4. Double-click on `CheckBox2` and add the following code to the `OnClick` event handler in the Code Editor:

```
void __fastcall TForm1::CheckBox2Click(TObject *Sender)
{
  TGridOptions options = StringGrid1->Options ;
  if (CheckBox2->Checked)
    options << goHorzLine ;
  else
    options >> goHorzLine ;
  StringGrid1->Options = options ;
}
```

5. Repeat the process for `CheckBox3`; modify its `OnClick` handler in the Code Editor so that it looks like this:

```
void __fastcall TForm1::CheckBox3Click(TObject *Sender)
{
  TGridOptions options = StringGrid2->Options ;
  if (CheckBox3->Checked)
    options << goVertLine ;
  else
    options >> goVertLine ;
  StringGrid2->Options = options ;
}
```

6. Double-click on `CheckBox4` and add the following code to its `OnClick` event handler:

```
void __fastcall TForm1::CheckBox4Click(TObject *Sender)
{
  TGridOptions options = StringGrid2->Options ;
  if (CheckBox4->Checked)
    options << goHorzLine ;
  else
    options >> goHorzLine ;
  StringGrid2->Options = options ;
}
```

7. Double-click on the Or button in the main code and add the following code to the `OnClick` handler that was created:

```
void __fastcall TForm1::Button1Click(TObject *Sender)
{
  TGridOptions options = StringGrid1->Options + StringGrid2->Options ;
  StringGrid3->Options = options ;
}
```

8. Finally, double-click on the And button and add the following code to the `OnClick` event handler:

```
void __fastcall TForm1::Button2Click(TObject *Sender)
{
  TGridOptions options = StringGrid1->Options * StringGrid2->Options ;
  StringGrid3->Options = options ;
}
```

9. Compile and test this program.

How It Works

There are two parts to a Set property in C++Builder. There is the range of values that can exist in the set, represented by an enumerated type, and the set type, created from a template class. In the case of the Options property for the TStringGrid class, VCL has an enumerated type called TGridOption that defines all the possible values that can be contained in the TGridOptions set type, which is the actual type for the property.

The VCL Set class implements the basic operations normally associated with sets. The most important operators and member functions for the Set classes are listed in Table 2-5.

Table 2-5 Major Set operators and member functions

OPERATOR	DESCRIPTION
<<	Adds a set member
>>	Removes a set member
+	Logical OR (Union) of two sets
*	Logical AND (Intersection) of two sets
-	Logical Difference of two sets
Contains()	Test for membership
Clear()	Makes the set a null set
==, !=	Comparison
+=, *=, -=	Assignment with Logical OR, AND, or Difference

The OnClick handlers for the check boxes add and remove values from the Options property using the << and >> operators. Notice that the event handlers operate on a copy of the Options property value and not on the property itself. The caution about using string properties in expressions (see How-To 2.1) applies to sets as well. Accessing the property fetches a copy of the property's value. The expression

```
StringGrid1->Options << goHorzLines ;
```

fetches the value of the Options property into temporary, then updates the temporary value with the property value remaining unchanged. This is why the application code uses a temporary variable to update the set property value like this:

```
TGridOptions options = StringGrid1->Options ;
if (CheckBox1->Checked)
  options << goVertLine ;
else
  options >> goVertLine ;
StringGrid1->Options = options ;
```

The << and >> operators for a **Set** are defined in a similar manner as they are for a stream so that it is easy to add more than one member to a set at a time. The expression:

```
options << goHorzLines << goVertLines ;
```

is equivalent to

```
options << goHorzLines ;
options << goVertLines ;
```

and

```
options >> goHorzLines >> goVertLines ;
```

is equivalent to

```
options >> goHorzLines ;
options >> goVertLines ;
```

The **OnClick** event handlers for the buttons on the Application's main form use the + and * operators to create a new set from the **Options** properties of the first two string grids. The new set is used to update the **Options** property of the third string grid.

Comments

Just as with strings, the best way to avoid problems when using **Set** properties is to use a lot of temporary variables. The only way you should ever modify a **Set** property is by using the = assignment operator. Use the VCL include files, help files, and documentation to determine how to declare the temporary variables.

A quick way to find the type declaration for **Set** property is to use the **GREP** program that comes with C++Builder. **GREP** searches for lines within files that match a string or pattern. If you open a DOS window and go to the C++Builder **Include** subdirectory, the command:

```
GREP -o -d TStringGrid *.hpp
```

will search all the **.HPP** files in all of the subdirectories for the string **TStringGrid**. The results of this command are shown in Figure 2-4; you can see that the **TStringGrid** class is declared in the file **GRIDS.HPP**.

To find the data type for the **Options** property, one more **GREP** command:

```
GREP -d Options GRID.HP
```

searches **GRID.HPP** for the string Options. Figure 2-5 shows the results from this command; the **Options** property is declared to be of the **TGridOptions** type.

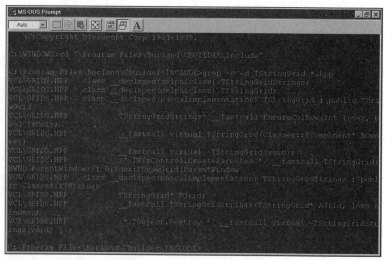

Figure 2-4 Results of using GREP to find the TStringGrid declaration

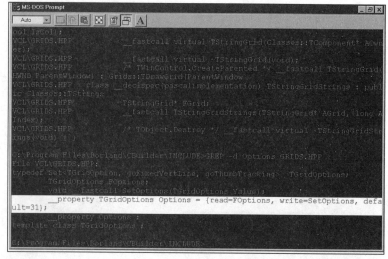

Figure 2-5 Results of using GREP to find the Options property declaration

2.3 How do I...
Create a Combo box that best matches user input?

Problem

Many applications, such as Quicken, use Combo boxes that update the edit window while the user types, with the item in the drop-down list that best matches the text typed in. The VCL Combo box control does not have any properties to control searching. How can I make a Combo box search as the user types?

Technique

The VCL Combo box control is based upon the standard Win32 Combo box. The Win32 Combo box responds to the CB_FINDSTRING message with the index of the item in the drop-down list that matches a specified text string. In the OnChange event of the Combo box, you can send the CB_FINDSTRING message to the Combo box using the text the user has already typed in so that the first matching list item is displayed in the edit window.

Steps

Run the SEARCHCOMBO.EXE shown in Figure 2-6. The Combo box at the top implements automatic searching while the one at the bottom does not. Try entering some text into the first Combo and notice how the Edit window gets updated as you type.

1. Select File|New Application from the main menu to create a new blank project. Select File|Save Project As and save the project as SearchCombo.

2. Add the properties and settings as shown in Table 2-6.

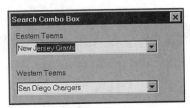

Figure 2-6 The SearchCombo program

Table 2-6 Components, properties, and settings for `SearchCombo`

COMPONENT	PROPERTY	SETTING
Form1	BorderStyle	bsDialog
	Caption	Search Combo Box
	Height	175
	Position	poDefaultPosOnly
	Width	340
Label1	Caption	Eastern Teams
	Left	0
	Top	10
Label2	Caption	Western Teams
	Left	10
	Top	80
ComboBox1	Height	24
	Items	Atlanta Falcons
		Baltimore Ravens
		Carolina Panthers
		Jacksonville Jaguars
		Miami Dolphins
		New England Patriots
		New Jersey Giants
		New Orleans Saints
		New York Jets
		Philadelphia Eagles
	Left	10
	Text	
	Top	40
	Width	275
	Sorted	True
ComboBox2	Height	24
	Items	Oakland Raiders
		San Diego Chargers
		San Francisco 49ers
		Seattle Seahawks
	Left	10
	Text	
	Top	105
	Width	275

3. Double-click on the top Combo box to create an `OnChange` handler for it. In the Code Editor add the following code to the `OnChange` handler:

```
void __fastcall TForm1::ComboBox1Change(TObject *Sender)
{
  String value = ComboBox1->Text ;

  // If the user tried to delete, he must not want to change anything.
  if (lastkey == '\b' || lastkey == VK_DELETE)
  {
    lastkey = 0 ;
    return ;
  }
  lastkey = 0 ;
  // Make sure the user is not typing something in the middle or else
  // proceeding will make the caret jump.
  if (ComboBox1->SelStart != value.Length ())
    return ;

  // Find the item matching text in the dropdown.
  int index = SendMessage (ComboBox1->Handle, CB_FINDSTRING, -1, (LPARAM)⇐
value.c_str ()) ;
  if (index >= 0)
  {
    // There was a match so now set up the selected text.
    ComboBox1->ItemIndex = index ;
    String newtext = ComboBox1->Text ;
    SendMessage (ComboBox1->Handle, CB_SETEDITSEL, 0, MAKELPARAM⇐
(value.Length (), -1)) ;
  }
}
```

4. On the application's main form select the first Combo box. Press [F11] to display the Object Inspector. Go to the Events page of the Object Inspector and double-click on the `OnKeyDown` event. Go to the Code Editor and add the following code to the event handler that was created:

```
void __fastcall TForm1::ComboBox1KeyDown(TObject *Sender, WORD &Key,
  TShiftState Shift)
{
  // Save the last key pressed.
  lastkey = Key ;
}
```

5. Select File|Open from the C++Builder main menu and open the file UNIT1.H. Add the definition of `lastkey` to the definition of `TForm1`.

```
class TForm1: public TForm
{
__published:
  TComboBox *ComboBox1;
  TLabel *Label1;
  TLabel *Label2;
  TComboBox *ComboBox2;
  void __fastcall ComboBox1Change(TObject *Sender);
```

```
void __fastcall ComboBox1KeyDown(TObject *Sender, WORD &Key,
  TShiftState Shift);
private:          // private user declarations
  WORD lastkey ;
public:           // public user declarations
  virtual __fastcall TForm1(TComponent* Owner);
};
```

6. Compile and test the project.

How It Works

Whenever the contents of the Combo box are changed, the `OnChanged` event handler `ComboBox1Change` gets called. The event handler calls the `SendMessage` API function to send a `CB_FINDSTRING` message to the underlying Win32 Combo box control, passing the contents of the edit string in the message. The `SendMessage` return value for this message is the index of the first matching item in the drop-down list.

If a match was found in the list, the event handler calls the `SendMessage` function again to send a `CB_SETEDITSEL` message to the Combo box control. While the Combo box control has `SelStart` and `SelLength` properties, they do not work correctly due to bugs in the VCL source code. Until these are corrected, you have to use `SendMessage`. The parameters to the `CB_SETEDITSEL` message specify that the text from the insertion point to the end of the string should be selected. The result is that all the text that gets selected is the text that was supplied for the user as a result of the search. If the user types another character, then the selected text will be deleted and the process will be repeated so that the drop-down list gets searched for the new text.

The process described above works fine when the user is typing in a string without pause. To make the editing more natural for the user, there are two situations in which the Combo box's `OnChange` event handler does not perform a search. If the user were to delete the selected text, it would not be desirable to have the search come right back and put the deleted text up again. To avoid this situation, no search is done when the last key the user entered was [BACKSPACE] or [DELETE]. Similarly, when the insertion point is not at the end of the string, the application assumes that the user is editing and does not want the text to be automatically updated.

Comments

When a VCL component is based on an existing Win32 control, like the `TComboBox` class is, the VCL class's interface includes the most commonly used features of the control. It would not be practical for VCL to include every possible feature of every Win32 control. However, all a standard control's features are available through Win32.

When you find that you would like to have a control do something that it does not appear able to do, check to see whether the control is a standard Win32 control. If so, then check Win32 documentation to see whether the standard control already has the feature you are interested in. Most standard features can be accessed using the `SendMessage` API function.

2.4 How do I...
Use drag-and-drop to move items from one list box to another?

Problem

Many applications allow the user to modify data by dragging items from one control to another. In my application I would like to be able to drag items from one list box to another. How can I do this using C++Builder?

Technique

VCL controls have the features needed to perform drag-and-drop built in. There are three main steps to handling drag-and-drop. The application needs to

1. Use the `BeginDrag` method to start the drag operation.

2. Give the user a visual clue when the mouse is over a point where an object can be dropped. This is done by providing an event handler for the `OnDragOver` event for controls that can have objects dropped on them. The event handler can change the mouse pointer to indicate that the control can be dropped.

3. Have an `OnDragDrop` handler for each control that can have objects dropped on it. This is where the actual dropping of an object is handled.

Steps

Run the **DRAGDROP.EXE** program shown in Figure 2-7. Use the mouse to drag a famous Roman from one column to another. Notice how the mouse cursor changes when you move over the list boxes and that the contents of both list boxes update automatically when you drop a name on a different list box.

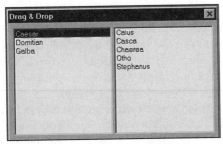

Figure 2-7 The `DragDrop` program

1. Select File|New Application from the main menu to create a new blank project. Select File|Save Project As and save the project as `DragDrop`.

2. Add the properties and settings as shown in Table 2-7.

Table 2-7 Components, properties, and settings for `DragDrop`

COMPONENT	PROPERTY	SETTING
Form1	BorderStyle	bsDialog
	Caption	Drag & Drop
	Height	250
	Position	poDefaultPosOnly
	Width	410
ListBox1	Height	200
	Items	Caesar
		Chaerea
		Galba
		Stephanus
	Left	10
	Sorted	true
	Top	10
	Width	190
ListBox2	Height	200
	Items	Caius
		Casca
		Domitian
		Otho
	Left	205
	Sorted	true
	Top	10
	Width	190

3. On the application's main form select the first list box; then press F11 to display the Object Inspector. Go to the Events page and double-click on the `OnMouseDown` event to create a handler for it. In the Code Editor add the following code to the event handler:

```
void __fastcall TForm1::ListBox1MouseDown(TObject *Sender,
  TMouseButton Button, TShiftState Shift, int X, int Y)
{
  if (Button != mbLeft)
    return ;
```

continued on next page

continued from previous page

```
  TListBox *listbox = (TListBox *) Sender ;
  // Make sure we are actually on an item on the list.
  if (listbox->ItemAtPos (Point (X, Y), true) >= 0)
    listbox->BeginDrag (false) ;
}
```

4. Go back to the Events page of the Object Inspector and make sure that
ListBox1 is still displayed in the Combo box at the top. Select the
OnDragOver event and double-click on it to create the event handler. In the
Code Editor modify the OnDragOver event handler to look like this:

```
void __fastcall TForm1::ListBox1DragOver(TObject *Sender,
  TObject *Source, int X, int Y, TDragState State, bool &Accept)
{
  // We can only accept drops from the list boxes.
  if (Source == ListBox1 || Source == ListBox2)
    Accept = true ;
  else
    Accept = false ;
}
```

5. Return the Object Inspector and create an OnDragDrop event handler for
ListBox1. Add this code to the event handler in the Code Editor:

```
void __fastcall TForm1::ListBox1DragDrop(TObject *Sender,
  TObject *Source, int X, int Y)
{
  // If we are dropping an item where it came from then do nothing.
  if (Sender == Source)
    return ;
  TListBox *sender = (TListBox *) Sender ;
  TListBox *source = (TListBox *) Source ;
  // Move the item from one list to the other.
  sender->Items->Add (source->Items->Strings [source->ItemIndex]) ;
  source->Items->Delete (source->ItemIndex) ;
}
```

6. Return to the main form and select the second list box. Press F11 and go to
the Events page of the Object Inspector. Select the OnMouseDown event but
do not double-click on it. Use the drop-down list and select
ListBox1MouseDown. The two list boxes now share the same OnMouseDown
event handler.

7. Remain on the Events page and go to the OnDragOver event. Select
ListBox1DragOver from the drop-down list. Do the same for the
OnDragDrop event but make ListBox1DragDrap the event handler.

8. Compile and test the project.

How It Works

Drag-and-drop is implemented in VCL by having one control dragged over and dropped on another. The control being dragged is referred to as the source and the control the source is dragged over or dropped onto is called the target. There can be only one source and target control at a time. A source can be dragged over any number of targets in sequence but it can only be dropped on one. If a control is dragged or dropped on itself, then the control is both the source and the target.

To handle drag-and-drop operations in your application, you create event handlers for the controls that you want to be involved in drag-and-drop operations. The sequence of drag-and-drop events is shown in Figure 2-8. Notice that some events are triggered in the source control and others occur in the target controls. Once a drag operation starts, all events for the source control get triggered but the target events may or may not get triggered depending on how the control is dragged.

In the `DragDrop` application, drag operations start in the `OnMouseDown` event handler shared by the list boxes. The `BeginDrag` member function is used to start a drag operation. In this example, the `Immediate` parameter is set to `false`, which delays the start of the drag operation until the user drags the mouse a small distance. Generally this value should be `false` unless you like the effect of having the mouse cursor blink at users each time they click on the control.

Because we want this application to appear to the user as though items in a list box are being dragged rather than the entire control, this application only allows a drag operation to occur when the mouse is clicked over an item in the list. The list box member function `ItemAtPos` is used to make sure that the mouse is not over an empty area of the list box before calling `BeginDrag`. An alternative method that would produce a different behavior would have been to check the `ItemIndex` property for a non-negative value. This would give the effect of dragging the List Box control rather than a line within the list box.

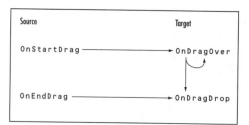

Figure 2-8 Drag-and-drop sequence of events

Once `BeginDrag` is called, the application goes into drag mode. While in drag mode, the application uses the source control's `DragCursor` property for the mouse pointer when the mouse is over a target control that is willing to accept the source and the `crNoDrop` cursor at other times. The different mouse pointers give users a visual clue as to where they can drop the object they are dragging.

A Target control indicates that it is willing to accept dragged items through the `OnDragOver` event handler. The value returned in the `Accept` parameter determines which icon is displayed. The `OnDragOver` event for list boxes is set up so that it only accepts drops from the two list boxes. As the application is written now, the check that determines whether the source is one of the two list boxes is redundant because only the list boxes can be dragged. It is a good practice to code defensively in these cases so that the code will not break if the capability to drag another control gets added to the application later on.

When a source control is dropped on a target that has accepted it in the `OnDragOver` event, the `OnDragDrop` event gets triggered in the target. It is not necessary to duplicate the tests in the `OnDragOver` method in the `OnDragDrop` as well because the `OnDragDrop` event can only be triggered for controls that have already been accepted. The `OnDragDrop` event in this application uses the list boxes' `Add` and `Delete` methods to move a list item from one list to the other.

Comments

An enhancement to this application that would be fairly easy to make would be to allow multiple items to be dragged at once. To do this, you would set the `MultiSelect` and `ExtendedSelect` properties to `true`. Before calling `BeginDrag`, you might use the `SelCount` property to determine how many items are being dragged so that you could use one drag cursor for dragging a single item and another for multiple items. In the `OnDragDrop` handler you would use the `Selected` property to determine which items needed to be moved.

In the Object Inspector you can see that most controls have a `DragMode` property that can be set to `dmAutomatic`. When a control is set up this way, any time the user moves the mouse with the button down, a drag operation is automatically started. In theory this makes drag-and-drop easier but it removes almost all control of the mouse from your application. In practice, setting the `DragMode` property to `dmAutomatic` is rarely useful.

COMPLEXITY
BEGINNING

2.5 How do I...
Add a horizontal scroll bar to a list box?

Problem

I have a list box in which most of the item strings are fairly short but it is possible for some of them to get quite long. I do not want to make the list box wider than necessary. Scrolling the list box would be the best solution but the control does not have a property to add a horizontal scroll bar. Is there any way to scroll the text in a list box horizontally in C++Builder?

Technique

The VCL list box is based on the standard Win32 list box control. This control uses the **LB_SETHORIZONTALEXTEND** message to set the virtual width of the text box. If this value is wider than the physical width of the control, the list box will display a horizontal scroll bar so the user can scroll the contents of the list box.

Steps

Run the program **SCROLLLISTBOX.EXE**. In Figure 2-9 you can see that some of the items in the list box extend beyond the right margin but that this list box has a horizontal scroll bar so you can view all the text. Try resizing the form. The scroll bar goes away when the list box is wide enough to show all the text.

1. Select File|New Application from the main menu to create a new blank project. Select File|Save Project As and save the project as **ScrollListBox**.

2. Add the properties and settings as shown in Table 2-8.

Figure 2-9 The
ScrollListBox program

Table 2-8 Components, properties, and settings for `ScrollListBox`

COMPONENT	PROPERTY	SETTING
Form1	Caption	Scrolling List Box
	Position	poDefaultPosOnly
ListBox1	Align	alClient
	Items	Barber Overture to The School for Scandal
		Bax Tintagel
		Beethoven Symphony #3
		Brahms A German Requiem
		Bruckner Symphony #9 (Finale completed by Carragan)
		Mendelsohn Elijah
		Mussorgsky/Gortchakov Pictures at an Exhibition
		Rachmaninoff Piano Concerto #4
		Scriabin Poem of Ecstacy
	Sorted	True

3. Press F11 to display the Object Inspector. Select `Form1` from the drop-down list at the top. Go to the events page and double click on the `OnCreate` event. Add the following code in the Code Editor:

```
void __fastcall TForm1::FormCreate(TObject *Sender)
{
  int maxwidth = 0 ;          // Maximum Text Width
  const int border = 3 ;
  // Find the width of the widest item in the list box.
  for (int ii = 0 ; ii < ListBox1->Items->Count ; ++ ii)
  {
    String text = ListBox1->Items->Strings [ii] ;
    int width = ListBox1->Canvas->TextWidth (text) ;
    if (width > maxwidth)
      maxwidth = width ;
  }
  SendMessage (ListBox1->Handle,
            LB_SETHORIZONTALEXTENT,
            maxwidth + 2 * border, 0) ;
}
```

4. Compile and test the project.

How It Works

If you look at the Win32 help file, you can see that the `LB_SETHORIZONTALEXTENT` message is used to set the width that a list box can be horizontally scrolled to—exactly what we want to do. All the application needs to do to make the list box display a horizontal scroll bar when the text is not entirely visible is to determine how much to allow the window to scroll and send the `SETHORIZONTALEXTENT` message to the list box.

The `OnCreate` event handler for the main form uses the `TextWidth` method for the list box's canvas to determine the width of the widest string in the list. This value is used to set the scrolling width. When the scrolling width is wider than the list box's window, the list box automatically displays a horizontal scroll bar.

Comments

If a control is defined in `STDCTRLS.HPP` or `COMCTRLS.HPP`, it is a standard Win32 control. In a situation where you have a standard control and a feature that you need but lack a VCL property or method, take a look in the Win32 help file and browse through the methods and functions for the control.

COMPLEXITY
INTERMEDIATE

2.6 How do I...
Add images to a list box?

Problem

In my application I would like to be able to display a graphical image in a list box. I know it is possible because I have seen other Win32 applications do this. How can it be done using C++Builder?

Technique

To draw graphics in a list box, your application needs to take responsibility for drawing the items in the list box. Setting a list box's `Style` property, `lbOwnerDrawVariable` tells the control that your application will draw the items in the `OnDrawItem` event. To make drawing the graphics easier, this application uses an image list control to store the bitmaps.

Steps

Run the program IMAGELISTBOX.EXE shown in Figure 2-10. Notice that each item in the list box has a graphic to the left and the text is centered with respect to the graphic.

1. Select File|New Application from the main menu to create a new blank project. Select File|Save Project As and save the project as ImageListBox.

2. Add the properties and settings as shown in Table 2-9.

Table 2-9 Components, properties, and settings for ImageListBox

COMPONENT	PROPERTY	SETTING
Form1	Caption	Image List Box
	Position	poDefaultPosOnly
ImageList1		
ListBox1	Align	alClient
	Items	Clock
		Calculator
		Calendar
		Maps
		Tools
	Style	lbOwnerDrawVariable

3. Go to the application's main form and double-click on the image control to display the Image List Editor. Click on the Add button and select the file CLOCK.BMP from the C++Builder Images/Buttons subdirectory. Go to the Transparent Color Combo box and select clOlive. Repeat this process using CALCULAT.BMP, CALENDAR.BMP, GLOBE.BMP, and GEARS.BMP.

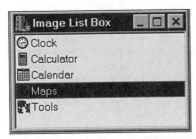

Figure 2-10 The
ImageListBox program

4. Switch to the Code Editor and select the file UNIT1.CPP. Go to the top of the file and add the definition of the constant margin.

```
#include <vcl\vcl.h>
#pragma hdrstop

#include "Unit1.h"
const margin = 2 ; // Margin around each bitmap
```

5. Return to the application's main form and select the list box. Press F11 and go to the Events page of the Object Inspector. Select the OnMeasureItem event and double-click on it. Add the following code to the event handler in the Code Editor:

```
void __fastcall TForm1::ListBox1MeasureItem(TWinControl *Control, int Index,
  int &Height)
{
  Height = ImageList1->Height + margin * 2 ;
}
```

6. Go back to the Object Inspector and make sure ListBox1 is selected in the Combo box at the top. Double-click on the OnDrawItem event and modify the event handler in the Code Editor so that it looks like this:

```
void __fastcall TForm1::ListBox1DrawItem(TWinControl *Control, int Index,
  TRect &Rect, TOwnerDrawState State)
{
  // Fill in the background.
  ListBox1->Canvas->FillRect (Rect) ;
  // Draw the graphic.
  ImageList1->Draw (ListBox1->Canvas, Rect.Left + margin, Rect.Top +⇐
margin, Index) ;

  // Draw the text.
  String text = ListBox1->Items->Strings [Index] ;
  // Center the text vertically in relation to the bitmap.
  int off = (Rect.Bottom - Rect.Top - ListBox1->Canvas->TextHeight (text))⇐
/ 2 ;
  ListBox1->Canvas->TextOut (Rect.Left + ImageList1->Width + 2 * margin,
                             Rect.Top + off,
                             text) ;
}
```

7. Compile and test the project.

How It Works

The first problem in drawing a graphic in a list box is where to store the graphics. One common method is to use the API function LoadBitmap to read the bitmap files at runtime. The problem with this method is that it requires the bitmap files to be distributed with the application. Managing applications that require a large

number of files is a nightmare, so it is better to place graphics within the application's executable file or grouped together in a DLL.

This application uses an image list control to store and manage the bitmaps. The major restriction of an image list control is that all the images must be the same size. If bitmaps of different sizes are required, the best solution would be to put them in a resource file. The image list control stores the images at design time, eliminating the need for separate bitmap files to run applications, and draws the images for the application at runtime.

With the `Style` property set to `LbOwnerDrawVariable`, the List Box control uses the `OnMeasureItem` event to determine an item's height and the `OnDrawItem` event to draw an item. In this example, all the items are the same height so setting the value of the `ItemHeight` property at design time could have been used instead of having an `OnMeasureItem` event handler. When you have images of different sizes, the `OnMeasureItem` event takes on greater importance. Here the list box's `OnMeasureMeasure` item gets the height of the bitmap from the image list control. The `OnDrawItem` event handler draws both the image and the text. The image list control takes care of drawing the bitmap and the list box's canvas draws the text.

Comments

This How-To shows how easy it is to create slick effects in an application. Using techniques like this will set your program apart from the ones that use plain text everywhere. You are not restricted to just using graphics when drawing your own list item. You can do any type of drawing you want, including using multiple fonts for the text.

This same technique can be applied to Combo boxes as well, and the procedure is identical. An interesting possibility for a Combo box would be a font selection dropdown where the font name is displayed using its own type face.

COMPLEXITY
INTERMEDIATE

2.7 How do I...
Create a Windows 95–style scroll bar?

Problem

In Windows 95, the scroll box (the movable part) in a scroll bar can expand and contract to give the user a visual clue as to the amount of data that is available to be scrolled. The scroll box of the `TScrollBar` class is a fixed size, just like in earlier versions of Windows. How can I adjust the size of the scroll box in a TScrollBar control?

Technique

The `GetScrollInfo` and `SetScrollInfo` API functions are used to control the range of values for a Scroll Bar control. The width of the scroll box is controlled by a value called `Page Size`.

Steps

Run the program `SCROLLBARPAGE.EXE` shown in Figure 2-11. Use the track bar control to adjust the page size of the control.

1. Select File|New Application from the main menu to create a new blank project. Select File|Save Project As and save the project as `ScrollBarPage`.

2. Add the properties and settings as shown in Table 2-10.

Table 2-10 Components, properties, and settings for `ScrollBarPage`

COMPONENT	PROPERTY	SETTING
Form1	BorderStyle	bsDialog
	Caption	Scroll Bar Page Size
	Height	160
	Position	poDefaultPosOnly
	Width	475
Label1	Caption	Page Size
	Left	10
	Top	20
Label2	Left	395
	Top	20
Label3	Left	395
	Top	85
ScrollBar1	Left	80
	Top	85
	Width	290
TrackBar1	Height	45
	Left	80
	Top	10
	Width	290

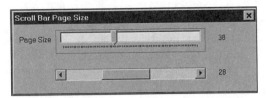

Figure 2-11 The ScrollBarPage program

3. Select the application's main form and double-click on it on any place not occupied by a control to create the OnCreate event handler for the form. Add the following code to the OnCreate handler in the Code Editor:

```
void __fastcall TForm1::FormCreate(TObject *Sender)
{
  UpdateLabels ();
}
```

4. Return to the main form and double-click on the scroll bar to create an OnChange handler for it. Modify the handler in Code Editor to look like this:

```
void __fastcall TForm1::ScrollBar1Change(TObject *Sender)
{
  UpdateLabels () ;
}
```

5. Double-click on the Track Bar control to create an OnChange handler for it. Add the following code in the Code Editor:

```
void __fastcall TForm1::TrackBar1Change(TObject *Sender)
{
  SCROLLINFO si ;
  memset (&si, 0, sizeof (si)) ;
  si.cbSize = sizeof (si) ;
  si.fMask = SIF_PAGE ;    // Change the page size.
  si.nPage = TrackBar1->Position ;
  SetScrollInfo (ScrollBar1->Handle, SB_CTL, &si, true) ;
  UpdateLabels () ;
}
```

6. Select the Code Editor then File|Open from the C++Builder main menu and open the file UNIT1.H. In the Code Editor, add the declaration of UpdateLabels to the definition of TForm1.

```
class TForm1 : public TForm
{
__published:
  TScrollBar *ScrollBar1;
  TTrackBar *TrackBar1;
  TLabel *Label1;
  TLabel *Label2;
```

```
  TLabel *Label3;
  void __fastcall ScrollBar1Change(TObject *Sender);
  void __fastcall TrackBar1Change(TObject *Sender);
  void __fastcall FormCreate(TObject *Sender);
private:        // private user declarations
  void UpdateLabels () ;
public:         // public user declarations
  virtual __fastcall TForm1(TComponent* Owner);
};
```

7. In the Code Editor, switch to the file UNIT1.CPP and add this definition of the member function UpdateLabels:

```
void TForm1::UpdateLabels ()
{
  TrackBar1->Min = ScrollBar1->Min ;
  TrackBar1->Max = ScrollBar1->Max ;
  Label2->Caption = String (TrackBar1->Position) ;
  Label3->Caption = String (ScrollBar1->Position) ;
}
```

8. Compile and test the project.

How It Works

When the Track Bar is moved, the OnChange event gets called that changes the page size. The API function SetScrollInfo adjusts the range values for a Win32 scroll bar. The scroll bar parameters are passed to this function in a SCROLLINFO structure. The fMask field of the structure contains flags that determine which scroll bar parameters should be updated. The value SIF_PAGE indicates that the page size is to be updated. If you need to update more than one parameter value, you can use a bitwise OR operator to set additional bits in the fMask field.

Comments

This technique for modifying the scroll bar can also be used with controls, such as the TStringGrid, where a fixed-size scroll box is used. In this case you would pass the handle of the control to SetScrollInfo and use SB_HORZ or SB_VERT in place of SB_CTL.

2.8 How do I...
Create a multipage dialog box?

Problem

I need to have a dialog box in which the user can enter several groups of values in sequence. Many applications implement a wizard where different pages are displayed on the same form. How can this be done easily in C++Builder?

Technique

The page control displays a set of pages on the same control. By disabling the tab on each page, you can force the user to change pages under program control.

Steps

Run the program MULTIPAGE.EXE shown in Figure 2-12. After filling the edit controls on each page, click on the Back or Next buttons to move among the pages. Try different values in the edit controls and see how they affect the results on the last page.

1. Select File|New Application from the main menu to create a new blank project. Select File|Save Project As and save the project as MultiPage.

2. Add a page control to the form. Click on the page control using the right mouse button to display the context menu and select New Page to create a Tab Sheet. Repeat this process and create a total of four Tab Sheets. Do not worry about the index tabs at this point.

3. Add the properties and setting as shown in Table 2-11.

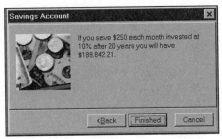

Figure 2-12 The MultiPage program

Table 2-11 Components, properties, and settings for `MultiPage`

COMPONENT	PROPERTY	SETTING
Form1	BorderStyle	bsDialog
	Caption	Savings Account
	Height	240
	Position	poScreenCenter
	Width	410
Panel1	Align	alBottom
	Caption	
	Height	45
Button1 (On Panel1)	Caption	<&Back
	Enabled	false
	Height	25
	Left	150
	Top	10
	Width	75
Button2 (On Panel1)	Caption	&Next>
	Default	true
	Height	25
	Left	230
	Top	10
	Width	75
Button3 (On Panel1)	Cancel	true
	Caption	Cancel
	Height	25
	Left	320
	Top	10
	Width	75
PageControl1	ActivePage	TabSheet1
	Align	alClient
TabSheet1		
Label1	Caption	Enter the interest rate.
	Left	130
	Top	15
Image1	Left	10
	Height	105

continued on next page

continued from previous page

COMPONENT	PROPERTY	SETTING
	PictureImages/	
	Splash/256color/	
	Finance.BMP	
	Top	15
	Width	105
MaskEdit1	EditMask	99 %;0;_
	Height	24
	Left	130
	Text	10
	Top	40
	Width	50
TabSheet2		
Label2	Caption	How much will you deposit each month?
	Left	130
	Top	15
MaskEdit2	EditMask	$ 9999;0;
	Height	24
	Left	130
	Text	250
	Top	40
	Width	120
TabSheet3		
Label3	Caption	How many years will you save?
	Left	130
	Top	15
MaskEdit3	EditMask	99;1;_
	Height	24
	Left	130
	Text	20
	Top	40
	Width	25
TabSheet4		
Label4	AutoSize	false
	Height	115

COMPONENT	PROPERTY	SETTING
	Left	130
	Top	15
	Width	250
	WordWrap	True

4. Select the file UNIT1.CPP in the Code Editor. Add the definition of the function ValidNumber below the declaration of Form1.

```
#pragma resource "*.dfm"
TForm1 *Form1 ;

static bool ValidNumber (String value)
{
  value = value.Trim () ;
  if (value == "")
    return false ;

  for (int ii = 1 ; ii <= value.Length () ; ++ ii)
  {
    if (! isdigit (value [ii]))
      return false ;
  }
  return true ;
}
```

5. Select File|Open from the C++Builder main menu and open the file UNIT1.H. Add these declarations to the private section of the TForm1 class definition:

```
private:          // private user declarations
  void SetButtons () ;
  int currentpage ;
public:           // public user declarations
  virtual __fastcall TForm1(TComponent* Owner);
};
```

6. Switch to the file UNIT1.CPP in the Code Editor and add the definition of SetButtons.

```
void TForm1::SetButtons ()
{
  // Move the splash image to the new page.
  Image1->Parent = PageControl1->ActivePage ;
  if (PageControl1->ActivePage == TabSheet1)
  {
    Button1->Enabled = false ;
    Button2->Caption = "&Next>" ;
    Button2->Enabled = ValidNumber (MaskEdit1->Text) ;
  }
  else if (PageControl1->ActivePage == TabSheet2)
  {
```

continued on next page

continued from previous page

```
    Button1->Enabled = true ;
    Button2->Caption = "&Next>" ;
    Button2->Enabled = ValidNumber (MaskEdit2->Text) ;
  }
  else if (PageControl1->ActivePage == TabSheet3)
  {
    Button1->Enabled = true ;
    Button2->Caption = "&Next>" ;
    Button2->Enabled = ValidNumber (MaskEdit3->Text) ;
  }
  else
  {
    Button1->Enabled = true ;
    Button2->Enabled = true ;
    Button2->Caption = "Finished" ;
  }
}
```

7. Modify the TForm1 constructor so that it initializes the currentpage member.

```
__fastcall TForm1::TForm1(TComponent* Owner) : TForm(Owner)
{
  currentpage = 0 ;
}
```

8. Select the application's main form and double-click on the Back button to create an OnClick event handler for it. Modify the event handler in the Code Editor like this:

```
void __fastcall TForm1::Button1Click(TObject *Sender)
{
  -- currentpage ;
  PageControl1->ActivePage = PageControl1->Pages [currentpage] ;
  SetButtons () ;
}
```

9. Go back to the main form and double-click on the Next button to create the OnClick event handler. Add the following code in the Code Editor:

```
void __fastcall TForm1::Button2Click(TObject *Sender)
{
  switch (currentpage)
  {
  case 3:
    // Moving forward from the last page means we are all done.
    Close () ;
    break ;
  case 2:
    // If we are moving to the last page then we need to calculate the⇐
values.
    if (PageControl1->ActivePage == TabSheet3)
    {
      long double rate = 1.0 + MaskEdit1->Text.ToDouble () / 100.00 /⇐
12.0 ;
```

```
      int periods = MaskEdit3->Text.ToInt () * 12 ;
      long double payment = MaskEdit2->Text.ToDouble () ;
      long double value = 0 ;
      for (int ii = 0 ; ii < periods ; ++ ii)
      {
        value *= rate ;
        value += payment ;
      }

      Label4->Caption = "If you save $" + String (MaskEdit2->Text) + "⇐
each "
                      + "month invested at " + MaskEdit1->Text + "%⇐
after "
                      + MaskEdit3->Text + " years you will have "
                      + String::FloatToStrF (value, String::sffCurrency,⇐
20, 2)
                      + "." ;
    }
    // fall through
  default:
    // Move to the next page.
    ++ currentpage ;
    PageControl1->ActivePage = PageControl1->Pages [currentpage] ;
    SetButtons () ;
  }
}
```

10. Return to the main form and double-click on the Cancel button to create an event handler for the `OnClick` event. Modify the event handler in the Code Editor to look like this:

```
void __fastcall TForm1::Button3Click(TObject *Sender)
{
  Close () ;
}
```

11. Double-click on the Mask Edit control on the first Tab Page to create the `OnChange` handler for the control. Add the following code to the event handler in the Code Editor:

```
void __fastcall TForm1::MaskEdit1Change(TObject *Sender)
{
  SetButtons () ;
}
```

12. Go to the second tab on the application's main form. Select the Mask Edit control and press F11 to display the Object Inspector. Go to the Events page and select, but do not double-click, the `OnChange` event. Select `MaskedEdit1Change` as the event handler from the drop-down list. Repeat this process for the Mask Edit control on the third tab page so that all three Mask Edit controls share the same `OnChange` handler.

13. Select the last index tab on the application's main form; then select the TabSheet4 control by clicking in the middle of the tab page. Press F11 to display the Object Inspector and go to the Properties page. Change the value of the `TabVisible` property to `false`. Working from back to front, repeat this process for all the tab pages until there are no more tabs visible on the Page Control.

14. Go to the Object Inspector and select `PageControl1` from the drop-down list at the top. Make sure the `ActivePage` property is set to `TabSheet1`.

15. Compile and test the project.

How It Works

This application uses a page control to create a multipage dialog box. The index tabs are removed so the changing of pages is managed entirely by the application. The application forces the user to go through the pages in the sequence defined by the application. The page sequence for this application is simply forward and backward, but you can make the page order in a dialog as elaborate as necessary.

The `currentpage` member variable maintains the index of the current page number. The `OnClick` event handlers for `Button1` and `Button2` move backward and forward through the tab sheets by decrementing and incrementing this value and assigning it to the page control's `ActivePage` property.

The code for `Button2`'s `OnClick` handler is a little more complex than the trivial one for `Button1`. The switch statement handles the two special cases that only occur when moving forward. If the user moves forward for the last page, the program exits and when it moves to the last page, the application calculates the new value for savings.

The `SetButtons` member function is called whenever a page changes or the user changes the data on a page. It updates the state of the buttons depending on the tab sheet displayed. This function prevents the user from advancing forward when the tab sheet being displayed has invalid data.

Comments

A common error when designing user interfaces is to have forms in which the valid values for one field on the form depend on the value already entered in another. Not only is this confusing to the user, but also it is complicated to implement. Such a design also creates the awkward situation where the user enters a value in a field, fills in the value of a dependent field, then goes back and modifies the first field so that the data already entered in the second field is now invalid.

A much better solution is to break down the information that the user has to enter into a sequence of steps. If a field on a form requires another to have been filled out, then the two fields should be in separate steps. Using the page control makes implementing this method very easy.

COMPLEXITY
BEGINNING

2.9 How do I...
Create a multipanel status bar?

Problem

Many applications have a status bar with multiple panels that display information about the state of an application. How do I create such a control in C++Builder?

Technique

The VCL TStatusBar class provides a wrapper around the standard Win32 status bar control. This class can be used to easily create professional-looking status bars for an application.

Steps

Run the program STATUSBAR.EXE shown in Figure 2-13. The status bar gets updated with the system time. Try entering some text into the memo control and notice how the status bar changes.

1. Select File|New Application from the main menu to create a new blank project. Select File|Save Project As and save the project as StatusBar.

2. Add the properties and settings as shown in Table 2-12.

Table 2-12 Components, properties, and settings for StatusBar

COMPONENT	PROPERTY	SETTING
Form1	Caption	Status Bar
	Position	poDefault
StatusBar1		
Memo1	Align	alClient
	Lines	
Timer1		

3. On the application's main form, select the status bar control and press F11 to display the Object Inspector. On the Properties page, select the Panels property and double-click on it to display the StatusBars Panels Editor. Click on the New button to create a new panel; then set its width to 300. Click on New again to create a second panel; then click on OK.

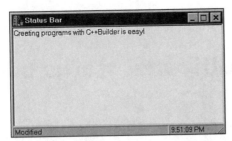

Figure 2-13 The StatusBar **program**

4. Go to the main form and create an OnChange handler for the memo control by double-clicking on it. Add the following code to the OnChange handler in the Code Editor:

```
void __fastcall TForm1::Memo1Change(TObject *Sender)
{
  if (Memo1->Modified)
    StatusBar1->Panels->Items [0]->Text = "Modified" ;
  else
    StatusBar1->Panels->Items [0]->Text = "" ;
}
```

5. Return to the main form and double-click on the time control. Modify the OnTimer event handler in the Code Editor to look like this:

```
void __fastcall TForm1::Timer1Timer(TObject *Sender)
{
 SYSTEMTIME time ;
 GetLocalTime (&time) ;

 String formattedtime ;
 formattedtime.SetLength (64) ;
 int length = GetTimeFormat (LOCALE_USER_DEFAULT,
                 0,                          // Flags
                 &time,
                 NULL,                       // Format
                 formattedtime.c_str (),
                 formattedtime.Length ()) ;
 formattedtime.SetLength (length) ;
 StatusBar1->Panels->Items [1]->Text = formattedtime ;
}
```

6. Compile and test the program.

How It Works

The status bar control maintains a list of panels, each of which contains a separate display area. The individual panels are accessed through the Items property of the status bar.

Comments

You can create a status bar with one text panel by setting the `SimplePanel` property to `true`. The `SimpleText` property controls the text displayed in a simple panel. This is easier than managing individual panels and for many applications this is all that is needed in a status bar.

It is also possible to display graphics in a panel. The technique is similar to that shown in How-To 2.6. In the StatusBars Panels Editor you can set the panel's style to Owner Draw. You draw the panel in the `OnDrawPanel` event of the status bar.

CHAPTER 3

TEXT CONTROLS

3

TEXT CONTROLS

How do I...

Rarely does one write a Windows program that does not require the user to enter text. This chapter shows you how to use some of the VCL text controls. Five of the How-To's deal with how to use the Rich Edit control. The features of this control are dealt with in separate How-To's so that they can be clearly demonstrated. The CD-ROM that accompanies this book contains the source for a program that puts all the Rich Edit control's features together.

3.1 Create a Simple Word Processor

The Rich Edit control is among the most powerful in the VCL library. This How-To demonstrates the basic file functions of the control as well as the File and Print Dialog controls.

3.2 Add Search and Replace Functions to My Word Processor

Using the `TFindDialog` and `TReplaceDialog` classes makes it easy to implement Search and Replace input functions in an application. This How-To shows how to use these controls with the Rich Edit control.

3.3 Use Different Fonts in My Word Processor

One of the most powerful features of the Rich Edit control is that it can display text that uses multiple fonts and paragraphs with different alignment attributes. Learn how to create an interface using the Font Dialog control, which implements these features.

3.4 Add Cut and Paste to My Word Processor

The Rich Edit control has member functions for cutting and pasting to the clipboard. An application can use these functions to implement clipboard operations without forcing the user to use keystroke combinations.

3.5 Implement Undo in a Word Processor

Mistakes sometimes happen, so having an application that allows the user to recover from mistakes is always a good idea. Learn how to undo the last edit a user made in a Rich Edit control.

3.6 Create a Right-Justified Edit Box

The Edit control always left-justifies its contents, but users are accustomed to having numbers right-justified. This How-To shows you how to create a single-line input control that is right-justified.

3.7 Create a Font Selection Combo Box

Many applications allow the user to choose a font by using a combo box. This How-To demonstrates how to find the fonts that are available and display them in a combo box's drop-down list.

3.8 Limit Text Entry to Certain Characters

Avoiding mistakes is a step on the path to creating robust applications. If a user must enter a number in a field, then why let him or her enter anything else?

COMPLEXITY
INTERMEDIATE

3.1 How do I...
Create a simple word processor?

Problem

In my application I need to be able to display text that contains multiple fonts. I would like something like the Memo control that can display more than one font at a time. How can I do this in C++Builder™?

Technique

The Rich Edit control can display and edit text containing formatting attributes such as multiple fonts and special effects. Its capabilities are similar to those in the WORDPAD program that comes with Windows. All you need to do to create a word processing application with the Rich Edit control is create the user interface to control it.

Steps

Use the WORDPAD program to create some text with multiple fonts and save the text into a Rich Text Format (RTF) file and not Word for Windows format. Then run the program WORDPROCESSOR.EXE, shown in Figure 3-1. Use the Open menu item to read in your RTF file. Your text should be formatted just as it was in Wordpad. Try editing the text and printing it.

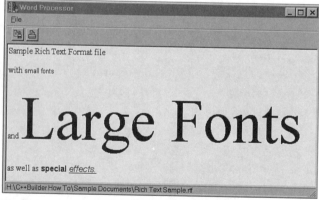

Figure 3-1 WordProcessor program

1. Select File|New Application from the main menu to create a new blank project. Select File|Save Project As and save the project as `WordProcessor`.

2. Add a Main Menu control to the form. Set the menu items to the Main Menu control as shown in Table 3-1.

Table 3-1 Menu design for the `WordProcessor` project

MENU	MENU ITEM
&File	&New
	&Open...
	&Save
	Save &As...
	-
	Print Set&up...
	&Print...
	-
	E&xit

3. Add the properties and settings as shown in Table 3-2. The bitmaps for the speed buttons can be found in C++Builder's `IMAGES\BUTTONS` subdirectory.

Table 3-2 Components, properties, and settings for `WordProcessor`

COMPONENT	PROPERTY	SETTING
Form1	Caption	Word Processor
	Menu	MainMenu1
	Position	poDefault
RichEdit1	Align	alClient
	Lines	
	PlainText	true
	ScrollBars	ssBoth
	WantTabs	true
Panel1	Align	alTop
	BevelOuter	bvNone
	Caption	
	Height	35
	ShowHint	true

COMPONENT	PROPERTY	SETTING
SpeedButton1 (On Panel1)	Glyph	FILESAVE.BMP
	Height	25
	Hint	Save
	Left	10
	Top	5
	Width	25
SpeedButton2 (On Panel1)	Glyph	PRINT.BMP
	Height	25
	Hint	Print
	Left	40
	Top	5
	Width	25
Bevel1 (On Panel1)	Align	alTop
	Height	5
	Shape	bsTopLine
StatusBar1		
OpenDialog1	Filter	DocumentFiles|*.TXT;*.RTF|Text Files|*.TXT|Rich TextFiles|* .RTF| All Files|*.*
	+Options	
	-ofPathMustExist	true
	-ofFileMustExist	true
	-ofShareAware	true
SaveDialog1	DefaultExt	TXT
	Filter	Document Files|*.TXT;*.RTF|Text Files|*.TXT|RichTextFiles| *.RTF|All Files|*.*
PrintDialog1		
PrinterSetupDialog1		

4. Select the Status Bar control on the application's main form and press F11 to display the Object Inspector. Double-click on the **Panels** property value to display the StatusBar Panels Editor. Click on the New button to create a panel; then click on the OK button to add the panel.

5. Make the Code Editor the active window; then select File|Open from the main menu and open the file **UNIT1.H**. Add the following declarations to the definition of **TForm1**:

```
class TForm1 : public TForm
{
__published:  // IDE-managed Components
  TMainMenu *MainMenu1;
  TMenuItem *File1;
  TMenuItem *New1;
  TMenuItem *Open1;
  TMenuItem *Save1;
  TMenuItem *SaveAs1;
  TMenuItem *N1;
  TMenuItem *PrintSetup1;
  TMenuItem *Print1;
  TMenuItem *N2;
  TMenuItem *Exit1;
  TRichEdit *RichEdit1;
  TPanel *Panel1;
  TSpeedButton *SpeedButton1;
  TSpeedButton *SpeedButton2;
  TStatusBar *StatusBar1;
  TBevel *Bevel1;
  TPrintDialog *PrintDialog1;
  TPrinterSetupDialog *PrinterSetupDialog1;
  TOpenDialog *OpenDialog1;
  TSaveDialog *SaveDialog1;
private:     // User declarations
  String Filename ;
  bool SaveFile () ;
  bool SaveFileAs () ;
  bool NewFile () ;
public:      // User declarations
  __fastcall TForm1(TComponent* Owner);
};
```

6. Switch to the file **UNIT1.CPP** in the Code Edit window and add the definitions of the **SaveFile**, **SaveFileAs**, and **NewFile** functions.

```
bool TForm1::SaveFile ()
{
  // This function saves the file. It returns true if the user cancels.

  // If there is no file name then get one from the user.
  if (Filename == "")
  {
    return SaveFileAs () ;
  }
  else
  {
    RichEdit1->Lines->SaveToFile (Filename) ;
    return false ;
  }
}
```

```
bool TForm1::SaveFileAs ()
{
  // This function lets the user enter a file name, then save the edit⇐
window to
  // this file.  It returns true if the user cancels.
  if (! SaveDialog1->Execute ())
    return true ;   // User clicked on cancel.

  Filename = SaveDialog1->FileName ;
  // If the file name indicates Rich Text, then save the formatting⇐
information.
  // otherwise save as text.
  if (Filename.SubString (Filename.Length () - 3, 4).UpperCase () ==⇐
".RTF")
    RichEdit1->PlainText = false ;
  else
    RichEdit1->PlainText = true ;

  StatusBar1->Panels->Items [0]->Text = Filename ;
  SaveFile () ;
  return false ;
}

bool TForm1::NewFile ()
{
  // This function  resets the edit window. It returns true if the user⇐
indicates
  // he does not want to discard changes made.

  // If the user has changed the text, then give him a chance to save it.
  if (RichEdit1->Modified)
  {
    switch (Application->MessageBox ("Do you wish to save your changes?",
                                     "Word Processor",
                                     MB_YESNOCANCEL))
    {
    case IDYES:
      if (SaveFile ())
        return true ;
      break ;
    case IDCANCEL:
      return true ;
    }
  }
  // Clear out the edit window and update the file names.
  RichEdit1->Text = "" ;
  RichEdit1->Modified = false ;
  Filename = "" ;
  StatusBar1->Panels->Items [0]->Text = "(Untitled)" ;
  return false ;
}
```

7. Go to the Object Inspector and select Form1 from the drop-down list at the top. Switch to the Events page; then double-click on OnCreate to create an event handler for the main form. Add this code to the `OnCreate` handler:

```
void __fastcall TForm1::FormCreate(TObject *Sender)
{
  NewFile () ;
}
```

8. Double-click on the first speed button. This will create a handler for the `OnClick` event. Add the following code to the `OnClick` event handler:

```
void __fastcall TForm1::SpeedButton1Click(TObject *Sender)
{
  SaveFile () ;
}
```

9. Double-click on the second speed button and modify its `OnClick` handler to look like this:

```
void __fastcall TForm1::SpeedButton2Click(TObject *Sender)
{
  RichEdit1->Print ("") ;
}
```

10. Go to the application's main form. Click on the New menu item to create an `OnClick` handler for it. Add the following code to the `OnClick` event handler:

```
void __fastcall TForm1::New1Click(TObject *Sender)
{
  NewFile () ;
}
```

11. Create an `OnClick` event handler for the Open menu item in the same manner as you did for the New item. In the Code Editor modify the `OnClick` handler so that it looks like this:

```
void __fastcall TForm1::Open1Click(TObject *Sender)
{
  if (NewFile ())
    return ;

  if (OpenDialog1->Execute ())
  { // User clicked on OK
    String file = OpenDialog1->FileName ;
    // See if the user selected a Rich Text File. If so, then treat the
    // contents as formatted text.
    if (file.SubString (file.Length () - 3, 4).UpperCase () == ".RTF")
      RichEdit1->PlainText = false ;
    else
      RichEdit1->PlainText = true ;
```

```
  RichEdit1->Lines->LoadFromFile (file) ;
  RichEdit1->Modified = false ;
  Filename = file ;
  StatusBar1->Panels->Items [0]->Text = file ;
  }
}
```

12. Using the same procedure, create `OnClick` handlers for the Save, Save As, Print, Print Setup, and Exit menu items that look like these:

```
void __fastcall TForm1::Save1Click(TObject *Sender)
{
  SaveFile () ;
}

void __fastcall TForm1::SaveAs1Click(TObject *Sender)
{
  SaveFileAs () ;
}

void __fastcall TForm1::PrintSetup1Click(TObject *Sender)
{
  PrinterSetupDialog1->Execute () ;
}

void __fastcall TForm1::Print1Click(TObject *Sender)
{
  if (PrintDialog1->Execute ())
    RichEdit1->Print ("") ;
}

void __fastcall TForm1::Exit1Click(TObject *Sender)
{
  Close () ;
}
```

13. Compile and test the project.

How It Works

The Rich Text Format (RTF) was created by Microsoft and is the most standard format for exchanging text created by different word processors. RTF is supported by almost every word processing program in existence. Help files are created from RTF documents.

The VCL `TRichEdit` class is based on the standard Rich Edit control. This control can display and edit formatted text. It can load and save text in the RTF format. (It is also possible for the Rich Edit control to use other file formats by defining a filter.) The Rich Edit control implements a subset of the features defined by the RTF format. When you create help files, you have to define many footnotes that, although supported by RTF, cannot be displayed in the Rich Edit control. The capabilities of the Rich Edit control are comparable to that of the `WORDPAD` program.

Designing an interface to the Rich Edit control is a matter of personal taste and common sense. The **WordProcessor** program's interface would not be unfamiliar to anyone who has used a Windows word processing program. All the program's functions can be accessed through the main menu but a few frequently used functions can be performed by using buttons on a speed bar. The **WordProcessor** program implements the following functions:

✔ Create a new file

✔ Open an existing file

✔ Save the text in the control

✔ Set up the printer

✔ Print the text in the control

The only nontrivial programming logic deals with prompting the user to save changes before destroying the contents of the control. All the rest of the work is handled by either the Rich Edit control or one of the standard dialog controls. The **Modified** property of the Rich Edit control is set to **true** whenever the user makes a change to the control's contents. Whenever the application is about to destroy the existing contents of the control, it checks the value of the **Modified** property and prompts the user to save the file if the contents have been changed.

The **WordProcessor** application demonstrates how to use four of the standard dialog box controls. To use a standard dialog box control, in most cases, you need to set various property values to control how the dialog appears to the user and then call **Execute** to display the dialog box. The return value of the **Execute** member function indicates whether the user used the OK button or the Cancel button to close the dialog. **true** means the user clicked on OK and **false** means the Cancel button was clicked. After the **Execute** method returns, the property values of the control can be inspected to determine the values the user entered.

The one dialog used here that does not follow this pattern is the Printer Setup dialog. This dialog has all the functionality for setting up the printer built into it. When the user clicks on the Printer Dialog control's OK button, the dialog sets up the printer on its own. All the application has to do with this dialog is use the **Execute** method to display it.

An important thing to remember about the Rich Edit control is that many of its features are built into its **Lines** property. The **Lines** property returns a pointer to the **TStrings** object that represents the text within the control. Notice that text is loaded and saved using the **LoadFromFile** and **SaveToFile** methods of the **TStrings** class, not by using **TRichEdit** member functions.

In general, a user should be able to access all an application's features using the menu. However, it has become common to provide speed buttons to access frequently used functions. The speed bar for holding these buttons is created using a Panel control, which is made to blend into the menu by eliminating its bevels. A Bevel control is used to create a more attractive division between the menu and the speed bar than would be created by a Panel control's bevel.

The behavior of the Print menu item and the Print button on the speed bar is deliberately different. The Print menu item displays the Print dialog box so that the user can select the printer before printing the Rich Edit control's contents. The speed button is supposed to be a quick function, so it prints the text immediately to the default printer.

If you have used other Windows programming tools, such as Visual Basic, you are probably accustomed to writing code to reposition your form's controls when it is resized; this defeats the purpose of visual development. In this application the controls resize automatically through the use of the **Align** property. When the size of the main form changes, the Panel and Status Bar controls remain the same height and the Rich Edit control sizes itself to fill the remaining area. Panel controls are useful for creating areas of a fixed size on a resizable control.

Comments

This How-To demonstrates the major file level options performed by the Rich Edit control as well as how to use several of the VCL dialog box controls. For a true word processing application you would need to implement more features. Although the application will display formatted RTF files, it does not allow the user to change fonts for new text. The next four How-To's address different features of the Rich Edit control, including how to allow a user to format text with different fonts.

COMPLEXITY

INTERMEDIATE

3.2 How do I...
Add Search and Replace functions to my word processor?

Problem

My application needs to allow the user to search for text strings and to replace one string with another in a Rich Edit control. How can I implement these features in C++Builder?

Technique

The Find Dialog and Replace Dialog controls in the VCL library are shells for the Windows Find and Replace dialog box classes. You can easily create an intuitive user interface for Search and Replace functions in the text editor with these controls. The **FindText** method of the Rich Edit control is used to search for text within the edit window.

Steps

Run the program **SEARCHREPLACE.EXE**. Either paste a text file into the Rich Edit control or type in some text. Select Find from the main menu to search for text or select Replace to replace text. Try out the various options on the Find and Replace dialog boxes. The main form of this application is shown in Figure 3-2.

1. Select File|New Application from the main menu to create a new blank project. Select File|Save Project As and save the project as `SearchReplace`.

2. Add a Main Menu control to the form. Set menu items to the Main Menu control as shown in Table 3-3.

Table 3-3 Menu design for the `SearchReplace` project

MENU	MENU ITEM	SHORTCUT
&File	E&xit	
&Edit	&Find	CTRL-F
	&Replace	CTRL-R

3. Add the properties and settings as shown in Table 3-4.

Table 3-4 Components, properties, and settings for `SearchReplace`

COMPONENT	PROPERTY	SETTING
Form1	Caption	Search & Replace
	Position	poDefault
	Menu	MainMenu1
RichEdit1	Align	alClient
	HideSelection	false
	Lines	
	ScrollBars	ssBoth
	WantTabs	true
FindDialog1		
ReplaceDialog1		
StatusBar1		

4. Click on the Exit menu item on the main form to create an `OnClick` event handler. Add code to the event handler in the Code Editor.

```
void __fastcall TForm1::Exit1Click(TObject *Sender)
{
  Close () ;
}
```

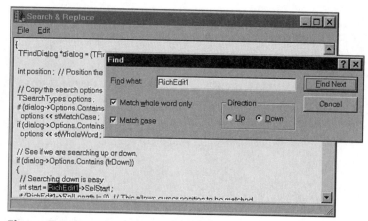

Figure 3-2 SearchReplace program

5. Click on the Find menu item and add the following code to the OnClick handler in the Code Editor:

```
void __fastcall TForm1::Find1Click(TObject *Sender)
{
  FindDialog1->Execute () ;
}
```

6. Click on Replace in the form's main menu and add this code to the OnClick handler in the Code Editor:

```
void __fastcall TForm1::Replace1Click(TObject *Sender)
{
  ReplaceDialog1->Execute () ;
}
```

7. Select the Find dialog on the main form. Press F11 to display the Object Inspector. Go to the Events page and double-click on the value for the OnFind event to create a handler for the event. Add this code to the event handler in the Code Editor:

```
void __fastcall TForm1::FindDialog1Find(TObject *Sender)
{
  TFindDialog *dialog = (TFindDialog *)(Sender) ;

  int position ;  // Position the string is found

  // Copy the search options from the dialog box.
  TSearchTypes options ;
  if (dialog->Options.Contains (frMatchCase))
    options << stMatchCase ;
  if (dialog->Options.Contains (frWholeWord))
    options << stWholeWord ;
```

continued on next page

continued from previous page

```
// See if we are searching up or down.
if (dialog->Options.Contains (frDown))
{
   // Searching down is easy.
   int start = RichEdit1->SelStart ;
   if (RichEdit1->SelLength != 0)  // This allows cursor position to be⇐
matched.
      ++ start ;
   position = RichEdit1->FindText (dialog->FindText,
                                   start,
                                   RichEdit1->Text.Length () -⇐
RichEdit1->SelStart-1,
                                   options) ;

}
else if (RichEdit1->SelStart > 0)
{
   // For searching down we have to loop until we find the previous⇐
match.
   int search = -1 ;
   do
   {
     position = search ;
     search = RichEdit1->FindText (dialog->FindText,
                                   search + 1,
                                   RichEdit1->SelStart - search - 1,
                                   options) ;

   } while (search >= 0) ;
}
else
{
   // We are searching up from the start of the buffer.
   position = -1 ;
}
// If found, then select the text.
if (position >= 0)
{
   RichEdit1->SelStart = position ;
   RichEdit1->SelLength = dialog->FindText.Length () ;
}
}
```

8. Select the Replace dialog control on the application's main form. Press F11 to display the Object Inspector. On the Events page select the `OnFind` event but do not double-click on it. Instead, use the drop-down list and select `FindDialog1Find` from the list.

9. Return to the Object Inspector and select the `OnReplace` event for the Replace dialog. Double-click on it to create the event handler; then add this code in the Code Editor:

```
void __fastcall TForm1::ReplaceDialog1Replace(TObject *Sender)
{
   if (ReplaceDialog1->Options.Contains (frReplaceAll))
```

```
{
  TSearchTypes options ;
  if (ReplaceDialog1->Options.Contains (frMatchCase))
    options << stMatchCase ;
  if (ReplaceDialog1->Options.Contains (frWholeWord))
    options << stWholeWord ;

  int position = RichEdit1->FindText (ReplaceDialog1->FindText, 0, -1,⇐
options) ;
  while (position >= 0)
  {
    RichEdit1->SelStart = position ;
    RichEdit1->SelLength = ReplaceDialog1->FindText.Length () ;
    RichEdit1->SelText = ReplaceDialog1->ReplaceText ;
    position = RichEdit1->FindText (ReplaceDialog1->FindText, 0, -1,⇐
options) ;
  }
}
else if (RichEdit1->SelLength > 0)
{
  RichEdit1->SelText = ReplaceDialog1->ReplaceText ;
}
}
```

10. Compile and test the project.

How It Works

Unlike all other standard dialogs, the Find and Replace dialogs are nonmodal. This means that when they are displayed, the other forms in your application can receive input focus. When a modal form such as the File Open dialog is displayed, no other form in the application can receive input focus until the modal form is closed or it displays another modal form. When the `Execute` method displays these dialogs nonmodally, the user can perform more than one search without closing the dialog and it allows the user to edit between searches.

Because the Find and Replace dialogs are nonmodal, their `Execute` methods return immediately and return no useful information. For the application to determine when the user wants to search for text, these dialog controls have an `OnFind` event that is called whenever the user clicks on the Find Next button. The Replace dialog control also has an `OnReplace` event that is called when the user clicks on the Replace or Replace All buttons.

When you created the application, you created only one `OnFind` handler that is shared by both the Find and Replace dialog controls. There is no sense in having two events with the exact same code and because the `TFindDialog` class is an ancestor of `TReplaceDialog`, a `TReplaceDialog` object can be used in the code anywhere there is a `TFindDialog`.

The `OnFind` event handler uses the Rich Edit control's `FindText` method to locate the text entered in the dialog. The options in the dialog match those handled by the `FindText` method with the exception of the search direction. The Find dialog

control has an option to search up or down, but the **FindText** method searches only down. To search upward, the event handler uses a loop to find the last matching position before the cursor position in the buffer.

The **OnReplace** event determines whether the user clicked the Replace or Replace All button by using the **Options** property of the dialog. If the Replace button was clicked, the text selected by the last Find operation is replaced. If the Replace All button was clicked, the handler uses a loop to replace all the matching text in the Rich Edit control.

Comments

This How-To demonstrates how to use the Find and Replace dialogs along with how to use the searching capabilities of the Rich Edit control. It also demonstrates how more than one control can share an event handler. Having two controls of exactly the same type share an event handler is easy. You should have controls of different types share event handlers when the event handler is restricted to using properties and methods from a common ancestor class.

COMPLEXITY
INTERMEDIATE

3.3 How do I...
Use different fonts in my word processor?

Problem

I have an application in which the user needs to be able to format text using different fonts and special effects. I know I can change the **Font** property, but that changes the font everywhere. How can I use different fonts in one window in C++Builder?

Technique

You can control the formatting of different sections of text in a Rich Edit control. You only need to implement the user interface to manipulate the Rich Edit control.

Steps

Run the program **CHANGEFONTS.EXE**. Try selecting some text, then use the items on the Edit menu or the speed bar to change the format. A sample demonstrating some of the possibilities is shown in Figure 3-3.

1. Select File|New Application from the main menu to create a new blank project. Select File|Save Project As and save the project as **ChangeFonts**.

Figure 3-3 ChangeFonts program

2. Add a Main Menu control to the form. Set menu items to the Main Menu control as shown in Table 3-5.

Table 3-5 Menu design for the ChangeFonts project

MENU	MENU ITEM
&File	E&xit
&Edit	&Left Justify
	&Center
	&Right Justify
	−
	&Bullets
	−
	&Font...

3. Add the properties and settings as shown in Table 3-6. The bitmap files are with the project source on the CD-ROM.

Table 3-6 Components, properties, and settings for `ChangeFonts`

COMPONENT	PROPERTY	SETTING
Form1	Caption	Change Fonts
	Menu	MainMenu1
	Position	poDefault
RichEdit1	Align	alClient
	Lines	
	ScrollBars	ssBoth
	WantTabs	true
Panel1	Align	alTop
	BevelOuter	bvNone
	Caption	
	Height	35
SpeedButton1 (On Panel1)	AllowAllUp	true
	Glyph	BULLETS.BMP
	GroupIndex	1
	Width	25
	Height	25
	Left	10
	Top	5
SpeedButton2 (On Panel1)	Glyph	ALIGNLEFT.BMP
	Height	25
	GroupIndex	2
	Left	55
	Top	5
	Width	25
SpeedButton3 (On Panel1)	Glyph	ALIGNCENTER.BMP
	GroupIndex	2
	Height	25
	Left	80
	Top	5
	Width	25
SpeedButton4 (On Panel1)	Glyph	ALIGNRIGHT.BMP
	Width	25
	Height	25
	Left	105
	Top	5
	GroupIndex	2

COMPONENT	PROPERTY	SETTING
Bevel1 (On Panel1)	Align	alTop
	Height	5
	Shape	bsTopLine
StatusBar1		
LeftJustify1 (Menu Item)	GroupIndex	1
	RadioItem	true
Center1 (Menu Item)	GroupIndex	1
	RadioItem	true
Rightjustify1 (Menu Item)	GroupIndex	1
	RadioItem	true
FontDialog1		

4. Double-click on the **SpeedButton1** speed button on the main form. Add this code to the **OnClick** event handler in the Code Editor:

```
void __fastcall TForm1::SpeedButton1Click(TObject *Sender)
{
  if (SpeedButton1->Down)
    RichEdit1->Paragraph->Numbering = nsBullet ;
  else
    RichEdit1->Paragraph->Numbering = nsNone ;
}
```

5. Double-click on the **SpeedButton2** speed button and add this code to its **OnClick** event handler:

```
void __fastcall TForm1::SpeedButton2Click(TObject *Sender)
{
  RichEdit1->Paragraph->Alignment = taLeftJustify ;
}
```

6. Double-click on the **SpeedButton3** speed button on the main form. Add this code to the **OnClick** event handler in the Code Editor:

```
void __fastcall TForm1::SpeedButton3Click(TObject *Sender)
{
  RichEdit1->Paragraph->Alignment = taCenter ;
}
```

7. Double-click on the **SpeedButton4** speed button and add this code to the **OnClick** event handler:

```
void __fastcall TForm1::SpeedButton4Click(TObject *Sender)
{
  RichEdit1->Paragraph->Alignment = taRightJustify ;
}
```

8. Select the Rich Edit control on the main form. Press F11 to display the Object Inspector. Go to the Events page and select the OnSelectionChanged event. Double-click on value for this event to create a handler for it and modify the handler in the Code Editor to look like the following:

```
void __fastcall TForm1::RichEdit1SelectionChange(TObject *Sender)
{
  // Select the alignment button matching the state of the current ⇐
selection.
  switch (RichEdit1->Paragraph->Alignment)
  {
  case taLeftJustify:
    SpeedButton2->Down = true ;
    break ;
  case taCenter:
    SpeedButton3->Down = true ;
    break ;
  case taRightJustify:
    SpeedButton4->Down = true ;
    break ;
  }
  // Set the state of the bullets button to match that of the current text.
  if (RichEdit1->Paragraph->Numbering == nsBullet)
    SpeedButton1->Down = true ;
  else
    SpeedButton1->Down = false ;
}
```

9. Click on the Exit menu item and add the following code to the OnClick handler:

```
void __fastcall TForm1::Exit1Click(TObject *Sender)
{
  Close () ;
}
```

10. Double-click on the Main Menu control to display the Menu Designer. Select the Edit menu item on the Form Designer; then press F11 to display the Object Inspector. Go to the Events page and double-click on the OnClick event. Add the following code to the event handler in the Code window:

```
void __fastcall TForm1::Edit1Click(TObject *Sender)
{
  // Make the state of the alignment menu match the selected text.
  switch (RichEdit1->Paragraph->Alignment)
  {
  case taLeftJustify:
    LeftJustify1->Checked = true ;
    break ;
  case taCenter:
    Center1->Checked = true ;
```

```
      break ;
   case taRightJustify:
     RightJustify1->Checked = true ;
     break ;
   }

   // Make the state of the bullets menu item match the selected text.
   if (RichEdit1->Paragraph->Numbering == nsBullet)
     Bullets1->Checked = true ;
   else
     Bullets1->Checked = false ;
}
```

11. On the application's main form, click on the Left Justify menu item to create an **OnClick** event handler for it. Add the following code to the event handler:

```
void __fastcall TForm1::LeftJustify1Click(TObject *Sender)
{
  if (Sender == LeftJustify1)
  {
    LeftJustify1->Checked = true ;
    RichEdit1->Paragraph->Alignment = taLeftJustify ;
  }
  else if (Sender == Center1)
  {
    Center1->Checked = true ;
    RichEdit1->Paragraph->Alignment = taCenter ;
  }
  else
  {
    RightJustify1->Checked = true ;
    RichEdit1->Paragraph->Alignment = taRightJustify ;
  }
  RichEdit1SelectionChange (RichEdit1) ;
}
```

12. Double-click on the Main Menu control to display the Menu Designer. Select the Center menu item and press F11 to display the Object Inspector. Go to the Events page and select—do not double-click—the **OnClick** event. Select ListJustify1Click from the drop-down list. Repeat this procedure for the Right Justify menu item.

13. Click on the Bullets menu item to create an **OnClick** event handler and add the following code to the event handler:

```
void __fastcall TForm1::Bullets1Click(TObject *Sender)
{
  Bullets1->Checked = ! Bullets1->Checked ;
  if (Bullets1->Checked)
    RichEdit1->Paragraph->Numbering = nsBullet ;
  else
    RichEdit1->Paragraph->Numbering = nsNone ;
  RichEdit1SelectionChange (RichEdit1) ;
}
```

14. Click on the Font Menu item. Add the following code to the `OnClick` event handler in the Code Editor:

```
void __fastcall TForm1::Font1Click(TObject *Sender)
{
  FontDialog1->Font->Assign (RichEdit1->SelAttributes) ;
  if (FontDialog1->Execute ())
    RichEdit1->SelAttributes->Assign (FontDialog1->Font) ;
}
```

15. Compile and test the project.

How It Works

The `TRichEdit` class has three properties that control how text is formatted within the control. The `SelAttributes` property controls the font attributes in the selected text in the control. The `DefAttributes` property is similar to the `SelAttributes` property except that it controls the font for any text that has not been assigned a font. It serves as the default attribute for the control. (Note that this application does not change the value for `DefAttributes`.) The `Paragraph` property controls the paragraph formatting for the selected text. This includes alignment, indentation, tabs, and bulleting.

The `ChangeFont` application allows the user to control the font, alignment, and bulleting by selecting text, using one of the menu items or speed buttons. One of the tricks in this application is that as the user moves the cursor, speed buttons and menu items are updated to reflect the formatting of the text containing the caret. The update of the button state is performed in the `OnSelectionChanged` event of the Rich Edit control, and the menu is updated in the `OnClick` event for the Edit1 menu item.

Comments

Two other features that may be of use to you are indenting and tab settings. These are controlled through the `Paragraph` property of the `TRichEdit` class.

 COMPLEXITY
BEGINNING

3.4 How do I...
Add Cut and Paste to my word processor?

Problem

I know that the user can cut and paste to the clipboard in a Rich Edit control using control keys, but I would like to add these features to menu items in my word processor. How is this possible?

Technique

The **TRichEdit** class contains methods for transferring text to and from the clipboard. All you have to do is implement the user interface.

Steps

Run the program **CUTPASTE.EXE**. Try typing in some text; then use the menu items to cut and paste text from the clipboard. Notice that the Cut and Copy menu items are not enabled when no text is selected and that the Paste menu item is not enabled when the clipboard does not contain text. The program's main form is shown in Figure 3-4.

1. Select File|New Application from the main menu to create a new blank project. Select File|Save Project As and save the project as **CutPaste**.

2. Add a Main Menu control to the form. Set menu items to the Main Menu control as shown in Table 3-7.

Table 3-7 Menu design for the **CutPaste** project

MENU	MENU ITEM
&File	E&xit
&Edit	Cu&t
	&Copy
	&Paste

3. Add the properties and settings as shown in Table 3-8.

Table 3-8 Components, properties, and settings for **CutPaste**

COMPONENT	PROPERTY	SETTING
Form1	Caption	Cut & Paste
	Menu	MainMenu1
	Position	poDefault
RichEdit1	Align	alClient
	Lines	
	ScrollBars	ssBoth
StatusBar1		

4. Click on the Exit menu item to create an **OnClick** event handler for it. Go to the Code Editor and add the following code to the handler:

```
void __fastcall TForm1::Exit1Click(TObject *Sender)
{
  Close () ;
}
```

5. Click the Cut menu item on the main form and add the following code to the **OnClick** event handler:

```
void __fastcall TForm1::Cut1Click(TObject *Sender)
{
  RichEdit1->CutToClipboard () ;
}
```

6. Click on the Copy menu item to create an **OnClick** handler for it. Add the following code to the event handler:

```
void __fastcall TForm1::Copy1Click(TObject *Sender)
{
  RichEdit1->CopyToClipboard () ;
}
```

7. Create an **OnClick** event handler for the Paste menu item by clicking on it. Modify the event handler to look like this:

```
void __fastcall TForm1::Paste1Click(TObject *Sender)
{
  RichEdit1->PasteFromClipboard () ;
}
```

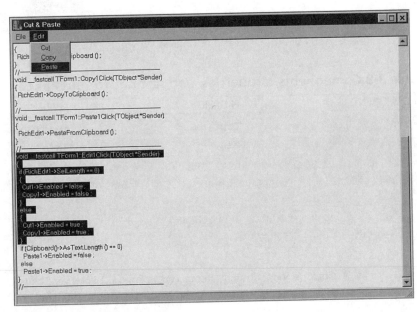

Figure 3-4 CutPaste program

8. Double-click on the Main Menu control to display the Menu Designer. Select the Edit menu item; then press [F11] to display the Object Inspector. Double-click on the value of the `OnClick` event to create a handler for it. Add the following to the event handler in the Code Editor:

```
void __fastcall TForm1::Edit1Click(TObject *Sender)
{
  if (RichEdit1->SelLength == 0)
  {
    Cut1->Enabled = false ;
    Copy1->Enabled = false ;
  }
  else
  {
    Cut1->Enabled = true ;
    Copy1->Enabled = true ;
  }
  if (Clipboard()->AsText.Length () == 0)
    Paste1->Enabled = false ;
  else
    Paste1->Enabled = true ;
}
```

9. Add the clipboard include file to `UNIT1.CPP`.

```
#include <vcl\vcl.h>
#include <vcl/clipbrd.hpp>
#pragma hdrstop
```

10. Compile and test the project.

How It Works

The `TRichEdit` class's `CopyToClipboard`, `CutToClipboard`, and `PasteFrom Clipboard` member functions allow an application to control Cut and Paste in a Rich Edit control. These operations are bound to items in the main menu.

The `OnClick` event for the Edit menu item gets called whenever the Edit menu is made visible. Here the Edit menu items are enabled or disabled depending upon whether they are applicable.

Comments

The state of the clipboard is represented in VCL by the `TClipboard` class. There is one `TClipboard` object per application and it is accessed by the `Clipboard` function. Your application should not attempt to delete the object returned by the `Clipboard` function. If you were to cast the address returned by `Clipboard` to a non-`const` pointer and then delete it, your application would produce unexpected results.

COMPLEXITY
ADVANCED

3.5 How do I...
Implement Undo in a word processor?

Problem

Most text processing applications allow the user to undo the last change by pressing the CTRL-Z key. I have looked at the documentation for the Rich Edit control and there is nothing about undo. How can I add Undo capabilities to my word processing application?

Technique

The **TRichEdit** class does not implement all the functionality of the underlying Win32 Rich Edit control. You can use the API function **SendMessage** to use the standard features of the Rich Edit control that are not implemented by the **TRichEdit** class.

Steps

Run the program **UNDO.EXE**, whose main form is shown in Figure 3-5. Try typing in some text; then press the CTRL-Z key. This will undo the last editing change you made. As you move the caret around the window, notice how the line number is updated in the status bar.

1. Select File|New Application from the main menu to create a new blank project. Select File|Save Project As and save the project as **Undo**.

2. Add a Main Menu Control to the form. Set menu items to the Main Menu Component as shown in Table 3-9.

Table 3-9 Menu design for the Undo project

MENU	MENU ITEM	SHORTCUT
&File	&Exit	
&Edit	&Undo	CTRL-Z

3. Add the properties and settings as shown in Table 3-10.

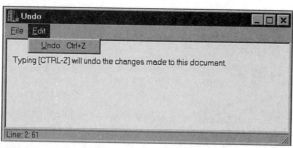

Figure 3-5 Undo program

Table 3-10 Components, properties, and settings for Undo

COMPONENT	PROPERTY	SETTING
Form1	Caption	Undo
	Menu	MainMenu1
	Position	poDefault
RichEdit1	Align	alClient
	Lines	
	ScrollBars	ssBoth
StatusBar1	SimplePanel	True

4. Click on the Exit button on the main form's menu to create an `OnClick` event handler.

```
void __fastcall TForm1::Exit1Click(TObject *Sender)
{
  Close () ;
}
```

5. Create an `OnClick` handler for the Undo menu item and modify it to look like this:

```
void __fastcall TForm1::Undo1Click(TObject *Sender)
{
  SendMessage (RichEdit1->Handle, EM_UNDO, 0, 0) ;
}
```

6. Double-click on the form's Main Menu Control to display the Menu Designer. Select the Edit menu item; then press F11 to display the Object Inspector. Go to the Events page and double-click on the value of the `OnClick` event to create a handler for it. Modify the `OnClick` event to look like this:

```
void __fastcall TForm1::Edit1Click(TObject *Sender)
{
  if (SendMessage (RichEdit1->Handle, EM_CANUNDO, 0, 0))
    Undo1->Enabled = true ;
  else
    Undo1->Enabled = false ;
}
```

7. Click on the Rich Edit control on the main form. Press F11 to display the Object Inspector. Go to the Events Page and double-click on the value for the OnSelectionChange event to create a handler for it. Add the following code to the event handler:

```
void __fastcall TForm1::RichEdit1SelectionChange(TObject *Sender)
{
  UpdateStatusBar () ;
}
```

8. Go to the Object Inspector and select the Form1 object from the drop-down list at the top. Go to the Events page and double-click on the OnCreate event and add this code to the handler in the Code Editor.

```
void __fastcall TForm1::FormCreate(TObject *Sender)
{
  UpdateStatusBar () ;
}
```

9. Return to the Object Inspector and create an OnResize handler for the main form.

```
void __fastcall TForm1::FormResize(TObject *Sender)
{
  const gutter = 10 ;
  RECT rect = { gutter,
          gutter,
          RichEdit1->ClientWidth - 2 * gutter,
          RichEdit1->ClientHeight - 2 * gutter} ;
  SendMessage (RichEdit1->Handle, EM_SETRECT, 0, (LPARAM) &rect) ;
}
```

10. Go to the Code Editor and select File|Open from the C++Builder menu and open the file UNIT1.H. Add the declaration for UpdateStatusBar to the definition of TForm1.

```
class TForm1 : public TForm
{
__published:
  TMainMenu *MainMenu1;
  TRichEdit *RichEdit1;
  TStatusBar *StatusBar1;
  TMenuItem *File1;
  TMenuItem *Edit1;
  TMenuItem *Undo1;
```

```
   TMenuItem *Exit1;
   void __fastcall Edit1Click(TObject *Sender);
   void __fastcall Undo1Click(TObject *Sender);

   void __fastcall RichEdit1SelectionChange(TObject *Sender);
   void __fastcall FormCreate(TObject *Sender);
   void __fastcall Exit1Click(TObject *Sender);
   void __fastcall FormResize(TObject *Sender);
private:          // private user declarations
   void UpdateStatusBar () ;
public:           // public user declarations
   virtual __fastcall TForm1(TComponent* Owner);
};
```

11. Switch to the file UNI1.CPP in the Code Editor and add this definition for UpdateStatusBar:

```
void TForm1::UpdateStatusBar ()
{
   // Get the line number.
   int line = SendMessage (RichEdit1->Handle,
                EM_LINEFROMCHAR,
                RichEdit1->SelStart,
                0) ;
   // Get the starting character position for the line.
   int lineindex = SendMessage (RichEdit1->Handle,
                EM_LINEINDEX,
                line,
                0) ;
   StatusBar1->SimpleText = String ("Line: ") + String (line + 1) + ": "
                + String (RichEdit1->SelStart - lineindex + 1);
}
```

12. Compile and test the project.

How It Works

As you saw in Chapter 2, "Standard Components and Classes," many controls in VCL are based upon standard Win32 controls. The VCL class is simply a wrapper around the standard control. Although VCL classes for standard controls implement the most important features of the controls, they do not implement all of them. The features of a standard control that are not implemented by VCL are always accessible using the Win32 API. The **Handle** property of the control returns the window handle that Win32 uses to identify the control. The handle can be passed to API functions to manipulate the control without using VCL.

The **Undo** application uses several features of the standard Rich Edit control that are not implemented by the VCL **TRichEdit** class. In addition to Undo processing, this program displays the position of the caret in the status bar and sets the margin so that text will not be right up against the edge of the control.

To undo the last editing operation in a Rich Edit control, you have to send an **EM_UNDO** message to the control using the **SendMessage** API function. The **WPARAM** and **LPARAM** values are not used for this message so they are set to zero.

In certain situations, such as when the control is created, it is not possible for a Rich Edit control to perform an Undo operation. The **EM_CANUNDO** message is used to determine whether a Rich Edit control is in a state where it can undo the last operation. The **Undo** program uses this message to determine whether the Undo menu item should be enabled. The application only enables this menu item when the Rich Edit control can undo.

This program also sends messages to the Rich Edit control to determine the current line number and column so that they can be displayed in the status bar. The current line number is obtained by the **EM_LINEFROMCHAR** message. When no characters are selected, the **SelStart** property marks the character offset of the caret. The **EM_LINEFROMCHAR** message translates this value to the line number. The line number is sent with an **EM_LINEINDEX** message, which returns the starting character position for a line. The difference between the value and the **SelStart** gives a zero-based column position.

Notice that the method for displaying text in the status bar is different from the application in How-To 3.1. In this application the **SimplePanel** property is set to **true**, which allows us to display text in the status bar using the **SimpleText** property. In How-To 3.1 you created a panel in the status bar and undated its text. The method here is easier but the earlier method is more flexible and allows more than one piece of information to be displayed.

The final feature of this application is that the main form's **OnResize** event offsets the text slightly from the edge of the control, making it easier to read. This is done using the **EM_SETRECT** message and passing it the address **RECT** structure containing the bounds for the text in the control.

Comments

A better title for this How-To might have been "How to Send Messages to a Rich Edit Control." It demonstrates several features of the Rich Edit control that can only be used by passing it messages through the Win32 API. The Rich Text control has many other features available only through the Win32 API. For more information on these you will have to check the Windows help files.

This is the last How-To on using the Rich Edit control. By combining the techniques in the last five How-To's you should be able to put together a powerful text processing application. A complete example putting together all the techniques of the previous five How-To's is included on the CD-ROM that comes with this book. The enlarged example also demonstrates a few Rich Edit controls not covered in the How-To's.

COMPLEXITY
BEGINNING

3.6 How do I...
Create a right-justified edit box?

Problem

I have an application in which the user has to enter numeric values. Usually numbers are right-justified but the Edit control has no properties to control alignment. How can I create an edit box that is right-justified in C++Builder?

Technique

The secret to creating a right-justified edit box is to use a Memo control. The Memo control has alignment properties, but to use it like an edit box, you need to prevent the text from wrapping over more than one line.

Steps

Run the program **RIGHTJUSTIFY.EXE**. Enter some text into the edit window. The text you enter should be right-justified, as shown in Figure 3-6.

1. Select File|New Application from the main menu to create a new blank project. Select File|Save Project As and save the project as **RightJustify**.

2. Add the properties and settings as shown in Table 3-11.

Table 3-11 Components, properties, and settings for **RightJustify**

COMPONENT	PROPERTY	SETTING
Form1	BorderStyle	bsDialog
	Caption	Right Justify
	Height	150
	Position	poScreenCenter
	Width	240
Memo1	Alignment	taRightJustify
	Height	25
	Left	20
	Lines	
	MaxLength	14
	Top	40
	Width	190

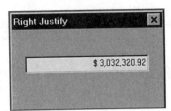

Figure 3-6 `RightJustify`
program

3. Double-click on the Memo control and add the following code to the
`OnChange` event handler in the Code Editor:

```
void __fastcall TForm1::Memo1Change(TObject *Sender)
{
  int caret = Memo1->SelStart ;
  String text = Memo1->Text ;
  for (int index = text.Pos ("\n") ; index != 0  ; index = text.Pos⇐
("\n"))
  {
    text.Delete (index, 1) ;
    -- caret ;
  }
  for (int index = text.Pos ("\r") ; index != 0  ; index = text.Pos⇐
("\r"))
  {
    text.Delete (index, 1) ;
    -- caret ;
  }
  if (caret != Memo1->SelStart)
  {
    Memo1->Text = text ;
    Memo1->SelStart = caret ;
  }
}
```

4. Compile and test the project.

How It Works

If you look at the VCL source for the Edit control and the Memo control, you
will see that they are fundamentally the same except that the Memo control has the
`ES_MULTILINE` window style bit set so that text in the Memo control can extend over
more than one line. Windows will only right-justify or center text in an edit box with
the `ES_MULTILINE` so if you want to right-justify text, you are forced to use a Memo
control.

The big problem you have to solve when using the Memo control is how to keep
the text on one line. The text in a memo will be wrapped if it is too wide to display

on one line or if it contains return characters. To keep the text from wrapping, the **MaxLength** property is set to a value small enough for the control's width. Preventing returns from being inserted into the control is a little tougher.

It would appear that one could set the **WantReturn** property to **false** to prevent the user from typing line breaks but there are still two holes. First of all the user could type CTRL-ENTER to create a line break. This could easily be handled by setting the **Key** parameter to zero in the **OnKeyPress** event when a line break is entered. However, that method would not handle the case of pasting from the clipboard. The solution used here is to strip all carriage return and line feed characters from the control's text in the **OnChange** event.

When new lines are deleted from the control in the **OnChange**, the insertion point marked by the caret will jump around. The **OnChange** handler uses the caret variable to keep the insertion point consistent with the user's typing.

Comments

Whenever you alter a control's basic behavior, you need to be rigorous about eliminating backdoor holes. Pasting from the clipboard is a hole that is frequently overlooked.

COMPLEXITY
INTERMEDIATE

3.7 How do I...
Create a font selection combo box?

Problem

Many applications allow the user to select a font using a combo box that displays the available fonts in the drop-down list. How can I create a combo box containing available fonts using C++Builder?

Technique

The **EnumFonts** Win32 API function returns all the fonts available for a device context. To get the fonts available for a device, you create a Device Context for the device and then call **EnumFonts**. The **Canvas** object for the **TForm** class has a Device Context that can be accessed through its **Handle** property. The application can use this Device Context rather than create a new one for the **EnumFonts** function.

Steps

Run the program **FONTSELECT.EXE**. As you select fonts from the combo box, you will see the name of the font displayed in the edit window below the combo box as shown in Figure 3-7.

Figure 3-7 `FontSelect` program

1. Select File|New Application from the main menu to create a new blank project. Select File|Save Project As and save the project as `FontSelect`.

2. Add the properties and settings as shown in Table 3-12.

Table 3-12 Components, properties, and settings for `FontSelect`

COMPONENT	PROPERTY	SETTING
Form1	Caption	Font Selection Combo
	Position	poDefault
Panel1	Align	alTop
	Caption	
	Height	40
ComboBox1 (On Panel1)	Height	24
	Left	8
	Style	csDropDownList
	Sorted	True
	Top	8
	Width	210
Memo1	Align	alClient
	Alignment	taCenter
	Lines	
	ReadOnly	True

3. Select the Code Editor; then click on File|Open in the C++Builder main menu and top the file `UNIT1.H`. Add the declaration of the `UpdateText` function to the definition of `TForm1` in the Code Editor.

```
class TForm1: public TForm
{
__published:
  TPanel *Panel1;
  TComboBox *ComboBox1;
  TMemo *Memo1;
private:  // private user declarations
```

```
   void UpdateText () ;
public:        // public user declarations
   virtual __fastcall TForm1(TComponent* Owner);
};
```

4. In the Code Editor, switch to the file **UNIT1.CPP** and add the definitions of the **UpdateText** and **EnumProc** functions to it. Note that the function **EnumProc** is not a member function.

```
void TForm1::UpdateText ()
{
   Memo1->Font->Name = ComboBox1->Text ;
   Memo1->Font->Size = 20 ;
   Memo1->Text = ComboBox1->Text ;
}

int CALLBACK EnumProc(LOGFONT *logfont, TEXTMETRIC  *textmetric, DWORD⇐
type, LPARAM  data)
{
   TComboBox *cb = (TComboBox *) data ;
   cb->Items->Add (String (logfont->lfFaceName)) ;
   return 1 ;
}
```

5. Go to the Object Inspector window and select **Form1** from the drop-down list at the top. Go to the events page and double-click on the **OnCreate** event to create a handler for it. Add this code to the form's **OnCreate** handler in the Code Editor:

```
void __fastcall TForm1::FormCreate(TObject *Sender)
{
   EnumFonts (Canvas->Handle, NULL, (FONTENUMPROC) EnumProc, (LPARAM)⇐
ComboBox1) ;
   ComboBox1->ItemIndex = ComboBox1->Items->IndexOf (Memo1->Font->Name) ;
   UpdateText () ;
}
```

6. Select the combo box on the main form. Press F11 to display the Object Inspector; then go to the Events page. Double-click on the **OnClick** event to create a handler for it. In the Code Editor, modify the combo box's **OnClick** handler to look like this:

```
void __fastcall TForm1::ComboBox1Click(TObject *Sender)
{
   UpdateText () ;
}
```

7. Compile and test the project.

How It Works

Almost all the work in this application is done in the main form's **OnCreate** event handler and the **EnumFonts** function. The **OnCreate** handler calls the Win32 API function **EnumFonts**. Notice that one of the arguments is the function that you created and named **EnumProc**. The **EnumFonts** function calls the function passed to it as a parameter once for each font available for the device context.

It is in the **EnumProc** function that you add the name of a font to the combo box's drop-down list. The problem here is that **EnumProc** is not a member function of the **TForm1** class so it does not have access to the combo box. The last parameter of the **EnumFonts** function is a value that gets passed to the enumeration function unmodified. The application can use it to pass any information it needs to. In this case, this parameter is used to pass the address of the combo box object to **EnumProc**. The **EnumProc** casts the parameter back to a pointer to a **TComboBox** so that the font name can be added to the drop-down list.

Comments

Many Win32 API functions, like **EnumFonts**, use an enumeration procedure to return information with a variable number of values. In C++ these functions are usually called from member functions so the main problem in using them is giving the enumeration procedure access to the object calling the API function.

Because of visibility, when calling an API function that uses an enumeration procedure, it is often desirable to create a member function to do all the processing and have it called from the enumeration function. Doing this in the class definition and enumeration procedure would look something like this:

```
Class TForm1 : public TForm
{
...
public:
   int EnumFonts (LOGFONT *logfont, TEXTMETRIC *textmetric, DWORD type) ;
...
} ;

int CALLBACK EnumProc(LOGFONT *logfont, TEXTMETRIC  *textmetric, DWORD⇐
type, LPARAM  data)
{
   TForm1 *form = (TForm1 *) data ;
   return form->EnumFonts (logfont, textmetrix, type) ;
}

void __fastcall TForm1::FormCreate(TObject *Sender)
{
   EnumFonts (Canvas->Handle, NULL, (FONTENUMPROC) EnumProc, (LPARAM) this)⇐
;
   ComboBox1->ItemIndex = ComboBox1->Items->IndexOf (Memo1->Font->Name) ;
   UpdateText () ;
}
```

COMPLEXITY
INTERMEDIATE

3.8 How do I...
Limit text entry to certain characters?

Problem

In my application I need to have some text boxes where the user enters numeric values. I would like to restrict the user to entering only numbers into these controls. The Masked Edit control works well for fixed-length data like ID numbers and postal codes, but it is awkward when entering data that can have a variable length like numbers. How can I create an Edit control that will only accept a number of any reasonable length?

Technique

The **OnChange** event of an Edit control is used to determine whether the text entered into the control is a valid number. If it is a valid number, the text is saved in a member field in the form object. If it is invalid, the last valid value is restored from the member field.

Steps

Run the program **MITTEXT.EXE** shown in Figure 3-8. Enter a number value into the Edit control. Notice that the Edit control will not allow you to enter a value that is not a number.

1. Select File|New Application from the main menu to create a new blank project. Select File|Save Project As and save the project as **LimitText**.

2. Add the properties and settings as shown in Table 3-13.

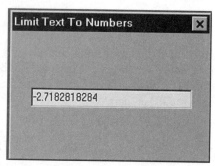

Figure 3-8 LimitText program

Table 3-13 Components, properties, and settings for `LimitText`

COMPONENT	PROPERTY	SETTING
Form1	BorderStyle	bsDialog
	Caption	Limit Text To Numbers
	Height	190
	Position	poScreenCenter
	Width	265
Edit1	Height	24
	Left	25
	Text	
	Top	70
	Width	210

3. Select the Code Editor; then click on File|Open in C++Builder's main menu and open the file **UNIT1.H**.

4. Add these private declarations to definition of **TForm1** in **UNIT1.H**:

```
class TForm1 : public TForm
{
__published:
  TEdit *Edit1;
private:      // private user declarations
  String lastvalue ;
  bool active ;
public:       // public user declarations
  virtual __fastcall TForm1(TComponent* Owner);
};
```

5. Switch to the file **UNIT1.CPP** in the Code Editor and modify **TForm1's** constructor to look like this:

```
__fastcall TForm1::TForm1(TComponent* Owner) : TForm(Owner)
{
  active = false ;
}
```

6. Go the application's main form and select the Edit control; then press F11 to display the Object Inspector. Go to the Events page and double-click on the **OnKeyDown** event to create a handler for it. In the Code Editor add the following code to the **OnKeyDown** handler:

```
void __fastcall TForm1::Edit1KeyPress(TObject *Sender, char &Key)
{
  if (! ((Key >= '0' && Key <= '9') || Key == '-' || Key == '.' || Key ==⇐
'\b'))
    Key = 0 ;
}
```

7. Go to the application's main form and double-click on the Edit control to create an `OnChange` handler. Modify the handler in the Code Editor to look like this:

```
void __fastcall TForm1::Edit1Change(TObject *Sender)
{
  // Prevent calls to this function while we are active.
  if (active)
    return ;
  active = true ;

  String newvalue = Edit1->Text ;
  int index = 1 ;

optionalsign: // Block lexing option minus sign
  if (index >= newvalue.Length ())
    goto end ;
  else if (newvalue [index] == '-')
   ++ index ;

integerpart:  // Block for lexing integer part of a real number
  if (index >= newvalue.Length ())
  {
    goto end ;
  }
  else if (newvalue [index] == '.')
  {
    ++ index ;
    goto fraction ;
  }
  else if (isdigit (newvalue [index]))
  {
   ++ index ;
   goto integerpart ;
  }
  else
  {
    goto error ;
  }

fraction:   // Block for lexing the fractional part of a real number.
  if (index >= newvalue.Length ())
  {
    goto end ;
  }
  else if (isdigit (newvalue [index]))
  {
   ++ index ;
   goto fraction ;
  }
  else
  {
    goto error ;
  }

end:  // Block for success in lexing
```

continued on next page

continued from previous page

```
    lastvalue = newvalue ;
    active = false ;
    return ;

error:   // Block for error in lexing.
    int caret = Edit1->SelStart - (newvalue.Length () - lastvalue.Length ())⇐
;
    Edit1->Text = lastvalue ;
    Edit1->SelStart = caret ;
    active = false ;
    return ;
}
```

8. Compile and test the project.

How It Works

The **LimitText** application only allows strings representing real numbers without exponents to be entered into its Edit control. The **OnKeyDown** event screens out all characters except for those that are legal in a number and the backspace key, by setting the value of the **Key** parameter to zero. When this value is set to zero in the **OnKeyDown**, the application discards the input character.

Unfortunately screening out characters this way only solves part of the problem. The user can still use the clipboard to paste any text into the control. In addition, the screening in the **OnKeyDown** event does not prevent the user from entering a string like "9.-9.-", which clearly is not a valid number. These problems are solved in the **OnChange** event for the Edit control.

The code in the **OnChange** event validates the text in the Edit control to make sure that it conforms to the format of a number. If the text is valid, it saves a copy in the **lastvalue** field of the **TForm1** class. If an invalid string is entered into the control, then the last valid value is retrieved from the **lastvalue** field and placed in the Edit box. The manipulations with the **SelStart** property restored the caret to its position before the text was changed to an invalid value.

The **active** field of the **TForm1** class is used to prevent multiple invocations of the **OnChange** handler from being active at once. This is possible because the **OnChange** event handler changes the value of the **Text** property, which in turn causes the **OnChange** handler to be called again.

Comments

If you frequently need to use a control for entering numbers, you may want to consider writing your own component for that purpose. In your own component you can intercept the message that causes text to be pasted from the clipboard, so you could do all the character screening then and when you receive the keystrokes. An elaborate **OnChange** handler like the one here would not be needed.

The programming style of the `OnChange` handler may appear to violate the rules of programming you have been taught because of its frequent use of **goto**. To determine whether the string in the Edit control is a valid number, processing the `OnChange` event handler uses a set of states and state transition rules. This type of processing is commonly used when writing lexical analyzers and it is much more clearly written using **goto**'s than with other constructs.

CHAPTER 4

MOUSE AND MENU

4

MOUSE AND MENU

How do I...

Windows handles mouse movement and menu selection behind the scenes. C++Builder™ makes it very easy to create basic menus and respond to mouse events. However, some applications need more than just basic functionality. Maybe you need a custom mouse cursor. Maybe you'd like to put pictures in your menus, or use a special font. The How-To's in this chapter will show those and other ways to use menus and the mouse to enrich your application's user interface.

4.1 Create and Use My Own Mouse Cursor

C++Builder makes it very easy to change the mouse cursor when it passes over certain controls and forms. Although it supports 21 standard cursors, there are still times you need to add a custom cursor to the list. This How-To shows you how to create a custom mouse cursor and use it in your C++Builder application.

4.2 Modify the Menu at Runtime

Many applications modify their menu based on the situation. For example, Microsoft Word's top-level menu contains only two submenus, File and Help, until a document is loaded. This How-To will show you the techniques necessary to add similar capabilities to your C++Builder applications. It also highlights the difference between main menus and menu items.

4.3 Display a File History List in a Menu

An application that works with files should include a list of the most recently opened items on the file menu. When the program is closed, it should save the history list so it can be restored the next time the program is run. This lets users open recent work without going through the file open dialog. This How-To takes you step-by-step through the creation of a simple object that you can reuse in your applications to provide this vital capability.

4.4 Put Pictures in Menus

User-interface researchers have proven again and again that the old saying "A picture is worth a thousand words" applies to computer programs. There is no denying that the graphical Windows environment is considerably easier to use than the old command-line interface that dominated the early days of the personal computer revolution. In fact, graphical interfaces have even revolutionized the way we program computers.

Even menu items sometimes benefit from a graphical treatment. A simple picture, used in place of a text caption, can sometimes tell the user much more about what action the menu item will trigger. This How-To will show you how you can add pictures to the menus in your C++Builder application.

4.5 Create and Use Custom Check Marks in Menus

Any Windows menu item can include a check mark to indicate the state of an option. For example, C++Builder's View menu includes toggles that allow you to turn the toolbar and component palette on and off. When they are displayed, a little check mark is displayed next to their respective menu items. When they are off, no check mark is displayed.

Although the standard Windows check mark is quite clear, it is pretty plain. You can, however, replace the rather boring default look with check marks that you create. This How-To will show you the proper techniques.

4.6 Use a Different Font in a Menu

Menu item captions are always displayed in the standard system font. Because C++Builder menu items do not include a Font property, you might conclude there is no way to change the font in a menu item. However, you can take over the drawing of a particular control if you want to do something special, like displaying a menu item caption in a particular font, by making it what Windows calls an Owner-Draw control. This How-To will show you how to accomplish this in your application.

4.7 Use a Popup Menu

The right mouse button is often used to pop up menus that apply to particular controls or windows. For example, if you select a block of text in Word for Windows and right-click, you'll get a menu of actions that can be taken on the currently selected block. This idea, which was pioneered on the Windows platform by Borland, is so good that Microsoft has made it a fundamental part of the new user interface on Windows 95 and Windows NT 4. This How-To will show you just how easy it is to add right-click menus to your C++Builder application.

COMPLEXITY
BEGINNING

4.1 How do I...
Create and use my own mouse cursor?

Problem

I'm writing an application that needs to display a special mouse cursor when the user selects a drawing tool from the toolbar. I know how to use the mouse cursors built into C++Builder, but none of them looks exactly like I want. How can I add a custom cursor to my application?

Technique

C++Builder manages to hide most of the mechanics of Windows programming. One of the things C++Builder hides is resource files— special binary files used to store application elements like icons, cursors, and bitmaps. Every time you create a form, C++Builder creates a resource file behind the scenes. In this How-To, you'll use the Image Editor included with C++Builder to create your own resource file that contains a custom mouse cursor. You'll also learn how to bind the resource to your application, load the mouse cursor it contains into your application, and make C++Builder controls use the custom mouse cursor.

Steps

Run **MYCURSOR.EXE**. When you move the cursor within the form's client area, the cursor looks like gun scope cross hairs as shown in Figure 4-1. If you move the cursor outside the form's client area, it will change into a standard windows cursor.

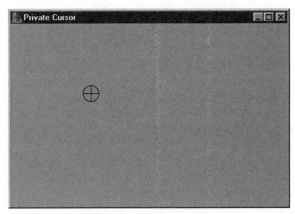

Figure 4-1 MYCURSOR displaying its custom
cursor

1. Use the image editor to create a custom resource file. Add a cursor named
"SCOPE". Save the resource file as **MYCURSOR.RES**.

2. Create a new project. Save the default unit as **MAIN.CPP** and the project as
CURSOR.MAK.

3. Change the caption of the form to "Private Cursor".

4. Just below the #include statements in **MAIN.CPP**, enter the following
code to define the constant that will be used to identify the new cursor:

```
#include "main.h"
//Define a constant to identify the custom cursor
const int crCrossHairs = 1;
```

5. Just below the first pragma resource statement, add a second one to
include the resource that contains the custom cursor.

```
#pragma resource "*.dfm"
//Bind the custom resource file into the executable
#pragma resource "mycursor.res"
```

6. On the events page of the Object Inspector, double-click the OnShow event
of the form and enter the following code to load the custom cursor and
assign it to Form1:

```
void __fastcall TForm1::FormShow(TObject *Sender)
{
  //Load new cursor into Screen object
  Screen->Cursors[crCrossHairs] = LoadCursor((void *)HInstance, "SCOPE");
  //Assign the cursor to the form
  Form1->Cursor = crCrossHairs;
}
```

7. Compile and run the application.

How It Works

As this How-To demonstrates, C++Builder makes it very easy to use custom cursors in your application. Once the cursor has been loaded and assigned to the `Cursors` array, it can be used just like C++Builder's built-in cursors.

Creating the Cursor

No matter what tool you use to create the cursor, you should save the custom cursor in a resource file (.RES extension) instead of a cursor file (.CUR). Resource files offer two advantages. First of all, resource files can contain multiple resources of many different types. For example, a single resource file can contain multiple cursors. Secondly, C++Builder makes it easy to link a resource file into the final executable file so you won't have to ship cursor files with your application.

Because C++Builder automatically creates a resource file with the same base name as your project name (for example `MYCURSOR.RES` is created for this How-To), you must name your custom resource file carefully. Otherwise, Borland C++Builder will overwrite your custom resource file without warning.

In C++Builder, the `pragma` resource statement is used to bind a custom resource to the executable. You can bind as many custom resource files to your executable as you want. However, keep in mind that resources contribute to the ultimate size of your executable file.

Loading the Cursor and Making It Available

The `LoadCursor` Windows API function is used to load the cursor from the executable file. The first parameter is the instance handle of your application, which C++Builder makes available in a global variable named `HInstance`. Note that the instance handle variable must be typecast for the call to `LoadCursor`. The second parameter passed to `LoadCursor` is the name of the resource.

C++Builder automatically creates a global `TScreen` pointer, named `Screen`, when an application starts. The `TScreen` object stores useful information like the screen size and information about the application's forms. It also manages cursor resources through a simple array called `Cursors`.

At application start-up, the `Cursors` array references the 18 standard cursors. The index values for the standard cursors start at -17 and end at position 0. Therefore, custom cursors can be added starting at position 1.

Once the cursor is included in the `Cursors` array, it can be assigned to the `Cursor` property of any control or form. The mouse cursor will then change to the custom cursor whenever it is moved over the form or control. When the application closes, your custom cursor will be removed from memory automatically because it is part of the `Cursors` array.

The entire process of loading the cursor, adding it to the **Cursors** array, and associating it with a form is accomplished in the two lines of code you added in step 6. The first line loads the cursor and adds it to the **Cursors** array. The second line assigns the custom cursor to the form's **Cursor** property. Because you are assigning an integer to an enumerated property, the compiler will generate a warning which can be safely ignored. It really is that simple.

Comments

The hardest part of using custom cursors in your application is drawing the cursor in the first place. Once you have a custom cursor in a resource file, it can be added to your application with just a few lines of code. If one of the standard cursors just doesn't fill your needs, you now know how to add your own.

COMPLEXITY
BEGINNING

4.2 How do I...
Modify the menu at runtime?

Problem

I'm creating an application in which, depending on the situation, I'd like to add or remove menu items in the main menu rather than just disabling or graying them. This would also make it possible to let the user customize the menu to some extent. How is this done in C++Builder?

Technique

All the methods and properties required for modifying menus at runtime are built into C++Builder. The example presented here demonstrates how to use the menu objects and helps clarify the differences between adding items to the **TMainMenu** and adding items to a **TMenuItem**. The methods shown here for **TMainMenu** also apply to the **TPopupMenu**.

Steps

Run **MODMENU.EXE**. Under the Edit menu, you will find four menu items. These menu items allow you to add and remove additional top-level items in the main menu, and add or remove additional menu items under the last top-level menu as shown in Figure 4-2. Experiment with these. Try selecting the new top-level menus and additional menu items you create.

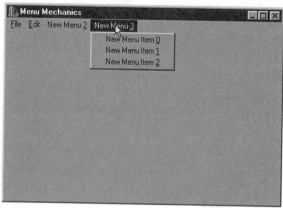

Figure 4-2 The MODMENU application displaying some new menu items

1. Create a new project. Save the default unit as **MODMENUMAIN.CPP** and the project as **MODMENU.MAK**.

2. Add a **TMainMenu** component to the form, and add the menus and menu items as shown in Table 4-1.

Table 4-1 Menu design for the MODMENU project

MENU	MENU ITEM
&File	E&Xit
&Edit	&Add Menu
	Add Menu &Item
	&Remove Menu
	Remove &Menu Item

3. Switch to the header file, **MODMENUMAIN.H**. Add the following declaration to **Form1**'s private section:

```
private:// User declarations
  void __fastcall DynaMenuClick(TObject *Sender);
```

4. Switch back to **MODMENUMAIN.CPP**. At the bottom of the file, add the actual **DynaMenuClick** function that will be the **OnClick** event handler for dynamically created menu items.

```
void __fastcall TForm1::DynaMenuClick(TObject *Sender)
{
```

continued on next page

continued from previous page

```
//Display a message box that contains the selected menu item's caption
Application->MessageBox(((TMenuItem *)Sender)->Caption.c_str(),
   "Menu Item Selected", IDOK);
}
```

5. Double-click on the form's `OnShow` event in the Object Inspector, and add the following code to initialize the enabled state of the items on the Edit menu:

```
void __fastcall TForm1::FormShow(TObject *Sender)
{
   //Disable menu actions that aren't allowed until a menu has been added
   AddMenuItem1->Enabled = FALSE;
   RemoveMenu1->Enabled = FALSE;
   RemoveMenuItem1->Enabled = FALSE;
}
```

6. Double-click on the Edit|Add menu item in the Menu Designer for `MainMenu1`. Add the following code to create a new top-level menu item:

```
void __fastcall TForm1::AddMenu1Click(TObject *Sender)
{
   TMenuItem *NewItem;

   //Create a new menu item with the main menu as owner
   NewItem = new TMenuItem(MainMenu1);
   //Create caption for new menu item
   NewItem->Caption = "New Menu &" + IntToStr(MainMenu1->Items->Count);
   //Assign an event handler
   NewItem->OnClick = DynaMenuClick;
   //Insert at end of main menu
   MainMenu1->Items->Insert(MainMenu1->Items->Count, NewItem);
   //Enabled menu items to remove a menu and to add a new menu item
   RemoveMenu1->Enabled = TRUE;
   AddMenuItem1->Enabled = TRUE;
   //Disable menu item to remove menu items because the new menu has none
   RemoveMenuItem1->Enabled = FALSE;
}
```

7. Double-click on Edit|Add Menu Item in the Menu Designer, and enter the following code to add a new menu item under the last top-level menu item:

```
void __fastcall TForm1::AddMenuItem1Click(TObject *Sender)
{
   TMenuItem *ToItem, *NewItem;

   //Don't add items to file or edit menus
   if (MainMenu1->Items->Count > 2)
   {
```

```
  //Get reference to last main menu item
  ToItem = MainMenu1->Items->Items[MainMenu1->Items->Count - 1];
  //Create new menu item with last main menu item as owner
  NewItem = new TMenuItem(ToItem);
  //Create caption relative to last main menu item's item count
  NewItem->Caption = "New Menu Item &" + IntToStr(ToItem->Count);
  //Assign an event handler
  NewItem->OnClick = DynaMenuClick;
  //Ensure ToItem has no event handler
  ToItem->OnClick = NULL;
  //Insert new menu item under last main menu item
  ToItem->Insert(ToItem->Count, NewItem);
  //Enable item removal
  RemoveMenuItem1->Enabled = TRUE;
  }
}
```

8. Double-click on the Edit|Remove Menu item in the Menu Designer, and
enter the code that removes the last top-level menu.

```
void __fastcall TForm1::RemoveMenu1Click(TObject *Sender)
{
  TMenuItem *ToItem;

  //Don't allow file or edit menu to be deleted
  if (MainMenu1->Items->Count > 2)
    //Delete the last item in the main menu
    MainMenu1->Items->Delete(MainMenu1->Items->Count - 1);

  //If there are no custom menu items
  if (MainMenu1->Items->Count == 2)
  {
    //Disable the menu commands that aren't allowed until a custom menu⇐
    exists
    AddMenuItem1->Enabled = FALSE;
    RemoveMenu1->Enabled = FALSE;
    RemoveMenuItem1->Enabled = FALSE;
  }
  //If there is a custom menu item left on the main menu
  else
  {
    //Get reference to last main menu item
    ToItem = MainMenu1->Items->Items[MainMenu1->Items->Count - 1];
    //If no more items in this menu
    if (ToItem->Count == 0)
      //Disable menu item removal
      RemoveMenuItem1->Enabled = FALSE;
    //Otherwise
    else
      //Enable item removal
      RemoveMenuItem1->Enabled = TRUE;
  }
}
```

9. Click on Edit|Remove Menu Item, and enter the code that removes the last item in the last top-level menu.

```
void __fastcall TForm1::RemoveMenuItem1Click(TObject *Sender)
{
  TMenuItem *ToItem;

  //Don't delete items from the file or edit menu
  if (MainMenu1->Items->Count > 2)
  {
    //Get reference to last main menu item
    ToItem = MainMenu1->Items->Items[MainMenu1->Items->Count - 1];
    //Make sure there is an item to delete
    if (ToItem->Count > 0)
      //Delete the last item in the main menu's last item
      ToItem->Delete(ToItem->Count - 1);

    //If no more items in this menu
    if (ToItem->Count == 0)
    {
      //Disable menu item removal
      RemoveMenuItem1->Enabled = FALSE;
      //Re-attach the event handler
      ToItem->OnClick = DynaMenuClick;
    }
  }
}
```

10. Click on File|Exit, and add the following line to terminate the application:

```
void __fastcall TForm1::Exit1Click(TObject *Sender)
{
  //End the program
  Close();
}
```

11. Compile and run the application.

How It Works

The basic mechanics of adding and removing menu items and checking for their presence are quite simple. They can, however, get confusing because there are differences between adding top-level menus to the TMainMenu component and adding menu items to a top-level menu.

The code to handle the OnShow event (step 5) disables the menu items that remove top-level menus, add menu items, and remove menu items. These options do not make sense until other events take place which create menus that could be modified. These menu items could just as easily have been disabled in the Object Inspector.

Adding Top-Level Menu Items

When Add Menu is selected, a new top-level menu item is added to the main menu. It is important to understand that all visible selections in a menu are **TMenuItem** components. The **TMainMenu** component represents the menu as a whole. The following code adds a new top-level menu item:

```
TMenuItem *NewItem;

//Create a new menu item with the main menu as owner
NewItem = new TMenuItem(MainMenu1);
//Create caption for new menu item
NewItem->Caption = "New Menu &" + IntToStr(MainMenu1->Items->Count);
//Assign an event handler
NewItem->OnClick = DynaMenuClick;
//Insert at end of main menu
MainMenu1->Items->Insert(MainMenu1->Items->Count, NewItem);
```

First, the new menu item is created, passing the main menu to the constructor to make this a top-level menu item. The new menu item's caption is built with a description and an accelerator key equal to the item's position on the menu. Then, **DynaMenuClick** is assigned as the new item's **OnClick** event handler. Finally, the new menu item is inserted at the end of the menu bar. At this point, the new item will appear as part of the menu. Selecting the new item from the menu will execute the **DynaMenuClick** function.

Although this example puts new top-level menu items at the end of the menu bar, you can, in fact, add menu items in any spot from the first or zero position to the last position. If you insert a menu item at any position except the last, existing menu items are pushed to the right after the new item is inserted.

Removing Top-Level Menu Items

Removing a top-level menu item is even easier.

```
//Don't allow file or edit menu to be deleted
if (MainMenu1->Items->Count > 2)
  //Delete the last item in the main menu
  MainMenu1->Items->Delete(MainMenu1->Items->Count - 1);
```

First, **MainMenu1** is checked to make sure it has at least one dynamically created top-level menu item. Because there is code elsewhere in the application to disable Edit|Remove Menu when there are no top-level items, this check is actually redundant, but it always pays to be safe.

The Delete method of **TMainMenu**'s **Items** property gets passed the position of the menu to be deleted where the first menu item is considered to be at position zero. In this case, the last top-level menu item is deleted. If you delete a menu item other than the last menu item, the remaining menu items shift left to fill the hole. For example, if you deleted the fifth item from a menu, the sixth item would become the fifth.

You do not have to check whether or not the top-level menu item contains sub-menu items. If there are any submenu items, they will be automatically deleted when the top-level menu item is deleted.

Adding Menu Items to a Top-Level Menu Item

The code to add a menu item to a top-level menu is slightly more complex because you must first retrieve a reference to the top-level menu item.

```
TMenuItem *ToItem, *NewItem;

//Don't add items to file or edit menus
if (MainMenu1->Items->Count > 2)
{
    //Get reference to last main menu item
    ToItem = MainMenu1->Items->Items[MainMenu1->Items->Count - 1];
    //Create new menu item with last main menu item as owner
    NewItem = new TMenuItem(ToItem);
    //Create caption relative to last main menu item's item count
    NewItem->Caption = "New Menu Item &" + IntToStr(ToItem->Count);
    //Assign an event handler
    NewItem->OnClick = DynaMenuClick;
    //Ensure ToItem has no event handler
    ToItem->OnClick = NULL;
    //Insert new menu item under last main menu item
    ToItem->Insert(ToItem->Count, NewItem);
```

Once again, a check is made to make sure the application is not attempting to add items before a dynamic top-level menu item has been created. This prevents new items from being added to the Edit menu. **ToItem** is assigned to reference the last top-level menu item in the main menu. This is the menu to which a new item will be added. A new menu item is then created as a child of the top-level menu item.

When the top-level menu item, referenced by **ToItem**, was first created, its **OnClick** event handler was assigned to the **DynaMenuClick** function. This way, something actually happened when you clicked on the top-level menu item. Now that the top-level menu contains subitems, the event handler must be removed to allow the pull-down menu containing the subitems to be displayed when you click on the top-level menu item. This is accomplished by setting the **OnClick** property of the top-level menu item to **NULL**.

Finally, the new item is inserted as the item in the menu. **TMenuItem**'s **Insert** method works the same way as the **Insert** method of **TMainMenu**'s **Items** property.

Removing Submenu Items

Removing a submenu item is almost as simple as removing a top-level menu item.

```
TMenuItem *ToItem;

//Don't delete items from the file or edit menu
if (MainMenu1->Items->Count > 2)
{
  //Get reference to last main menu item
  ToItem = MainMenu1->Items->Items[MainMenu1->Items->Count - 1];
  //Make sure there is an item to delete
  if (ToItem->Count > 0)
    //Delete the last item in the main menu's last item
    ToItem->Delete(ToItem->Count - 1);
```

In order to protect the required functionality of the application, a check is made to ensure there is at least one dynamic top-level menu item. As in adding a new submenu item, a reference must first be made to the desired top-level menu item. The top-level menu item referenced by **ToItem** is checked to make sure it contains at least one submenu item. If it has at least one, then the last one is deleted using the **Delete** method of **TMenuItem**. Once again, it should be noted that any submenu item can be removed using the **Delete** method. If you delete any item but the last, all following items are moved up to fill the empty position.

Housekeeping for the Sample Application

If you look at the actual functions that handle adding top-level menus, adding top-level menu items, removing top-level menus, and removing top-level menu items, you'll probably notice that quite a few lines of code were not described in detail. This housekeeping code should be easy to understand now that you understand how adding and deleting top-level menu items and submenu items works.

Comments

Real-world applications often use more complex menus. For example, a top-level menu item could have submenu items that, in turn, have submenu items of their own. The techniques used in the **AddMenuItem1** and **RemoveMenuItem1** functions can be adapted to work with more deeply nested menus. Only the statement that sets the **ToItem** variable needs to be changed to reference the proper parent menu item. For example, for a third level of menu items the reference would be

```
//Get reference to last main menu item for a third level item
ToItem = MainMenu1->Items->Items->Items[MainMenu1->Items->Count - 1];
```

4.3 How do I...
Display a file history list in a menu?

Problem

Many applications provide a history of the most recently opened files on the file menu. Over the last several years, this has become a common feature of most applications that have a file menu. In fact, Microsoft made file history a required part of any Windows 95 logo application. How can I implement this user interface feature in my C++Builder applications?

Technique

This How-To demonstrates how to create a reusable object to manage the file history list. The object uses a **TStringList** to store the history items, and changes the file menu at runtime to display the history items.

Steps

Run **HISTORY.EXE**. The file menu has the typical menu selections you see in file-oriented applications. Experiment with the New, Open, Save, and Save As menu entries and watch what happens to the file menu. Because the application only simulates opening and saving files, you don't have to worry about corrupting anything on your hard drive.

Figure 4-3 shows the file menu after a few files have been opened in succession. **HISTORY.EXE** will allow up to nine history items in the history list. Note that when a file already on the list is opened, either by selecting it from the history list or by opening it from the File|Open menu item, it will disappear from the list.

Close **HISTORY.EXE** after there are a few files on the history list. Run the program again. If you click on the file menu, you'll notice that the program remembered the history list from the last time you ran the program.

1. Create a new project. Save the default unit as **HISTORYMAIN.CPP** and the project as **HISTORY.MAK**.

2. Add the components, properties, and settings as shown in Table 4-2.

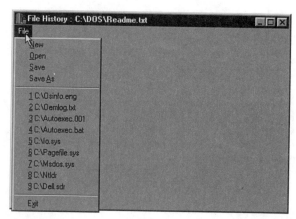

Figure 4-3 HISTORY.EXE with some file history items shown

Table 4-2 Components, properties, and settings of the History project

COMPONENT	PROPERTY	SETTING
TForm	Caption	File History
TMainMenu		
TOpenDialog	Filter	All Files (*.*) | *.*
TSaveDialog	Filter	All Files (*.*) | *.*

3. Start the Menu Designer for the MainMenu1 component, and add the menu items as shown in Table 4-3.

Table 4-3 Menu design for the project

MENU	MENU ITEM
File	&New
	&Open
	&Save
	Save &As
	—
	E&xit

4. Add a new unit to the application by picking File|New Unit from the C++Builder menu. Save the new unit as FILEHISTORY.CPP.

5. Switch to the header file for the new unit, and add the following class declaration after the **define** statement:

```
#define FileHistoryH
//-----------------------------------------------------------
class TFileHistory
{
private:
  // String list to hold the history file names
  TStringList *HistoryList;
  // Menu separators that will mark the beginning and end of the history
  TMenuItem *TopSeperator, *BottomSeperator;
  // The file that is currently open by the application
  String LastFile;
  //The file menu
  TMenuItem *FileMenu;
  //Holds maximum number of history items allowed
  int MaxHistoryItems;
  //Holds name of the file that contains history file names
  String HistoryFileName;
  //Callback function that opens a particular file
  void (__closure *OpenFileFunc) (String FileName);
  //Function that rebuilds the history list
  void RebuildHistory(void);
  //Function to handle click event on file history items
  void __fastcall HistoryItemClick(TObject *Sender);

public:
  // Construct the file history object
  TFileHistory(int theMaxHistoryItems,
               String theHistoryFileName,
               TMenuItem *theFileMenu,
               TMenuItem *theSeperator,
               void (__closure *theOpenFileFunc) (String FileName));
  //Destructor
  ~TFileHistory(void);
  //Function for menu item click event handlers to call
  void MaintainHistory(String OldFile);
               };
```

6. Switch back to FILEHISTORY.CPP. Add the following code, which is the TFileHistory object's constructor, after the **include** statement:

```
#include "FileHistory.h"
//------------------------------------------------------------------------
//Constructor
TFileHistory::TFileHistory(int theMaxHistoryItems,
                           String theHistoryFileName,
                           TMenuItem *theFileMenu,
                           TMenuItem *theSeperator,
                           void (__closure *theOpenFileFunc) (String⇐
                           FileName))
{
```

```
//Assign defaults from values passed
MaxHistoryItems = theMaxHistoryItems;
HistoryFileName = theHistoryFileName;
FileMenu = theFileMenu;
OpenFileFunc = theOpenFileFunc;
LastFile = "";

//Assign values of top separator to existing separator
TopSeparator = theSeperator;
//Bottom separator doesn't exist yet so set it to NULL
BottomSeperator = NULL;

//Initialize the file history list
HistoryList = new TStringList;

//Attempt to open the file and load history items
//If the attempt fails, ignore the error
try
{
  HistoryList->LoadFromFile(HistoryFileName);
  //If the history file was found, set up the menu
  RebuildHistory();
}
catch (...)
{
}
}
```

7. Add the object's `Destructor` function just beneath the constructor.

```
//Destructor
TFileHistory::~TFileHistory(void)
{
  MaintainHistory("");
  //Save the history list to the file
  //If something goes wrong, display an error message
  try
  {
    //Save the history list
    HistoryList->SaveToFile(HistoryFileName);
  }
  catch (...)
  {
    //Display an error message
    MessageBox(NULL, "Could not save history file", "Error",
      MB_ICONERROR | MB_OK);
  }
  //Destroy the history list
  HistoryList->Free();
}
```

8. After the `Destructor`, add the function that actually changes the file menu to display the history items.

```
//Function actually  changes the file menu to show the history items
void TFileHistory::RebuildHistory(void)
{
    TMenuItem *MenuItem;
    int Pos, HistoryStart, HistoryEnd;

    //History appears after existing separator
    HistoryStart = FileMenu->IndexOf(TopSeperator) + 1;

    // If BottomSeperator is not NULL, then there are history items
    if (BottomSeperator != NULL) {
        // Use position of BottomSeperator as end of history range
        HistoryEnd = FileMenu->IndexOf(BottomSeperator);
        // Delete all history elements including bottom separator
        for (Pos = HistoryStart; Pos <= HistoryEnd; Pos++)
            FileMenu->Delete(HistoryStart);
    }

    //Trim list, if required, to maximum items allowed
    if (HistoryList->Count > MaxHistoryItems)
        for (Pos = MaxHistoryItems; Pos < HistoryList->Count; Pos++)
            HistoryList->Delete(MaxHistoryItems);

    //If there are history items, then build menu items
    if (HistoryList->Count > 0) {
        //For each file in the history list
        for (Pos = 0; Pos < HistoryList->Count; Pos++) {
            //Create a new menu item
            MenuItem = new TMenuItem(FileMenu);
            //Use position number as accelerator in front of file name
            MenuItem->Caption = "&" + IntToStr(Pos + 1) + " " +
                HistoryList->Strings[Pos];
            //Assign event handler
            MenuItem->OnClick = HistoryItemClick;
            //Insert into file menu
            FileMenu->Insert(HistoryStart + Pos, MenuItem);
        }
        //Create and insert a separator following the last item
        BottomSeperator = new TMenuItem(FileMenu);
        BottomSeperator->Caption = "-";
        FileMenu->Insert(HistoryStart + HistoryList->Count,
BottomSeperator);
    }
}
```

9. Below the `RebuildHistory` function, add the event handler that takes care of mouse clicks on file history items.

```
//Event handler for clicks on the history items
void __fastcall TFileHistory::HistoryItemClick(TObject *Sender)
{
```

```
    int Pos;
    String NewName;

    //Calculate position in history list
    //from relative position of selected file name
    Pos = FileMenu->IndexOf((TMenuItem *)Sender) -
      FileMenu->IndexOf(TopSeperator) - 1;
    //Get file name from history list
    NewName = HistoryList->Strings[Pos];
    //Call back to owner form function to open the file
    OpenFileFunc(NewName);
}
```

10. After the `HistoryItemClick` function, add the public function that the main application will call to maintain the history list.

```
//Called by the main application to maintain the
//history list
void TFileHistory::MaintainHistory(String NewFile)
{
    int Pos;

    //If the last file was not a new file
    if (LastFile != "")
      //Add the file to the top of the history list
      HistoryList->Insert(0, LastFile);

    //If the file the application is telling us about is not a new file
    if (NewFile != "")
    {
      //Try to find the file name in the history list
      Pos = HistoryList->IndexOf(NewFile);
      //If the file was found
      if (Pos != -1)
        //Delete the file from the history list
        HistoryList->Delete(Pos);
    }

    //Save the name of the file
    LastFile = NewFile;

    //Rebuild the file history menu items
    RebuildHistory();
}
```

11. Return to `HISTORYMAIN.CPP`, and switch to the header file. Add an additional `include` in the same area as the other `include` statements, which makes the `THistoryList` object available to `HISTORYMAIN`.

```
#include <vcl\Dialogs.hpp>
//Make TFileHistory available to the main unit
#include "FileHistory.h"
```

12. Add the following declarations to the header file:

```
private:// User declarations
    //History list
    TFileHistory *FileHistory;
    //File currently open by the application
    String CurrentFileName;
    //Window caption of the main window
    String ApplicationTitle;
public:// User declarations
    virtual __fastcall TForm1(TComponent* Owner);
    //Function that opens a file.
    void OpenFile(String FileName);
};
```

13. Switch to HISTORYMAIN.CPP. Open the Menu Designer for MainMenu1, and double-click on the New menu item. Add the following code to simulate creating a new file:

```
void __fastcall TForm1::New1Click(TObject *Sender)
{
  //Tell the file history object that a new file is being opened
  FileHistory->MaintainHistory("");
  //Set the caption to indicate a new file
  Caption = ApplicationTitle + " : [untitled]";
}
```

14. Double-click on the Open item, and add the code that brings up the standard file open dialog and simulates opening the file selected by the user.

```
void __fastcall TForm1::Open1Click(TObject *Sender)
{
  //Pop up a file open dialog
  if (OpenDialog1->Execute())
    //Open the file
    OpenFile(OpenDialog1->FileName);
}
```

15. Add the code for the OpenFile function beneath the Open1Click event handler.

```
void TForm1::OpenFile(String FileName)
{
  //Tell FileHistory about the newly opened file
  FileHistory->MaintainHistory(FileName);
  //Update the caption
  Caption = ApplicationTitle + " : " + FileName;
}
```

16. Double-click on File|Save, and add the code to simulate the file save operation.

```
void __fastcall TForm1::Save1Click(TObject *Sender)
{
  //Check to see if this was a new file
  if (CurrentFileName == "")
  {
    //Open the save dialog so user can set a name
    if (SaveDialog1->Execute())
    {
      //Tell FileHistory about the name
      FileHistory->MaintainHistory(SaveDialog1->FileName);
      //Update the caption
      Caption = ApplicationTitle + " : " + SaveDialog1->FileName;
    }
  }
}
```

17. Double-click on the File|Save As menu entry, and add the code to simulate saving the file under a different name.

```
void __fastcall TForm1::SaveAs1Click(TObject *Sender)
{
  //Pop up the save dialog
  if (SaveDialog1->Execute())
  {
    //Tell the FileHistory object about the new name
    FileHistory->MaintainHistory(SaveDialog1->FileName);
    //Update the caption
    Caption = ApplicationTitle + " : " + SaveDialog1->FileName;
  }
}
```

18. Double-click on the Exit menu item, and add the code to close the application.

```
void __fastcall TForm1::Exit1Click(TObject *Sender)
{
  //Close the application
  Close();
}
```

19. Double-click the form's **OnCreate** event in the Object Inspector, and add the code that creates the file history object and initializes some defaults:

```
void __fastcall TForm1::FormCreate(TObject *Sender)
{
  //Initialize the file history object
  FileHistory = new TFileHistory(9, "History", File1, N1, &OpenFile);
  //Save the application's title
  ApplicationTitle = Caption;
  //Set the caption to indicate a new file
  Caption = ApplicationTitle + " : [untitled]";
}
```

20. Go to the Object Inspector and double-click on the form's `OnDestroy` event. Add the following code to destroy the file history object:

```
void __fastcall TForm1::FormDestroy(TObject *Sender)
{
  //Destroy the file history object
  delete FileHistory;
}
```

21. Compile and run the application.

How It Works

The `HISTORY` application has two parts. `FILEHISTORY.CPP` does all the real work of maintaining the history list, updating the file menu, and handling file history item clicks. `HISTORYMAIN.CPP` simulates a file-oriented application and demonstrates how to use the `TFileHistory` object.

The File History Object

`FILEHISTORY.H` (step 3) defines a variety of private data elements. A `TStringList`, called `HistoryList`, is used to store the list of recently opened files. Two `TMenuItem` objects are declared to store the menu separators at the top and bottom of the file history list. Another `TMenuItem` is declared to hold the file menu object from the main application. `MaxHistoryItems` holds the maximum number of history items that should be placed on the file menu. `HistoryFileName` stores the name of the disk file used to store the history list when the application is closed. Finally, a closure, `OpenFileFunc`, is used to store a pointer to the member function in the main form responsible for opening a disk file.

The code for the constructor, found in step 6, is very simple. First, the member variables of the `TFileHistory` object are initialized. Some get values from the parameters passed in the constructor, while some are initialized to default values. Finally, the constructor attempts to load the file history list from the disk file. If the file does not exist, the call to `LoadFromFile` will fail, and C++Builder will raise an exception. This error is ignored by the empty `catch( )` block, because it is nonfatal and may simply indicate that the program is running for the first time.

`TFileHistory`'s destructor (step 7) starts by calling the `MaintainHistory` function to save the currently open file, if there is one, to the history list. It then attempts to save the history list to disk. If it fails, an error message is displayed to the user. Finally, the file history list is removed from memory.

`RebuildHistory`, added in step 8, adds the file history list to the file menu. Because the history list can change in so many ways, it removes all the history items from the menu and then adds the items found in the file history list back into the menu.

RebuildHistory starts by calculating the starting position of history items on the menu as one past the position of the top separator. It then checks to see whether there are history items by checking for the existence of the bottom separator. If there is a bottom separator, its location in the file menu is found by calling the **IndexOf** function which returns the numeric position of a given item in the menu. A loop is used to delete everything from the first history item up to and including the bottom separator.

The next three lines of code make sure the history list does not contain more than the maximum number of items passed in the constructor. If there are too many, then the oldest files, the ones at the end of the list, are deleted.

The last block of code in the **RebuildHistory** function adds the file history items to the menu. For each item in the file history list, a new **TMenuItem** is created and inserted into the file menu. The **HistoryItemClick** function is assigned as the **OnClick** event handler. The file menu is the parent of the new menu item, so the new menu item will be automatically destroyed when the application terminates. After all the history items are placed on the menu, a separator is added at the bottom of the history list. The bottom separator is stored for later use.

The **HistoryItemClick** function, assigned as the **OnClick** event handler for file history items, starts by calculating the position of the clicked history file name in the file history list as the position of the clicked item on the menu minus the position of the top separator. One more is subtracted to make the result relative to zero just like the index in the file history string list. The filename is then retrieved from the history list.

Once the filename is known, **HistoryItemClick** calls back, through the **OpenFileFunc** function pointer which was passed to the object in the constructor, to a routine in the main form that knows how to open a file. This somewhat complex mechanism is necessary because each application that uses the **TFileHistory** object may need to do different things when a file is opened. Because **TFileHistory** is designed to be application-independent, the function for opening a new file must be part of the calling application.

The last function defined in **FILEHISTORY.CPP**, **MaintainHistory**, is the function that updates the history list as files are opened, saved, and renamed. It starts by checking to see whether the last file opened by the calling application was a new file; if it was not, then that filename is added to the history list.

If the file being opened is not a new file, the history list is examined to see whether the file already is part of the history list by using the **IndexOf** function. If it is, the name is removed from the history list. Finally, the new filename is saved, and the **RebuildHistory** function is called.

The Main Form

As noted earlier, **HISTORYMAIN** is a test rig to demonstrate the use of the **TFileHistory** object. All file operations are simulated. This description will focus on the interface code and will not describe the simulation code.

The TFileHistory object, declared as FileHistory in HISTORYMAIN.H, is initialized in the form's OnCreate event handler (step 18). In this example, there will be a maximum of nine files allowed in the file history list. The file name that stores history items will be called HISTORY, the file menu object is File1, the separator that will be the top separator for the file history list is N1, and the function that opens files is named OpenFile.

The calls to FileHistory->MaintainHistory in the event handlers for clicks on File|New (step 13), File|Save (step 16), and File|Save As (step 17) tell the file history object the name of the newly opened or saved file to add to the history list. The call to MaintainHistory for the File|Open menu item is contained in the OpenFile function you added in step 15. In all cases, the new filename is passed to the MaintainHistory function. New files are indicated by passing an empty string to MaintainHistory.

The FileHistory object is destroyed in the OnDestroy event handler you added in step 20. As described earlier, the FileHistory's destructor takes care of adding the currently open file to the history list and saving the history list to disk.

Comments

The TFileHistory object created in this How-To can be used to add a file history list to any SDI application you create with a minimum of work. Just add the unit to your project, add a few lines of code, and you're done.

The TFileHistory object can be improved in several ways. Better error checking could be added. Support for MDI applications would be useful. The file history could be stored in the registry instead of in a file. Finally, you could use the How-To's in Chapter 15, "Custom Components," to convert the TFileHistory object into a VCL component.

COMPLEXITY
BEGINNING

4.4 How do I...
Put pictures in menus?

Problem

I've seen some applications that use pictures instead of text in menus. I find that the pictures often work better than a small text label to indicate the purpose of the menu item. How can I add pictures to the menu in my C++Builder application?

Technique

Windows provides a simple API function that can be used to replace menu text with a bitmap image. This How-To shows you how to use this API function.

Steps

Run **BITMAPMENU**. Click the Options menu. The only available selection is a picture that toggles between two states. At program start-up, the picture is a large musical note with a big red x through it to indicate that selecting the menu option will turn the music off (Figure 4-4). When the music is turned off, the menu item changes to indicate that selecting the menu option will turn the music back on.

1. Create a new project. Save the default unit as **BITMAPMENUMAIN.CPP** and the project as **BITMAPMENU.MAK**.

2. Create the bitmaps shown in Figure 4-5. Save them in a resource file named **BITMAP.RES**.

3. Add a **TMainMenu** component to the form, and use the Menu Designer to add the menu items as shown in Table 4-4.

Table 4-4 Menu design for the **BITMAPMENU** project

MENU	MENU ITEM
&Options	Sound

4. Switch to the header file, **BITMAPMENUMAIN.H**. Add the following declarations used to store the bitmaps and the menu state to the private section of the form:

```
private:// User declarations
  //Bitmap storage
  HBITMAP SoundOnBitmap, SoundOffBitmap;
  //Holds menu state
  BOOL SoundOn;
```

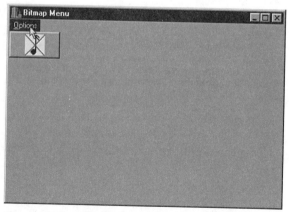

Figure 4-4 BITMAPMENU showing the sound menu in its default state

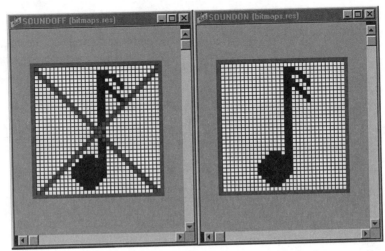

Figure 4-5 Bitmap resources for BITMAPMENU in the Image
Editor

5. Switch back to **BITMAPMENUMAIN.CPP**. Add the following statement after
the **pragma** statement near the top of the file to bind the resource file you
created in step 2 to the application:

```
#pragma resource "*.dfm"
#pragma resource "bitmaps.res"
```

6. Double-click the **OnCreate** event for **Form1** in the Object Inspector, and
add the following code to load the menu bitmaps and initialize the Sound
menu item:

```
void __fastcall TForm1::FormCreate(TObject *Sender)
{
  //Load sound bitmaps from bitmap resource
  SoundOnBitmap = LoadBitmap((void *)HInstance, "SOUNDON");
  SoundOffBitmap = LoadBitmap((void *)HInstance, "SOUNDOFF");

  //Sound is on by default
  ModifyMenu(MainMenu1->Handle, Sound1->Command, MF_BYCOMMAND | MF_BITMAP,
    Sound1->Command, (char *)SoundOffBitmap);
  SoundOn = TRUE;
}
```

7. Double-click the **OnDestroy** method, and add the code to remove the
bitmaps from memory.

```
void __fastcall TForm1::FormDestroy(TObject *Sender)
{
  //Remove bitmaps from memory
  DeleteObject(SoundOnBitmap);
  DeleteObject(SoundOffBitmap);
}
```

8. Open the Menu Designer for the main menu component. Double-click on the sound menu item, and add the code that will toggle the menu picture and the sound state.

```
void __fastcall TForm1::Sound1Click(TObject *Sender)
{
  //Check to see if sound is on
  if (SoundOn)
  {
    //Change to the sound off bitmap
    ModifyMenu(MainMenu1->Handle, Sound1->Command, MF_BYCOMMAND |
MF_BITMAP,
      Sound1->Command, (char *)SoundOnBitmap);
    //Record that sound is off
    SoundOn = FALSE;
  }
  else
  {
    //Change to the sound on bitmap
    ModifyMenu(MainMenu1->Handle, Sound1->Command, MF_BYCOMMAND |
MF_BITMAP,
      Sound1->Command, (char *)SoundOffBitmap);
    //Record that sound is on
    SoundOn = TRUE;
  }
}
```

9. Compile and run the application.

How It Works

Although C++Builder supplies VCL components to handle the most common menu functions, you'll have to turn to the Windows API if you want more than standard text menus. This How-To demonstrates how to use the `ModifyMenu` function.

`ModifyMenu` is very flexible. With it you can control menu states, toggle between menu text and bitmaps, or change the bitmap associated with a menu item. It will even allow you to combine multiple changes in a single call as long as the changes do not conflict with one another.

Loading the Bitmaps

As discussed in How-To 4.1, the `pragma` resource directive (step 5) tells C++Builder to bind the named resource file to the application's executable. The `LoadBitmap` Windows API function (step 6) loads a named bitmap resource into memory. The first parameter is the instance handle of your application, which C++Builder makes available in a global variable named `HInstance`. Note that the instance handle variable must be type cast for the call to `LoadBitmap`. The second parameter is the name of the resource.

The bitmap handles returned by **LoadBitmap** are stored in two of **Form1**'s private members. The memory associated with the bitmaps is released when the program terminates by calling the **DeleteObject** Windows API function (step 7).

Using the **ModifyMenu** Windows API Function

After the bitmaps are loaded, the bitmap that represents turning the sound off is assigned to the **Sound1** menu item using the **ModifyMenu** Windows API function. The first parameter passed to **ModifyMenu** is the menu handle which is found, naturally enough, in the handle property of **MainMenu1**.

The second parameter identifies the menu item to be changed. **ModifyMenu** lets you identify the menu item by either its command ID or by its position on the menu. Because **TMenuItem** stores the command ID in its command property, it is easiest to pass the menu item's command ID in the second parameter. Note that the fourth parameter should be the same as the second parameter to preserve the command ID.

The third parameter is a set of flags that tells **ModifyMenu** how the menu item is identified and what operation or operations it should perform. In this case, the **MF_BYCOMMAND** flag tells **ModifyMenu** that the menu item is identified by command ID, and the **MF_BITMAP** flag specifies that **ModifyMenu** is being used to change the menu item text to a bitmap.

The last parameter passed to **ModifyMenu** depends on the command flags. In the case of **MF_BITMAP**, **ModifyMenu** expects a bitmap handle. This parameter must be cast to a character pointer to satisfy the compiler.

Handling Menu Selections

The code you added in step 8 handles mouse clicks on the **Sound1** menu item. The sound state is reversed, and the proper bitmap is placed on the menu using the **ModifyMenu** function.

Comments

Adding pictures to menus is not hard once you know how to use the **ModifyMenu** function. This How-To demonstrates how to change a menu item to a picture. It also illustrates how to use multiple pictures to indicate different menu states.

COMPLEXITY
BEGINNING

4.5 How do I...
Create and use custom check marks in menus?

Problem

I've seen some applications that use a custom check mark in place of the standard Windows check mark. How do I do this in my C++Builder application?

Technique

You'll have to dip into the Windows API to use a custom check mark bitmap in place of the standard Windows check mark. In fact, Windows allows you to assign two different custom bitmaps, one for the checked state and one for the unchecked state, with the `SetMenuItemBitmaps` function.

Steps

Run `MENUCHECK.EXE`. Your screen will look like Figure 4-6. Select the sound menu item a few times and note how the custom check mark toggles between a green circle, used to indicate that sound is on, and a red circle, used to indicate that sound is off.

1. Create a new project. Save the default unit as `MENUCHECKMAIN.CPP` and the project as `MENUCHECK.MAK`.

2. Create the bitmaps shown in Figure 4-7. Save them in a resource file named `CHECKMARKS.RES`.

3. Add a `TMainMenu` component to the form, and create the menu item as shown in Table 4-5.

Table 4-5 Menu design for the `MENUCHECK` project

MENU	MENU ITEM
&Test	Sound

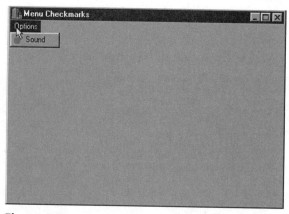

Figure 4-6 `MENUCHECK` displaying custom check mark in default state

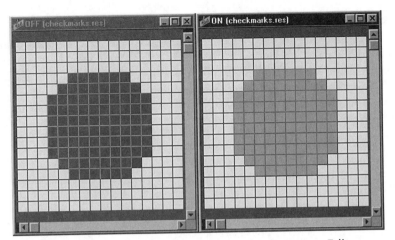

Figure 4-7 Bitmap resources for MENUCHECK in Image Editor

4. Switch to MENUCHECKMAIN.H. Add the following declarations to the private section of the Form1 object:

```
private:// User declarations
  HBITMAP OnBitmap, OffBitmap;
```

5. Switch back to MENUCHECKMAIN.CPP, and add the pragma resource directive to bind your custom resource file to the application.

```
#pragma resource "*.dfm"
#pragma resource "checkmarks.res"
```

6. In the Object Inspector, double-click the OnCreate event for Form1, and add the code that loads the bitmaps from the resource and tells Windows to use them as the check marks for the menu item.

```
void __fastcall TForm1::FormCreate(TObject *Sender)
{
  //Load the on bitmap
  OnBitmap = LoadBitmap((void *)HInstance, "ON");
  //Load the off bitmap
  OffBitmap = LoadBitmap((void *)HInstance, "OFF");
  //Assign the custom on and off check marks
  SetMenuItemBitmaps(MainMenu1->Handle, Sound1->Command, MF_BYCOMMAND,
    OffBitmap, OnBitmap);
  //Initially set the menu item checked (sound on)
  Sound1->Checked = TRUE;
}
```

7. Double-click Form1's **OnDestroy** event, and add the code that removes the bitmaps from memory.

```
void __fastcall TForm1::FormDestroy(TObject *Sender)
{
  //Delete the custom check marks
  DeleteObject(OnBitmap);
  DeleteObject(OffBitmap);
}
```

8. In the Menu Designer for **MainMenu1**, double-click on the Sound item, and add the code that toggles its checked state.

```
void __fastcall TForm1::Sound1Click(TObject *Sender)
{
  //Toggle the checked status
  Sound1->Checked = !Sound1->Checked;
}
```

9. Compile and run the application.

How It Works

As in How-To 4.4, the bitmaps are stored in a resource file bound to the executable by the **pragma** resource directive. The **LoadBitmap** function is used to load the bitmaps into memory (step 6), and the **DeleteBitmap** function is used to delete the bitmaps from memory when the program ends (step 7). How-To 4.4 explains the parameters passed to the **LoadBitmap** function.

Assigning the Check Marks

Once the bitmaps are loaded, the **SetMenuItemBitmaps** Windows API function is called to assign the bitmaps to the menu item (step 6). The first parameter passed is the menu handle found in the handle property of **MainMenu1**.

SetMenuItemBitmaps lets you identify the menu item by either its command ID or by its position on the menu. Because **TMenuItem** stores the command ID in its command property, it is easiest to pass the menu item's command ID in the second parameter.

The third parameter tells **SetMenuItemBitmaps** how the menu item is identified. In this case, the **MF_BYCOMMAND** flag tells **SetMenuItemBitmaps** that the menu item is identified by command ID.

The last two parameters are handles to bitmaps that Windows will use to indicate the unchecked and checked states, respectively, of the menu item. In this How-To, a bitmap handle is passed for both the unchecked and checked states. However, you can pass zero for either the checked or unchecked states to indicate that Windows should use its default method to indicate the menu item's state. For example, if the fourth parameter was zero, Windows would not display a bitmap to indicate the unchecked state. If the fifth parameter was zero, Windows would use its default check mark bitmap to indicate the checked state.

Windows only allows a certain amount of space on the menu for custom check mark bitmaps. The space allowed depends on the system font. If the bitmap you use as a check mark is too large, Windows will truncate the part that won't fit. A 12×14 pixel bitmap will work regardless of system font, or, if you want to be very precise, create two bitmaps (12×14 pixels and 12×20 pixels) and determine which to display by getting the menu check mark size from the `GetSystemMetrics` Windows API function.

Displaying the Check Marks

Once you've assigned custom check marks to the menu item using the `SetMenuItemBitmaps` function, Windows takes care of displaying the proper bitmap based on the checked or unchecked state of the menu item. The `OnClick` event handler for the `Sound1` menu item (step 8) simply reverses the checked state of the menu item and lets Windows do the rest.

Comments

As you've seen in this How-To and How-To 4.4, Windows provides several ways to customize the way it draws menus. If you need even more control, you need to take over the task of drawing the menu. The next How-To will demonstrate how that is accomplished.

COMPLEXITY
ADVANCED

4.6 How do I...
Use a different font in a menu?

Problem

I'd like to include a menu item in my application that lets the user change fonts. I think it would be really cool if I could display the menu item in the user's selected font. Can I do this in my C++Builder application?

Technique

C++Builder's `TMenuItem` object does not give you control over the font used to display a menu item's caption. Unfortunately, Windows doesn't let you change a menu item's font either. However, Windows does provide a sort of back door that will let you do what you want.

This How-To will show you how to use the owner-draw technique on a menu item. Instead of telling Windows what to draw, your application will tell Windows to let it do the drawing. Using this method, you can do just about anything you want, including changing a menu item's font.

Steps

Run FONTMENU.EXE. Select Test|Font from the menu, and select something other than the standard system font and size from the font dialog that appears. When you open the test menu again, you'll notice the Font menu item is using the font you selected earlier. An example is shown in Figure 4-8.

1. Create a new project. Save the default unit as FONTMENUMAIN.CPP and the default project as FONTMENU.MAK.

2. Add a MainMenu and a FontDialog component to the form. Add menu items to the MainMenu component as shown in Table 4-6.

Table 4-6 Menu design for the FONTMENU project

MENU	MENU ITEM	SHORTCUT
&Test	&Disable Font	
	&Enable Font	
	&Font	CTRL-F

3. Switch to FONTMENUMAIN.H, and add the following declarations to Form1's private section:

```
private:// User declarations
  //Working area for font size calculations
  Graphics::TBitmap *WorkBitmap;
  //Copy of the font menu item caption
  String FontCaption;
  //Message maps to tie windows events to certain functions
  BEGIN_MESSAGE_MAP
  MESSAGE_HANDLER(WM_MEASUREITEM, TMessage, WMMeasureItem)
  MESSAGE_HANDLER(WM_DRAWITEM, TMessage, WMDrawItem)
  END_MESSAGE_MAP(TForm)
  //Function to handle the WM_MEASUREITEM event
  void __fastcall WMMeasureItem(TMessage& Message);
  //Function to handle the WM_DRAWITEM event
  void __fastcall WMDrawItem(TMessage& Message);
```

Figure 4-8 Font menu
item shown in 16pt Bold
Times New Roman

4. Double-click `Form1`'s `OnCreate` event handler in the Object Inspector, and add the code that initializes the variables, font dialog, and menu.

```
void __fastcall TForm1::FormCreate(TObject *Sender)
{
  //Initialize the working area
  WorkBitmap = new Graphics::TBitmap;
  //Initialize current font to the standard menu text color
  FontDialog1->Font->Color = GetSysColor(COLOR_MENUTEXT);
  //Tell windows that the menu item is owner-draw
  ModifyMenu(MainMenu1->Handle, Font1->Command, MF_BYCOMMAND | MF_OWNERDRAW,
    Font1->Command, NULL);
  //Make a copy of the font caption
  FontCaption = Font1->Caption;
  //Add on the shortcut if there is one
  if (Font1->ShortCut != 0)
    FontCaption = FontCaption + "\t" + ShortCutToText(Font1->ShortCut);
}
```

5. Double-click the `OnDestroy` event handler, and enter the code that cleans up after the application is finished.

```
void __fastcall TForm1::FormDestroy(TObject *Sender)
{
  //Dispose of work area
  WorkBitmap->Free();
}
```

6. Just below the `FormDestroy` method, add the function that handles the `WM_MEASUREITEM` Windows message.

```
void __fastcall TForm1::WMMeasureItem(TMessage& Message)
{
  TMeasureItemStruct *Measures;
```

```
//Copy structure into a working variable for easy access
Measures = (TMeasureItemStruct *)(Message.LParam);
//Is message for a menu item?
if (Measures->CtlType == ODT_MENU)
{
  //Is message for font menu item?
  if (Measures->itemID == Font1->Command)
  {
    //Assign currently selected font to workspace
    WorkBitmap->Canvas->Font = FontDialog1->Font;
    //Calculate needed height for current font
    Measures->itemHeight = WorkBitmap->Canvas->TextHeight(FontCaption);
    //Calculate needed width
    Measures->itemWidth = WorkBitmap->Canvas->TextWidth(FontCaption) +
      GetSystemMetrics(SM_CXMENUCHECK) + 8;
    //Tell Windows the event is handled
    Message.Result = 1;
  }
}
}
```

7. After the WMMeasureItem function, enter the function that handles the WM_DRAWITEM message sent from Windows.

```
void __fastcall TForm1::WMDrawItem(TMessage& Message)
{
  HFONT OldFont;
  TDrawItemStruct *DrawItem;

  //Create a working variable for draw item structure
  DrawItem = (TDrawItemStruct *)(Message.LParam);
  //Is message for a menu item?
  if (DrawItem->CtlType == ODT_MENU)
  {
    //Is message for the font menu item?
    if (DrawItem->itemID == Font1->Command)
    {
      //Select current font into menu's device context
      OldFont = SelectObject(DrawItem->hDC, FontDialog1->Font->Handle);
      //Set correct background color
      if ((DrawItem->itemState & ODS_SELECTED) != 0)
        WorkBitmap->Canvas->Brush->Color = clHighlight;
      else
        WorkBitmap->Canvas->Brush->Color = clMenu;

      //Paint the background
      FillRect(DrawItem->hDC, &(DrawItem->rcItem),
        WorkBitmap->Canvas->Brush->Handle);
      //Adjust left bound of caption
      DrawItem->rcItem.left += (GetSystemMetrics(SM_CXMENUCHECK) + 8);
      //Set text color according to state
      if (((DrawItem->itemState & ODS_DISABLED) != 0) ||
        ((DrawItem->itemState & ODS_GRAYED) != 0))
```

continued on next page

continued from previous page

```
    {
      //Use systems grayed color
      SetTextColor(DrawItem->hDC, GetSysColor(COLOR_GRAYTEXT));
    }
    else if ((DrawItem->itemState & ODS_SELECTED) != 0)
    {
      //Use reverse of current font color
      SetTextColor(DrawItem->hDC, ~FontDialog1->Font->Color);
    }
    else
    {
      //Use selected font color
      SetTextColor(DrawItem->hDC, FontDialog1->Font->Color);
    }

    //Allow background color to surround characters
    SetBkMode(DrawItem->hDC, TRANSPARENT);
    //Draw the menu's caption
    DrawText(DrawItem->hDC, FontCaption.c_str(), FontCaption.Length(),
      &(DrawItem->rcItem), DT_TOP | DT_SINGLELINE | DT_EXPANDTABS);
    //Release current font handle
    SelectObject(DrawItem->hDC, OldFont);
    //Tell windows the message is handled
    Message.Result = 1;
    }
  }
}
```

8. In the Menu Designer for **Test1**, double-click on the **Enable** item, and add the code that makes the Font menu item active.

```
void __fastcall TForm1::EnableFont1Click(TObject *Sender)
{
  //Tell windows that the font command is enabled
  ModifyMenu(MainMenu1->Handle, Font1->Command,
    MF_BYCOMMAND | MF_ENABLED | MF_OWNERDRAW, Font1->Command, NULL);
}
```

9. Double-click on Test|Disable Font, and enter the code that disables the Font menu option.

```
void __fastcall TForm1::DisableFont1Click(TObject *Sender)
{
  //Tell windows that the font command is disabled
  ModifyMenu(MainMenu1->Handle, Font1->Command,
    MF_BYCOMMAND | MF_GRAYED | MF_OWNERDRAW, Font1->Command, NULL);
}
```

10. Double-click on Test|Font, and enter the code that brings up the font selection dialog and sends a **WM_MEASUREITEM** message to the application.

```
void __fastcall TForm1::Font1Click(TObject *Sender)
{
```

```
//Bring up the font dialog and check to see if the font was changed
if (FontDialog1->Execute())
   //Fool windows into sending another WM_MEASUREITEM message
   // so menu items can be sized for new font
   ModifyMenu(MainMenu1->Handle, Font1->Command, MF_BYCOMMAND |  ⇐
   MF_OWNERDRAW,
      Font1->Command, NULL);
}
```

11. Compile and run the application.

How It Works

The key to using the owner-draw technique on a menu item is responding to a couple of Windows messages. Unless you tell C++Builder that you want to process these messages, they will not be passed on to your application, and you'll end up with a blank menu item. You tell C++Builder that you want to process a certain Windows message with a certain function by creating a message map.

The message map and the associated messages-handling function for this How-To look like this:

```
//Message maps to tie windows events to certain functions
BEGIN_MESSAGE_MAP
MESSAGE_HANDLER(WM_MEASUREITEM, TMessage, WMMeasureItem)
MESSAGE_HANDLER(WM_DRAWITEM, TMessage, WMDrawItem)
END_MESSAGE_MAP(TForm)
//Function to handle the WM_MEASUREITEM event
void __fastcall WMMeasureItem(TMessage& Message);
//Function to handle the WM_DRAWITEM event
void __fastcall WMDrawItem(TMessage& Message);
```

To understand what a message map does, you have to understand a little bit about Windows messages. A message is a notification of some occurrence. For example, when the user clicks the mouse on a control, Windows generates several messages and sends them to the application. C++Builder processes most Windows messages in the background and automatically turns some of them into events. For example, a mouse click on a control ends up firing the **OnClick** event handler for that control.

The **MESSAGE HANDLER** statements associate a member function to a Windows message. When a message-mapped Windows message occurs, C++Builder assembles the information about the message into a **TMessage** structure and passes that information on to the function hooked to the message in the message map. For example, the first **MESSAGE HANDLER** statement tells C++Builder to call the **WMMeasureItem** function whenever the **WM_MEASUREITEM** Windows message is received. Message handling functions must be members of the object that contain the message map and should be declared as shown in this How-To.

Preparing for Owner-Draw

A few things need to be done in order to prepare for painting the menu item (step 4). First, a **TBitmap** component is created to serve as a working area. Next, the font color of the **TFontDialog** component is initialized.

When a **TFontDialog** is created, it defaults to the system font and size also used to draw menu items. However, the font color is not correct and must be changed to reflect the color Windows uses to draw menu items. This color, set by the user in the Display Properties, is retrieved with a call to the **GetSysColors** Windows API function.

The **ModifyMenu** API function is then used to tell Windows that the application will take care of painting the Font menu item. This is done by adding the **MF_OWNERDRAW** item to the flags passed in the third parameter. Once **ModifyMenu** has been called with the **MF_OWNERDRAW** flag, Windows will start sending **WM_MEASUREITEM** and **WM_DRAWITEM** messages to the application. More information on the **ModifyMenu** function can be found in How-To's 4.4 and 4.5.

Finally, the Font menu item caption is saved for later use. **Font1**'s **Shortcut** property is checked to see whether a shortcut exists. If it does, the **ShortCutToText** function is used to append a text description of the shortcut to the caption. A single tab character separates the menu item text from the shortcut text.

Handling the **WM_MEASUREITEM** Event

Windows generates the **WM_MEASUREITEM** event when an API function is called to make a control owner-draw. The function that handles the **WM_MEASUREITEM** event calculates how big the control is supposed to be and passes that information back to Windows by modifying the measurement item structure pointed to by the **LParam** of the message.

Using the measure item structure passed by Windows is a little tricky. Windows places a measure item structure pointer in the **LParam** field of the message. Unfortunately, **LParam** is defined as a long integer. In order to access the fields of the measure item structure, the **LParam** field has to be typecast and de-referenced. The code would end up quite ugly. For example, the code to access the **itemHeight** field of the structure would look like this:

```
((TMeasureItemStruct *)(Message.Lparam))->itemHeight = 20
```

WMMeasureItem gets around this potential problem by creating a working variable called **Measure** and using it throughout the function. The first two lines of code you added in step 7 assign the measure item structure passed by Windows to the working variable.

Next, **WMMeasureItem** checks to make sure the control to be measured is the Font menu item by checking the **CtlType** and **itemID** fields of the measure item structure. This is not strictly necessary in this example because there is only one owner-draw control. If, however, your application has more than one owner-draw control, Windows will send a **WM_MEASUREITEM** message for each control and the **WMMeasureItem** function will have to know how to measure each one.

After `WMMeasureItem` determines that it is measuring the font item, the font of the working area's canvas is set to the font selected by the user. The Font menu's height is calculated using the `TextHeight` method of `TCanvas`. The item's width is calculated as the width of the caption plus the width of a menu check mark plus eight, because Windows always reserves space for check marks on the menu, and the check mark is placed eight pixels to the left of the menu item's caption. Finally, the `Result` field of the message is set to one to tell Windows that the application handled the message.

Painting the Menu Item

Windows sends a `WM_DRAWITEM` message each time an owner-control needs to be painted. The draw item structure, passed by Windows in the `LParam` field of the message, contains three important fields. `HDC` is a device context supplied by Windows for you to paint on, `ItemState` tells you how the item should be painted, and `rcItem` is the rectangular area within the device context where you should perform the painting.

`WMDrawItem` performs the same preparatory steps that `WMMeasureItem` performs. A working variable is created to hold the structure passed in the `LParam` message variable, but this time it is a draw item structure. It then checks to make sure the control in question is the Font menu item.

Next, the current font, stored in `FontDialog1`, is selected into the device context using the `SelectObject` API function. The font being replaced is saved in `OldFont`. The background of the menu item is prepared next. `ItemState` is used to determine what color the background should be, and the brush color of the working bitmap's `TCanvas` object is set accordingly. The background is painted using the `FillRect` Windows API method.

Once the background is painted, the starting position of the Font menu item text is calculated as the left edge of the drawing rectangle, plus the size of a menu check mark, plus eight pixels for the space between the check mark and the item caption.

`ItemStates` is consulted again to determine the correct text color for the menu item. In this How-To, an item in the normal state is painted in the font color, an item in the selected state is painted in the inverse of the font color, and disabled and grayed items are painted in the system's gray text color. Windows, on the other hand, paints disabled menu items with the same font color as normal menu items.

When you draw text or lines in Windows, you are using a pen resource. A pen has a foreground or text color, which you've already set with the `SetTextColor` API function. Its background color, used for painting the area behind the text or in the spaces of patterned lines, can be set using the `SetBkColor` API function. However, if you want the background color to match the color of the surface on which the text or lines are drawn, you should use the `SetBkMode` function passing the `TRANSPARENT` constant, as `WMDrawItem` does. This tells Windows to make the background color transparent so the surface color can show through.

Finally, the function is ready to paint the menu item text. This is done using the very powerful and flexible `DrawText` Windows API function. `DrawText` is passed

the device context to draw on, the string to be drawn, the string length, the rectangle in which to draw, and instructions on how to draw. In this case, drawing will be aligned with the top of the rectangle, the text will be truncated if it does not fit on a single line, and tabs will be expanded into the appropriate number of spaces. `DrawText` uses all the other attributes assigned to the device context.

After the text is drawn, the font that was assigned to the device context (before `DrawText` changed it) is reassigned to the device context with a call to `SelectObject`. The last line of code tells Windows that the application processed the `WM_DRAWTEXT` message.

Handling Menu Clicks

The event handlers for clicks on Test|Enable Font (step 8) and Test|Disable Font (step 9) are very simple. The `ModifyMenu` API function is called to enable, or gray, the Font menu item as appropriate. Windows then sends a `WM_MEASUREITEM` message to the application.

The event handler for clicks on the Font item is a little more complex. The font dialog is opened, and, if the user makes a selection and presses the OK button, `ModifyMenu` is called with no changes specified to fool Windows into sending another `WM_MEASUREITEM` message to the application. If the `ModifyMenu` call was not made, the application would not have a chance to adjust the size of the menu to fit the font item's caption properly. For example, if the font the user selected was bigger, part of the font item's caption would be truncated.

Comments

C++Builder handles Windows messages behind the scenes. It also frees you from having to call Windows API functions directly to perform basic functions. This makes C++Builder a very productive programming environment. However, Borland could not build in support for every little thing and still make the environment easy to use. Therefore,C++Builder gives you the flexibility to dip into the Windows API and handle Windows messages yourself when you need to accomplish something it does not support directly.

COMPLEXITY
BEGINNING

4.7 How do I...
Use a popup menu?

Problem

I like the way the right-mouse button is used to bring up context-sensitive menus in some applications. I also like the way the right-mouse button works on my Windows 95 desktop. How can I add menus that pop up on right-mouse button clicks to my C++Builder application?

Technique

This How-To will show you how to create a popup menu, attach it to two different components, and figure out which component the user right-clicked on to bring up the menu. The **TPopupMenu** component provided by C++Builder makes this very easy.

Steps

Run **POPUP.EXE**. Right-click on either label and a simple menu will pop up. Click on the font menu item and change the font. Notice that the font of the label you right-clicked on will change to the font you selected. An example is shown in Figure 4-9.

1. Create a new project. Save the default unit as **POPUPMAIN.CPP** and the project as **POPUP.MAK**.

2. Add the components, properties, and settings as shown in Table 4-7.

Table 4-7 Components, properties, and settings for the **POPUP** project

COMPONENT	PROPERTY	SETTING
TForm	Caption	Popup
TFontDialog		
TPopupMenu		
TLabel	PopupMenu	PopupMenu1
TLabel	PopupMenu	PopupMenu1

3. Start the menu designer for the **PopupMenu** component, and add the menu items as shown in Table 4-8.

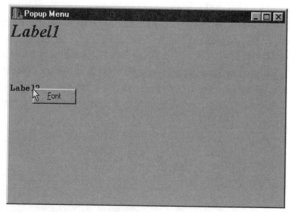

Figure 4-9 The POPUP application with its popup menu showing

Table 4-8 Menu design for the popup menu

POPUP MENU ITEM
&Font

4. Open the Menu Designer for `PopupMenu1`. Double-click on the Font menu item, and add the code that lets the user select a font.

```
void __fastcall TForm1::Font1Click(TObject *Sender)
{
  //Set the font dialog's font to the font of the label that was clicked
  FontDialog1->Font = ((TLabel *)(PopupMenu1->PopupComponent))->Font;
  //If the user pressed the font dialog's OK button
  if (FontDialog1->Execute())
    //Set the font of the label
    ((TLabel *)(PopupMenu1->PopupComponent))->Font = FontDialog1->Font;
}
```

5. Compile and run the application.

How It Works

C++Builder includes everything you need to add right-click popup menus to any component. In this example, most of the hard work is performed with C++Builder's visual design tools. The popup menu is created in the Menu Designer and attached to the label components by setting their popup menu property in the Object Inspector. Once the popup menu property of the component is assigned, C++Builder takes care of the details of popping up the menu when the right-mouse button is clicked.

The `PopupComponent` property of the popup menu contains a reference to the component on which the user right-clicked to bring up the menu. This property is used in the `OnClick` event handler of the Font menu item (step 3) to figure out which label was right-clicked by the user.

`Font1Click` starts by assigning the label's current font to the font dialog's font. If the user presses the OK button on the font dialog, the label's font is changed to the font selected in the dialog. Note that the `PopupComponent` property is cast to a `TLabel` object before the font property is accessed because the `PopupComponent` is declared as a `TComponent` and `TComponent` does not have a font property. This cast is legal because the `TPopupMenu` component inherits from `TComponent`.

Comments

Right-click menus should only perform certain functions. The Font item used in this sample application directly affects the properties of the control the user right-clicked, so it is a good item to have on the popup menu. Right-click menus should not generally be used for global functions, like terminating the application. The best way to learn what items should be on a right-click menu is to take a close look at the Windows 95 desktop interface. You might also want to look at quality commercial applications like Microsoft Word for Windows.

CHAPTER 5
GRAPHICS

5

GRAPHICS

How do I...

Quality graphics have become an essential ingredient in many Windows 95 applications, but the Win32 API makes coding graphical programs more daunting than it needs to be. C++Builder™ provides a multitude of components, classes, and functions that simplify the production of graphically intense applications. For example, **TImage** allows you to load and display bitmaps, metafiles, and icons with a single function call. **TPaintBox** provides a rectangular region on which to draw, and it also gives you a canvas to draw with. **TBitmap** makes it easy to load bitmaps from files and perform graphical operations in memory.

The How-To's in this chapter demonstrate how to harness the graphical power of C++Builder. Several How-To's point out how the Win32 API and the VCL can be used together in the same program. But perhaps the most important feature of this chapter is that it shows you how to do some downright cool stuff.

5.1 Use a Canvas to Draw on a Form

Programmers with Windows experience may be familiar with device contexts and the Windows **WM_PAINT** message. C++Builder provides a class called **TCanvas** that encapsulates the Windows device context. You have already used the **TCanvas** class in other sections of the book. How-To 1.6 used a canvas to draw on an MDI background, and How-To 1.7 painted the title bar of a form using canvas functions. C++Builder forms provide a nifty way of responding to **WM_PAINT** messages via their **OnPaint** handler. This How-To illustrates how **OnPaint** and **TCanvas** can work together to paint graphics on a form.

5.2 Visualize the Pen Mode Settings

Every **TCanvas** object contains a **TPen** member. **TPen** encapsulates the Windows **HPEN**. **TPen** contains a property called **Mode** that determines the raster operation (ROP) code of the pen. You can use the **Mode** property to achieve powerful effects, but knowing which mode to use can be difficult. This How-To helps you visualize what each pen mode does.

5.3 Draw a Bounding Box with the Mouse

In many applications, the user must select a particular area of a form by dragging the mouse. This selection may determine the size of an object, or it may group objects together. In this How-To, you create a bounding box with the mouse by utilizing a rubber-band effect. Windows uses rubber-banding when you size a header control or when you use the mouse to select a group of folders on the desktop. This How-To demonstrates how you can achieve the same bounding box effect using the **Mode** property of **TPen**.

5.4 Create Hot Spots in Pictures

Pictures can convey information and spice up an application. Pictures can also act as intuitive controls. For example, a multimedia program might display a map of midwestern states. Clicking on a particular state might cause the program to take action. C++Builder's **TPaintBox** makes a terrific invisible hot spot that can be placed

on top of an image in order to trigger events when the mouse passes over it or when the user clicks on the image.

5.5 Load Icons from a Resource File and Display Them on a Form

This How-To shows how to paint an icon on your form. You can use any of the stock Windows icons or you can use your own icon from a resource file. This How-To also demonstrates how to overcome limitations in some of Win32 API functions that load and draw icons.

5.6 Create Animation

In this How-To, you create an animated spaceship that hops around the galaxy at warp speed. The program shows how C++Builder allows you to perform graphics operations in memory before displaying an image on the screen. This eliminates screen flicker and optimizes performance. C and C++ programmers from other development environments should be pleased with C++Builder's encapsulation of memory DCs. If you thought creating graphical games would be too complicated in Windows, this How-To may change your mind.

5.7 Fade One Picture into Another

Some of the most popular applications today are presentation packages such as Microsoft PowerPoint. These programs include the ability to perform gradual transitions between images. This How-To presents a technique that allows you to gradually fade from one picture to another. In addition, the example can fade an image to blackness and fade it back again.

5.8 Fade Text In and Out over a Background

In this How-To, you build on the code in How-To 5.7 to smoothly fade text into and out of an image. Presentation programs often utilize this effect.

5.9 Draw with a True Cartesian Coordinate System

Windows employs a screen coordinate system that graphics functions must use to paint on the screen. By default, Windows places the origin of the coordinate system in the upper-left corner of the screen with the positive Y axis pointing down. This upside-down Y axis makes it difficult to paint graphs and charts. This How-To describes how to use API functions to flip the Y axis back around so the positive Y axis points up. You can then paint graphs using a traditional Cartesian coordinate system.

5.10 Translate a System Color into an Actual Color

Most of the time, you can use system colors, such as `clActiveCaption`, `clWindowText`, and `clButtonFace`, without regard for the actual color represented by the setting. However, sometimes you need to know what the actual color is. In this How-To, you learn how to convert the system color to an actual color using the API `GetSysColor` function.

5.11 Draw a Bitmap with a Transparent Background

You may run across situations where you need to draw an image transparently. This How-To loads a bitmap that contains a white background. The program converts the white background to the background color of the form. This makes the image's background appear transparently.

5.12 Autosize a Form to Fit a Picture and Autosize a Picture to Fit a Form

This How-To teaches a simple technique for displaying bitmaps. When you load a bitmap, the form resizes itself to fit the size of the picture. Once displayed, the picture stretches to fit the form as the user resizes the main window.

5.13 Write a Screen Saver

It's time to put your graphical knowledge to the test. In this How-To, you learn how to work with the operating system to create a simple screen saver.

COMPLEXITY
BEGINNING

5.1 How do I...
Use a canvas to draw on a form?

Problem

I would like to draw on my forms. I've written traditional Windows C++ programs that use API functions and a **WM_PAINT** handler to draw on my windows and dialog boxes. How do I paint on a form using C++Builder?

Technique

TForm has an **OnPaint** event property that parallels the **WM_PAINT** handler in traditional C/C++ programs. You can use a **TCanvas** object to draw on the screen from inside the **OnPaint** handler.

Steps

Run **CANVAS.EXE**. Figure 5-1 shows **CANVAS** at runtime. Step through the sequence of drawing functions using the Next button. Experiment by changing the pen and brush attributes using the **UpDown** control and the Combo boxes. The Color grid allows you to change the pen and brush colors. Click the Color grid with the left mouse button to change the pen color, and use the right mouse button to change the brush.

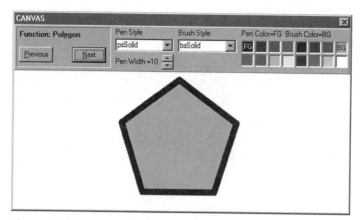

Figure 5-1 CANVAS at runtime

This How-To utilizes the Color grid sample control provided with C++Builder. You can install the C++Builder sample controls by following the directions listed in the README.TXT file in the \EXAMPLES\CONTROLS directory.

1. Create a new project. Name the unit **MAINFORM.CPP**, and name the project **CANVAS.MAK**.

2. Place controls on the form so it matches the picture in Figure 5-1. Change properties to match Table 5-1.

Most of the controls can be automatically named by C++Builder. Four of the controls (two Combo boxes, the label that says Polygon in Figure 5-1, and the label next to the UpDown control) have been renamed for code readability in later steps.

In this step, you can save a lot of time by copying controls from the project on the CD-ROM. Open MAINFORM.CPP from the CANVAS project on the CD-ROM. Choose Edit|Select All from the menu. Push CTRL-C to copy. Move to your own form, and push CTRL-V to paste.

Table 5-1 Components, properties, and settings for `Form1` in the CANVAS project

COMPONENT	PROPERTY	SETTING
Form1	ClientWidth	555
	ClientHeight	295
	BorderStyle	bsDialog
	Color	clWhite
Panel1	Align	alTop
	Caption	""
	Height	75
Button1	Caption	&Previous
Button2	Caption	&Next
UpDown1	Min	1
	Max	15
	Position	1
Label1	Caption	Function
	Font->Style	fsBold
Label2	Caption	Pen Style
Label3	Caption	Brush Style
Label4	Caption	Pen Color=FG Brush Color=BG
FunctionLabel	(position)	(right of Label1)
	Font->Color	clNavy
	Font->Style	fsBold
PenWidthLabel	(position)	(left of UpDown1)
Bevel1		
PenStyleComboBox	(position)	(under Label2)
	Items(TStrings)	psSolid, psDash, psDot,
		psDashDot, psDashDotDot,
		psClear, psInsideFrame
	Style	csDropDownList
BrushStyleComboBox	(position)	(under Label3)
	Items(TStrings)	bsSolid, bsClear,
		bsHorizontal, bsVertical,
		bsFDiagonal, bsBDiagonal,
		bsCross, bsDiagCross
	Style	csDropDownList
ColorGrid1	BackgroundIndex	9
	ForegroundIndex	0
	GridOrdering	go8x2

3. Open **MAINFORM.CPP**, and add the following constant declarations. The code will use the strings in **FunctionNames** to display the current canvas function. **FunctionCount** keeps track of how many functions the program displays. **PolyPoints** is used in the **Polygon** and **PolyLine** function calls.

NOTE

The **PenStyles** and **BrushStyles** arrays correspond to the Combo box strings in Table 5-1.

```
#include <vcl\vcl.h>
#pragma hdrstop

#include "MAINFORM.h"
const int FunctionCount = 14;
const AnsiString FunctionNames[FunctionCount]={
     "Arc","Chord","DrawFocusRect","Ellipse","FillRect","FrameRect",
     "LineTo","Pie","Polygon","PolyLine","Rectangle","RoundRect",
     "TextOut","TextRect"};
const TPenStyle PenStyles[]={psSolid,psDash,psDot,psDashDot,psDashDotDot,⇐
                            psClear,psInsideFrame};
const TBrushStyle BrushStyles[]={bsSolid,bsClear,bsHorizontal,bsVertical,
bsFDiagonal,bsBDiagonal,bsCross,bsDiagCross};
const POINT PolyPoints[]={{275,85},{370,154},{334,265},{216,265},{180,154}};
```

4. Open **MAINFORM.H**, and add a declaration to **TForm1** for an indexing variable.

```
private:     // User declarations
   int       FunctionIndex;
```

5. Select **Form1** into the Object Inspector. Click the Events tab, and locate the **OnPaint** event. Create an **OnPaint** handler, and type in this code:

```
void __fastcall TForm1::FormPaint(TObject *Sender)
{
   // c contains the center coordinates of the client area
   TPoint c=Point(ClientWidth/2,
                 (ClientHeight-Panel1->Height)/2+Panel1->Height);

   // Initialize pen, font, and brush of the Form's canvas
   Canvas->Pen->Style = PenStyles[PenStyleComboBox->ItemIndex];
   Canvas->Pen->Width = UpDown1->Position;
   Canvas->Pen->Color = ColorGrid1->ForegroundColor;
   Canvas->Font->Color = ColorGrid1->ForegroundColor;
   Canvas->Brush->Color = ColorGrid1->BackgroundColor;
   Canvas->Brush->Style = BrushStyles[BrushStyleComboBox->ItemIndex];
```

continued on next page

continued from previous page

```
// Draw using one canvas function, determined by index variable
switch(FunctionIndex)
{
    case 0:
        Canvas->Arc(c.x-100,c.y-100,c.x+100,c.y+100,c.x,0,ClientWidth,c.y);
        break;
    case 1:
        Canvas->Chord(c.x-100,c.y-100,c.x+100,c.y+100,ClientWidth,c.y,c.x,0);
        break;
    case 2:
        Canvas->DrawFocusRect(Rect(c.x-100,c.y-50,c.x+100,c.y+50));
        break;
    case 3:
        Canvas->Ellipse(c.x-100,c.y-50,c.x+100,c.y+50);
        break;
    case 4:
        Canvas->FillRect(Rect(c.x-100,c.y-50,c.x+100,c.y+50));
        break;
    case 5:
        Canvas->FrameRect(Rect(c.x-100,c.y-50,c.x+100,c.y+50));
        break;
    case 6:
        Canvas->MoveTo(c.x-100,c.y-50);
        Canvas->LineTo(c.x+100,c.y+50);
        break;
    case 7:
        Canvas->Pie(c.x-50,c.y-50,c.x+50,c.y+50,c.x,0,ClientWidth,c.y-15);
        break;
    case 8:
        Canvas->Polygon(PolyPoints,sizeof(PolyPoints)/sizeof(POINT)-1);
        break;
    case 9:
        Canvas->Polyline(PolyPoints,sizeof(PolyPoints)/sizeof(POINT)-1);
        break;
    case 10:
        Canvas->Rectangle(c.x-100,c.y-50,c.x+100,c.y+50);
        break;
    case 11:
        Canvas->RoundRect(c.x-100,c.y-50,c.x+100,c.y+50,25,25);
        break;
    case 12:
        Canvas->TextOut(c.x-50,c.y,"TextOut function call");
        break;
    case 13:
        Canvas->TextRect(Rect(c.x-75,c.y,c.x+75,c.y+15),c.x-75,c.y,"TextRect⇐
        function call");
        break;
    }
}
```

The second argument to `Polygon` and `PolyLine` determines how many points are in the shape. Set this argument to one less than the number of points in the `PolyPoints` array. `sizeof(PolyPoints)/sizeof(POINT)-1` ensures that the proper number gets passed to the function, regardless of how many points are in the array.

6. Create an `OnClick` handler for the Next button, and insert this code:

```
void __fastcall TForm1::Button2Click(TObject *Sender)
{
  // Check location in the array. Wrap around
  // if index is at the end.
  if(FunctionIndex==FunctionCount-1)
    FunctionIndex=0;
  else
    FunctionIndex++;
  FunctionLabel->Caption=FunctionNames[FunctionIndex];
  Invalidate();
}
```

7. Now add an `OnClick` handler for the Previous button.

```
void __fastcall TForm1::Button1Click(TObject *Sender)
{
  // Check location in the array. Wrap around
  // if index is at the end.
  if(FunctionIndex==0)
    FunctionIndex=FunctionCount-1;
  else
    FunctionIndex--;
  FunctionLabel->Caption=FunctionNames[FunctionIndex];
  Invalidate();
}
```

8. Select `UpDown1` into the Object Inspector. The `OnPaint` handler for `Form1` already knows how to use the position of `UpDown1`, but the form must be repainted when `UpDown1` changes position. Create an `OnClick` handler for `UpDown1` that invalidates the screen and updates the `PenWidthLabel`.

```
void __fastcall TForm1::UpDown1Click(TObject *Sender, TUDBtnType Button)
{
  PenWidthLabel->Caption="Pen Width =" + AnsiString(UpDown1->Position);
  Invalidate();
}
```

9. The `OnPaint` handler already knows about the Combo boxes. Create an `OnChange` handler for each Combo box that invalidates the screen.

```
void __fastcall TForm1::PenStyleComboBoxChange(TObject *Sender)
{
  Invalidate();
}
//----------------------------------------------------------------
void __fastcall TForm1::BrushStyleComboBoxChange(TObject *Sender)
{
  Invalidate();
}
```

10. The `OnPaint` handler also knows how to deal with the Color grid values. Add an `OnChange` handler for `ColorGrid1` that invalidates the screen so the new color selection will be drawn.

```
void __fastcall TForm1::ColorGrid1Change(TObject *Sender)
{
  Invalidate();
}
```

11. Make an `OnCreate` handler for `Form1`, and type in this code. The `OnCreate` handler initializes the Combo boxes and the label controls.

```
void __fastcall TForm1::FormCreate(TObject *Sender)
{
  FunctionIndex=0;
  PenStyleComboBox->ItemIndex=0;
  BrushStyleComboBox->ItemIndex=0;
  PenWidthLabel->Caption="Pen Width =" + AnsiString(UpDown1->Position);
  FunctionLabel->Caption=FunctionNames[FunctionIndex];
}
```

12. Compile and test the program.

How It Works

The core of this How-To lies within the `OnPaint` handler of `Form1`. The `OnPaint` handler utilizes the drawing classes of C++Builder to paint a shape on the form.

The `OnPaint` Handler

The `OnPaint` handler (step 5) executes every time Windows sends the form a **WM_PAINT** message. This occurs when the form is displayed for the first time, when the form is uncovered from beneath another window, or when other parts of the code (steps 6–10) call `Invalidate` to request a repaint.

TIP

Invalidate tells Windows that the form needs to be repainted. Windows responds by placing a WM_PAINT message in the form's message queue. The form repaints when it gets a chance to process the WM_PAINT message. You could force the form to repaint immediately by calling the Update method after calling Invalidate.

The OnPaint handler begins by configuring the Pen, Brush, and Font properties of the form's Canvas. The Color grid supplies the colors for these properties. UpDown1 provides the pen width, and the two Combo boxes supply pen and brush styles. After configuring the Canvas, the OnPaint handler checks the value of FunctionIndex and then executes a TCanvas drawing function based on the value.

The VCL Graphics Classes

The OnPaint handler utilizes several VCL classes to draw on the form. The most important class is TCanvas. TForm contains a Canvas property that allows you to paint on the form. TCanvas encapsulates a Windows device context handle (HDC). The drawing methods of TCanvas have API counterparts; however, the TCanvas functions are much easier to use than the raw API functions. Additionally, TCanvas contains three properties that simplify the use of pens, brushes, and fonts.

TIP

You must supply a DC handle when calling the GDI functions of the Windows API. The functions of TCanvas work like their API counterparts, except that you can drop the HDC argument. Additionally, some API functions require a pointer to a RECT structure, whereas their TCanvas counterparts use TRect objects by reference.

Windows uses pens, brushes, and fonts as part of the GDI system. The VCL encapsulates pens, brushes, and fonts using the TPen, TBrush, and TFont classes. TPen affects the appearance of lines drawn using a Canvas object. TBrush, on the other hand, controls how areas are filled in. TFont only plays a role when drawing text. Some functions, such as Chord, Ellipse, and Rectangle, use a pen to draw the boundary of the shape and then fill in the object using the brush. FillRect uses only the brush, while other functions (Arc, FrameRect, PolyLine) use only the pen. To make matters really fun, DrawFocusRect ignores both the pen and the brush.

Working with VCL pens, brushes, and fonts is significantly simpler and more intuitive then working with the API counterparts (HPEN, HBRUSH, HFONT). For example, examine these two code statements:

```
Canvas->Brush->Color = clBlue;
Canvas->Pen->Color = clGreen;
```

The first line sets the brush color to blue, while the second statement sets the pen color to green. This is much simpler than equivalent API code involving **CreatePen**, **SelectObject**, and **DeleteObject**.

Comments

You may have noticed that **TCanvas** does not contain a replacement for the API **DrawText** function. **DrawText** includes a handy argument for centering and justifying text. You can call **DrawText**, or any other API GDI function, by using the **Canvas->Handle** property as the **HDC** argument. You might want to add a **DrawText** call to this How-To to get a feel for how this works. Add this code to the **OnPaint** handler (after the switch block).

```
AnsiString test="DrawText test";
RECT r;
r.left=50; r.top=c.y-50; r.right=450; r.bottom=c.y+50;
DrawText(Canvas->Handle,test.c_str(),test.Length(),
         &r,DT_SINGLELINE|DT_VCENTER);
```

COMPLEXITY
INTERMEDIATE

5.2 How do I...
Visualize the pen mode settings?

Problem

I know that **TPen** objects have a **Mode** property, but these modes have all sorts of weird names, and I don't know what they mean. How can I visualize what these modes do?

Technique

TPen::Mode can be set to one of 16 possible values. The best way to find the right mode for a particular situation is by testing each of the modes until you run across the one that does what you want. This How-To creates a program that allows you to select a pen color and a pen mode with which to draw. The code uses an **OnPaint** handler to draw a series of vertical stripes, each of a different color. The **OnPaint** handler then draws a large X across the stripes using the pen mode setting.

Steps

Run **PENMODE.EXE**. Figure 5-2 shows the program in action. Choose different pen modes using the Radio buttons on the right-hand panel. Vary the pen color using the Color grid. Study the results of different color and mode combinations. Note that some of the pen modes, such as **pmXor** and **pmNot**, perform neat operations, while others don't seem to do anything too useful at all.

1. Create a new project. Save the unit as **MAINFORM.CPP** and save the project as **PENMODE.MAK**.

2. Drop controls onto **Form1** so it resembles Figure 5-2. Rename the Radio buttons **BlackRadio**, **MergeRadio**, **XorRadio**, and so on. Change properties to match Table 5-2.

TIP

C++Builder can help you place the RadioButton controls quickly. Press and hold SHIFT, and then click on the RadioButton icon in the Component Palette. You can now place the RadioButton controls in rapid succession without reclicking on the Component Palette.

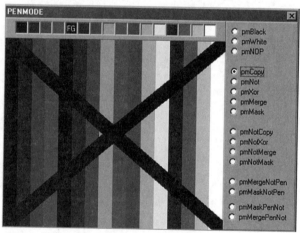

Figure 5-2 PENMODE at runtime

Table 5-2 Components, properties, and settings for `Form1` in the `PENMODE` project

COMPONENT	PROPERTY	SETTING
Form1	ClientWidth	488
	BorderStyle	bsDialog
Panel1	Align	alRight
	Caption	""
	Width	120
BlackRadio	Caption	pmBlack
	Checked	true
WhiteRadio	Caption	pmWhite
NOPRadio	Caption	pmNOP
CopyRadio	Caption	pmCopy
NotRadio	Caption	pmNot
XorRadio	Caption	pmXor
MergeRadio	Caption	pmMerge
MaskRadio	Caption	pmMask
NotCopyRadio	Caption	pmNotCopy
NotXorRadio	Caption	pmNotXor
NotMergeRadio	Caption	pmNotMerge
NotMaskRadio	Caption	pmNotMask
MergeNotPenRadio	Caption	pmMergeNotPen
MaskNotPenRadio	Caption	pmMaskNotPen
MergePenNotRadio	Caption	pmMergePenNot
MaskPenNotRadio	Caption	pmMaskPenNot
Panel2	Caption	""
	Height	33
ColorGrid1	Height	21
	Width	336
	GridOrdering	go16x1
	BackgroundEnabled	false

3. Open `MAINFORM.CPP`, and add an array of colors that can be used by a `for` loop.

```
#include <vcl\vcl.h>
#pragma hdrstop

#include "MAINFORM.h"
```

```
const TColor Colors[]={clBlack,clMaroon,clGreen,clOlive,clNavy,clPurple,
  clTeal,clSilver,clGray,clRed,clLime,clYellow,
                       clBlue,clFuchsia,clAqua,clWhite};
```

4. Open MAINFORM.H. Add a declaration to TForm1 for a private variable that can store a pen mode setting from the Radio buttons.

```
private:   // User declarations
    TPenMode PenMode;
```

5. Go back to MAINFORM.CPP, and modify the TForm1 constructor to initialize the PenMode variable.

```
_fastcall TForm1::TForm1(TComponent* Owner)
  : TForm(Owner),
    PenMode(pmBlack)
{
}
```

6. The program needs to assign a new value to PenMode every time the user checks a different Radio button. Leave the Code Editor, and go back to the Form Designer. Press and hold CTRL. Select all the Radio buttons by drawing a box around them using the mouse. Release CTRL after you draw the box. Each Radio button should be selected. You can now create a single OnClick handler for all 16 Radio buttons. Click the Events tab of the Object Inspector, create an OnClick event handler called RadioClick, and type in this code:

```
void __fastcall TForm1::RadioClick(TObject *Sender)
{
  // Determine which radio button is checked,
  // and set the pen mode accordingly.
  if      (Sender==BlackRadio)       PenMode = pmBlack;
  else if(Sender==WhiteRadio)        PenMode = pmWhite;
  else if(Sender==NOPRadio)          PenMode = pmNop;
  else if(Sender==CopyRadio)         PenMode = pmCopy;
  else if(Sender==NotRadio)          PenMode = pmNot;
  else if(Sender==XorRadio)          PenMode = pmXor;
  else if(Sender==MergeRadio)        PenMode = pmMerge;
  else if(Sender==MaskRadio)         PenMode = pmMask;
  else if(Sender==NotCopyRadio)      PenMode = pmNotCopy;
  else if(Sender==NotXorRadio)       PenMode = pmNotXor;
  else if(Sender==NotMergeRadio)     PenMode = pmNotMerge;
  else if(Sender==NotMaskRadio)      PenMode = pmNotMask;
  else if(Sender==MergeNotPenRadio)  PenMode = pmMergeNotPen;
  else if(Sender==MaskNotPenRadio)   PenMode = pmMaskNotPen;
  else if(Sender==MergePenNotRadio)  PenMode = pmMergePenNot;
  else if(Sender==MaskPenNotRadio)   PenMode = pmMaskPenNot;

  // Request a redraw using the new pen mode.
  Invalidate();
}
```

7. The program should redraw the screen when the user selects a different color from the Color grid. Make an **OnChange** handler for **ColorGrid1**, and use **Invalidate** to update the screen.

```
void __fastcall TForm1::ColorGrid1Change(TObject *Sender)
{
  Invalidate();
}
```

8. Now add the guts of the program. Create an **OnPaint** handler for **Form1** that will draw the vertical stripes, select the pen mode setting, and then draw the big X.

```
void __fastcall TForm1::FormPaint(TObject *Sender)
{
  // Calculate width of vertical stripes.
  int cw=(ClientWidth-Panel1->Width)/16;

  // Draw the vertical stripes, this uses the normal
  // pmCopy mode.
  Canvas->Pen->Width = cw;
  Canvas->Pen->Mode  = pmCopy;
  // Loop through and draw each stripe.
  for(int i=0;i<sizeof(Colors)/sizeof(TColor);i++)
  {
    Canvas->Pen->Color = Colors[i];            // Set color
    // Position line start based on stripe number.
    // Note that Panel2 will clip the top of the stripes.
    Canvas->MoveTo(i*cw+cw/2,0);
    Canvas->LineTo(i*cw+cw/2,ClientHeight);  // Draw vertical line
  }

  // Now select the chosen pen mode and draw a big
  // X on the screen using the foreground color from
  // the color grid.
  Canvas->Pen->Mode = PenMode;
  Canvas->Pen->Color = ColorGrid1->ForegroundColor;
  Canvas->MoveTo(0,Panel2->Height);
  Canvas->LineTo(Panel1->Left,ClientHeight);
  Canvas->MoveTo(Panel1->Left,Panel2->Height);
  Canvas->LineTo(0,ClientHeight);
}
```

9. Compile and test the program.

How It Works

The **OnPaint** handler for **Form1** (step 8) starts by painting 16 vertical stripes using different colors. The pen color is then changed to match the color grid, and the pen mode is changed to the value determined by the radio buttons. Finally, the **OnPaint** handler paints a giant X across the 16 stripes to reveal how the selected pen mode affects the screen.

Comments

The pen mode determines how existing pixels on the screen should be mixed with the pen color to produce a result. Some modes, such as `pmNot`, don't use the pen color, while others, such as `pmCopy`, don't depend on the contents of the screen before the operation takes place. `pmBlack` ignores both the screen and the pen color, while most of the other modes use a combination of the two. Believe it or not, each of the pen mode names describes what the mode actually does. Table 5-3 explains each mode.

Table 5-3 Pen mode settings and descriptions

MODE	RESULT	COMMENT
pmBlack	DEST = black	Ignores pen color and draws using black.
pmWhite	DEST = white	Ignores pen color and draws using white.
pmNOP	DEST = DEST	Leaves screen unchanged.
pmCopy	DEST = PEN	Ignores screen contents and draws using the pen color.
pmNot	DEST = ~DEST	Inverts pixels on the screen ~black = white. If you invert a pixel twice, it will be unchanged.
pmXor	DEST = PEN ^ DEST	XORs pen with the screen. XOR'ing with white inverts pixels. XOR'ing with black leaves the pixels unchanged. XOR'ing a color with itself results in black.
pmMerge	DEST = PEN | DEST	ORs the pen and screen. Results tend to be whiter. OR'ing with black leaves pixels unchanged.
pmMask	DEST = PEN & DEST	ANDs the pen and screen. Results get darker. AND'ing with black equals black.
pmNotCopy	DEST = ~PEN	Equivalent to doing a `pmCopy` followed by a `pmNot`.
pmNotXor	DEST = ~(PEN ^ DEST)	Equivalent to `pmXOR`'ing followed by `pmNot`.
pmNotMerge	DEST = ~(PEN | DEST)	NOR operation. Same as `pmMerge` followed by `pmNot`.
pmNotMask	DEST = ~(PEN & DEST)	NAND operation. Same as `pmMask` followed by `pmNot`.
pmMergePenNot	DEST = PEN | ~DEST	Same as `pmNot` followed by `pmMerge`.
pmMaskPenNot	DEST = PEN & ~DEST	Same as `pmNot` followed by `pmMask`.
pmMergeNotPen	DEST = ~PEN | DEST	Same as `pmMerge` using the inverse of the pen color. `pmMergeNotPen` with black pen is same as `pmMerge` with white pen.
pmMaskNotPen	DEST = ~PEN & DEST	Same as `pmMask` using the inverse of the pen color.

Only a few of the 16 modes serve a purpose that you might actually need, but it is nice to know what each mode does just in case. **pmXor** and **pmNot** are probably the two most useful modes outside the normal **pmCopy**. You can use these modes to invert screen pixels as you pass over them and you can restore the pixels by drawing over them again. The next How-To shows how **TPen::Mode** can be put to use.

COMPLEXITY
BEGINNING

5.3 How do I...
Draw a bounding box with the mouse?

Problem

I would like to let users create a bounding box by dragging the mouse from one point to another in my form. How can I add this feature to my C++Builder program?

Technique

The bounding box effect is sometimes referred to as "rubber-banding". You create a bounding box by responding to mouse events and drawing a rectangle with the **pmNot** pen mode. This mode inverts every pixel the frame passes over, which ensures that the user can see the box regardless of the background colors. As the bounding box grows, you must restore altered pixels to their original condition. Redrawing the box with the **pmNot** pen mode flips the pixels back to their original color.

Steps

Run **BOUNDBOX.EXE**. Figure 5-3 shows what the program looks like. Click anywhere on the form, and drag the mouse to a new location. **BOUNDBOX** creates a box between the point where you first clicked the mouse and the current mouse location. The boundary disappears when you release the mouse button.

1. Create a new project. Name the unit **MAINFORM.CPP**, and name the project **BOUNDBOX.MAK**.

2. Place a handful of different colored shapes on the form using the **Shape** control from the Additional tab of the Component Palette. Create a form that resembles Figure 5-3. You can change the color of the shapes by altering the **Brush->Color** property in the Object Inspector.

3. The **Shape** controls can respond to mouse events on their own, but this feature only gets in the way for what this program will do. Set the **Enabled** property to **false** for each **Shape** control that you added in step 2.

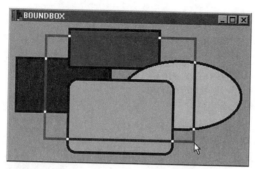

Figure 5-3 BOUNDBOX at runtime

4. Open **MAINFORM.H**, and add these private variables to the **TForm1** class:

```
private:  // User declarations
  TPoint AnchorPoint;
  TPoint CurrentPoint;
  bool   Bounding;
```

5. Make sure that **Form1** is selected in the Object Inspector. Create an **OnMouseDown** event handler, and insert this code:

```
void __fastcall TForm1::FormMouseDown(TObject *Sender, TMouseButton Button,
    TShiftState Shift, int X, int Y)
{
  // Only draw a bounding box if the user has
  // clicked the left mouse button.
  if (Button != mbLeft)
    return;

  // Initialize point variables
  AnchorPoint.x=CurrentPoint.x=X;
  AnchorPoint.y=CurrentPoint.y=Y;
  Bounding=true;
}
```

6. Create an **OnMouseMove** handler for **Form1** that will draw the bounding box as the mouse drags across the form.

```
void __fastcall TForm1::FormMouseMove(TObject *Sender, TShiftState Shift,
    int X, int Y)
{
  // Check for Bounding is important; it ensures that the
  // mouse button was pressed within the form and that it
  // is still down.
  if (Bounding == true)
  {
```

continued on next page

continued from previous page

```
// First, erase the old bounding box
Canvas->Pen->Mode  = pmNot;
Canvas->Pen->Width = 4;
Canvas->Brush->Style=bsClear;
Canvas->Rectangle(AnchorPoint.x,AnchorPoint.y,
                  CurrentPoint.x,CurrentPoint.y);
// Update location and redraw the box
CurrentPoint.x=X;
CurrentPoint.y=Y;
Canvas->Rectangle(AnchorPoint.x,AnchorPoint.y,
                  CurrentPoint.x,CurrentPoint.y);
  }
}
```

7. Add an `OnMouseUp` handler to `Form1` that will erase the bounding box when the user lets go of the mouse button.

```
void __fastcall TForm1::FormMouseUp(TObject *Sender, TMouseButton Button,
    TShiftState Shift, int X, int Y)
{
  if ((Bounding==true) && (Button == mbLeft))
  {
    // Turn off bounding, and then erase the bounding box
    // by drawing it again using pmNot.
    Bounding=false;
    Canvas->Pen->Mode  = pmNot;
    Canvas->Pen->Width = 4;
    Canvas->Brush->Style=bsClear;
    Canvas->Rectangle(AnchorPoint.x,AnchorPoint.y,
                      CurrentPoint.x,CurrentPoint.y);
  }
}
```

8. Compile and test the program.

How It Works

As you can see, the rubber-banding effect can be achieved without doing too much hard core programming. The `OnMouseDown` handler (step 5) stores the coordinates of the mouse cursor in `AnchorPoint` whenever the user clicks in the form with the left mouse button. The `OnMouseDown` handler also initializes the `CurrentPoint` variable by setting it equal to the `AnchorPoint`. Finally, the handler sets the boolean `Bounding` flag to `true`, which tells subsequent mouse events that bounding is in effect.

Windows fires `WM_MOUSEMOVE` messages at your form as the user sweeps the mouse cursor across it. The `OnMouseMove` handler (step 6) reacts to these messages and updates the bounding box if bounding has been activated. The code erases the old bounding box by redrawing it with the `pmNot` pen. This inverts the pixels for a second time, which places them in their original state. Next, the `OnMouseMove` handler saves the new mouse coordinates in `CurrentPosition` and draws the new bounding box.

TIP

Recall that pmNot inverts screen pixels: DEST = ~DEST. If you do this twice then DEST = ~ (~DEST), which is the same as DEST = DEST. This explains why inverting a pixel twice leaves it unchanged.

The OnMouseUp handler (step 7) removes the bounding box from the screen and resets the Bounding flag to false. OnMouseUp uses the same erasure technique from step 6 to clean up the screen. Once the OnMouseUp handler erases the bounding box, the form reverts to its original appearance.

NOTE

The mouse handlers draw the bounding box using the Rectangle function of TCanvas. Normally, Rectangle fills its interior using the brush color, but this would cover up the form. Setting Canvas->Brush->Style to bsClear prevents the brush fill from occurring.

Comments

Windows 95 allows left-handed users to swap the meaning of the left and right mouse buttons. You will be relieved to know that this swapping is transparent to your code. Windows 95 performs the button swapping for you. You can test this out for yourself by changing the settings for the mouse using the control panel. Change the button configuration to left-handed and run the program again. The right mouse button now activates the bounding box even though the code checks for mbLeft in the OnMouseDown handler (step 5). Windows 95 converts the right mouse click to a normal left mouse click before sending you the OnMouseDown event.

The code from this How-To works pretty well, but it does have a downfall. Run the program again. Press the mouse button, and create a box. Keep the mouse button down and [ALT]-[TAB] to another program. Now [ALT]-[TAB] back to **BOUNDBOX**, and release the mouse button. A bounding box gets permanently drawn and won't go away until the form completely repaints. One way to fix this is to turn off bounding whenever the form receives a **WM_PAINT** message. You could create an **OnPaint** handler that looks like this:

```
void __fastcall TForm1::FormPaint(TObject *Sender)
{
  if (Bounding)
  {
    MessageBeep(0);      // Beep for testing
    Bounding = false;
    Invalidate();        // Invalidate to redraw all
  }
}
```

The technique of handling the three mouse events (down, move, and up) is common to many programs. You could use code similar to the code in this How-To to move items around on the screen or actually draw lines and shapes. This could come in handy as you create custom controls.

COMPLEXITY
BEGINNING

5.4 How do I...
Create hot spots in pictures?

Problem

I want to display a picture in my form that has hot spots. Clicking on a hot spot should launch an `OnClick` handler. I'd also like to pop up a Hint box and change the mouse cursor whenever the mouse passes over the hot spot to let users know they can click on the image. This is difficult to do in other development environments. Is there an easy way to do this in C++Builder?

Technique

You can embed hot spots in a picture by using the `PaintBox` component located on the System controls tab. `PaintBox` controls are transparent unless you paint something in them, but this does not mean they are disabled. You can use the invisible `PaintBox` to change the mouse cursor, show the hint box, and respond to `OnClick` events.

Steps

Run `HOTSPOT.EXE`. Move the mouse cursor over the surface of the earth. Hint boxes should appear as you pass over different geographic locations. Figure 5-4 shows the program at runtime. Notice that the cursor changes to a pointing finger when you move the mouse over a hot spot. Click on Northern Africa with the left mouse button to launch an `OnClick` handler that pops up a message box.

1. Create a new project. Name the unit `MAINFORM.CPP`, and name the project `HOTSPOT.MAK`.

2. Locate `EARTH.BMP` and `HANDCURSOR.RES` on the CD-ROM, and copy them to the directory where you saved the project. The bitmap contains a picture of the earth, and the resource file contains a mouse cursor.

NOTE

You could create the mouse cursor yourself using the Image Editor. How-To 4.1 explains how.

Figure 5-4 HOTSPOT at runtime

3. Size **Form1** using the values from Table 5-4. Locate the **Image** control on the Additional component tab, and place one on **Form1**. Set its properties as shown in Table 5-4.

> **NOTE**
>
> The ClientWidth and ClientHeight properties from Table 5-4 were calculated to match the dimensions of the bitmap picture.

Table 5-4 Components, properties, and settings for **Form1** in the HOTSPOT project

COMPONENT	PROPERTY	SETTING
Form	ClientWidth	318
	ClientHeight	238
	BorderStyle	bsDialog
	Scaled	false
Image	Align	alClient
	AutoSize	false
	Stretch	false
	Picture (TBitmap)	(EARTH.BMP)
PaintBox	Hint	Africa (north)
	ParentShowHint	false
	ShowHint	true
PaintBox	Hint	Africa (south)
	ParentShowHint	false
	ShowHint	true

continued on next page

continued from previous page

COMPONENT	PROPERTY	SETTING
PaintBox	Hint	Antarctica
	ParentShowHint	false
	ShowHint	true
PaintBox	Hint	Atlantic Ocean (south)
	ParentShowHint	false
	ShowHint	true
PaintBox	Hint	Atlantic Ocean (north)
	ParentShowHint	false
	ShowHint	true
PaintBox	Hint	South America
	ParentShowHint	false
	ShowHint	true
PaintBox	Hint	Europe
	ParentShowHint	false
	ShowHint	true

4. Double-click on **Image1** to launch the Picture Editor. Click the Load button; then, find and select **EARTH.BMP**.

5. Place a **PaintBox** component on each major geographical region of the picture. This How-To uses seven **PaintBox** controls, but you can vary the number if you want.

6. Fill in the **Hint** text for each **PaintBox**, and set each control's **ShowHint** property to **true**, otherwise the hint will not display.

NOTE

C++Builder automatically sets ParentShowHint to false when you set the ShowHint property to true. The hints will not appear if ParentShowHint is true.

7. That's all you need to do to display hints for each hot spot. The next two steps change the mouse cursor when it passes over a hot spot. Open **MAINFORM.CPP**, and insert a constant **TCursor** declaration and a **#pragma** statement for a new resource file.

```
#include <vcl\vcl.h>
#pragma hdrstop

#include "MAINFORM.h"
//-------------------------------------------------------------
```

```
#pragma resource "*.dfm"
#pragma resource "HANDCURSOR.res"    // New resource file for mouse cursor
const TCursor crHandCursor=1;        // ID for hand type cursor.
```

8. The VCL contains a global instance of **TScreen** called **Screen**. **Screen** contains an array of mouse cursors available to the program. You must add custom cursors to this array before you can assign them to a control. Create an **OnCreate** handler function for **Form1**, and add code that will load the custom cursor into the array of mouse cursors. Once the cursor has been loaded, it can be assigned to each of the **PaintBox** controls.

```
void __fastcall TForm1::FormCreate(TObject *Sender)
{
  // Load the cursor.
  Screen->Cursors[crHandCursor]=LoadCursor(HInstance,"HAND");

  // Set the cursor for all TPaintBox controls
  for(int j=0;j<ControlCount;j++)
  {
    if(Controls[j]->ClassNameIs("TPaintBox"))
      Controls[j]->Cursor = crHandCursor;
  }
}
```

9. Choose one of the hot spot **PaintBox** controls that covers Africa. Create an **OnClick** handler using the Object Inspector, and type in code to pop up a Message box.

```
void __fastcall TForm1::PaintBox1Click(TObject *Sender)
{
  Application->MessageBox("You clicked on Africa",
                          "Hot Spot Click",MB_OK);
}
```

10. Compile and test the program.

How It Works

This How-To utilizes invisible **PaintBox** controls to produce the hot spot effect. Creating hot spots requires placing **PaintBox** controls, setting hint properties, changing the mouse cursor, and creating **OnClick** event handlers.

Using PaintBox Controls As Hot Spots

In step 5, you placed a **PaintBox** control on each geographical region of the earth bitmap. By default, **PaintBox** components are completely invisible. They don't appear unless you paint something in them. Even though **PaintBox** components cannot be seen, they still function like a normal component. This means they can have hints, respond to mouse movements, and launch event handlers.

Using Hints

All visual components, including **TPaintBox**, have a **Hint** property. The **Hint** string can contain up to 255 characters of text. In this How-To, the **Hint** property contains the name of the hot spot region (step 6). Setting the control's **ShowHint** property to **true** activates the hint. When the program runs, the hints notify the user which hot spot the mouse is over.

By default, hints appear with a yellow background defined by the system color **clInfoBk**. You can change the hint background color by altering the **HintColor** property of **TApplication**.

```
Application->HintColor=clAqua;
```

When you move the mouse cursor over a hot spot, there is a delay before the hint pops up. The amount of delay can be controlled by changing the **HintPause** property of **TApplication**.

```
Application->HintPause= 250; // time base in milli-seconds
```

You may need to alter **HintColor** and **HintPause** to improve how the hot spot text appears in your application.

Changing the Mouse Cursor

PaintBox controls can change the mouse cursor whenever the mouse passes over their air space. The Object Inspector allows you to change a control's **Cursor** to any of the stock Windows cursors. This How-To requires a custom cursor provided by a resource file, so you must load the cursor yourself. The **OnCreate** handler for **Form1** (step 8) loads the cursor by calling the API **LoadCursor** function. **LoadCursor** returns an **HCURSOR** handle, which you place in the array of cursors contained in **Screen**. After the cursor has been loaded, the **OnCreate** handler loops through the **Controls** array looking for **PaintBox** controls. Each **PaintBox** has its **Cursor** property set to the ID of the custom cursor.

Creating OnClick Handlers

Hot spots don't do much good unless clicking them causes something to happen. Once again, the **PaintBox** control can perform this task by launching an **OnClick** event. The code from step 9 creates an **OnClick** handler for one hot spot. You could create similar handlers for the remaining hot spot **PaintBox** controls.

Comments

This How-To ended up being pretty simple, but you might have noticed one annoying aspect of using **PaintBox** controls as a hot spot detector. **PaintBox** controls must be rectangular, which makes it difficult to design a curved hot spot contour. You can partially overcome this by splitting a hot spot among two or more **PaintBox** components. The Atlantic Ocean and Africa hot spots employ this technique by combining two **PaintBox** controls into one irregularly shaped hot spot.

5.5 How do I...

Load icons from a resource file and display them on a form?

Problem

I would like to be able to display icons in my applications. I know how to do this using other C++ development tools. How can I load and display icons in a C++Builder program?

Technique

TIcon encapsulates the Windows **HICON** handle. It provides member functions that simplify loading and saving icons from .ICO files, copying icon objects, drawing icons, and cutting and pasting icons to the clipboard. **TIcon** also deletes the icon handle for you when you delete the **TIcon** object. This How-To uses a mix of API and VCL functions to load 16×16 and 32×32 icons into **TIcon** objects and display the icons on the form. The code also displays the Windows 95 stock icons.

Steps

Run **ICON.EXE**. Figure 5-5 shows the program during execution. Choose an icon to display from the Source Combo box, and choose the icon's display size using the Icon Size Combo box. The Source Combo box gives you the choice to display either a custom icon or a standard Windows icon.

1. Create a new project. Name the unit **MAINFORM.CPP**, and name the project **ICON.MAK**.

2. Add two **ComboBox** controls and two **Label** controls to **Form1** so it resembles Figure 5-5. Set properties using Table 5-5.

Figure 5-5 ICON at runtime

Table 5-5 Components, properties, and settings for `Form1` in the `ICON` project

COMPONENT	PROPERTY	SETTING
Form	ClientWidth	185
	ClientHeight	200
	BorderStyle	bsDialog
Label	Caption	Source
Label	Caption	IconSize
ComboBox	Name	SourceComboBox
	Style	csDropDownList
	Items (TStrings)	ICON16(res), ICON32(res),
		IDI_APPLICATION,IDI_ASTERISK,
		IDI_EXCLAMATION,IDI_HAND,
		IDI_QUESTION, IDI_WINLOGO
ComboBox	Name	SizeComboBox
	Style	csDropDownList
	Items (TStrings)	16x16, 32x32, 48x48, 64x64

3. The program needs a couple of custom icons. You can get these from the CD-ROM if you want. Copy `ICONS.RES` from the CD-ROM to your project directory. Then add a `#pragma` statement for the resource in `MAINFORM.CPP`.

```
#include "MAINFORM.h"
//---------------------------------------
#pragma resource "*.dfm"
#pragma resource "ICONS.res"
```

NOTE

Follow these steps if you want to create your own icons for this How-To:

✔ Open the Image Editor.

✔ Choose File|New Resource.

✔ Use Resource|New to add two icons to the resource file. Make one icon a 16×16 icon and name it `ICON16`. Make the other icon 32×32 and name it `ICON32`.

✔ Save the resource file as `ICONS.RES`.

4. Open **MAINFORM.H**, and add a declaration for a **TIcon** array to the private section of **TForm1**.

```
private:   // User declarations
  Graphics::TIcon *Icons[8];
```

5. Create an **OnCreate** handler for **Form1**, and type in code to initialize the icon objects.

```
void __fastcall TForm1::FormCreate(TObject *Sender)
{
  // Create each pointer in the array.
  for(int j=0;j<8;j++)
    Icons[j] = new Graphics::TIcon;

  // Load in the icons. The 16x16 icon (first in the array)
  // must be loaded using win32 LoadImage. The 32x32 icons
  // can be loaded using LoadIcon.
  Icons[0]->Handle=LoadImage(HInstance,
                             "ICON16",
                             IMAGE_ICON,
                             16,16,
                             LR_LOADREALSIZE);
  Icons[1]->Handle=LoadIcon(HInstance,"ICON32");
  Icons[2]->Handle=LoadIcon(0,IDI_APPLICATION);
  Icons[3]->Handle=LoadIcon(0,IDI_ASTERISK);
  Icons[4]->Handle=LoadIcon(0,IDI_EXCLAMATION);
  Icons[5]->Handle=LoadIcon(0,IDI_HAND);
  Icons[6]->Handle=LoadIcon(0,IDI_QUESTION);
  Icons[7]->Handle=LoadIcon(0,IDI_WINLOGO);

  // Initialize the Combo boxes.
  SourceComboBox->ItemIndex = 0;
  SizeComboBox->ItemIndex   = 1;
}
```

6. You need to delete the icons when the program terminates. Create an **OnDestroy** handler for **Form1**, and insert code that loops through the array of pointers and delete each one.

```
void __fastcall TForm1::FormDestroy(TObject *Sender)
{
  for(int j=0;j<8;j++)
    delete Icons[j];
}
```

7. Create an **OnPaint** handler for **Form1** that displays the selected icon in its proper size.

```
void __fastcall TForm1::FormPaint(TObject *Sender)
{
  int x;

  // Act based on the size requested. Icons that are not
  // 32x32 must use Win32 DrawIconEx (even if no scaling is
```

continued on next page

continued from previous page

```
// required) 32x32 icons can just use the canvas draw method
// Use DrawIconEx to stretch both 16x16 and 32x32 icons to
// 48x48 and 64x64
switch(SizeComboBox->ItemIndex)
{
  case 0:                                    // Draw 16x16 icon
    x = (Width-16)/2;                        // Calculate center
    DrawIconEx(Canvas->Handle,x,100,         // and draw
               Icons[SourceComboBox->ItemIndex]->Handle,
               16,16,0,NULL,DI_NORMAL);
    break;
  case 1:                                    // Draw 32x32
    x = (Width-32)/2;
    Canvas->Draw(x,100,Icons[SourceComboBox->ItemIndex]);
    break;
  case 2:                                    // Draw 48x48
    x = (Width-48)/2;
    DrawIconEx(Canvas->Handle,x,100,
               Icons[SourceComboBox->ItemIndex]->Handle,
               48,48,0,NULL,DI_NORMAL);
    break;
  case 3:                                    // Draw 64x64
    x = (Width-64)/2;
    DrawIconEx(Canvas->Handle,x,100,
               Icons[SourceComboBox->ItemIndex]->Handle,
               64,64,0,NULL,DI_NORMAL);
    break;
  }
}
```

8. The program should repaint when the Combo boxes change position. Create an `OnChange` handler for both Combo boxes and, insert a call to `Invalidate` in each handler.

```
void __fastcall TForm1::SourceComboBoxChange(TObject *Sender)
{
  Invalidate();
}
//----------------------------------------------------------------
void __fastcall TForm1::SizeComboBoxChange(TObject *Sender)
{
  Invalidate();
}
```

9. Compile and test the program.

How It Works

Displaying an icon is a two-step process. First, the icon must be loaded into a `TIcon` object. You then display the icon using either `TCanvas` or API functions.

Loading Icons

The OnCreate handler of Form1 (step 5) constructs an array of TIcon pointers. After being constructed, each pointer has an icon loaded into it. You load an icon by assigning a Windows HICON handle to the Handle property of TIcon. The API LoadImage and LoadIcon functions provide the HICON handles. LoadImage fetches the 16×16 icon and LoadIcon loads the 32×32 resource icon and the 32×32 stock Windows icons. The process of loading an icon can be summarized with two code statements.

```
Icon = new Graphics::TIcon;                    // Construct pointer
Icon->Handle = LoadIcon(0,IDI_EXCLAMATION);    // Load icon into Handle
```

> **NOTE**
>
> LoadIcon can only load 32×32 icons. If you load a 16×16 icon using LoadIcon, the icon will stretch to 32×32.

Displaying Icons

Icons can be displayed once they have been loaded. The OnPaint handler (step 7) checks the Combo boxes and draws the selected icon using DrawIconEx or TCanvas::Draw. Draw paints the icon if the user has selected 32×32 using SizeComboBox. The API DrawIconEx draws the icon if any other size was selected. Both Draw and DrawIconEx stretch the icon to fit the selected size.

> **NOTE**
>
> TCanvas::Draw calls the API DrawIcon function when you paint icons. DrawIcon can only draw 32×32 icons. If you paint a 16×16 icon using Draw, the icon will stretch to 32×32.

> **TIP**
>
> In Windows 95, LoadIcon and DrawIcon produce icons whose height and width match the SM_CXICON and SM_CYICON values returned by GetSystemMetrics. Normally this is 32×32. To avoid stretching, load 16×16 icons using the LoadImage function and paint them with DrawIconEx.

Comments

Icons work well as graphical notes to users. In addition to representing programs and shortcuts with icons, Windows 95 uses icons in many of its configuration dialog boxes. For example, the dial-up networking dialog uses a series of icon pictures to portray a modem connection. This How-To demonstrates how you can use icons in your forms just as Windows 95 does.

5.6 How do I...
Create animation?

Problem

I would like to spice up some of my programs by showing animated graphics. Naturally, performance is a big concern. Can I create professional-looking animated graphics using C++Builder?

Technique

Most forms of animation utilize one of two core methods: sprite-based animation and frame-based animation. Frame-based animation uses a sequence of frames that combine to give the appearance of smooth motion. This mimics how video clips and cartoons work. The logo in Netscape Navigator employs frame-based animation. Sprite animation involves moving an object, such as a spaceship, across a background that never changes. Some high performance programs combine the two methods.

Both animation methods rely on the same basic principles: Prepare the image in memory and then move the pixels to the screen. Preparing the image in memory speeds processing because operations in system memory execute faster than the same operations performed in video memory. This technique also reduces screen flicker because intermediate images never make it to the screen.

This How-To uses the power of C++Builder to demonstrate sprite-based techniques, but the lessons of this section could easily be adapted to produce frame-based graphics. C++Builder reduces the complexity of creating animated graphics by providing a set of well-designed classes that encapsulate much of the work. **TCanvas**, **TBitmap**, and **TPaintBox** simplify the task of loading images, performing the animation operations in memory, and moving images to the screen.

Steps

Run **ANIMATION.EXE**. Figure 5-6 shows the program at runtime. Play with the horizontal and vertical Track bars to control how fast the spaceship moves across the screen. Concentrate on the background image and observe that no screen flicker occurs.

1. Create a new project. Name the unit **MAINFORM.CPP** and name the project **ANIMATION.MAK**.

2. Place components on **Form1** so it resembles Figure 5-6 at design time. Set properties to match Table 5-6, Table 5-7, and Table 5-8.

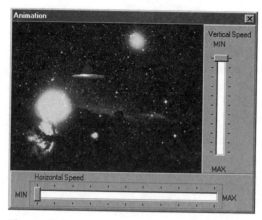

Figure 5-6 ANIMATION at runtime

Table 5-6 Components, properties, and settings for Form1 in the ANIMATION project

COMPONENT	PROPERTY	SETTING
Form	ClientWidth	403
	ClientHeight	298
	BorderStyle	bsDialog
Panel	Name	Panel1
	Align	alBottom
	Caption	""
	Height	60
Panel	Name	Panel2
	Align	alRight
	Caption	""
	Width	85
PaintBox	Name	PaintBox1
	Align	alClient
	Width	318
	Height	238
Timer	Interval	5

NOTE

Make sure the height and width values of PaintBox1 match the values in Table 5-6. The background bitmap is 318×238 and PaintBox1 should be the same dimension.

NOTE

The Windows 95 timer can go no faster than 55ms. The Windows NT timer pegs out at 10ms. Setting the `Interval` property to 5ms doesn't result in 5ms intervals, but it does produce more consistent 55ms intervals in Windows 95. Setting the `Interval` to 55ms causes skipping because Windows treats the timer as a low priority event. For more reliable timing, consider using the multimedia timer.

Table 5-7 Components, properties, and settings for `Panel1` in the `ANIMATION` project

COMPONENT	PROPERTY	SETTING
Trackbar	Name	XSpeedBar
	Orientation	trHorizontal
	Frequency	1
	Position	1
	Min	0
	Max	10
	TickMarks	tmBoth
	TickStyle	tsAuto
Label	Caption	Horizontal Speed
Label	Caption	MIN
Label	Caption	MAX

Table 5-8 Components, properties, and settings for `Panel2` in the `ANIMATION` project

COMPONENT	PROPERTY	SETTING
Trackbar	Name	YSpeedBar
	Orientation	trVertical
	Frequency	1
	Position	1
	Min	0
	Max	10
	TickMarks	tmBoth
	TickStyle	tsAuto
Label	Caption	Vertical Speed
Label	Caption	MIN
Label	Caption	MAX

3. The project needs some bitmap pictures for the sprite background and the moving object. Copy **PICTURES.RES** from the CD-ROM to your project directory if you want to use the same pictures shown in Figure 5-6. Add this #pragma statement to **MAINFORM.CPP** so **PICTURES.RES** will get linked with the project:

```
#include "MAINFORM.h"
//-------------------------------------------------
#pragma resource "*.dfm"
#pragma resource "PICTURES.res"
```

4. Open **MAINFORM.H**, and insert declarations for private variables and functions into the **TForm1** class.

```
private:  // User declarations
   Graphics::TBitmap *Ship,        *ShipMask,
                     *Background, *SavedBackgroundRegion;
   void PatchBackground(void);
   void DrawShipOnBackground(void);
   void MoveBitmapToScreen(void);
   void MoveShipLocation(void);
   TPoint Location;
   int XSpeed;
   int YSpeed;
   int XDirection;
   int YDirection;
   TRect ShipRect;
```

5. Select **Form1** into the Object Inspector. Create an **OnCreate** event handler, and type in this code to initialize data members and load in bitmap resources:

```
void __fastcall TForm1::FormCreate(TObject *Sender)
{
   // Construct each bitmap.
   Ship                  = new Graphics::TBitmap;
   ShipMask              = new Graphics::TBitmap;
   Background            = new Graphics::TBitmap;
   SavedBackgroundRegion = new Graphics::TBitmap;

   // Load the three bitmaps from resource.
   Ship      ->LoadFromResourceName((int)HInstance,"SHIP");
   ShipMask  ->LoadFromResourceName((int)HInstance,"SHIPMASK");
   Background->LoadFromResourceName((int)HInstance,"STARS");

   // SavedBackgroundRegion will store the portion of the background
   // that gets destroyed when the ship is copied in. Make it the same
   // size as the ship.
   SavedBackgroundRegion->Width = Ship->Width;
   SavedBackgroundRegion->Height= Ship->Height;
```

continued on next page

continued from previous page

```
// Program starts with the ship in the upper left hand corner
// of the screen, initialize members, and draw the ship there.
XSpeed=XSpeedBar->Position;      // Initialize speed values
YSpeed=YSpeedBar->Position;      // to match the Track bars.
XDirection=1;                    // Set directions to
YDirection=1;                    // right and down.
Location.x=0;                    // Set location to 0,0
Location.y=0;
ShipRect = Rect(0,0,         // Size of ship never changes, calculate its
            SavedBackgroundRegion->Width,    // size once for use⇐
            in many
            SavedBackgroundRegion->Height); // functions.

// Parameters are ready, draw the ship in its initial location
// and move the image to the screen
DrawShipOnBackground();
MoveBitmapToScreen();
            }
```

6. Create an `OnDestroy` handler for `Form1`, and insert code to delete each bitmap pointer when the program closes.

```
void __fastcall TForm1::FormDestroy(TObject *Sender)
{
  delete Ship;
  delete ShipMask;
  delete Background;
  delete SavedBackgroundRegion;
}
```

7. The `Timer` control drives the animation. Create an `OnTimer` event for the `Timer` control in `Form1`, and type this code:

```
void __fastcall TForm1::Timer1Timer(TObject *Sender)
{
  PatchBackground();
  MoveShipLocation();
  DrawShipOnBackground();
  MoveBitmapToScreen();
}
```

8. The Track bars control the speed of the flying spaceship. Create an `OnChange` handler for each track bar, and add code to copy the track bar position into the private data variables.

NOTE

The track bar changes take effect after the next timer event occurs.

```
void __fastcall TForm1::XSpeedBarChange(TObject *Sender)
{
  XSpeed = XSpeedBar->Position;
}
//----------------------------------------------------------
void __fastcall TForm1::YSpeedBarChange(TObject *Sender)
{
  YSpeed = YSpeedBar->Position;
}
```

9. Now you can code the meat of the animation. A new animation step occurs on every timer tick. You must first patch the background region where the spaceship is currently located. Open **MAINFORM.CPP**, and type the function body for **PatchBackground** which will perform this task.

> **NOTE**
>
> DrawShipOnBackground (step 11) saves the background region before it copies the spaceship into its new location.

```
void TForm1::PatchBackground(void)
{
  // Get coordinates of ship location on screen.
  TRect LocationRect = Rect(Location.x,Location.y,
                           Location.x+Ship->Width,Location.y+Ship->⇐
                           Height);

  // Need to copy (cmSrcCopy) pixels from the saved bknd bitmap
  // to the background. This restores the background bitmap to
  // its original state (no spaceship)
  Background->Canvas->CopyMode = cmSrcCopy;
  Background->Canvas->CopyRect(LocationRect,
                           SavedBackgroundRegion->Canvas,
                           ShipRect);
}
```

10. Stay in **MAINFORM.CPP**, and code the function that calculates new spaceship coordinates.

```
void TForm1::MoveShipLocation(void)
{
  // Calculate new location.
  Location.x+=XSpeed*XDirection; // Direction is
  Location.y+=YSpeed*YDirection; // either 1 or -1

  // Must detect when the ship hits the wall. Easy calculation
  // on the left, on the right, must account for ship's width
  if (Location.x < 0 || Location.x > Background->Width-ShipRect.Right)
  {
```

continued on next page

continued from previous page

```
    XDirection *= -1;    // If wall collision detected, change direction
    if(Location.x<0)     // Bounce the ship back into the client area
      Location.x *= -1;  // Bounce the ship back in as far as it would
    else                 // have travelled without the wall.
      Location.x=2*Background->Width-2*ShipRect.Right-Location.x;
  }

  // Detect up down wall collisions the same way
  if (Location.y < 0 || Location.y > Background->Height-ShipRect.Bottom)
  {
    YDirection *= -1;
    if(Location.y<0)
      Location.y *= -1;
    else
      Location.y=2*Background->Height-2*ShipRect.Bottom-Location.y;
  }
}
```

11. Code the function that draws the spaceship on the background memory bitmap.

```
void TForm1::DrawShipOnBackground(void)
{
  // Get coordinates of ship relative to the background
  TRect LocationRect = Rect(Location.x,
                            Location.y,
                            Location.x+Ship->Width,
                            Location.y+Ship->Height);

  // We destroy a portion of the background when we draw
  // the ship. Save the contents of this region so it can
  // be patched back in later.
  SavedBackgroundRegion->Canvas->CopyRect( ShipRect,
                                           Background->Canvas,
                                           LocationRect);

  // Now draw on the background. Start by using the mask
  // bitmap to punch out the region where the ship will be
  Background->Canvas->CopyMode = cmSrcAnd;  // DEST = SRC AND DEST
  Background->Canvas->CopyRect(LocationRect,
                               ShipMask->Canvas,
                               ShipRect);

  // Now OR in the ship. Pixels that were punched out get
  // replaced with pixels from the ship.
  Background->Canvas->CopyMode = cmSrcPaint;  // DEST = SRC OR DEST
  Background->Canvas->CopyRect(LocationRect,
                               Ship->Canvas,
                               ShipRect);

}
```

12. The memory bitmap can be moved to the screen once the background has been patched and the ship has been moved. Add the function body for the `MoveBitmapToScreen` function to `MAINFORM.CPP`.

```
void TForm1::MoveBitmapToScreen(void)
{
    // Move the image from the memory bitmap
    // to the PaintBox
    PaintBox1->Canvas->Draw(0,0,Background);
}
```

13. Compile and test the program.

How It Works

The `OnCreate` handler of `Form1` (step 5) creates four bitmap objects. The handler then initializes private data variables and draws the ship in its initial location. Once the initialization is complete, subsequent timer events execute the animation of the spaceship using the animation functions `PatchBackground`, `MoveShipLocation`, `DrawShipOnBackground`, and `MoveBitmapToScreen`.

Bitmap Resources—An Image, a Mask, and a Background

Common to any sprite-based animation are objects that move and a background surface to move them on. This How-To gives you a head start by providing these ingredients for you in `PICTURES.RES`. This animation utilizes four bitmaps. Three of them, the spaceship, the spaceship mask, and the background, come from the resource file. The fourth bitmap functions as the saved background region.

The background picture is the simplest image to understand. It's just a bitmap without any restrictions. It can have 16- or 256-color resolution. As this How-To illustrates, it can also have its own color palette, which makes the bitmap a device-independent bitmap (DIB). The background bitmap serves as a drawing board for the animation. Each animation step paints the spaceship onto the background bitmap, and then draws the result on the screen.

The spaceship bitmap contains the ship as it will appear on the screen during animation. The spaceship is not a simple rectangle, so you must paint it using a masking technique to achieve transparency. The masking technique requires that the background of the spaceship be black. The mask bitmap has the same shape as the spaceship except that the interior of the spaceship is black and the exterior is white. Figure 5-7 shows the background bitmap, the spaceship bitmap, and the spaceship mask.

> **NOTE**
>
> White pixels in the mask become transparent pixels when the image is displayed. Black pixels in the mask get filled in with pixels from the spaceship.

Figure 5-7 Bitmaps used in the ANIMATION project

TIP

If the animation object contains black regions, those regions must also be black in the mask. Otherwise, the pixels will end up being transparent.

Animation Steps—Patch, Move, and Draw

An animation step executes each time the program receives a timer tick. First, the background must be patched where the ship currently resides. `PatchBackground` (step 9) handles this by copying pixels from the saved background region into the background bitmap. Copying occurs at the spaceship's location, and only enough pixels to erase the spaceship are copied. `PatchBackground` completely restores the background image to its original form.

The spaceship's coordinates can be moved after the background bitmap has been patched. The `MoveShipLocation` function (step 10) calculates a new position for the spacecraft. `MoveShipLocation` uses the speed and direction variables to determine a new ship location. The new location is stored in the private `Location` variable.

After calculating a new ship location, `DrawShipOnBackground` (step 11) copies the spaceship bitmap onto the background bitmap at the new coordinates. The function stores a portion of the background image before it draws the spaceship onto the background. The saved background region will be used by the next `PatchBackground` call to erase the ship from the background. `DrawShipOnBackground` then uses the mask bitmap to draw the spaceship on the background transparently. Once the spaceship has been painted on the background, `MoveBitmapToScreen` (step 12) copies the composite image into the `PaintBox`.

NOTE

`MoveBitmapToScreen` could have been a little smarter about moving the image from memory to the screen. The function doesn't need to copy all the pixels from the background bitmap to the screen. Instead, it could save time by only copying the regions changed by `PatchBackground` and `DrawShipOnBackground`. The screen saver in How-To 5.13 utilizes this technique to improve performance.

Painting the Spaceship Transparently

This How-To employs a simple technique for drawing a complex image transparently (step 11). The process involves two steps: First, punch out a region in the background where the spaceship will go, and second, draw the spaceship using a copy mode that will merge (OR) the images.

Punching out a region in the background means blackening out pixels in the background where the ship will be drawn. This step uses the mask bitmap and the `cmSrcAnd` copy mode. Recall that the mask contains only white and black pixels. The black pixels represent pixels from the spaceship, and the white pixels represent the transparent regions of the image. The `cmSrcAnd` copy mode ANDs the mask with the existing background pixels. Any background pixel that gets AND'ed with a white pixel from the mask remains unchanged. Background pixels that get AND'ed with a black pixel from the mask get wiped out and become black themselves.

TIP

The `CopyMode` property of `TCanvas` determines how pixels from the source canvas will be mixed with pixels from the destination canvas when you call the `CopyRect` function. `cmSrcAnd` tells `TCanvas` to logically AND the source image with the existing destination image. When drawing the mask, remember that any COLOR & WHITE = COLOR and that any COLOR & BLACK = BLACK. The punch step creates a shadow of the spaceship on the background image.

The next step is to move the spaceship into the shadow, without harming background pixels that surround the shadow. The `smSrcPaint` copy mode merges, or ORs, the spaceship bitmap with the background bitmap. OR'ing the black shadow pixels with the spaceship's pixels safely copies the spaceship pixels into the image. Likewise, OR'ing the black pixels from the spaceship with nonshadow pixels from the background leaves the background pixels unharmed.

TIP

Recall that `COLOR | BLACK = COLOR`.

Figure 5-8 illustrates the masking process. The first slide shows the initial background image. The second image shows the background after AND'ing the background with the ship mask. Notice the shadow image of the spaceship. The last slide illustrates how the spaceship ORs into the shadow in the background.

`Tbitmap`—The Easy Way to Work with Memory DCs

Both `PatchBackground` and `DrawShipOnBackground` copy images onto `BackgroundBitmap`. These operations occur in memory, and cannot be seen on the screen. Processing the graphics operations in system memory before moving pixels to the screen improves performance. System memory is slightly faster than video memory, which results in faster processing of the `CopyRect` commands. In addition, the screen never gets erased. The new image gets blasted to the screen directly on top of the existing image. This reduces flicker because most of the pixels remain unchanged and the user cannot tell that the image was just redrawn. Finally, moving the image to the screen in its final form means that no intermediate images make it to the screen. Imagine how the screen would look if `PatchBackground` literally patched the screen. The ship would appear dimmer than usual and might appear with a funky haze.

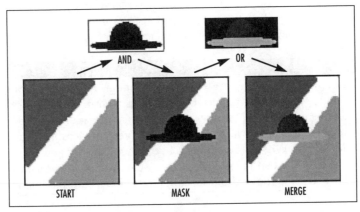

Figure 5-8 The masking process

Drawing in memory involves memory DCs (memory device contexts). The `Canvas` property of `TBitmap` encapsulates a memory DC. In fact, the `Canvas` hides the memory DC so well you usually don't have to worry about the underlying memory DC. `TBitmap` creates the memory DC and calls the API `SelectObject` function for you. `TBitmap::Canvas` allows you to draw on a bitmap in memory using the same technique you used to paint on a form's canvas.

NOTE

Calls to `BackgroundBitmap->Canvas->CopyRect` end up as Win32 `StretchBlt` calls. The `CopyMode` setting becomes the `dwROP` (raster operation) argument to `StretchBlt`.

TIP

You can interact with `TBitmap::Canvas` after setting the `Height` and `Width` properties of `TBitmap`, or after you load a bitmap image using `LoadFromResourceName`.

Comments

If you are serious about animation, you will want to take much of the code presented here and build it into components. This way, you will not have to rewrite the same graphics code for every program you write. A collection of such controls is often called a Sprite library. You may want to search the World Wide Web for commercial and shareware sprite controls for Delphi and C++Builder.

If you actually want to earn a taxable income as a game designer, then you will want to investigate DirectX and DirectDraw graphics. DirectX can be used with C++Builder. You can download the DirectX libraries and the games SDK from the Microsoft Web site at **www.microsoft.com**.

COMPLEXITY
ADVANCED

5.7 How do I...
Fade one picture into another?

Problem

I have two pictures that I want to display and I'd like to create the effect of a gradual transition from one picture to the other rather than a sudden jump. How can I create this type of effect using C++Builder?

Technique

You can fade images by employing some of the same techniques used in the animation program of How-To 5.6. This time, the code uses patterned brushes to perform the task that the mask bitmap handled in How-To 5.6. The patterned brushes mask out pixels from the two pictures, after which the two pictures can be OR'ed together.

Steps

Run **FADE.EXE**. You will see a form with a picture displayed as shown in Figure 5-9. Press the Fade To Next Image button, and watch the old picture fade out and the new picture fade in. Try the Fade To Black and Fade From Black buttons; observe how the image gradually fades out and in.

1. Create a new project, and save the unit as **MAINFORM.CPP** and the project as **FADE.MAK**.

2. Add a **Panel** component to **Form1**. Place three Button controls onto the **Panel**. Use Figure 5-9 as a reference. Check that properties match Table 5-9.

Figure 5-9 FADE at runtime

Table 5-9 Components, properties, and settings for `Form1` in the FADE project

COMPONENT	PROPERTY	SETTING
Form	ClientWidth	318
	ClientHeight	280
	BorderStyle	bsDialog
Panel	Name	Panel1
	Caption	""
	Align	alTop
	Height	42
PaintBox	Name	PaintBox1
	Align	alClient
	Width	318
	Height	238
Button	Name	FadeToBlackButton
	Caption	Fade To Black
Button	Name	FadeFromBlackButton
	Caption	Fade From Black
	Enabled	false
Button	Name	FadeToNextButton
	Caption	Fade To Next Image
Timer	Name	Timer1
	Interval	20
	Enabled	false

3. Place a `PaintBox` control and a `Timer` control on `Form1`; match their settings to Table 5-9. Both the `Timer` and the `PaintBox` can be found on the System tab in the Component Palette.

4. The project needs bitmaps to display and some brushes to use in the transformations. Copy `PICTURES.RES` from the CD-ROM (same directory as `FADE.EXE`) to the project directory. Open `MAINFORM.CPP`, and type a `#pragma` for the new resource file.

```
#include "MAINFORM.h"
//----------------------------------------------------
#pragma resource "*.dfm"
#pragma resource "PICTURES.RES"
```

> **NOTE**
>
> You will have to create a resource file yourself if you decide not to use the one from the CD-ROM. The brushes are 8×8 black and white bitmaps. You only need to create the positive brushes because the code creates the negative brushes from the positive brushes. Figure 5-10 illustrates the eight brushes used in this How-To.

5. Open `MAINFORM.H` and add these private declarations and the function prototype to the `TForm1` class. The program uses a couple of utility enumeration types and a constant, so insert these items above the `TForm1` class declaration:

```
enum TSpecialEffects {None, FadeToBlack, FadeFromBlack, FadeToImage};
enum TCurrentDrawing {Stars, Nebula};

const int BRUSHCOUNT = 8;

class TForm1 : public TForm
{
__published: // IDE-managed Components
...
private:  // User declarations
  TRect BitmapRect;
  TBrush *PositiveMasks[BRUSHCOUNT];
  TBrush *NegativeMasks[BRUSHCOUNT];
  TBrush *SolidBlackBrush;
  Graphics::TBitmap *StarBitmap;
  Graphics::TBitmap *NebulaBitmap;
  Graphics::TBitmap *WorkSpaceBitmap;
  Graphics::TBitmap *TempBitmap;
  int Progress;
  TSpecialEffects CurrentEffect;
  TCurrentDrawing CurrentDrawing;
  void ProcessFadeToBlackStep(void);
  void ProcessFadeFromBlackStep(void);
  void ProcessFadeToImageStep(void);

public:  // User declarations
    virtual __fastcall TForm1(TComponent* Owner);
};
```

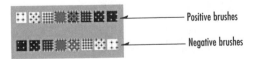

———— Positive brushes

———— Negative brushes

Figure 5-10 The custom brushes used in image transformations

6. Make an `OnCreate` handler for `Form1`, and add code that constructs the bitmaps and brushes, loads them from the resource file, and initializes data variables.

```
void __fastcall TForm1::FormCreate(TObject *Sender)
{
  AnsiString MaskName; // String used for loading brushes.
  RECT BrushRect;       // Windows rect used in Win32 InvertRect.
  BrushRect.left = BrushRect.top = 0;
  BrushRect.right= BrushRect.bottom=8;

  // Loop through and load each brush and its bitmap. The
  // negative masks are created by inverting the positive mask.
  for (int j=0; j<BRUSHCOUNT;j++)
  {
    MaskName = "BRUSH" + AnsiString(j);
    PositiveMasks[j] = new TBrush;
    NegativeMasks[j] = new TBrush;

    PositiveMasks[j]->Bitmap = new Graphics::TBitmap;
    NegativeMasks[j]->Bitmap = new Graphics::TBitmap;
    PositiveMasks[j]->Bitmap->LoadFromResourceName((int)HInstance,
                                                     MaskName);
    NegativeMasks[j]->Bitmap->Assign(PositiveMasks[j]->Bitmap);
    InvertRect(NegativeMasks[j]->Bitmap->Canvas->Handle, &BrushRect);
  }
  SolidBlackBrush = new TBrush;          // Need a solid black brush
  SolidBlackBrush->Style = bsSolid;      // when the image has faded
  SolidBlackBrush->Color = clBlack;      // to black.

  // Create each bitmap.
  StarBitmap      = new Graphics::TBitmap;
  NebulaBitmap    = new Graphics::TBitmap;
  WorkSpaceBitmap = new Graphics::TBitmap;
  TempBitmap      = new Graphics::TBitmap;

  // Load the two images from resource
  StarBitmap  ->LoadFromResourceName((int)HInstance,"STARS");
  NebulaBitmap->LoadFromResourceName((int)HInstance,"NEBULA");
  WorkSpaceBitmap->Width  = StarBitmap->Width;    //Create mem bitmap by
  WorkSpaceBitmap->Height = StarBitmap->Height;   //setting height & width.
  WorkSpaceBitmap->Canvas->Draw(0,0,StarBitmap);  //Copy initial image
  TempBitmap->Width  = StarBitmap->Width;         //Temp is also same size
  TempBitmap->Height = StarBitmap->Height;
  CurrentDrawing = Stars;                         //Init status variables
  CurrentEffect  = None;
  Progress = 0;
  BitmapRect = Rect(0,0,StarBitmap->Width,StarBitmap->Height);
}
```

7. Don't forget to include code to delete the bitmaps and brushes when the program closes. Create an **OnDestroy** handler for the form, and add this code. The brushes are deleted just as they were created.

```
void __fastcall TForm1::FormDestroy(TObject *Sender)
{
  for (int j=0;j<BRUSHCOUNT;j++)
  {
    // Delete the brush bitmap, and then delete
    // the actual brush.
    delete PositiveMasks[j]->Bitmap;
    delete NegativeMasks[j]->Bitmap;
    delete PositiveMasks[j];
    delete NegativeMasks[j];
  }
  // Delete the bitmaps.
  delete SolidBlackBrush;
  delete StarBitmap;
  delete NebulaBitmap;
  delete WorkSpaceBitmap;
  delete TempBitmap;
}
```

8. The program sits idle until a button press occurs. Create **OnClick** handlers for the three buttons, and type in this code. Make sure that each function body corresponds to the proper button.

```
void __fastcall TForm1::FadeToBlackButtonClick(TObject *Sender)
{
  // Don't start a new fade in the middle
  // of an existing transition.
  if (CurrentEffect == None)
  {
    FadeToBlackButton  ->Enabled = false; // Enable and disable buttons
    FadeFromBlackButton->Enabled = true;  // to match state of the image.
    Timer1->Enabled = true;               // Turn on the process timer.
    CurrentEffect = FadeToBlack;          // Set the current effect and
    Progress = 0;                         // progress value; then
                                          // perform
    ProcessFadeToBlackStep();             // first step in the effect.
  }
}
//----------------------------------------------------------
void __fastcall TForm1::FadeFromBlackButtonClick(TObject *Sender)
{
  // Don't start a new fade in the middle
  // of an existing transition.
  if (CurrentEffect == None)
  {
    FadeFromBlackButton ->Enabled = false; // Set buttons to match
    FadeToBlackButton   ->Enabled = true;  // the image.
    Timer1->Enabled = true;                // Start the timer.
```

```
      CurrentEffect = FadeFromBlack;        // Set variables.
      Progress = 0;
      ProcessFadeFromBlackStep();           // Perform first step.
   }
}
//-------------------------------------------------------------
void __fastcall TForm1::FadeToNextButtonClick(TObject *Sender)
{
  // Don't start a new fade in the middle
  // of an existing transition.
  if (CurrentEffect == None)
  {
    FadeFromBlackButton  ->Enabled = false; // Set buttons to match
    FadeToBlackButton    ->Enabled = true;  // the image.
    Timer1->Enabled = true;                 // Start process timer.
    CurrentEffect = FadeToImage;            // Set variables.
    Progress = 0;
    ProcessFadeToImageStep();               // Perform first step.
  }
}
```

9. Each timer tick should process one step in the fade transformation. Create an `OnTimer` handler for the `Timer1` control of `Form1`. Insert this code to determine the current transformation, and execute the proper stepping function:

```
void __fastcall TForm1::Timer1Timer(TObject *Sender)
{
  // Execute the proper stepping function based on
  // the current effect
  if(CurrentEffect == FadeToBlack)
    ProcessFadeToBlackStep();
  else if(CurrentEffect == FadeFromBlack)
    ProcessFadeFromBlackStep();
  else if(CurrentEffect == FadeToImage)
    ProcessFadeToImageStep();
}
```

10. Open `MAINFORM.CPP`, and code the functions that step through each transformation. Each function contains the same basic structure.

```
void TForm1::ProcessFadeToBlackStep(void)
{
  // Has each brush been used? If so, the transformation is done
  // Reset variables, turn off the timer, and use a solid black
  // brush to fill in the image.
  if (Progress == BRUSHCOUNT)
  {
    CurrentEffect =  None;
    Progress = 0;
    Timer1->Enabled = false;
    WorkSpaceBitmap->Canvas->Brush = SolidBlackBrush;
    WorkSpaceBitmap->Canvas->FillRect(BitmapRect);
```

continued on next page

continued from previous page

```
    }
    else    // Else, must use a brush to pattern out the picture.
    {       // Choose a brush from the positive masks.
      WorkSpaceBitmap->Canvas->Brush = PositiveMasks[Progress];
      // copymode 0xA000C9 → DEST = BRUSH & DEST, no SOURCE bitmap
      WorkSpaceBitmap->Canvas->CopyMode=0xA000C9;
      WorkSpaceBitmap->Canvas->Draw(0,0,WorkSpaceBitmap); // Redraw workspace
                                                          // using pattern brush
      Progress++;                                         // and update progress.
    }
    PaintBox1->Canvas->Draw(0,0,WorkSpaceBitmap);
// Move pixels from
}                                                   // memory to screen.



void TForm1::ProcessFadeFromBlackStep(void)
{
    // Has each brush been used? If so, transformation is done.
    // Reset variables, kill timer, and draw the final image.
    if (Progress == BRUSHCOUNT)
    {
      CurrentEffect = None;
      Progress = 0;
      Timer1->Enabled = false;
      WorkSpaceBitmap->Canvas->CopyMode=cmSrcCopy;
      if(CurrentDrawing == Stars)
        WorkSpaceBitmap->Canvas->Draw(0,0,StarBitmap);
      else
        WorkSpaceBitmap->Canvas->Draw(0,0,NebulaBitmap);
    }
    else
    { // Else, must pattern out part of the image.
      // Fading in uses the negative masks, which start out
      // mostly black and gradually become all white.
      WorkSpaceBitmap->Canvas->Brush = NegativeMasks[Progress];
      // The WorkSpaceBitmap has been destroyed with black pixels, must
      // recover the original bitmap. Use cmMergeCopy to AND the original
      // image with the brush, result goes into WorkSpaceBitmap
      WorkSpaceBitmap->Canvas->CopyMode=cmMergeCopy; // DEST = SRC & BRUSH
      if(CurrentDrawing == Stars)                    // Choose correct img.
        WorkSpaceBitmap->Canvas->Draw(0,0,StarBitmap);
      else
        WorkSpaceBitmap->Canvas->Draw(0,0,NebulaBitmap);
      Progress++;                                    // Inc progress var.
    }
    PaintBox1->Canvas->Draw(0,0,WorkSpaceBitmap);    // Move pixels to
}                                                    // screen.



void TForm1::ProcessFadeToImageStep(void)
{
```

```
// Has each brush been used? If so, transformation is done.
// Reset variables, kill timer, and draw the final image.
if (Progress == BRUSHCOUNT)
{
  CurrentEffect = None;
  Progress = 0;
  Timer1->Enabled = false;
  WorkSpaceBitmap->Canvas->CopyMode=cmSrcCopy;
  // CurrentDrawing = old image, check its value.
  // Draw the new image, and update CurrentDrawing.
  if(CurrentDrawing == Stars)
  {
    WorkSpaceBitmap->Canvas->Draw(0,0,NebulaBitmap);
    CurrentDrawing = Nebula;
  }
  else
  {
    WorkSpaceBitmap->Canvas->Draw(0,0,StarBitmap);
    CurrentDrawing = Stars;
  }
}
else // Else, use the brushes to pattern the images.
{
  // First, knock out some pixels from the existing image
  // contained in the work space bitmap. Similar to how
  // ProcessFadeToBlackStep does it.
  WorkSpaceBitmap->Canvas->Brush = PositiveMasks[Progress];
  WorkSpaceBitmap->Canvas->CopyMode=0xA000C9;  // DEST = DEST & BRUSH
  WorkSpaceBitmap->Canvas->Draw(0,0,WorkSpaceBitmap);

  // Wipe out pixels from the image that is being transformed to
  // store results in temp bitmap; don't want to alter original.
  // Want to knock out pixels that didn't get knocked out from the
  // workspace bitmap, so use the inverted brushes
  TempBitmap->Canvas->Brush = NegativeMasks[Progress];
  TempBitmap->Canvas->CopyMode=cmMergeCopy;            // DEST = SRC &
BRUSH
  if(CurrentDrawing == Stars)                     // Choose the correct
    TempBitmap->Canvas->Draw(0,0,NebulaBitmap);   // image, (not the
  else                                            // current image) and
    TempBitmap->Canvas->Draw(0,0,StarBitmap);     // copy pixels to⇐
temp.

  // WorkSpaceBitmap and TempBitmap can now be combined into
  // one image that is half stars and half nebula.
  WorkSpaceBitmap->Canvas->Brush = PositiveMasks[Progress];
  WorkSpaceBitmap->Canvas->CopyMode=cmSrcPaint;  // DEST = DEST | SRC
  WorkSpaceBitmap->Canvas->Draw(0,0,TempBitmap);
  Progress++;                                  // Update progress
}
PaintBox1->Canvas->Draw(0,0,WorkSpaceBitmap);  // Move pixels to screen
}
```

11. The `PaintBox` will need repainting if part of the window gets covered by another program. Click on the `PaintBox1` component in `Form1`. Create an `OnPaint` handler and add this code:

```
void __fastcall TForm1::PaintBox1Paint(TObject *Sender)
{
  // The workspacebitmap always holds the contents of
  // what should be displayed. Copy it to the screen.
  PaintBox1->Canvas->Draw(0,0,WorkSpaceBitmap);
}
```

> **NOTE**
>
> The `OnPaint` handler is only needed during idle time. During transformations, the timer tick continuously repaints the `PaintBox`.

12. Compile and test the program.

How It Works

The `OnCreate` handler for `Form1` (step 6) constructs an array of `TBrush` pointers that help fade the images. The `OnCreate` handler then constructs the bitmaps and loads images from the resource file. The rest of `FormCreate` initializes private data variables to set the initial state of the program.

The `OnClick` handlers for the three pushbuttons (step 8) launch the image transformation process. The `OnClick` handlers enable the `Timer` control, disable the appropriate pushbuttons, and execute the first step in the fade effect. The `Timer` control then spaces out each subsequent step in the fade by calling `ProcessFadeToBlackStep`, `ProcessFadeFromBlackStep`, or `ProcessFadeToImageStep`. The `OnTimer` handler must determine which function should be called (step 9). The code in the processing functions disables the timer when the effect has finished (step 10).

Fading to Black and Fading from Black

Fading an image to black and fading an image in from black both use the same principle. A picture can be darkened by sprinkling black dots all over it. Fading to black means that you sprinkle a few dots at first and then keep adding more and more dots until the image disappears. Fading an image in from black works in reverse—you start by globbing on tons of black sprinkles and then gradually remove them until the image shows through completely.

The patterned brushes provide the sprinkling capability needed to darken an image. A light brush, one that is more white than black, darkens an image slightly. An image can be darkened more by using a brush that is more black than white. To fade an image to black, you sprinkle black dots on the image using a progression of increasingly dark brushes. You fade an image in from black by starting with the darkest brushes and moving toward the lighter brushes.

In How-To 5.6 you learned how to punch a black hole in an image using a bitmap mask. Sprinkling an image with black dots utilizes the same technique. Setting the bitmap copy mode to `0xA000C9` (step 10) tells `Canvas->Draw` that you want to AND the brush with the existing bitmap. The brush is AND'ed with the image using a step and repeat technique. This means that the brush, which is only 8×8 pixels, gets swept across the entire picture. Pixels in the bitmap that get AND'ed with a white pixel from the brush remain intact. Pixels that get AND'ed with a black pixel from the brush become one of the black sprinkles.

Each timer tick event executes one step in the fade process. Each fade step uses a new brush to further darken or lighten the existing image. The image transformation is complete when the last available brush has been used. Figure 5-11 illustrates fading an image to black.

Fading from One Image to Another

If you understand fading an image to black, then fading one image into another should be a breeze. Instead of sprinkling black dots, you sprinkle pixels from the second image onto the existing image. The code globs on more and more pixels from the second image until the original image cannot be seen anymore.

Once again, the custom brushes provide the sprinkling mechanism. Each fade transition performs the same sequence of actions.

1. Use the positive brush and copy mode `0xA000C9` (DEST = DEST & BRUSH) to mask out part of the original image by sprinkling it with black dots.

2. Switch to the negative brush and mask out the destination image using copy mode `cmMergeCopy` (DEST = SRC & BRUSH). Store the result in a temporary bitmap so as not to corrupt the destination bitmap.

3. OR the two images together using copy mode `cmSrcPaint` (DEST = DEST | SRC) to create one image that contains portions of both images.

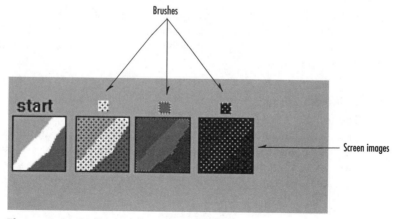

Figure 5-11 Fading an image to black

The **Progress** variable (step 10) determines which brush gets used. When **Progress** is less than 3, the original image shows through more than the destination image. The destination image becomes more and more prevalent as the last brushes get used. Finally, the destination image is copied directly into the work space bitmap after the last brush has been used. The original bitmap has disappeared completely after this step.

Comments

This How-To produces some pretty awesome effects. **TBitmap**, **TBrush**, and **TCanvas** provide the horsepower behind the effects. As with How-To 5.6, **TBitmap** encapsulates much of the dirty work relating to memory DCs. **TBrush** simplifies creation of custom brushes.

The fading effects could be performed without using the VCL classes. Each call to **Bitmap->Canvas->Draw** could be replaced with a Win32 call to **PatBlt** or **BitBlt**. However, **TCanvas::Draw** is easier to understand and just as powerful as the equivalent API functions. Likewise, **TBrush** allows you to load a custom brush with just a single function call, while the API equivalent would require several lines. The code presented in this How-To demonstrates how good object-oriented design and solid runtime performance can coincide in the same program.

COMPLEXITY
INTERMEDIATE

5.8 How do I...
Fade text in and out over a background?

Problem

Placing text over an image is easy, but it would be really cool if I could have the text fade in gradually instead of just appearing suddenly. While I'm at it, it would be neat if I could gradually fade text out of the image, too. How can I achieve these effects using C++Builder?

Technique

The technique used to fade text in and out of an image closely resembles the process of fading from one image to another. To tell you the truth, the two methods are identical. Instead of fading from one picture to the next, you fade from one image to the same image with text written on it. The background image remains mostly intact as the patterning and merging of the images takes place.

Steps

Run **FADETEXT.EXE**. You will see a form that looks like Figure 5-12. Press the Fade Text In button and watch the words **Hello World** fade into the picture. Click Fade Text Out to watch the message disappear.

1. Create a new project, and save the unit as **MAINFORM.CPP** and the project as **FADETEXT.MAK**.

2. Place a **Panel**, a **PaintBox**, and a **Timer** control on **Form1**. Then place two **Button** controls on **Panel1**. Set properties to match Table 5-10. Both the **Timer** and the **PaintBox** can be found on the System tab in the Component Palette.

Table 5-10 Components, properties, and settings for **Form1** in the FADETEXT project

COMPONENT	PROPERTY	SETTING
Form	ClientWidth	318
	ClientHeight	280
	BorderStyle	bsDialog
Panel	Name	Panel1
	Caption	""
	Align	alTop
	Height	42
PaintBox	Name	PaintBox1
	Align	alClient
	Width	318
	Height	238
Button	Name	FadeTextOutButton
	Caption	Fade Text Out
	Enabled	false
Button	Name	FadeTextInButton
	Caption	Fade Text In
Timer	Name	Timer1
	Interval	20
	Enabled	false

Figure 5-12 FADETEXT at runtime

3. Once again, you will need to use a resource file that provides bitmaps for the brushes and the image. Copy **PICTURES.RES** from the CD-ROM to your project directory. Make sure to get the file from the directory that contains this How-To. Add a **#pragma** statement for the resource file to **MAINFORM.CPP**.

```
#include "MAINFORM.h"
//-------------------------------------------------
#pragma resource "*.dfm"
#pragma resource "PICTURES.res"
```

> **NOTE**
>
> PICTURES.RES contains the same brush resources that were used in How-To 5.7.

4. Insert these private declarations, enumerated types, and constants into **MAINFORM.H**:

```
enum TSpecialEffects {None, FadeTextOut, FadeTextIn};

const int BRUSHCOUNT = 8;

class TForm1 : public TForm
{
...
private: // User declarations
  TRect BitmapRect;
  TBrush *PositiveMasks[BRUSHCOUNT];
  TBrush *NegativeMasks[BRUSHCOUNT];
```

```
      Graphics::TBitmap *WorldBitmap;
      Graphics::TBitmap *TextBitmap;
      Graphics::TBitmap *WorkSpaceBitmap;
      Graphics::TBitmap *TempBitmap;
      int Progress;
      TSpecialEffects CurrentEffect;
      void ProcessFadeStep(void);
public:  // User declarations
      virtual __fastcall TForm1(TComponent* Owner);
};
```

5. Make an `OnCreate` handler for `Form1`, and add code that constructs the bitmaps and brushes, loads them from the file, and initializes data variables. This function also draws text on top of one of the bitmaps.

```
void __fastcall TForm1::FormCreate(TObject *Sender)
{
  // Load in the brushes.
  AnsiString MaskName;
  RECT BrushRect;      // Windows RECT for API InvertRect.
  BrushRect.left = BrushRect.top = 0;
  BrushRect.right= BrushRect.bottom=8;

  // Loop around and construct and load in each bitmap.
  for (int j=0; j<BRUSHCOUNT;j++)
  {
    MaskName = "BRUSH" + AnsiString(j);
    PositiveMasks[j] = new TBrush;
    NegativeMasks[j] = new TBrush;

    PositiveMasks[j]->Bitmap = new Graphics::TBitmap;
    NegativeMasks[j]->Bitmap = new Graphics::TBitmap;
    PositiveMasks[j]->Bitmap->LoadFromResourceName((int)HInstance,MaskName);
    NegativeMasks[j]->Bitmap->Assign(PositiveMasks[j]->Bitmap);
    InvertRect(NegativeMasks[j]->Bitmap->Canvas->Handle, &BrushRect);
  }

  // Create the bitmap objects
  WorldBitmap     = new Graphics::TBitmap;
  TextBitmap      = new Graphics::TBitmap;
  WorkSpaceBitmap = new Graphics::TBitmap;
  TempBitmap      = new Graphics::TBitmap;

  // Load images from resource.
  WorldBitmap ->LoadFromResourceName((int)HInstance,"EARTH");
  TextBitmap  ->LoadFromResourceName((int)HInstance,"EARTH");
  TempBitmap->Width        = WorldBitmap->Width;   // Size temp bitmap and
  TempBitmap->Height       = WorldBitmap->Height;  // the work space.
  WorkSpaceBitmap->Height = WorldBitmap->Height;
  WorkSpaceBitmap->Width  = WorldBitmap->Width;
  WorkSpaceBitmap->Canvas->Draw(0,0,WorldBitmap); // Initialize workspace.
```

continued on next page

continued from previous page

```
// Write some text on the text bitmap
TextBitmap->Canvas->Font->Name="Arial";
TextBitmap->Canvas->Font->Size = 60;
TextBitmap->Canvas->Font->Style =
TextBitmap->Canvas->Font->Style<< fsItalic<<fsBold;
TextBitmap->Canvas->Font->Color = clWhite;
SetBkMode(TextBitmap->Canvas->Handle,TRANSPARENT);
TextBitmap->Canvas->TextOut(0,0,"Hello");
TextBitmap->Canvas->Font->Color = clFuchsia;
TextBitmap->Canvas->TextOut(0,
                    TextBitmap->Canvas->TextHeight("Hello"),
                    "World");
TextBitmap->Canvas->Refresh(); // Restore canvas to defaults.

// Initialize the rest of the variables.
Progress=0;
CurrentEffect = None;
BitmapRect = Rect(0,0,WorldBitmap->Width,WorldBitmap->Height);
}
```

6. Create an `OnDestroy` handler for `Form1`, and add code to delete the allocated resources when the program closes.

```
void __fastcall TForm1::FormDestroy(TObject *Sender)
{
  // Delete the array of brush pointers the same way
  // it was constructed.
  for (int j=0;j<BRUSHCOUNT;j++)
  {
    delete PositiveMasks[j]->Bitmap;
    delete NegativeMasks[j]->Bitmap;
    delete PositiveMasks[j];
    delete NegativeMasks[j];
  }

  delete WorldBitmap;
  delete TextBitmap;
  delete WorkSpaceBitmap;
  delete TempBitmap;
}
```

7. As with How-To 5.7, the program sits idle until a button press occurs. Create `OnClick` handlers for the buttons, and type in this code:

```
void __fastcall TForm1::FadeTextOutButtonClick(TObject *Sender)
{
  // Don't start a new fade in the middle
  // of an existing transition.
  if (CurrentEffect == None)
  {
    FadeTextOutButton->Enabled = false; // Set button states.
    FadeTextInButton ->Enabled = true;
    Timer1->Enabled = true;              // Activate timer.
    CurrentEffect = FadeTextOut;
```

```
      Progress = 0;
      ProcessFadeStep();                    // Perform first step.
    }
}
//-------------------------------------------------------------
void __fastcall TForm1::FadeTextInButtonClick(TObject *Sender)
{
   // Don't start a new fade in the middle
   // of an existing transition.
   if (CurrentEffect == None)
   {
     FadeTextInButton  ->Enabled = false; // Set button states.
     FadeTextOutButton ->Enabled = true;
     Timer1->Enabled = true;               // Activate timer.
     CurrentEffect = FadeTextIn;
     Progress = 0;
     ProcessFadeStep();                    // Perform first step.
   }
}
```

8. Each timer tick should execute a step in the transform. Create an `OnTimer` event for `Timer1`, and insert this code:

```
void __fastcall TForm1::Timer1Timer(TObject *Sender)
{
   // Process one step in the transform.
   ProcessFadeStep();
}
```

9. Now add the body for the `ProcessFadeStep` function to `MAINFORM.CPP`. Each function call executes one step in the transformation.

```
void TForm1::ProcessFadeStep(void)
{
   // Is the transform done? If so, copy in the correct bitmap,
   // reset the variables, and kill the timer.
   if (Progress == BRUSHCOUNT)
   {
     WorkSpaceBitmap->Canvas->CopyMode=cmSrcCopy;
     if(CurrentEffect == FadeTextOut)
       WorkSpaceBitmap->Canvas->Draw(0,0,WorldBitmap);
     else
       WorkSpaceBitmap->Canvas->Draw(0,0,TextBitmap);
     CurrentEffect =  None;
     Progress = 0;
     Timer1->Enabled = false;
   }
   else // Otherwise perform an intermediate transform step.
   {
     // First, knock out some pixels from the existing image
     WorkSpaceBitmap->Canvas->Brush = PositiveMasks[Progress];
     WorkSpaceBitmap->Canvas->CopyMode=0xA000C9;   // DEST = DEST & BRUSH
     WorkSpaceBitmap->Canvas->Draw(0,0,WorkSpaceBitmap);

     // Next, knock out some pixels from the image that will be combined
```

continued on next page

continued from previous page

```
// with the workspace. Store result in a temp bitmap, don't alter
// the original images.
TempBitmap->Canvas->Brush = NegativeMasks[Progress];
if(CurrentEffect == FadeTextOut) // Use bitmap with no text.
{
    TempBitmap->Canvas->CopyMode=cmMergeCopy; // DEST = SRC & BRUSH.
    TempBitmap->Canvas->Draw(0,0,WorldBitmap);
}
else   // Use bitmap with text.
{
    // Want to do DEST = SRC & BRUSH, but must do it in two steps
    // because we cannot cmMergeCopy a modified bitmap.
    TempBitmap->Canvas->CopyMode = cmSrcCopy;   // DEST = SRC.
    TempBitmap->Canvas->Draw(0,0,TextBitmap);
    TempBitmap->Canvas->CopyMode=0xA000C9;      // DEST = DEST & BRUSH.
    TempBitmap->Canvas->Draw(0,0,TempBitmap);
}

// Now combine the two images that have had holes punched in them.
WorkSpaceBitmap->Canvas->CopyMode=cmSrcPaint;  // DEST = SRC | DEST.
WorkSpaceBitmap->Canvas->Draw(0,0,TempBitmap);
Progress++;                                    // Update progress.
}
PaintBox1->Canvas->Draw(0,0,WorkSpaceBitmap);  // Move pixels to screen.
}
```

10. PaintBox1 will need to be repainted if another window covers it up. Click on PaintBox1, create an OnPaint handler, and insert this code:

```
void __fastcall TForm1::PaintBox1Paint(TObject *Sender)
{
    // The workspace bitmap always holds the contents of
    // what should be displayed. Copy it to the screen.
    PaintBox1->Canvas->Draw(0,0,WorkSpaceBitmap);
}
```

11. Compile and test the program.

How It Works

This How-To works exactly like How-To 5.7. The OnCreate, OnDestroy, OnClick, and OnTimer events resemble the handlers from How-To 5.7. Only one difference exists between the two programs. This How-To fades from a picture of the earth to another picture of the earth with text on it, rather than fading between entirely different pictures. It appears that only the text fades in and out, because the two images are nearly identical.

To visualize how this How-To works, imagine that the program is running and that `WorkSpaceBitmap` contains a copy of `TextBitmap`, the bitmap with `Hello World` written on it. Pretend that the user has just pressed the Fade Text Out button. `ProcessFadeStep` (step 9) executes one time. It starts by sprinkling black dots on `WorkSpaceBitmap` using a positive brush. Then the function selects a negative brush and sprinkles dots on `WorldBitmap`, the picture with no text written on it. Pixels that get blackened out in `WorldBitmap` are left intact on `WorkSpaceBitmap`, and vice versa. `ProcessFadeStep` then merges (ORs) the two bitmaps using `cmSrcPaint`. Many of the pixels in `WorkSpaceBitmap` get replaced with pixels from `WorldBitmap`. However, most of the pixels in both bitmaps are identical, so the overall appearance of the image remains the same. Only `WorkSpaceBitmap` pixels that were part of the `Hello World` text actually change. Some of these text pixels get replaced with `WorldBitmap` pixels. The net result is that the `Hello World` message has lost some of its pixels and now looks dimmer.

Each subsequent `OnTimer` event (step 8) erases more and more pixels from the `Hello World` message until finally the message has had all its pixels wiped from the face of the planet. Fading the text back in repeats this process in reverse.

TIP

For experimentation purposes, you may want to set `Timer1->Interval` to a larger number (1000). This would allow you to run the program in slow motion. You should be able to see the text message gradually losing pixels until it completely disappears.

Comments

`TCanvas::CopyMode` has carried the workload for How-To's 5.6, 5.7, and 5.8. Each of these How-To's has utilized `CopyMode` to first mask (AND) out a region of one image and then combine two images using an OR'ing technique. These techniques arm you with the same powerful graphical weapons used by professional applications, such as Microsoft's PowerPoint presentation program. PowerPoint allows users to fade images using the same sprinkling technique demonstrated in How-To's 5.7 and 5.8.

5.9 How do I...
Draw with a true Cartesian coordinate system?

Problem

Normally, I don't have a problem with the way the Windows graphics coordinate system works. I can usually handle having Y=0 at the top of the screen and bigger Y values at the bottom. However, this coordinate system just gets in the way when I need to use the screen to graph mathematical functions. It would be nice if I could graph with a regular Cartesian coordinate system where the positive Y axis points up. Can I flip the coordinate system around to make graphing easier?

Technique

The designers of Windows probably knew that programmers would want to use the screen as a mathematical scratch pad. For this reason, and many others, they provided API functions that allow you to alter a device context's coordinate system. You can use these functions to change the mapping mode, move the graph's origin, and make the positive Y axis point upward.

Steps

Run **VERTICAL.EXE**. A graph of a sine wave should appear as depicted in Figure 5-13. Play with the vertical track bar to alter the Y axis scaling.

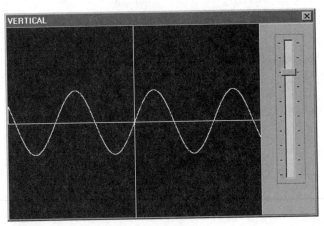

Figure 5-13 VERTICAL at runtime

1. Create a new project. Name the unit as **MAINFORM.CPP**, and name the project **VERTICAL.MAK**.

2. This How-To only uses three controls: a **Panel**, a **TrackBar**, and a **PaintBox**. Place the **Panel** and the **PaintBox** on **Form1**, and set their properties to match Table 5-11. Then place a **TrackBar** on **Panel1**, and set its properties.

Table 5-11 Components, properties, and settings for **Form1** in the VERTICAL project

COMPONENT	PROPERTY	SETTING
Form	ClientWidth	475
	ClientHeight	288
	BorderStyle	bsDialog
Panel	Name	Panel1
	Caption	""
	Align	alRight
	Width	85
PaintBox	Name	PaintBox1
	Align	alClient
TrackBar	Name	TrackBar1
	Min	1
	Max	10
	Position	5
	Orientation	trVertical
	TickMarks	tmBoth
	TickStyle	tsAuto

3. Open **MAINFORM.H**, and add these declarations to the **TForm1** class:

```
private:   // User declarations
  TRect   DrawingRect;
  void    InitializeViewPort(void);
  void    DrawGraph(void);
```

4. The graphing functions will use the floating point **sin** function. Open **MAINFORM.CPP**, and insert a **#include** for the math libraries.

```
#include <vcl\vcl.h>
#pragma hdrstop

#include <math.h>
#include "MAINFORM.h"
```

5. Make an OnCreate handler for Form1 that initializes the DrawingRect variable.

```
void __fastcall TForm1::FormCreate(TObject *Sender)
{
  // DrawingRect holds size of the drawing region in logical units.
  // Drawing units must be ints, we would rather graph in floats.
  // Use integer = float * 1000 as a conversion
  DrawingRect.Left    = -10000; // Left  = -10.0.
  DrawingRect.Right   =  10000; // Right =  10.0.
  DrawingRect.Top     =   1000 * TrackBar1->Position; //Trackbar starts at
  5.
  DrawingRect.Bottom  =  -1000 * TrackBar1->Position; //Top = 5.0 bottom =
  -5.0.
}
```

6. Two functions work together to draw the graph. InitializeViewPort sets the mapping mode, origins, and window extents for the Canvas property of PaintBox1. DrawGraph then paints a set of axes and draws the graph of the sine wave. Open MAINFORM.CPP, and type the function bodies for these two functions.

```
void TForm1::InitializeViewPort(void)
{
  // Calculate the drawing width and height.
  int DrawingWidth = DrawingRect.Right - DrawingRect.Left;
  int DrawingHeight= DrawingRect.Top - DrawingRect.Bottom;

  // Set the map mode to MM_ANISOTROPIC.
  SetMapMode(PaintBox1->Canvas->Handle,MM_ANISOTROPIC);

  // Now size the window to match the drawing width. The width is always
20.0
  // (+- 10), represented by an integer width of 20000. The height varies
  // according to the trackbar.
  SetWindowExtEx(PaintBox1->Canvas->Handle,
                 DrawingWidth,
                 DrawingHeight,
                 NULL);

  // Set the ViewPort. The negative argument flips the Y Axis.
  SetViewportExtEx(PaintBox1->Canvas->Handle,
                   PaintBox1->Width,
                   -PaintBox1->Height,
                   NULL);

// Window origin should be the point 0,0.
  SetWindowOrgEx(PaintBox1->Canvas->Handle,
                 0,
                 0,
                 NULL);
```

```
// Viewport origin is the pixel where the window origin should be drawn.
// This is the middle of the paint box.
SetViewportOrgEx(PaintBox1->Canvas->Handle,
                 PaintBox1->Width/2,
                 PaintBox1->Height/2,
                 NULL);
}


void TForm1::DrawGraph(void)
{
  // Fill in a black background.
  PaintBox1->Canvas->Brush->Color=clBlack;
  PaintBox1->Canvas->FillRect(DrawingRect);

  // Select a white pen and draw the X and Y axes.
  PaintBox1->Canvas->Pen->Color=clWhite;
  PaintBox1->Canvas->Pen->Width=1;
  PaintBox1->Canvas->MoveTo(DrawingRect.Left,0);
  PaintBox1->Canvas->LineTo(DrawingRect.Right,0);
  PaintBox1->Canvas->MoveTo(0,DrawingRect.Top);
  PaintBox1->Canvas->LineTo(0,DrawingRect.Bottom);

  // Now draw a graph of Y=SinX. Need to divide by 1000 before
  // calling sin() to convert from our integers to a float. Then
  // multiply by 1000 afterwards to convert back to ints.
  PaintBox1->Canvas->MoveTo(DrawingRect.Left,0);
  for(int j=DrawingRect.Left;j<=DrawingRect.Right;j+=5)
    PaintBox1->Canvas->LineTo(j,(int)(1000*sin(float(j)/1000)));
}
```

> **NOTE**
>
> If the program seems slow when you run it, try changing the
> j+= 5 part of the for loop to j+=50. This results in fewer sine
> wave points that must be plotted on the screen. Additionally, the
> sine wave results never change, so you could optimize the code by
> storing the numbers in an array.

7. Create an OnPaint handler for **PaintBox1** that redraws the graph using the two functions from step 6.

```
void __fastcall TForm1::PaintBox1Paint(TObject *Sender)
{
  InitializeViewPort();
  DrawGraph();
}
```

8. Create an `OnChange` event handler for `Trackbar1`. This function alters the drawing rectangle size and then repaints the graph.

```
void __fastcall TForm1::TrackBar1Change(TObject *Sender)
{
  // Change top and bottom values. This scales the
  // y axis with the trackbar.
  DrawingRect.Top    =   1000 * TrackBar1->Position;
  DrawingRect.Bottom =  -1000 * TrackBar1->Position;

  InitializeViewPort();
  DrawGraph();
}
```

9. Compile and test the program.

How It Works

`InitializeViewPort` (step 6) contains the important code for this How-To. `InitializeViewPort` sets the mapping mode for `PaintBox1`'s `Canvas` and must be called each time before drawing because canvases don't retain their mapping mode settings. `DrawGraph` paints a sine wave after `InitializeViewPort` configures the drawing window. Notice how the `for` loop in `DrawGraph` works. The `sin` function call uses locations along the X axis as its argument. The `sin` result becomes the Y location in a `LineTo` call. The reconfigured mapping mode greatly simplifies the graphing code.

The Windows Mapping Modes

You realign the Y axis by changing the Windows mapping mode for the device context that you draw the graph on. Windows supports eight different mapping modes, which are listed in Table 5-12. This How-To utilizes the `MM_ANISOTROPIC` mapping mode. As Table 5-12 points out, `MM_ANISOTROPIC` allows you to have an ascending vertical axis and it permits you to arbitrarily define the logical width and height of a window. This made the Y axis scaling possible.

Table 5-12 The eight mapping modes of Windows

MODE	LOGICAL UNIT	INCREASING X	INCREASING Y	NOTES
MM_TEXT	Pixel	Right	Down	Default mapping mode
MM_LOMETRIC	.1 mm	Right	Up	
MM_HIMETRIC	.01 mm	Right	Up	
MM_LOENGLISH	.01 inch	Right	Up	
MM_HIENGLISH	.001 inch	Right	Up	
MM_TWIPS	1/1440 inch	Right	Up	

MODE	LOGICAL UNIT	INCREASING X	INCREASING Y	NOTES
MM_ISOTROPIC	Arbitrary	Either	Either	Logical units must have same physical dimension in both axes
MM_ANISOTROPIC	Arbitrary	Either	Either	Scaling of logical units can vary

NOTE

SetWindowExtEx and SetViewportEx can only be called in conjunction with the MM_ISOTROPIC and MM_ANISOTROPIC modes.

TIP

Physical units deal with actual screen pixels. Logical units simplify drawing by hiding the details of physical units from you. For example, MM_LOMETRIC uses tenths of millimeters as its logical unit. You can use MM_LOMETRIC to draw a 1cm x 1cm box at any screen resolution by calling Rectangle(0,0,10,10). Windows converts from logical units to physical units when it draws the square on the screen.

Configuring the Mapping Mode

Configuring the mapping mode for a device context must be done carefully. InitializeViewPort (step 6) calls the following functions in order:

✔ **SetMapMode**. Changes the mapping mode to MM_ANISOTROPIC.

✔ **SetWindowExtEx**. Tells Windows the height and width of the graphing region in logical units. Widening a canvas using SetWindowExtEx doesn't take up more screen space. Instead, it determines how many logical units must squish into a canvas's extents. This How-To contains an X axis that ranges from -10.0 to +10.0. Since floats can't be passed to SetWindowExtEx, the code employs a conversion factor of 1000 to 1 to convert from floats to ints. Hence, one horizontal logical unit in this How-To equates to a floating point value of .001.

✔ **SetViewportExtEx**. The SetWindowExtEx call told Windows that the canvas was 20000 logical units wide (-10.0 to +10.0). SetViewportExtEx determines how many screen pixels the 20000 logical units can actually consume. The SetViewportExtEx values determine how much the

logical units must shrink in order to fit within the allowed size. The negative sign in front of the height argument tells Windows to draw the graph with the positive Y axis pointing up.

✔ `SetWindowOrgEx`. Tells Windows the location of the graph's origin in logical units. This How-To uses the point 0,0 as its origin. The entire graph can shift up, down, or sideways by altering the origin point.

✔ `SetViewPortOrgEx`. Tells Windows where on the screen it should place the origin that was set using `SetWindowOrgEx`. `SetViewPortOrgEx` sets a screen pixel location. This How-To sets the middle of `PaintBox1` as the screen location for the origin of the graph.

Comments

It may be difficult to understand the API calls utilized by `InitializeViewPort`. You may want to play with the arguments of these functions to get a feel for what each function does. Try any or all of the following steps individually as an educational exercise.

✔ Shrink the X axis by a factor of 10 by using `DrawingWidth/10` in the `SetWindowExtEx` call.

✔ Make the positive Y axis point down by removing the negative sign from the height argument to `SetViewportExtEx`.

✔ Shift the entire graph down by 1.0 (1000 logical units) by altering the `SetWindowOrgEx` call.

```
SetWindowOrgEx(PaintBox1->Canvas->Handle,
               0,
               1000,
               NULL);
```

✔ Move the graph origin to the lower left corner of `PaintBox1`. Business charts usually place the origin here.

```
SetViewportOrgEx(PaintBox1->Canvas->Handle,
                 0,
                 PaintBox1->Height,
                 NULL);
```

You may have noticed excessive screen flicker as you changed the Y axis scaling using `Trackbar1`. This How-To was designed to explain how you can draw with the positive Y axis pointing up, so screen flicker was not a concern. You will certainly want to eliminate this flicker in your graphing programs. You can combine the lessons from this How-To with the power of `TBitmap` to produce flicker-free scaling. Set the mapping mode of the bitmap's canvas, and then draw the graph on the bitmap's canvas. Move the graph to the screen using the `Draw` method of `PaintBox1->Canvas`.

COMPLEXITY
BEGINNING

5.10 How do I...
Translate a system color into an actual color?

Problem

Sometimes I need to know the actual color of a system color. For example, the Choose Font common dialog does not understand system colors (it ignores them and just uses black instead). Also, sometimes I have different colored text on the same window, and I want to make sure that the reader can see all the text. I want to check the actual color of the form to make sure my text isn't the same color. How can I calculate the actual color of a system color?

Technique

The Windows API provides a `GetSysColor` function that converts a system color into an RGB color. The `GetSysColor` function does not work with the `clXXXX` system color constants (such as `clBtnFace`, `clWindowText`) of C++Builder directly, but you can circumvent the problem by modifying the `clXXXX` constant before calling `GetSysColor`.

Steps

Run `TRANSLATE.EXE`. Figure 5-14 shows the program during execution. Choose a system color from the Combo box. The color of the Memo text and the `PaintBox` color will adapt based on your setting. The program assigns the Memo color directly to the system color, while the `PaintBox` uses an actual color calculated from the system color. Select a non-black system color, and click the font button to launch the Choose Font dialog. Observe that the dialog chooses the proper color when it initializes its Color Combo box.

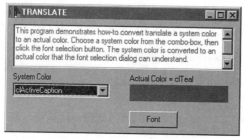

Figure 5-14 TRANSLATE at runtime

1. Create a new project by selecting File|New Application. Name the unit `MAINFORM.CPP`, and name the project `TRANSLATE.MAK`.

2. Add components to `Form1` using Figure 5-14 as a guideline. The shaded region underneath the Actual Color label is a `PaintBox` control. Set component properties to match Table 5-13.

Table 5-13 Components, properties, and settings for `Form1` in the TRANSLATE project

COMPONENT	PROPERTY	SETTING
Form	BorderStyle	bsDialog
Label	Caption	SystemColor
Label	Name	ActualColorLabel
	Caption	Actual Color =
ComboBox	Style	csDropDownList
Memo	Color	clWhite
	ScrollBars	ssVertical
PaintBox	Width	150
Button	Caption	Font
FontDialog		

3. Edit the `Lines` property of `Memo1`, and type some text. You can use the same text displayed in Figure 5-14, if you want.

4. Open `MAINFORM.CPP`, and type in these constant declarations:

```
#pragma resource "*.dfm"
TForm1 *Form1;

const TColor SystemColors[]={
clScrollBar,clBackground,clActiveCaption,clInactiveCaption,clMenu,clWindow,
clWindowFrame,clMenuText, clWindowText,clCaptionText,clActiveBorder,
clInactiveBorder,clAppWorkSpace, clHighlight,clHighlightText,clBtnFace,
clBtnShadow,clGrayText,clBtnText,clInactiveCaptionText,clBtnHighlight,
cl3DDkShadow,cl3DLight,clInfoText,clInfoBk,
};

const TColor ActualColors[]={
clBlack,clMaroon,clGreen,clOlive,clNavy,clPurple,clTeal,clGray,clSilver,⇐
clRed,
clLime,clYellow,clBlue,clFuchsia,clAqua,clWhite,clNone};

const int ActualColorCount=17;

const AnsiString ActualColorNames[]={
"clBlack","clMaroon","clGreen","clOlive","clNavy","clPurple","clTeal","⇐
clGray",
"clSilver","clRed","clLime","clYellow","clBlue","clFuchsia","clAqua",⇐
"clWhite",
"NONE"};
```

5. ComboBox1 should contain strings that correspond to the `SystemColors` constant in step 4. Edit the `Items` property of `ComboBox1`, and add a string for every color listed in the `SystemsColors` constant (`clScrollBar, clBackground, ..., clInfoText, clInfoBk`). Make sure you enter the strings in the same order as they appear in the constant declaration. Put each string on its own line.

6. Open `MAINFORM.H`, and add a function prototype to `TForm1`. This function will convert the system color from the Combo box into an RGB color. Add private data variables for storing the color and an array index.

```
private: // User declarations
  int     ActualColorIndex;
  TColor ActualColor;
  void ConvertSystemColor(void);
public:  // User declarations
  virtual __fastcall TForm1(TComponent* Owner);
};
```

7. Type the function body for `ConvertSystemColor` in `MAINFORM.CPP`. The key part of the function is the `GetSysColor` statement.

```
void TForm1::ConvertSystemColor(void)
{
  // Get the RGB value for the selected system color. GetSysColor uses
  // Win32 defined constants (COLOR_WINDOWTEXT,COLOR_ACTIVECAPTION)
  // C++Builder's system color constants (clWindowText, clActiveCaption)
  // equal the Win32 constant bitwised or'd with 0x80000000. To use
  // GetSysColor, mask out the leading bit.
  unsigned ConvertedColor = SystemColors[ComboBox1->ItemIndex] & 0x7FFFFFFFL
  ActualColor = (TColor)GetSysColor(ConvertedColor);

  // See which actual color matches the color returned from GetSysColor.
  // If no match found, just use clNone.
  for(int j=0;j<ActualColorCount;j++)
  {
    if ( (j == ActualColorCount - 1   ) ||
         (ActualColor == ActualColors[j])      )
    {
      ActualColorIndex = j;
      break;
    }
  }

  // Fill in the PaintBox with the ActualColor value.
  PaintBox1->Canvas->Brush->Color = ActualColor;
  PaintBox1->Canvas->FillRect(Rect(0,0,PaintBox1->Width,PaintBox1->Height));

  ActualColorLabel->Caption = "Actual Color = " +
                          ActualColorNames[ActualColorIndex];
```

continued on next page

continued from previous page

```
  // Some system colors may be white. If so, the text
  // in the memo will disappear. Detect and fix this
  if(ActualColor ==  clWhite)
    Memo1->Color = clBlack;
  else
    Memo1->Color = clWhite;
}
```

8. Combo box changes should update the color drawn in **PaintBox1**. Select **ComboBox1**, and create an **OnChange** handler. Add this code to change **Memo1**'s text color and to convert the new system color:

```
void __fastcall TForm1::ComboBox1Change(TObject *Sender)
{
   // Set the memo color directly to the system color
   // and paint the paintbox with the actual color. if
   // the code works, they should appear as the same color
   Memo1->Font->Color = SystemColors[ComboBox1->ItemIndex];
   ConvertSystemColor();
}
```

9. The program needs to repaint **PaintBox1** occasionally. Create an **OnPaint** handler for **PaintBox1** that repaints the region with the **ActualColor** value.

```
void __fastcall TForm1::PaintBox1Paint(TObject *Sender)
{
   PaintBox1->Canvas->Brush->Color = ActualColor;
   PaintBox1->Canvas->FillRect(Rect(0,0,PaintBox1->Width,PaintBox1->Height));
}
```

10. Create an **OnCreate** handler for **Form1** that will initialize **ComboBox1** and convert the first system color.

```
void __fastcall TForm1::FormCreate(TObject *Sender)
{
   ComboBox1->ItemIndex = 8;
   ConvertSystemColor();
}
```

11. Create an **OnClick** handler for **Button1**. Insert code that launches the Choose Font dialog box.

```
void __fastcall TForm1::Button1Click(TObject *Sender)
{
   FontDialog1->Font->Assign(Memo1->Font);
   FontDialog1->Font->Color = ActualColor;

   if(FontDialog1->Execute())
     Memo1->Font->Assign(FontDialog1->Font);
}
```

12. Compile and test the program. You can safely ignore the warning of "Negating unsigned value" generated by the `SystemColors` constant.

How It Works

The `GetSysColor` API call from step 7 is the beef of this How-To; everything else is just pudding that helps illustrate how `GetSysColor` can be implemented. `GetSysColor` takes an argument that tells it which system color to look up. The `INCLUDE\WIN32\WINUSER.H` file contains the valid arguments to `GetSysColor`. Two possibilities are `COLOR_WINDOWTEXT` (8) and `COLOR_ACTIVECAPTION` (2). The C++Builder system color constants (`clWindowText`, `clActiveCaption`) can't be fed directly into `GetSysColor` without some modification.

You can find the C++Builder constants in this include file: `\INCLUDE\VCL\GRAPHICS.HPP`. Take a look at the value for `clWindowText`. You should find that `clWindowText` equals -2147483640. This number doesn't mean a whole lot until you look at it in hexadecimal format: 0x80000008. The C++Builder constants equal the Windows constants bitwise OR'ed with 0x8000000. Compare some of the other system color constants to prove that the relationship holds for each one. Now that you know the secret relationship between the C++Builder system colors and the Windows constants, it's just a matter of clearing the leading bit from the C++Builder constant before passing the value on to `GetSysColor`. A bitwise AND with 0x7FFFFFFF nukes the leading bit. This code statement shows how the bitwise AND works.

```
TColor ActualColor = (TColor) GetSysColor(clBtnFace & 0x7FFFFFFFL);
```

The return value from `GetSysColor` can be used like the built-in `clBlue`, `clWhite`, and other values provided by C++Builder. `clBlue`, `clWhite`, and friends all have values, and those values are RGB colors. In fact, all `TColor` objects are RGB colors. The `ConvertSystemColor` function stores the `GetSysColor` result in a `TColor` variable called `ActualColor`. `ActualColor` is then assigned to `PaintBox1`'s brush color and the font color of the Choose Font dialog.

NOTE

The result from the `GetSysColor` call gets cast to a `TColor` type. This prevents the compiler from complaining about assigning integers to `TColor` objects.

TIP

You may be wondering how C++Builder knows when a `TColor` variable represents an actual color (`clBlue`) or a system color (`clBtnFace`). The actual colors are RGB values. RGB values use the lower three bytes of a four-byte integer to store the actual color. The largest RGB value is 0x00FFFFFF (`clWhite`). The system colors hide 0x80 in the leading byte to differentiate them from normal RGB colors.

Comments

This How-To shows how to convert a C++Builder constant to a Win32 constant for use in an API function call. You may need to do this in other situations when working with the API. Most of the C++Builder constants should relate easily to their API buddies, so don't hesitate to check the header files. The designers of C++Builder probably had API integration on their minds when they chose values for VCL constants.

COMPLEXITY
INTERMEDIATE

5.11 How do I...
Draw a bitmap with a transparent background?

Problem

I know how to draw bitmaps on a form, but they always seem to appear using the background of the bitmap. Sometimes it looks goofy if the bitmap has a white background while the form has a gray background. How can I draw the bitmap so it has a transparent background?

Technique

You can attack this problem in several ways. The animation example in How-To 5.6 demonstrated how to paint a spaceship transparently on another background bitmap. This works well if both the source bitmap and its mask are available. This How-To shows how to confront the problem without using a mask. **TCanvas** provides a function called **BrushCopy** that can take a color argument and convert it to the brush color of the destination canvas. All the pixels in the bitmap that match the color argument will be drawn transparently. **TImageList** also provides the tools needed to draw an image transparently. This How-To describes both methods.

Steps

Run **TRANSPARENT.EXE**. Figure 5-15 shows the program's main window. The program transparently displays the logo for "Bob's Software" using two different techniques. Click on the Change Background Color button and select a different background color. Observe how the background color of the two company logos adapts to whatever color you select.

1. Create a new project. Name the unit **MAINFORM.CPP**, and name the project **TRANSPARENT.MAK**.

2. Place controls on the form so it matches the picture in Figure 5-15. The logos are drawn using **PaintBox** controls. Set properties to match Table 5-14.

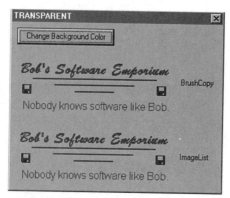

Figure 5-15 TRANSPARENT at runtime

Table 5-14 Components, properties, and settings for `Form1` in the TRANSPARENT project

COMPONENT	PROPERTY	SETTING
Form1	ClientWidth	325
	ClientHeight	250
	BorderStyle	bsDialog
Button1	Caption	Change Background Color
Label1	Caption	BrushCopy
Label2	Caption	ImageList
PaintBox1	Width	250
	Height	100
PaintBox2	Width	250
	Height	100
ImageList1	Width	250
	Height	100
	Masked	true
	DrawingStyle	dsTransparent
ColorDialog	Color	clBtnFace

3. Copy `LOGO.RES` and `LOGO.BMP` from the CD-ROM to your project directory. Open `MAINFORM.CPP`, and type in the `#pragma` statement needed to link the resource file to the project.

```
#include "MAINFORM.h"
//----------------------------------------------------------
#pragma resource "*.dfm"
#pragma resource "LOGO.res"
```

4. Double-click on `ImageList1` to launch the Image List editor. Click the Add button and load in `LOGO.BMP`. The logo for Bob's Software uses white for its background. Set the Transparent Color Combo box to `clWhite` after the bitmap has been loaded and click OK.

5. Open `MAINFORM.H`, and add a private declaration to `TForm1` for a bitmap object.

```
private:   // User declarations
  Graphics::TBitmap *LogoBitmap;
```

6. Make an `OnCreate` handler for `Form1`, and type code to create the bitmap pointer.

```
void __fastcall TForm1::FormCreate(TObject *Sender)
{
  // New the pointer, load the resource, and match
  // the paint box dimensions to the bitmap.
  LogoBitmap = new Graphics::TBitmap;
  LogoBitmap->LoadFromResourceName((int)HInstance,"LOGO");
}
```

> **NOTE**
>
> `PaintBox1` was sized to match the size of the logo bitmap. Sometimes you may need to display an image whose size is unknown. If so, add statements to size the `PaintBox` controls to match size of the logo bitmap.
>
> ```
> PaintBox1->Height = LogoBitmap->Height;
> PaintBox1->Width = LogoBitmap->Width;
> ```

7. Create an `OnClick` handler for the push button. Add code to display the Choose Color dialog, and assign the form's background color to the result.

```
void __fastcall TForm1::Button1Click(TObject *Sender)
{
  ColorDialog1->Execute();
  Color = ColorDialog1->Color;
}
```

8. Make an `OnPaint` handler for `Form1`. This code draws the bitmap transparently using `TCanvas::BrushCopy` and `TImageList::Draw`.

```
void __fastcall TForm1::FormPaint(TObject *Sender)
{
  TRect BitmapRect = Rect(0,0,LogoBitmap->Width,LogoBitmap->Height);
  // First use BrushCopy to paint the logo into PaintBox1.
```

```
// BrushCopy will convert transparent pixels to the brush
// color of PaintBox1, so set brush color first.
PaintBox1->Canvas->Brush->Color = Color;
PaintBox1->Canvas->BrushCopy(BitmapRect,LogoBitmap,BitmapRect,clWhite);

// Next, use the ImageList to draw the logo into PaintBox2.
ImageList1->Draw(PaintBox2->Canvas,0,0,0);
}
```

9. Compile and test the program.

How It Works

This How-To displays a bitmap image in two **PaintBox** controls. This isn't anything new. You have painted bitmaps into **PaintBox** controls all through this chapter. This How-To utilizes a different technique for copying the image into the **PaintBox**. Instead of just calling **PaintBox1->Canvas->Draw**, the **OnPaint** handler (step 8) uses two different methods. The first method replaces **Canvas->Draw** with **Canvas ->BrushCopy**. The second technique lets **TImageList** handle the drawing.

Transparent Drawing with BrushCopy

BrushCopy contains four arguments. The **BrushCopy** call in step 8 looks like this:

```
PaintBox1->Canvas->BrushCopy(BitmapRect,LogoBitmap,BitmapRect,clWhite);
```

The first three arguments resemble the arguments to **TCanvas::CopyRect** (except that **BrushCopy** uses a source bitmap whereas **CopyRect** needs a source canvas). The difference between **BrushCopy** and **CopyRect** lies in the last argument to **BrushCopy**. This parameter is a **TColor** value that determines the transparent color of the source bitmap. **BrushCopy** locates pixels that match the transparent color and changes their color to match the brush color of the destination canvas.

LogoBitmap contains a white background, so the code from step 8 passes **clWhite** as the transparent color argument to **BrushCopy**. **BrushCopy** then converts white pixels in the bitmap to match the brush color of **PaintBox1**. Before calling **BrushCopy**, the **OnPaint** handler assigns the form's color to the brush color of **PaintBox1**. This allows the **BrushCopy** call to convert the logo's white background to the form's background color.

Transparent Drawing with TImageList

TImageList does half of its work at design time (step 4). You specify a transparent color when you add images to an **ImageList** control. **TImageList** then generates a mask bitmap based on the transparent color and the image that was loaded in. **TImageList::Draw** (step 8) uses the mask to draw the image transparently using the same technique employed in the animation program in How-To 5.6.

TIP

Here are some tips on using ImageList components.

✔ Specify clNone as the transparent color when you first load in an image if you want to display the image as is without any color masking.

✔ TImageList::Draw will draw the image as is if no transparent color was specified. The dsNormal and dsTransparent DrawingStyles, the BkColor, and Masked property will have no effect if the transparent color is clNone.

✔ The ImageList editor converts the transparent color to black as soon as you click OK. It also generates the mask.

✔ The dsSelected and dsFocused DrawingSytles work with the BlendColor to draw focused items. This has more to do with ListView and TreeView controls.

✔ There are two ways to draw transparently if a transparent color was given. You can either set DrawingStyle to dsTransparent, or you can leave it at dsNormal and set BkColor to clNone.

✔ You can paint the image with any background color by setting DrawingStyle to dsNormal and by setting BkColor to the desired background color.

Comments

This How-To demonstrates two methods for painting a standard bitmap transparently. C++Builder includes **BrushCopy** mainly for backward compatibility, so you should use **TImageList** whenever possible.

TIP

To use the ImageList exclusively, skip steps 3, 5, and 6, and remove the BrushCopy code from step 8.

COMPLEXITY
BEGINNING

5.12 How do I...
Autosize a form to fit a picture and autosize a picture to fit a form?

Problem

I want to create a program that displays pictures, but I don't know how large the pictures will be until runtime. Can I make a C++Builder form automatically size itself to the size of the picture? Once the picture has been loaded, I would like it to stretch as the user resizes the window. How can I make the picture do that?

Technique

`TImage` can be used to load and display pictures. You can adjust the `ClientWidth` and `ClientHeight` properties of `TForm` to size the form to match the picture. Once the picture has been loaded, it's easy to stretch an image to fill the client area of a form. `TImage` can stretch automatically if you set the `Alignment` property to `alClient` and set `Stretch` to `true`.

Steps

Run `AUTOSIZE.EXE`. Only a tiny form appears at first. Select File|Load to locate and display a bitmap. The form will immediately resize itself to match the size of the picture. Figure 5-16 shows the program after loading the image. Now resize the form and observe how the image stretches to fill the available client area of the form.

1. Create a new project. Choose File|Save Project As; name the unit `MAINFORM.CPP`, and name the project `AUTOSIZE.MAK`.

Figure 5-16
AUTOSIZE at
runtime

2. Place an **Image** control and an **OpenDialog** control on **Form1**. Set properties to match Table 5-15.

Table 5-15 Components, properties, and settings for **Form1** in the AUTOSIZE project

COMPONENT	PROPERTY	SETTING
Form1	AutoScroll	false
	Position	poScreenCenter
	Scaled	false
Image1	Align	alClient
	AutoSize	true
	Stretch	true
MainMenu1	MenuItem	&File
	MenuItem	&Load
OpenDialog1	Filter	Bitmap files (*.bmp) | *.bmp
	+Options	
	-ofPathMustExist	true
	-ofFileMustExist	true

3. Place a **MainMenu** control on **Form1**. Add a **File** menu item and a **Load** subitem. Create an **OnClick** handler for the **Load** menu item, and insert code to launch the File Open dialog and load in a bitmap.

```
void __fastcall TForm1::Load1Click(TObject *Sender)
{
  if(OpenDialog1->Execute())
  {
    Image1->Picture->LoadFromFile(OpenDialog1->FileName);
    ClientWidth  = Image1->Picture->Width;
    ClientHeight = Image1->Picture->Height;
  }
}
```

4. Make an **OnCreate** handler for **Form1** that initially sizes the form when the program starts.

```
void __fastcall TForm1::FormCreate(TObject *Sender)
{
  ClientHeight = 0;
  ClientWidth = 200;
}
```

5. Compile and test the program.

How It Works

There certainly isn't any brain surgery involved in this How-To. The File|Load `OnClick` handler (step 3) launches a File Open common dialog, and then asks the `Image1 ->Picture` to load the selected file. The code then resizes the `ClientWidth` and `ClientHeight` of the form based on the dimensions of the picture.

The properties of `TImage` play a critical role in making this How-To work. `Image1` has its `Alignment` property set to `alClient`, which causes the image to resize itself to fit the client area of the screen when the form gets resized. The `TImage` component stretches the picture because its `Stretch` property is `true`. The `AutoSize` property of `TImage` also plays an important role. It tells `TImage` that it should resize itself when it loads a new picture. If `AutoSize` was `false`, `Image1->Picture->Width` and `Image1->Picture->Height` would stay the same regardless of the size of images that get loaded.

Comments

The `TImage` component is extremely powerful, flexible, and easy to use. You will typically need very little, if any, code to use this component to its maximum advantage.

COMPLEXITY
ADVANCED

5.13 How do I...
Write a screen saver?

Problem

Now that I know how to use the graphics abilities of C++Builder, I would like to put my knowledge to work by coding a screen saver. Can I use C++Builder to make a screen saver?

Technique

A Windows 95 screen saver has many responsibilities for responding to various system messages. Describing each of these responsibilities would take tons of code and could fill a small book by itself. This How-To explains only the very basics of writing a Windows 95 screen saver using C++Builder.

Screen savers are really just programs that know which messages to respond to. This How-To describes these messages and how your program should handle them. The VCL classes of C++Builder make it an excellent programming environment for coding a screen saver.

Steps

Run SCREENSAVER.EXE. A simple screen saver should appear that looks like
Figure 5-17. Let it run for a while, and then move the mouse to shut the screen saver
down and return to Windows.

1. Create a new project; save the unit as MAINFORM.CPP, and save the project
as SCREENSAVER.MAK.

2. Add a Timer control to Form1. This is the only component that Form1
needs. Set properties to match Table 5-16.

Table 5-16 Components, properties, and settings for Form1 in the
SCREENSAVER project

COMPONENT	PROPERTY	SETTING
Form1	BorderStyle	bsNone
Timer1	Enabled	false
	Interval	20

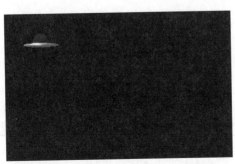

Figure 5-17 SCREENSAVER at runtime

3. Open `MAINFORM.H` and type function prototypes, variable declarations, and message maps in the private section of `TForm1`.

```
class TForm1 : public TForm
{
__published:  // IDE-managed Components
...
...
private:  // User declarations
    void __fastcall CreateParams(TCreateParams &Params);
    void __fastcall WMEraseBkgnd(TWMEraseBkgnd &Msg);
    void __fastcall WMActivate(TWMActivate &Msg);
    void __fastcall WMSysCommand(TWMSysCommand &Msg);
    TPoint AnchorPoint;
    Graphics::TBitmap *ScreenBitmap;
    Graphics::TBitmap *SpaceShipBitmap;
    void DrawShipOnBackground(void);
    void MoveBitmapToScreen(void);
    void MoveShipLocation(void);
    void PatchBackground(void);
    TPoint Location;
    TPoint OldLocation;
    TRect LocationRect;
    int XSpeed;
    int YSpeed;
    int XDirection;
    int YDirection;
    TRect ShipRect;
public:  // User declarations
    virtual __fastcall TForm1(TComponent* Owner);

BEGIN_MESSAGE_MAP
    MESSAGE_HANDLER(WM_ERASEBKGND,TWMEraseBkgnd,WMEraseBkgnd)
    MESSAGE_HANDLER(WM_ACTIVATE,TWMActivate,WMActivate)
    MESSAGE_HANDLER(WM_SYSCOMMAND,TWMSysCommand,WMSysCommand)
END_MESSAGE_MAP(TForm)
};
```

4. The screen saver needs to be on top of all other windows. Override the `CreateParams` function to modify the window style when the program starts. Type this function in `MAINFORM.CPP`.

```
void __fastcall TForm1::CreateParams(TCreateParams &Params)
{
    TForm::CreateParams(Params);       // Call base class first,
    Params.ExStyle |= WS_EX_TOPMOST; // then modify the style.
}
```

5. The screen saver uses the same spaceship from the animation How-To. Copy `PICTURES.RES` from the screen saver directory on the CD-ROM to your project directory. Then type this `#pragma` statement in `MAINFORM.CPP`. Also type in a constant declaration that will be used for measuring mouse movement.

```
#include "MAINFORM.h"
//-------------------------------------------
#pragma resource "*.dfm"
#pragma resource "PICTURES.res"

const int MouseMoveDistance = 10;
```

6. Create an `OnCreate` handler for `Form1`. Type in code to resize the form to fit the entire screen, hide the mouse cursor, and set up the memory bitmaps.

```
void __fastcall TForm1::FormCreate(TObject *Sender)
{
  Left = 0;                   // Make the form fill
  Top  = 0;                   // the whole screen.
  Width = Screen->Width;
  Height= Screen->Height;
  Cursor = crNone;            // Hide the cursor.

  POINT WinPoint;             // Find the mouse cursor
  GetCursorPos(&WinPoint);    // using api function. Store
  AnchorPoint.x=WinPoint.x;   // result for measuring
  AnchorPoint.y=WinPoint.y;   // mouse movement.

  ScreenBitmap    = new Graphics::TBitmap; // Memory bitmap for the
  SpaceShipBitmap = new Graphics::TBitmap; // screen and a spaceship.
  ScreenBitmap->Width  = Width;            // Size the screenbitmap.
  ScreenBitmap->Height = Height;           // Load spaceship from resource
  SpaceShipBitmap->LoadFromResourceName((int)HInstance,"SHIP");

  ShipRect = Rect(0,0,        // Size of ship never changes, calculate its
              SpaceShipBitmap->Width,    // size once for use in many
              SpaceShipBitmap->Height); // functions

  XSpeed     = YSpeed     = 2;    // Initialize data members.
  XDirection = YDirection = 1;
  Location.x = Location.y = 0;
  OldLocation = Location;
  Timer1->Enabled = true;

  // Blackout the memory bitmap.
  ScreenBitmap->Canvas->Brush->Color = clBlack;
  ScreenBitmap->Canvas->FillRect(Rect(0,0,Width,Height));
}
```

7. Create an `OnDestroy` handler for `Form1`, and insert code to delete the resources allocated when the program started.

```
void __fastcall TForm1::FormDestroy(TObject *Sender)
{
  Timer1->Enabled = false;
  delete SpaceShipBitmap;
  delete ScreenBitmap;
}
```

8. Key presses, mouse button presses, and mouse movement should all close down the screen saver. Create `OnKeyDown`, `OnMouseDown`, and `OnMouseMove` event handlers for `Form1`, and add code to close the program.

```
void __fastcall TForm1::FormKeyDown(TObject *Sender, WORD &Key,
  TShiftState Shift)
{
  Close();
}
//-------------------------------------------------------------------
void __fastcall TForm1::FormMouseDown(TObject *Sender, TMouseButton Button,
  TShiftState Shift, int X, int Y)
{
  Close();
}
//-------------------------------------------------------------------
void __fastcall TForm1::FormMouseMove(TObject *Sender, TShiftState Shift,
  int X, int Y)
{
  // Calculate how far the mouse has been moved
  // from its original point.
  int XDistance = X - AnchorPoint.x;
  int YDistance = Y - AnchorPoint.y;

  if ((XDistance < -MouseMoveDistance) ||
      (XDistance > MouseMoveDistance)          )
    Close();
  else if ((YDistance < -MouseMoveDistance) ||
           (YDistance > MouseMoveDistance)         )
    Close();
}
```

9. The screen saver needs to react directly to a handful of Windows messages. The function prototypes for these handler functions were added to `TForm1` in step 3. Now type the function bodies into `MAINFORM.CPP`.

```
void __fastcall TForm1::WMEraseBkgnd(TWMEraseBkgnd &Msg)
{                         // Tell windows to never mind about the
  Msg.Result = false;   // background; we've got it covered.
}


void __fastcall TForm1::WMActivate(TWMActivate &Msg)
{
  if(Msg.Active == false) // If we are deactivated for
    Close();              // some reason, close down.
}
void __fastcall TForm1::WMSysCommand(TWMSysCommand &Msg)
{                              // SC_SCREENSAVE means that
  if(Msg.CmdType == SC_SCREENSAVE) // Windows is trying to start the
    Msg.Result = true;         // screensaver twice, don't let it
  else
    TForm::Dispatch(&Msg);     // Other system commands can be
}                              // handled as usual.
```

> **TIP**
>
> The WMEraseBkgnd function prevents the background of the form from painting itself. You may want to temporarily remove this function as you debug your screen savers.

10. The previous steps simply lay the groundwork for how a screen saver should interact with the operating system. The subsequent steps handle the chores of painting on the screen. Create an OnTimer handler for the Timer control on Form1. Type in these statements:

```
void __fastcall TForm1::Timer1Timer(TObject *Sender)
{
    PatchBackground();       // Repair the memory bitmap.
    MoveShipLocation();      // Calculate new location of ship.
    DrawShipOnBackground();  // Paint ship on memory bitmap.
    MoveBitmapToScreen();    // Copy pixels from memory to screen.
}
```

> **TIP**
>
> For smoother graphics performance you may want to consider using threads or a multimedia timer instead of a system timer. Chapter 12, "Threads," contains information on multithreaded programs.

11. The OnTimer handler in step 10 calls four functions that drive the animation for the screen saver. Stay in **MAINFORM.CPP**, and insert the code for these drawing functions:

```
void TForm1::PatchBackground(void)
{
    // Blacken in pixels where the ship is
    // currently located.
    ScreenBitmap->Canvas->Brush->Color = clBlack;
    ScreenBitmap->Canvas->FillRect(LocationRect);
}


void TForm1::MoveShipLocation(void)
{
    // Save old location.
    OldLocation = Location;
    // Calculate new location.
    Location.x+=XSpeed*XDirection; // Direction is
    Location.y+=YSpeed*YDirection; // either 1 or -1.
```

```
   // Must determine when the ship hits the walls. Easy calculation
   // on the left, on the right, must take into account ship's width
   if (Location.x < 0 || Location.x > ScreenBitmap->Width-ShipRect.Right)
   {
      XDirection *= -1;    // If wall collision detected, change direction
      if(Location.x<0)     // Bounce the ship back into the client area
        Location.x *= -1;  // Bounce the ship back in as far as it would
      else                 // have travelled if there was no wall.
        Location.x=2*ScreenBitmap->Width-2*ShipRect.Right-Location.x;
   }
   // Detect up down wall collisions just like left right collisions.
   if (Location.y < 0 || Location.y > ScreenBitmap->Height-ShipRect.Bottom)
   {
      YDirection *= -1;
      if(Location.y<0)
        Location.y *= -1;
      else
        Location.y=2*ScreenBitmap ->Height-2*ShipRect.Bottom-Location.y;
   }

   // Update the rect variable.
   LocationRect = Rect(Location.x,Location.y,
                        Location.x+SpaceShipBitmap->Width,
                        Location.y+SpaceShipBitmap->Height);
}


void TForm1::DrawShipOnBackground(void)
{
   // Copy the ship into its new location
   // in the memory bitmap.
   ScreenBitmap->Canvas->CopyMode = cmSrcCopy; // DEST = SRC
   ScreenBitmap->Canvas->CopyRect(LocationRect,
                                  SpaceShipBitmap->Canvas,
                                  ShipRect);
}


void TForm1::MoveBitmapToScreen(void)
{
   // The screen is big. Rather than move all pixels from
   // memory to the screen, it s more effecient to only
   // move the regions that have changed. For example, an
   // 800x600 screen has 480,000 pixels. This code copies
   // only 2*(57*23) = 2622 pixels rather than all 480,000.

   // First copy in the pixels where the ship used to be.
   TRect OldRect = Rect(OldLocation.x,OldLocation.y,
                        OldLocation.x+SpaceShipBitmap->Width,
                        OldLocation.y+SpaceShipBitmap->Height);
   Canvas->CopyRect(OldRect,
                    ScreenBitmap->Canvas,
                    OldRect);
```

continued on next page

continued from previous page

```
// Then copy in pixels where the ship is now.
Canvas->CopyRect(LocationRect,
                    ScreenBitmap->Canvas,
                    LocationRect);
}
```

12. The form will receive a single `WM_PAINT` message when the screen saver starts. This is a good time to move pixels from the memory bitmap to the screen, which effectively blacks out the display. Create an `OnPaint` handler for `Form1`, and add code to copy the entire memory bitmap to the screen.

```
void __fastcall TForm1::FormPaint(TObject *Sender)
{
   Canvas->Draw(0,0,ScreenBitmap);
}
```

TIP

To prove that the `OnPaint` handler almost never gets called, put a `MessageBeep(0);` statement after the call to `Canvas->Draw`. This How-To will only beep once when the screen saver starts. The `OnPaint` handler becomes more important in screen savers that support password dialogs.

13. Well, it's almost ready to go. In fact, compile and test the program now if you want. This step takes care of a detail with how Windows activates a screen saver. Windows starts your screen saver with a **/s** command line argument when it wants you to run your screen saver in full screen mode. Windows uses other command line arguments to tell your screen saver to run in preview mode or to show its options dialog box. This How-To doesn't implement these features, so it should not run for command line arguments other than **/s**. Open **SCREENSAVER.CPP**, and edit **WinMain** to detect the proper command line argument.

```
WINAPI WinMain(HINSTANCE, HINSTANCE, LPSTR, int)
{
   try
   {
      // Check the command line argument, if it s not /s
      // return now without running. (a complete screensaver
      // would handle each command line possibility)
      if (ParamStr(1) != "/s")
         {
         MessageBeep(0);  // Beep for educational purposes.
         return 0;
         }
```

```
    Application->Initialize();
    Application->CreateForm(__classid(TForm1), &Form1);
    Application->Run();
}
catch (Exception &exception)
{
    Application->ShowException(&exception);
}
return 0;
}
```

> **WARNING**
>
> You can skip step 13 if you just want to test the screen saver executable. If you intend to test the program as your real Windows screen saver, then you must code step 13. Neglecting this step will lead to big time funkiness when you try to set the screen saver in the Control Panel.

14. Compile and test the program.

> **TIP**
>
> Before you run the program, select Run|Parameters and type in /s. Otherwise, the program won't start due to the code that was added in step 13.

How It Works

This How-To can be split into two code sections: code that makes the program act like a Windows screen saver and code that paints the screen saver graphics. The screen saver graphics in this How-To were stolen from the animation program in How-To 5.6. The only new graphical feature is how `MoveBitmapToScreen` (step 11) updates the screen on each timer tick. Screen savers take up the entire screen. The code in `MoveBitmapToScreen` uses `CopyRect` to update portions of the display, instead of using `Draw` to overwrite every pixel on the screen.

Acting like a screen saver more or less means responding to Windows events. The screen saver has the responsibility of knowing when to shut down, hiding the mouse cursor, and many other details. Table 5-17 lists the details that must be handled by the program.

Table 5-17 Events and functions needed to make a well-behaved screen saver

EVENT/FUNCTION	RESPONSIBILITY
CreateParams	Make the screen saver the topmost program.
OnCreate	Hide the mouse cursor, set the mouse anchor point, and initialize other variables.
WM_ERASEBACKGROUND	Windows is telling the program to repaint its background. The background of Form1 should never be displayed, so swallow this message without processing it.
WM_KEYDOWN	Close the screen saver.
WM_MOUSEDOWN	Close the screen saver.
WM_MOUSEMOVE	Close the screen saver, but first check that the mouse has moved a considerable distance.
WM_ACTIVATE	Exit the program if the program has been deactivated.
WM_SYSCOMMAND	Prevent two occurrences of the screen saver from running.

Comments

This How-To won't win Screen Saver of the Year award, but it does describe the basics of how a screen saver must act. You can make this screen saver your Windows screen saver by following these steps:

✔ Rename the program so it has a long filename (the long filename is important) and a **.SCR** extension. How about **MY CPPBUILDER SCREEN SAVER.SCR**?

✔ Copy the .SCR file to your **\WINDOWS\SYSTEM** directory. This step isn't actually necessary, but it's the easiest way to ensure that Windows can find your file.

✔ Right-click on the desktop and choose Properties to bring up the display properties. Click on the Screen Saver tab. Use the Combo box to locate your .SCR file.

✔ Click the OK button, or click Preview to run the screen saver now.

Windows will now launch the screen saver after a period of activity. Wait around and verify that the program starts.

This How-To explains how to create a very simple screen saver. The screen saver does work and can function as the main screen saver on your PC. However, this screen saver is definitely not ready for prime time. It should implement a Password dialog box if the user wants one. The screen saver should know how to run in preview mode so it will fit in the little monitor box located on the Screen Saver tab of the Display Properties dialog. It should also provide a configuration dialog and use the registry to save settings. All of these prime-time features were left out of this example.

The CD-ROM contains a demo of Lucian Wischik's scrPlus screen saver library. This library is the best way to code a fully functional screen saver. The CD-ROM also contains sample screen savers with source code and a Windows help file that explains undocumented API features, the screen saver command line arguments, password dialogs, and much more. You should definitely make use of these resources if you plan on writing a real Windows screen saver.

CHAPTER 6
ENVIRONMENT AND SYSTEM

6

ENVIRONMENT AND SYSTEM

How do I...

6.13 Determine which programs are running?

6.14 Find out which disk drives are available and how much disk space there is?

It is rare for an application to be run only on systems with identical configurations. Most applications will be run on systems with different hardware and software configurations. Almost any significant application will need to get information about its environment at runtime. The Win32 API contains many functions for retrieving information about the system configuration. The How-To's in this chapter show how to use these functions in C++Builder™ applications.

6.1 List Files as in File Manager

Applications frequently need the user to select files, directories, or disk drives. C++Builder includes components that display the available choices and allows the user to select from them.

6.2 Run Another Program from My Application

You can create an application that runs other programs to perform tasks. If the application needs to, it can wait for the other program to finish.

6.3 Restart Windows

If an application, such as a setup program, makes changes to the system configuration, the system may need to be rebooted for the changes to take effect. An application can call the Win32 API function ExitWindowsEx to shut down the system and reboot.

6.4 Search an Entire Disk for a File

Searching a directory for a file is easy but what about searching a directory tree or an entire disk? That is a little trickier. This How-To will show you how to use the FindFirst and FindNext API functions to do recursive wildcard searching.

6.5 Disable the Windows Screen Saver

If an application needs to do lengthy calculations or database lookups, the user may leave the computer alone for a while. If the screen saver comes on, its processing requirements will slow down the application and make the user's wait even longer. Fortunately, it is possible for the active application to prevent the screen saver from cutting in on it.

6.6 Prevent Multiple Instances of My Program from Being Loaded

Some applications will not function property if more than one instance of the program is running simultaneously. Learn how to use the synchronization mechanisms built into Windows to prevent more than one copy of a program from being run at a time.

6.7 Determine the Directory Where Windows Is Located

An application may expect to find files in the directory where the operating system is located. For networked systems, the operating system may not be in the default location. The `GetWindowsDirectory` and `GetSystemDirectory` API functions show exactly where the operating system is located.

6.8 Determine How Much System Memory Is Available

Nothing affects the performance of a system more than the amount of memory available. This How-To shows how to use `GlobalMemoryStatus` API function to find out what memory resources are available on a system.

6.9 Determine What Version of Windows Is Running

There are several different flavors of Windows and different versions of each type. If your application runs on different operating system versions, and a user has a problem, you may need to know exactly what type of system he or she is running.

6.10 Display an Icon in the Windows Tray

Applications that run in the background frequently display an icon in the "tray" at the bottom right of the desktop. Applications with icons in the tray can respond to mouse events over their icon.

6.11 Find and Set Environment Variables

While the Registry has replaced environment variables to a large extent, they are still used and play an important role. Learn how to find the environment variables that have been defined for a process and how to change their values.

6.12 Drag and Drop Files

Many applications allow the user to open a file by dragging its icon, then dropping it on the application. This How-To shows how to add this functionality to your applications.

6.13 Determine Which Programs Are Running

On Windows 95, applications run in separate processes. An application can use the `Toolhelp` API functions to find out what programs are running on the system.

6.14 Find Out Which Disk Drives Are Available and How Much Disk Space There Is

The Win32 API has functions that return information about the number and types of disk drives available. These functions can be used to determine the amount of free disk space available on each disk drive.

COMPLEXITY
BEGINNING

6.1 How do I...
List files as in File Manager?

Problem

I have a program where the user needs to select files to be processed by the application. The user should be able to choose a disk, then see what directories and files of a given type exist, as you can with the File Manager program. I know I can use the Win32 API to search for files and directories but is there an easier way?

Technique

The VCL library has four controls designed to work together that make selecting files in an application simple. The Drive Combo Box control is a Combo box that contains an entry in the drop-down list for each disk drive on the system. The Directory List Box control displays the directories on a disk drive in a tree format. The File List box shows a list of files within a directory and it can be used with a Filter Combo Box control to restrict the types of files displayed.

Steps

Run the program **FILEMANAGER.EXE**. A view of its screen is shown in Figure 6-1. Try changing the Drive and Filter Combo boxes while selecting files using the Directory and File List boxes.

1. Select File|New Application from the main menu to create a new blank project. Select File|Save Project As, and save the project as **FileManager**.

2. Add the properties and settings as shown in Table 6-1.

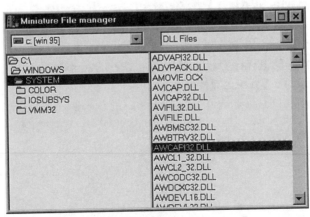

Figure 6-1 FILEMANAGER program

Table 6-1 Components, properties, and settings for FILEMANAGER

COMPONENT	PROPERTY	SETTING
Form1	Caption	Miniature File manager
	Height	320
	Position	poDefault
	Width	500
Panel1	Align	alTop
	Caption	
	Height	40
FileListBox1	Align	alLeft
	Width	255
DirectoryListBox1	Align	alClient
	FileList	FileListBox1
DriveComboBox1 (On Panel1)	DirList	DirectoryListBox1
	Height	22
	Left	8
	Top	8
	Width	220
FilterComboBox1 (On Panel1)	FileList	FileListBox1
	Filter	All files
		(*.*)|*.*|Program
		Files|*.exe|DLL
		Files|*.DLL;*.OCX;*.VBX
	Height	24
	Left	255
	Top	8
	Width	220

The property value is

```
All files (*.*)|*.*|Program Files|*.exe|DLL⇐ Files|*.DLL;*.OCX;*.VBX
```

The strange formatting is required by Windows. The string has to be a list of field pairs separated by vertical bars. The first string in the pair is a description that gets displayed; the second string is a pattern to match files matching the description. If there are multiple patterns, then they are separated by semicolons.

When displayed, it looks something like

```
All files (*.*)
Program Files
DLL Files
```

continued on next page

continued from previous page

```
All files (*.*), When selected Matches *.* or any file
Program Files When selected matches *.exe or application files.
DLL Files When selected matches the threes types *.DLL OR *.OCX OR *.VBX
```

3. Compile and test the project.

How It Works

The interesting aspect of this application is that it is created using no custom code at all. The VCL `TDriveComboBox`, `TDirectoryListBox`, `TFileListBox`, and `TFilterCombo` classes are all designed to work together, so you do not have to write event handlers that tell the other controls when the value of another has changed. The secret is knowing how to use the properties that link these components together.

The `TDriveComboBox`'s `DirList` property can be used to link it to a `TDirectoryListBox` object. Whenever the drive selection changes in the Combo box, the Directory List box gets notified of the change and automatically updates itself. Similarly, the `TDirectoryListBox` class's `FileList` property links a Directory List box to a `TFileListBox` object and the `TFilterCombo` class's `FileList` property can link it to a File List Box control.

Comments

This is about as easy as it gets to do Win32 programming. While any nontrivial C++Builder program will require you to write some code, there are many places where the VCL library will save you a lot of time and effort.

Keep in mind that, while the controls demonstrated in this example can work together automatically, you do not have to use them this way. If an application needed to do some special processing, it could set up an `OnClick` handler for a Drive Combo box, and, within the handler, it could set the value of the `Drive` property in a directory List box.

Each of these controls can be used without any of the others. If you only need to select a disk drive in your application, then you could use a Drive Combo Box control all by itself, or you could use a Drive Combo Box with a Directory List Box, if the program only needed to select a directory. The only exception to this is that while the Filter Combo Box control can be used by itself, it is of very little practical value, unless it is linked to a File List Box control.

COMPLEXITY
INTERMEDIATE

6.2 How do I...
Run another program from my application?

Problem

I need to be able to run another program from a C++Builder application. My program needs to wait until the other application finishes before it continues processing. How can I do this with C++Builder?

Technique

The `ShellExecuteEx` and `CreateProcess` functions in the Win32 API can be used to execute another application. There are advantages to using either function in different situations. `CreateProcess` gives you more control over low level attributes, such as security, and is better for creating background processes while `ShellExecuteExe` is easier to use for programs that will run in the foreground. You can use the `WaitForSingleObject` function to wait until the other program finishes.

Steps

Run `RUNPROGRAM.EXE`. Select an executable file using the Drive Combo box and the Directory and File List boxes as shown in Figure 6-2. Double-click on a file or click on the Run button to run the application. Try passing parameters to an application by entering them in the edit window. See what happens when you check the Don't Wait Check box.

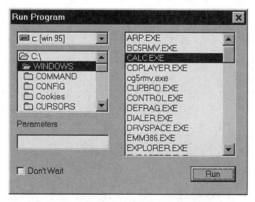

Figure 6-2 RUNPROGRAM application

1. Select File|New Application from the main menu to create a new blank project. Select File|Save Project As, and save the project as **RunProgram**.

2. Add the components and set their properties as shown in Table 6-2.

Table 6-2 Components, properties, and settings for RUNPROGRAM

COMPONENT	PROPERTY	SETTING
Form1	BorderStyle	bsDialog
	Caption	Run Program
	Height	300
	Position	poScreenCenter
	Width	400
FileListBox1	Height	200
	Left	190
	Mask	*.EXE
	Top	10
	Width	185
DirectoryListBox1	FileList	FileListBox1
	Height	100
	Left	10
	Top	40
	Width	155
DriveComboBox1	DirList	DirectoryListBox1
	Height	22
	Left	10
	Top	10
	Width	155
Label1	Caption	Parameters
	Left	10
	Top	150
Edit1	Height	24
	Left	10
	Text	
	Top	175
	Width	155
CheckBox1	Caption	Don't Wait
	Left	10
	Top	225

COMPONENT	PROPERTY	SETTING
Button1	Caption	Run
	Enabled	false
	Height	25
	Left	300
	Top	225
	Width	75

3. Go to the Code Editor; then select File|Open from the main menu to open the file **UNIT1.H**. Add the following declaration to the definition of TForm1:

```
class TForm1 : public TForm
{
__published:   // IDE-managed Components
  TFileListBox *FileListBox1;
  TDirectoryListBox *DirectoryListBox1;
  TDriveComboBox *DriveComboBox1;
  TLabel *Label1;
  TEdit *Edit1;
  TCheckBox *CheckBox1;
  TButton *Button1;
private:   // User declarations
    void RunProgram () ;
public:   // User declarations
  __fastcall TForm1(TComponent* Owner);
};
```

4. Switch to the file **UNIT1.CPP** and edit it to include the Shell API definitions.

```
#include <vcl\vcl.h>
#include <shellapi.h>
#pragma hdrstop
```

5. Add this code for the **RunProgram** member function to **UNIT1.CPP**:

```
void   TForm1::RunProgram ()
{
  // Select the program and how it will be run.
  SHELLEXECUTEINFO execinfo ;
  memset (&execinfo, 0, sizeof (execinfo)) ;
  execinfo.cbSize = sizeof (execinfo) ;
  execinfo.lpVerb = "open" ;
  execinfo.lpFile = FileListBox1->FileName.c_str () ;
  execinfo.lpParameters = Edit1->Text.c_str () ;
  execinfo.fMask = SEE_MASK_NOCLOSEPROCESS ;
  execinfo.nShow = SW_SHOWDEFAULT ;

  // Run the program.
```

continued on next page

continued from previous page

```
if (! ShellExecuteEx (&execinfo))
{
  ShowMessage ("Could not create process") ;
  return ;
}
if (! CheckBox1->Checked)
{
  Application->Minimize () ;
  WaitForSingleObject (execinfo.hProcess, INFINITE) ;
  Application->Restore () ;
}
}
```

6. Double-click on the application's main form to create an event handler for the `OnCreate` event; then functions add this code to the event handler in `UNIT1.CPP`:

```
void __fastcall TForm1::FormCreate(TObject *Sender)
{
  DriveComboBox1->Drive = 'C' ;
  DirectoryListBox1->Directory = "\\" ;
}
```

7. Select the File List box on the application's main form; then, go the Events page in the Object Inspector. Double-click on the entry for `OnDblClick` to create a handler for the event. Add the following code to the event handler:

```
void __fastcall TForm1::FileListBox1DblClick(TObject *Sender)
{
  RunProgram () ;
}
```

8. Return to the Events page of the Object Inspector, and add the following `OnClick` event handler for the File List box:

```
void __fastcall TForm1::FileListBox1Click(TObject *Sender)
{
  Button1->Enabled = true ;
}
```

9. Select the Directory List box on the application's main form. Go the Events page of Object Inspector, and add an `OnChange` handler that looks like this:

```
void __fastcall TForm1::DirectoryListBox1Change(TObject *Sender)
{
  Button1->Enabled = false ;
}
```

10. Double-click on the Run button and add the following code to the `OnClick` event handler:

```
void __fastcall TForm1::Button1Click(TObject *Sender)
{
```

```
    RunProgram () ;
}
```

11. Compile and test the project.

How It Works

The core of this How-To is the `RunProgram` member function. All the rest of the code is for selecting the file run by this function. The file selection is done using the method demonstrated in How-To 6.1. `RunProgram` calls the `ShellExecuteEx` API function which runs the other application. This function returns `true` if it is successful.

The only parameter to the `ShellExecuteEx` function is the address of a `SHELLEXECUTEINFO` structure. All the information needed to run the other application is stored in this structure. The `cbSize` field holds this size of the structure. Having this value allows the structure to be enlarged over time while maintaining compatibility with older programs. The `RunProgram` application fills in several other fields of this structure required to start the application. A pointer to the string constant "open" is stored in the `lpVerb` field to indicate that we want to run an executable file. The `lpFile` and `lpParameters` fields are initialized with pointers to the file to execute and the command line parameters. The `nShow` field specifies how the application's main window is to be displayed and can be filled in with any `SW_` values listed in the documentation for the `ShowWindow` API function. If this value is left as zero, the application's window is not displayed. The only field whose purpose is not obvious is the `fMask` field. This field is a bit mask used to specify options for running the application. The `SEE_MASK_NOCLOSEPROCESS` bit in this field needs to be set in order to allow `RunProgram` to determine when the other application terminates.

After calling `ShellExecuteEx` to run the program, the state of the Check box determines whether `RunProgram` waits for it to finish by calling `WaitForSingleObject`. The parameters to `WaitForSingleObject` are the object to wait for and the number of milliseconds to wait before timing out. `WaitForSingleObject` suspends the thread that called it until either the object becomes signaled or the timeout occurs. `WaitForSingleObject` can wait for several types of objects including mutexes, semaphores, threads, and processes. Each instance of an application runs in a separate process and a process is signaled when it terminates. The `ShellExecuteEx` function returns the handle of the process created to run the application in the `hProcess` field of the `SHELLEXECUTEINFO` structure. This value is passed to the `WaitForSingleObject` function. For more information on threads and processes, refer to Chapter 12, "Threads."

During the `WaitForSingleObject` call, the application is not able to repaint itself. If the application's window was to become hidden and then exposed during this period, it would get pretty ugly. To avoid this problem, `RunProgram` calls the `Minimize` and `Restore` methods so that its window will remain hidden while it waits for the other application.

Comments

The `ShellExecuteEx` function can be used for more than just starting executable programs. It can be used to open or print any type of document that has been registered with the system. Try changing the `Mask` property of the File List box from `*.EXE` to an empty string and running this program. If you select a .TXT file, run it; you should see the file loaded in Notepad or some other text editor. To print a file, set the `lpVerb` field in the `SHELLEXECUTEINFO` structure to `print`.

COMPLEXITY
BEGINNING

6.3 How do I...
Restart Windows?

Problem

I have an installation program for my application. After the application is installed, the system needs to be rebooted in order to run the application. I would like to give the user the opportunity to reboot the system as part of the installation procedure. How can I do this within a C++Builder application?

Technique

The Windows API function `ExitWindowsEx` is used to shut down Windows. You can control how the shutdown is performed through the parameter values passed to this function.

Steps

Before you start, make sure you do not have any programs with unsaved work already running. Next, run the program `RESTART.EXE`. The main form for this program is shown in Figure 6-3. Try selecting different options before clicking on the Shutdown button.

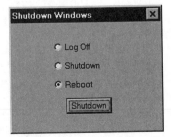

Figure 6-3 The RESTART application

1. Select File|New Application from the main menu to create a new blank project. Select File|Save Project As, and save the project as **Restart**.

2. Add the components to the main form and set their properties as shown in Table 6-3.

Table 6-3 Components, properties, and settings for RESTART

COMPONENT	PROPERTY	SETTING
Form1	BorderStyle	bsDialog
	Caption	Shutdown Windows
	Height	205
	Position	poScreenCenter
	Width	255
RadioButton1	Caption	Log Off
	Checked	true
	Left	70
	Top	30
RadioButton2	Caption	Shutdown
	Checked	false
	Left	70
	Top	60
RadioButton3	Caption	Reboot
	Checked	false
	Left	70
	Top	90
Button1	Caption	Shutdown
	Height	25
	Left	90
	Top	120
	Width	75

3. Double-click on the button, and add the following code to the **OnClick** handler:

```
void __fastcall TForm1::Button1Click(TObject *Sender)
{
  UINT flags ;
  if (RadioButton1->Checked)
    flags = EWX_LOGOFF ;
  else if (RadioButton2->Checked)
    flags = EWX_SHUTDOWN ;
```

continued on next page

continued from previous page

```
else
   flags = EWX_REBOOT ;
ExitWindowsEx (flags, 0) ;
}
```

4. Compile and run the program.

How It Works

The `ExitWindowsEx` functionon is used to shut down or log out of Windows. Although this function has two parameters, only the first one is used. This parameter is a set of flags that determines how the shutdown is to be performed. When `Button1` is clicked, the value of the shutdown flag is determined by checking the radio buttons. The result is that either the user is logged out, the system is shut down, or the system is rebooted.

Comments

Shutting down the system through an application is generally useful only for an installation program or for a system management utility. If you need to have a program run after you reboot, you can add the path to a program as a value to the Registry key `HKEY_LOCAL_MACHINE\SOFTWARE\Microsoft\Windows\CurrentVersion\RunOnce`. Your program will automatically be removed from the Registry once it is run.

COMPLEXITY

ADVANCED

6.4 How do I...
Search an entire disk for a file?

Problem

I have an application that needs to be able to do a wildcard search for a file. I have found functions that search a directory for a file, but I need to be able to search an entire disk. How do I do this in C++Builder?

Technique

The Win32 API functions `FindFirst` and `FindNext` allow you to search for files within a directory. To find all the files on a disk, you have to create a recursive procedure to search all the subdirectories.

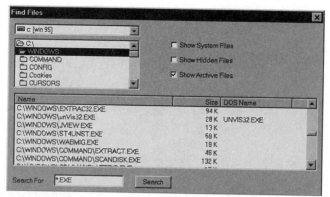

Figure 6-4 The FINDFILES program displaying application files in the WINDOWS directory and subdirectories

Steps

Run the program **FINDFILES.EXE**. Select a disk drive and the directory where you want to start searching. Enter the name of a file you want to search for (you can use an asterisk to match any characters); then, click on the Search button. The application is shown in Figure 6-4.

1. Select File|New Application from the main menu to create a new blank project. Select File|Save Project As, and save the project as **FindFiles**.

2. Add the components, and set their properties as shown in Table 6-4.

Table 6-4 Components, properties, and settings for FINDFILES

COMPONENT	PROPERTY	SETTING
Form1	BorderStyle	bsDialog
	Caption	Find Files
	Height	380
	Position	poScreenCenter
	Width	665
DirectoryListBox1	Height	100
	Left	10
	Top	40
	Width	265
DriveComboBox1	DirList	DirectoryListBox1
	Height	22
	Left	10

continued on next page

continued from previous page

COMPONENT	PROPERTY	SETTING
	Top	10
	Width	265
ListView1	Height	150
	Left	10
	Top	150
	ViewStyle	vsReport
	Width	640
Label1	Caption	Search For:
	Left	10
	Top	320
Edit1	Height	24
	Left	100
	Text	
	Top	315
	Width	145
Button1	Caption	Search
	Height	25
	Left	270
	Top	315
	Width	75
CheckBox1	Caption	Show System Files
	Checked	false
	Left	340
	Top	40
	Width	140
CheckBox2	Caption	Show Hidden Files
	Checked	false
	Left	340
	Top	70
	Width	140
CheckBox3	Caption	Show Archive Files
	Checked	true
	Left	340
	Top	100
	Width	140

3. Select the List View control on the main form with the mouse; then, press F11 to display the Object Inspector. Double-click on the value of the Columns property to display the List View Columns Editor. Add three columns with the properties shown in Table 6-5.

Table 6-5 List View column properties

COLUMN NAME	ALIGNMENT	WIDTH
Name	Left Justify	300
Size	Right Justify	100
DOS Name	Left Justify	150

4. Go to the Code Editor, and select File|Open from the main menu to open the file UNIT1.H. Add the declaration of the member function FindFilesInDirectory to the definition of TForm1.

```
class TForm1 : public TForm
{
__published: // IDE-managed Components
  TDirectoryListBox *DirectoryListBox1;
  TDriveComboBox *DriveComboBox1;
  TListView *ListView1;
  TLabel *Label1;
  TEdit *Edit1;
  TButton *Button1;
  TCheckBox *CheckBox1;
  TCheckBox *CheckBox2;
  TCheckBox *CheckBox3;
private: // User declarations
  void FindFilesInDirectory (const String &directory) ;
public:  // User declarations
  __fastcall TForm1(TComponent* Owner);
};
```

5. Switch to the file UNIT1.CPP and add this definition of the member function FindFilesInDirectory:

```
void TForm1::FindFilesInDirectory (const String &directory)
{
  // This method searches the directory specified by the parameter and all
  // of its subdirectories for the file matching the value in Edit1.
  // The directory name is assumed to end with a backslash.

  WIN32_FIND_DATA filedata ;  // Structure for file data
  HANDLE filehandle ;         // Handle for searching

  // Pass 1 - Search for the files within the directory.
  filehandle = FindFirstFile ((directory + Edit1->Text).c_str (),⇐
  &filedata) ;
  if (filehandle != INVALID_HANDLE_VALUE)
```

continued on next page

continued from previous page

```
{
  do
  {
    // Here we skip files that don't meet the attributes selected on⇐
    the screen.
    if ((filedata.dwFileAttributes & FILE_ATTRIBUTE_SYSTEM) != 0 && !⇐
    CheckBox1->Checked)
      continue ;
    if ((filedata.dwFileAttributes & FILE_ATTRIBUTE_HIDDEN) != 0 && !⇐
    CheckBox2->Checked)
      continue ;
    if ((filedata.dwFileAttributes & FILE_ATTRIBUTE_ARCHIVE) != 0 && !⇐
    CheckBox3->Checked)
      continue ;

    // Display the file name.
    TListItem *li = ListView1->Items->Add () ;
    li->Caption = directory + filedata.cFileName ;

    // Display the file size.
    if (filedata.nFileSizeHigh == 0)
    {
      li->SubItems->Add (String ((int) ((filedata.nFileSizeLow +⇐
      1023)/1024)) + " K") ;
    }
    else
    {
      // If nFileSizeHigh is non-zero then this is a **HUGE** file.
      double filesize = (MAXDWORD * filedata.nFileSizeHigh) +
filedata.nFileSizeLow ;
      li->SubItems->Add (String (filesize / 1024.0) + " K") ;
    }

    // Display the MS-DOS name for the file.
    li->SubItems->Add (String (filedata.cAlternateFileName)) ;

    Application->ProcessMessages () ;

  } while (FindNextFile (filehandle, &filedata)) ;
  FindClose (filehandle) ;
}

// Pass 2 - Search for all the subdirectories within this directory
String dir = directory + "*.*" ;
filehandle = FindFirstFile ((directory + "*.*").c_str (), &filedata) ;
if (filehandle != INVALID_HANDLE_VALUE)
{
  do
  {
    if ((filedata.dwFileAttributes & FILE_ATTRIBUTE_DIRECTORY) != 0
        && String (filedata.cFileName) != "."
        && String (filedata.cFileName) != "..")
    {
```

```
    if ((filedata.dwFileAttributes & FILE_ATTRIBUTE_SYSTEM) != 0 && !⇐
    CheckBox1->Checked)
      continue ;
    if ((filedata.dwFileAttributes & FILE_ATTRIBUTE_HIDDEN) != 0 && !⇐
    CheckBox2->Checked)
      continue ;
    if ((filedata.dwFileAttributes & FILE_ATTRIBUTE_ARCHIVE) != 0 &&⇐
    ! CheckBox3->Checked)
      continue ;
    // Recursive call here
    FindFilesInDirectory (directory + filedata.cFileName + "\\") ;
  }

  Application->ProcessMessages () ;
  } while (FindNextFile (filehandle, &filedata)) ;
  FindClose (filehandle) ;
}

  Application->ProcessMessages () ;
  return ;
}
```

6. Double-click on the Search button, and add the following code to the
OnClick event:

```
void __fastcall TForm1::Button1Click(TObject *Sender)
{
  // Prevent a call to this method while one is already active.
  Button1->Enabled = false ;
  Cursor = crHourGlass ;

  ListView1->Items->Clear () ;
  // The root directory is returned from the directory list as D:\. All
  // others are returned as D:\A\B...\Z. Here we make them consistent with
  // a trailing backslash.
  String directory = DirectoryListBox1->Directory ;
  if (directory [directory.Length () - 1] != '\\')
    directory = directory + "\\" ;

  // Do the search here.
  FindFilesInDirectory (directory) ;

  // Put things back the way they were.
  Button1->Enabled = true ;
  Cursor = crDefault ;
}
```

7. Compile and test the program.

How It Works

This program uses a Drive Combo box linked to a Directory List box to select the
directory to start the file search from. The technique is the same as shown in

How-To 6.1. The only difference is that in this program a File List box is not needed.

When the Search button is clicked, it determines the starting directory for the file search, formats it, and then passes it to the `FindFilesInDirectory` function which is the core of the whole program. This function searches a directory and all its subdirectories for the file entered in the edit control. The only argument to the function is the name of the directory to search.

The `FindFirstFile` and `FindNextFile` API functions are used to search a directory for files that match a pattern that may contain wildcard characters. The `FindFirstFile` function, as the name suggests, finds the first file in a directory that matches a file specification. The arguments to this function are the file to search for (including the directory path) and the address of a `WIN32_FIND_DATA` that is used to return details about the matching files. If the `FindFirstFile` function finds a match, it returns a handle to context information for finding any other matching files in the directory.

The `FindNextFile` function finds any other matching files in the directory. The arguments to `FindNextFile` are the context handle returned by `FindFirstFile` and a pointer to a `WIN32_FIND_DATA`. The `FindNextFile` returns **true** if it finds a match and **false** if no match is found. `FindNextFile` is called repeatedly until no more matches are found. Notice that the filename is not passed to `FindNextFile`. This is because the context handle maintains the name of the file being searched for as well as the current search position in the directory. This ensures that each `FindNextFile` call will begin its search at the correct point in the directory.

Because `FindFirstFile` allocates a handle that contains resources, the handle needs to be freed when the search is complete. The `FindClose` function is used for this purpose. Its only argument is the handle allocated by `FindFirstFile`.

The trick to `FindFilesInDirectory` is that it makes two search passes through the directory. In the first pass, it searches for all the files that match the name entered in the edit control. The attributes of the matching files returned in the `dwFileAttributes` field of the `WIN32_FIND_DATA` structure are compared to the setting of the Check boxes. This allows the application to filter out file types, such as hidden files, that a user might not want displayed. The files not filtered out are displayed with a few file attributes in the List View control.

After finding the matching files in the directory, the second pass looks for all the subdirectories. This time when `FindFirstFile` is called, the search string is changed to the directory name with `*.*` appended. `FindFilesInDirectory` calls itself for each of the directories found in the search. This causes a recursive search of the directory tree so the subdirectory and all its subdirectories continue to be searched until `FindFilesInDirectory` is called for a directory with no subdirectories or all the subdirectories have been searched.

Two issues have to be dealt with in the second pass. Searching for `*.*` results in all files in the directory being returned in the search when, at this point, we are only concerned with finding directories. The method for identifying a directory is that

the `FILE_ATTRIBUTE_DIRECTORY` bit is set in the `dwFileAttributes` of the `WIN32_FIND_DATA` structure. In the second pass through the directory, all files that do not have this bit set are ignored. The `dwFileAttributes` value is also compared to the settings of the Combo boxes again so that system directories, such as the recycle bin, are screened out of the search.

The second issue is not obvious. Just like UNIX, every directory (except for the disk's root directory) contains entries for the directories "." and "..". The "." entry in a directory is a link to itself. This means that `C:\WINDOWS` and `C:\WINDOWS\.` refer to the same directory. The `..` entry in a directory is a link to a directory's parent. `C:\WINDOWS\..` and `C:\` reference the same directory. These two special directories are ignored in `FindFilesInDirectory`'s second pass because including them would result in infinite recursion. If a search began with the directory `C:\WINDOWS`, then the `FindFilesInDirectory` would eventually be calling itself with directories like `C:\WINDOWS\.\.\.\.\.` or `C:\WINDOWS\..\WINDOWS\..\WINDOWS` until either the maximum path length was reached or the program ran out of stack space.

Because searching an entire disk could be a lengthy task, the `FindFilesInDirectory` function makes frequent calls to `Application->ProcessEvents`. This allows the application to perform such tasks as repainting itself while the search is underway. A C++Builder application should generally call `ProcessEvents` when it is performing tasks that take an extended period of time.

A possibly undesirable side effect of calling `ProcessEvents` is that it allows the application's controls to operate. An application that calls `ProcessEvents` may need to disable user input. This is why the program disables the search button while a search is in progress. Otherwise, a frustrated user could cause multiple searches to be active simultaneously by repeatedly clicking on the Search button.

This application uses a List View control to display the matching files and their attributes in neat columns. The List View control is similar to the one that the Windows shell uses to display files. The `ViewStyle` property controls how the items are displayed in the control. The possible values of the `ViewStyle` property correspond to the Small Icons, Large Icons, List, and Details setting under the View menu in the Windows shell.

Comments

Searching tree structures is a common task in programming. Directory structures are the most frequently encountered example but anything that can be organized into a hierarchical structure, including insurance policies and computer programs, is often stored as trees. The main issue in searching trees is how to deal with loops such as the ones caused by ".." and "." directory entries.

The next logical extension of this program is to search all drives on an entire system. How-To 6.14 shows how to find all the disk drives on the system.

6.5 How do I...
Disable the Windows screen saver?

Problem

I have a C++Builder application that takes a while to do some processing. Occasionally the delay is long enough to allow the Windows screen saver to start. If this happens, my processing can really get slowed down. I know how to turn off the screen saver on my computer but this is a pain and is beyond the capabilities of most of my users. Is there a way I can automatically stop the screen saver from coming on while my application is running?

Technique

Windows posts a **WM_SYSCOMMAND** message to the active application prior to starting the screen saver. You can handle this message using the **OnMessage** event handler of the **TApplication** class. Returning a nonzero value in response to this message prevents the screen saver from running.

Steps

Enable the screen saver on your system and set the wait time to as small a value as possible. Run **DISABLESCREENSAVER.EXE** without clicking on the Check box. The form is shown in Figure 6-5. Time the period required for the screen saver to start. Now click on the Check box and wait again for the screen saver to start. As long as the **DISABLESCREENSAVER** application is the active program, the screen saver will not come on. Try making another program, such as Notepad, active, and see what happens.

1. Select File|New Application from the main menu to create a new blank project. Select File|Save Project As, and save the project as **DisableScreenSaver**.

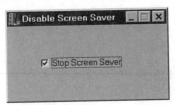

Figure 6-5 DISABLESCREENSAVER program

2. Add components and set their properties as shown in Table 6-6.

Table 6-6 Components, properties, and settings for DISABLESCREENSAVER

COMPONENT	PROPERTY	SETTING
Form1	+BorderIcons	
	-biMaximize	false
	BorderStyle	bsSingle
	Caption	Disable Screen Saver
	Height	150
	Position	poScreenCenter
	Width	27
CheckBox1	Caption	Stop Screen Saver
	Left	50
	Top	50
	Width	150

3. Go to the Code Editor; then open the file **UNIT1.H**. Add the declaration for the member function **ProcessMessage** to the definition of **TForm1**.

```
class TForm1 : public TForm
{
__published:
  TCheckBox *CheckBox1;
private:          // private user declarations
  void __fastcall ProcessMessage (TMsg &message, bool &handled) ;
public:           // public user declarations
  virtual __fastcall TForm1(TComponent* Owner);
};
```

4. Switch to the file **UNIT1.CPP**. Add the following definition of ProcessMessage to the end of the file:

```
void __fastcall TForm1::ProcessMessage (TMsg &message, bool &handled)
{
  if (message.message == WM_SYSCOMMAND
      && message.wParam == SC_SCREENSAVE
      && CheckBox1->Checked)
  {
    handled = true ;
  }
  else
  {
    handled = false ;
  }
}
```

5. Move to the top of the file **UNIT1.CPP** and add the following code to the **TForm1** constructor:

```
fastcall TForm1::TForm1(TComponent* Owner) : TForm(Owner)
{
   Application->OnMessage = ProcessMessage ;
}
```

6. Compile and test the project.

How It Works

Windows constantly watches the system for user activity, such as moving the mouse or hitting keystrokes. If the system senses no activity for a specified period of time, Windows begins to initiate the screen saver. Windows runs the screen saver by sending a **WM_SYSCOMMAND** message with the **WPARAM** parameter set to **SC_SCREENSAVE** to the active application. The default processing for this message is to start the screen saver.

You can respond to messages that are sent to your application by creating a handler for the **OnMessage** event of the **Application** object. When the **Application** object has an **OnMessage** handler, it gets called each time the **Application** receives a message and before the message gets processed. If you set the **handled** parameter to **true** after receiving a message, then no further processing occurs for the message. In this example, when the message to start the screen saver is received, the application eats it so the screen saver does not get started up.

Comments

You need to be somewhat careful when using an **OnMessage** handler for the application. If you are careless, you can get some unexpected side effects. Try creating a handler that does nothing but set **handled** to **true**. The other thing you have to watch out for is that every message sent to your application will go through this event handler, so you need to make sure that you do not add any unnecessary overhead or else your application's performance will suffer.

6.6 How do I...
Prevent multiple instances of my program from being loaded?

Problem

I have an application that will not work properly if more than one instance is running at the same time. In order to protect the user from causing a problem, I would like to prevent multiple instances of the application from being started. In 16-bit Windows I used to be able to check a previous instance value but this does not seem to work with C++Builder. How can I solve this problem?

Technique

Each 32-bit Windows application runs in its own address space so there is no concept of a previous instance of an application as in Win16. A good way to prevent more than one instance of your program from running is to use one of the Win32 API synchronization objects. One of these is called a mutex (MUTually EXclusive).

Steps

Run the program **SINGLEINSTANCE.EXE**. The first instance should run successfully. Now try to run a second instance of the program. You will get an error message, and the second instance will terminate. Figure 6-6 shows the result when you try to run more than one instance of the application.

1. Select File|New Application from the main menu to create a new blank project. Select File|Save Project As, and save the project as `SingleInstance`.

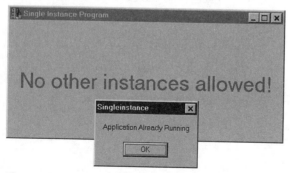

Figure 6-6 Result of multiple `SingleInstance` instances

2. Add the components, and set their properties as shown in Table 6-7.

Table 6-7 Components, properties, and settings for SINGLEINSTANCE

COMPONENT	PROPERTY	SETTING
Form1	BorderStyle	bsDialog
	Caption	Single Instance Program
	Height	250
	Position	poScreenCenter
	Width	540
Label1	Caption	No other instances allowed!
	+Font	
	−Size	24
	−Color	clRed
	Left	20
	Top	90

3. From the main menu select View|Project Source. Add the following code to WinMain in SINGLEINSTANCE.CPP:

```
WINAPI WinMain(HINSTANCE, HINSTANCE, LPSTR, int)
{
   HANDLE mutex ;
   try
   {
      const char mutexname [] = "SingleInstanceProgram" ;
      // See if the mutex already exists.
      mutex = OpenMutex (0, false, mutexname) ;
      if (mutex == NULL)
      {
         // The mutex is not there. This means another instance of the
program is
         // not already running. Create the mutex so any other instance of
the
         // program will know that this one is already running.
         mutex = CreateMutex (NULL, true, mutexname) ;
      }
      else
      {
         // The mutex exists so another instance of the program is running
         // OR some other program created a mutex called
"SingleInstanceProgram".
         ShowMessage ("Application Already Running") ;
         // Returning from WinMain terminates the program.
         return 0 ;
      }

      Application->Initialize();
```

```
    Application->CreateForm(__classid(TForm1), &Form1);
    Application->Run();
  }
  catch (Exception &exception)
  {
    Application->ShowException(&exception);
  }
  ReleaseMutex (Mutex) ;
  return 0;
}
```

4. Compile and test the project.

How It Works

When the single SINGLEINSTANCE program starts, the first thing it does is attempt to access the mutex called "SingleInstanceProgram" using the OpenMutex API function. The mutex name argument is case-sensitive and is global to all applications running on the system. The return value of OpenMutex is a handle to the mutex. If the mutex cannot be opened, the return value is NULL.

If the SingleInstance cannot open the mutex, this means another instance is not already running. The program immediately creates a mutex with the CreateMutex function. If another instance of the program is run, the OpenMutex function will succeed, and the program will terminate.

Comments

Mutexes are used to restrict access to a shared resource to one thread of execution. In this case, the resource is the application itself. We could have used any global object, even a file, in place of the mutex. A mutex is convenient in this instance, because it is easy to create and destroy. If you wanted to limit an application to a fixed number of instances, then you could use a semaphore in place of the mutex.

COMPLEXITY
BEGINNING

6.7 How do I...
Determine the directory where Windows is located?

Problem

During the start up phase of one of my C++Builder applications I need to determine whether certain files exist. These files are normally located in the C:\WINDOWS and C:\WINDOWS\SYSTEM directories but, if the operating system has not been installed with the default settings, these directories could have different names. How can I find where the operating system is without searching the entire disk drive?

Technique

The Win32 API contains the functions `GetWindowsDirectory` and `GetSystemDirectory` that return the path to the WINDOWS and SYSTEM directories.

Steps

Run the program WINDOWSDIRECTORY.EXE. It should correctly display the locations of your WINDOWS and SYSTEM directories as shown in Figure 6-7.

1. Select File|New Application from the main menu to create a new blank project. Select File|Save Project As, and save the project as WindowsDirectory.

2. Add the components, and set their properties as shown in Table 6-8.

Table 6-8 Components, properties, and settings for WINDOWSDIRECTORY

COMPONENT	PROPERTY	SETTING
Form1	BorderStyle	bsDialog
	Caption	Windows Directories
	Height	250
	Position	poScreenCenter
	Width	300
Label1	Autosize	true
	Left	
	Top	10
Label2	Autosize	true
	Left	10
	Top	40

3. Double-click on the form to display the Code Editor. Add the following to the `FormCreate` member function of the form:

```
void __fastcall TForm1::FormCreate(TObject *Sender)
{
  String path ;
  path.SetLength (MAX_PATH) ;
  path.SetLength (GetWindowsDirectory (path.c_str (), path.Length ())) ;
  Label1->Caption = String ("Windows Directory:  ") + path ;
  path.SetLength (MAX_PATH) ;
  path.SetLength (GetSystemDirectory (path.c_str (), path.Length ())) ;
  Label2->Caption = String ("System Directory:  ") + path ;
}
```

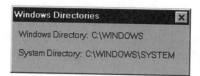

Figure 6-7 WINDOWSDIRECTORY
program

4. Compile and test the program.

How It Works

The GetWindowsDirectory and the GetSystemDirectory API functions return
the path of the WINDOWS and SYSTEM directories. The arguments to these functions
are the address of the buffer to return the directory path and the size of the buffer.
The return value of these functions is the length of the string returned. The application uses the return value in a call to the String member function SetLength
to adjust the length of the string's internal length. See How-To 2.1 for more information on using the String type.

Comments

While on most computers the WINDOWS and SYSTEM directories are in their traditional locations, it is not uncommon, especially among networked systems, to have
WINDOWS or SYSTEM directories in a different, possibly remote, location. It is best
not to assume the locations of these directories.

COMPLEXITY
ADVANCED

6.8 How do I...
Determine how much system memory is available?

Problem

I know that available memory is one of the most important factors in system performance. How can I tell how much memory is available on my system and how much
is being used?

Technique

The Win32 API function **GlobalMemoryStatus** is used to determine memory usage. By using a Timer control, the memory status of the system can be updated regularly.

Steps

Run the program **MEMORY.EXE**. The appearance of this program is shown in Figure 6-8. Try loading a large program like a word processor or compiler while it is running, and see how the values change.

1. Select File|New Application from the main menu to create a new blank project. Select File|Save Project As, and save the project as **Memory**.

2. Add components and set their properties as shown in Table 6-9.

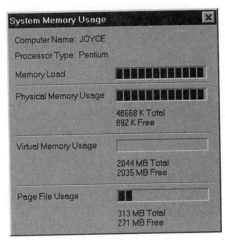

Figure 6-8 MEMORY application

Table 6-9 Components, properties, and settings for MEMORY

COMPONENT	PROPERTY	SETTING
Form1	BorderStyle	bsDialog
	Caption	System Memory Usage
	Height	360
	Position	poScreenCenter
	Width	350
Label1	Caption	Memory Load
	Left	10
	Top	65
Label2	Caption	Physical Memory Usage
	Left	10
	Top	100
Label3	Caption	Virtual Memory Usage
	Left	10
	Top	180
Label4	Caption	Page File Usage
	Left	10
	Top	260
Label5	Left	10
	Top	10
Label6	Left	10
	Top	35
Label7	Left	175
	Top	130
Label8	Left	175
	Top	145
Label9	Left	175
	Top	210
Label10	Left	175
	Top	225
Label11	Left	175
	Top	290
Label12	Left	175
	Top	305
Timer1	Enabled	true
	Interval	1000

continued on next page

continued from previous page

COMPONENT	PROPERTY	SETTING
TProgressBar1	Height	20
	Left	175
	Width	150
	Top	65
TProgressBar2	Height	20
	Left	175
	Top	100
	Width	150
TProgressBar3	Height	120
	Left	175
	Top	180
	Width	150
TProgressBar4	Height	20
	Left	175
	Top	260
	Width	150
Bevel1	Height	5
	Left	10
	Shape	bsTopLine
	Top	90
	Width	320
Bevel2	Height	5
	Left	10
	Shape	bsTopLine
	Top	170
	Width	320
Bevel3	Height	5
	Left	10
	Shape	bsTopLine
	Top	250
	Width	320

3. Select the Code Editor; then, open the file **UNIT1.H**. Add the declaration of the member function **UpdateUsage** to the definition of **TForm1** as shown below:

```
class TForm1 : public TForm
{
__published: // IDE-managed Components
```

```
    TLabel  *Label1;
    TLabel  *Label2;
    TLabel  *Label3;
    TLabel  *Label4;
    TLabel  *Label5;
    TLabel  *Label6;
    TLabel  *Label7;
    TLabel  *Label8;
    TLabel  *Label9;
    TLabel  *Label10;
    TLabel  *Label11;
    TLabel  *Label12;
    TTimer  *Timer1;
    TProgressBar  *ProgressBar1;
    TProgressBar  *ProgressBar2;
    TProgressBar  *ProgressBar3;
    TProgressBar  *ProgressBar4;
private:   // User declarations
    void UpdateUsage () ;
public:   // User declarations
    __fastcall TForm1(TComponent* Owner);
};
```

4. Switch to the file UNIT1.CPP and add the definition of the UpdateUsage member function to the end of the file as shown below:

```
void TForm1::UpdateUsage ()
{
  MEMORYSTATUS memory ;

  memory.dwLength = sizeof (memory) ;
  GlobalMemoryStatus (&memory) ;

  ProgressBar1->Position = (float) memory.dwMemoryLoad ;

  // Physical Memory Usage
  ProgressBar2->Position = 100.0 * (memory.dwTotalPhys -⇐
  memory.dwAvailPhys) /
                                    (float) memory.dwTotalPhys ;

  Label7->Caption = String ((int) (memory.dwTotalPhys / 1024)) + ⇐
  " K Total" ;

  Label8->Caption = String ((int) (memory.dwAvailPhys / 1024))
                        + " K Free" ;

  // Virtual Memory Usage
  ProgressBar3->Position =
    100.0 * (memory.dwTotalVirtual - memory.dwAvailVirtual)/
                (float) memory.dwTotalVirtual ;

  Label9->Caption = String ((int) (memory.dwTotalVirtual /  1048576.0))
                        + " MB Total" ;
```

continued on next page

continued from previous page

```
   Label10->Caption = String ((int) (memory.dwAvailVirtual /  1048576.0))
                     + " MB Free" ;

   // Page File Usage
   ProgressBar4->Position =
     100.0 * (memory.dwTotalPageFile - memory.dwAvailPageFile) /
       (float) memory.dwTotalPageFile ;

   Label11->Caption = String ((int) (memory.dwTotalPageFile /  1048576.0))
                     + " MB Total" ;

   Label12->Caption = String ((int) (memory.dwAvailPageFile /  1048576.0))
                     + " MB Free" ;
}
```

5. Select the application's main form, and double-click on it to create a handler for the **OnCreate** event. Add the following code to the event handler:

```
void __fastcall TForm1::FormCreate(TObject *Sender)
{
  // Get the system name
  String computername ;
  computername .SetLength (MAX_COMPUTERNAME_LENGTH + 1) ;
  DWORD size ;
  size = computername.Length () ;
  if (GetComputerName (computername.c_str (), &size))
    Label5->Caption = String ("Computer Name:  ") + computername ;
  else
    Label5->Caption = "Computer Name:  Unavailable" ;

  // Get the processor type
  SYSTEM_INFO systeminfo ;
  GetSystemInfo (&systeminfo) ;
  switch (systeminfo.dwProcessorType)
  {
  case PROCESSOR_INTEL_386:
    Label6->Caption = "Processor Type:   i386" ;
    break ;
  case PROCESSOR_INTEL_486:
    Label6->Caption = "Processor Type:   i486" ;
    break ;
  case PROCESSOR_INTEL_PENTIUM:
    Label6->Caption = "Processor Type:   Pentium" ;
    break ;
  case PROCESSOR_MIPS_R4000:
    Label6->Caption = "Processor Type:   MIPS" ;
    break ;
  case PROCESSOR_ALPHA_21064:
    Label6->Caption = "Processor Type:   Alpha" ;
    break ;
  default:
    Label6->Caption = "Processor Type:   Unknown" ;
    break ;
  }
  // Display the memory usage.
  UpdateUsage () ;
}
```

6. Return to the form, and double-click on the Timer control to add an `OnTimer` event handler. Add the following code to the handler:

```
void __fastcall TForm1::Timer1Timer(TObject *Sender)
{
   UpdateUsage () ;
}
```

7. Compile and test the program.

How It Works

Basic information about the system is displayed in the main form's `OnCreate` event. The first thing it does is call the `GetComputerName` Win32 API to retrieve the computer name. This function has two arguments: the address of a buffer to store the computer name and the address of a `DWORD` containing the size of the buffer. You have to pass the address of the size parameter because `GetComputerName` overwrites this value with the length of the computer name.

Next, it calls the Win32 API function `GetSystemInfo` in order to determine the processor type. The only argument to `GetSystemInfo` is the address of a `SYSTEM_INFO` structure. This structure contains several fields that hold information about such system details as the number of processors and the system page size. The only field the `MEMORY` program uses is `dwProcessorType`, which contains a code for the processor type. The program translates this code to a string and then displays it in a label.

Before returning, `FormCreate` calls the `UpdateUsage` function to display memory details. `UpdateUsage` calls the API function `GlobalMemoryStatus` to get details about the current memory usage. The only parameter to this function is the address of a `MEMORYSTATUS` structure, with the `dwLength` field initialized to the size of the structure, which is used to return the information.

The rest of the `UpdateUsage` function is involved with formatting the information that is returned. The first piece of information displayed is the memory load returned in the `dwMemoryLoad` field. This is a value from 0 to 100, which is supposed to give a rough idea of the current memory usage.

The next piece of information is the amount of physical memory installed on the machine. The `dwTotalPhys` and `dwAvailPhys` fields return the amount of memory installed on the system and the amount that is free. These values are the most important ones for gaining an idea of what is going on in a system.

The `dwTotalVirtual` and `dwAvailVirtual` fields return information about the amount of user-mode virtual memory. Because Win32 uses 32-bit addressing, these values will be much larger (unless you have a mighty powerful system) than the amount of physical memory. The virtual address space size will not be 2^{32} because the system divides virtual memory between kernel mode and user mode and these values only deal with user mode.

Finally the `dwTotalPageFile` and `dwAvailPageFile` fields return information about page file usage. The `dwTotalPageFile` field returns the total number of bytes that can be stored in the page file and `dwAvailPage` file is the number of additional bytes that can be stored in the page file. Because the size of the page file can change, these values do not reflect the physical size of the file but the size of the paging disk.

The application uses a timer control to get a regular update of the memory state on the system. The timer control's `OnTimer` event gets called at the interval specified by the `Interval` property in milliseconds. The `MEMORY` application has this value set at 1000 so the `OnTimer` event gets called every second. The `OnTimer` event handler for this program simply calls the `UpdateUsage` member function to redisplay the memory status.

Comments

This How-To demonstrates how to get a great deal of information about a system in addition to memory usage. To get more information about a system, you might want to look at the other information returned by the `GetSystemInfo` or at some of the other system information API functions.

The most useful pieces of information returned by `GlobalMemoryState` are the physical memory usage and the page file usage. If there is very little page file space available, then it is probably time to do some cleaning up on the system disk. If your system is running slowly, and there is very little physical memory, it may be time for a hardware upgrade.

COMPLEXITY
BEGINNING

6.9 How do I...
Determine what version of Windows is running?

Problem

My application is supposed to run on all 32-bit Windows platforms but there is Windows 95, Windows NT, and even Win32s. On top of that, there are multiple versions of each and there are serious incompatibilities among them. There seems to be a new version of NT out every week. When a user reports a problem, I need to know exactly what version of Windows is being used. How can I create a form that will tell the user what version of Windows is running?

Technique

The Win32 API function `GetVersionEx` returns detailed information about the operating system version in use. By interpreting the information returned by this function, you can determine the exact version of the operating system your program is running on.

Steps

Run the program `WINDOWSVERSION.EXE`. It should look similar to Figure 6-9. The four labels contain the name of the operating system, the major and minor version numbers, the build number, and a string of system information that, in this case, is empty.

1. Select File|New Application from the main menu to create a new blank project. Select File|Save Project As and save the project as `WindowsVersion`.

2. Add the components and set their properties as shown in Table 6-10.

Table 6-10 Components, properties, and settings for `WINDOWSVERSION`

COMPONENT	PROPERTY	SETTING
Form1	BorderStyle	bsxDialog
	Caption	Windows Version
	Height	125
	Position	poScreenCenter
	Width	230
Label1	Left	10
	Top	10
Label2	Left	10
	Top	30
Label3	Left	10
	Top	50
Label4	Left	10
	Top	70

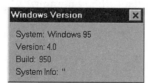

Figure 6-9 The `WINDOWSVERSION` application displaying the operating system version

3. Double-click on the application's main form to create a handler for the
`OnCreate` event. Add the following code to the event handler in
`UNIT1.CPP`:

```
void __fastcall TForm1::FormCreate(TObject *Sender)
{
  OSVERSIONINFO info ;
  info.dwOSVersionInfoSize = sizeof (info) ;
  GetVersionEx (&info) ;

  switch (info.dwPlatformId)
  {
  case VER_PLATFORM_WIN32s:
    Label1->Caption = "System:   Windows Win 32s" ;
    break ;
  case VER_PLATFORM_WIN32_WINDOWS:
    Label1->Caption = "System:   Windows 95" ;
    break ;
  case VER_PLATFORM_WIN32_NT:
    Label1->Caption = "System:   Windows NT" ;
    break ;
  default:
    Label1->Caption = "System:   Unknown" ;
    break ;
  }

  Label2->Caption = String ("Version: ")
    + String ((int) info.dwMajorVersion) + "." +⇐
    String((int)info.dwMinorVersion) ;
  Label3->Caption = String ("Build:   ") + String ((int) ⇐
  (info.dwBuildNumber & 0xFFFF)) ;
  Label4->Caption = String ("System Info:  '") + info.szCSDVersion + "'" ;
}
```

4. Compile and test the program.

How It Works

The `GetVersionEx` function returns information about the operating system version running in an `OSVERSIONINFO` structure. The highest level of differentiation
is the product (NT, Windows 95, or Win32s). The next division is the major and
minor version numbers. In "Windows 3.1" the major version number is 3 and the
minor version is 1. Finally there is something called the build number. Presumably
the build number is incremented each time the operating system is rebuilt with major
and minor versions being assigned to a particular build number.

Comments

Notice that the version number of Windows 95 is 4.0. One thing that may complicate your task in the future is the relatively new trend of assigning year numbers to products rather than version numbers. If the version field is "8.0", your application will have no way to display the version number. Does "8.0" mean Windows 8.0 or is it Windows 20 or even Windows 25? The world would be a better place with fewer marketing people.

COMPLEXITY

ADVANCED

6.10 How do I...
Display an icon in the Windows tray?

Problem

Many applications, such as Norton AntiVirus, place an icon in the "tray" at the right or bottom of the taskbar. Tray icons let the user know that a background program is running and provide a quick way to change system settings. How can I create a C++Builder application with its taskbar icon located in the tray?

Technique

The "tray" is technically known as the "Taskbar Notification Area." Because this part of the taskbar remains visible even when the other icons are scrolled, an application can place an icon in this area to notify the user of some event or to provide for an icon that should always remain visible.

The `Shell_NotifyIcon` function adds, deletes, or modifies icons in the tray. The icon can be set up so the Windows shell will send the application notification of mouse events that occur when the mouse is placed over the icon. This allows the application to know, for example, when the user clicks on the icon in the tray.

Steps

Run `ICONTRAY.EXE`. The window for this application will not be visible. The application's icon will be visible in the icon tray as shown in Figure 6-10. If you place the mouse pointer on the application's icon and let it remain there for a few seconds, you will see the amount of free physical memory displayed in a tip window. To close the application, double-click on its icon in the tray.

1. Select File|New Application from the main menu to create a new blank project. Select File|Save Project As, and save the project as `IconTray`.

2. Add the components and set their properties as shown in Table 6-11.

Figure 6-10 The
ICONTRAY program in
the notification area

Table 6-11 Components, properties, and settings for ICONTRAY

COMPONENT	PROPERTY	SETTING
Timer1	Enabled	true
	Interval	1000

3. Go to the Code Editor; then select File|Open from the C++Builder main menu. Open the file UNIT1.H and add these declarations to the definition of TForm1:

```
class TForm1 : public TForm
{
__published: // IDE-managed Components
  TTimer *Timer1;
private: // User declarations
  unsigned int iconmessage ;
  void AddTrayIcon () ;
  void RemoveTrayIcon () ;
protected:
  virtual void __fastcall WndProc(Messages::TMessage &Message) ;
public:  // User declarations
  __fastcall TForm1(TComponent* Owner);
};
```

4. Switch to the file UNIT1.CPP. Move to the top of the file, and add the shellapi header file.

```
#include <vcl\vcl.h>
#include <shellapi.h>
#pragma hdrstop

#include "unit1.h"
```

5. Using the Code Editor, add these definitions of `AddTrayIcon`, `RemoveTrayIcon`, and `WndProc` to `UNIT1.CPP`:

```
void TForm1::AddTrayIcon ()
{
  // This function adds an icon to the tray.

  // Initialize the structure for Sell_NotifyIcon
  NOTIFYICONDATA icondata ;
  memset (&icondata, 0, sizeof (icondata)) ;
  icondata.cbSize = sizeof (icondata) ;

  icondata.hWnd = Handle ;   // Handle of the window to receive notification
  // Set up the Tip displayed when the mouse is over the icon.
  strncpy (icondata.szTip, "Time Unknown", sizeof (icondata.szTip)) ;
  // Use the application's icon for the tray.
  icondata.hIcon = Application->Icon->Handle ;
  // Tell the shell the value to use for the notification message.
  icondata.uCallbackMessage = iconmessage ;
  // Tell what we are modifying (everything in this case).
  icondata.uFlags = NIF_MESSAGE | NIF_ICON | NIF_TIP ;
  // Add the icon.
  Shell_NotifyIcon (NIM_ADD, &icondata) ;
}
void TForm1::RemoveTrayIcon ()
{
  // This function removes the icon from the tray.
  NOTIFYICONDATA icondata ;
  memset (&icondata, 0, sizeof (icondata)) ;
  icondata.cbSize = sizeof (icondata) ;

  icondata.hWnd = Handle ;
  Shell_NotifyIcon (NIM_DELETE, &icondata) ;
}

void __fastcall TForm1::WndProc(Messages::TMessage &Message)
{
  // If the window receives a notification message from the shell, then
  // pass it to the ProcessIconMessage function. Otherwise, let the default
  // processing for the message take place.
  if (Message.Msg == iconmessage)
  {
    if (Message.LParam == WM_LBUTTONDBLCLK)
    {
      Application->Terminate () ;
    }
    return ;
  }
  TForm::WndProc (Message) ;
}
```

6. Go to the application's main form, and double-click on it to create a handler for the **OnCreate** event. Modify the handler to look like this:

```
void __fastcall TForm1::FormCreate(TObject *Sender)
{
  // Create a unique message number.
  iconmessage = RegisterWindowMessage ("IconNotify") ;

  AddTrayIcon () ;
}
```

7. Select the main form in the form designer; then, press F11 to display the Object Inspector. Go to the Events page. Double-click on the value for the **OnDestroy** event to create a handler for it. Add the following code to the **OnDestroy** handler in **UNIT1.CPP**:

```
void __fastcall TForm1::FormDestroy(TObject *Sender)
{
  RemoveTrayIcon () ;
}
```

8. Double-click on the Timer control on the main form to create a handler for the control's **OnTimer** event. Add the following code to the event handler:

```
void __fastcall TForm1::Timer1Timer(TObject *Sender)
{
  ModifyTrayIcon () ;
}
```

9. Select View|Project Source from the C++Builder menu. This displays the file **ICONTRAY.CPP** in the Code Editor. Modify **WinMain** in **ICONTRAY.CPP** so that it looks like this:

```
WINAPI WinMain(HINSTANCE, HINSTANCE, LPSTR, int)
{
  try
  {
    Application->Initialize();
    ShowWindow (Application->Handle, SW_HIDE);
    Application->ShowMainForm = false ;
    Application->CreateForm(__classid(TForm1), &Form1);
    Application->Run();
  }
  catch (Exception &exception)
  {
    Application->ShowException(&exception);
  }
  return 0;
}
```

10. Compile and test this project.

How It Works

In addition to creating an icon in the tray, this How-To demonstrates how to remove an application's icon from the taskbar and how to subclass a VCL object by overriding its **WinProc** virtual function.

Like most applications that display an icon in the tray the entire time they run, the **IconTray** application does not display an icon in the taskbar. The code for removing the application's icon from the taskbar is in the **WinMain** function in **ICON-TRAY.CPP**. The call to **ShowWindow** with the **SW_HIDE** parameter hides the icon. The next line, where the application's **ShowMainWindow** is set to **false**, prevents the main window from getting displayed.

The application in How-To 1.6 used the **SetWindowLong** function to subclass the client window of an MDI form. The **IconTray** application, in effect, subclasses the **TForm** class by overriding the **WndProc** function in the **TForm1** class. All VCL classes that descend from **TWinControl** have a **WndProc** function. This function is called to dispatch the messages that the control's associated window receives. The **WndProc** function is defined as a virtual function so that a descendant class can define its own **WndProc** function to replace the one defined by an ancestor class. The MDI client window does not have an associated VCL class so it does not have a **WndProc** function to override. This is why the example in How-To 1.6 was forced to use the more complicated method of calling **SetWindowLong**.

The general flow of a new **WndProc** function should be very similar to a window function set up by **SetWindowLong**. It should only handle those messages where special processing needs to be added. The direct ancestor's **WndProc** should be called to process the remaining messages (which should be the vast majority).

The reason this application goes through the trouble of subclassing is that the Window shell notifies the application of mouse events for its tray icon by sending a message to the application. What is unusual when you create a tray icon is that the application defines the value of the notification message rather than the system. The shell usage is the value the application selects to notify it of events in the notification area.

There are a couple of legal ways to select your own message value. The system does not define any messages with values greater than **WM_USER**. We could have picked one of these values to use for the message. This would have allowed us to use a message map (see How-To 6.12) instead of overriding **WndProc**. The problem is, if you have an application with a large number of components and third-party tools picking message numbers, you could get a conflict.

The **ICONTRAY** program gets a message number by calling **RegisterWindowMessage** in the **FormCreate** function. This API function creates a unique message number so the application can be certain of having no conflicts.

After creating the message number, **FormCreate** calls **AddTrayIcon** to add an icon to the tray. The **Shell_NotifyIcon** function maintains icons in the tray. Its only parameters are a constant to tell the operation to be performed (**NIM_ADD**, **NIM_MODIFY**, or **NIM_DELETE**) and a **NOTIFYICONDATA** structure.

The cbSize field in the NOTIFYICONDATA structure has to be initialized with the size of the structure and the handle of the associated window has to be stored in the hWnd field. The rest of the fields are optional. The other information fields used here are the icon (hIcon) to be displayed, a tip string (szTip), and the notification message number (uCallbackMessage). The uFlags field is used to identify the fields that have values to be changed.

The Timer control is set to trigger an OnTimer event every second. The event handler calls ModifyTray icon. This function calls Shell_NotifyIcon using the value NIM_MODIFY to update the tip string with the amount of free physical memory. How-To 6.8 has more information on how to determine memory usage on a system.

The WndProc that TForm1 sets up checks for the notify message and calls ProcessIconMessage when it receives one. The LPARAM value of the notify message contains a message code for the mouse event and the WPARAM value contains the value of uID field in the NOTIFYICONDATA structure. ProcessIconMessage terminates the application when the user double-clicks on the icon.

The FormDestroy member function calls Shell_NotifyIcon to remove the icon from the tray. If your application terminates without removing the icon, the icon remains in the tray, so be sure to clean up after yourself.

Comments

This How-To demonstrates most of the features of the Shell_NotifyIcon function other than using the uID field of the NOTIFYICONDATA structure to process messages from more than one icon in the tray. The icon tray is the proper place to put icons that must be displayed at all times and to provide notification about events. You should be conservative about placing icons in the tray. Far too many applications put icons in the tray that do not really need to be there.

COMPLEXITY
INTERMEDIATE

6.11 How do I...

Find and set environment variables?

Problem

For the most part, environment variables have been replaced by the Registry. There are some cases, most notably the PATH, where environment variables are still used. How can I find and change the definitions of environment variables from a C++Builder application?

Technique

It is easy to set and retrieve the value of an environment variable using the API functions GetEnvironmentVariable and SetEnvironmentVariable. The GetEnvironmentStrings function returns all the environment strings that have been defined for the application.

Steps

Run the program ENVIRONMENT.EXE. A sample screen is shown in Figure 6-11. When you select an environment variable from the List Box control, its value is displayed in the Edit control. Try editing a value, and, then, click on the Change button to update the variable's value.

1. Select File|New Application from the main menu to create a new blank project. Select File|Save Project As, and save the project as Environment.

2. Add the components, and set their properties as shown in Table 6-12.

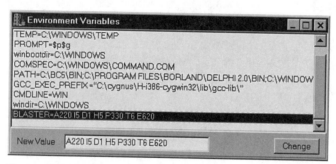

Figure 6-11 ENVIRONMENT application

Table 6-12 Components, properties, and settings for ENVIRONMENT

COMPONENT	PROPERTY	SETTING
Form1	Caption	Environment Variables
	Position	poDefault
Panel1	Align	alBottom
	Caption	
	Height	40
Panel2 (On Panel1)	Align	alLeft
	BevelOuter	bvNone
	Caption	
	Width	350
Label1 (On Panel1)	Caption	New Value
	Left	10
	Top	12
Edit1 (On Panel1)	Height	24
	Left	90
	Text	
	Top	8
	Width	240
Panel3 (On Panel1)	Align	alRight
	BevelOuter	bvNone
	Caption	
	Width	95
Button1 (On Panel3)	Caption	Change
	Enabled	false
	Height	25
	Left	10
	Top	8
	Width	75
ListBox1	Align	alClient

3. Go to the Code Editor, then select File|Open from the C++Builder main menu. Open the file **UNIT1.H** and add the following declarations to the definition of **TForm1**:

```
class TForm1 : public TForm
{
__published: // IDE-managed Components
  TPanel *Panel1;
  TLabel *Label1;
  TEdit *Edit1;
```

```
    TButton *Button1;
    TListBox *ListBox1;
private: // User declarations
    void DisplayEnvironment () ;
    String CurrentSymbol () ;
public:  // User declarations
    __fastcall TForm1(TComponent* Owner);
};
```

4. Switch to the file UNIT1.CPP in the Code Editor, and add the following definition of the DisplayEnvironment and CurrentSymbol member functions:

```
void TForm1::DisplayEnvironment ()
{
  ListBox1->Items->Clear () ;
  char *strings = GetEnvironmentStrings () ;
  for (int index = 0 ; strings [index] != 0 ; index += strlen (&strings⇐
  [index]) + 1)
    ListBox1->Items->Add (&strings [index]) ;

  FreeEnvironmentStrings (strings) ;
}
String TForm1::CurrentSymbol ()
{
  if (ListBox1->ItemIndex < 0)
    return "" ;

  String result = ListBox1->Items->Names [ListBox1->ItemIndex] ;
  return result ;
}
```

5. Return to the main form, and double-click on the List box control to create an OnClick event handler. Modify the OnClick handler in UNIT1.CPP to look like this:

```
void __fastcall TForm1::ListBox1Click(TObject *Sender)
{
  String symbol = CurrentSymbol () ;
  const int valuesize = 512 ;
  String value ;
  value.SetLength (valuesize) ;
  int length = GetEnvironmentVariable (symbol.c_str (), value.c_str (),⇐
  valuesize) ;
  value.SetLength (length) ;
  Edit1->Text = value ;
  Button1->Enabled = True ;
}
```

6. Compile and test the project.

How It Works

The `DisplayEnvironment` member function displays the definitions of all the process's environment variables. It calls the API function `GetEnvironmentStrings` to allocate a buffer that contains all the definitions. The layout of the data returned by `GetEnvironmentStrings` is shown in Figure 6-12. The environment strings are stored as a sequence of null-terminated strings. The last string in the sequence contains two null characters in sequence.

The environment strings are separated and added to the List box in the for loop. On iteration of the loop, the value of `index` is set to the offset of the first character of an environment string within the buffer referenced by the variable string.

The `GetEnvironmentStrings` function allocates memory to hold the data returned. The `FreeEnvironmentStrings` function is used to free these resources.

When the user clicks on an entry in the List box, the `OnClick` handler calls the function `CurrentSymbol` to return the symbol name for the line that is selected. This function only returns the characters up to the equal sign in the string. We could have done this using `ListBox1->Items->Strings [index]` but the `Items` property is a `TStrings` object which has the `Names` property that does just what we want. The `Names` property returns the part of the string up to the equal sign.

Next, the List box's `OnClick` calls the API function `GetEnvironmentVariable` to return the environment variable's value. The parameters to this function are the name of the variable, a buffer for the value to be returned in, and the size of the buffer. The function return value is the number of characters in the variable's value. After getting the value of the symbol, it is displayed in the Edit box so the user can modify it.

When the button is clicked to update the value of a variable, the `OnClick` event handler is called. The event handler calls the `SetEnvironmentVariable` API function to change the variable's value. This function's two parameters are the name of the variable and the new value for the variable. After the value is set, the `DisplayEnvironment` member function is called to update the list with the current environment values.

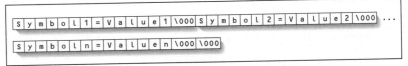

Figure 6-12 Format of data returned by `GetEnvironmentStrings`

Comments

This application only allows you to update the values of existing environment variables but not to create new ones. You could easily modify it to create new environment variables because the `SetEnvironmentVariable` function can create new variables as well as update existing ones. When an application modifies or creates an environment variable using `SetEnvironmentVariable`, the change only applies to the current process. The environment for the other processes on the system remains the same.

In the List box's `OnClick` handler, we could have used `ListBox1->Items ->Values[]` to return the value of the environment instead of calling `GetEnvironmentVariable`. We chose to demonstrate the API function because most applications are not going to have a ready-made List box full of environment variables.

COMPLEXITY
ADVANCED

6.12 How do I...
Drag and drop files?

Problem

I have an application that allows the user to view files. I would like the user to be able to view a file by dragging its icon from the desktop to my application just like Notepad and other similar programs do. How can I do this in C++Builder?

Technique

Three steps are required to implement dragging and dropping files into an application. Your application needs to call the API function `DragAcceptFiles` to tell the system that it is interested in receiving dropped files. Next, your application needs to set up a handler for the `WM_DROPFILES` message. Finally, the application needs to retrieve the names of the files that were dropped when it receives the `WM_DROPFILES` message.

Steps

Run the program `DRAGFILES.EXE`. Select the icons of one or more .TXT files, drag them over the application's main window, and drop them. A sample view of the `DRAGFILES` application is shown in Figure 6-13.

1. Select File|New Application from the main menu to create a new blank project. Select File|Save Project As, and save the project as `DragFiles`.

2. Add a main menu component to the form. Set menu items to the main menu component as shown in Table 6-13.

Table 6-13 Menu design for the DRAGFILES project

MENU	MENU ITEM	SHORTCUT
&File	E&xit	

3. Set the properties for Form1 as shown in Table 6-14.

Table 6-14 Components, properties, and settings for DRAGFILES main form

COMPONENT	PROPERTY	SETTING
Form1	Caption	Drag & Drop Files
	FormStyle	fsMDIForm
	Position	poScreenCenter
	Menu	MainMenu1

4. Select File|New Form from the main menu to create a new blank form for the project. Select File|Save from the main menu, and save the new form in the file UNIT2.CPP.

5. Add the components to the new form, and set their properties as shown in Table 6-15.

Table 6-15 Components, properties, and settings for the child form

COMPONENT	PROPERTY	SETTING
Form2	FormStyle	fsMDIChild
	Position	poDefault
RichEdit1	Align	alClient

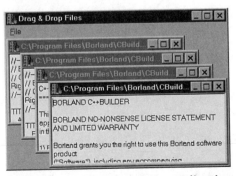

Figure 6-13 The DRAGFILES application displaying some text files dropped on it

6. Go to the Code Editor; then, select File|Open from the C++Builder main menu. Open the file **UNIT1.H** and modify the definition of **TForm1** so that it looks like the following:

```
class TForm1 : public TForm
{
__published: // IDE-managed Components
  TMainMenu *MainMenu1;
  TMenuItem *File1;
  TMenuItem *Exit1;
private: // User declarations
  void virtual __fastcall WMDropFiles (TWMDropFiles &message);
public: // User declarations
  __fastcall TForm1(TComponent* Owner);
BEGIN_MESSAGE_MAP
MESSAGE_HANDLER(WM_DROPFILES,TWMDropFiles,WMDropFiles)
END_MESSAGE_MAP (TForm) ;
};
```

7. Select the file **UNIT1.CPP** in the Code Editor window, and modify the top of the file to include the declarations for the child form.

```
#include <vcl\vcl.h>
#pragma hdrstop

#include "unit1.h"
#include "unit2.h"
```

8. Add the code for the member function **WMDropFiles** to the end of UNIT1.CPP.

```
void __fastcall TForm1::WMDropFiles (TWMDropFiles &message)
{
  // Get a count of the number of files being dropped.
  UINT filecount = DragQueryFile ((HDROP) message.Drop, 0xFFFFFFFF, NULL,⇐
  0) ;
  for (UINT ii = 0 ; ii < filecount ; ++ ii)
  {
    // Get the path of one file.
    String filename ;
    filename.SetLength (MAX_PATH) ;
    int length = DragQueryFile ((HDROP) message.Drop,
                                ii,
                                filename.c_str (), filename.Length ())
                                ;
    filename.SetLength (length) ;

    // Extract the file extension.
    String extension ;
    extension = filename.UpperCase ().SubString (filename.Length⇐
    () - 3, 4) ;
```

continued on next page

continued from previous page

```
    // Ignore all but .TXT files.
    if (extension == ".TXT")
    {
      // View the file.
      TForm2 *child = new TForm2 (Application) ;
      child->Caption = filename;
      child->RichEdit1->Lines->LoadFromFile (filename) ;
      child->Show () ;
    }
  }
  DragFinish ((HDROP) message.Drop) ;
}
```

9. Double-click on **Form1** in the Form Designer to create an **OnCreate** handler for the form. Add the following code to the event handler in the Code Editor:

```
void __fastcall TForm1::FormCreate(TObject *Sender)
{
  DragAcceptFiles (Handle, True) ;
}
```

10. Go to application's main form in the Form Designer. Click on the Exit item on the File menu to create an **OnClick** handler for the menu item. Add the code to the **OnClick** handler.

```
void __fastcall TForm1::Exit1Click(TObject *Sender)
{
  Close () ;
}
```

11. Go to Object Inspector and select **Form2** from the drop-down list at the top. Go the Events page and double-click on the value of the **OnClose** event to create a handler for it. In the Code Editor, add the following code to the **OnClose** hander in the file **UNIT2.CPP**:

```
void __fastcall TForm2::FormClose(TObject *Sender, TCloseAction &Action)
{
  Action = caFree ;
}
```

12. Select Options|Project on the C++Builder main menu, and remove **Form2** from the list of Auto-create forms.

13. Compile and test the project.

How It Works

The **OnCreate** handler for **TForm1** calls the function **DragAcceptFiles**, passing it the handle of the window that can accept dropped files and the value **True** to indicate that it can accept files. Calling this function with **False** indicates that the window no longer wants dropped files.

In the definition of **TForm1** in the file **UNIT1.H**, you set up a message handler for the **WM_DROPFILES** message by using a message map. A message map associates a message number with a member function that handles the message. A message map is placed in the definition of a window component class. It begins with an expansion of the macro **BEGIN_MESSAGE_MAP**, which has no arguments, and ends with **END_MESSAGE_MAP**. The only argument to the **END_MESSAGE_MAP** macro is the name of the parent class for the component. (Be sure not to use the class name or you will get a stack overflow.) The only things that you can put between the **BEGIN_MESSAGE_MAP** and **END_MESSAGE_MAP** are references to the **MESSAGE_HANDLER** macro.

The **MESSAGE_HANDLER** macro associates a message handler with a message number. **MESSAGE_HANDLER** has three arguments: the message number, the type of message structure that the message handler uses, and the name of the message handler function for the message number. In **TForm1**, the message map associates the **WM_DROPFILES** message with the **WMDropFiles** member function.

There are a few things to keep in mind when creating a message map.

✔ There can be only one message map per class definition.

✔ There can be only one handler per message number. (You can associate the same handler to more than one message.)

✔ The message number must be a constant.

✔ The message handler must have one argument, which must be a reference to the type specified in the **MESSAGE_MAP** macro.

✔ The message map must be placed after all the member functions it references.

With the form set up to accept dropped files, when the user drops one or more files on the main form, the application receives a **WM_DROPFILES** message that gets handled by the **WMDropFiles** method. Within the message handler, the API function **DragQueryFile** gets called to retrieve the paths for the files that have been dropped.

The first parameter for **DragQueryFile** is a handle that gets sent to the application with a **WM_DROPFILES** message. This handle serves as the link to the filenames. The second parameter specifies the index of the file to be returned. The last two parameters are the address of a buffer where **DragQueryFile** stores the file's path and the size of the buffer. The return value of the function is the length of the path. If **DragQueryFile** is called with the file index set to **0xFFFFFFFF**, the function returns the number of files that have been dropped.

The first thing that the **WMDropFiles** member function does is call **DragQueryFile** to find out how many files have been created. It then uses a **for** loop to retrieve the path to each file. The file extension is extracted and checked to see whether it is a .TXT file. (The only reason for this is to prevent binary files from being displayed.) It then creates an MDI child window and displays the file's contents in a Rich Edit control on the form. Before **WMDropFiles** exits, it calls the function **DragFinish** to free the memory resources used to store the paths to the dropped files.

Comments

In addition to showing how to drop files into an application, this How-To also demonstrates how to use a message map to add special handling for a message. It would have been possible to override the **WndProc** virtual function to intercept the message as was done in How-To 6.10, but using a message map is generally the better method to use because you can tell from looking at the class definition what the handler for a particular message is. Note, however, that we could not have used a message map in How-To 6.10 because the message value must be a constant.

COMPLEXITY
ADVANCED

6.13 How do I...
Determine which programs are running?

Problem

I am writing a program on Windows 95 that implements some features that were absent in a large software package my company bought. The program I wrote cannot be run when the software package runs. How can I tell what programs are running on my system?

Technique

The Win32 API function **CreateToolhelpSnapshot** is used to create a handle to a structure containing a "snapshot" of the processes running on the system at an instant in time. The API functions **Process32First** and **Process32Next** are used to access the individual processes within the snapshot.

Steps

Run the program **PROCESSES.EXE**. A sample image of this program is shown in Figure 6-14.

1. Select File|New Application from the main menu to create a new blank project. Select File|Save Project As, and save the project as **Processes**.

2. Add the components, and set their properties as shown in Table 6-16.

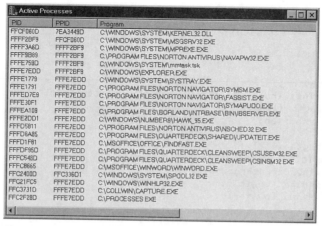

Figure 6-14 The PROCESSES program showing active processes on the system

Table 6-16 Components, properties, and settings for PROCESSES

COMPONENT	PROPERTY	SETTING
Form1	Caption	Active Processes
	Position	poDefault
ListView1	Align	alClient
	Columns	1-Caption:"PID", Width:100
		2-Caption:"PPID", Width:100
		3-Caption:"Program", Width:1000
	ViewStyle	vsReport

3. Go to the Object Inspector, and select **Form1** from the drop-down list at the top. Go to the Events page, and double-click on the value of the **OnCreate** event to create a handler for it. Add the following code to the **OnCreate** handler in the Code Editor:

```
void __fastcall TForm1::FormCreate(TObject *Sender)
{
  // Find each process and display it.
  HANDLE snapshot ;
  PROCESSENTRY32 processinfo ;
  processinfo.dwSize = sizeof (processinfo) ;
  snapshot = CreateToolhelp32Snapshot (TH32CS_SNAPPROCESS, 0) ;
  if (snapshot == NULL)
    return ;

  bool status = Process32First (snapshot, &processinfo) ;
  while (status)
```

continued on next page

continued from previous page

```
{
    TListItem *li = ListView1->Items->Add () ;

    String buffer ;
    int length ;
    buffer.SetLength (512) ;
    length = sprintf (buffer.c_str (), "%08X", processinfo.th32ProcessID) ;
    buffer.SetLength (length) ;
    li->Caption = buffer;

    buffer.SetLength (512) ;
    length = sprintf (buffer.c_str (), "%08X",⇐
    processinfo.th32ParentProcessID) ;
    buffer.SetLength (length) ;
    li->SubItems->Add (buffer) ;

    li->SubItems->Add (processinfo.szExeFile) ;

    status = Process32Next (snapshot, &processinfo) ;
    }
}
```

4. Move to the top of UNIT1.CPP, and include the file TLHELP32.H.

```
#include <vcl\vcl.h>
#include <tlhelp32.h>
#pragma hdrstop
```

5. Compile and test the program.

How It Works

The CreateToolhelp32Snapshot creates a "snapshot" of the system at the time it was called. The TH32CS_SNAPPROCESS parameter value tells the function to make a snapshot of the processes running on the system. (It is also possible to create a snapshot of threads, modules, and heaps. The second parameter is not used in a processes snapshot so it is set to zero.) The return value is a handle to the snapshot that was created. The Process32First and Process32Next functions are used to walk through the snapshot and retrieve the information about each process.

The Process32First and Process32Next functions return information about a process in a PROCESSENTRY32. The OnCreate event handler extracts the information about each process and displays it in a List View control. When there are no more processes, these functions return false.

Keep in mind that, when you create a snapshot, it reflects the state of the system when the snapshot was made. If you took a snapshot of the processes on the system, then waited 20 minutes before using Process32First and Process32Next to retrieve the process information, the data would almost certainly not reflect the state of the system. As with any other system resource, a snapshot should be freed when it is no longer needed.

Comments

This program will only run on Windows 95. It will not even load on Windows NT. The reason is that the **Process32First** and **Process32Next** functions are not available on NT so the program loader cannot resolve their addresses. It is unfortunate, but the various flavors of Windows are just as incompatible as the different versions of UNIX.

If you must create a program that can run on NT and 95 but needs a function that only exists on one system or another, you can use what is known as dynamic linking. The procedure is to use the **LoadLibrary** API function to load the DLL containing the functions you need, then use the **GetProcAddress** function to find the address where the function you wanted was loaded. You store the procedure address in a pointer to a function variable and dereference the pointer to call the function. While this does not solve the problem of system incompatibility, it does allow your program to at least run. Your application would then have to call different functions based upon the system that was running. The CD-ROM that accompanies this book contains a version of this application modified to use dynamic linking.

Imagine if you had to explicitly load the address of every API function into a pointer when your program started up. It would be a maintenance nightmare. So, in general, dynamic linking is something to avoid. Unless you have some marketing or business reason, you are probably better off simply writing your applications for one system or the other.

COMPLEXITY
ADVANCED

6.14 How do I...

Find out which disk drives are available and how much disk space there is?

Problem

I am writing a system management utility. One of the features I would like to include is a display that shows how much free disk space there is. How can I determine which disk drives are available on a system and the amount of free disk space on each?

Technique

The Windows API contains several functions that return information about the disk drives on a system. **GetLogicalDrives** returns the disk drives that are present, **GetDriveType** is used to determine the kind of device a drive letter is assigned to, **GetVolumeInformation** gets information about the file system on the disk, and **GetDiskFreeSpace** returns information about the size, layout, and available

space on a disk. By using these functions, you can create an application that can determine most of the attributes of a disk drive.

Steps

Run the program **DISKDRIVES.EXE**. Select a disk drive; then click on the Select button to view the drive details form shown in Figure 6-15. Different types of drive information are shown on the tab pages in the details form.

1. Select File|New Application from the main menu to create a new blank project. Select File|Save Project As, and save the project as **DiskDrives**.

2. Add the components, and set their properties as shown in Table 6-17.

Table 6-17 Components, properties, and settings for **DiskDrives**

COMPONENT	PROPERTY	SETTING
Form1	Position	poDefault
Panel1	Align	alBottom
	Caption	
	Height	40
Panel2 (On Panel1)	Align	alRight
	BevelOuter	bvNone
	Caption	
	Width	95
Button1 (On Panel2)	Caption	Select
	Enabled	false
	Height	25
	Left	5
	Top	8
	Width	10
ListBox1	Align	alClient

3. From the main menu select File|New Form, and create a new blank form. Save the form as **UNIT2.CPP**.

4. Add the components, and set their properties as shown in Table 6-18.

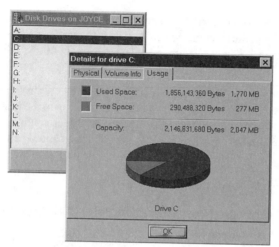

Figure 6-15 The DISKDRIVES program showing drive details

Table 6-18 Components, properties, and settings for Details

COMPONENT	PROPERTY	SETTING
Form2	BorderStyle	bsDialog
	Height	360
	Position	poScreenCenter
	Width	400
Panel1	Align	alBottom
	BevelOuter	bvNone
	Caption	
	Height	40
Button1 (On Panel1)	Caption	&OK
	Default	true
	Height	25
	Left	160
	ModalResult	mrOK
	Top	8
	Width	75
PageControl1	Align	alClient

5. Use the mouse to select the Page control. Click on the left mouse button to display the context menu. Select New Page to create a new Tab Sheet in the Page control. Repeat the process to create a total of three Tab Sheet controls.

6. Click on the first tab on the Page control; then, click on the Tab Sheet control that was brought to the top. Add the components to the first tab sheet, and set their properties as shown in Table 6-19. Be certain that you have selected the Tab Sheet control and not the Tab Page control. If you put a control on the Tab Page control, it will be visible no matter what tab is selected.

Table 6-19 Components, properties, and settings for `TabSheet1`

COMPONENT	PROPERTY	SETTING
TabSheet1	Caption	Physical
Label1	Alignment	taRightJustify
	AutoSize	false
	Caption	Drive Type:
	Left	70
	Top	10
	Width	120
Label2	Alignment	taRightJustify
	AutoSize	false
	Caption	Sectors Per Cluster:
	Left	70
	ToUp	30
	Width	120
Label3	Alignment	taRightJustify
	AutoSize	false
	Caption	Bytes Per Sector:
	Left	70
	Top	50
	Width	120
Label4	Alignment	taRightJustify
	AutoSize	false
	Caption	Clusters:
	Left	70
	Top	70
	Width	120
Label5	Left	195

COMPONENT	PROPERTY	SETTING
	Top	10
Label6	Left	195
	Top	30
Label7	Left	195
	Top	50
Label8	Left	195
	Top	70

7. Click on the second tab on the Page control; then click on the Tab Sheet control at the top. Add the components to the second Tab Sheet, and set their properties as shown in Table 6-20.

Table 6-20 Components, properties, and settings for `TabSheet2`

COMPONENT	PROPERTY	SETTING
TabSheet2	Caption	Volume Info
Label9	Alignment	taRightJustify
	AutoSize	false
	Caption	Label:
	Left	70
	Top	10
	Width	120
Label10	Alignment	taRightJustify
	AutoSize	false
	Caption	Serial Number:
	Left	70
	Top30	
	Width120	
Label11	Alignment	taRightJustify
	AutoSize	false
	Caption	File System:
	Left	70
	Top	50
	Width120	
Label12	Alignment	taRightJustify
	AutoSize	false
	Caption	Long File Names:

continued on next page

continued from previous page

COMPONENT	PROPERTY	SETTING
	Left	70
	Top	70
	Width	120
Label13	Left	195
	Top	10
Label14	Left	195
	Top	30
Label15	Left	195
	Top	50
Label16	Left	195
	Top	70

8. Click on the third tab on the Page control; then, click on the Tab Sheet control that was brought to the top. Add the components to the third Tab Sheet, and set their properties as shown in Table 6-21.

Table 6-21 Components, properties, and settings for `TabSheet3`

COMPONENT	PROPERTY	SETTING
TabSheet3	Caption	Usage
Label17	Caption	Used Space:
	Left	50
	Top	12
Label18	Caption	Free Space:
	Left	50
	Top	40
Label19	Caption	Capacity:
	Left	50
	Top	80
Label20	Alignment	taRightJustify
	AutoSize	false
	Left	140
	Top	12
	Width	160
Label21	Alignment	taRightJustify
	AutoSize	false
	Left	140

COMPONENT	PROPERTY	SETTING
	Top	40
	Width	160
Label22	Alignment	taRightJustify
	AutoSize	false
	Left	140
	Top	80
	Width	160
Label23	Alignment	taRightJustify
	AutoSize	false
	Left	305
	Top	12
	Width	60
Label24	Alignment	taRightJustify
	AutoSize	false
	Left	305
	Top	40
	Width	60
Label25	Alignment	taRightJustify
	AutoSize	false
	Left	305
	Top	80
	Width	60
Label26	Alignment	taCenter
	AutoSize	false
	Left	160
	Top	230
	Width	60
PaintBox1	Height	110
	Left	105
	Top	110
	Width	175
Bevel1	Height	5
	Left	20
	Shape	bsTopLine
	Top	70
	Width	345

continued on next page

continued from previous page

COMPONENT	PROPERTY	SETTING
Panel2	BevelInner	bvLowered
	BevelOuter	bvLowered
	Caption	
	Color	clBlue
	Height	20
	Left	20
	Top	10
	Width	20
Panel3	BevelInner	bvLowered
	BevelOuter	bvLowered
	Caption	
	Color	clFuchsia
	Height	20
	Left	20
	Top	40
	Width	20

9. Go to the Code Editor; then, select File|Open from the C++Builder main menu. Open the file **UNIT1.H**, and add the declaration of **ShowDetails** to the definition of **TForm1**.

```
class TForm1 : public TForm
{
__published: // IDE-managed Components
  TPanel *Panel1;
  TPanel *Panel2;
  TButton *Button1;
  TListBox *ListBox1;
private: // User declarations
  void ShowDetails () ;
public: // User declarations
  __fastcall TForm1(TComponent* Owner);
};
```

10. Switch to the file **UNIT1.CPP**, and include the file **UNIT2.H** at the top.

```
#include <vcl\vcl.h>
#pragma hdrstop

#include "Unit1.h"
#include "Unit2.h"
```

11. Add the definition of the member function **ShowDetails** to the end of the file UNIT1.CPP.

```
void TForm1::ShowDetails ()
{
   String drive = ListBox1->Items->Strings [ListBox1->ItemIndex] ;
   Form2->ShowDrive (drive) ;
}
```

12. Select File|Open from the main menu, and open the file UNIT2.H. Add these declarations to the definition of TForm2:

```
class TForm2 : public TForm
{
__published: // IDE-managed Components
   TPageControl *PageControl1;
   TPanel *Panel1;
   TButton *Button1;
   TTabSheet *TabSheet1;
   TTabSheet *TabSheet2;
   TTabSheet *TabSheet3;
   TLabel *Label1;
   TLabel *Label2;
   TLabel *Label3;
   TLabel *Label4;
   TLabel *Label5;
   TLabel *Label6;
   TLabel *Label7;
   TLabel *Label8;
   TLabel *Label9;
   TLabel *Label10;
   TLabel *Label11;
   TLabel *Label12;
   TLabel *Label13;
   TLabel *Label14;
   TLabel *Label15;
   TLabel *Label16;
   TPaintBox *PaintBox1;
   TLabel *Label17;
   TLabel *Label18;
   TLabel *Label19;
   TLabel *Label20;
   TLabel *Label21;
   TLabel *Label22;
   TLabel *Label23;
   TLabel *Label24;
   TLabel *Label25;
   TLabel *Label26;
   TPanel *Panel2;
   TPanel *Panel3;
   TBevel *Bevel1;
private: // User declarations
   // Saved here for use when painting
   int diskbytes ;
   int freebytes ;
```

continued on next page

continued from previous page

```
public: // User declarations
    __fastcall TForm2(TComponent* Owner);
    void ShowDrive (String &Drive) ;
};
```

13. Switch to the file UNIT2.CPP in the Code Editor. Add the definition of the functions Format3, FormatLong, and ShowDrive to the end of the file.

```
// The format Long Function converts a number to a string in the format
// 111,111,111,111. Format3 is a helper function.
static inline String Format3 (int value)
{
    String result ;
    if (value < 10)
        result = "00" + String (value) ;
    else if (value < 100)
        result = "0" + String (value) ;
    else
        result = String (value) ;
    return result ;
}

static String FormatLong (long value)
{
    int billions = value / 1000000000L ;
    int millions = (value % 1000000000) / 1000000; ;
    int thousands = (value % 1000000) / 1000 ;
    int hundreds = value % 1000 ;
    String result ;
    if (billions != 0)
        result = String (billions) + "," ;

    if (result != "")
        result += Format3 (millions) + "," ;
    else if (millions != 0)
        result = String (millions) + "," ;

    if (result != "")
        result += Format3 (thousands) + "," ;
    else if (thousands != 0)
        result = String (thousands) + "," ;

    if (result != "")
        result += Format3 (hundreds) ;
    else
        result = String (hundreds) ;

    return result ;
}

// Display Drive Information
void TForm2::ShowDrive (String &drive)
{
    Caption = String ("Details for drive ") + drive ;

    String path = drive + "\\" ;
```

```
String volume ;
volume.SetLength (256) ;
DWORD serialnumber ;
DWORD maxcomponentlength ;
DWORD flags ;
String filesystem ;
filesystem.SetLength (256) ;
if (GetVolumeInformation (path.c_str (),
                              volume.c_str (),
                              volume.Length (),
                              &serialnumber,
                              &maxcomponentlength,
                              &flags,
                              filesystem.c_str (),
                              filesystem.Length ()))
{
  Label13->Caption = volume ;
  Label14->Caption = String ((int)serialnumber) ;
  Label15->Caption = filesystem ;
  if (filesystem == "FAT" && maxcomponentlength != 255)
    Label16->Caption = "No" ;
  else
    Label16->Caption = "Yes" ;

  UINT drivetype = GetDriveType (path.c_str ()) ;
  switch (drivetype)
  {
  case 1:
    Label5->Caption = "Does not exist" ;
    break ;
  case DRIVE_REMOVABLE:
    Label5->Caption = "Removable" ;
    break ;
  case DRIVE_FIXED:
    Label5->Caption = "Fixed" ;
    break ;
  case DRIVE_REMOTE:
    Label5->Caption = "Remote" ;
    break ;
  case DRIVE_CDROM:
    Label5->Caption = "CD ROM" ;
    break ;
  case DRIVE_RAMDISK:
    Label5->Caption = "RAM Disk" ;
    break ;
  default:
    Label5->Caption = "Unknown" ;
    break ;
  }

  DWORD sectorspercluster ;
  DWORD bytespersector ;
  DWORD clusters ;
  DWORD freeclusters ;
  GetDiskFreeSpace (path.c_str (),
```

continued on next page

continued from previous page

```
                             &sectorspercluster,
                             &bytespersector,
                             &freeclusters,
                             &clusters) ;
   Label6->Caption = FormatLong (sectorspercluster) ;
   Label7->Caption = FormatLong (bytespersector) ;
   Label8->Caption = FormatLong (clusters) ;

   diskbytes = clusters * sectorspercluster * bytespersector ;
   freebytes = freeclusters * sectorspercluster * bytespersector ;
   Label20->Caption = FormatLong (diskbytes - freebytes)  + " Bytes" ;
   Label21->Caption = FormatLong (freebytes) + " Bytes" ;
   Label22->Caption = FormatLong (diskbytes) + " Bytes" ;

   Label23->Caption = FormatLong ((diskbytes - freebytes)/(1<<20))  + "⇐
MB" ;
   Label24->Caption = FormatLong (freebytes/(1<<20)) + " MB" ;
   Label25->Caption = FormatLong (diskbytes/(1<<20)) + " MB" ;

   Label26->Caption = String ("Drive ") + drive [1] ;
   ShowModal () ;
 }
 else
 {
   ShowMessage ("Can't Get Drive Information") ;
 }
}
```

14. Move to the top of the file UNIT2.CPP and include MATH.H.

```
#include <vcl\vcl.h>
#include <math.h>
#pragma hdrstop

#include "Unit2.h"
```

15. Select the application's main form then press F11 to display the Object Inspector. Select **Form1** from the drop-down list at the top. Go to the Events page and double-click on the value for the **OnCreate** event to create a handler for it. Using the Code Editor, add the following code to the body the **OnCreate** handler in UNIT1.CPP:

```
void __fastcall TForm1::FormCreate(TObject *Sender)
{
  // Create the caption for the form.
  String system ;
  DWORD length = 256 ;
  system.SetLength (length) ;
  GetComputerName (system.c_str (), &length) ;
  Caption = String ("Disk Drives on ") + system ;

  // Find the drives and see which ones are there.
  DWORD drivemask = GetLogicalDrives () ;
  for (int ii = 0 ; ii < 'Z' - 'A' ; ++ ii)
  {
```

```
    if ((drivemask & (1 << ii)) != 0)
    {
      String drive ("_:") ;
      drive [1] = (char) ('A' + ii) ;
      ListBox1->Items->Add (drive) ;
    }
  }
}
```

16. Return to `Form1` in the form designer and double-click on the List Box
control to create a handler for the `OnClick` event. Add the following code
to the `OnClick` handler:

```
void __fastcall TForm1::ListBox1Click(TObject *Sender)
{
  Button1->Enabled = true ;
}
```

17. Select the List Box control on `Form1`; then press F11 to go to the Object
Inspector. Go to the Events page; then, double-click on the value for
`OnDblClick` to create the event handler. Add the following code to the
event handler in the Code Editor:

```
void __fastcall TForm1::ListBox1DblClick(TObject *Sender)
{
  ShowDetails () ;
}
```

18. Double-click on `Button1` on `Form1` to edit the `OnClick` event handler.
Edit the handler in `UNIT1.CPP` to look like this:

```
void __fastcall TForm1::Button1Click(TObject *Sender)
{
  ShowDetails () ;
}
```

19. Use the mouse to select the Paint Box control on `Form2`'s Usage Tab Sheet
control. Press F11 to display the Object Inspector. Go to the Events page
and double-click on the value of the `OnPaint` event to create the event
handler. Add the following code to `UNIT2.CPP`:

```
void __fastcall TForm2::PaintBox1Paint(TObject *Sender)
{
  const int ydelta = 15 ;   // Space between ellipses
  const int xborder = 5 ;
  const int yborder = 5 ;

  // Ellipse Radii
  int xradius = PaintBox1->Width / 2 - xborder ;
  int yradius = PaintBox1->Height / 2 - yborder - ydelta ;

  // Center of the top ellipse
  int centerx = xborder + xradius ;
```

continued on next page

continued from previous page

```
  int centery = yborder + yradius   ;

  PaintBox1->Canvas->Pen->Style = psSolid ;
  PaintBox1->Canvas->Pen->Color = clBlack ;
  PaintBox1->Canvas->Brush->Style = bsSolid ;

  // Draw the outline for the bottom ellipse
  PaintBox1->Canvas->Arc (centerx - xradius, centery - yradius + ydelta,
                          centerx + xradius, centery + yradius + ydelta,
                          centerx - xradius, centery + ydelta,
                          centerx + xradius, centery + ydelta) ;

  // Draw the top ellipse
  PaintBox1->Canvas->Brush->Color = clFuchsia ;
  PaintBox1->Canvas->Ellipse (centerx - xradius, centery - yradius,
                              centerx + xradius, centery + yradius) ;

  // Draw the vertical lines between the ellipses
  PaintBox1->Canvas->MoveTo (centerx - xradius, centery) ;
  PaintBox1->Canvas->LineTo (centerx - xradius, centery + ydelta) ;

  PaintBox1->Canvas->MoveTo (centerx + xradius - 1, centery) ;
  PaintBox1->Canvas->LineTo (centerx + xradius - 1, centery + ydelta) ;

  // Determine how much of the ellipse is used.
  double angle = (diskbytes - freebytes)*(2.0 * M_PI)/diskbytes + M_PI ;
  int wedgex = (int) (centerx + xradius * cos (angle)) ;
  int wedgey = (int) (centery + yradius * sin (angle)) ;

  // Draw the used wedge area on the top ellipse.
  PaintBox1->Canvas->Brush->Color = clBlue ;

  // Special case of empty disk. Draw the smallest possible sliver.
  if (centerx - wedgex == xradius)
  {
    ++ wedgex ;
    -- wedgey ;
  }

  if (freebytes > 0)
  {
    PaintBox1->Canvas->Pie (centerx - xradius, centery - yradius,
                            centerx + xradius, centery + yradius,
                            wedgex, wedgey,
                            centerx - xradius, centery - 1) ;

  }
  else
  {
    PaintBox1->Canvas->Ellipse (centerx - xradius, centery - yradius,
                                centerx + xradius, centery + yradius) ;

  }
  // If not hidden draw a vertical line from the wedge on the top ellipse
to the
  // bottom ellipse.
  if (wedgey > centery || freebytes == 0)
```

```
{
    PaintBox1->Canvas->MoveTo (wedgex, wedgey) ;
    PaintBox1->Canvas->LineTo (wedgex, wedgey + ydelta) ;

    // Fill in the bottom ellipse using a shading color.
    // We are doing a poor man's FloodFill here. Unfortunately FloodFill
    // doesn't work so well when doing a partial repaint.
    PaintBox1->Canvas->Pen->Color = clPurple ;
    for (int ii = 1 ; ii < ydelta ; ++ ii)
    {
        PaintBox1->Canvas->Arc (centerx - xradius, centery - yradius + ii,
                                centerx + xradius, centery + yradius + ii,
                                centerx - xradius, centery + ii,
                                centerx + xradius, centery + ii) ;
    }

    // Fill in the used wedge using a shading color.

    PaintBox1->Canvas->Pen->Color = clNavy ;
    for (int ii = 1 ; ii < ydelta ; ++ ii)
    {
        PaintBox1->Canvas->Arc (centerx - xradius, centery - yradius + ii,
                                centerx + xradius, centery + yradius + ii,
                                wedgex, wedgey + ii,
                                centerx + xradius, centery + ii) ;
    }

}
else
{
    // Fill in the used wedge using a shading color.
    PaintBox1->Canvas->Pen->Color = clPurple ;
    for (int ii = 1 ; ii < ydelta ; ++ ii)
    {
        PaintBox1->Canvas->Arc (centerx - xradius, centery - yradius + ii,
                                centerx + xradius, centery + yradius + ii,
                                centerx - xradius, centery + ii,
                                centerx + xradius, centery + ii) ;
    }
}
}
```

20. Compile and test the project.

How It Works

Although this How-To is rather lengthy, it demonstrates how to use the drive information functions and how to display the information in an attractive manner. It also gives you a good excuse to review some trigonometry. The application that results from this How-To is a fairly close copy of the Windows 95 device properties display.

Finding the Drives on the System

The application's main form (Form1) displays the names of the disk drives that are on the system in a List box. The list of drives is created in the form's OnCreate event. The GetLogicalDrives API function is used to determine which drives are available on the system. This function returns a bit mask where each bit position corresponds to a drive letter with drive A: being bit zero. When a bit is set, the corresponding drive is available. The GetLogicalDrives returns a 32-bit DWORD so it can represent all the letters in the English alphabet.

The OnCreate event handler uses this loop:

```
DWORD drivemask = GetLogicalDrives () ;
for (int ii = 0 ; ii < 'Z' - 'A' ; ++ ii)
{
  if ((drivemask & (1 << ii)) != 0)
  {
    String drive ("_:") ;
    drive [1] = (char) ('A' + ii) ;
    ListBox1->Items->Add (drive) ;
  }
}
```

to determine which drives are present. The loop executes 26 times and uses the left shift operator (<<) to a create a bit mask for each drive letter. This bit mask is compared with the value returned by GetLogicalDrives using the bitwise And operator (&) to see whether the two bit masks are mutually exclusive. The value (X & (1<<Y)) is non-zero only when bit Y is set in X. If GetLogicalDrives were to return the value five [5 = (1<<0)|(1<<2)], it would mean that the system had disk drives assigned to letters A: and C:.

Getting the Drive Details

The ShowDetails function is called when the user clicks on the Select button or double-clicks on a drive in the List box. The ShowDetails function displays the details form (Form2). The ShowDrive member function calls several API functions to retrieve the information about the disk. Then it formats the information and displays it.

The first parameter to all the API drive information functions is a string containing the path to the root directory of the drive. This name needs to end with a backslash. If you only supply a drive letter followed by a colon (for example: "C:" instead of "C:\"), the function will succeed only if the current directory for the drive is the root. If you omit the backslash, the API will work most of the time, but your application will be more reliable if you remember to include the backslash.

The first API function called by ShowDrive is GetVolumeInformation, which returns information about the file system on the disk. This function returns a string containing the volume label, the volume serial number, the maximum component length, a set of information flags, and the name of the file system. The only value whose significance is not obvious is the maximum component length. This

value gives the only indication that a FAT file system can support long filenames. On a DOS file system, this value is 8+3 while, on a Windows 95 file system, it is 255.

The `ShowDrive` member function calls `GetDriveType` to determine what type of disk the user selected. This function returns a numeric code that identifies the drive type (for example: Fixed, Floppy, or CD-ROM). `ShowDrive` uses a `switch` statement to translate this value to a string.

The last function that `ShowDrive` uses to get information about the disk drive is `GetFreeDiskSpace`. This function returns the number of sectors per cluster, bytes per sector, clusters, and free clusters — a lot more information than the function name implies.

Disk drives are read from and written to in units called *sectors*. A sector on a disk is analogous to a byte in memory. When a disk drive is read from or written to, an entire sector is transferred. The sector size is fixed for a disk but can vary among drive types depending upon how the manufacturer designed the drive. Typically, sectors are multiples of 512 bytes.

A *cluster* is the smallest unit that can be allocated for a file on a disk drive, and its size is expressed as a number of sectors. The cluster size is determined by the file system created on the disk. The number of bytes in a cluster is the product of the number of sectors per cluster and the number of bytes per sector. By multiplying this value by either the number of clusters or free clusters, you get the number of bytes on the disk or the number of free bytes.

Drawing the Pie Chart

The last major piece of code in this project is the `OnPaint` handler for the Paint Box control. This code paints a pie chart that shows the amount of free and used space on a disk drive in a format similar to that of the properties page for a disk drive in the Windows shell. The pie chart is drawn using basic trigonometry and the `TCanvas` class's drawing methods. The `OnPaint` handler draws the pie chart using the values of the member variables `diskbytes` and `freebytes`, which are updated by the `ShowDrive` function.

In order to give the pie chart perspective, the pie chart is represented as a circle that has been rotated slightly along the X-axis to form an ellipse. The angle representing a complete path around a circle is **2o** so the angle for the pie slice representing the used disk space is

```
2o(UsedDiskSpace) / (TotalDiskSpace)
```

The `TCanvas` class's `Arc` and `Pie` member functions used to draw the pie slices require the X/Y coordinates of the points on the ellipse. The following functions translate an angle **h** to the X/Y coordinate of a point on a ellipse with its center at (X=0, Y=0):

```
X = Rx cos (h)
Y = Ry sin (h)
```

In these functions, R_x is the radius of the ellipse along the X-axis and R_y is the radius along the Y-axis. The `OnPaint` handler translates these coordinates to take

into account the fact that the origin of the ellipse is not at zero and that the reference line for the angle is at $(X=-R_x, Y=0)$ rather than $(X=R_x, Y=0)$.

The elements of the pie chart are drawn using the `Ellipse`, `Arc`, and `Pie` member functions of the `TCanvas` class. Review Chapter 5, "Graphics," for more information on how to use `TCanvas`.

Comments

Typically, a file system maintains a bitmap on the disk with one bit for each cluster on the disk used to mark which clusters are in use by files. The smaller the cluster size, the more space on the disk the bitmap occupies. Unfortunately, a major flaw with the FAT file system is that the cluster size is set based on the size of the disk partition. The cluster size for a 2GB FAT partition is 32K (2K would probably be ideal). This means that the smallest file, even an 800-byte `AUTOEXEC.BAT` file, actually takes up 32K bytes on the disk.

A possible project would be to calculate the amount of wasted space on a disk. Determine the cluster size of a disk in bytes; then, use the technique shown in How-To 6.4 to find all the files on the disk. The amount of wasted space per file is file-size % cluster-size.

Another follow-up project would be to create a program that graphically displays the percentage of a disk a given directory and all of its subdirectories occupies. You could create such a program by combining the techniques shown in this How-To with the ones shown in How-To 6.4.

CHAPTER 7
PERIPHERALS

7

PERIPHERALS

How do I...

What good would that new Pentium Pro computer on your desk be if it wasn't for its peripherals? How would you connect to the outside world? How would you produce hard-copy program listings? How would you store all those powerful C++Builder™ applications you're going to develop?

The How-To's in this chapter show you some very useful techniques for using the peripherals attached to your system. The first two deal with modems, which are among the most powerful peripherals you can connect to your computer. This chapter also provides How-To's that cover disk drives, displays, and printers.

7.1 Use the Modem to Dial a Voice Call

The modem is one of the most useful peripherals on a PC since it gives you the ability to communicate with the rest of the world. This How-To shows you just how easy it is to use the most basic function in the Telephony API (TAPI) to tell your modem to dial the phone for you.

7.2 Send and Receive Data Through a Serial Port

Here, you will learn how to use a combination of TAPI functions and standard file functions to build a rudimentary terminal emulator. Data communications are handled in the background by separate threads using overlapped I/O to make sure the user interface stays responsive. Incidentally, the file handling techniques demonstrated in this How-To also apply to regular disk files.

7.3 Determine Whether There Is a Disk in a Floppy or CD-ROM Drive

This How-To will show you how to use a simple Windows API function to determine whether there is a disk in a drive that has removable media. Along the way, you'll learn how to get other useful information about the logical drive devices attached to your computer.

7.4 Determine the Color Capabilities of a Monitor or Printer

In the real world, not every computer has attached devices with the same capabilities. Some computers have color printers attached, while others have only black and white available. Some computer displays support essentially unlimited colors, while others are limited to 256. This How-To shows you how to use a couple of Windows API functions to determine the color capabilities of the screen and the default printer. The techniques demonstrated can be extended to many other situations.

COMPLEXITY
BEGINNING

17.1 How do I...
Use the modem to dial a voice call?

Problem

I'm building an address book into my application, and I would like to add a button that would let the user dial the currently displayed contact through their computer modem. How do I do this in C++Builder?

Technique

The Telephony API, TAPI for short, is a set of functions to interface computer applications with communication peripherals. TAPI includes a single, easy-to-use function that allows you to add voice-call dialing to any application.

Steps

Run **DIAL.EXE**. You will see a display similar to Figure 7-1. Enter a phone number and press the dial button. You'll hear the modem dial, the phone will ring, and,

hopefully, someone will answer at the other end. By the way, the computer knows this is a voice call, so the person who picks up will not hear any of those loud, annoying screeching sounds modems use to get connected.

1. Create a new project. Save the default form as **DIALMAIN.CPP** and the project as **DIAL.MAK**.

2. Add the components, and set their properties as shown in Table 7-1. Lay out the controls as shown in Figure 7-1.

Table 7-1 Components, properties, and settings for the **DIAL** project

COMPONENT	PROPERTY	SETTING
TForm	Caption	Dialer
TLabel	Caption	Phone Number:
TLabel	Caption	Person Called:
TLabel	Caption	Reason:
TButton	Name	bCall
	Caption	Call
	Default	True
TEdit	Name	ePhone
	Tab Order	0
	Text	None
TEdit	Name	ePerson
	Tab Order	1
	Text	None
TEdit	Name	eReason
	Tab Order	2
	Text	None

Figure 7-1 DIAL.EXE after a number has been entered

3. Add the following statement to include the TAPI headers right after the other #include statements in DIALMAIN.MAK:

```
#include "dialmain.h"
//Un-comment the following line if you receive a linker error:
//Undefined symbol tapiRequestMakeCallA
//#define TAPI_CURRENT_VERSION 0x00010004
#include <tapi.h>
```

4. Double-click on the call button, and add the following code that actually makes the phone call:

```
void __fastcall TForm1::bCallClick(TObject *Sender)
{
  //If the user entered something in the phone edit box,
  if (ePhone->Text.Length())
  {
    //Disable the call button.
    bCall->Enabled = FALSE;
    //Ask TAPI to make a call using the phone dialer.
    tapiRequestMakeCall(ePhone->Text.c_str(), "Dial",
                        ePerson->Text.c_str(), eReason->Text.c_str());
    //Call is done, enable the call button.
    bCall->Enabled = TRUE;
  }
}
```

5. Open the Object Inspector for Form1. Double-click on the OnShow event, and add the code that sets the input focus on the edit box.

```
void __fastcall TForm1::FormShow(TObject *Sender)
{
  //Put the cursor in the phone number edit box.
  ePhone->SetFocus();
}
```

6. Compile and run the application. If you receive a linker error, then you have an earlier version of TAPI on your system. Un-comment the following define statement located near the top of DIALMAIN.CPP:

```
#include "dialmain.h"
//Un-comment the following line if you receive a linker error:
//Undefined symbol tapiRequestMakeCallA
#define TAPI_CURRENT_VERSION 0x00010004
#include <tapi.h>
```

How It Works

As you will see in How-To 7.2, the Telephony API can get quite complicated. This How-To, on the other hand, uses assisted telephony which is designed to allow applications to make telephone calls without needing to be aware of the details of the Telephony API. The whole secret to the application is contained in a single line of code:

```
tapiRequestMakeCall(ePhone->Text.c_str(), "Dial", ePerson->⇐
Text.c_str(), eReason->Text.c_str());
```

The first parameter is the phone number as a standard null-terminated C string. Since the `Text` property of an edit box is a `String` object, the `c_str()` method of `String` is used to make the necessary conversion. The last three parameters, app name, called party, and a comment, are used by the registered TAPI call-control application to log information about the call.

The default call-control application shipped with TAPI is the phone dialer application found in the Accessories folder. You should notice that the phone dialer opens when you press the Call button. You can check out the information it logs about your call by selecting Tools|Show Log from its menu. A more sophisticated call-control application would record more information about the call.

Comments

Assisted Telephony makes it very easy to add basic calling capability to your application. One function call does all the work. If you want to go further with communications, you have to journey into the full TAPI API to gain the sort of control you'll need. How-To 7.2 maps the first steps of that journey.

COMPLEXITY

ADVANCED

7.2 How do I...
Send and receive data through a serial port?

Problem

An application I'm writing needs to be able to dial into another computer and exchange data. How do I accomplish this with C++Builder?

Technique

This How-To shows you all the techniques you'll need to build applications that exchange data over dial-up serial connections. The Telephony API is used to make and manage the phone connection. File-handling functions from the standard Windows API handle data exchange. The application smoothly handles user input, receiving data and transmitting data at the same time by using overlapped I/O and multiple threads to manage the communications link.

Although most of the work is performed by standard Windows API functions, this How-To introduces the `TThread` VCL object that makes it very easy to add multithreading to your application. Chapter 12, "Threads," covers the use of the `TThread` object in more detail.

Steps

Run **TERM.EXE**. Enter the phone number of a local dial-up server, like the number of your Internet Service Provider. If you dial your ISP, you will be able to enter your user name and password, but you will not be able to complete the Internet connection unless you have a simple UNIX shell account. Press the Call button. You'll hear the modem dial, and you'll see progress messages in the status box located in the upper right corner of the window. Once the computer at the other end connects, you'll see the message "Connected: Dialer" in the status box, and the cursor will move into the input window. You can send data to the remote computer by typing text into the input window and pressing (ENTER). Messages from the remote computer will appear in the output window. You can disconnect from the remote computer by pressing the Hang Up button. Figure 7-2 shows **TERM.EXE** after it has connected to my ISP (note that the phone number has been changed to protect the innocent).

1. Create a new project. Save the default form as **TERMMAIN.CPP** and the default project as **TERM.MAK**.

2. Add the components, and set their properties as shown in Table 7-2. Lay out the controls as shown in Figure 7-2.

Table 7-2 Components, properties, and settings for **TERM**

COMPONENT	PROPERTY	SETTING
TForm	Caption	Term
TLabel	Caption	Phone Number:
TLabel	Caption	Input:
TLabel	Caption	Output:
TLabel	Caption	Status:
TMemo	Name	mMessage
	Readonly	True
	Scrollbars	ssVertical
	Lines	None
TButton	Name	bCall
	Caption	Call
	Default	True
TMemo	Name	mInput
	Scrollbars	ssVertical
	Lines	None
TMemo	Name	mOutput
	ReadOnly	True
	Scrollbars	ssVertical
	Lines	None

COMPONENT	PROPERTY	SETTING
TButton	Name	bHangUp
	Caption	Hang Up
	Enabled	False

3. Add the following declarations in TERMMAIN.H right after the system generated #includes:

```
#include <vcl\Forms.hpp>
//Un-comment thefollowing line if you receive a linker error
//Undefined symbol lineGetCallInfoA (and several others)
//#define TAPI_CURRENT_VERSION 0x00010004
//Include the TAPI headers
#include <tapi.h>
#define BUFSIZE 255
//---------------------------------------------------------------------
//Basic file event handling thread
class TFileThread : public TThread
{
  private:
    //Internal routine that will update screen with error message
    void __fastcall ShowError(void);

  protected:
    //Handles for the communications file and an event
    HANDLE hFileEvent, hCommDevice;
    //Overlap structure for overlapped i/o
    OVERLAPPED oOverlap;
    //Holding area for the last error message
    String ErrorMess;
    //Buffer for communications data
    char Buffer[BUFSIZE];

    //Actual error routine
    void __fastcall Error(String ErrMess);

  public:
    //Override constructor, destructor and terminate method
    virtual __fastcall TFileThread(HANDLE CommFile);
    virtual __fastcall ~TFileThread(void);
    void __fastcall Terminate(void);
};

//Thread to manage writing data to comm file
class TFileWriteThread : public TFileThread
{
private:
  //Holding area for string to write
  String WriteString;
  //Critical section used to protect the write string
  CRITICAL_SECTION CriticalSection;
```

continued on next page

continued from previous page

```
  //Override TThread main loop
  void __fastcall Execute(void);
public:
  //Override constructor and destructor
  __fastcall TFileWriteThread(HANDLE CommFile);
  __fastcall ~TFileWriteThread(void);
  //Called by main thread to write data to communications device
  void __fastcall WriteData(String s);
};

//Object to manage reading from comm file
class TFileReadThread : public TFileThread
{
private:
  //Override TThread main loop
  void __fastcall Execute(void);
  //Routine to update main window display
  void __fastcall UpdateWindow(void);
public:
  //Override constructor
  __fastcall TFileReadThread(HANDLE);
};

//Structure to hold information on comm device returned by TAPI
typedef struct modem_info_tag {
  VARSTRING vs;
  HANDLE hComm;
  char szDeviceName[255];
} MODEM_INFO, FAR *LPMODEM_INFO;
```

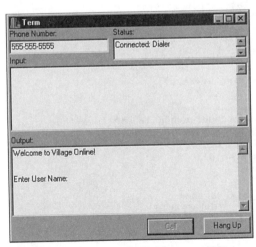

Figure 7-2 TERM connected to an ISP

4. Add the following lines of code to `Form1`'s declaration in `TERMMAIN.H`:

```
private: // User declarations
  //Handle to TAPI DLL connection
  HLINEAPP LineApp;
  //Handle to TAPI line
  HLINE Line;
  //Handle to TAPI call
  HCALL Call;
  //Parameters of call
  LINECALLPARAMS CallParams;
  //Communications file handle
  HANDLE hCommDevice;
  //Pointers to the file reading and file writing threads
  TFileWriteThread *FileWriteThread;
  TFileReadThread *FileReadThread;
  //Holds state of terminal
  bool TerminalConnected;

public: // User declarations
  virtual __fastcall TForm1(TComponent* Owner);
  //Function to start up terminal after modem has connected
  void __fastcall ConnectTerminal(void);
  //Function to shut down terminal when modem has disconnected
  void __fastcall ShutdownTerminal(void);
};
```

5. Add the definition of the TAPI callback function near the bottom of the header file.

```
extern TForm1 *Form1;

//Function called by TAPI functions when events occur
void CALLBACK lineCallback(DWORD hDevice, DWORD dwMsg, DWORD⇐
dwCallbackInstance,
                          DWORD dwParam1, DWORD dwParam2, DWORD⇐
dwParam3);

//--------------------------------------------------------------
#endif
```

6. Switch to `TERMMAIN.CPP`. Add the TAPI callback function near the top of the file.

```
TForm1 *Form1;

void CALLBACK lineCallback(DWORD hDevice, DWORD dwMsg, DWORD⇐
dwCallbackInstance
                          , DWORD dwParam1, DWORD dwParam2, DWORD⇐
dwParam3)
{
  String s;
  HCALL hCall;
  char LineCallBuf[1024];
```

continued on next page

continued from previous page

```
switch (dwMsg)
{
   //Replies to asynchronous function calls
   // < 0 is an error
   case LINE_REPLY:
     if (dwParam2 < 0)
       Form1->mMessage->Lines->Add("Reply error");
     else
       Form1->mMessage->Lines->Add("LINE_REPLY OK");
     break;
   //Status of call has changed
   case LINE_CALLSTATE:
     //Call is specified in the hDevice parameter
     hCall = (HCALL)hDevice;
     switch (dwParam1)
     {
        //Call has gone idle
        case LINECALLSTATE_IDLE:
          if (hCall)
          {
             //Free the memory associated with the call
             lineDeallocateCall(hCall);
             //Tell the user that the call memory was freed
             Form1->mMessage->Lines->Add("Idle -- Call deallocated");
             //Adjust the buttons
             Form1->bCall->Enabled = TRUE;
             Form1->bHangUp->Enabled = FALSE;
             //if the terminal is connected, shut it down
             Form1->ShutdownTerminal();
          }
          break;
        //Call has connected
        case LINECALLSTATE_CONNECTED:
          if (hCall)
          {
             //Start the connected message off with this string
             s = "Connected: ";
             //Tell the line call status buffer its total size
             ((LPLINECALLINFO)LineCallBuf)->dwTotalSize =⇐
sizeof(LineCallBuf);
             //Get the call status (0 indicates success)
             if (lineGetCallInfo(hCall, (LPLINECALLINFO)LineCallBuf) == 0)
             {
                //Check to see if there is an application name associated
                //with the call.
                if (((LPLINECALLINFO)LineCallBuf)->dwAppNameSize > 0)
                {
                   //Add the application name to the message
                   s = s + (LineCallBuf +
                     ((LPLINECALLINFO)LineCallBuf)->dwAppNameOffset);
                   //Display the message
                   Form1->mMessage->Lines->Add(s);
                }
                //Open the communications port
                Form1->ConnectTerminal();
             }
          }
```

```
         break;
      //Dialing is complete and the call is on the way
      case LINECALLSTATE_PROCEEDING:
         Form1->mMessage->Lines->Add("Proceeding");
         break;
      //Phone is dialing
      case LINECALLSTATE_DIALING:
         Form1->mMessage->Lines->Add("Dialing");
         //Set up the buttons
         Form1->bCall->Enabled = FALSE;
         Form1->bHangUp->Enabled = TRUE;
         break;
      //Line was busy
      case LINECALLSTATE_BUSY:
         Form1->mMessage->Lines->Add("Busy");
         break;
      //Call has disconnected
      case LINECALLSTATE_DISCONNECTED:
         //Start the disconnected message
         s = "Disconnected: ";
         //Why did the call disconnect?
         switch (dwParam2)
         {
            //Normal disconnect
            case LINEDISCONNECTMODE_NORMAL:
               s = s + "normal";
               break;
            //Line was busy and disconnected
            case LINEDISCONNECTMODE_BUSY:
               s = s + "busy";
               break;
         }
         //Tell the user about the disconnect
         Form1->mMessage->Lines->Add(s);
         //Disconnect the call if required
         if (hCall)
            LineDrop(hCall, NULL, 0);
         //Set up the buttons
         Form1->bCall->Enabled = TRUE;
         Form1->bHangUp->Enabled = FALSE;
         //If the terminal is connected, shut it down
         Form1->ShutdownTerminal();
         break;
      }
      break;
   }
}
```

7. Add the code that initializes the `TerminalConnected` flag to `Form1`'s constructor.

```
__fastcall TForm1::TForm1(TComponent* Owner)
   : TForm(Owner)
{
   //Initialize the state of the terminal
   TerminalConnected = FALSE;
}
```

8. Open the Object Inspector for **Form1**. Double-click the **OnCreate** event handler, and add the following code, which initializes the connection to the TAPI library:

```cpp
void __fastcall TForm1::FormCreate(TObject *Sender)
{
  DWORD nDevs, tapiVersion;
  LINEEXTENSIONID extid;

  //Initialize the call parameters
  strnset((LPSTR)&CallParams, '0', sizeof(CallParams));

  //Set the total size of the structure
  CallParams.dwTotalSize = sizeof(CallParams);
  //This is a voice telephone line
  CallParams.dwBearerMode = LINEBEARERMODE_VOICE;
  //Modems will be speaking on the line
  CallParams.dwMediaMode = LINEMEDIAMODE_DATAMODEM;

  //Initialize connection to TAPI (Return < 0 indicates an error)
  if (lineInitialize(&LineApp, HInstance, lineCallback, "Dialer", &nDevs)⇐
< 0)
  {
    //Indicate the error to this application
    LineApp = 0;
  }
  //Make sure there are some TAPI devices
  else if (nDevs == 0)
  {
    //Close the connection to TAPI
    lineShutdown(LineApp);
    //Indicate the error to this application
    LineApp = 0;
  }
  //Application and TAPI negotiate to agree on a TAPI version
  //< 0 indicates error
  else if (lineNegotiateAPIVersion(LineApp, 0, 0x00010000, 0x00090000,
                                   &tapiVersion, &extid) < 0)

  {
    //Close the connection to TAPI
    lineShutdown(LineApp);
    //Indicate the error to this application
    LineApp = 0;
  }
  //Open the line using a device that supports the
  //parameters in the CallParams parameter(< 0 indicates failure)
  else if (lineOpen(LineApp, LINEMAPPER, &Line, tapiVersion, 0, 0,
                    LINECALLPRIVILEGE_NONE, 0, &CallParams) < 0)

  {
    //Close the connection to TAPI
    lineShutdown(LineApp);
    //Indicate the error to this application
    LineApp = 0;
    Line = 0;
  }
```

```
//If an error occurred above, tell the user
if (Line == 0)
  mMessage->Lines->Add("Error");
}
```

9. Double-click the `OnDestroy` event in the Object Inspector for `Form1`, and add the code that cleans up the TAPI connection and the communication threads before the program ends.

```
void __fastcall TForm1::FormDestroy(TObject *Sender)
{
  //Close the line if it is open
  if (Line)
    lineClose(Line);

  //Close the connection to TAPI if it is open
  if (LineApp)
    lineShutdown(LineApp);

  //Close the terminal if it is open
  if (TerminalConnected)
    ShutdownTerminal();
}
```

10. Double-click on the Form's `OnShow` event in the Object Inspector, and add the code that puts the cursor in the phone number edit box.

```
void __fastcall TForm1::FormShow(TObject *Sender)
{
  //Put the cursor in the phone number edit box
  Edit1->SetFocus();
}
```

11. Double-click on the Form's Call button, and add the code that initiates a call.

```
void __fastcall TForm1::bCallClick(TObject *Sender)
{
  //If the user entered something in the number edit box
  if (Edit1->Text.Length())
  {
    //Clear the status memo box
    mMessage->Lines->Clear();
    //Make a call on the line (< 0 is an error)
    if (lineMakeCall(Line, &Call, Edit1->Text.c_str(), 0, &CallParams) < 0)
      //Indicate the error
      mMessage->Lines->Add("Could not initiate call");
  }
}
```

12. Double-click on the Hang Up button, and add the code to disconnect the call.

```
void __fastcall TForm1::bHangUpClick(TObject *Sender)
{
  //If a call is open
  if (Call)
    //Drop it (return < 0 is an error)
    if (LineDrop(Call, NULL, 0) < 0)
      //If an error occurs, report it
      Form1->mMessage->Lines->Add("Error on drop call " +
IntToStr(GetLastError()));
}
```

13. Open the Object Inspector for the input memo control (`mInput`). Double-click the `OnKeyPress` event, and add the code that sends lines of input to the serial output thread.

```
void __fastcall TForm1::mInputKeyPress(TObject *Sender, char &Key)
{
  //When the user presses [ENTER]
  if (Key == 13)
    //Write the last memo line to the communications file
    //(Append the carriage return)
    FileWriteThread->
      WriteData(mInput->Lines->Strings[mInput->Lines->Count - 1] + "\r");
}
```

14. Immediately after the code you added in step 13, add the function that starts terminal communications.

```
//Start the dumb terminal
void __fastcall TForm1::ConnectTerminal(void)
{
  DCB dcb;
  COMMTIMEOUTS ct;
  MODEM_INFO ModemInfo;

  //If the terminal is already running return
  if (TerminalConnected)
    return;

  //Set the total size of the modem information buffer
  ModemInfo.vs.dwTotalSize = sizeof(MODEM_INFO);
  //Set the format of the buffer
  ModemInfo.vs.dwStringFormat = STRINGFORMAT_BINARY;

  //Clear the input and output memos
  mInput->Lines->Clear();
  mOutput->Lines->Clear();

  //Get the device information of the line which is connected to a modem
  //and put the information into ModemInfo.
  //Result < 0 indicates an error
  if (lineGetID(Line, 0, 0, LINECALLSELECT_LINE, (LPVARSTRING)&ModemInfo,
                "comm/datamodem") < 0)
  {
    //Report the error, and return, because we cannot connect to the comm
  file
```

```
    mMessage->Lines->Add("Error on line get id " +⇐
IntToStr(GetLastError()));
    return;
  }

  //The file handle to the communications device is contained in ModemInfo
  hCommDevice = ModemInfo.hComm;

  //If this is not a valid file handle
  if (hCommDevice == INVALID_HANDLE_VALUE) {
    //Report the error and return
    mMessage->Lines->Add("Error on open " + IntToStr(GetLastError()));
    return;
  }

  //Get the config of the modem connection
  GetCommState(hCommDevice, &dcb);

  //Set to 8 bits, no parity, 1 stopbit
  dcb.ByteSize = 8;
  dcb.Parity = NOPARITY;
  dcb.StopBits = ONESTOPBIT;

  //Actually set the config
  SetCommState(hCommDevice, &dcb);

  //Get timeout information for the communications channel
  GetCommTimeouts(hCommDevice, &ct);

  //Set the timeout to 1 second so that a pending read
  //will complete when more that 1 second has elapsed between the arrival
  //of two consecutive characters.
  ct.ReadIntervalTimeout = 1000;

  //Set the new timeout value
  SetCommTimeouts(hCommDevice, &ct);

  //Put the input focus on the input memo box
  mInput->SetFocus();

  //Start the threads that actually read and write the communications file
  FileWriteThread = new TFileWriteThread(hCommDevice);
  FileReadThread = new TFileReadThread(hCommDevice);

  //Terminal status is connected
  TerminalConnected = TRUE;
}
```

15. Add the function that stops terminal communications right after the
ConnectTerminal function.

```
//Stop the dump terminal
void __fastcall TForm1::ShutdownTerminal(void)
{
  //If the terminal is connected
  if (TerminalConnected)
```

continued on next page

continued from previous page

```
  {
    //Shutdown the writing thread if it exists
    if (FileWriteThread)
      FileWriteThread->Terminate();

    //Shutdown the reading thread if it exists
    if (FileReadThread)
      FileReadThread->Terminate();

    //Close the communications channel
    CloseHandle(hCommDevice);
  }
  //The terminal is now disconnected
  TerminalConnected = FALSE;
}
```

16. After the ShutdownTerminal function, add the code for the communication thread objects.

```
//------------------------------------------------------------------------
//TFileThread

//Basic functionality for file reading and file writing threads

//Constructor
__fastcall TFileThread::TFileThread(HANDLE CommFile)
    : TThread(True)

{
  //Initialize an event object
  hFileEvent = CreateEvent(NULL,  //no security attribute
                           FALSE, //Auto-reset event
                           FALSE, //initial state unsignaled
                           NULL); //Unnamed
  //Assign the communications file handle
  hCommDevice = CommFile;
  //Assign the auto-reset event to the event field of the structure
  //used by overlapped i/o calls
  oOverlap.hEvent = hFileEvent;
  //Initialize the error message
  ErrorMess = "";
}

//Destructor
__fastcall TFileThread::~TFileThread(void)
{
  //Close the event object
  CloseHandle(hFileEvent);
}

//Error routine to call
void __fastcall TFileThread::Error(String ErrMess)
{
  //Set the current error message
```

```
  ErrorMess = ErrMess;
  //Call ShowError in the context of the main thread
  Synchronize(ShowError);
  //Clear the error message
  ErrorMess = "";
}


//Internal error routine
//Must always be called with synchronize
void __fastcall TFileThread::ShowError(void)
{
  //Display the current error message in the message memo
  Form1->mMessage->Lines->Add(ErrorMess);
}


//Tell the thread to terminate
void __fastcall TFileThread::Terminate(void)
{
  //Call the parent's terminate event to set the termination flag
  TThread::Terminate();
  //Raise the file event so that the thread will actually terminate
  //See the execute method of TFileWriteThread and TFileReadThread
  //for more info.
  SetEvent(hFileEvent);
}
//----------------------------------------------------------------
//TFileWriteThread

//Manage writing the communications file

//Constructor
__fastcall TFileWriteThread::TFileWriteThread(HANDLE hCommFile)
    : TFileThread(hCommFile)

{
  //Create the critical section
  InitializeCriticalSection(&CriticalSection);
  //Start execution of the thread which was started in the suspended state
  Resume();
}


//Destructor
__fastcall TFileWriteThread::~TFileWriteThread(void)
{
  //Free the memory associated with the critical section
  DeleteCriticalSection(&CriticalSection);
}


//Main loop
void __fastcall TFileWriteThread::Execute(void)
{
  DWORD BytesWritten, ErrCode;

  //As long as the thread is supposed to run
  while (!Terminated)
```

continued on next page

continued from previous page

```
{
  //If there is data waiting to write
  if (WriteString != "")
  {
    //Initialize the write buffer
    strnset(Buffer, '\0', sizeof(Buffer));
    //Start the critical section
    EnterCriticalSection(&CriticalSection);
    //Copy the data to the write buffer
    strcpy(Buffer, WriteString.c_str());
    //Clear the data
    WriteString = "";
    //End critical section
    LeaveCriticalSection(&CriticalSection);
    //Start a pending write operation
    if (!WriteFile(hCommDevice, Buffer, strlen(Buffer),
                   &BytesWritten, &oOverlap))
      //If an error occurred get the error code
      //if the error code is not ERROR_IO_PENDING
      if ((ErrCode = GetLastError()) != ERROR_IO_PENDING)
        //Report the error
        Error("Error on write file " + IntToStr(ErrCode));
  }

    //Otherwise wait for the IO to finish (which will raise this event) or
    //for the user to enter a line of information (event will be raised by
    //the WriteData method), or for the thread to be terminated (which will
    //also raise the event).
    WaitForSingleObjectEx(hFileEvent, INFINITE, TRUE);
  }
}

void __fastcall TFileWriteThread::WriteData(String s)
{
  //Start the critical section
  EnterCriticalSection(&CriticalSection);
  //Set the data to be written
  WriteString = s;
  //End the critical section
  LeaveCriticalSection(&CriticalSection);
  //Raise the event so that the waiting data can be written
  SetEvent(hFileEvent);
}
//---------------------------------------------------------------------
//TFileReadThread

//Handle reading the communications file

__fastcall TFileReadThread::TFileReadThread(HANDLE hCommFile)
    : TFileThread(hCommFile)

{
  //Start the thread which was born in the suspended state
  Resume();
}
```

```
void __fastcall TFileReadThread::UpdateWindow(void)
{
  //Write data to the output window in the context of the main thread
  Form1->mOutput->Lines->Add(Buffer);
}

void __fastcall TFileReadThread::Execute(void)
{
  DWORD BytesRead, ErrCode;

  //While the thread is not terminated
  while (!Terminated)
  {
    //Initialize the buffer
    strnset(Buffer, '\0', sizeof(Buffer));
    //Start a pending read operation
    if (!ReadFile(hCommDevice, Buffer, BUFSIZE, &BytesRead, &oOverlap))
    {
      //If an error occurred get the error code
      //If the error code is not ERROR_IO_PENDING
      if ((ErrCode = GetLastError()) != ERROR_IO_PENDING)
        //Report the error
        Error("Error on read file " + IntToStr(ErrCode));
      //Otherwise
      else
      {
        //Wait for the IO to complete or for the thread to terminate
        WaitForSingleObjectEx(hFileEvent, INFINITE, TRUE);
        //If there is some data in the buffer
        if (strlen(Buffer))
        {
          //Write it to the output window
          Synchronize(UpdateWindow);
        }
      }
    }
  }
}
//------------------------------------------------------------------------
```

17. Compile and run the application.

How It Works

Before you dig into the details of TERM, it is important to understand how the user interface, TAPI, and the two background threads work together to make a connection and send data back and forth. Figure 7-3 shows the overview.

Making the Connection to TAPI

The code you added to the OnCreate event of the form (step 8) initializes the connection to the TAPI DLL and opens a line to the first modem device connected to your computer. The first four lines of code initialize the parameters of the call. These

parameters are stored in the `CallParams` private member variable of `TForm1`. The code assumes your modem is connected to a normal analog telephone line which TAPI calls a voice line. Look up the `LINECALLPARAMS` structure in the WIN32 help file to get a complete list of the valid values for `dwBearerMode`.

The call to `lineInitialize` is used to connect to the TAPI DLL. Like most TAPI functions, a return value less than zero indicates an error. The first parameter is a pointer to an `HLINEAPP` handle and, if the call to `lineInitialize` succeeds, will represent `Form1`'s connection to TAPI. The next parameter is the application instance handle, which C++Builder stores in the global `HInstance` variable. The third parameter is a function pointer to the TAPI callback function; this will be discussed a little later. The fourth parameter is the application name, and the last parameter is a `DWORD` pointer, which will store the number of TAPI devices configured in the system.

If the call to `lineInitialize` succeeds, and there is at least one TAPI device connected to the system, the application negotiates with the TAPI DLL on a compatible API version by calling `lineNegotiateAPIVersion`. The first parameter is the application's connection to TAPI. The second parameter is the device ID to negotiate with. In this case, the application assumes that the only TAPI device connected to the computer is a modem.

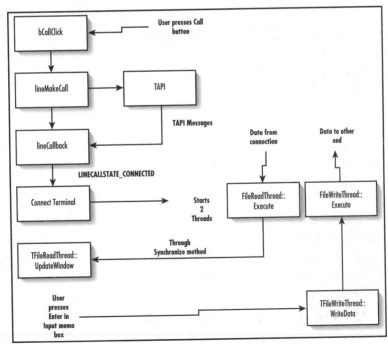

Figure 7-3 Overview of TERM connecting to a remote computer and running the dumb terminal

The third and fourth parameters are the least-recent and most-recent versions of TAPI the application will accept. Version numbers are of the form `<major version number>.<minor version number>` and are passed with the major version number in the high-order word and the minor version in the low-order word. In this How-To, the application will accept any TAPI version between 1.0 and 9.0.

If the application and TAPI agree on a common version, the application calls `lineOpen` to make a connection to the modem device. The first parameter is the application's connection to TAPI. The second parameter is the device to connect, or the special value `LINEMAPPER` that tells TAPI to connect to the first device that supports the properties specified in the `LINECALLPARAMS` parameter which was set up in the `FormCreate` method and is passed as the last parameter to `lineOpen`. The third parameter is `HLINE` that will be the application's connection to the selected device if the call succeeds. The fourth parameter is the TAPI version that was agreed upon in the call to `lineNegotiateAPIVersion`. The next parameter is the agreed-upon TAPI extension version that is only used with certain vendor-specific drivers and can be ignored when using basic TAPI devices like the modem. The sixth parameter is for instance-specific data that will be passed to the callback function by TAPI. This is not needed here, so it is set to zero.

The seventh parameter tells TAPI what sort of rights the application wants for calls it is notified for. Since this application is only interested in the call it is making, this parameter is set to `LINECALLPRIVILEDGE_NONE`. More sophisticated applications can monitor or even take ownership of inbound calls if the appropriate devices are attached to the computer. The next parameter is ignored by TAPI when the seventh parameter is set to `LINECALLPRIVELDGE_NONE`.

Making the Call

Once the application has connected to the proper TAPI device, making the call is very easy. The code you added to the `OnClick` event of the Call button in step 11 checks to make sure the user entered a phone number, clears the status memo box, and makes the call using the `LineMakeCall` function.

`LineMakeCall` gets passed the line connection created by the `LineOpen` call, an `HCALL` variable that will store a handle to this call, the phone number to call, and the parameters of the call which were set in the `FormCreate` method. If the function returns an error value, the application reports the error to the user.

Monitoring the Call

To make things run smoothly, many TAPI functions are asynchronous. The application requests a service by making a function call, but TAPI does not make the application wait until the request completes before allowing program execution to continue. For example, when the application calls `LineMakeCall`, TAPI starts the process of making the call and immediately returns control to the application. Instead of waiting, the application passes TAPI a pointer to a function in the `lineInitialize` function, which TAPI calls to notify the application of certain TAPI events.

This application's callback function was added in step 6. It handles a variety of message types through a big switch statement. The **LINE_REPLY** message is sent to report the success or failure of asynchronous function calls. This application will receive a **LINE_REPLY** message to report the results of the **lineCall** function. **LINE_REPLY** messages place a value less than zero to indicate failure in **dwParam2**.

A **LINE_CALLSTATE** message is sent each time the status of a call has changed. Several **LINE_CALLSTATE** messages will be received as the call progresses. The value passed in **dwParam1** indicates the new call state. When the call goes idle, as indicated by a **dwParam1** value of **LINECALLSTATE_IDLE**, the application cleans up the call and shuts down the communications terminal. When the call connects, **dwParam1** is **LINECALLSTATE_CONNECTED**, and the application retrieves status information about the call and starts the communications terminal. When the call is proceeding through the phone system, dialing, or a busy signal is received, the application simply reports status to the user. If the value of **dwParam1** is **LINECALLSTATE_DISCONNECTED**, the application checks the value of **dwParam2** to determine why the call disconnected, reports the reason to the user, and shuts down the communications terminal.

The Communications Threads

Once the line is connected, the program has to start monitoring the serial port for data from the other end of the connection. At the same time, the application has to let the user key data into the input memo box, and when the user presses (ENTER), it must send that data out the serial port. Since the application has to remain responsive to the user and incoming data at all times, background threads and overlapped I/O are used to manage the communications.

A total of three threads is used by this application. The main thread, which is automatically created by Windows at application start-up, handles the user interface and the TAPI connection. The other two threads, which are started once the modem connection is made, are used to manage serial port input and output, respectively.

The object hierarchy of the communication thread objects is shown in Figure 7-4. The **TThread** object supplied by C++Builder provides the basic functionality, **TFileThread** adds the functionality common to reading and writing files, **TFileReadThread** adds the specifics of reading a communications file and updating the output memo box, and **TFileWriteThread** handles the specifics of getting user input and writing it to the serial port. You added all the code for the thread objects in step 16.

TFileThread's constructor starts by calling its parent's constructor with the parameter **True**. This starts the thread in a suspended state. It then initializes several critical member variables which will be discussed later. **TFileThread**'s destructor cleans up the WIN32 event object created in the constructor.

The **Error** method places its **ErrMess** parameter in a private variable and calls **ShowError** through **Synchronize** to update the screen. The **ShowError** method is used to update the status memo box with error information. Since it is updating the screen, it must be called with **TThread**'s **Synchronize** method to avoid multithread conflicts. If you try to update the screen directly from a separate thread of

execution, you may get some very strange results because the VCL is not thread-safe. The **Synchronize** method is discussed in more detail in How-To 12.2.

TFileThread's **Terminate** method starts off by calling **TThread**'s terminate method. It then raises **hFileEvent** to insure that any pending wait state in the communication threads will end so the threads can terminate. The use of **hFileEvent** will be discussed in more detail a little later. For now, just remember that when a **TFileThread** is terminated, the **hFileEvent** is raised.

File-Writing Thread

TFileWriteThread's constructor initializes a critical section object that will be used to protect some data that needs to be shared between the main thread and the file-writing thread. It then starts execution of the thread, which was started in the suspended state, by calling the **Resume** method.

The **WriteData** method is designed to be called from the user-interface thread and uses a critical section to protect the assignment of the **WriteString** data element. A critical section is a small section of code that requires exclusive access to some shared data. Critical sections allow only one thread at a time to gain access to the code protected by the critical section. For now, just keep in mind that access to **WriteString** in **WriteData** is protected by a critical section. The *why* will be explained a little later. After **WriteData** has set the value of **WriteString**, it raises the **hFileEvent** so that the main loop will be able to write the data.

The **Execute** method is the thread's main loop. As long as the thread is active, the **Terminated** member variable will be **False**, and the **while** loop will continue to run.

If there is user input waiting in **WriteString**, **Execute** copies **WriteString** into a buffer. Notice that the manipulation of **WriteString** is protected by the same critical section used in the **WriteData** method. This ensures that the file-writing thread cannot access **WriteString** at the same time that the user-interface thread is changing **WriteString** in **WriteData**. If this were allowed to happen, the application would crash or perform erratically. More detail on critical sections can be found in How-To 12.3.

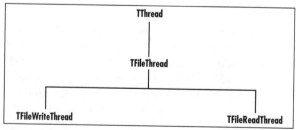

Figure 7-4 Object hierarchy of thread objects for TERM project

Execute then calls the **WriteFile** method passing the communications file handle, the buffer to write, the amount of data to write, a variable to hold the amount of data written and the **oOverlapped** structure that includes a pointer to **hFileEvent**. Therefore, when **WriteFile** is called, it will return immediately even if the write has not completed. It will then raise the **hFileEvent** when the write completes. Communication files opened by TAPI are automatically configured to work this way.

If the call to **WriteFile** returns **False**, the thread tests the value returned by **GetLastError** to see if the I/O is still pending. If it is not, the error number is reported to the user. If the I/O is pending, the thread assumes that the **WriteFile** operation will finish successfully.

The call to **WaitForSingleObjectEx** tells the thread to wait an infinite amount of time for **hFileEvent** to be raised. It can be raised in one of three ways: the **WriteFile** operation finishes and Windows raises **hFileEvent** because it is part of the **oOverlap** structure passed to **WriteFile**, the user inputs data and **hFileEvent** is set to the signaled state by the **WriteData** method, or the thread is terminated and **hFileEvent** is raised by the **Terminate** method. Using an event object this way lets the thread wait quietly for something to happen. While the thread waits, it is not consuming any processor time so other important activities, like user-input, get full attention. Once the event is signaled, **WaitForSingleObjectEx** returns, and execution continues in the **while** loop. Since the event was created with the auto-reset option, Windows automatically sets the event to the unsignaled state after **WaitForSingleObjetEx** returns. You can find more information about Win32 event objects in How-To 12.5.

When the thread terminates, C++Builder automatically destroys it, and the destructor deletes the critical section.

File-Reading Thread

The **TFileReadThread** object is actually a little simpler than the **TFileWriteThread** object because it doesn't need to accept data from the user-interface thread. Its constructor only has to resume the execution of the thread. The **UpdateWindow** method writes the data most recently read from the communications file, and must be called through the **Synchronize** method because it updates the user interface.

The **Execute** method of **TFileReadThread** uses the same **while** loop used in **TFileWriteThread**'s **Execute** method to make sure the thread runs until the **Terminate** method is called. A buffer is initialized, and then **ReadFile** is called with the communications file handle, a buffer to put data in, the size of the buffer, a variable to hold the number of bytes actually read, and the **oOverlap** structure. Error checking on the **ReadFile** call is the same as that for the **WriteFile** call found in the **TFileWriteThread**.

The thread is then put in a wait state with a call to **WaitForSingleObjectEx**. The thread will continue to wait until the read operation completes, the read operation times out, or the **Terminate** method is called, as these events will set

hFileEvent to the signaled state. Then, if some data was read, it is added to the output memo box by calling **UpdateWindow** through the **Synchronize** method.

Starting the Communications Terminal

Form1's **ConnectTerminal** method (step 14) gets the communications file handle from TAPI, sets a few connection parameters, and then starts the file-reading and -writing threads. It starts off by checking a private member variable, **TerminalConnected** which was set to **True** in **FormCreate**, to see if the terminal is already running. If it is, the function returns.

Next, the program needs to get a file handle to the communications file opened by TAPI. This is done by calling **LineGetId** that, as the TAPI documentation says, "returns a device ID for the specified device class associated with the selected line, address, or call." It may not sound like that would include a communications file handle—I know it didn't to me the first dozen times I read it—but in the crazy world of the Windows API it will, if the device in question is a modem.

The secret is in the funny way **LineGetId** returns information. The calling program passes either a handle to a line in the first parameter, or a handle to a TAPI address on an open line in the second parameter, or a handle to an open call in the third parameter. The fourth parameter tells **LineGetId** which of the first three parameters the calling program wants it to use. Then the fun begins.

The TAPI help file describes the fifth parameter as "a pointer to a memory location of type **VARSTRING**, where the device ID is returned." It turns out that, for devices of class **comm/datamodem** specified in the last parameter to **LineGetId**, a couple of extra fields of information get tacked on to the end of the **VARSTRING** structure returned by **LineGetId**. The final definition is

```
//Structure to hold information on comm device returned by TAPI
typedef struct modem_info_tag {
   VARSTRING vs;
   HANDLE hComm;
   char szDeviceName[255];
} MODEM_INFO, FAR *LPMODEM_INFO;
```

As you can see, the extra information includes a handle to the communications file opened by TAPI.

If the call to **LineGetID** succeeded, the function checks to make sure the file handle TAPI gave it is valid. If it is, the **GetCommState** Windows API function is called to fill a **DCB** structure with information about the current communications settings. **TERM** then sets a couple of parameters just to show how it's done and changes the communications settings by calling the **SetCommState** function, passing the modified **DCB** structure. A real-world program would have some sort of configuration function that would let the user select these settings.

GetCommTimeouts is called next to retrieve the current serial port time-out settings and place them in a **COMMTIMEOUTS** structure. The program then sets the **ReadIntervalTimeout** member of the **COMMTIMEOUTS** structure to one second and updates the time-out settings by calling **SetCommTimeouts**.

The `ReadIntervalTimeout` field of `COMMTIMEOUTS` is very important because it defines the maximum interval allowed between the receipt of two consecutive characters on the communications port. Pending reads will be terminated once the time-out limit is exceeded. `TReadFileThread` depends on this time-out to terminate the `ReadFile` operation after receiving a burst of data from the host computer. If the `ReadIntervalTimeout` was not set in this manner, the `ReadFile` operation would continue until `BUFSIZE` characters were read from the communications port, which would make for a very unresponsive terminal.

Finally, input focus is moved to the input memo box and the communications threads, one to read the communications file and one to write to the communications file, are started. The function then sets the `TerminalConnected` flag to `true`.

Shutting Down the Communications Terminal

Form1's `ShutDownTerminal` function (step 15) tests the `TerminalConnected` flag to see if the terminal was started earlier. If it was, it checks the communications threads to see if they are running and shuts them down if they are by calling their `Terminate` methods. The communications file is then closed and the `TerminalConnected` flag is set to `false`.

Comments

This How-To demonstrates the use of a variety of important Win32 programming techniques. Once you master the information presented in this How-To, you will be ready to tackle almost anything in the Windows API.

Because this How-To covers such complex material and the example was already so long, some critical error checking has been left out. For example, real-world programs would check the return values from functions like `SetCommState` and `SetCommTimeouts`. If you develop routines based on the example in this How-To, make sure to check the Win32 help file for information on error returns.

COMPLEXITY
INTERMEDIATE

7.3 How do I...

Determine whether there is a disk in a floppy or CD-ROM drive?

Problem

My program needs a way to tell whether there is a removable disk in a drive. How do I do this with C++Builder?

Technique

The Windows API provides a set of functions for finding out information about the logical disk devices connected to a system along with statistics about the media inside.

This How-To will show you how to use these functions to create a simple tool that finds all the logical devices in your system and lets you find out, among other things, whether a disk is in your CD-ROM drive.

Steps

Run **DRIVEINFO.EXE**. You will see a dialog like that shown in Figure 7-5. Make sure there is not a disk in your CD-ROM drive, and pick your CD-ROM device path from the logical path drop-down list. The program will report that the device is a CD-ROM drive and the drive is not ready.

1. Create a new project. Save the form as **DRIVEINFOMAIN.CPP**. Save the project as **DRIVEINFO.MAK**.

2. Add the components and set their properties as shown in Table 7-3. Lay out the controls as shown in Figure 7-5.

Table 7-3 Components, properties, and settings of Form1 in DRIVEINFO

COMPONENT	PROPERTY	SETTING
TForm	Caption	Get Disk Info
TLabel	Caption	Logical Drive Path
TLabel	Caption	Information
TComboBox	Name	cbPath
	Style	cbDropDownList
TMemo	Name	mInfo
	ScrollBars	ssVertical
	Lines	None

Figure 7-5 DRIVEINFO showing the status of an empty CD-ROM drive

3. Switch to the header file, DRIVEINFOMAIN.H. Add the declaration for the GetDriveInfo function to TForm1's private section.

```
private:// User declarations
  void __fastcall GetDriveInfo(void);
```

4. Open Form1's Object Inspector, and double-click on the OnCreate event handler. Add the code that fetches the list of logical drives in the system and initializes the display.

```
void __fastcall TForm1::FormCreate(TObject *Sender)
{
  DWORD dwSize;
  char *lpDrives, *lpItem;

  //Determine how big a buffer is needed to hold all the logical device
paths
  dwSize = GetLogicalDriveStrings(0, NULL);
  //Initialize a buffer of the proper size
  lpDrives = new char[dwSize];
  //Get the logical drives
  GetLogicalDriveStrings(dwSize, lpDrives);
  //Initialize a working variable
  lpItem = lpDrives;
  //While there are more items in the list
  //(end of list is indicated by a 0 length string)
  while (strlen(lpItem) != 0)
  {
    //Add the current item to the path list
    cbPath->Items->Add(lpItem);
    //Increment the pointer to the next path item in the list
    lpItem += strlen(lpItem) + 1;
  }

  //If there areto some logical device paths,
  if (cbPath->Items->Count)
  {
    //make the first item the default.
    cbPath->ItemIndex = 0;
    //Load the drive info for the default device path
    GetDriveInfo();
  }

  //Free the memory allocated for the device paths
  delete [] lpDrives;
}
```

5. Switch to the cbPath combo box in the Object Inspector. Double-click on the OnChange method and add the code that updates the display to reflect the newly selected logical device path.

```
void __fastcall TForm1::cbPathChange(TObject *Sender)
{
  //User changed the combo box selection. Update the display
  GetDriveInfo();
}
```

6. Move to the bottom of DISKINFOMAIN.CPP, and add the GetDriveInfo function.

```cpp
void __fastcall TForm1::GetDriveInfo(void)
{
  UINT Type;
  String s;
  char lpVolumeName[255], lpFileSystemName[100], szBuffer[512];
  DWORD dwVolumeSerialNumber, dwMaximumComponentLength, dwFileSystemFlags;

  //Clear the info display
  mInfo->Clear();

  //Get the drive type
  Type = GetDriveType(cbPath->Items->Strings[cbPath->ItemIndex].c_str());
  //Update the display according to the drive type
  switch (Type)
  {
    case 0:
      s = "Unknown";
      break;
    case 1:
      s = "Does not exist";
      break;
    case DRIVE_REMOVABLE:
      s = "Removable Disk Drive";
      break;
    case DRIVE_FIXED:
      s = "Fixed Disk Drive";
      break;
    case DRIVE_REMOTE:
      s = "Network Drive";
      break;
    case DRIVE_CDROM:
      s = "CD ROM Drive";
      break;
    case DRIVE_RAMDISK:
      s = "RAM Disk";
  }

  mInfo->Lines->Add("Device Type: " + s);

  //Check the volume information. Returns TRUE on success
  if (GetVolumeInformation(cbPath->Items->Strings[cbPath←
->ItemIndex].c_str(),
                           lpVolumeName,
                           255,
                           &dwVolumeSerialNumber,
                           &dwMaximumComponentLength,
                           &dwFileSystemFlags,
                           lpFileSystemName,
                           100))
  {
    //Update the display with the information
    wsprintf(szBuffer, "Volume Name: %s", lpVolumeName);
```

continued on next page

continued from previous page

```
    mInfo->Lines->Add(szBuffer);
    wsprintf(szBuffer, "Serial Number: %u", dwVolumeSerialNumber);
    mInfo->Lines->Add(szBuffer);
    wsprintf(szBuffer, "File System: %s", lpFileSystemName);
    mInfo->Lines->Add(szBuffer);
  }
  //GetVolumeInformation failed
  else
    //No disk in removable drive or drive not ready
    mInfo->Lines->Add("DRIVE IS NOT READY");
}
```

7. Compile and run the application.

How It Works

The application retrieves the logical device paths using the `GetLogicalDriveStrings` function (step 4). Logical devices include hard drives, CD-ROM drives, floppy drives, tape drives, zip drives, network drives, and any other sort of mapping that ends up assigning a drive letter (like the DOS SUBST command). The first call to `GetLogicalDriveStrings` retrieves the length of the buffer necessary to hold all the drive strings. Then the application allocates a buffer of the proper size and calls the `GetLogicalDriveStrings` again, passing the buffer size and the buffer itself.

The returned buffer contains all the logical device paths separated by **null** characters. The end of the list is marked with a pair of **null** characters. The buffer returned on a system with three logical devices would look like

a:\<null>c:\<null>d:\<null><null>

To retrieve the individual device paths from the buffer, the function uses some pointer arithmetic and a **while** loop. First, a working variable called **lpItem** is set to point at the beginning of the buffer. The **while** loop checks to make sure that **lpItem** does not point to the zero-length string (`<null><null>`) that marks the end of the buffer. If it does not, the logical drive path it points to is added to the combo box, and **lpItem** is incremented to point to the beginning of the next logical drive path in the buffer. This process continues until all the logical drive paths have been added to the combo box.

If there is at least one logical drive path, the first item in the combo box is made the default and information about the device is retrieved by calling the `GetDriveInfo` function, which is described later. Finally, the buffer used to hold the logical device paths is deleted.

Getting the Drive Information

The `GetDriveInfo` function (step 6) is called when the application first starts (from `FormCreate`) and whenever the selection in the combo box is changed by the user (from `cbPathChange` added in step 7). It retrieves information about the currently selected logical device path by calling a couple of Windows API functions. Since the **ItemIndex** property of a combo box holds the list index of the

currently selected item, and **cbPath->Items->Strings** is the array of items in the combo box, a **String** object containing the currently selected logical device string is returned by

```
cbPath->Items->Strings[cbPath->ItemIndex]
```

Since this value is a **String** object and the Windows API functions used in **GetDriveInfo** require a logical path as a standard C string, the application uses the **c_str()** method of the returned **String** object to convert the logical path to a C-style string.

First, the **GetDriveType** Windows API function is called to return the drive type. The **switch** statement converts the numeric result returned by **GetDriveType** into a human-readable message and then the information is added to the **mInfo** memo box.

Once the drive type is displayed, **GetVolumeInfo** is called to retrieve information about the logical volume. For removable devices, this call will fail if there is no disk in the drive. If the call succeeds, the returned information is formatted and displayed in the information memo box. If the call fails, the system reports "DRIVE NOT READY."

Comments

Obviously, this How-To demonstrates more than just a routine to determine whether there is a disk in a floppy or CD-ROM drive. However, you can use the techniques outlined here to build such a function, and you have the tools to do even more.

COMPLEXITY

INTERMEDIATE

7.4 How do I...

Determine the color capabilities of a monitor or printer?

Problem

Many of the applications I write use color on screens and on printed documents. Is there an easy way to find out the color capabilities of the user's screen and printer without asking?

Technique

The Windows API includes a function that lets you find out all about the supported capabilities of the printers and the display attached to a computer. This How-To uses that API function, with a little help from C++Builder VCL objects, to find out basic color information about the display and the current default printer.

Steps

Run COLORCAPS.EXE. You will see a display similar to Figure 7-6. My computer happens to be running a 16-bit high color display, so that is the capability information shown. Pull down the device combo box and select the default printer. As long as you have an attached printer, the display will change to show the basic color capabilities of your printer.

1. Create a new project. Save the form as COLORCAPSMAIN.CPP and the project as COLORCAPS.MAK.

2. Add the components and set their properties as shown in Table 7-4. Lay out the controls as shown in Figure 7-6.

Table 7-4 Components, properties, and settings for COLORCAPS

COMPONENT	PROPERTY	SETTING
TForm	Caption	Device Capabilities
TLabel	Caption	Device
TComboBox	Name	cbDevice
	Style	csDropDownList
	Items	Screen
		Default Printer
TMemo	Name	mCaps
	ReadOnly	True

3. Switch to COLORCAPSMAIN.H, and add the following private declarations to TForm1:

```
private:// User declarations
    void __fastcall GetDeviceColorCaps(HDC hDC, long int &iBitsPerPixel,
                                       long int &iColorPlanes,
                                       long int &iTotalColors);
    void __fastcall DisplayScreenColorCaps(void);
    void __fastcall DisplayDefaultPrinterColorCaps(void);
```

4. Go back to COLORCAPSMAIN.CPP, and add the following include statements near the top of the file:

```
#include <vcl\vcl.h>
#include <vcl\printers.hpp>
#include <math.h>
```

Figure 7-6 COLORCAPS
showing screen color
capabilities

5. Under Form1's constructor, add the function that looks up the color capabilities of a device context.

```
//Gets color capabilities from given display context
void __fastcall TForm1::GetDeviceColorCaps(HDC hDC, long int &iBitsPerPixel,
                                           long int &iColorPlanes,
                                           long int &iTotalColors)
{
  int BitsPerPixel, ColorPlanes;
  long int TotalColors, TotalColorShades;

  //Determine the number of bits per pixel;
  BitsPerPixel = GetDeviceCaps(hDC, BITSPIXEL);
  //Determine number of color shades
  TotalColorShades = pow(2, BitsPerPixel);
  //Number of color planes
  ColorPlanes = GetDeviceCaps(hDC, PLANES);
  //Total Colors
  TotalColors = pow(TotalColorShades, ColorPlanes);
  //Return the results
  iTotalColors = TotalColors;
  iBitsPerPixel = BitsPerPixel;
  iColorPlanes = ColorPlanes;
}
```

6. Next, add the function that displays the color capabilities of the screen.

```
//Display color capabilities of screen
void __fastcall TForm1::DisplayScreenColorCaps(void)
{
  long int TotalColors, ColorPlanes, BitsPerPixel;

  //Clear the display
  mCaps->Clear();
```

continued on next page

continued from previous page

```
//Get the color capabilities of the screen
GetDeviceColorCaps(Form1->Canvas->Handle, BitsPerPixel, ColorPlanes,
  TotalColors);

//Update the display
if (TotalColors < 3)
   mCaps->Lines->Add("Monochrome display");
else
   mCaps->Lines->Add("Color display (" + IntToStr(TotalColors) + "⇐
Colors)");

  mCaps->Lines->Add("Color Planes: " + IntToStr(ColorPlanes));
  mCaps->Lines->Add("Bits Per Pixel: " + IntToStr(BitsPerPixel));
}
```

7. Underneath `DisplayScreenColorCaps`, add the function to display the color capabilities of the default printer.

```
//Display color capabilities of default printer
void __fastcall TForm1::DisplayDefaultPrinterColorCaps(void)
{
  long int TotalColors, ColorPlanes, BitsPerPixel, iMode;
  HDC hDC;
  char szDevice[100], szDriver[100], szPort[100];

  //Clear the display
  mCaps->Clear();

  //Get the color capabilities
  Printer()->GetPrinter(szDevice, szDriver, szPort, iMode);
  hDC = CreateDC(NULL, szDevice,
                 NULL, NULL);
  if (hDC)
  {
     GetDeviceColorCaps(hDC, BitsPerPixel, ColorPlanes,
       TotalColors);
     DeleteDC(hDC);
     //Update the display
     if (TotalColors < 3)
        mCaps->Lines->Add("Monochrome printer");
     else
        mCaps->Lines->Add("Color printer (" + IntToStr(TotalColors) + "⇐
Colors)");

     mCaps->Lines->Add("Color Planes: " + IntToStr(ColorPlanes));
     mCaps->Lines->Add("Bits Per Pixel: " + IntToStr(BitsPerPixel));
  }
  else
     mCaps->Lines->Add("Could not get device context");
}
```

8. Open the Object Inspector for `Form1`. Double-click the `OnCreate` event and add the following code to make the program show the color capabilities of the screen when the program starts:

```
//Default to displaying color capabilities of screen
void __fastcall TForm1::FormCreate(TObject *Sender)
{
  //Make screen the default;
  cbDevice->ItemIndex = 0;
  //Display the screen capabilities
  DisplayScreenColorCaps();
}
```

9. Open the Object Inspector for the combo box, and double-click on the OnChange event. Add the code that changes the display to reflect the new selection in the combo box.

```
//User changed choice in combo box
void __fastcall TForm1::cbDeviceChange(TObject *Sender)
{
  if (cbDevice->ItemIndex == 0)
    DisplayScreenColorCaps();
  else
    DisplayDefaultPrinterColorCaps();
}
```

10. Compile and run the application.

How It Works

The key to this How-To is the GetDeviceCaps Windows API function, which returns various capability information on a given device context. Of course, before you call this function you must obtain a handle to the device context.

Getting a Device Context

The VCL makes it very easy to get the device context for the screen. In fact, the device context you need is stashed in the Handle property of the Form's Canvas property.

```
Form1->Canvas->Handle
```

Things are just a little trickier when it comes to printers, because the VCL provides a device context for a printer only when the application is preparing a print document. If the program tried to use this method to obtain the printer's device context, it would have to print a blank page on the printer. Since that wouldn't be very nice, this How-To uses a slightly different approach.

The TPrinter VCL object includes a method, called GetPrinter, that will retrieve information about the currently selected printer, including the device name. The CreateDC Windows API function can then be used to create a device context for the printer, as shown below:

```
#include (vcl\printers.hpp>
HDC hDC
char szDevice[100], szDriver[100, szPort[100];
int iMode;
```

continued on next page

continued from previous page

```
//Call GetPrinter to retrieve the device name
Printer()->GetPrinter(szDevice, szDriver, szPort, iMode);
//Create a device context for the printer
hDC = CreateDC(NULL, szDevice, NULL, NULL);
//Make sure the device context is valid
if (hDC)
{
    //hDC is valid and can be used for things
    //Code that works with hDC goes here
    //Delete the device context when done
    DeleteDC(hDC);
}
```

Getting the Color Capabilities of a Device

In step 5 you added the `GetDeviceColorCaps` function that does the work of calling `GetDeviceCaps` to retrieve the color capabilities of a given device. `GetDeviceColorCaps` receives four parameters: a handle to a device context, a reference to a variable that will hold the bits per pixel, a reference to a variable that will hold the number of color planes, and a reference to a variable that will hold the total number of supported colors. In traditional C/C++ programs, the variables designed to return information would have been defined as pointers. The advantage of reference variables is you don't have to remember to pass pointers, and the code to put the return values in the variables is much easier to read.

Calculating color information is a bit complicated. The number of bits per pixel determines how many shades of color are possible by raising 2 to the `BitsPerPixel` power. The number of colors a device can display is calculated by raising the shades of color to the color plane's power.

Now that you understand the basic issues, the code should be straightforward. First, it looks up the number of bits per pixel with `GetDeviceCaps`. It then calculates how many shades of a color are possible based on the value of `BitsPerPixel`. `GetDeviceCaps` is called again, this time to fetch the number of color planes. The total possible display colors are calculated, and then the return values are assigned.

Comments

`GetDeviceCaps` is a very powerful function. Armed with the techniques shown in this How-To, you can find out all sorts of useful information about the output devices attached to a computer.

C H A P T E R 8

INTERNET

8

INTERNET

How do I...

The mainstreaming of the Internet is the biggest thing to hit the computer industry since the release of the original IBM PC. What used to be a home for academics and hard-core technical people now plays host to everybody from your Aunt Jodi to Reebok. Terms like Java and surfing are popping up in everyday conversations, and you cannot escape the URLs that are becoming part of the advertising for every media outlet.

This chapter shows you the basics of creating applications that browse the Web, send Internet mail, interact with HTTP requests at the Web server, and transmit data over the Internet. Armed with the tools from this chapter, you will be ready to start your assault on programming cyberspace-enabled applications.

8.1 Create a Basic HTML Browser

C++Builder™ includes an HTML control that can be used to create a basic Web browser with just a few lines of code. This How-To shows you the basics of using the HTML control, and gives you a framework application that can be expanded into a fully featured Web browser or even an HTML file viewer.

8.2 Send Mail Through the Internet

Simple Mail Transport Protocol, SMTP, is the standard Internet method for sending email. This How-To demonstrates the basics of the SMTP client control included with C++Builder to format and send Internet mail.

8.3 Create a Basic CGI Application

This How-To will show you how to write an application that interacts with a Web server to handle data input from HTML forms. The common gateway interface, CGI, will be used to get information from the Web server sent from the client, and to send data back to the client. The example shown here will work with any Web server running on a Win32 platform.

8.4 Create a Basic ISAPI Application

CGI has several weaknesses. Most importantly, each request has to start a separate process, which makes CGI a fairly expensive activity, especially under heavy loads. Microsoft, in concert with a few other Web server vendors, came up with the Internet Server API, ISAPI for short, that attempts to solve some of the problems with CGI. ISAPI extensions work almost the same way as CGI scripts do, but, because they are DLLs, they run inside the same process as the Web server. Multiple requests are served by creating multiple threads of execution which are far less expensive than processes. This How-To will show you the basics of ISAPI extension programming. The demonstrated techniques will work with any ISAPI-compliant Web server running on a Win32 platform.

8.5 Communicate Between Programs over the Internet

This How-To will show you how to use the TCP socket controls included with C++Builder to send data between two programs on the Internet. Along the way, you'll learn a little about how Internet protocols like FTP, Telnet, and HTTP are built on top of TCP/IP sockets.

COMPLEXITY
BEGINNING

8.1 How do I...
Create a basic HTML browser?

Problem

I know that with all the excitement surrounding the Internet, I'm going to need to know how to make my applications work with the Internet. How can I embed Web browser capabilities in my application?

Technique

Whether you want to build a true Web browser or a local HTML file viewer, the HTML control shipped with C++Builder can do the trick. This How-To will show you how to use the HTML control to build a very simple Web browser.

Steps

Run **SIMPBROWSE.EXE** while you are connected to the Internet. Enter the URL of a site you like and press (ENTER). After a short wait, the site will start to appear in the large window. You can now browse the site exactly as you would in the Web browser you normally use. Figure 8-1 shows the Borland Web site as seen in the **SIMPBROWSE** window.

1. Create a new project. Save the default form as **SIMPBROWSEMAIN.CPP** and the project as **SIMPBROWSE.MAK**.

2. Add the components and set their properties as shown in Table 8-1. Lay out the controls as shown in Figure 8-1.

Figure 8-1 SIMPBROWSE displaying http://www.borland.com

Table 8-1 Components, properties, and settings for the SIMPBROWSE project

COMPONENT	PROPERTY	SETTING
TForm	Caption	Simple Browser
TPanel	Name	panel1
	Align	alTop
	Caption	None
TStatusBar	SimplePanel	true
TPanel	Name	panel2
	Align	alClient
	Caption	None
TLabel (On panel1)	Caption	URL:
TEdit (On panel1)	Name	eURL
	Text	None
TButton (On panel1)	Caption	Stop
	Name	bStopClick
THTML (On panel2)	Align	alClient

3. Open the Object Inspector for the URL edit box. Double-click on the OnKeyPress event, and add the following code, which tries to fetch the indicated URL when (ENTER) is pressed:

```
void __fastcall TForm1::eURLKeyPress(TObject *Sender, char &Key)
{
  //When user presses <ENTER> key on URL edit box
  if (Key == 13)
  {
    //Get the document
    HTML1->RequestDoc(eURL->Text);
    //Update the status bar
    StatusBar1->SimpleText = "Requesting " + eURL->Text;
  }
}
```

4. In the Object Inspector for the HTML control, double-click on the OnError event, and add the code that reports HTML errors.

```
void __fastcall TForm1::HTML1Error(TObject *Sender, short Number,
                              AnsiString &Description, int Scode,⇐
const AnsiString Source,
                 const AnsiString HelpFile, int HelpContext,⇐
WordBool &CancelDisplay)
{
  //Report the error
  StatusBar1->SimpleText = "Could not retrieve document";
```

```
    //Document is not being retrieved, disable stop button
    bStop->Enabled = FALSE;
}
```

5. Double-click on HTML1's `OnBeginRetrieval` event, and add the code that enables the stop button and reports that document retrieval is in progress.

```
void __fastcall TForm1::HTML1BeginRetrieval(TObject *Sender)
{
    //Document is being fetched, update status bar
    StatusBar1->SimpleText = "Retrieving " + HTML1->URL;
    //Update the URL box with the fully qualified URL
    eURL->Text = HTML1->URL;
    //Enable stop button
    bStop->Enabled = TRUE;
}
```

6. Double-click the `OnEndRetrieval` event, and add the code that disables the stop button and reports that document retrieval is completed.

```
void __fastcall TForm1::HTML1EndRetrieval(TObject *Sender)
{
    //Document retrieval is complete, update status bar
    StatusBar1->SimpleText = "Done";
    //Disable the stop button
    bStop->Enabled = FALSE;
}
```

7. Double-click the `OnTimeout` event, and add the code that disables the stop button and reports that a time-out has occurred.

```
void __fastcall TForm1::HTML1Timeout(TObject *Sender)
{
    //Document retrieval has timed out
    StatusBar1->SimpleText = "Time-out";
    //Disable the stop button
    bStop->Enabled = FALSE;
}
```

8. Double-click on Form1's Stop button, and add the code that cancels document retrieval.

```
void __fastcall TForm1::bStopClick(TObject *Sender)
{
    //Cancel document retrieval
    HTML1->Cancel("");
}
```

9. Compile and run the application.

How It Works

Because the HTML control supplied with C++Builder does all the hard work, there just isn't a great deal of code in this How-To. The process starts when the user types a URL and presses ENTER. **eURLKeyPress** (step 3) waits for ENTER to be pressed and then calls the **RequestDoc** method of the HTML control to start the retrieval of the URL the user typed in the edit box. Finally, it updates the Status Bar control to indicate that the document is being retrieved.

The key to using the HTML control is understanding that the **RequestDoc** method returns after starting document retrieval, not after the document is retrieved. Various events will occur as document retrieval progresses, and you must add code to handle these events if you want to tell whether the document is retrieved successfully or not.

The **OnError** event handler (step 4) is called by the HTML control when an error occurs during document retrieval. The HTML control passes several parameters to the event handler including the error number (**Number**), the error message (**Description**), and a boolean reference variable called **CancelDisplay**. In this How-To, a generic error message is put in the status bar, and the Stop button is disabled. Because **CancelDisplay** is not set to **true** in the event handler, the HTML control will pop up a dialog box to report the error. If **CancelDisplay** had been set to **true**, the dialog box would not appear.

The **OnBeginRetrieval** event handler (step 5) is called when document retrieval begins. A message indicating that document retrieval is in process is placed on the status bar, the URL edit box is updated to display the URL being retrieved, and the Stop button is enabled so the user can cancel document retrieval. The URL Edit box is updated because, when this event occurs, **HTML1->URL** contains the fully qualified URL. For example, if the user typed **www.mysite.com** into the Edit box, the **URL** property will be something like **http://www.mysite.com**.

HTML1EndRetrieval (step 6) handles **OnEndRetrieval** events. Because the document has been retrieved successfully, the status bar is updated with the word **Done** and the Stop button is disabled.

The HTML control does not channel all errors to the **OnError** event. When a time-out occurs, the **OnTimeout** event is triggered instead. The **HTML1Timeout** function (step 7) puts a message indicating that the time-out occurred on the status bar and disables the Stop button. The time-out interval is stored in the **Time-out** property of the HTML control and has a default value of 30 seconds. Time-outs can be disabled by setting the **Time-out** property to zero.

Finally, the **OnClick** event handler for the Stop button (step 8) calls HTML1's **Cancel** method to stop document retrieval. The parameter passed to **Cancel** is supposed to be appended to the end of the partially retrieved document. However, during my work on this How-To, I was unable to make the message appear as the documentation claims it should. Therefore, I left the parameter blank.

Comments

Although the HTML control included with C++Builder is very powerful, it just is not capable enough to serve as the basis of a full-fledged Web browser that can compete with Explorer. For example, it does not support Java, HTTP authentication, document caching, or cookies. However, if you need to embed a basic Web browser in an application, or you want to build an HTML document viewer that integrates with a database system, the HTML control is the right tool for the job.

COMPLEXITY
INTERMEDIATE

8.2 How do I...
Send mail through the Internet?

Problem

My company is dropping our expensive mail system and replacing it with Internet mail. Sometimes I need to give users the ability to send mail from inside an application. How can I do this with C++Builder?

Technique

Simple mail transport protocol, or SMTP, is the Internet standard for sending mail. This How-To will show you how to use the SMTP control included with C++Builder to send Internet mail.

Steps

Run `SIMPMAIL.EXE` while connected to the Internet or your corporate Intranet. You'll see a screen something like Figure 8-2. Fill in the To and From fields with your email address, add a subject, and type in a message. Put the address of your SMTP mail server in the My Mail Server Edit box and press the Send button. Wait a minute or so and then check your email with your normal email reader. You should see the message you sent from `SIMPMAIL` in your mailbox.

1. Create a new project. Save the default form as `SIMPMAILMAIN.CPP` and the project as `SIMPMAIL.MAK`.

2. Add the components and set their properties as shown in Table 8-2. Lay out the controls as shown in Figure 8-2.

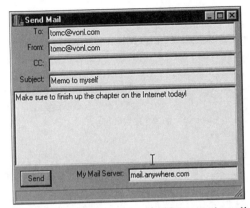

Figure 8-2 SIMPMAIL ready to send mail

Table 8-2 Components, properties, and settings of SIMPMAIL

COMPONENT	PROPERTY	SETTING
TForm	Caption	Send Mail
TLabel	Alignment	taRightJustify
	Caption	To:
TLabel	Alignment	taRightJustify
	Caption	CC:
TLabel	Alignment	taRightJustify
	Caption	Subject:
TLabel	Alignment	taRightJustify
	Caption	From:
TLabel	Caption	My Mail Server:
TSMTP		
TButton	Name	bSendMail
	Caption	Send
	Default	true
TEdit	Name	eTo
	Text	None
TEdit	Name	eFrom
	Text	None
TEdit	Name	eCC
	Text	None
TEdit	Name	eSubject
	Text	None

COMPONENT	PROPERTY	SETTING
TMemo	Name	mMessage
	Lines	None
TEdit	Name	eMailServer
	Text	None
TStatusBar	SimplePanel	true

3. Double-click the Send button, and add the code that actually sends an email message.

```cpp
void __fastcall TForm1::bSendMailClick(TObject *Sender)
{
  //Make sure to address and mail server address have been filled in
  if (eMailServer->Text == "")
  {
    ShowMessage("You must specify your mail server name or address!");
    return;
  }

  if (eTo->Text == "")
  {
    ShowMessage("You must specify an address to send to");
    return;
  }

  //Disable the send button
  bSendMail->Enabled = FALSE;

  //Set the mail server address
  SMTP1->RemoteHost = eMailServer->Text;

  //Clear the headers
  SMTP1->DocInput.OlePropertyGet("Headers").OleProcedure("Clear");
  //Add the to address
  SMTP1->DocInput.OlePropertyGet("Headers").
    OleProcedure("Add", "To", eTo->Text.c_str());
  //If from is provided, add the from address
  if (eFrom->Text != "")
    SMTP1->DocInput.OlePropertyGet("Headers").
      OleProcedure("Add", "From", eFrom->Text.c_str());

  //If carbon copy address is provided, add the CC
  if (eCC->Text != "")
    SMTP1->DocInput.OlePropertyGet("Headers").
      OleProcedure("Add", "CC", eCC->Text.c_str());

  //Add the subject even if it is a blank subject
  SMTP1->DocInput.OlePropertyGet("Headers").
    OleProcedure("Add", "Subject", eSubject->Text.c_str());
  //Send the message
  SMTP1->SendDoc(0, SMTP1->DocInput.OlePropertyGet("Headers"),
                 mMessage->Text, 0, 0);
}
```

4. Open the Object Inspector for the SMTP control. Double-click the `OnError` event, and add the code that reports an error.

```
void __fastcall TForm1::SMTP1Error(TObject *Sender, short Number,
AnsiString &Description, int Scode, const AnsiString Source,
const AnsiString HelpFile, int HelpContext, WordBool &CancelDisplay)
{
  //Show the error on the status bar and in a message box
  StatusBar1->SimpleText = Description;
  ShowMessage(Description);
}
```

5. Double-click the `OnStateChanged` event, and add the code that reports the current state to the user.

```
void __fastcall TForm1::SMTP1StateChanged(TObject *Sender, short State)
{
  //Update the status bar depending on the connection state
  switch (State)
  {
    case 0:
      StatusBar1->SimpleText = "Connecting to host...";
      break;
    case 1:
      StatusBar1->SimpleText = "Resolving host...";
      break;
    case 2:
      StatusBar1->SimpleText = "Resolved host";
      break;
    case 3:
      StatusBar1->SimpleText = "Connected to host";
      break;
    case 4:
      StatusBar1->SimpleText = "Disconnecting from host...";
      break;
    case 5:
      StatusBar1->SimpleText = "Disconnected from host";
      bSendMail->Enabled = TRUE;
      break;
  }
}
```

6. Compile and run the application.

How It Works

SMTP is not a very complex protocol, but it still amazes me that this tiny program can send Internet mail. The SMTP control hides all the nasty details of connecting to the server and communicating with the SMTP protocol. All you have to do is give the control some header information and a message to send.

The `OnClickEvent` handler for the Send button (step 3) first makes sure that the user has provided the address to send mail to, and the address of the SMTP mail

server. If either of these items is blank, the application displays an error message and returns. If the information was provided, the Send button is disabled, and the SMTP mail server's address is put in **SMTP1**'s **RemoteHost** property. The function then sets up the mail headers.

The mail headers are stored in a **DocHeader** collection. The **DocInput** property of the SMTP control includes a **DocHeader** collection that it stores in its **Headers** property. You might think that you'd access the **DocHeaders** collection with code that looks like this:

```
SMTP1->DocInput.Headers
```

Unfortunately, properties of OLE controls are returned as variants. To get a property of a variant that happens to be an OLE object, you use the **OlePropertyGet** function like this:

```
SMTP1->DocInput.OlePropertyGet("Headers")
```

Because the **Headers** property is also a variant, **OleProcedure** is used to call methods of the **DocHeaders** collection like this:

```
SMTP1->DocInput.OlePropertyGet("Headers").OleProcedure("Clear")
```

The application uses the method shown above to clear the **DocHeaders** collection by calling the **Clear** procedure of the **Headers** property. It then adds the mail headers for the To address, the From address, the Carbon-Copy address, and the Subject by calling the **Add** procedure of the **Headers** property. The **Add** procedure is passed the header name and the header text as a C-style string.

Finally, the **SendDoc** method of **SMTP1** is called to send a message in the simplest way possible. The use of the first parameter is not made clear in the documentation and can always be ignored. The second parameter is a **DocHeaders** collection containing the mail headers. The third parameter is the message body as a static text buffer. The fourth parameter is the name of a file that contains the document body. This parameter comes in handy when you want to send an existing document through email, but, because **SIMPMAIL** is just sending a message typed at the computer, this parameter is set to zero. The fifth parameter is the name of a file that will hold a reply document for protocols that send reply documents like HTTP. SMTP does not send reply documents, so this parameter can be ignored.

When you call **SendDoc,** the SMTP control starts the process of connecting to the SMTP server and sending the mail message. As the process progresses, events are fired that let you report the progress and handle errors.

The **OnError** event (step 4) is called whenever an error occurs. The SMTP control passes several parameters to the event handler including the error number, the error message, and the **CancelDisplay** flag. Unlike the HTML control covered in How-To 8.1, the SMTP control does not pop up an error dialog under any circumstances, and the **CancelDisplay** flag has no apparent effect. Therefore, **SMTP1Error** puts the error message on the status bar, displays an error dialog, and enables the Send button.

The `OnProtocolStateChanged` event handler (step 5) is called whenever the protocol state changes. The `SMTP1StateChanged` function displays a descriptive protocol state message in the status bar. In addition, the Send button is enabled when the SMTP control disconnects from the host and is ready to send another message.

Comments

Do not assume that your message will be delivered just because the `OnError` event handler is not called. The SMTP server only checks to make sure the message has syntactically correct headers. Because of the way Internet mail works, you will not know that the mail could not be delivered until you get an email message, sent to the From address, saying that it could not be delivered.

COMPLEXITY
INTERMEDIATE

8.3 How do I...
Create a basic CGI application?

Problem

My company runs a small Web site. We want to add a page that would have fields where someone could enter his name, address, and phone number so we can send him more information. I know how to use the database features in C++Builder, but how do I get the information from the form?

Technique

This How-To will show you how to write a very basic program that interacts with the Web server through the common gateway interface, or CGI, to retrieve information from Web form fields. Such applications are called CGI programs.

This How-To assumes that you have access to the document and CGI directories of a Web server running on a Win32 platform like Windows NT or Windows 95.

Steps

Unlike most of the example programs in this book, you should not run this program on its own. You must install it on your Web server, create a test page, and run it by accessing the test page's URL from your Web browser. Steps six through eight show you how to install and test the program.

1. Create a new console application by selecting File|New... and picking Console App from the dialog that appears (see Figure 8-3). Save the resulting file as `CGI.CPP`.

2. Create a new Unit by selecting File|New Unit, and save the new unit as `URLENCODE.CPP`.

Figure 8-3 File|New... dialog with Console App selected

3. Switch to the header file for the **URLENCODE** unit, **URLENCODE.H**, and add the following declarations:

```
#define urlencodeH
//-------------------------------------------------------------------
#define must_encode(c)  !isalnum(c)
#ifndef _ASCII_non_Portable_
#    define X2C(x)   ((x) >= 'A' ? (((x) & 0xDF) - 'A')+10 : ((x) - '0'))
#else
     const char xc[] = "0123456789ABCDEF";
     const char xv[] = { 0,1,2,3,4,5,6,7,8,9,10,11,12,13,14,15 };
#    define X2C(x)   xv[strcdx(xc,toupper(x))]
#endif

static char x2c(char *hex);
char* str2url(char *buf, char *str);
char* url2str(char *url);
#endif
```

4. Switch back to **URLENCODE.CPP**. Add the functions necessary to encode and decode URL strings.

```
#include "urlencode.h"
//-------------------------------------------------------------------
//****************************************************************************
*
//Function to URL encode and decode.
//****************************************************************************
*
```

continued on next page

continued from previous page

```
//url encode a string
char* str2url(char *buf, char *str)
{
    char *t;
    int c;
    for (t = buf; *str; str++) {
        if ((c = *str) == ' ')
            *t++ = '+';
        else if (must_encode(c)) {
            sprintf(t, "%%%2X", c);
            t += 3;
        } else {
            *t++ = (char)c;
        }
    }
    *t = '\0';
    return buf;
}


//un-encode a url encoded string

char* url2str(char *url)
{
    int x, y;
    for (x = 0, y = 0; url[y] != '\0'; ++x, ++y) {
        if ((url[x] = url[y]) == '%') {
            url[x] = x2c(url + y + 1);
            y += 2;
        } else if (url[x] == '+')
            url[x] = ' ';
    }
    url[x] = '\0';
    return url;
}

//Turn hex encoded character into a character
static char x2c(char *hex)
{
    return (char)(X2C(hex[0]) * 16 + X2C(hex[1]));
}
```

5. Switch to `CGI.CPP`, and add the main function and the statement to include the declarations in `URLENCODE.H`.

```
#include "urlencode.h"
//----------------------------------------------------------------
int main(int argc, char **argv)
{
    char *Method, *StrLen, *Buffer, *UserAgent, *Host;
    char *FoundAmpersand, *WorkString, *QueryString;
    long ContentLength;
```

```
//Get the request method CGI variable
Method = getenv("REQUEST_METHOD");
//Send the most basic content header to the browser
printf("Context-Type: text/html\n\n");
//If the request method did not exist
//Most likely the application is being run from the command line
//instead of through a CGI request
if (Method == NULL)
{
  //Issue error message to the browser and quit
  printf("This was not called from a web browser!\n");
  return 0;
}
//If the method was GET
else if (strcmp(Method, "GET") == 0)
{
  //Get the query string variable
  QueryString = getenv("QUERY_STRING");
  //If there was a query string
  if (QueryString)
  {
    //Allocate a buffer of sufficient size
    Buffer = new char [strlen(QueryString) + 1];
    //Copy the query string into the parameter buffer
    strcpy(Buffer, QueryString);
  }
  //No query string on GET request (this SHOULD not happen)
  else
  {
    //Issue error message and quit
    printf("Could not process GET request");
    return 0;
  }
}
//If the method was POST
else if (strcmp(Method, "POST") == 0)
{
  //Get the content length
  StrLen = getenv("CONTENT_LENGTH");
  //If there was a content length
  if (StrLen)
  {
    //Convert the content length to a number
    ContentLength = strtol(StrLen, NULL, 0);
    //If there is some content
    if (ContentLength > 0)
    {
      //Allocate a buffer big enough to hold the data and a NULL
      Buffer = new char [ContentLength + 1];
      //Read the content from stdin into the buffer
      fread((void *)Buffer, ContentLength, 1, stdin);
      //Put a NULL character at the end to make it a legal C string
      Buffer[ContentLength] = '\0';
```

continued on next page

continued from previous page

```
    }
    //Content length was 0
    else
    {
      //No input data, issue error message and quit
      printf("Content length was not specified!\n");
      return 0;
    }
  }
  //No content length on GET (this SHOULD not happen)
  else
  {
    //Issue error message and quit
    printf("Content length was not specified\n");
    return 0;
  }
}
//Method was something other than GET or POST
else
{
  //Don't know what to do, issue error message and quit
  printf("Unrecognized method\n");
  return 0;
}

//Output some basic data
printf("***Some HTTP Headers***\n");
//User agent identifies the browser software in use
UserAgent = getenv("HTTP_USER_AGENT");
if (!UserAgent)
  printf("HTTP_USER_AGENT = Unknown\n");
else
  printf("HTTP_USER_AGENT = %s\n", UserAgent);

//Host is IP address of host
Host = getenv("HTTP_HOST");
if (!Host)
  printf("HTTP_HOST = Unknown\n");
else
  printf("HTTP_HOST = %s\n", Host);

//Headers for input variables
printf("\n***Information from form ***\n");
printf("Method: %s\n", Method);

//URL Decode the buffer
Buffer = url2str(Buffer);
//Assign it to a working variable
WorkString = Buffer;
//Find the location of the first &
FoundAmpersand = strchr(WorkString, '&');
//If a & was found
while (FoundAmpersand)
```

```
{
  //Change it to a NULL
  FoundAmpersand[0] = '\0';
  //Output up to where the first & was
  printf("%s\n", WorkString);
  //Move past where the & was. Is the next input variable
  WorkString += (FoundAmpersand - WorkString + 1);
  //Look for the next & and loop
  FoundAmpersand = strchr(WorkString, '&');
}

//Output the last input variable (there isn't a & at the end of the⇐
last var)
if (strlen(WorkString))
  printf("%s\n", WorkString);

//Free the buffer allocated to hold the input data
delete [] Buffer;

return 0
}
//----------------------------------------------------------------------
```

6. Compile the program and move the resulting executable file to your Web server's CGI directory. If you are not sure how to do this, ask your Webmaster.

7. Create the following test form and save it in the Web server's document root directory as **TEST.HTML**. This example assumes that your CGI directory is **SCRIPTS** (the default for Microsoft's Internet Information server). You will have to change the CGI directory name in the HTML file if your CGI directory is not called **SCRIPTS**. If you are not sure how to do this, ask your Webmaster.

```
<FORM ACTION="/scripts/cgi.exe"  METHOD="GET">
<B>First Name:</B><BR>
<INPUT TYPE="TEXT" NAME="FIRST"><BR>
<BR>
<B>Last Name:</B><BR>
<INPUT TYPE="TEXT" NAME="LAST"><BR>
<BR>
<B>EMail:</B><BR>
<INPUT TYPE="TEXT" NAME="EMAIL"><BR>
<BR>
<INPUT TYPE="submit" NAME="Submit" BORDER=0 VALUE="Submit it!"></FORM>
```

8. Open your Web browser and access http://<your server name>/ test.html. The form will look something like Figure 8-4. Fill in some information and press the submit button. The browser will now display the page returned from the CGI program (see Figure 8-5).

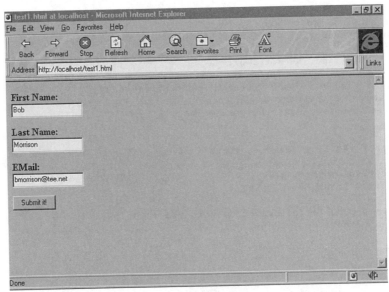

Figure 8-4 Microsoft Explorer displaying a sample Web page

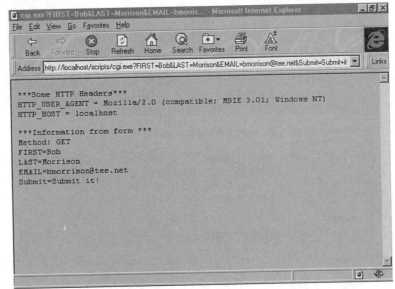

Figure 8-5 Output of the CGI application developed in this How-To

How It Works

The first thing you need to understand is that Web servers communicate with Web browsers using the HTTP protocol. HTML is just a formatting language commonly used to create Web documents. CGI is part of HTTP, not HTML.

HTTP is built around a fairly simple model. The HTTP client, commonly a Web browser, requests documents from an HTTP server, commonly a Web server. The Web server processes the request and sends back the proper document. The HTTP client is responsible for formatting the document and displaying it to the user. It is important to note that the HTTP server does not have to know anything about HTML to process the request.

CGI in Theory

CGI, part of HTTP, provides a standard way for an application to participate, with the help of a Web server, in Web requests. First, the HTTP server must be configured to recognize one or more directories as CGI directories. When the user presses the submit button, the HTTP client sends a request to the HTTP server just like normal. However, because the URL of the request refers to a CGI directory, the HTTP server starts the CGI program and hands it a set of environment variables that contain information about the request. The CGI program looks at the environment variables, reads additional information from the Web server on **stdin** if necessary, and sends a document back through **stdout** to the HTTP server. The HTTP server then passes the document back to the client to satisfy the request that started the whole process.

The **REQUEST_METHOD** environment variable tells the CGI program how to get the form information from the Web server. If **REQUEST_METHOD** is **POST**, the data submitted by the Web client can be read from **stdin**, and the amount of data sent by the client is stored in the **CONTENT_LENGTH** environment variable. If the **REQUEST_METHOD** is **GET**, the data submitted by the Web client is appended to the URL after a "?" character and can also be found in the **QUERY_STRING** environment variable. **GET** is used most of the time because the submitted data appears as part of the URL. Because of this, **GET** requests can be reloaded from most Web browsers. **POST** should be used when there is a significant amount of data on the form. For example, **POST** is the right method for an HTML form that includes a big text box to accept user comments.

In all cases, the data from the form is sent back in the form:

```
<Field Name>=<Field Value>
```

The form information is always URL-encoded, which means that spaces are turned into "+" characters, name/value pairs are separated by "&" characters, and non-alphanumeric characters are represented as a % sign followed by an ASCII code in hexadecimal. For example, the query string returned by the example HTML form will look something like this:

```
FIRST=Tom&LAST=Cabanski&Email=tomc@vonl.com
```

Regardless of the request method, additional information about the request is stored in various environment variables. For example, a description of the Web browser used by the requesting user can be found in the **USER_AGENT** environment variable. A full list of common CGI variables can be found off the home page of the World Wide Web Committee, which maintains the HTTP and HTML standards, at **http://www.w3c.org**.

The CGI program sends a complete document back to the Web server through **stdout**. The document should include the necessary HTTP headers in addition to the body of the document. The example in this How-To sends only the most basic header which tells the Web browser the format of the document. A complete list of HTTP headers can be found off the home page of the W3C.

Once the program is finished sending the document to **stdout**, it simply terminates. The Web server takes care of the details of sending the data to the client over the Internet.

CGI in Practice

Because this is a console application, the program starts by calling the **main** function (step 5). The **stdout** device can be accessed with the **printf** function or through the special file variable **stdout**. The **stdin** file can be read with **scanf** or through the special file variable **stdin**. The program will end when the **main** function returns.

The application writes the most basic HTTP header using **printf** to make sure it is the first thing sent to the Web browser. This header tells the browser that the document is in text format. The pair of newline characters at the end of the header tell the Web browser that this is the last document header.

The **main** function starts by attempting to get the **REQUEST_METHOD** environment variable by calling **getenv**. **Getenv** will return either a pointer to the named environment variable, or **NULL** if the environment variable does not exist. If the **REQUEST_METHOD** did not exist, this is probably not a CGI request, so **main** prints an error message to **stdout** and exits. If you run **CGI.EXE** from the command line, you will see the document header, a blank line, and an error message telling you that you did not run this program through a CGI request.

If the method is **GET**, **main** attempts to read the **QUERY_STRING** environment variable to get the form data. If the query string does exist in the environment, **main** allocates a buffer using the new function and copies the query string into the buffer. If the query string does not exist, the program prints an error message and exits.

If the method is **POST**, the application attempts to read the **CONTENT_LENGTH** environment variable. If the content length environment variable exists, and it is greater than zero, a buffer big enough to hold the content plus a **NULL** terminator is allocated. The **fread** function is used to read one element of **CONTENT_LENGTH** characters into the newly allocated buffer. A **NULL** terminator is then added to the end of the buffer. If the content length does not exist, or is zero, **main** prints an error message and exits.

If the request method environment variable exists, but is not **GET** or **POST**, the program prints an error message and quits. To handle form input, CGI programs

only need to deal with **GET** and **POST** requests. There are, however, other request methods defined in the HTTP protocol. Check out the W3C Web site for more information on this subject.

Once the variable buffer holds the information sent from the user request, the program attempts to fetch two of the standard CGI variables and display them on the Web page. **Getenv** is used exactly as it was to fetch the other environment variable.

This program performs a simple dump of the field name/value pairs in the last part of **main**. First, the buffer is URL decoded by calling the **url2str** function—**+** characters are turned into spaces and **%xxx** markers are turned into the proper ASCII characters. I won't go into detail of how **url2str** works here because it is just ugly, low-level stuff that I got off the Internet years ago. You can use the **url2str** and **str2url** functions in the programs you write without ever worrying about how they work. If you want to learn how to decode and encode URL strings yourself, you can study the code.

To understand the **while** loop that actually prints out the name-value pairs, you must remember how the data sent from the user looks. Field name/value pairs are separated by ampersands, but the last name-value pair does not end with an ampersand. For example:

```
<field name1>=<field value>&<field name2>=<field value>& &<field
namen>=<field value>
```

First, **WorkString** is set to point at the beginning of the data as shown below:

```
buffer: <field name1>=<value>&<field name2>=<value>&...&<field namen>=<value>
        ^
        WorkString
```

The **strchr** function will make **FoundAmpersand** point at the first ampersand character in the string, or it will return **NULL** if the ampersand was not found. For the example data shown above, things will end up as shown below:

```
buffer: <field name1>=<value>&<field name2>=<value>&...&<field namen>=<value>
        ^                     ^
        WorkString            FoundAmpersand
```

As long as **FoundAmpersand** points at an ampersand character, the ampersand will be replaced with a **NULL** terminator:

```
buffer: <field name1>=<value>\0<field name2>=<value>&...&<field namen>=<value>
        ^                     ^
        WorkString            FoundAmpersand
```

When **WorkString** is output to **stdout**, only the first name/value pair will be printed because the **NULL** terminator marks the end of **WorkString** as far as **printf** is concerned. **WorkString** is then moved to point at the next name-value pair:

```
buffer: <field name1>=<value>\0<field name2>=<value>&...&<field namen>=<value>
                               ^
                               WorkString
```

The loop continues until there are no more ampersand characters left. The remaining portion of **WorkString** is then sent to **stdout**, the data buffer is released, and the program terminates.

Comments

Once you understand the basics of processing **GET** and **POST** requests through CGI, you are ready to build all kinds of interactive Web applications. The techniques shown in this How-To, combined with powerful database tools, make C++Builder an excellent choice for building sophisticated Web applications.

COMPLEXITY
ADVANCED

8.4 How do I...
Create a basic ISAPI application?

Problem

Now I know how to build CGI applications (How-To 8.3), but my Webmaster told me that CGI applications are expensive in terms of performance. Is there a more efficient way to process the data from Web forms?

Technique

If you're using Microsoft's Internet Information Server, or some other compatible Web server, you can build a DLL that works almost exactly like a CGI script except it runs as part of the Web server. Performance is generally better, especially under heavy load, because requests are handled in threads which are much cheaper to create than the full-fledged processes that CGI requires.

Steps

Unlike most of the example programs in this book, you cannot run this program on its own. You must install it on your Web server, create a test page and run it by accessing the test page's URL from your Web browser. Steps 6 through 8 show you how to install and test the program.

This How-To assumes that you have read How-To 8.2 which covers standard CGI programming.

1. Create a new DLL by selecting File|New... and picking DLL from the dialog that appears. Save the resulting file as **SIMPLEISAPI.CPP**.

2. Add the **URLENCODE.CPP** file you created in How-To 8.2 to the project by using the Add button in the Project Manager.

3. Add the following **#include** statements near the top of **SIMPLEISAPI.CPP**.

```
#include <vcl\vcl.h>
#include <vcl\isapi.hpp>
#include "urlencode.h"
#pragma hdrstop
```

4. Add the `GetExtension` function at the end of `SIMPLEISAPI.CPP`.

```
//Negotiate version with ISAPI
extern "C" __declspec(dllexport) BOOL __stdcall GetExtensionVersion(⇐
THSE_VERSION_INFO  *pVer )
{
    //Version is current version
    pVer->dwExtensionVersion = MAKELONG( HSE_VERSION_MINOR,
                                         HSE_VERSION_MAJOR );
    //Send version back to ISAPI
    lstrcpyn( pVer->lpszExtensionDesc,
              "This is a sample Web Server Application",
              HSE_MAX_EXT_DLL_NAME_LEN );
    //Everything is OK
    return TRUE;
}
```

5. After `GetExtensionVersion`, add the code for the `WriteClient` function.

```
//Helper function to write data to client
void WriteClientData(TEXTENSION_CONTROL_BLOCK *lpEcb, char *WriteBuffer)
{
  int Count;

  //Get length of buffer
  Count = strlen(WriteBuffer);
  //Write it out via ISAPI function
  lpEcb->WriteClient(lpEcb->ConnID, (void *)WriteBuffer, Count, 0);
}
```

6. After `WriteClient`, add the code for `HttpExtensionProc`.

```
//This is the body of the ISAPI extension. This function does the actual⇐
work.
//Since there can be multiple requests working at the same time, this⇐
function
//must access global data in a thread-safe manner.
extern "C" __declspec(dllexport) DWORD __stdcall HttpExtensionProc( ⇐
TEXTENSION_CONTROL_BLOCK  *lpEcb )
{
  char *Buffer, InBuffer[255], OutBuffer[1024], *WorkString,⇐
*FoundAmpersand;
  int BufferSize;

  //Send standard headers
  lpEcb->ServerSupportFunction(lpEcb->ConnID, HSE_REQ_SEND_RESPONSE_HEADER,⇐
NULL, 0, 0);
  //And tack on the content type
  WriteClientData(lpEcb, "Content-type: text/plain\n\n");
```

continued on next page

continued from previous page

```
//Is this a GET request?
if (strcmp(lpEcb->lpszMethod, "GET") == 0)
{
  //Allocate a buffer big enough to hold the data
  Buffer = new char [strlen(lpEcb->lpszQueryString + 1)];
  //Copy the query string into the buffer
  strcpy(Buffer, lpEcb->lpszQueryString);
}
//Is this a POST request?
else if (strcmp(lpEcb->lpszMethod, "POST") == 0)
{
  //Was there some data sent from the client?
  if (lpEcb->cbAvailable > 0)
  {
    //Allocate a buffer big enough to hold the data
    Buffer = new char [lpEcb->cbAvailable + 1];
    //Copy the data into the buffer
    memcpy((void *)Buffer, (void *)lpEcb->lpbData, lpEcb->cbAvailable);
    //Tack a NULL onto the end of the buffer
    Buffer[lpEcb->cbAvailable] = '\0';
  }
  //No data sent from the client
  else
  {
    //Issue error message to the client
    WriteClientData(lpEcb, "Content length not specified\n");
    //Exit, the process is complete
    return HSE_STATUS_SUCCESS;
  }
}
//Method other than POST or GET
else
{
  //Issue error message to the client
  WriteClientData(lpEcb, "Unrecognized Method\n");
  //Exit, the process is complete
  return HSE_STATUS_SUCCESS;
}

//Write a couple of HTTP variables to the client
WriteClientData(lpEcb, "***Some HTTP Headers***\n");

//Set the buffer size
BufferSize = 255;
//If the HTTP_USER_AGENT variable is retrieved
if (lpEcb->GetServerVariable(lpEcb->ConnID, "HTTP_USER_AGENT",
                             InBuffer, BufferSize))
  //Output it to a buffer
  wsprintf(OutBuffer, "HTTP_USER_AGENT = %s\n", InBuffer);
//The variable was not returned
else
  //Output an error message to the buffer
  strcpy(OutBuffer, "HTTP_USER_AGENT = Unknown\n");
```

```
//Send the buffer to the client
WriteClientData(lpEcb, OutBuffer);

//HTTP_HOST retrieval works as above
if (lpEcb->GetServerVariable(lpEcb->ConnID, "HTTP_HOST",
                                    InBuffer, BufferSize))
  wsprintf(OutBuffer, "HTTP_HOST = %s\n", InBuffer);
else
  strcpy(OutBuffer, "HTTP_HOST = Unknown\n");

WriteClientData(lpEcb, OutBuffer);

//Write the field data to the client
WriteClientData(lpEcb, "\n***Information from form ***\n");

//Method
wsprintf(OutBuffer, "Method: %s\n", lpEcb->lpszMethod);
WriteClientData(lpEcb, OutBuffer);

//URL decode the buffer of data from the client
Buffer = url2str(Buffer);
//Assign a work string
WorkString = Buffer;
//Find the first & which is used to separate data elements
FoundAmpersand = strchr(WorkString, '&');
//As long as we found a &
while (FoundAmpersand)
{
  //Replace the & with a NULL
  FoundAmpersand[0] = '\0';
  //Write the client data element to a buffer
  wsprintf(OutBuffer, "%s\n", WorkString);
  //Send the buffer to the client
  WriteClientData(lpEcb, OutBuffer);
  //Move past the location of the & we found, that makes
  //WorkString point at the next data element
  WorkString += (FoundAmpersand - WorkString + 1);
  //Look for an & again and repeat
  FoundAmpersand = strchr(WorkString, '&');
}

//If there was a data element left over
//(HTTP does not put an & after the last data element)
if (strlen(WorkString))
{
  //Send it to the client
  wsprintf(OutBuffer, "%s\n", WorkString);
  WriteClientData(lpEcb, OutBuffer);
}

//Delete the client data buffer
delete [] Buffer;

//Process is complete, return
return HSE_STATUS_SUCCESS;
}
```

7. Compile the DLL and move the resulting executable file to your Web server's CGI directory. If you are not sure how to do this, ask your Webmaster.

8. Create the following test form and save it in the Web server's document root directory as **TEST.HTML**. This example assumes that your CGI directory is **SCRIPTS** (the default for Microsoft's Internet Information server). You will have to change the CGI directory name in the HTML file if your CGI directory is not called **SCRIPTS**. If you are not sure how to do this, ask your Webmaster.

```
<FORM ACTION="/scripts/simpleisapi.dll"  METHOD="GET">
<B>First Name:</B><BR>
<INPUT TYPE="TEXT" NAME="FIRST"><BR>
<BR>
<B>Last Name:</B><BR>
<INPUT TYPE="TEXT" NAME="LAST"><BR>
<BR>
<B>EMail:</B><BR>
<INPUT TYPE="TEXT" NAME="EMAIL"><BR>
<BR>
<INPUT TYPE="submit" NAME="Submit" BORDER=0 VALUE="Submit it!"></FORM>
```

9. Open your Web browser and access `http://<your server name>/test.html`. The form will look something like Figure 8-4. Fill in some information and press the submit button. The browser will now display the page returned from the ISAPI DLL (see Figure 8-5).

How It Works

An ISAPI extension is a high-performance alternative to a standard CGI program. When a standard CGI request is received, the Web server starts the CGI program in its own process. Each time the CGI program is called, the system must again pay the overhead of starting a new process. ISAPI extensions, on the other hand, are DLLs that get loaded the first time they are called and remain loaded until the Web server is shut down. User requests are processed in threads which are far less expensive to start than processes.

An ISAPI extension DLL must have two exported functions. The Web server calls **GetExtensionVersion** to make sure the Web server and the extension can agree upon a common version of ISAPI. Each time a user request is received, the Web server starts a thread and calls **HttpExtensionProc** from the context of the thread to process the user request. In C++Builder you indicate that a DLL function should be exported by adding the **declspec(dllexport)** modifier to the declaration of the function.

GetExtensionVersion (step 4) modifies two fields in the **HSE_VERSION_INFO** structure to let the Web server know the version of the API it wants and a description of itself. First, the **MAKELONG** macro is used to put the current ISAPI version into

the dwExtensionVersion field. Then, lstrcpyn is used to put a description, no longer than HSE_MAX_EXT_DLL_NAME_LEN characters, into the lpszExtensionDesc field. Lstrcpyn will truncate the description if it is too long.

HttpExtensionProc (step 5) actually services the requests from the user. ISAPI passes in a pointer to an EXTENSION_CONTROL_BLOCK structure that contains the fields shown in Table 8-3.

Table 8-3 EXTENSION_CONTROL_BLOCK structure

FIELD	DESCRIPTION
cbSize	Size of the structure
dwVersion	ISAPI version
ConnID	Connection context number
dwHttpStatusCode	HTTP status code
lpszLogData[HSE_LOG_BUFFER_LEN]	Log information for this DLL
lpszMethod	REQUEST_METHOD CGI Variable
lpszQueryString	QUERY_STRING CGI variable
	Holds user data when lpszMethod is GET
lpszPathInfo	PATH_INFO CGI variable
lpszPathTranslated	PATH_TRANSLATED CGI variable
cbTotalBytes	Total bytes indicated from client
cbAvailable	Corresponds to CGI CONTENT_LENGTH
	Holds number of bytes to read
	when method is POST
lpbData	Holds user data when method is POST
GetServerVariable	Function to get additional CGI
	variables for this request
ReadClient	Function to read data from client
	for this request
ServerSupportFunction	Function to perform miscellaneous functions for this request
WriteClient	Function to write data to client for this request

HttpExtensionProc starts by using the ServerSupportFunction to send a set of standard HTTP headers to the client. Note that ServerSupportFunction must be called through the EXTENSION_CONTROL_BLOCK pointer passed into HttpExtensionProc because it is part of the EXTENSION_CONTROL_BLOCK structure. This is true for calls to GetServerVariable, WriteClient, and ReadClient as well. The extension control block also includes the context number of the connection which must be passed to certain ISAPI functions.

Next, **WriteClientData**, a helper function described later, is used to send the content-type header to the client. The two newline characters ("\n") tell the client that this is the last HTTP header. If the request method is **GET**, a buffer big enough to hold **lpszQueryString** plus a **NULL** terminator is allocated. The query string is then copied into the buffer using **strcpy** which appends a **NULL** terminator to the end of the string.

If the request method is **POST**, **HttpExtensionProc** checks to make sure there is some form data to process. If there is, a buffer is allocated to hold the data, and **memcpy** is used to copy the data from **lpbData** to the new buffer. A **NULL** terminator is tacked onto the end of the buffer to make it a legitimate C-style string. If there is no form data, the application sends an error message to the client and returns **HSE_STA-TUS_SUCCESS** to indicate that it has finished processing the request.

Next, **HttpExtensionProc** gets and prints the values of a couple of CGI variables. If this was a regular CGI program, this information would be retrieved with **getenv**. In ISAPI, though, the **GetServerVariable** function is used instead.

GetServerVariable takes the context number of the connection, a variable name, a buffer to hold the data, and a variable that holds the size of the buffer. If successful, **GetServerVariable** will return **true**, the variable data will be held in the buffer, and the size of the actual data will be stored in the buffer size variable. If **GetServerVariable** fails, it will return **false**.

After the **HTTP_USER_AGENT** and **HTTP_HOST** variable information is output, the form data is parsed and output exactly as it was in How-To 8.3. In fact, if you examine both **HttpExtensionProc** and the main function from How-To 8.3, you should notice that they are very similar.

The **WriteClientData** function takes an **EXTENSION_BLOCK_POINTER** and a string. It gets the length of the string by calling **strlen**, and then calls the **WriteClient** function to send output to the Web client. **WriteClient** takes the context number, the buffer to write, a variable that holds the length of the buffer, and an extra parameter that should be ignored by basic extension DLLs like this one. If **WriteClient** fails, it will return **false**, and if it succeeds it will return **true**. **WriteClientData** simply assumes that **WriteClient** will succeed.

Comments

You must carefully test ISAPI extensions before running them on a production Web server. Because ISAPI extensions are DLLs that get loaded by the Web server the first time a request is made, you have to shut down the Web server to free the DLL once it is loaded. I have also seen cases where a poorly written ISAPI extension crashes the Web server.

You should also note that because ISAPI extensions stay loaded between requests, you can use global data elements to store context information or statistics about requests. You must always remember, however, that the **HttpExtensionProc** can be called

from multiple threads of execution. As a result, you must access global data elements in a thread-safe manner as discussed in Chapter 12, "Threads."

COMPLEXITY
ADVANCED

8.5 How do I...
Communicate between programs over the Internet?

Problem

I am developing a program that needs to communicate with other instances of itself over the Internet. I don't think FTP is the right solution because that would require an FTP server at both ends. Is there an easy way to make two programs communicate directly over the Internet with C++Builder?

Technique

This How-To shows you how to use the TCP control included with C++Builder to create applications that know how to communicate over the Internet. The sample application you'll create knows how to act as a server or a client, and, when acting as a server, can handle requests from several clients at once.

Steps

Run **PINGPONG.EXE** twice. On the first (or server) copy, type **111** into the port field and press the Listen button. On the second (or client) copy, type the IP address of your machine into the Host field, type **111** into the port field, and press the Connect button. The server copy's status bar should indicate that a connection has been accepted. Press the Ping button on the Client copy and your screen should look something like Figure 8-6. Notice that pressing the Ping button on the client displays a Ping message on the server and that the Pong message that appears on the client was sent by the server after it received the Ping message. Experiment by opening additional clients, connecting them, closing them, and closing the server copy while clients are connected.

1. Create a new application. Save the form as **PINGPONGMAIN.CPP** and the project as **PINGPONG.MAK**.

2. Add the components and set their properties as shown in Table 8-4. Lay out the controls as shown in Figure 8-6.

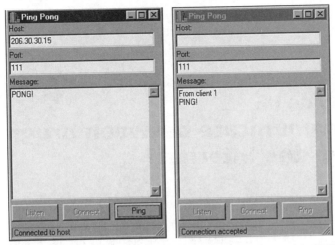

Figure 8-6 Client PINGPONG connected to server PINGPONG after Ping button has been pressed

Table 8-4 Components, properties, and settings for PINGPONG

COMPONENT	PROPERTY	SETTING
TForm	Caption	Ping Pong
TLabel	Caption	Port:
TLabel	Caption	Host:
TLabel	Caption	Message:
TTCP		
TButton	Name	bListen
	Caption	Listen:
	Enabled	True
TButton	Name	bConnect
	Caption	Connect
	Enabled	True
TButton	Name	bPing
	Caption	Connect
	Enabled	False
TEdit	Name	eHost
	Text	None
TEdit	Name	ePort
	Text	None
TMemo	Name	mStatus
	Lines	None

COMPONENT	PROPERTY	SETTING
	ReadOnly	True
	ScrollBars	ssVertical
TStatusBar	SimplePanel	True

3. Switch to **PINGPONGMAIN.H**, and add the following declarations to TForm1's private section:

```
private:// User declarations
  TList *TCPList;
  bool Listening;
  int NextConnectionID;
```

4. Open Form1's Object Inspector. Double-click on the **FormCreate** event, and add the code that initializes the private variables.

```
void __fastcall TForm1::FormCreate(TObject *Sender)
{
  //Initialize the list to hold client connections
  TCPList = new TList;
  //When application starts it is not listening
  Listening = FALSE;
  //First client will get ID number 1
  NextConnectionID = 1;
}
```

5. Double-click on the Connect button, and add the code that attempts to connect to a listening server.

```
void __fastcall TForm1::bConnectClick(TObject *Sender)
{
  //Application needs host and port to connect
  if ((eHost->Text == "") || (ePort->Text == ""))
  {
    //Show the error and return
    ShowMessage("You must indicate host and port to connect to");
    return;
  }

  //Update the status bar
  StatusBar1->SimpleText = "Attempting to connect to host...";
  //Disable the connect and listen buttons
  bConnect->Enabled = FALSE;
  bListen->Enabled = FALSE;
  //Error in the TRY block will transfer control to the catch(...)
  try
  {
    //Attempt to connect to the given host and port
    TCP1->Connect(eHost->Text.c_str(), ePort->Text.c_str());
```

continued on next page

continued from previous page

```
  }
  //Errors in try caught here
  catch (...)
  {
    //Error occurred, client not connected, reset buttons
    bConnect->Enabled = TRUE;
    bListen->Enabled = TRUE;
  }
}
```

6. Double-click on the Ping button, and add the code that sends a message to a connected server.

```
void __fastcall TForm1::bPingClick(TObject *Sender)
{
  //Send ping command to host
  TCP1->SendData("PING!");
}
```

7. Double-click on the Listen button, and add the code to make the program become a listening server.

```
void __fastcall TForm1::bListenClick(TObject *Sender)
{
  //Need port to listen on, server is always on this machine's IP
  if (ePort->Text == "")
  {
    //show the error and return
    ShowMessage("Port must be specified to listen");
    return;
  }

  //Set the listening port
  TCP1->LocalPort = StrToInt(ePort->Text);
  //Try to listen
  TCP1->Listen();
  //If the listen attempt succeeded
  if (TCP1->State == sckListening)
  {
    //Update the status bar
    StatusBar1->SimpleText = "Listening on port " + ePort->Text;
    //Set the application's listening flag
    Listening = TRUE;
    //Disable listen and connect buttons
    bListen->Enabled = FALSE;
    bConnect->Enabled = FALSE;
  }
}
```

8. Open the Object Inspector for the TCP control. Double-click on the OnConnectionRequest button, and add the code that connects the server to a client requesting a connection.

```
//Someone is knocking on the door. Let them in.
void __fastcall TForm1::TCP1ConnectionRequest(TObject *Sender, int⇐
requestID)
{
  TTCP *WorkTCP;

  //Update the status bar
  StatusBar1->SimpleText = "Connection request received";
  //Create a new TCP control owned by the form.
  WorkTCP = new TTCP(Form1);
  //Add the new TCP control to the TCPList
  TCPList->Add(WorkTCP);
  //Accept the connection on the new TCP control
  WorkTCP->Accept(requestID);
  //Assign the OnDataArrival event
  WorkTCP->OnDataArrival = TCP1DataArrival;
  //Assign the OnClose event
  WorkTCP->OnClose = TCP1Close;
  //Assign the Tag to identify the client
  WorkTCP->Tag = NextConnectionID;
  //Increment the connection ID
  NextConnectionID++;
  //Update the status bar
  StatusBar1->SimpleText = "Connection accepted";
}
```

9. Double-click the `OnConnect` event, and add the code that enables the Ping button when a client gets a connection to a server.

```
//Connection accepted
void __fastcall TForm1::TCP1Connect(TObject *Sender)
{
  //Update status bar
  StatusBar1->SimpleText = "Connected to host";
  //Since we're connected, enable the ping button
  bPing->Enabled = TRUE;
}
```

10. Double-click the `OnDataArrival`, and add the code to handle incoming data for a client or a server.

```
//Data has arrived
void __fastcall TForm1::TCP1DataArrival(TObject *Sender, int bytesTotal)
{
  Variant Data;

  //Get the data from the TCP control that sent the message
  //For the client there is only one control but for the
  //server there is one for each client connection
  ((TTCP *)Sender)->GetData(Data, VT_BSTR, bytesTotal);
  //if this is the server
  if (Listening)
    //write the client ID first
    mStatus->Lines->Add("From client " + IntToStr(((TTCP *)Sender)->Tag));
```

continued on next page

continued from previous page

```
//Write the data to a line in the memo box
mStatus->Lines->Add(Data);

//If this is a server
if (Listening)
  //Reply with PONG!
  ((TTCP *)Sender)->SendData("PONG!");
}
```

11. Double-click the `OnError` event, and add the code to handle errors from the TCP control.

```
//Error occurred
void __fastcall TForm1::TCP1Error(TObject *Sender, short Number,
  AnsiString &Description, int Scode, const AnsiString Source,
  const AnsiString HelpFile, int HelpContext, WordBool &CancelDisplay)
{
  //Set buttons to default state
  bConnect->Enabled = TRUE;
  bListen->Enabled = TRUE;
  bPing->Enabled = FALSE;
}
```

12. Double-click the `OnClose` event, and add the code that is executed when the connection is closed by the program at the other end of the connection.

```
//Connection closed
void __fastcall TForm1::TCP1Close(TObject *Sender)
{
  int i;
  TTCP *WorkTCP;

  //If this is the server
  if (Listening)
  {
    //Find the connection in the list
    i = TCPList->IndexOf(Sender);
    //If the connection was found in the list (it's a client connection)
    if (i != -1)
    {
      //Free the TTCP control
      ((TTCP *)TCPList->Items[i])->Free();
      //Delete it from the list
      TCPList->Delete(i);
    }
  }
  //This is the client
  else
  {
    //The following code works around a bug in the OCX
    //When the server closes the socket, the client socket closes
    //as it should but something in the control is corrupted.
```

```
//This code destroys the corrupted control, creates a new one with
//the proper event handlers and assigns the new control to TCP1
TCP1->Free();
WorkTCP = new TTCP(Form1);
WorkTCP->OnConnectionRequest = TCP1ConnectionRequest;
WorkTCP->OnConnect = TCP1Connect;
WorkTCP->OnDataArrival = TCP1DataArrival;
WorkTCP->OnError = TCP1Error;
WorkTCP->OnClose = TCP1Close;
TCP1 = WorkTCP;
//Set buttons to default state
bConnect->Enabled = TRUE;
bListen->Enabled = TRUE;
bPing->Enabled = FALSE;
  }

//Indicate that the connection is closed
StatusBar1->SimpleText = "Connection closed";
}
```

13. Open the Object Inspector for **Form1**. Double-click on the **OnDestroy** event, and add the code that closes the open connection and frees any allocated memory just before the program terminates.

```
void __fastcall TForm1::FormDestroy(TObject *Sender)
{
  int x;

  //If the primary socket is open, close it.
  if (TCP1->State == sckOpen)
    TCP1->Close();

  //If this is the server
  if (Listening)
  {
    //Iterate through the client connection list
    for (x = 0; x < TCPList->Count; x++)
    {
      //Close the client connection
      ((TTCP *)TCPList->Items[x])->Close();
      //Free the TCP control
      ((TTCP *)TCPList->Items[x])->Free();
    }
  }

  //Free the client connection list
  TCPList->Free();
}
```

14. Compile and run the application.

How It Works

This program is actually two programs in one. If you press the Listen button, the program acts as a server that accepts connections from clients, and responds to PING requests from connected clients. If, on the other hand, you press the Connect button, the program acts as a client and can send PING requests to the server.

PINGPONG Server

The FormCreate function (step 4) initializes a TList to hold client connections, a boolean variable called Listening that will be set to true when the user presses the Listen button, and a variable to hold the ID number that will be assigned to the next connecting client.

The bListenClick function (step 7) turns the program into a server. A TCP server listens for incoming connections on a particular port. This allows multiple servers for different purposes to run on the same machine. The Internet services you're probably already used to work by listening on the ports shown in Table 8-5.

Table 8-5 Ports for common Internet services

PORT	SERVICE
21	FTP
23	Telnet
25	SMTP (Send mail)
80	HTTP (Web)
123	NNTP (News)

If you have installed TCP/IP networking on your machine, the SERVICES file found in your WINDOWS directory contains a complete list of standard services and ports. Port numbers range from 1 to 65,536.

The bListenClick function checks to make sure the user has selected a port and prints an error message if one was not provided. It then assigns the port number to the TCP control's LocalPort property, and calls the Listen method to start the server listening on the LocalPort. If the TCP control is listening, the status bar is updated, the Listening flag is set to true, and the Listen and Connect buttons are disabled. If, for some reason, the server could not listen, for example networking is not installed, the function does nothing special because the error will be handled by the TCP control's OnError event handler, which will be described later.

When a client tries to connect, the TCP control will call its OnConnectionRequest event handler (step 8). TCP1ConnectionRequest updates the status bar to say that a connection request was received and then creates a new TCP control, WorkTCP, to service the client. This is very important because the original TCP control is dedicated to listening for client requests and cannot service a client at the same time as it is listening. After WorkTCP is created, it is added to the list of client TCP controls so that all the open connections can be cleaned up when the program ends. Next,

the `Accept` method of `WorkTCP` is called to connect the client request identified by the `requestID` variable passed into the event handler, the event handlers for `OnDataArrival` and `OnClose` are set, the `Tag` property of the new TCP control is assigned the `NextConnectionID` for identification purposes, the `NextConnectionID` is incremented, and the status bar is updated to reflect that a client has just connected.

The `OnDataArrival` event handler, `TCP1DataArrival` (step 10), is called whenever one of the TCP controls that is serving a client receives data. The `Sender` variable which was passed into the event handler is a pointer to the TCP control that received the data. Because Sender is a `TObject` pointer, it must be cast to a TTCP pointer before it is used to access properties or methods of the TTCP control.

`TCP1DataArrival` gets the data from the control by calling its `GetData` method. `GetData` is passed a variant variable to hold the data, the type to retrieve, and the number of bytes to retrieve. Because the client application is sending string data, `GetData` is told to retrieve a `VT_BSTR` and the `bytesTotal` variable passed into this event is passed on to `GetData`.

Because `TCP1DataArrival` is used both for the server and the client, `TCP1DataArrival` checks the `Listening` flag to see whether this is the server. If it is, the client ID, stored in the `Tag` member of the TCP control servicing the client, is output to the Status Memo box. Then, for client and server, the data sent by the other end of the connection is output to the Memo box. Finally, if this is the server, a PONG message is sent back to the client.

The TCP control's `OnClose` event handler (step 12) is called whenever the other end of the connection closes. This gives the application a chance to clean things up when the other end of the connection is shut down. For the server, `TCP1Close` looks for the TCP control in the list of TCP controls servicing client. If it is found, the control is freed and removed from the list.

For both client and server, the `FormDestroy` method (step 13) closes the primary socket if it is open. Then, if this is the server, `FormDestroy` iterates through the client connection list, closes each client connection, and then frees each client control. This step is very important because a `TList` object simply stores a list of pointers. Releasing the memory associated with a `TList` does not release the memory associated with objects referenced by the pointers in the list. Furthermore, if you do not call a TCP control's `Close` method, there is no guarantee that the other end of the connection will close properly. Finally, for both server and client, the memory associated with the client connection list is released.

PINGPONG Client

Once you understand the server, the client portion of `PINGPONG` is pretty simple. The `bConnectClick` function (step 5) checks to make sure a host name (or address) and a port have been specified. If both are not provided, the function displays an error message and exits. If both are specified, the Connect and Listen buttons are disabled, and the TCP control attempts to initiate a connection to the specified server address and port by calling the `TCP1's` `Connect` method. The `Connect` method will throw an exception if the address or port specified is in an invalid format. Because

the call to **Connect** is in a **Try** block, if any exception occurs, control will be transferred to the **Catch(...)** block, and the Connect and Listen buttons will be re-enabled.

The **bPingClick** function (step 6) simply sends a PING command to the connected server. Note that the Ping button will not be active unless the client is currently connected to a server.

The **OnConnect** event handler (step 9) will be called when the connection, initiated with the TCP control's **Connect** method, is actually accepted by a server. In this case, the status bar is updated, and the Ping button is enabled. If the connection is not accepted, the **OnError** event handler will be called instead.

The **OnClose** event handler for the client is a little ugly because of a bug in the TCP control. When a connection is closed from the remote end using the **Close** method, the client's TCP control is sometimes left in an unstable state. To work around this, **TCP1Close** frees the existing TCP control, creates a new TCP control, sets up the proper event handlers, and assigns the new TCP control to **TCP1**. This allows the client to initiate a connection with another server without causing funny GPF errors.

Comments

This How-To demonstrates how to use the TCP control to create clients, and servers that can handle multiple client connections. The techniques shown in this How-To can be used to build standard servers and clients for protocols like HTTP and FTP, or custom servers and clients for protocols you invent. If you understand how to use the TCP control, you have a basic understanding of the foundation of all the Internet services.

CHAPTER 9
MULTIMEDIA

9

MULTIMEDIA

How do I...

9.1 **Determine whether a system has a sound card?**

9.2 **Play wave and MIDI files?**

9.3 **Play video files in my form?**

9.4 **Play an audio CD?**

9.5 **Detect and use a joystick in my application?**

9.6 **Display JPEG and GIF files?**

The popularity of multimedia programs has exploded over the past couple of years. Virtually all new computers come equipped with a sound card, powerful graphics, and a high speed CD-ROM. Pentium and Pentium Pro grade machines can execute complex multimedia programs without straining a muscle. In addition, users of older PCs are quickly upgrading their systems with multimedia-capable hardware.

Multimedia includes sight and sound. Sight consists of pictures, animation, video, and even live, real-time motion. Sound includes sound effects, music, and voice recordings. Games are the best examples of multimedia use. They combine user interaction with just about every aspect of multimedia. Today's hardware allows games and other applications, such as online encyclopedias, to feature smooth, full motion video at 15 frames per second.

This chapter presents a few basics on playing and controlling different forms of multimedia. Most of the How-To's make extensive use of C++Builder™'s `MediaPlayer` control. `TMediaPlayer` simplifies most multimedia chores by encapsulating the Media Control Interface (MCI) of Windows 95.

9.1 Determine Whether a System Has a Sound Card

There aren't too many reasons to play audio files if your users do not have a sound card in their system. This How-To shows you how to detect if a machine can play audio.

9.2 Play Wave and MIDI Files

This How-To uses the `MediaPlayer` component to play music and other sounds stored as wave files or MIDI sequences. Playing audio is simple, but tracking the progress of a long audio clip takes more effort. In addition to playing sound, this How-To also describes how you can display the progress of the audio clip.

9.3 Play Video Files in My Form

Playing AVI video files is also a piece of cake. `TMediaPlayer` does all the work. However, it will normally spawn a new window in which to play the video clip. This How-To shows how you can play the video file right in your own form.

9.4 Play an Audio CD

This How-To configures the `MediaPlayer` component to play an audio CD. The `MediaPlayer` control allows users to navigate from track to track on the CD. The program also displays a list of audio tracks and the progress of the CD as it plays.

9.5 Detect and Use a Joystick in My Application

The best multimedia programs are generally games. Many games use a joystick, if it's present, as the main input device for the program. Windows encapsulates the joystick with the rest of the MCI section of the API. This How-To shows how you can add joystick support to your programs.

9.6 Display JPEG and GIF Files

The World Wide Web allows access to thousands of JPEG and GIF images. Currently, Windows 95 does not offer built-in support for displaying JPEG and GIF images. This How-To employs a custom control to handle the chores of displaying JPEG and GIF files in a form.

COMPLEXITY
INTERMEDIATE

9.1 How do I...
Determine whether a system has a sound card?

Problem

I want to add neat sound effects and audio capability to some of my programs, but I know that some of my users don't have sound cards in their PCs. How can I detect whether or not a system has a sound card at runtime?

Technique

Determining the presence of a sound card can be split into two items: detecting wave support and detecting MIDI support. Usually the two go together, but not always. The Media Control Interface, or MCI, provides API functions for determining how many wave and MIDI devices are present on a system. If no devices exist, then you know the user doesn't have a sound card installed.

Steps

Run SOUNDCARD.EXE. A window will appear that resembles Figure 9-1. The label at the top of the form indicates whether the system contains a sound card. If your system has a sound card, you can use the UpDown controls to scroll through each of the wave and MIDI devices provided by the sound card.

NOTE

A single sound card may contain several wave and MIDI devices. For example, a Yamaha OPL-3 sound card provides three MIDI devices.

1. Create a new project. Name the unit MAINFORM.CPP and name the project SOUNDCARD.MAK.

2. You only need to use Label and UpDown controls in this project. Place the controls on Form1 and set properties to match Table 9-1. Figure 9-2 shows what the form should look like at design time.

NOTE

C++Builder will automatically change the Caption of a Label if you change its Name property.

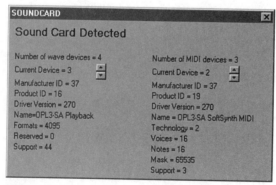

Figure 9-1 SOUNDCARD at runtime

TIP

You can save time by copying controls from the files on the CD-ROM. Open SOUNDCARD's main form, copy the controls, and then move to your form and paste the controls in.

Table 9-1 Components, properties, and settings for Form1 in the SOUNDCARD project

COMPONENT	PROPERTY	SETTING
Form	ClientWidth	410
	ClientHeight	235
	BorderStyle	bsDialog
UpDown	Name	WaveUpDown
	Position	0
	Min	0
UpDown	Name	MidiUpDown
	Position	0
	Min	0
Label	Name	Detected
	+Font	
	-Size	12
	-Style	fsBold
Label	Name	WaveCount
Label	Name	WaveIndex
Label	Name	WaveMid
Label	Name	WavePid
Label	Name	WaveDriver
Label	Name	WaveName
Label	Name	WaveFormats
Label	Name	WaveReserved
Label	Name	WaveSupport
Label	Name	MidiCount
Label	Name	MidiIndex
Label	Name	MidiMid
Label	Name	MidiPid

COMPONENT	PROPERTY	SETTING
Label	Name	MidiDriver
Label	Name	MidiName
Label	Name	MidiTech
Label	Name	MidiVoices
Label	Name	MidiNotes
Label	Name	MidiMask
Label	Name	MidiSupport

3. The MCI function prototypes reside in **MMSYSTEM.H**. Open **MAINFORM.CPP** and add an **#include** statement for this header file.

```
#include <vcl\vcl.h>
#pragma hdrstop

#include <mmsystem.h>
#include "MAINFORM.h"
```

4. Open **MAINFORM.H** and add these declarations to the private section of the **TForm1** class:

```
private:   // User declarations
  int WaveOutputDeviceCount;   // Holds the number of wave devices.
  int MidiOutputDeviceCount;   // Number of Midi devices.
  void UpdateStatusInfo(void); // Updates labels with new info.
```

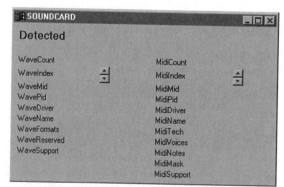

Figure 9-2 SOUNDCARD's main form at design time

5. Make an `OnCreate` handler for `Form1` and type in this code. The actual detection of the sound card occurs in the first two lines.

```
void __fastcall TForm1::FormCreate(TObject *Sender)
{
  // Count the number of wave and MIDI devices available.
  WaveOutputDeviceCount = (int)waveOutGetNumDevs();
  MidiOutputDeviceCount = (int)midiOutGetNumDevs();

  // If no devices were detected then no sound card is
  // present. Set some captions, and deactivate the
  // UpDown controls.
  if ( (WaveOutputDeviceCount == 0) &&
       (MidiOutputDeviceCount == 0)    )
  {
    Detected->Caption = "Sound Card Not Detected!";
    MidiUpDown->Enabled = false;
    WaveUpDown->Enabled = false;
    WaveCount->Caption = "No wave devices";
    MidiCount->Caption = "No MIDI devices";
  }
  // Else, some sound support is present. Set the limits on
  // the UpDown controls and set some captions.
  else
  {
    Detected->Caption = "Sound Card Detected";
    // Set max limits on UpDown controls. It's possible that one but
    // not both, of the Count vars is 0, so check before blindly
    // setting the UpDown max value to a negative value.
    if(MidiOutputDeviceCount !=0)
      MidiUpDown->Max = (short)(MidiOutputDeviceCount -1);
    else
      MidiUpDown->Enabled = false;
    if(WaveOutputDeviceCount != 0)
      WaveUpDown->Max = (short)(WaveOutputDeviceCount -1);
    else
      WaveUpDown->Enabled = false;
    WaveCount->Caption = "Number of wave devices = " +
                         IntToStr(WaveOutputDeviceCount);
    MidiCount->Caption = "Number of MIDI devices = " +
                         IntToStr(MidiOutputDeviceCount);
  }

  // Fill in the rest of the labels by calling
  // the update function.
  UpdateStatusInfo();
}
```

6. Stay in `MAINFORM.CPP` and type the code for the `UpdateStatusInfo` function. This function uses `midiOutGetDevCaps` and `waveOutGetDevCaps` to fetch more information about the sound devices on the system.

```
void TForm1::UpdateStatusInfo(void)
{
```

```
// Were there any wave devices. If so, find out which device the
// user wants information on, then call waveOutGetDevCaps and
// display the information in the labels.
if(WaveOutputDeviceCount != 0)
{
  WAVEOUTCAPS WaveOutCaps;
  waveOutGetDevCaps(WaveUpDown->Position,
                    &WaveOutCaps,
                    sizeof(WAVEOUTCAPS));
  WaveIndex->Caption = "Current Device = " +IntToStr(WaveUpDown⇐
  ->Position);
  WaveMid->Caption = "Manufacturer ID = " + IntToStr(WaveOutCaps.wMid);
  WavePid->Caption = "Product ID = " + IntToStr(WaveOutCaps.wPid);
  WaveDriver->Caption = "Driver Version = " +
                        IntToStr(WaveOutCaps.vDriverVersion);
  WaveName->Caption = "Name=" + AnsiString(WaveOutCaps.szPname);
  WaveFormats->Caption = "Formats = " + IntToStr(WaveOutCaps.dwFormats);
  WaveReserved->Caption = "Reserved = "⇐
  +IntToStr(WaveOutCaps.wReserved1);
  WaveSupport->Caption = "Support = " + IntToStr(WaveOutCaps.dwSupport);
}
else   // Else, there were no wave devices
{
  WaveIndex->Caption = "Current Device = NONE";
  WaveMid->Visible = false;
  WavePid->Visible = false;
  WaveDriver->Visible = false;
  WaveName->Visible = false;
  WaveFormats->Visible = false;
  WaveReserved->Visible = false;
  WaveSupport->Visible = false;
}


// Were there any MIDI devices, if so, display the information
// (just like wave info above)
if(MidiOutputDeviceCount !=0)
{
  MIDIOUTCAPS MidiOutCaps;
  midiOutGetDevCaps(MidiUpDown->Position,
                    &MidiOutCaps,
                    sizeof(MIDIOUTCAPS));
  MidiIndex->Caption = "Current Device = " +IntToStr(MidiUpDown⇐
  ->Position);
  MidiMid->Caption = "Manufacturer ID = " + IntToStr(MidiOutCaps.wMid);
  MidiPid->Caption = "Product ID = " + IntToStr(MidiOutCaps.wPid);
  MidiDriver->Caption = "Driver Version = " +
                        IntToStr(MidiOutCaps.vDriverVersion);
  MidiName->Caption = "Name = " + AnsiString(MidiOutCaps.szPname);
  MidiTech->Caption = "Technology = " +⇐
  IntToStr(MidiOutCaps.wTechnology);
  MidiVoices->Caption = "Voices = " + IntToStr(MidiOutCaps.wVoices);
  MidiNotes->Caption = "Notes = " + IntToStr(MidiOutCaps.wNotes);
  MidiMask->Caption = "Mask = " + IntToStr(MidiOutCaps.wChannelMask);
  MidiSupport->Caption = "Support = " + IntToStr(MidiOutCaps.dwSupport);
}
else // Else, no wave devices in sight.
```

continued on next page

continued from previous page

```
{
    MidiIndex->Caption = "Current Device = NONE";
    MidiMid->Visible = false;
    MidiPid->Visible = false;
    MidiDriver->Visible = false;
    MidiName->Visible = false;
    MidiTech->Visible = false;
    MidiVoices->Visible = false;
    MidiNotes->Visible = false;
    MidiMask->Visible = false;
    MidiSupport->Visible = false;
    }
}
```

7. Use the Object Inspector to create `OnClick` handlers for the `UpDown` controls. Insert a call to `UpdateStatusInfo` in each handler. This updates the labels with new device information when an `UpDown` control changes position.

```
void __fastcall TForm1::WaveUpDownClick(TObject *Sender, TUDBtnType Button)
{
    UpdateStatusInfo();
}
//-----------------------------------------------------------
void __fastcall TForm1::MidiUpDownClick(TObject *Sender, TUDBtnType Button)
{
    UpdateStatusInfo();
}
```

8. Compile and test the program. Try to run the program on a system that does not have a sound card to verify that your code detects the missing hardware.

How It Works

This How-To was more icing than cake. The first two lines in the `OnCreate` handler detect the sound card (step 5). `waveGetNumDevs` and `midiGetNumDevs` tell you how many wave and MIDI devices are present in the system. The machine does not have a sound card if both numbers equal zero.

NOTE

Most, if not all, sound cards provide both MIDI and wave support. Some hardware devices, such as voice modems and voice mail devices, provide wave support but not MIDI support. For this reason, you may want to simply use the number of MIDI devices to indicate whether or not a sound card is present.

The `UpdateStatusInfo` function (step 6) illuminates the information provided by `waveOutGetDevCaps` and `midiOutGetDevCaps`. Each click of an `UpDown`

control updates this information using a new device number. The user can scroll through and inspect the capabilities of each wave or MIDI device.

Comments

This How-To demonstrates how you can quickly determine whether a PC supports wave and MIDI sound by using the MCI functions of the API. This information can be very useful in multimedia programs. First, you can avoid playing sound when no sound device exists. Second, you can allow users to select a different playback device. For example, the various MIDI devices provided by a sound card each produce their own distinct type of sound. By checking the value returned by `midiOutGetNumDevs`, you could allow the user to select a different device for playback.

You may want to open `\INCLUDE\MMSYSTEM.H` and look around. It explains the meaning of the `MIDIOUTCAPS` and `WAVEOUTCAPS` structures used in step 6. Also look at `\INCLUDE\WIN32\MMREG.H`. It contains a list of product and manufacturer IDs. The Windows MCI supports several other functions for determining multimedia capability. Table 9-2 lists some of the functions and their purposes.

Table 9-2 MCI functions for determining system capabilities

FUNCTION	PURPOSE
waveOutGetDevCaps	Wave output (playing) capability
waveInGetDevCaps	Wave input (recording) capability
midiOutGetDevCaps	MIDI playing capability
midiInGetDevCaps	MIDI recording capability
auxGetDevCaps	Capabilities of an auxillary device
joyGetDevCaps	Joystick capability

COMPLEXITY
BEGINNING

9.2 How do I...
Play wave and MIDI files?

Problem

I would like users to be able to play wave sounds and MIDI sequences from within my application. They should be able to select the file they want to play at runtime. It would also be cool to display the progress of the file as it plays. How can I do this with C++Builder?

Technique

You may have turned to this How-To expecting to find tons of hard-core, low-level code. Think again. C++Builder's **MediaPlayer** component encapsulates the details of the Windows 95 MCI. **TMediaPlayer** can play wave and MIDI files, AVI video files, and audio CDs. **TMediaPlayer** also provides information on the progress of the media being played. About the only thing **TMediaPlayer** can't do is play 8-track cassettes, which is probably a blessing. This How-To demonstrates how you can use the **MediaPlayer** control to play wave and MIDI files. You will be surprised at how easy it is.

TIP

You might want to verify that your system can play wave and MIDI files before you continue. Use the Windows 95 media player to test your system.

Steps

Run **WAVEPLAY.EXE**. Figure 9-3 shows the program during execution. Click the Open button and locate a .WAV, an .MID, or a .RMI file (.RMI files are also MIDI files). Select the file, push the triangular Play button, and listen as **TMediaPlayer** does its job (it helps if you have a sound card). Try both wave and MIDI files.

1. Create a new project. Save the unit as **MAINFORM.CPP** and save the project as **WAVEPLAY.MAK**.

2. Place controls on **Form1** using Figure 9-3 as a guideline for placement. You can find the **MediaPlayer** control on the System tab of the Component Palette. Set properties to match Table 9-3.

TIP

You can center a control by right-clicking on it in the Form Designer and selecting Align from the popup menu. The Center In Window Radio button allows you to quickly center the control in the form.

Figure 9-3 WAVEPLAY
at runtime

Table 9-3 Components, properties, and settings for `Form1` in the WAVEPLAY project

COMPONENT	PROPERTY	SETTING
Form	ClientWidth	180
	ClientHeight	125
	BorderStyle	bsDialog
Button	Caption	&Open
MediaPlayer	DeviceType	dtAutoSelect
	+VisibleButtons	
	−btPlay	true
	−btPause	true
	−btStop	true
	−everybody else	false
OpenDialog	+Options	·
	−ofFileMustExist	true
	Filter	MIDI Sequence(*.mid *.rmi)
		|*.mid;*.rmi Audio Wave File (*.wav)
		|*.wav All Files(*.*) |*.*
ProgressBar	Min	0
	Max	100
	Position	0
Timer	Enabled	false
	Interval	200

3. Make an `OnClick` handler for **Button1** and type in this code. This function pops up the File Open dialog box and then opens the media file using the `Open` method of `TMediaPlayer`.

> **TIP**
>
> Calling `TMediaPlayer::Open` does not play the file, it just opens it. `TMediaPlayer::Play` actually starts the music.

```
void __fastcall TForm1::Button1Click(TObject *Sender)
{
  // Pop up the common file dialog.
  if(OpenDialog1->Execute())
  {
    MediaPlayer1->FileName=OpenDialog1->FileName;
    // Open raises an exception if something acts up. Use a try
    // catch block to detect an error.
    try
```

continued on next page

continued from previous page

```
    {
        MediaPlayer1->Open();
    }
    catch (...)
    {
        // Should Application->Terminate if an exception occurs.
        Application->MessageBox("Error opening file",mtWarning,⇐
        MB_ICONWARNING|MB_OK);
    }
  }
}
```

4. TMediaPlayer is ready to rock and roll after it opens the file. TMediaPlayer can respond to its buttons without our interference, but the program needs to start the progress timer when the Play button gets pushed. Likewise, the timer needs to shut down when the user pushes Stop. Create an OnClick handler for MediaPlayer1 and insert this code:

```
void __fastcall TForm1::MediaPlayer1Click(TObject *Sender, TMPBtnType
Button,
    bool &DoDefault)
{
    // Find out which button was pressed; if Play, then start
    // the timer, if Stop then disable it. The timer will just
    // run if pause was pushed.
    if(Button == btPlay)
        Timer1->Enabled = true;
    else if (Button == btStop)
        Timer1->Enabled = false;

    // Set DoDefault to true so the MediaPlayer will do
    // what it normally does for the button press.
    DoDefault = true;
}
```

5. The code from step 4 activates a timer that will tick every 200 ms while the media plays. Create an OnTimer event for Timer1 that will update ProgressBar1 during playback.

```
void __fastcall TForm1::Timer1Timer(TObject *Sender)
{
    // Update position using properties of TMediaPlayer. Need to cast because
    // TProgressBar is 16 bits while TMediaPlayer is 32. Division ensures⇐
    that
    // number will be between 0 and 100.
    ProgressBar1->Position = (TProgressRange)(MediaPlayer1->Position * 100 /
                                              MediaPlayer1->Length);

    // If media has finished then shut off the timer.
    if(ProgressBar1->Position == 100)
        Timer1->Enabled = false;
}
```

6. Compile and test your new audio player.

How It Works

As promised, you did not have to type low-level code to play audio files. The fine folks at Borland have encapsulated most of the work for you via the `TMediaPlayer` class. Your only responsibility is finding a file to play and then telling `MediaPlayer1` what file was selected. `OpenDialog1` (step 3) handles the first step by popping up the Windows File Open dialog box. After the user selects a file, the code assigns the selected file to `MediaPlayer1->FileName`. `TMediaPlayer::Open` then opens the media file so it can be played.

Since `TMediaPlayer` can play the file on its own, the `Open` call would suffice by itself if you just wanted to play the audio file. This How-To goes a little further by demonstrating how `TMediaPlayer` can help you track the progress of the media being played. `TMediaPlayer::Length` calculates the length of the audio file, and `TMediaPlayer::Position` tells how much of the media has been played. The timer event (step 5) updates the progress bar by recalculating a percentage formula using `Length` and `Position`.

TIP

`TMediaPlayer::TimeFormat` determines the unit of measurement for the `Position` and `Length` properties. Consult the online help for a list of possible time formats.

TIP

This How-To utilizes only a handful of the buttons provided by `TMediaPlayer`. `TMediaPlayer` also provides buttons that can rewind, fast forward, and step through a media. It also contains an Eject button.

Comments

This How-To dealt with playing audio files, but there is no reason to restrict the power of `TMediaPlayer`. Run the program again, click the Open button, and change the file filter in the file open dialog to read "All files (*.*)". Now locate an AVI video, select it, and push Play on the `MediaPlayer` control. A separate window should appear that plays the video. `TMediaPlayer` automatically detects the type of media selected because you set `DeviceType` to `dtAutoSelect` in step 2. The next How-To will show you how to move the video into your form instead of having a separate window pop up.

Perhaps you need to play media files without providing buttons for the user to push. With C++Builder you have two choices. First, you could work directly with the MCI portion of the API. This would involve calling the mighty `mciSendCommand` function. Alternatively, you could just hide the `MediaPlayer` control. You would start and stop a sound file by calling the `Play` and `Stop` member functions directly.

COMPLEXITY
BEGINNING

9.3 How do I...
Play video files in my form?

Problem

I want my application to play video files. I know that the **MediaPlayer** control can play these just as easily as it plays sound files, but it puts the videos in a separate window. How can I play the videos directly in my form?

Technique

TMediaPlayer operates by communicating with the MCI functions of the Windows API. By default, the MCI creates a separate window to play videos, so this is also the default for **TMediaPlayer**. However, you can specify your own window handle for playing back video. Any component that contains a valid window handle can be used for playback, but using forms and panels makes the most sense. Panels work well because they have beveled edges that surround the video with an attractive frame.

TIP

Before you continue, make sure your system can play AVI video using the built-in Windows 95 media player.

Steps

Run **VIDEO.EXE**. Click the Open button and hunt down a video (*.AVI) file. Select it, and then push Play to view the video within the form. The form will resize to accommodate the height and width of the video. Figure 9-4 shows **VIDEO** while it's playing an AVI file.

1. Create a new project. Name the unit **MAINFORM.CPP** and name the project **VIDEO.MAK**.

2. Place a **Button**, a **MediaPlayer**, an **OpenDialog**, and a **Panel** on **Form1**. Use Figure 9-4 to help place the controls. Set properties to match Table 9-4.

Table 9-4 Components, properties, and settings for **Form1** in the **VIDEO** project

COMPONENT	PROPERTY	SETTING
Form	ClientWidth	275
	ClientHeight	275

COMPONENT	PROPERTY	SETTING
	BorderStyle	bsDialog
Button	Caption	&Open
Panel	Caption	""
	Visible	false
MediaPlayer	DeviceType	dtAVIVideo
	Display	Panel1
	+VisibleButtons	
	–btPlay	true
	–btPause	true
	–btStop	true
	–btNext	true
	–btPrev	true
	-btStep	true
	-btBack	true
	–everybody else	false
OpenDialog	+Options	
	–ofFileMustExist	true
	Filter	Video Files (*.avi)	*.avi

Figure 9-4 VIDEO at runtime

3. You can knock out this entire How-To in one event handler. Create an
OnClick handler for Button1. Insert code that loads an AVI file and then
repositions the form and its controls.

```
void __fastcall TForm1::Button1Click(TObject *Sender)
{
  if(OpenDialog1->Execute())
  {
    // Loading AVI files can be slow. Repaint form now (so it doesn't
    // look dead), then set the cursor to the hourglass.
    Update();
    Screen->Cursor = crHourGlass;
    MediaPlayer1->FileName=OpenDialog1->FileName;  // Set filename and
    try                                            // try to open file.
    {
      MediaPlayer1->Open();
    }
    catch (...)
    {
      Application->MessageBox("Error opening file",mtWarning,MB_ICON-
WARNING|MB_OK);
    }
    Screen->Cursor = crArrow;                      // Reset cursor.

    // Use DisplayRect to autosize the MediaPlayer.
    MediaPlayer1->DisplayRect = Rect(4,4,0,0);

    // Re-adjust the controls. Use temp varables during calculations. Note
    // that DisplayRect.Right = AVI width and DisplayRect.Bottom = Height.
    int TempPanelWidth  = MediaPlayer1->DisplayRect.Right  + 8; // Four
pixels
    int TempPanelHeight = MediaPlayer1->DisplayRect.Bottom + 8; // on each
side
    int TempPanelLeft;
    int TempPanelTop;
    int TempFormWidth;
    int TempFormHeight;
    int TempMediaPlayerLeft;

    // Determine the form's width based on the widest control on the form.
    if(TempPanelWidth < MediaPlayer1->Width)    // If MediaPlayer1 is⇐
    widest,                                          // make the form 4
    {
pixels wider
      TempFormWidth = MediaPlayer1->Width + 4; // than MediaPlayer1.
      TempMediaPlayerLeft = 2;                 // Place MP 2 pixels in, and
      TempPanelLeft = TempMediaPlayerLeft +    // center the panel.
                  (MediaPlayer1->Width - TempPanelWidth)/2;
    }
    else                                              // Else, panel is wider.
    {                                                 // Make form 4 pixels
      TempFormWidth = TempPanelWidth + 4;        // wider than panel.
      TempPanelLeft = 2;
      TempMediaPlayerLeft = (TempFormWidth -     // Center MediaPlayer.
```

```
                                MediaPlayer1->Width)/2;
     }
     TempPanelTop = MediaPlayer1->Top + MediaPlayer1->Height + 15;
     TempFormHeight = TempPanelTop + TempPanelHeight +2;

     ClientWidth       = TempFormWidth;        // Copy temps into their
     ClientHeight      = TempFormHeight;       // corresponding properties.
     Panel1->Left      = TempPanelLeft;        // Every control should be
     Panel1->Width     = TempPanelWidth;       // centered when finished.
     Panel1->Top       = TempPanelTop;         // Video should fit nicely
     Panel1->Height    = TempPanelHeight;      // on form and panel.
     MediaPlayer1->Left = TempMediaPlayerLeft;
     Panel1->Visible = true;                   // Display the panel.
     Button1->Left = (ClientWidth-Button1->Width) / 2;
   }
 }
```

4. Compile and test the program.

How It Works

The most important piece of this How-To is setting the **Display** property of **MediaPlayer1** (step 2). This assignment tells **TMediaPlayer** that you want to play video within **Panel1**. The MCI will use **Panel1**'s window handle to display images when the video clip runs.

The runtime assignment to **DisplayRect** also plays a critical role in making this How-To work. The code from step 3 sets **DisplayRect** every time the user opens an AVI file.

```
MediaPlayer1->DisplayRect = Rect(4,4,0,0); // autosize display
```

This statement determines how much space the video can consume. It looks more appealing to play video files in their natural size rather than contorting them to fit the dimensions of the form. Using zeroes as the **Right** and **Bottom** values in **DisplayRect** tells **TMediaPlayer** that you want to play the video in its natural size. The VCL then replaces the zeroes with the width and height of the video frame. You can then access the new **DisplayRect** values to resize the form and its controls.

NOTE

The VCL source for adjusting **DisplayRect** can be found in the **\SOURCE\VCL\MPLAYER.PAS** file (if you have the professional edition of C++Builder). Look for the **SetDisplayRect** function. Notice that **DisplayRect.Right** stores the width of the video, and likewise, **DisplayRect.Bottom** contains its height.

The code must resize and reposition **Form1** and its controls after the video's size has been auto-calculated (step 3). **Panel1** resizes such that it provides a constant, four-pixel border around the video. **Form1** resizes so it can accommodate the

widest control in the form (either **MediaPlayer1** or **Panel1**). The remaining controls are centered in the form. The code uses temporary variables in the positioning calculations. Properties are set after all the math has been resolved. Resizing and repositioning the controls in succession results in a smooth transformation of the form.

Comments

Once again **TMediaPlayer** has made life pretty simple. Most of the code in this How-To dealt with sizing the form and its control. Only a property setting was needed to direct the video output to the panel component.

COMPLEXITY
ADVANCED

9.4 How do I...
Play an audio CD?

Problem

I would like to create an application that can play audio CDs. I need to be able to display information about the CD as it plays. How can I do this using C++Builder?

Technique

As with sound and video files, the **MediaPlayer** component has no problem playing audio CDs. In fact, you can compile a program that plays audio CDs without writing any code. **TMediaPlayer** can be geared for CDs at design time by changing a few of its properties. Playing a CD is actually easier than playing audio files because you don't have to worry about selecting the file.

While **TMediaPlayer** can play a compact disc on its own, it won't display any information about the CD. This makes it difficult for users to select the song they want to listen to. Displaying track and length information about a CD mandates some coding effort, but **TMediaPlayer** provides the information you need by encapsulating the details of the Windows MCI. This How-To utilizes **TMediaPlayer** and a timer control to update information about the CD as it plays.

NOTE

This How-To requires that you have a sound card, a CD player, a connection between the two, and an audio CD. Verify that your machine can play an audio CD using the Windows 95 media player.

Steps

Place an audio CD in your disk drive. If Windows 95 launches its own media player, stop the music and close down that program to keep it from interfering with ours. Launch **CDPLAY.EXE**. A media program should appear that allows you to play music from the CD. Figure 9-5 shows the program. Click Open to read in the CD's information. The labels in the application display information about the CD and its first track. Play the first song and notice how the labels display the progress of the CD. Use the **MediaPlayer** control to change tracks and observe that the information in the program updates to match your selection.

1. Create a new project. Name the unit **MAINFORM.CPP** and name the project **CDPLAY.MAK**.

2. Plop controls on to **Form1** using Tables 9-5 through 9-8 as guidelines. Position the controls according to Figure 9-5.

Table 9-5 Components, properties, and settings for **Form1** in the **CDPLAY** project

COMPONENT	PROPERTY	SETTING
Form	ClientWidth	170
	ClientHeight	210
	BorderStyle	bsDialog
BitBtn	Caption	&Open
	Kind	bkCustom
	Glyph	\IMAGES\BUTTONS\CDDRIVE.BMP
MediaPlayer	DeviceType	dtCDAudio
	+VisibleButtons	
	-btPlay	true
	-btPause	true
	-btStop	true
	-btNext	true
	-btPrev	true
	-btEject	true
	everybody else	false
Timer	Enabled	false
	Interval	250
Panel	Caption	""

Figure 9-5 CDPLAY
at runtime

Table 9-6 Components, properties, and settings for Panel1 in the CDPLAY project

COMPONENT	PROPERTY	SETTING
GroupBox	Name	TrackGroup
	Caption	Track Info
GroupBox	Name	CDGroup
	Caption	CD Info

Table 9-7 Components, properties, and settings for TrackGroup in the CDPLAY project

COMPONENT	PROPERTY	SETTING
Label	Caption	Track Number:
Label	Caption	Track Length:
Label	Caption	Current Time:
Label	Name	TrackNumber
	Alignment	taRightJustify
	AutoSize	false
	Caption	0
	Width	32
	Left	112
	Top	15
	Font	Courier, bold
Label	Name	TrackLength
	Alignment	taRightJustify
	AutoSize	false

COMPONENT	PROPERTY	SETTING
	Caption	00:00
	Width	58
	Left	86
	Top	30
	Font	Courier, bold
Label	Name	TrackTime
	Alignment	taRightJustify
	AutoSize	false
	Caption	00:00
	Width	58
	Left	86
	Top	45
	Font	Courier, bold
	Font Color	clNavy

Table 9-8 Components, properties, and settings for `CDGroup` in the `CDPLAY` project

COMPONENT	PROPERTY	SETTING
Label	Caption	Tracks:
Label	Caption	Total Time:
Label	Caption	Current Time:
Label	Name	TrackCount
	Alignment	taRightJustify
	AutoSize	false
	Caption	0
	Width	32
	Left	112
	Top	15
	Font	Courier, bold
Label	Name	TotalTime
	Alignment	taRightJustify
	AutoSize	false
	Caption	00:00
	Width	58
	Left	86
	Top	30

continued on next page

continued from previous page

COMPONENT	PROPERTY	SETTING
	Font	Courier, bold
Label	Name	CDTime
	Alignment	taRightJustify
	AutoSize	false
	Caption	00:00
	Width	58
	Left	86
	Top	45
	Font	Courier, bold
	Font Color	clNavy

3. Open **MAINFORM.H** and add custom members to the private section of the TForm1 class.

```
private:  // User declarations
  bool CheckForDisc(void);
  void UpdateCDInfo(void);
  void UpdateTrackInfo(void);
  void UpdatePositions(void);
  int  CurrentTrack;
```

4. The MCI section of the Windows API contains some macros that will simplify life later on. Open **MAINFORM.CPP** and type in an `#include` statement so our code can to access the macros.

```
#include <vcl\vcl.h>
#pragma hdrstop

#include <mmsystem.h>
#include "MAINFORM.h"
```

5. Even though an audio CD is not a file, **TMediaPlayer** must still open it via its **Open** method. Create an **OnClick** handler for the **Open** button, and type in code to open the audio CD.

```
void __fastcall TForm1::BitBtn1Click(TObject *Sender)
{
  Screen->Cursor = crHourGlass; // Loading can be slow so change cursor.
  MediaPlayer1->FileName = "";   // Use null string when opening CDs.
  MediaPlayer1->Wait = true;     // Wait before moving on.

  try
    {
    MediaPlayer1->Open();        // Open the CD.
    }
  catch (...)
    {
    // Should terminate app using Application->Terminate
```

```
        Application->MessageBox("Error opening compact disc",mtWarning,MB_OK);
      }

    Screen->Cursor = crArrow;        // Restore cursor after opening.

    // Check that a disc is in the drive.
    if (!CheckForDisc())
    {
      Application->MessageBox("No disc in CD-ROM drive.\n"
                              "Insert disc and push Open again",
                              "ERROR",MB_OK);
      MediaPlayer1->Close();
    }
    else
    {
      UpdateCDInfo();             // Update static information about CD.
      Timer1->Enabled = true;    // Turn on the timer that will track the CD.
    }
}
```

6. Create an `OnTimer` event, and add function calls to update the information contained in the position labels.

```
void __fastcall TForm1::Timer1Timer(TObject *Sender)
{
  // Check that the CD was not ejected by the user. If it was,
  // set all captions to zeroes, shut off the timer, and close
  // the media player.
  if (!CheckForDisc())
  {
    Timer1->Enabled = false;
    MediaPlayer1->Close();
    TrackNumber ->Caption = "0";
    TrackLength ->Caption = "00:00";
    TrackTime   ->Caption = "00:00";
    TrackCount  ->Caption = "0";
    TotalTime   ->Caption = "00:00";
    CDTime      ->Caption = "00:00";
  }
  else  // CD was not ejected, update information.
  {
    UpdateTrackInfo();
    UpdatePositions();
  }
}
```

7. The `UpdateCDInfo` function displays the number of tracks and the total length of a CD. Add the code for this function to `MAINFORM.CPP`.

```
void TForm1::UpdateCDInfo(void)
{
  // This function updates the  number of tracks
  // and the total length of the CD.

  // Put the media player into track mode (tracks, minutes, seconds).
```

continued on next page

continued from previous page

```
// This is the normal mode for a CD player.
MediaPlayer1->TimeFormat = tfTMSF;
int CDTrackCount      = MediaPlayer1->Tracks; // Track count.

// Get length of media. Length does not use TMSF mode due to
// the MCI functions it encapsulates. Result is in MSF format.
// Use MCI_MSF macros from MMSYSTEM.H to decode Length.
int CDLengthMinutes = MCI_MSF_MINUTE(MediaPlayer1->Length);
int CDLengthSeconds = MCI_MSF_SECOND(MediaPlayer1->Length);

TrackCount->Caption = IntToStr(CDTrackCount);
TotalTime->Caption  = IntToStr(CDLengthMinutes) + ":" +
                      IntToStr(CDLengthSeconds/10) +
                      IntToStr(CDLengthSeconds%10);
}
```

TIP

`IntToStr(X/10) + IntToStr(X%10)` forces a leading zero into the string when X < 10. Hence, if X equals 7 the string will contain 07 rather than 7. This looks better when you display time information.

8. Add the function body for the `UpdateTrackInfo` function to `MAINFORM.CPP`. This function updates the track number and track size when the CD player moves from one song to the next.

```
void TForm1::UpdateTrackInfo(void)
{
  // Make sure media player is in track mode (tracks, minutes, seconds).
  MediaPlayer1->TimeFormat = tfTMSF;
  int TrackIndex = MCI_TMSF_TRACK(MediaPlayer1->Position); // Get track⇐
  number.

  // Has the track number changed since last time? If so, update the
  // static information about the song; if not, then don't bother.
  if(CurrentTrack != TrackIndex)
  {
    CurrentTrack = TrackIndex;                    // Update indexing variable.

    // Just like Length, TrackLength will not use TMSF format due to the
    // underlying MCI function, interpret results using MSF format.
    int LengthValue = MediaPlayer1->TrackLength[TrackIndex];
    int LengthMinutes  = MCI_MSF_MINUTE(LengthValue); // Decode return⇐
    value
    int LengthSeconds  = MCI_MSF_SECOND(LengthValue); // using macros.

    TrackNumber->Caption = IntToStr(TrackIndex);       // Update captions.
    TrackLength->Caption = IntToStr(LengthMinutes) + ":" +
                           IntToStr(LengthSeconds/10)+  // Display⇐
                           leading 0.
                           IntToStr(LengthSeconds%10);
  }
}
```

9. Add the function body for `UpdatePositions` to `MAINFORM.CPP`. This function updates the time meters as a song plays.

```
void TForm1::UpdatePositions(void)
{
  // Ensure track mode (TMSF). This way, Position will return
  // values relative to the position in the current track.
  MediaPlayer1->TimeFormat = tfTMSF;
  int PositionValue    = MediaPlayer1->Position;      // Get position⇐
                                                      // DWord.
  int TPositionMinutes= MCI_TMSF_MINUTE(PositionValue); // Decode result
  int TPositionSeconds= MCI_TMSF_SECOND(PositionValue); // using macros.

  TrackTime->Caption   = IntToStr(TPositionMinutes) + ":" +
                         IntToStr(TPositionSeconds/10) +
                         IntToStr(TPositionSeconds%10);

  // Now get out of track mode and check Position again. This time
  // it will read relative to the beginning of the CD.
  MediaPlayer1->TimeFormat = tfMSF;
  PositionValue    = MediaPlayer1->Position;
  int CDLengthMinutes = MCI_MSF_MINUTE(PositionValue);
  int CDLengthSeconds = MCI_MSF_SECOND(PositionValue);
  CDTime->Caption   = IntToStr(CDLengthMinutes) + ":" +
                      IntToStr(CDLengthSeconds/10)      +
                      IntToStr(CDLengthSeconds%10);

  // Return to track mode; media player buttons don't work right
  // if we are not in track mode.
  MediaPlayer1->TimeFormat = tfTMSF;
}
```

10. Finally, type the `CheckForDisc` function into `MAINFORM.CPP`. This function checks for a disc in the CD-ROM drive.

```
bool TForm1::CheckForDisc(void)
{
  // Use MCI API function to check that a CD is present.
  MCI_STATUS_PARMS Status;
  Status.dwItem = MCI_STATUS_MEDIA_PRESENT;
  mciSendCommand(MediaPlayer1->DeviceID,
                 MCI_STATUS,
                 MCI_STATUS_ITEM|MCI_WAIT,
                 (DWORD) (LPMCI_STATUS_PARMS) &Status);
  return (bool)Status.dwReturn;
}
```

11. Compile and test the program.

How It Works

This How-To can be split into two separate tasks: playing the CD and displaying its size and track information.

Playing the CD

Playing the CD is the easy part because `TMediaPlayer` does most of the work. The code that opens the CD resides in the `OnClick` handler for `BitBtn1` (step 5). Here are the code steps for opening the CD.

```
MediaPlayer1->DeviceType = dtCDAudio;
MediaPlayer1->FileName = "";
MediaPlayer1->Wait = true;
MediaPlayer1->Open();
```

First, `DeviceType` must be set explicitly to read an audio CD (`dtCDAudio`). This was done in step 2 at design time, so the code from step 5 doesn't actually contain this statement. Next, `FileName` is set to a null string. These first two steps tell `TMediaPlayer` that it will be dealing with an audio CD instead of a file. The third statement sets `Wait` to `true`, which tells the `Open` call to wait until the CD has finished opening before it returns. This is important because opening a CD takes time, and accessing the `Length` and `Position` members raises an exception if you read them before the CD has finished opening. Finally, the code calls `Open` after `DeviceType`, `FileName`, and `Wait` have been set.

The rest of the `OnClick` handler (step 5) performs auxiliary functions. Opening CDs can be slow, so changing the cursor to an hourglass gives users a visual hint that they should be patient. The `Open` method executes from within a `try-catch` block since it can raise an exception. The code restores the mouse cursor and activates the timer once `Open` has finished. The last section of the `OnClick` handler checks that the CD drive contains a disc. The code prompts the user for a CD if no disc is found.

Retrieving CD Information

This How-To contains three functions for retrieving information about the CD: `UpdateCDInfo`, `UpdateTrackInfo`, and `UpdatePositions`. These functions retrieve CD information and display it on the screen. `UpdateCDInfo` runs when a CD is first opened (step 5). `UpdateTrackInfo` and `UpdatePositions` execute during each `OnTimer` event (step 6). Each of these functions will produce garbage results on the screen if they are called while the CD drive is empty. The `CheckForDisc` function (step 10) prevents this garbage by ensuring that the CD drive contains a disc.

`UpdateCDInfo` (step 7) displays the total time and track count for the entire CD. The code only needs to call `UpdateCDInfo` each time the user opens a CD because a CD's length and track count do not change. The `Tracks` property of `TMediaPlayer` returns the number of tracks on the CD, and `Length` returns the length of the CD. The `Length` return value works differently for CDs than it does for wave files. `Length` encodes its return value in MSF (minutes, seconds, frames) format. The `MCI_MSF_XXXX` macros decode this format into separate variables for minutes and seconds.

`UpdateTrackInfo` (step 8) displays the track number and track length for the current track selection. You only need to update the track information when the track selection changes, but the code does not really know when this happens. `UpdateTrackInfo` executes on each timer tick (step 6). It uses a private variable to compare the current track with the track during the last timer tick. The function updates its labels when a new track begins. `UpdateTrackInfo` uses

TMediaPlayer::TrackLength to determine the length of the current track. Once again, TMediaPlayer encodes the value using the packed MSF format.

UpdatePositions (step 9) uses TMediaPlayer::Position to display the position of the current track. The Position value depends on the current TimeFormat setting. Position returns a value relative to the start of the current track if TimeFormat has been set to tfTMSF (tracks, minutes, seconds, frames). If TimeFormat equals tfMSF (minutes, seconds, frames), then Position returns a value relative to the start of the CD.

NOTE

Setting the timer interval to 250 ms (step 2) results in smooth ticking of the position labels. Setting the interval higher can result in visual skipping.

TIP

A hefty mciSendCommand call executes each time you access the Position, TrackLength, and Length properties of TMediaPlayer. Optimize your code by storing these results in integer variables if the result will be used more than once. This minimizes the number of times TMediaPlayer has to call the potentially sluggish mciSendCommand function.

Comments

TMediaPlayer::TimeFormat determines whether MSF or TMSF format is used when accessing the Position property (step 9). You may have noticed the use of both MCI_MSF_XXXX and MCI_TMSF_XXXX macros (note the additional T). The MSF macros unpack a value that was returned in MSF format. Likewise, the TMSF macros work on TMSF formatted numbers. Both formats pack multiple values into a 32-bit number. MSF places the minutes value in the lowest byte of the 32-bit number, while TMSF puts the track number in the lowest byte. Unfortunately, the macros are not type safe, so using the wrong macro will simply lead to bad numbers at run-time.

To complicate matters further, it can be confusing trying to determine how TimeFormat affects the Position, Length, and TrackLength values of TMediaPlayer. You may have noticed that MSF macros were used in step 7 and 8 even when TimeFormat was set to tfTMSF. TimeFormat always determines how Position works, as shown in the UpdatePositions function (step 9). TrackLength (step 8) always returns track information in MSF format, and it doesn't seem to care whether TimeFormat is tfMSF or tfTMSF. However, it does care if TimeFormat is something totally different, such as tfMilliseconds. Length (step 7) works the same way. It always returns its values in MSF format as long as TimeFormat is set

to either `tfTMSF` or `tfMSF`. Changing `TimeFormat` to `tfMilliseconds` will force `Length` and `TrackLength` to use milliseconds instead of MSF format. These complexities result from the raw MCI API functions embedded within `TMediaPlayer`.

You may have noticed some latency when changing tracks on the CD. Changing tracks is inherently slow, but you can improve the response of the program by overriding the `OnClick` handler for `TMediaPlayer`. This would allow you to change the screen cursor, hold the media buttons down until the function completes, or otherwise modify the default behavior of the program.

COMPLEXITY
ADVANCED

9.5 How do I...
Detect and use a joystick in my application?

Problem

I am working on a game using C++Builder, and I would like to add joystick support to my program. How can I detect the presence of a joystick and then use it if it's connected?

Technique

Adding joystick support means working directly with the MCI portion of the API. The MCI provides functions to detect a joystick, determine the joystick's capabilities, and retrieve position and button information. This How-To demonstrates each task.

Steps

Run `JOYSTICK.EXE`. If possible, try to connect a joystick to the system first; otherwise the program will seem pretty boring. A window will appear that looks like Figure 9-6. Move the joystick around and notice how the gun sight tracks your movement. The labels along the left side continuously update as you move the joystick and press its buttons.

1. Create a new project. Name the unit `MAINFORM.CPP` and name the project `JOYSTICK.MAK`.

2. Place the components listed in Table 9-9 onto `Form1`. The main form in this How-To contains a gaggle of labels used to display system information about the joystick. Make sure that the `Name` property for each label matches Table 9-9.

NOTE
You can save time by copying controls from the source file on the CD-ROM and pasting them into your form.

Table 9-9 Components, properties, and settings for `Form1` in the `JOYSTICK` project

COMPONENT	PROPERTY	SETTING
Form	WindowState	wsMaximized
Label	Caption	Joystick Device Information
	Font	16 pt, bold, MS Sans Serif
Label	Name	JoystickCount
Label	Name	JoysticksConnected
Label	Name	JoystickMid
Label	Name	JoystickPid
Label	Name	JoystickName
Label	Name	JoystickXMin
Label	Name	JoystickXMax
Label	Name	JoystickYMin
Label	Name	JoystickYMax
Label	Name	JoystickNumButtons
Label	Name	JoystickMinPoll
Label	Name	JoystickMaxPoll
Label	Caption	Joystick Status Information
	Font	16 pt, bold, MS Sans Serif
Label	Name	JoystickXPosition
Label	Name	JoystickYPosition
Label	Name	JoystickButton1
Label	Name	JoystickButton2
Label	Name	JoystickButton3
Label	Name	JoystickButton4
ImageList	Width	76
	Height	76
	DrawingStyle	dsTransparent
Timer	Interval	2000

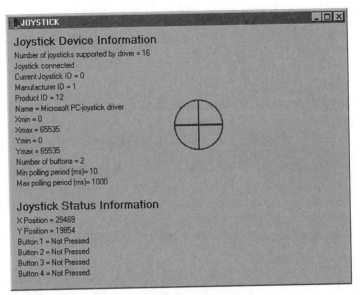

Figure 9-6 JOYSTICK at runtime

3. ImageList1 holds a bitmap that will act as the gun sight for the joystick. Double-click ImageList1 to launch the Image List Editor. Click Add and browse for GUNSIGHT.BMP on the CD-ROM. After loading the bitmap, set the Transparent Color Combo box to clWhite and click OK.

TIP

Make sure you set the Width and Height properties of ImageList1 before you try to load the picture.

4. Open MAINFORM.H and add private declarations and message maps to the TForm1 class. Don't forget to add an #include for MMSYSTEM.H. MMSYSTEM.H contains the constants for the joystick messages.

```
#include <mmsystem.h>

//------------------------------
class TForm1 : public TForm
{
__published:            // IDE-managed Components
...
...
private:   // User declarations
   TPoint Position;
   int DriverCount;
   bool Connected;
   int JoystickID;
   JOYCAPS JoyCaps;
```

```
    int YDivider;
    int XDivider;
    void ShowDeviceInfo(void);
    void ShowStatusInfo(void);
    void __fastcall JMButtonUpdate(TMessage &msg);
    void __fastcall JMMove(TMessage &msg);
public:   // User declarations
    virtual __fastcall TForm1(TComponent* Owner);

BEGIN_MESSAGE_MAP
  MESSAGE_HANDLER(MM_JOY1BUTTONDOWN,TMessage,JMButtonUpdate)
  MESSAGE_HANDLER(MM_JOY1BUTTONUP,TMessage,JMButtonUpdate)
  MESSAGE_HANDLER(MM_JOY1MOVE,TMessage,JMMove)
  MESSAGE_HANDLER(MM_JOY2BUTTONDOWN,TMessage,JMButtonUpdate)
  MESSAGE_HANDLER(MM_JOY2BUTTONUP,TMessage,JMButtonUpdate)
  MESSAGE_HANDLER(MM_JOY2MOVE,TMessage,JMMove)
END_MESSAGE_MAP(TForm)
};
```

5. Create an `OnCreate` handler for `Form1` and type in this code to detect the joystick at start up:

```
void __fastcall TForm1::FormCreate(TObject *Sender)
{
  // Find out how many joysticks the driver supports.
  DriverCount = joyGetNumDevs();

  Connected = false;
  MMRESULT JoyResult;
  JOYINFOEX JoyInfo;
  // The joystick could be disconnected even if the driver is
  // loaded. Use joyGetPosEx to detect if a joystick is connected.
  // It returns JOYERR_NOERROR if the joystick is plugged in.
  if(DriverCount != 0)      // Can any joysticks be supported?
  {
    // Test for joystick1.
    JoyResult = joyGetPosEx(JOYSTICKID1,&JoyInfo);
    if(JoyResult == JOYERR_NOERROR )
    {
      Connected = true;
      JoystickID = JOYSTICKID1;
    }
    // INVALIDPARAM means something is bad. Quit now without
    // checking for joystick 2.
    else if(JoyResult == MMSYSERR_INVALPARAM)
      Application->MessageBox("An error occured while calling joyGetPosEx",
                              "Error", MB_OK);
    // If joystick1 is unconnected, check for joystick2.
    else if((JoyResult=joyGetPosEx(JOYSTICKID2,&JoyInfo)) == JOYERR_NOERROR)
    {
      Connected = true;
      JoystickID = JOYSTICKID2;
    }
  }
  ShowDeviceInfo(); // Initialize the labels.
  ShowStatusInfo();
}
```

6. Stay in `MAINFORM.CPP` and type in the function bodies for the `ShowDeviceInfo` and `ShowStatusInfo` functions. `ShowDeviceInfo` displays information obtained via `joyGetDevCaps`, whereas `ShowStatusInfo` initializes the joystick position and button states.

NOTE

Most of `ShowDeviceInfo` just sets `Caption` properties. Pay particular attention to the `joyGetDevCaps` and `joySetCapture` function calls.

```
void TForm1::ShowDeviceInfo(void)
{
  // Use joyGetDevCaps to display information from JOYCAPS structure.
  // Note that not all of the information from joyGetDevCaps is shown
  // here. Consult the win32 SDK help file for a full description of
  // joyGetDevCaps.
  joyGetDevCaps(JoystickID,&JoyCaps, sizeof(JOYCAPS));

  JoystickCount->Caption = "Number of joysticks supported by driver = " +
                           IntToStr(DriverCount);

  if(Connected)
    JoysticksConnected->Caption = "Joystick connected";
  else
    JoysticksConnected->Caption = "Joystick not plugged in";
  CurrentJoystick->Caption = "Current Joystick ID = " +
                           IntToStr(JoystickID);
  JoystickMid->Caption = "Manufacturer ID = " +
                           IntToStr(JoyCaps.wMid);
  JoystickPid->Caption = "Product ID = " +
                           IntToStr(JoyCaps.wPid);
  JoystickName->Caption = "Name = " + AnsiString(JoyCaps.szPname);
  JoystickXMin->Caption = "Xmin = " + IntToStr(JoyCaps.wXmin);
  JoystickXMax->Caption = "Xmax = " + IntToStr(JoyCaps.wXmax);
  JoystickYMin->Caption =  "Ymin = " + IntToStr(JoyCaps.wYmin);
  JoystickYMax->Caption = "Ymax = " + IntToStr(JoyCaps.wYmax);
  JoystickNumButtons->Caption = "Number of buttons = "+
                           IntToStr(JoyCaps.wNumButtons);
  JoystickMinPoll->Caption = "Min polling period (ms)= " +
                           IntToStr(JoyCaps.wPeriodMin);
  JoystickMaxPoll->Caption = "Max polling period (ms)= " +
                           IntToStr(JoyCaps.wPeriodMax);

  // Tell Windows we want to receive joystick events.
  // Handle = receiver, JoystickID = joystick we're using.
  // 3rd arg = how often MM_JOYMOVE events happen.
  if(Connected)
    joySetCapture(Handle,JoystickID,2*JoyCaps.wPeriodMin,FALSE);

  // Calculate ratios to divide down the joystick value to a
  // screen value.
  XDivider = (JoyCaps.wXmax - JoyCaps.wXmin)/ Width;
  YDivider = (JoyCaps.wYmax - JoyCaps.wYmin)/ Height;
}
```

```
void TForm1::ShowStatusInfo(void)
{
  if(Connected)
  {
    JOYINFO JoyInfo;
    joyGetPos(JoystickID,&JoyInfo); // Get the initial joystick pos.
    Position.x = JoyInfo.wXpos;      // Save values,
    Position.y = JoyInfo.wYpos;      // and update each caption.
    JoystickXPosition->Caption = "X Position = " + IntToStr(Position.x);
    JoystickYPosition->Caption = "Y Position = " + IntToStr(Position.y);

  // The bits of wButtons tell which buttons have been pressed. AND
  // wButtons with JOY_BUTTONX to determine if a button X is pressed.
  // Buttons that are not present are reported as not pressed.
    if(JoyInfo.wButtons & JOY_BUTTON1)
      JoystickButton1->Caption = "Button 1 = Pressed";
    else
      JoystickButton1->Caption = "Button 1 = Not Pressed";
    if(JoyInfo.wButtons & JOY_BUTTON2)
      JoystickButton2->Caption = "Button 2 = Pressed";
    else
      JoystickButton2->Caption = "Button 2 = Not Pressed";
    if(JoyInfo.wButtons & JOY_BUTTON3)
      JoystickButton3->Caption = "Button 3 = Pressed";
    else
      JoystickButton3->Caption = "Button 3 = Not Pressed";
    if(JoyInfo.wButtons & JOY_BUTTON4)
      JoystickButton4->Caption = "Button 4 = Pressed";
    else
      JoystickButton4->Caption = "Button 4 = Not Pressed";
  }
  else
  {
    JoystickXPosition->Visible = false;
    JoystickYPosition->Visible = false;
    JoystickButton1->Visible   = false;
    JoystickButton2->Visible   = false;
    JoystickButton3->Visible   = false;
    JoystickButton4->Visible   = false;
    JoystickButton4->Visible   = false;
  }
}
```

7. Now you're ready to type in the functions that will respond to joystick events. Type the function bodies for **JMMove** and **JMButtonUpdate** in **MAINFORM.CPP**.

```
void __fastcall TForm1::JMMove(TMessage &msg)
{
  // Find where the gunsight used to be, and fill in that
  // region with the background color of the form.
  Canvas->Brush->Color=Color;
  // Calculate screen points from joystick points. First half of equation
does
```

continued on next page

continued from previous page

```
    // the conversion. The subtraction centers the gunsights on the
    // joystick location.
    int ScreenX = (Position.x-JoyCaps.wXmin)/XDivider - ImageList1->Width/2;
    int ScreenY = (Position.y-JoyCaps.wYmin)/YDivider - ImageList1->Height/2;
    Canvas->FillRect(Rect(ScreenX,ScreenY,
                                ImageList1->Width+ScreenX,
                                ImageList1->Height+ScreenY));

    // Save new position values. Joystick coordinates are passed to us
    // in the high and low words of LPARAM. Values are 16 bit ints.
    Position.x = msg.LParamLo;
    Position.y = msg.LParamHi;
    // Calculate new screen coordinates.
    ScreenX = (Position.x-JoyCaps.wXmin)/XDivider - ImageList1->Width/2;
    ScreenY = (Position.y-JoyCaps.wYmin)/YDivider - ImageList1->Height/2;

    JoystickXPosition->Caption = "X Position = " + IntToStr(Position.x);
    JoystickYPosition->Caption = "Y Position = " + IntToStr(Position.y);
    ImageList1->Draw(Canvas,ScreenX,ScreenY,0);
}

void __fastcall TForm1::JMButtonUpdate(TMessage &msg)
{
    // This event only happens when a button changes state.
    // You could find out which button was toggled by ANDing
    // with JOY_BUTTONXCHG where X is the button number.
    // Instead, this function simply polls the state of
    // each button.
    if(msg.WParam & JOY_BUTTON1)
        JoystickButton1->Caption = "Button 1 = Pressed";
    else
        JoystickButton1->Caption = "Button 1 = Not Pressed";
    if(msg.WParam & JOY_BUTTON2)
        JoystickButton2->Caption = "Button 2 = Pressed";
    else
        JoystickButton2->Caption = "Button 2 = Not Pressed";
    if(msg.WParam & JOY_BUTTON3)
        JoystickButton3->Caption = "Button 3 = Pressed";
    else
        JoystickButton3->Caption = "Button 3 = Not Pressed";
    if(msg.WParam & JOY_BUTTON4)
        JoystickButton4->Caption = "Button 4 = Pressed";
    else
        JoystickButton4->Caption = "Button 4 = Not Pressed";
}
```

8. Each call to `joySetCapture` should be paired with a call to `joyReleaseCapture`. Create an `OnDestroy` handler, and insert the `joyReleaseCapture` call.

```
void __fastcall TForm1::FormDestroy(TObject *Sender)
{
if(Connected)
    joyReleaseCapture(JoystickID);
}
```

9. For the most part, the program is ready to go. Unfortunately the gun sight will get drawn on top of the labels when you move the joystick around. You can use a timer to periodically update each **Label** control to patch up any damage that may occur. Create an **OnTimer** event for **Timer1** and add this code.

```
void __fastcall TForm1::Timer1Timer(TObject *Sender)
{
for (int j=0; j< ControlCount;j++)
  Controls[j]->Refresh();
}
```

10. Compile and test the program.

How It Works

The program must first detect the presence of a joystick. Detecting a joystick involves checking for driver support and verifying that the joystick is connected to the system (step 5). You can verify that the system has a game port and driver by calling **joyGetNumDevs**. The PC has no joystick capability if the result equals zero. If **joyGetNumDevs** returns a nonzero value, then the system can support a joystick. **joyGetNumDevs** does not verify the joystick's connection. You verify the connection by calling **joyGetPosEx** and checking that no errors occurred.

NOTE

joyGetNumDevs generally returns sixteen for PCs that have a game port.

You can receive joystick messages once you have determined that the joystick is connected. **joySetCapture** (step 6) tells Windows where to send joystick messages and how often it should send them.

```
joySetCapture(Handle,JoystickID,2*JoyCaps.wPeriodMin,FALSE);
```

The first argument to **joySetCapture** tells Windows who gets the messages, and the second argument determines which joystick the program wants to receive messages from. The third argument determines how frequently you want to receive **JM_MOVE** messages (in milliseconds). You will receive **JM_MOVE** messages at this frequency whether the joystick has moved or not.

NOTE

The fourth argument to **joySetCapture** allows you to only receive messages if the joystick has moved a specified distance. The distance is set by using **joySetThreshold**.

Your form will receive joystick events after **joySetCapture** has been called. **MM_JOYxMOVE** (x = joystick id) events flow in at the time interval specified by

joySetCapture. MM_JOYxBUTTONUP and MM_JOYxBUTTONDOWN events stream in only when a button changes state. The joystick events trigger handlers that update the status labels (step 7). The move messages also repaint the gun sight in its new location. The program calls joyReleaseCapture (step 8) to tell Windows that it's finished using the joystick.

Comments

The purpose of this How-To was to demonstrate joystick principles. Consequently, the graphics portions of the code (step 7) are somewhat crude. You could improve the appearance of the program by painting the gun sight using the animation code from How-To 5. 6. This would reduce flicker as the joystick's gun sight sweeps across the screen.

You may notice that the gun sight jitters when you run the program. You can reduce jitter by filtering the joystick positions. One common technique involves setting a joystick threshold. With this technique, the JMMove function would not redraw the gun sight unless the user moved the joystick farther than the threshold value.

This How-To demonstrates how you can go straight to the Windows API when C++Builder does not provide built-in support for a particular item. While the MCI joystick functions may not be perfect, working with the joystick in Windows is easier than reading a joystick in a DOS program.

COMPLEXITY
INTERMEDIATE

9.6 How do I...
Display JPEG and GIF files?

Problem

Bitmaps are cool, but the Eighties are over. I want to display images that use the newer GIF and JPEG compression formats. TImage and TBitmap don't support these types of files. How can I display JPEGs and GIFs in my program?

Technique

The JPEG and GIF file formats can be obtained via the World Wide Web. You could write your own routines for decompressing the files and displaying the pictures. But this work has already been done by thousands of other programmers, so there isn't much point redoing it yourself. This How-To uses a freeware OCX control (TwistedPixel by Alex Lerner) to display GIF and JPEG files. This approach fits the component model of C++Builder. After all, you don't have to concern yourself with the file format of bitmaps because TBitmap and Windows take care of that for you. Likewise, you should not have to worry about the details of GIF and JPEG files just to display them. The OCX control minimizes your coding effort by utilizing the work of other programmers.

Steps

You must register the **TwistedPixel** OCX control before you can run the sample program. The easiest way to do this is by installing the control into C++Builder, which you have to do anyway. You can install the control by following these steps.

1. Create a new subdirectory called **TWISTEDPIXEL** in the **\OCX** directory of C++Builder. Copy the **TwistedPixel** OCX files from the CD-ROM into this subdirectory.

2. Run C++Builder. Select Component|Install.

3. Click the ActiveX button.

4. Click the Register button in the Import OLE Control dialog. Select the **TWISTEDPIXEL.OCX** file.

5. When you close the Choose File dialog, C++Builder registers the OCX control and returns you to the Import OLE Control dialog. Now highlight "Twisted Pixel OLE Control module" in the Registered Controls List box.

6. Change the Unit File Name Edit box from **$(BCB)\LIB\Unnamed.pas** to **$(BCB)\LIB\TwistedPixel.pas** (the key is changed from **UNNAMED.PAS** to **TWISTEDPIXEL.PAS**).

7. Make sure the Class Names Edit box says **TTwistedPixel**. The Palette Page Edit box should say ActiveX. Figure 9-7 shows what you should now see.

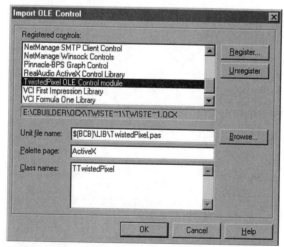

Figure 9-7 Installing the TwistedPixel OCX control

8. Click OK to close the Import OLE Control dialog. Then click OK again to install the component. C++Builder will then rebuild the Component Library and add the **TwistedPixel OCX** to the Component Palette.

After installing the OCX control, run **JPEGVIEWER.EXE** (start the program from outside the C++Builder IDE). Click File|Load and locate either a .JPG or a .GIF file. The program will load the image and display it in the main form of the program. Figure 9-8 shows **JPEGVIEWER** during execution. Test the program on both file formats.

1. Create a new project. Name the unit **MAINFORM.CPP** and name the project **JPEGVIWER.MAK**.

2. The **TwistedPixel OCX** should have been added to the ActiveX tab in the Component Palette when you installed the component. Locate the control and plop one onto the form. The OCX contains a ton of properties, but only a few really matter for this How-To. Table 9-10 lists the property settings and the other controls you should add to the form.

Table 9-10 Components, properties, and settings for `Form1` in the `JPEGVIEWER` project

COMPONENT	PROPERTY	SETTING
Form	AutoScroll	false
TwistedPixel	Left	0
	Top	0
OpenDialog	Filter	JPEG (*.jpg) |*.jpg
		GIF (*.gif) |*.gif
	+Options	true
	−ofFileMustExit	true
	−ofPathMustExist	true
MainMenu	MenuItem	&File
	MenuItem	&Load
	MenuItem	E&xit

3. If you have not already done so, place a **MainMenu** control on **Form1**. Make a **File** menu item, and add two subitems: **Load** and **Exit**. Create an **OnClick** handler for the **Exit** subitem, and use the **Close** method to shut down the program.

```
void __fastcall TForm1::Exit1Click(TObject *Sender)
{
  Close();
}
```

Figure 9-8 JPEGVIEWER at runtime

4. Now make an OnClick handler for the **Load** menu item. This handler contains code for loading the image. Use the function provided by the OCX to open the file. Consult the OCX documentation on the CD for more information.

```
void __fastcall TForm1::Load1Click(TObject *Sender)
{
    // Load the image. First arg is a char* with the file name.
    // Second arg is ignored for JPEGS and GIFS.
    TwistedPixel1->Load(OpenDialog1->FileName.c_str(),0);
    // Size the OCX to match the image.
    TwistedPixel1->Width = TwistedPixel1->ImageWidth;
    TwistedPixel1->Height= TwistedPixel1->ImageHeight;
    // Size the Form to match the image.
    ClientWidth = TwistedPixel1->ImageWidth;
    ClientHeight = TwistedPixel1->ImageHeight;
    }
}
```

5. Compile and test the program.

> **NOTE**
>
> Run the program from outside the C++Builder IDE. The OCX will trip breakpoints in the C++Builder debugger if you execute it using DebuglRun (you can use F9 to step through the breakpoints if you need to).

How It Works

The real work in this How-To resides inside the OCX control. Displaying the images turned out to be quite simple. In fact, by reusing an existing control, loading JPEGs and GIFs is almost as easy as loading native bitmap files.

The OnClick handler of step 4 pops up an Open dialog box when the user clicks Load from the menu. When the user selects a file, OpenDialog1->FileName is passed to the OCX so it can open the file. The OCX performs its voodoo and magically displays the image. The OnClick handler then resizes the form to fit the image that was loaded.

Comments

This How-To illustrates the benefits of component reuse. The OCX allows you to accomplish the task at hand without concerning yourself with low-level, file formatting details. This is object-oriented programming to the max.

One downfall of using an OCX is that it must be registered on the user's system in order for the program to run. Fortunately, C++Builder comes with InstallShield. InstallShield can automatically register OCX controls when it installs your program. As an alternative to the TwistedPixel OCX, the CD-ROM also contains a freeware JPEG/GIF DLL called NViewLib (provided by K. Nishita). The DLL has an advantage in that it allows you to statically link the decompression code to your executable, which simplifies program distribution. The OCX offers the advantage of looking and acting like a normal VCL control that you can manipulate at design time. Both products simplify your efforts by handling the murky details of JPEG and GIF decompression for you.

CHAPTER 10
PRINTING

10

PRINTING

How do I...

Do you remember when we all talked about the paperless office? Documents would be created, exchanged, and read electronically, and, as a result, millions of trees would be saved each year. In reality, computers have made it easier than ever before to generate beautiful documents that get printed, duplicated, and distributed the old fashioned way.

Whether you are working with plain text, formatted text, or database records, your users will demand a way to put stuff on paper. The How-To's in this chapter cover all the basic techniques you'll need. You'll learn about the VCL objects that help you use the standard print setup and print dialog boxes. You'll see how the `TPrinter` object helps you format and put text on paper. Finally, you'll use the basic functionality of the Quick Reports VCL objects to create a simple database report which can be previewed on the screen and printed on paper.

10.1 Print Simple Text Documents

Printing from a Windows application can get a little involved. You have to let the user select a printer, possibly set options for that printer, and then, because Windows lets you do things like print fancy fonts, you have to do more that just send the text to the printer device. Fortunately, C++Builder™ provides plenty of support to make what used to be a complex job into a fairly simple one.

This How-To will demonstrate how to use the standard Windows Print Setup dialogs from your application. It will also show you how to format and send your text to the printer allowing for multiple copies and collation if the user selects those options from the Print Setup dialog.

10.2 Allow the User to Select a Page Range to Print

Sometimes the user doesn't want to print the whole document. This How-To builds on the functionality in How-To 10.1 to give the user the ability to select a page range to print through the Print Setup standard dialog.

10.3 Maintain the Same Appearance on the Printed Page as on the Screen

Windows is supposed to be a WYSIWYG environment: What you see is supposed to be what you get. Unfortunately, the printer and the screen rarely have the same resolution. This How-To shows you how to adjust the printer's font size to make the printed output look more like the screen.

10.4 Show Print Spooler Status

Printers are slow devices. Even a good quality laser printer is not able to keep up with an application's ability to send data. If your application had to wait for the printer, it would end up waiting a long time and the user would not be very happy.

Windows takes care of this problem by buffering (spooling) the data you send to the printer on your disk or on some network disk if you are printing to a shared printer. You can watch the status of the spooler by opening a printer from Start|Printers, and sending it a document. This How-To shows you how to add such a spooler status window to your C++Builder application. In addition, you'll learn how to build an application that can deal with situations where the Windows 95 and Windows NT APIs differ.

10.5 Create a Simple Report Using Quick Reports

Because C++Builder makes it easy to build applications that manipulate databases, you'd expect it to include powerful tools for putting together database reports. You won't be disappointed by the Quick Reports components. This How-To shows you the basics you'll need to get started.

COMPLEXITY
INTERMEDIATE

10.1 How do I...
Print simple text documents?

Problem

I have written an application that includes a little Text Editor. I want to give the user the capability to print from the editor. How can I do this with C++Builder?

Technique

C++Builder includes VCL objects that make it easy to add standard Print Setup and Print dialog boxes to your application. Unfortunately, even with the help of the **TPrinter** class, the actual job of printing is a little more difficult. This How-To will show you the basics.

Steps

Run **PRINT1.EXE**. Type some information into the Memo box. Select File|Print from the menu, and the application will print a hard copy of what you typed. Experiment with the File|Print Setup and Edit|Font menu options to see how they affect the application's printed output. Figure 10-1 shows **PRINT1.EXE** after the File|Print option has been selected from the menu.

1. Create a new project. Save the default form as **PRINT1MAIN.CPP** and the project as **PRINT1.MAK**.

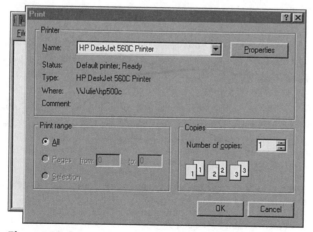

Figure 10-1 PRINT1.EXE displaying Windows' . standard Print dialog box

2. Add the components, and set their properties as shown in Table 10-1. Lay out the controls as shown in Figure 10-1.

Table 10-1 Components, properties, and settings for the `PRINT1` project

COMPONENT	PROPERTY	SETTING
TForm	Caption	Print1
TMemo	Name	mEdit
	Align	alClient
	Lines	None
TFontDialog		
TPrintDialog		
TPrinterSetupDialog		
TMainMenu		

3. Add the menu items shown in Table 10-2.

Table 10-2 Menu items for the `TMainMenu` component

MENU CAPTION	MENU ITEM CAPTION
&File	&Print
	Printer &Setup
	—
	E&xit
&Edit	&Font

4. Add the following `#include` statement near the top of `FORM1MAIN.CPP`:

```
#include <vcl\vcl.h>
#include <vcl\printers.hpp>
```

5. Open the Object Inspector for `Form1`. Double-click on the `FormCreate` event and add the code that makes sure the printer, the Font dialog, and the Memo edit box are all using the same font.

```
void __fastcall TForm1::FormCreate(TObject *Sender)
{
  //Make sure the Font dialog starts with the same font as the Memo box
  FontDialog1->Font = mEdit->Font;
  //Make sure the printer starts with the same font as the Memo box
  Printer()->Canvas->Font = mEdit->Font;
}
```

6. Click on the `Form1`'s Exit menu item, and add the code to close the program.

```
void __fastcall TForm1::Exit1Click(TObject *Sender)
{
  Close();
}
```

7. Click on `Form1`'s Font menu item, and add the code that brings up the Font dialog box to allow the user to change the font.

```
void __fastcall TForm1::Font1Click(TObject *Sender)
{
  //If the user pressed OK on the Font dialog
  if (FontDialog1->Execute())
  {
    //Change the font of the Memo box
    mEdit->Font = FontDialog1->Font;
    //Change the font of the printer
    Printer()->Canvas->Font = FontDialog1->Font;
  }
}
```

8. Click on `Form1`'s Printer Setup menu item, and add the code that brings up the Printer Setup dialog box.

```
void __fastcall TForm1::PrinterSetup1Click(TObject *Sender)
{
  //Bring up the print setup dialog box
  PrinterSetupDialog1->Execute();
  //Change the printer's font just in case the user changed printers
  Printer()->Canvas->Font = FontDialog1->Font;
}
```

9. Click on `Form1`'s Print menu item. Add the code that brings up the Print dialog box and actually prints the document.

```
void __fastcall TForm1::Print1Click(TObject *Sender)
{
  int Iterations, Copies, LineOnPage, LinesPerPage;
  int StartLine, EndLine;
  int x, y, z, PageNumber;
  bool NewPageRequired;

  //If the user did not press OK on the printer dialog, return
  if (!PrintDialog1->Execute())
    return;

  //Change the printer's font just in case the user changed fonts
  Printer()->Canvas->Font = FontDialog1->Font;
```

continued on next page

continued from previous page

```
//Printer will start at the top of a new page
//So we don't have to issue a new page before printing the
//first page
NewPageRequired = FALSE;
//Calculate number of lines that can fit on a page
LinesPerPage = (Printer()->PageHeight /
  Printer()->Canvas->TextHeight("W"));

//If the user did not ask for collation
if (!PrintDialog1->Collate)
{
  //Loop through all the pages once
  Iterations = 1;
  //Print as many copies of each page as the user requested
  Copies = PrintDialog1->Copies;
}
//User wants to collate
else
{
  //Loop through all the pages enough times
  //to make all the copies the user requested
  Iterations = PrintDialog1->Copies;
  //Print each page once per iteration
  Copies = 1;
}

//Set the title used in the print manager to identify this job
Printer()->Title = "C++ Builder How-To Printer Example 1";
//Start the printing job
Printer()->BeginDoc();

//Start with the first line
LineOnPage = 0;

//Outer loop runs only once unless user requested collation
for (x = 0; x < Iterations; x++)
{
  //Always start at the first page
  PageNumber = 1;
  //Loop runs until we run out of pages to print
  do
  {
    //Loop to print multiple copies of a page (if required)
    for (y = 0; y < Copies; y++)
    {
      //If a new page is required
      if (NewPageRequired)
      {
        //Print a new page
        Printer()->NewPage();
        //Reset the line count
        LineOnPage = 0;
```

```
    }
    //Must always print a new page
    //for pages after the first
    NewPageRequired = TRUE;

    //Calculate the Memo line that prints at the top of this page
    StartLine = ((PageNumber - 1) * LinesPerPage);
    //Calculate the Memo line that prints at the bottom of this page
    EndLine = LinesPerPage + ((PageNumber - 1) * LinesPerPage) - 1;

    //Asjust the ending line count for the last page (which may not⇐
    be full)
    if (EndLine >= mEdit->Lines->Count)
      EndLine = mEdit->Lines->Count;

    //For each Memo line that will appear on this page
    for (z = StartLine; z < EndLine; z++)
    {
      //Print out a line
      Printer()->Canvas->TextOut(20,
        Printer()->Canvas->TextHeight(mEdit->Lines->Strings[z]) *⇐
        LineOnPage,
          mEdit->Lines->Strings[z].c_str());
      //Increment the line count
      LineOnPage++;
    }
  }
  //Required copies of page are printed
  //Increment the page number
  PageNumber++;
//Keep going until we're out of lines to print
} while (EndLine < mEdit->Lines->Count);
}

//Close the document
Printer()->EndDoc();
}
```

10. Compile and run the application.

How It Works

The application starts in the **FormCreate** function (step 5). **FormCreate** makes sure that the Font dialog and the printer object start with the same font as the Memo box. The **Printer()** function returns a pointer to the default printer object automatically created whenever you include the Printers module. Note that the **TPrinter** object returned will always be the current selected printer. The **Canvas** property of the default printer object is a **TCanvas** object, which the application will draw on to send data to the printer. The **Font** property of the **TCanvas** object is, therefore, the currently selected printer's font.

`Font1Click` (step 7), which executes when the user selects Edit|Font from the main menu, and `PrinterSetup1Click` (step 8), which executes when the user selects File|Printer Setup, are very simple functions. `Font1Click` displays the Font dialog. If the user presses OK, `FontDialog1->Execute` will return `true`, and the font of the Memo box and the printer will be set to match the font selected by the user. `PrinterSetup1Click` just displays the Printer Setup dialog by calling `PrinterSetupDialog1`'s `Execute` method. Because the user can change the current printer from the Printer Setup dialog, the default printer object's font is set to match the font selected in the `FontDialog1`.

Printing

`Print1Click` (step 9), which is the event handler for the File|Print menu option, does all the hard work. It starts by calling `PrintDialog1`'s `Execute` method to display the standard Print dialog. If the user did not press the OK button, `Execute` will return `false`, and the function will return because the user does not want to print the document. Because the user can change the current printer from the Print Setup dialog, which can be accessed from the Print dialog, the default printer object's font is set to match the font selected in the `FontDialog1`.

If `Execute` returns `true`, the function performs a little setup. First, the `NewPageRequired` flag is set to `false` because the application will not have to issue a page feed before printing the first page because the printer should be positioned at the top of a page at this point. The number of lines that will print on a page is then calculated by dividing the height of a printer page in pixels by the pixel height of a W printed using the current font. A W is used because it is as tall as any other upper-case character. The page height in pixels comes from the `PageHeight` property of the default printer object. The pixel height of a W printed with the current font is returned from the `TextHeight` method of the default printer object's `TCanvas` object. Because `LinesPerPage` is an integer, it will end up holding the whole number of lines that will fit on the page even if a fraction of a line can fit at the bottom of the page.

Next, the `Collate` property of the Print dialog is checked to see whether the user wants multiple copies collated. If the user wants to collate copies, the application must loop through the whole document enough times to print the desired number of copies. For example, to collate three copies of a three page document, the application must print page one, then page two, then page three, and it must repeat that operation three times. If the user does not check collate, the application can print three copies of page one, then three copies of page two, and then three copies of page three. `Iterations` holds the number of times the application must print the entire document while `Copies` holds the number of times each page will be printed on each pass through the document. If the user wants to collate, `Iterations` will be equal to the number of copies selected in the Print dialog, and `Copies` will be one. If the user does not want to collate, `Copies` will be equal to the number of copies selected in the Print dialog, and `Iterations` will be one.

The next two lines of code actually start the printing process. The `BeginDoc` method of the default `Printer` object actually starts the print job. `LineOnPage` holds the

row number where the next line of text will be printed. It is initialized to zero so printing will start at the top of the page.

The outer loop controls iterations through the entire document. `PageNumber` is initialized to one at the start of the loop because this application always starts at page one. The `do...while` loop that comes next runs until the application has printed the entire document. The `for` loop inside the `do` loop controls printing copies of a single page.

Page Processing

The application is now ready to print a page. If this is not the first page of the document, `NewPageRequired` will be `true`, and the `NewPage` method of the default printer object is called to start a new page. Because this is a new page, `LineOnPage` is once again set to zero so printing will start at the top of the page.

Next, the memo start line and memo end line for the current page are calculated. `StartLine` is calculated as the current page number minus one times the number of lines that fit on a page. For example, `StartLine` on page one will be zero, and, if 60 lines fit on a page, `StartLine` on page two will be 60. `EndLine` is calculated as `LinesPerPage` plus the calculation of `StartLine` minus 1. For example, the `EndLine` for page one, assuming 60 lines per page, is 59. Because the calculation of `EndLine` assumes a full page, it is adjusted to make sure it does not exceed the number of lines contained in the Memo control. This is necessary because there may not be enough lines in the Memo to fill the last page.

The next `for` loop actually controls the printing of text on the printer. It loops through each line that is supposed to appear on the printer and draws it on the default printer object's canvas by calling the `TextOut` method. `TextOut` takes three parameters: the column in pixels, the row in pixels, and the string to draw on the canvas. The column is a constant 20 in this application. The row is calculated as the height of the printed string in pixels times the current line number. For example, the first line of text will be printed at row 0 because `LineOnPage` starts at zero, while the fifth row of text will be printed at row four times the height of the string in pixels.

After the required number of copies of the current page are printed, `PageNumber` is incremented and the application prints the next page if there is one. If the application is out of pages to print, it will print additional copies of the document if necessary. Finally, when all the iterations are completed, the default printer object's `EndDoc` method is called to close the print job.

Comments

Unfortunately, you have to manage more than a few details to print from your C++Builder application. Your application must know where to put text, where to end pages, and how to handle copies and collation. Fortunately, as shown in this How-To, there is nothing particularly hard about managing those details.

COMPLEXITY
BEGINNING

10.2 How do I...
Allow the user to select a page range to print?

Problem

Sometimes the user won't want to print the whole text document. How do I turn on the page range portion of the Print dialog box, and, if the user does select a range of pages, how can I make my program print only that set of pages?

Technique

Adding this capability to How-To 10.1 is not difficult at all. First, you have to tell the Print dialog box the lowest and highest page numbers so it can validate the user's input. You then have to add some logic to the print routine to print only the selected range of pages.

Steps

Run PRINT2.EXE. Load a long text document (at least two pages) into Notepad, copy it to the clipboard, and paste it into PRINT2 by clicking in the Memo control and pressing CTRL-V. Select Print from the File menu and enter a print range as shown in Figure 10-2. The printed document will only include the page range you selected.

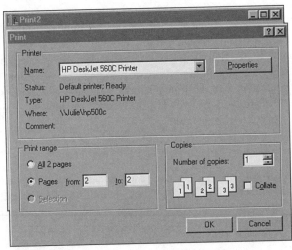

Figure 10-2 PRINT2.EXE with a page range selected in the Print dialog

1. Open PRINT1.MAK from How-To 10.1. Save Form1 as PRINT2MAIN.CPP, and the project as PRINT2.MAK.

2. Change the component properties as shown in Table 10-3.

Table 10-3 Component properties modified for PRINT2

COMPONENT	PROPERTY	SETTING
Form1	Caption	Print 2
PrintDialog1	Options	[poPageNums]

3. Replace the Print1Click function from How-To 10.1 with the version shown here.

```
void __fastcall TForm1::Print1Click(TObject *Sender)
{
  int Iterations, Copies, LineOnPage, LinesPerPage;
  int StartLine, EndLine, PagesInDoc, FromPage, ToPage;
  int x, y, z, PageNumber;
  bool NewPageRequired;

  //Printer will start at the top of a new page
  //So we don't have to issue a new page before printing the
  //first page
  NewPageRequired = FALSE;
  //Calculate number of lines that can fit on a page
  LinesPerPage = (Printer()->PageHeight /
    Printer()->Canvas->TextHeight("W"));
  //Calculate number of whole pages in the document
  PagesInDoc = mEdit->Lines->Count / LinesPerPage;
  //If there are any lines left over, add one more page
  //(that will be a partial page)
  if ((mEdit->Lines->Count % LinesPerPage) > 0)
    PagesInDoc++;

  //Tell the printer dialog the maximum page number
  PrintDialog1->MaxPage = PagesInDoc;

  //If the user did not press OK on the printer dialog, return
  if (!PrintDialog1->Execute())
    return;

  //If the user did not ask for collation
  if (!PrintDialog1->Collate)
  {
    //Loop through all the pages once
    Iterations = 1;
    //Print as many copies of each page as the user requested
    Copies = PrintDialog1->Copies;
```

continued on next page

continued from previous page

```
    }
    //User wants to collate
    else
    {
      //Loop through all the pages enough times
      //to make all the copies the user requested
      Iterations = PrintDialog1->Copies;
      //Print each page once per iteration
      Copies = 1;
    }

    //If the user did not select a page range
    if (PrintDialog1->PrintRange == prAllPages)
    {
      //Print from page 1
      FromPage = 1;
      //To the last page
      ToPage = PagesInDoc;
    }
    //The user picked a range
    else
    {
      //Set up to print the page range
      FromPage = PrintDialog1->FromPage;
      ToPage = PrintDialog1->ToPage;
    }

    //Set the title used in the print manager to identify this job
    Printer()->Title = "C++ Builder How-To Printer Example 2";
    //Start the printing job
    Printer()->BeginDoc();

    //Start with the first line
    LineOnPage = 0;

    //Outer loop runs only once unless user requested collation
    for (x = 0; x < Iterations; x++)
    {
      //Always start at the first page
      PageNumber = FromPage;
      //Loop runs until we run out of pages to print
      do
      {
        //Loop to print multiple copies of a page (if required)
        for (y = 0; y < Copies; y++)
        {
          //If a new page is required
          if (NewPageRequired)
          {
            //Print a new page
            Printer()->NewPage();
            //Reset the line count
```

```
        LineOnPage = 0;
    }
    //Must always print a new page
    //for pages after the first
    NewPageRequired = TRUE;

    //Calculate the Memo line that prints at the top of this page
    StartLine = ((PageNumber - 1) * LinesPerPage);
    //Calculate the Memo line that prints at the bottom of this page
    EndLine = LinesPerPage + ((PageNumber - 1) * LinesPerPage);

    //Adjust the ending line count for the last page (which may not⇐
    be full)
    if (EndLine >= mEdit->Lines->Count)
      EndLine = mEdit->Lines->Count;

    //For each Memo line that will appear on this page
    for (z = StartLine; z < EndLine; z++)
    {
      //Print out a line
      Printer()->Canvas->TextOut(20,
        Printer()->Canvas->TextHeight(mEdit->Lines->Strings[z]) *⇐
        LineOnPage,
          mEdit->Lines->Strings[z].c_str());
      //Increment the line count
      LineOnPage++;
    }
  }
  //Required copies of page are printed
  //Increment the page number
  PageNumber++;
  //Keep going until we're out of pages to print
} while (PageNumber <= ToPage);
}

//Close the document
Printer()->EndDoc();

}
```

4. Compile and run the application.

How It Works

Because this How-To builds on the functionality already in How-To 10.1, this section will focus on the changes made to the **Print1Click** function to handle printing a page range (step 3). First of all, before printing can start, the application must calculate the total number of pages in the document. This is accomplished by the following three lines of code:

```
PagesInDoc = mEdit->Lines->Count / LinesPerPage;
if ((mEdit->Lines->Count % LinesPerPage) > 0)
  PagesInDoc++;
```

The number of lines in the Memo box are divided by the number of lines that can fit on the page and be placed in **PagesInDoc**. Because **PagesInDoc** is an integer, this calculation only determines the number of complete pages in the document. The **if** statement that follows tests for an additional partial page and increments **PagesInDoc** if one exists. The number of pages in the document is then assigned to the Print dialog component's **MaxPage** property so the Print dialog can validate the page range entered by the user. The **MinPage** property is not assigned here because it defaults to one, which makes perfect sense for this application.

After checking for collation, **Print1Click** tests the Print dialog's **PrintRange** property to see whether the user selected a page range. If not, **PrintRange** will be **prAllPages**, and the application assigns **FromPage** and **ToPage** to indicate that all pages will be printed. If the user did select a page range, **FromPage** and **ToPage** are assigned the values provided by the user. Note that the page range provided by the Print dialog is guaranteed to be valid as long as the **MaxPage** and **MinPage** properties of the Print dialog are set to valid values before the Print dialog's **Execute** method is called.

The rest of the changes involve the nested loops that print the document. Just inside the outer loop, the **PageNumber** is set to the first page in the page range instead of always being set to one, as in How-To 10.1. Finally, the **while** condition that makes printing continue through all the pages tests to make sure printing ends after the last page in the page range is printed.

Comments

Once you know how to use the **TPrinter** object, adding additional capabilities is easy. For fun you might want to try adding a dialog box that lets the user adjust the margins of the document.

COMPLEXITY
BEGINNING

10.3 How do I...
Maintain the same appearance on the printed page as on the screen?

Problem

Because the resolution of the printer and screen may be very different, the hardcopy often does not look like what is on the screen. Is there a way to make the printed output look more like the screen version?

Technique

With the help of the screen's **TCanvas** and the **TCanvas** that is part of the **TPrinter** object, it is a simple matter to adjust the font size of the printer to account for the resolution difference between the two devices.

Steps

Run **PRINT3.EXE**. Type in some text, and print it. You should notice that the printed output is much closer in appearance to the text on the screen than the same text printed from **PRINT2.EXE** (How-To 10.2).

1. Open **PRINT2.MAK** from How-To 10.2. Save the form as **PRINT3MAIN.CPP** and the project as **PRINT3.MAK**.

2. Change the form's **Caption** property to **"Print 3"**.

3. Switch to **PRINT3MAIN.H**, and add the following declaration to **Form1**'s private section:

```
private:// User declarations
  void __fastcall ScalePrinterFont(void);
```

4. Switch back to **PRINT3MAIN.CPP**. Add the following **#include** statement:

```
#include <vcl\printers.hpp>
#include <math.h>
```

5. Add the call to **ScalePrinterFont** to the **Print1Click** function.

```
void __fastcall TForm1::Print1Click(TObject *Sender)
{
  int Iterations, Copies, LineOnPage, LinesPerPage;
  int StartLine, EndLine, PagesInDoc, FromPage, ToPage;
  int x, y, z, PageNumber;
  bool NewPageRequired;

  //Adjust the printer font to make the output look more   like the screen
  ScalePrinterFont();

  //Printer will start at the top of a new page
  //So we don't have to issue a new page before printing the
  //first page
  NewPageRequired = FALSE;
...
```

6. Add the body of the **ScalePrinterFont** function to the bottom of **PRINT3MAIN.CPP**.

```
void __fastcall TForm1::ScalePrinterFont(void)
{
   double ScreenCharacterWidth, PrinterCharacterWidth, ScalingFactor;

   //Calulate the width of a chracter on the screen
   ScreenCharacterWidth = Canvas->TextWidth("W");
   //Calculate the width of a character on the printer
   PrinterCharacterWidth = Printer()->Canvas->TextWidth("W");

   //Calulate the scaling factor for the printer font
   //floor rounds down to the largest integer not greater
   //than the parameter. By adding .5, floor ends up rounding
   //to the nearest integer
   //e.g floor(1.4 + .5) = 1
   //    floor(1.5 + .5) = 2
   //    floor(1.8 + .5) = 2
   ScalingFactor = floor((Printer()->Canvas->Font->Size *
     (ScreenCharacterWidth / PrinterCharacterWidth)));

   //If screen characters are smaller, then printer characters3
   if (ScreenCharacterWidth < PrinterCharacterWidth)
     Printer()->Canvas->Font->Size += ScalingFactor;
   else
     Printer()->Canvas->Font->Size -= ScalingFactor;
}
```

7. Compile and run the application.

How It Works

The key to this How-To is the `ScalePrinterFont` function that you added in step 6. Its job is to adjust the printer font to compensate for the resolution differences between the screen and the printer. First, the width of a W character in pixels is calculated by calling the `TextWidth` function for the screen's canvas and the printer's canvas. A W is used because it is the widest possible character. `ScalingFactor` is then calculated as the biggest integer not greater than the current printer's font size times the ratio of the screen character width and the printer character width. This integer value represents the approximate amount that the printer's font should be adjusted to compensate for the resolution difference between the screen and the printer. If the width of a screen character is less than that of a printer character, the size of the printer font is increased by the scaling factor because the printer has greater resolution. Otherwise, the printer's font size is reduced because the printer has less resolution than the screen.

Comments

This is not a technique you should generally use with text. If the user picks a 10-point font, you should probably use a 10-point font on the screen and the printer. The general technique of adjusting print dimensions by a scaling factor really

becomes important when you want to print graphics that look the same as they do on the screen. The basic calculation presented here will work in either case.

COMPLEXITY
ADVANCED

10.4 How do I...
Show print spooler status?

Problem

My corporate network is very busy, and it can take a few minutes for a print job to make it to the printer. An impatient user will sometimes print the job again because he or she thinks something went wrong. Is there any way to show users the status of jobs in the spooler so they know how their print job is progressing?

Technique

The Windows API provides a couple of functions that allow applications to monitor the status of a print spooler. Both Windows 95 and Windows NT provide the functions to actually check the spooler status. Under Windows NT, there is even an easy way to tell the operating system to notify your program when the status of the print spooler changes. Unfortunately, under Windows 95, your application will have to poll the print spooler at regular intervals.

Because this kind of problem crops up from time to time when you are trying to build applications that will perform optimally under both Windows NT and Windows 95, this How-To also shows you how an application can identify the operating system and adjust its functionality based on that information.

Steps

Shut off your default printer, and then try to print something to it. Run **SPOOL.EXE**. You should get a screen that looks something like Figure 10-3. The job status is "offline printing" because the printer is turned off. Turn the printer back on. The job should print and eventually disappear from the spooler monitor screen.

1. Create a new project. Save the form as **SPOOLMAIN.CPP** and the project as **SPOOL.MAK**.

2. Add the components, and set their properties as shown in Tables 10-4 and 10-5. Lay out the controls as shown in Figure 10-3.

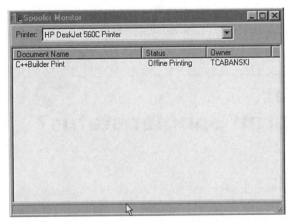

Figure 10-3 SPOOL.EXE showing a job in the spooler

Table 10-4 Components, properties, and settings for SPOOL

COMPONENT	PROPERTY	SETTING
TForm	Caption	Spooler Monitor
TStatusBar	SimplePanel	True
TPanel	Align	alTop
	Caption	None
	Name	Panel1
TPanel	Align	alClient
	BevelOuter	bvNone
	Caption	None
	Name	Panel2
TLabel (On Panel1)	Caption	Printer:
TComboxBox (On Panel1)	Name	cbPrinter
	Style	csDropDownList
TListView (On Panel2)	Name	lvSpoolInfo
	Align	alClient
	Columns	(See Table 10-5)
	ReadOnly	True
	ViewStyle	vsReport

Table 10-5 Items, properties, and settings of `lvSpoolInfo`'s `Columns` property

ITEM	PROPERTY	SETTING
0	Caption	Document Name
	Width	200
1	Caption	Status
	Width	100
2	Caption	Owner
	Width	100

3. Switch to SPOOLMAIN.H. Add the following declarations:

```
#include <vcl\printers.hpp>
//-----------------------------------------------------------------
class TMonitorThread : public TThread
{
private:
  HANDLE hEvent;
  bool OsIsNT;

  void __fastcall Execute(void);
  void __fastcall UpdateUI(void);
public:
  __fastcall TMonitorThread(HANDLE Event);
};

class TForm1 : public TForm
{
__published:// IDE-managed Components
  TStatusBar *StatusBar1;
  TPanel *Panel1;
  TPanel *Panel2;
  TListView *lvSpoolInfo;
  TLabel *Label1;
  TComboBox *cbPrinter;
  void __fastcall FormCreate(TObject *Sender);
  void __fastcall FormClose(TObject *Sender, TCloseAction &Action);
  void __fastcall cbPrinterChange(TObject *Sender);
private:// User declarations
  HANDLE hPrinter, hChange;
  TMonitorThread *MonitorThread;
  bool OsIsNT;

  void __fastcall OpenPrinterMonitor(int PrinterIndex);
  void __fastcall ClosePrinterMonitor(void);
public:// User declarations
  fastcall TForm1(TComponent* Owner);
  void __fastcall UpdateMonitor(void);
};
```

4. Open the Object Inspector for **Form1**. Double-click on the **OnCreate** event, and add the code that initializes the screen display.

```
void __fastcall TForm1::FormCreate(TObject *Sender)
{
  int x;
  char Buffer[255], *FoundOn;
  OSVERSIONINFO VersionInfo;

  for (x = 0; x < Printer()->Printers->Count; x++)
  {
    strcpy(Buffer, Printer()->Printers->Strings[x].c_str());
    FoundOn = strstr(Buffer, " on ");
    if (FoundOn)
      FoundOn[0] = '\0';

    cbPrinter->Items->Add(Buffer);
  }

  VersionInfo.dwOSVersionInfoSize = sizeof(OSVERSIONINFO);
  if (!GetVersionEx(&VersionInfo))
    OsIsNT = FALSE;
  else
    if (VersionInfo.dwPlatformId == VER_PLATFORM_WIN32_NT)
      OsIsNT = TRUE;
    else
      OsIsNT = FALSE;

  cbPrinter->ItemIndex = Printer()->PrinterIndex;
  OpenPrinterMonitor(cbPrinter->ItemIndex);
}
```

5. Double-click the **OnClose** event, and add the code that cleans up just before the program ends.

```
void __fastcall TForm1::FormClose(TObject *Sender, TCloseAction &Action)
{
  ClosePrinterMonitor();
}
```

6. Add the code for the **OpenPrinterMonitor** function at the bottom of SPOOLMAIN.CPP.

```
void __fastcall TForm1::OpenPrinterMonitor(int PrinterIndex)
{
  ClosePrinterMonitor();

  try
  {
    if (!OpenPrinter(cbPrinter->Items->Strings[PrinterIndex].c_str(),
                     &hPrinter, NULL))
      throw new Exception("Could not open printer " +
        IntToStr(GetLastError()));
```

```
    UpdateMonitor();

    if (OsIsNT)
    {
      hChange = FindFirstPrinterChangeNotification(hPrinter,
        PRINTER_CHANGE_ALL, 0, NULL);
      if (hChange == INVALID_HANDLE_VALUE)
        throw new Exception("Could not set printer notification " +
          IntToStr(GetLastError()));
    }

    MonitorThread = new TMonitorThread(hChange);
  }
  catch (Exception &E)
  {
    ShowMessage(E.Message);
  }
}
```

7. Directly beneath `OpenPrinterMonitor`, add the `ClosePrinterMonitor` function.

```
void __fastcall TForm1::ClosePrinterMonitor(void)
{
  if (MonitorThread)
    MonitorThread->Terminate();

  if (hChange)
    FindClosePrinterChangeNotification(hChange);

  if (hPrinter)
    ClosePrinter(hPrinter);
}
```

8. Next, add the function that is called to update the monitor status display.

```
void __fastcall TForm1::UpdateMonitor(void)
{
  DWORD NumOfBytes, NumOfStructures;
  unsigned int x;
  BYTE *Buffer;
  JOB_INFO_1 *ji;
  String s;
  bool UsepStatus;

  lvSpoolInfo->Items->Clear();

  EnumJobs(hPrinter, 0, 2000, 1, NULL, 0, &NumOfBytes, &NumOfStructures);
  try
  {
    Buffer = new BYTE[NumOfBytes];
    if (!EnumJobs(hPrinter, 0, 2000, 1, Buffer, NumOfBytes,
      &NumOfBytes, &NumOfStructures))
```

continued on next page

continued from previous page

```
      throw new Exception("Could not get job info " +
        IntToStr(GetLastError()));

  for (x = 0; x < NumOfStructures; x++)
  {
    ji = ((JOB_INFO_1 *)Buffer);
    lvSpoolInfo->Items->Add();
    lvSpoolInfo->Items->Item[x]->Caption = ji->pDocument;
    if (ji->pStatus)
      if (strcmp(ji->pStatus, "") == 0)
        UsepStatus = FALSE;
      else
        UsepStatus = TRUE;
    else
      UsepStatus = FALSE;

    if (UsepStatus)
      lvSpoolInfo->Items->Item[x]->SubItems->Add(ji->pStatus);
    else
    {
      s = "";
      if (ji->Status & JOB_STATUS_DELETING)
        s = s + " Deleting";
      if (ji->Status & JOB_STATUS_ERROR)
        s = s + " Error";
      if (ji->Status & JOB_STATUS_OFFLINE)
        s = s + " Offline";
      if (ji->Status & JOB_STATUS_PAPEROUT)
        s = s + " Paper Out";
      if (ji->Status & JOB_STATUS_PAUSED)
        s = s + " Paused";
      if (ji->Status & JOB_STATUS_PRINTED)
        s = s + " Printed";
      if (ji->Status & JOB_STATUS_PRINTING)
        s = s + " Printing";
      if (ji->Status & JOB_STATUS_SPOOLING)
        s = s + " Spooling";
      if (ji->Status & JOB_STATUS_USER_INTERVENTION)
        s = s + "User intervention required";
      lvSpoolInfo->Items->Item[x]->SubItems->Add(s);
    }
    lvSpoolInfo->Items->Item[x]->SubItems->Add(ji->pUserName);
  }

  delete [] Buffer;
}
catch (Exception &E)
{
  if (Buffer)
    delete [] Buffer;

  ShowMessage(E.Message);
}
}
```

9. After `UpdateMonitor`, add the constructor for the thread object used to actually monitor the spooler for activity.

```
__fastcall TMonitorThread ::TMonitorThread(HANDLE Event) : TThread(TRUE)
{
  OSVERSIONINFO VersionInfo;

  hEvent = Event;

  VersionInfo.dwOSVersionInfoSize = sizeof(OSVERSIONINFO);
  if (!GetVersionEx(&VersionInfo))
    OsIsNT = FALSE;
  else
    if (VersionInfo.dwPlatformId == VER_PLATFORM_WIN32_NT)
      OsIsNT = TRUE;
    else
      OsIsNT = FALSE;

  Resume();
}
```

10. Add the monitor thread's main loop beneath its constructor.

```
void __fastcall TMonitorThread::Execute(void)
{
  DWORD dw;

  while (!Terminated)
  {
    if (!OsIsNT)
      Sleep(5000);
    else
      WaitForSingleObject(hEvent, INFINITE);

    if (!Terminated)
    {
      Synchronize(UpdateUI);
      if (OsIsNT)
        FindNextPrinterChangeNotification(hEvent, &dw, NULL, NULL);
    }
  }
}
```

11. Beneath the main loop, add the function that the monitor thread calls to update the spooler status display.

```
void __fastcall TMonitorThread::UpdateUI(void)
{
  Form1->UpdateMonitor();
}
```

12. Open the Object Inspector for the Printer Combo box. Double-click the `OnChange` event, and add the code that updates the status display when the user selects a different printer.

```
void __fastcall TForm1::cbPrinterChange(TObject *Sender)
{
   OpenPrinterMonitor(cbPrinter->ItemIndex);
}
```

13. Compile and run the application.

How It Works

The `FormCreate` function (step 4) starts by populating the Combo box with all the printers currently recognized by the computer. C++Builder makes this easy because the `TPrinter` object stores the list of descriptive printer names in a `TStringList` called printers. Printer names that refer to shared printers on other computers include an additional description of the remote computer that the application does not want. The computer name is always tacked on the end after the word *on*. For example, "HP Laserjet 5P on Julie." `FormCreate` strips off the additional description before adding the printer name to the Combo box.

After the printer names are added to the Combo box, `FormCreate` calls `GetVersionEx` to determine whether it is running on NT or not. `GetVersionEx` takes a pointer to an `OSVERSIONINFO` structure that must have its `dwOsVersionInfoSize` field set to `sizeof(OSVERSIONINFO)`. `GetVersionEx` fills in the rest of the fields of the `OSVERSIONINFO` structure with information about the operating system. `FormCreate` checks the `dwPlatformId` field to see whether the operating system is NT and sets the `OsIsNt` flag appropriately.

After the operating system is identified, `FormCreate` sets the selected item in the Combo box to be the current system printer. Finally, it passes the current printer name to the `OpenPrinterMonitor` function to begin monitoring the spooler on the current printer. The `FormClose` function, which is called just before the application terminates, stops print spooler monitoring by calling the `ClosePrintMonitor` function.

Opening and Closing the Printer Monitor

`OpenPrinterMonitor` (step 6) starts the monitoring function. It starts by calling `ClosePrinterMonitor`, which will stop the monitoring function if it is already running. It then calls the `OpenPrinter` Windows API function to open the printer. `OpenPrinter` is passed the name of the printer, a pointer to a handle that will be used by the application to access the printer, and a third parameter that should always be `NULL`. `OpenPrinter` returns `true` if it succeeds; otherwise it returns `false`. If it does fail, `OpenPrinterMonitor` raises an exception that will transfer control to the `catch` block a little further down in the function. If the `OpenPrinter` succeeds, `UpdateMonitor` is called to update the display to show information about the newly opened printer.

Next, if the operating system is Windows NT, the application takes advantage of the `FindFirstPrinterChangeNotification` API function. `FindFirstPrinterChangeNotification` is passed the printer set by `OpenPrinter`, a flag that tells NT what events should trigger a notification, a zero, and a pointer to a printer options structure that can be `NULL` if a flag is specified in the second parameter. The `PRINTER_CHANGE_ALL` flag passed to `FindFirstPrinterChangeNotification` tells NT to notify this application whenever anything happens to the printer. `FindFirstPrinterChangeNotification` returns a handle to a WIN32 event that will be described a little later. If `FindFirstPrinterChangeNotification` fails, the returned event handle will be `INVALID_HANDLE_VALUE` and an exception will be raised that transfers control to the `catch` block.

If everything worked, `OpenPrinterMonitor` starts a background thread to monitor the spooler. If anything went wrong, a description of the error message will be displayed by the `ShowMessage` function.

`ClosePrinterMonitor` (step 7) does three things. First, if a background thread is monitoring a spooler, it is terminated. If `FindFirstPrinterChange` returned an event handle, it is closed by calling the `FindClosePrinterChangeNotification` API function. Finally, if the printer handle is open, it is closed by calling the `ClosePrinter` Windows API function.

Updating the Display

`UpdateMonitor` (step 8) starts by clearing the screen display. The display is managed by a `TListView` object called `lvSpoolInfo`. The `Items` property of a `TListView` is a `TListItems` object called `Items` that holds the list items. `UpdateMonitor` calls the `Clear` method of the `TListItems` object to erase all the items and clear the display.

The `EnumJobs` Windows API function returns information about the jobs in an open printer's spooler. The first parameter passed to `EnumJobs` is the printer handle opened by an earlier call to `OpenPrinter`. The second and third parameters are used to specify the range of jobs to return information on. The fourth parameter tells `EnumJobs` what information to return. The fifth parameter is a pointer to a buffer that `EnumJobs` will fill with information. If the fifth parameter is `NULL`, `EnumJobs` will simply return information on how big a buffer is needed. The sixth parameter is a `DWORD` pointer that will hold the number of bytes read or required. Finally, the seventh parameter is a `DWORD` pointer that will hold the number of job information structures returned. In this case, `UpdateMonitor` passes a `1` as the type of data requested so that `EnumJobs` will return a set of `JOB_INFO_1` structures. Information is requested for jobs 0 to 2000. Because `NULL` is passed as the buffer, `EnumJobs` will return the size of the required data buffer in the `NumOfBytes` variable.

A `BYTE` buffer of the proper size is then allocated with the `new` operator. In the second call to `EnumJobs`, the buffer is passed to receive the data. If the call fails, `EnumJobs` returns `false`, and the application throws an exception to transfer control to the `catch` block.

If the call to **EnumJobs** succeeds, **UpdateMonitor** loops through the returned structures and updates the screen. First, the buffer returned from **EnumJobs** is cast to a **JOB_INFO_1** pointer and assigned to a working variable so the rest of the code will be easier to read. A new **TListItem** is added to **lvSpoolInfo's TListItems** object by calling its **Add** method. The new item's caption is then set to the **pDocument** field of the **JOB_INFO_1** structure.

The **JOB_INFO_1** structure's **pStatus** field is then checked to see whether it contains a status description. If **pStatus** is not **NULL**, and it is not the null string (""), then **UsepStatus** is set to **true**. If **UsepStatus** is **true**, the status string is added to the **SubItem TStringList** of the **TListItem** by calling **TStringList's Add** method. If **UsepStatus** is **false**, the **Status** field of the **JOB_INFO_1** structure must be checked to determine the job status. Each bit in the **Status** field has a different meaning and multiple bits can be set. Therefore, **UpdateMonitor** uses the bitwise AND operator (**&**) to check each possible flag and builds a descriptive string that includes all the information. The resulting description is then added to the **SubItem** list.

After the status string is set, **UpdateMonitor** adds the **pUseName** field of the **JOB_INFO_1** structure to the sub-item list. The screen is now fully updated and the buffer can be deallocated with the **delete** operator. The **catch** block at the bottom of the function traps exceptions that get raised within the **try** block and shows the error message to the user.

The Background Thread

The constructor of the background thread (step 9) passes **true** to **TThread's** constructor so the thread starts in a suspended state. The event handler passed to the constructor is then assigned to a private member variable for later use, the thread's **OsIsNT** flag is set by calling the **GetVersionEx** function, and the **Resume** function is called to start the thread's execution.

The **Execute** method (step 10) is the main loop of the thread. The **while** loop will keep the thread running until it is terminated. If the application is running on NT, the **WaitForSingleObject** Windows API function is called to make the thread sleep forever or until the indicated event is signaled. In this case, the event **Execute** is waiting for is controlled by NT and was returned from **FindFirstPrinterChangeNotification**. Whenever a printer event occurs, NT will signal the event and **WaitForSingleObject** will return. This is very efficient because the thread uses no resources while it is waiting for the event to be signaled. If, on the other hand, this is not NT, the thread simply pauses for 5000 milliseconds by calling the **Sleep** Windows API function. This means that under Windows 95 the window will be updated roughly every five seconds regardless of whether or not it needs to be updated.

If the thread was not asked to terminate while it was waiting, the **UpdateUI** method (step 10) is called through **Synchronize** to update the display. **Synchronize** makes sure the screen update happens in the context of the main thread to avoid any multithreading conflicts. See How-To 12.2 for more information.

Finally, if the application is running on NT, the notification event has to be reset by calling **FindNextPrinterChangeNotification**. The first parameter is the event

handle, the second is a pointer to a **DWORD**, and the last two can be **NULL** when using the function to reset the event. Note that **FindNextPrinterChangeNotification** is a flexible function that can be used to determine precisely what caused NT to raise the event in the first place. Refer to the Win32 API help file for more information.

Comments

This is a very simple example that displays a minimal amount of information to the user. There is other data available in the **JOB_INFO_1** structure that you might want to display. In addition, you can get even more data from **EnumJobs** by asking for other structures. Refer to the Win32 API help for more information on the **JOB_INFO_1** structure and the **EnumJobs** function.

COMPLEXITY
INTERMEDIATE

10.5 How do I...
Create a simple report using Quick Reports?

Problem

I'd like to create a simple report of database records that can be displayed on the screen or printed on paper. What's the easiest way to do this in my C++Builder?

Technique

C++Builder includes Quick Reports, a set of components that work together to let you build simple and complex reports. This How-To will show you how to build a very simple detail report that includes page headers, column headers, page footers, and print preview capability.

Steps

Run **SIMPLEREPORT.EXE**. Press the Preview button to display the report on your screen (Figure 10-4). If you like, you can print the report by pressing the small printer button on the preview screen, or by pressing the Print button on the main form.

1. Create a new project. Save the default form as **SIMPLEREPORTMAIN.CPP** and the project as **SIMPLEREPORT.MAK**.

2. Add the components, and set their properties as shown in Table 10-6.

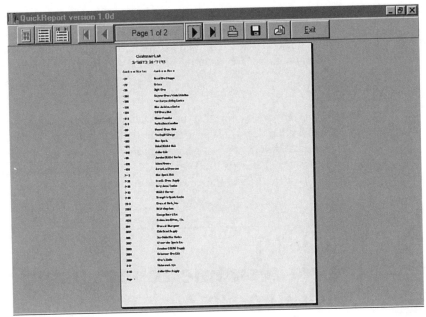

Figure 10-4 SIMPLEREPORT showing a print preview

Table 10-6 Components, properties, and settings of
SIMPLEREPORTMAIN.CPP

COMPONENT	PROPERTY	SETTING
TForm	Caption	Simple Report
TButton	Caption	Print
TButton	Caption	Preview

3. Add a new form to the project by selecting File|New Form. Save the new form as REPORT.CPP.

4. Add the components, and set their properties as shown in Table 10-7. Lay out the controls as shown in Figure 10-5.

Table 10-7 Components, properties, and settings for REPORT.CPP

COMPONENT	PROPERTY	SETTING
TTable	Active	true
	DatabaseName	BCDEMOS
	TableName	CUSTOMER.DB
TDataSource	DataSet	Table1

COMPONENT	PROPERTY	SETTING
TQuickReport	DataSource	DataSource1
	DisplayPrintDialog	true
TQRBand	Name	HeaderBand1
	BandType	rbPageHeader
TQRLabel (On HeaderBand1)	Name	Header1
	Alignment	taCenter
	Caption	Customer List
	Font	Arial Bold 12
TQRBand	Name	HeaderBand2
	BandType	rbPageHeader
TQRSysData (On HeaderBand2)	Name	Header2
	Alignment	taCenter
	Data	qrsDateTime
	Font	Arial Bold 12
TQRBand	Name	HeaderBand3
	BandType	rbColumnHeader
TQRLabel (On HeaderBand3)	Name	Header3
	Caption	Customer Number
	Font	Arial Bold 8
TQRLabel (On HeaderBand3)	Name	Header4
	Caption	Customer Name
	Font	Arial Bold 8
TQRBand	Name	DetailBand1
	BandType	rbDetail
TQRDBText (On DetailBand1)	Name	Detail1
	DataSource	DataSource1
	DataField	CustNo
TQRDBText (On DetailBand1)	Name	Detail2
	DataSource	DataSource1
	DataField	Company
TQRBand	Name	FooterBand1
	BandType	rbPageFooter
TQRLabel (On FooterBand1)	Name	Footer1
	Caption	Page:
TQRSysData (On FooterBand1)	Name	Footer2
	Data	qrsPageNumber

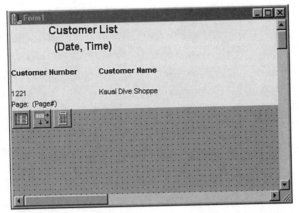

Figure 10-5 Screen layout for REPORT.CPP

5. Switch to **SIMPLEREPORTMAIN.CPP**. Add the following **include** statement near the top of the file.

```
#include "SimpleReportMain.h"
#include "Report.h"
```

6. Switch to **SIMPLEREPORTMAIN.CPP**. Double-click the Print button, and add the code that prints a report.

```
void __fastcall TForm2::Button1Click(TObject *Sender)
{
  Form1->QuickReport1->Print();
}
```

7. Double-click the Preview button, and add the code that brings up the print preview screen.

```
void __fastcall TForm2::Button2Click(TObject *Sender)
{
  Form1->QuickReport1->Preview();
}
```

8. Compile and run the application.

How It Works

Obviously, the three lines of code you added to the project are not the key to understanding how to use Quick Reports in your applications. In reality, the most important part of this How-To is understanding how the Quick Report components work together to produce the report.

The first step is connecting the **TQuickReport** component to a **TDataSource**. This tells Quick Reports where the data is coming from. Because the connection is made through a **TDataSource**, Quick Reports can work with any table or query supported by C++Builder. In this How-To, the data comes from the **CUSTOMER.DB** table which is included with C++Builder (BCDEMOS BDE Alias). Note that a single C++Builder form can contain only one **TQuickReport** component. In other words, the form is the report definition and only one report can be defined on a form.

Next, you have to understand the concept of report bands. A report band is a horizontal slice of a report. For example, the report in this How-To contains a couple of page header bands, a column header band, a detail band, and a page footer band. Quick Reports prints the contents of report bands as appropriate. For example, the page header bands will be printed at the top of each page, and the detail band will be printed for each data record.

The rest should be pretty simple. Report data fields, labels, and system fields, like the current date and time, are placed on report bands. Whenever a band is printed, the fields on the band are printed as well. You print the report to the screen by calling **TQuickReport**'s Preview method, and you call the Print method of the **TQuickReport** to send the report to the printer.

Comments

This How-To only scratches the surface of what Quick Reports can do. Additional band types, like sort group headers and footers, can be used to handle more complex reporting needs. In addition, the Quick Report components include events that let you add code that participates in the report creation process. This How-To gives you the tools you need to explore further.

CHAPTER 11
DATABASE

11

DATABASE

How do I...

C++Builder™ includes a powerful set of components that make it an excellent tool for creating front-end display programs for database systems. In fact, the Component Palette in C++Builder contains three tabs devoted entirely to database programming (Data Access, Data Controls, and QReport). From simple Paradox or dBASE tables

to complex client/server SQL queries, C++Builder has built-in components that automate the process of displaying and editing database information.

The How-To's in this chapter discuss how you can link forms to record-oriented and SQL-type databases, how to utilize the data-aware components of C++Builder, and how to encapsulate the messy details of a database using the data access controls. This chapter also covers techniques for controlling the layout of database displays, both at design time and at runtime.

This chapter is written at a more basic level than some of the other chapters in the book. This is due to the unique way C++Builder simplifies database programming through visual programming, object-oriented design, and compiled runtime programming. The end result is a database development environment like no other. Because of the way C++Builder makes database programming a breeze, this chapter focuses on getting you acquainted with the database controls provided by C++Builder.

11.1 View the Contents of a Database

C++Builder provides a powerful component called `TTable` that connects to record-based databases (such as Paradox or dBASE). This How-To demonstrates how to connect a `TTable` with a `TDataSource` and how to connect the `TDataSource` with a `TDBGrid` that will automatically display database information in a familiar grid control.

11.2 View the Contents of a Database Using SQL

Single user databases, such as Paradox tables, tend to be record-oriented. Larger, more complex databases utilize a query language to keep the data in sets instead of records. SQL (Structured Query Language) provides a standard way to access query-based data. C++Builder provides a `TQuery` component that provides SQL access in much the same way that `TTable` works for simple databases. This How-To guides you through the steps of setting up `TQuery` to retrieve data using SQL.

11.3 Use VCL Components to Automatically Display and Edit Database Information

C++Builder provides data-aware controls that help display and edit database information. Imagine how much code you would have to write if you wanted to display information from a database in a List box or an Edit control. The data-aware controls allow you to automate this process. Most of the standard Windows controls have a data-aware counterpart. How-To 11.3 shows how to use some of these data-aware controls.

11.4 Use VCL Components to Navigate a Database

Navigating through records in a database is typically a tedious chore. C++Builder reduces your coding effort by providing a `DBNavigator` control that can navigate the database for you.

11.5 Search a Database

Searching for information is the principal reason for having databases. `TTable` encapsulates this task for you, and allows easy access to the searching capabilities of the underlying database.

11.6 Edit a Database Without Using Data-Aware Controls

The data-aware controls can normally handle your database editing chores, but sometimes you just need to get down and work with `TTable` directly. This How-To demonstrates how you can use `TTable` to edit records in a database.

11.7 Control the Layout of Database Table Displays at Design Time

It can be difficult to display information from a database that contains many fields. Sometimes displaying all the information at once will just confuse the user. C++Builder has a tool called the Fields Editor that allows complete control over which fields are displayed in a form.

11.8 Control the Layout of Database Table Displays at Runtime

The Fields Editor works great, but it can only be employed at design time. This How-To shows how you can achieve the same effect at runtime by manipulating the field objects created by the Fields Editor.

11.9 Use Lookup Controls in a Relational Database

Relational databases use a master/detail configuration to store related data in separate tables. This How-To exposes you to C++Builder's lookup controls that can help connect relational databases in your programs.

11.10 Create a BDE Alias at Runtime

This How-To shows you how to use the Borland Database Engine (BDE) to create aliases at runtime. This comes in handy when you need to hunt down and work with database files on a user's machine without knowing where the files will be.

COMPLEXITY
BEGINNING

11.1 How do I...

View the contents of a database?

Problem

I need to create a quick application that displays data from a Paradox or dBASE database, but I have virtually no experience in database programming. I know that C++Builder comes with database tools. How do I use them to display the contents of a database?

Technique

The **TTable** component automates the process of opening and obtaining data from a desktop database, but it has no ability to display the data. **TDBGrid** handles the task of displaying records from a database, but it has no database connectivity ability. **TDBGrid** and **TTable** can work together to display database information. **TDataSource** links the two together. Once the connection between visual and non-visual controls has been made, database information automatically appears in the grid control. This How-To utilizes **TTable**, **TDataSource**, and **TDBGrid** to display records from one of the sample databases supplied with C++Builder.

> **NOTE**
>
> You must install the BDE before you can compile and run any of the examples used in this chapter. This chapter uses the sample databases provided with C++Builder. You can check for the presence of these sample databases by running the Database Explorer utility supplied with the BDE.

Steps

Run **TABLE.EXE**. Figure 11-1 illustrates what the program should look like. The program uses a grid control to display the entire contents of **ORDERS.DB**, a Paradox table supplied with C++Builder. You can scroll through the database using the mouse or keyboard, but notice that you cannot edit the contents of the database.

1. Create a new project using File|New Application. Save the unit as **MAINFORM.CPP** and save the project as **TABLE.MAK**.

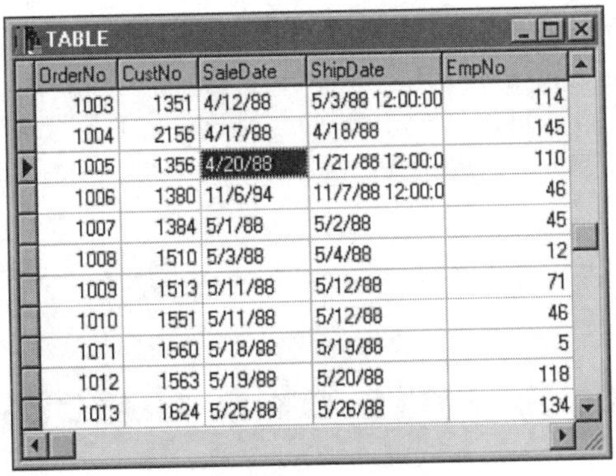

Figure 11-1 TABLE at runtime

2. Table 11-1 lists the controls employed by the program. Start by placing a `Table` control on `Form1` and setting its properties. The `Table` control, and all the other nonvisual database controls, can be found on the Data Access tab in the Component Palette.

NOTE

Set `Table1`'s `DatabaseName` property before you set `TableName`. The Combo box in the `TableName` box of the Object Inspector relies on the setting in `DatabaseName`.

Table 11-1 Components, properties, and settings for `Form1` in the TABLE project

COMPONENT	PROPERTY	SETTING
Table1	DatabaseName	BCDEMOS
	ReadOnly	true
	TableName	ORDERS.DB
	Active	false
DataSource1	DataSet	Table1
DBGrid1	Align	alClient
	DataSource	DataSource1
	Options->dgEditing	false

3. Now place a `DataSource` control on `Form1` and set its properties. The `DataSet` property needs to point to `Table1`, so you should place the `Table` control first. The `DataSource` control has no visual function, so it can also be found on the Data Access tab.

4. Plop a `DBGrid` control grid onto `Form1`. The `DBGrid` control resides on the Data Controls tab with the rest of the visual database components. `DBGrid1` needs to point to `DataSource1`, so the `DataSource` control should be placed on the form first.

NOTE

You can actually place the controls in any order. You won't be able to set `TDataSource::DataSet` until you place the `Table` control. Likewise, you can't set `TDBGrid::DataSource` until you put a `DataSource` control on the form.

TIP

You may want to toggle the `Active` property of `Table1` after you finish setting all the properties. This will fill in `DBGrid1` with database information before you compile. This can help prove that the `DBGrid->DataSource->Table` connection is correct without having to run the program.

5. Create an `OnCreate` handler for `Form1`, and add this code to open the database when the program starts:

```
void __fastcall TForm1::FormCreate(TObject *Sender)
{
  // Open the table, could also open by
  // using Table1->Active = true;
  Table1->Open();
}
```

NOTE

You don't need to call `Table1->Open` if you set `Table1->Active` to `true` at design time. Also, you can open a table by either calling the `Open` method or by setting the `Active` property to `true` in code.

6. Compile and test the program.

How It Works

The simplicity of this How-To might make you think that displaying database information takes little effort. Actually it takes quite a lot of work, but fortunately, the components provided with C++Builder do practically all the work for you. Your job involves setting properties to correctly establish a connection between a visual control and the underlying database file.

Understanding `TTable`

`TTable` is quite simply a database workhorse. It allows you to connect to, access, and modify a record-oriented table. It performs these tasks by interacting with a variety of BDE drivers.

The `DatabaseName` property of `TTable` normally contains a BDE alias. The BDE converts the alias to a directory path so the database file can be accessed. The actual path to a set of database files will probably vary from user to user. Utilizing aliases relieves your code from worrying about the location of database files by shifting this burden onto the BDE. In step 2, you set `Table1`'s `Alias` to `BCDEMOS`. You can run the Database Explorer utility to determine the path that corresponds to the `BCDEMOS`

alias. You don't have to use aliases if you don't want to. You could have set `TTable::DatabaseName` to the path that contains the database files.

The `TableName` property of `TTable` contains the name of the database file. You set `Table1->TableName` to `ORDERS.DB` in step 2. `TTable` automatically configures itself depending on the file extension entered into `TableName`. You can turn off auto-detection by setting the `TableType` property to something other than `ttDefault`. For example, you could read in a comma-separated file with any file extension by explicitly setting `TableType` to `ttAscii`.

`TTable` has some other properties that deserve some explanation. When `true`, the `Active` property allows you to open a table at design time. This allows you to view database information in your form before you run the program. Setting `Active` to `true` at design time also means the table will automatically be opened when the program starts. If `Active` is `false`, you must explicitly call `TTable::Open` in code. The code from step 5 calls the `Open` function, but you can skip this step when `Active` is `true`.

The `ReadOnly` property determines whether or not a table can be written to. It's important to set `TTable::ReadOnly` if a table's contents must be preserved. Note that setting the `ReadOnly` property of a data-aware control, such as `DBGrid1`, only prevents that control from changing the table. It does not prevent other controls or your code from changing the table.

`TTable` also provides direct access to the information contained in a database. You can use the `TTable::Fields` array to access the field names and `TTable::FieldValues` allows you to read or set the values in a record. You can navigate the database using the `Prev`, `Next`, `First`, and `Last` functions. You can also `Insert`, `Delete`, and `Edit` records. Many of these properties and functions will be used throughout this chapter. Consult the C++Builder help files for more information.

The Role of `TDataSource`

Although `TTable` provides complete access to a database table, it has no way of displaying data to the user. `TDataSource` acts as a bridge between a dataset and one or more data-aware visual controls. The VCL encapsulates datasets through the `TDataSet` and `TDBDataSet` abstract classes, and both `TTable` and `TQuery` derive much of their functionality from these base classes. You assigned the `DataSet` property of `DataSource1` to `Table1` back in step 3. This binds `DataSource1` to `Table1`. Any visual control that accesses `DataSource1` will actually be interacting with `Table1`. `TDataSource` can point to either a `TTable` or a `TQuery`.

The `AutoEdit` property of `TDataSource` helps automate changes to a database through a data-aware control. You must call `TTable::Edit` before you can alter a table. Setting `AutoEdit` to `true` tells `TDataSource` to call the `Edit` method for you whenever a data-aware control, such as `DBGrid1`, receives the input focus. `AutoEdit` did not play a role in this How-To because you made `Table1` `ReadOnly` in step 2, but it will come into play in the subsequent How-To's. `TDataSource` also contains a property called `Enabled`. Normally you will want to just let `Enabled` default to

true. Setting **Enabled** to **false** disconnects and blanks out data-aware controls from the underlying dataset.

TDataSource's only job is to help data-aware controls connect to a database. One or more visual controls can attach to one **TDataSource** control, but **TDataSource** can only point to one underlying dataset. You don't need a **TDataSource** control if you don't use any data-aware visual controls.

Data-Aware Controls

The Data Controls tab lists the data-aware visual controls that you can use in your database programs. This How-To utilizes the **DBGrid** component to display records from **Table1**. All data-aware controls have a **DataSource** property that must point to a **TDataSource** component. You assigned **DBGrid1**'s **DataSource** property to **DataSource1** back in step 4. This tells **DBGrid1** where to obtain data that it can display. **DBGrid1** automatically determines how many columns to display, fetches the database information, and then draws the data in its grids. This happens behind the scenes and does not require you to write any code.

TDBGrid displays all the fields in a database. Most of the other data-aware controls only display data from a single field. For example, **TDBEdit** contains a **DataField** property that determines which field it interacts with. You will use the **DataField** property in subsequent How-To's.

Comments

This How-To did not require you to write much code. In fact, you would not have needed any code at all if **Table1**'s **Active** property had been **true**. Many of the How-To's in this chapter may leave you wondering "Where's the code?" Database programming does require code, but the classes and controls of C++Builder handle a lot of tasks for you. As a result, you can write a simple database editor without writing a single line of code. You may want to peruse the VCL source code to see just how much work C++Builder does for you.

COMPLEXITY
INTERMEDIATE

11.2 How do I...
View the contents of a database using SQL?

Problem

I want to access a database using SQL statements rather than accessing it using the **TTable** control. How can I perform SQL queries in C++Builder?

Technique

The **TQuery** control provides three properties, **SQL**, **Params**, and **DataSource**, for executing SQL statements. You use **TQuery** in place of **TTable** when you need to interact with a database using SQL. **TDataSource** and **TDBGrid** connect to a **TQuery** just as they connect to a **TTable**.

Steps

Run **QUERY.EXE**. The program should appear as shown in Figure 11-2. **QUERY** accesses two different tables. A **Table** control fetches information from **CUSTOMER.DB**, and a **Query** control accesses data from **ORDERS.DB**. The **ORDERS** table contains information about orders placed by customers in the **CUSTOMER** table. The **Query** control retrieves information on orders placed by the currently selected customer. Click on the upper grid control and navigate around using the mouse or the keyboard. Notice how the lower grid adapts based on the position of the upper grid.

NOTE

The grid that attaches to the **Query** control displays three columns. Open **ORDERS.DB** using the Database Explorer and note that it has more than three fields. **TQuery** can access a subset of the available fields in a table. While **TTable** can hide its fields, it cannot access a subset of the fields in a table.

1. Create a new project. Name the unit **MAINFORM.CPP**. Name the project **QUERY.MAK**.

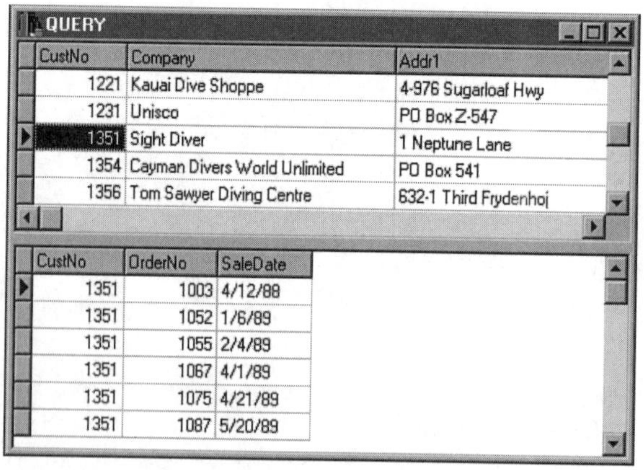

Figure 11-2 QUERY at runtime

2. Table 11-2 lists the controls used in the program. You can start by placing the `Table` (`CustomerTable`) control and its accompanying `DataSource` (`CustomerDataSource`) and `DBGrid` (`CustomerGrid`).

Table 11-2 Components, properties, and settings for `Form1` in the `QUERY` project

COMPONENT	PROPERTY	SETTING
Table	Name	CustomerTable
	DatabaseName	BCDEMOS
	TableName	CUSTOMER.DB
	Active	true
DataSource	Name	CustomerDataSource
	DataSet	CustomerTable
DBGrid	Name	CustomerGrid
	Align	alTop
	DataSource	CustomerDataSource
Query	Name	OrdersQuery
	DatabaseName	BCDEMOS
	SQL	select CustNo,OrderNo,SaleDate from
		Orders where Orders.CustNo =: CustNo
	DataSource	CustomerDataSource
	Params	Parameter Name=CustNo
		Data Type=Float
		Value=(leave blank)
		Null Checkbox=unchecked
	Active	true
DataSource	Name	OrdersDataSource
	DataSet	OrdersQuery
DBGrid	Name	OrdersGrid
	Align	alClient
	DataSource	OrdersDataSource

3. Place a `Query` control on `Form1`. Set its properties in this order: `Name`, `DatabaseName`, `SQL`, `DataSource`, `Params`, and then `Active`. You must fill in `SQL` before you can fill in the `Params` values or set `Active` to `true`. You can fill in the `Params` command by double-clicking next to `Params` in the Object Inspector. `CustNo` should be highlighted in the Parameter Name List box. Change the Data Type to Float and click on the OK button (leave Value blank and Null Value unchecked).

> **NOTE**
>
> You enter the SQL statement by clicking on the ellipsis button (...) next to the SQL box in the Object Inspector. Type the command all on one line, and hit return at the end of the line.

> **NOTE**
>
> The Active property of TQuery reverts back to false when you change certain properties, such as the SQL command string.

4. Add the DataSource (OrdersDataSource) and DBGrid (OrdersGrid) controls that connect to the Query control. Set properties to match Table 11-2. Set up the OrdersDataSource and then set properties for OrdersGrid.

5. Compile and test the program.

How It Works

You can split the functionality of this How-To into two parts. In step 2 you configured a TTable/TDataSource/TDBGrid connection using exactly the same technique discussed in How-To 11.1. These controls work on their own, and really don't care too much about the TQuery group of controls placed below them. Steps 3 and 4 configured the TQuery control and its TDataSource and TDBGrid controls. You set the DataSource property of TQuery using the same technique which set a TTable's DataSource.

Crash Course in SQL

The SQL property of TQuery plays a critical role in how the component acts. The SQL command in this How-To fetches records for display. In step 3 you entered this command into the SQL property:

```
select CustNo, OrderNo, SaleDate from Orders where Orders.CustNo =:CustNo
```

select tells TQuery you want to retrieve a dataset for display. The three arguments after select (CustNo, OrderNo, SaleDate) tell TQuery which fields you want to see. from Orders indicates that the three fields should come from the ORDERS.DB database table. You can prove that ORDERS.DB actually contains these fields by inspecting it using the Database Explorer.

Everything between select and from Orders relates to which fields should be returned. The rest of the SQL command determines which records to return. where Orders.CustNo =:CustNo indicates that the command should return all the records in ORDERS.DB whose CustNo value matches the CustNo value from the current record in CUSTOMER.DB.

Table 11-3 describes some of the different ways you can formulate an SQL command. Notice that the **select** SQL command follows the syntax of

```
select (these fields) from (what table) where (this statement is true)
```

For example:

```
select SaleDate from Orders where CustNo > 1000
```

The other common SQL commands, **update**, **insert**, and **delete**, use a similar but slightly different syntax.

Table 11-3 Crash course description of some common SQL commands

STATEMENT	FUNCTION	EXAMPLES
select	Retrieves a set of records for display	select * from Orders
		select (ItemsTotal*1.07) from Orders
		select ItemsTotal from Orders where ItemsTotal > 1000
		select * from Orders where Order No. is between 1100 and 1150
insert	Inserts records into a table	insert into Industry values (4811,"Semi","Semiconductors")
		insert into Orders (OrderNo,CustNo,EmpNo,ItemsTotal) values (1318,1231,138,4250.12)
update	Alters existing records in a table	update Orders set ItemsTotal=5450 where OrderNo=1005
delete	Deletes records from a table	delete from Industry (deletes whole table!)
		delete from Orders where CustNo=1380

TIP

You can test these SQL commands using the Database Explorer (Client/Server only). Open a table and then click the SQL tab in the left half of the main window. Type an SQL statement from Table 11-3 into the Edit box. Click the speed button with the lightning rod image to execute the command.

While the SQL language is nothing to be scared of, it does deserve more coverage than will fit in the confines of this book. Visit these Web sites to learn more about SQL:

✔ http://www.inquiry.com/techtips/thesqlpro/index.html

✔ http://w3.one.net/~jhoffman/sqltut.htm

Configuring a TQuery Control

The TQuery control revolves around its SQL property. The SQL property determines how a TQuery will behave. For this reason, you should make entering the SQL command one of the first steps in setting up a TQuery control.

TQuery contains two other properties, DataSource and Params, that provide support for the SQL command. DataSource and Params fill in variables in the SQL statement with actual values. Simple queries may not need any variables. For example, you could have typed this statement into the SQL property: select * from Orders. This SQL command doesn't use any variables, so the DataSource and Params properties wouldn't need to be filled in.

This How-To utilizes a variable in the where portion of the SQL command:

```
where Orders.CustNo = :CustNo
```

Either TQuery::DataSource or TQuery::Params must provide a value for the CustNo variable in the SQL command. The goal of this How-To is to fill in the OrdersGrid with a list of orders placed by the selected record in the CustomerGrid. This means that CustNo should come from CustomerDataSource. Setting TQuery::DataSource to CustomerDataSource connects the CustNo variable in the SQL command to the CustNo field of CustomerTable (step 4).

NOTE

The leading : in the SQL command signals that the following word is a variable.

The Params property configures variables used in the SQL command. In this How-To, the Params property determines the data type of the SQL variable, but the actual value for the variable comes from the DataSource property. Params can also supply values to the SQL command. For example, what if you only wanted to display orders where the ItemsTotal was more than $4500? You could hard code a where ItemsTotal > 4500 right into the SQL command. However, using a variable in conjunction with the Params property offers some run-time flexibility in case the user wants to change the limit to $1000.

Configuring the Params property in this mode takes two steps. First, add a variable to the SQL command string. Then configure the variable using the Params property dialog box. If you want to practice these steps, open the project back up and change the SQL command string to this (type all on one line):

```
select CustNo, OrderNo, SaleDate, ItemsTotal from Orders
where Orders.CustNo =:CustNo and Orders.ItemsTotal > :Limit
```

Click the ... next to the Params property in the Object Inspector to launch the Params dialog box. Highligh Limit in the Parameter Name List box. Set the Data Type to

Currency and type 4500 into the Value box. Close the dialog and set the Active property of OrdersQuery back to true. You should see your changes in Form1.

The Params dialog box shows all the variables used by the SQL command. Even the CustNo variable appears despite the fact that CustNo comes from the DataSource. Notice that the Value box is empty for the CustNo parameter. This is important. You can override the DataSource by explicitly giving CustNo a value in the Params dialog box. Leave the Value box empty for variables that should be set by the DataSource control.

Comments

There are many reasons why you might want to use TQuery and SQL database access in place of TTable. For starters, SQL access reduces network traffic when database files reside on a remote server. Secondly, the versatility of SQL allows you to combine data from two tables into one result set. The TTable control can only interact with one table whereas TQuery can work with multiple tables. Finally, both the TTable and TQuery controls can work with record-oriented desktop databases, such as Paradox and dBASE tables, but using TTable with large, set-oriented databases doesn't work that well. The database help file (BCBDADG.HLP) contains extensive coverage of TQuery and provides guidelines that explain when you should and should not choose SQL over the TTable component.

COMPLEXITY
BEGINNING

11.3 How do I...
Use VCL components to automatically display and edit database information?

Problem

The DBGrid control is pretty cool, but I would like to display database information in other controls. Can I do this using C++Builder without having to write tons of code?

Technique

The Data Controls tab of the Component Palette contains a collection of visual controls designed to display and edit database information without forcing you to write any code. If you look at the Data Controls tab now you should see DBListBox, DBEdit, DBText, DBComboBox, DBMemo, and a few others. You utilize these

data-aware controls in the same way that the `DBGrid` control was used in the previous two How-To's. The only difference is that most of the data-aware controls only display information from a single field, or column, of a database, whereas the `DBGrid` control displays several fields.

Steps

Run `VCLDISPLAY.EXE`. Figure 11-3 shows what you should see. The controls at the top of the form update as you navigate the database using the grid control. Try editing a value from the `ShipVia` column in the grid. Notice that the List box automatically changes to reflect the new value. Reverse the process by changing a value in the List box and observe that the grid control adapts to match the new List box selection. Test this using the other controls, too.

NOTE

Changes made through the `DBEdit` control, the `DBListBox`, or the `DBComboBox` don't get written to the database until you focus on a different control. This may cause a delay when looking for changes to appear in the `DBGrid` control.

---

1. Create a new project. Name the unit `MAINFORM.CPP`. Name the project `VCLDISPLAY.MAK`.

2. Table 11-4 lists the controls used in the program. Place the `Table` control first, set its values, and then move on to the `DataSource` control and `DBGrid` control.

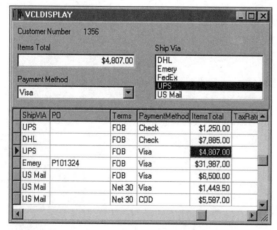

Figure 11-3 VCLDISPLAY at runtime

Table 11-4 Components, properties, and settings for `Form1` in the `VCLDISPLAY` project

COMPONENT	PROPERTY	SETTING
Form1	ClientHeight	300
Panel1	Align	alTop
	Caption	""
	Height	130
Table1	DatabaseName	BCDEMOS
	ReadOnly	false
	TableName	ORDERS.DB
	Active	true
DataSource1	DataSet	Table1
DBGrid1	Align	alClient
	DataSource	DataSource1
	+Options	
	-dgTabs	false
DBText1	DataSource	DataSource1
	DataField	CustNo
DBEdit1	DataSource	DataSource1
	DataField	ItemsTotal
DBComboBox1	DataSource	DataSource1
	DataField	PaymentMethod
	Items	AmEx
		Credit
		Check
		COD
		MC
		Visa
DBListBox1	DataSource	DataSource1
	DataField	ShipVIA
	IntegralHeight	true
	Items	DHL
		Emery
		FedEx
		UPS
		US Mail
Label1	Caption	Customer Number

COMPONENT	PROPERTY	SETTING
Label2	Caption	Items Total
Label3	Caption	Ship Via
Label4	Caption	Payment Method

3. The remaining controls each go on top of **Panel1**, so make sure the panel is in place. Put the **DBText**, **DBEdit**, **DBListBox**, and **DBComboBox** controls on the panel and set properties for each. Use Figure 11-3 as a guideline for placement. Each data-aware control has two critical properties, **DataSource** and **DataField**, that determine which table and which field it will display information from. The **DataField** property relies on the **DataSource** setting, so set the **DataSource** property first.

4. Changes made to a record don't get posted, or written, to the database until you focus on a different control. This has the annoying side effect that you lose changes if you edit a record and then close the program without first tabbing to a different control. **TTable** provides the tools to overcome this hiccup. Create an **OnClose** handler for **Form1** and enter this code:

```
void __fastcall TForm1::FormClose(TObject *Sender, TCloseAction &Action)
{
  // Check to see if the table is in edit mode. If so, then an unfinished
  // entry exists. Ask the user if they want to save the changes
  if(Table1->State == dsEdit)
  {
    if(Application->MessageBox("Your changes have not been saved.\n"
                               "Do you want to save them?", "Save⇐
                               changes?",
                               MB_YESNO|MB_ICONQUESTION) == ID_YES)
      Table1->Post();
  }
}
```

5. Compile and test the program.

How It Works

Setting up a **TTable/TDataSource/TDBGrid** connection should be old hat by now, because you performed this task in the previous How-To's. This How-To introduces some of the data-aware controls that bind themselves to a single field of a dataset. These single field controls automatically display and edit data without requiring you to write any code.

Binding Single Field Data-Aware Controls to a DataSource

TDBGrid displays multiple fields, or columns, of the dataset it connects to. The other data-aware controls in this How-To only display information from a single field. You

can call these controls single field data-aware controls. Configuring these single field controls (`TDBText`, `TDBEdit`, `TDBListBox`, and `TDBComboBox`) requires an additional step.

Luckily, the setup routine for one single field control works for the rest of the single field controls, so you only have to memorize one routine. The first step is to set the `DataSource` property. This How-To uses several data-aware controls that connect to the `ORDERS.DB` database. In step 3 you set the `DataSource` property of each single field control to `DataSource1`. The next step is to set the `DataField` property of each single field control. As you may have guessed, `DataField` binds a control to an actual field within a dataset. You set the `DataField` property of `DBText1` to the `CustNo` field back in step 3. When the program runs, `DBText1` displays the `CustNo` text of the currently selected record. The other single field controls display different fields.

Getting to Know `TDBText`, `TDBEdit`, `TDBListBox`, and `TDBComboBox`

`TDBText` is probably the simplest data-aware control. This variation of `TLabel` can bind itself to any field in a database. It doesn't matter if the field contains strings, floats, integers, or currency values. `TDBText` has enough brain power to convert numbers into strings. This How-To utilizes a `TDBText` control to display the `CustNo` field, so you can see the number-to-string conversion happening at runtime. `TDBText` usually displays a field that the user won't want to change, or that they shouldn't change.

`TDBEdit` functions as a data-aware variant of `TEdit`. `TDBEdit` also inherits some masking capability from `TCustomMaskEdit`. `TDBEdit` allows you to edit the contents of a record. Like `TDBText`, `TDBEdit` doesn't give a hoot about the underlying datatype of the field it interacts with. `TDBEdit` will convert the data to a string for display. When you edit the value, `TDBEdit` converts your text back into the format desired by the table. Because `TDBEdit` is a descendant of `TCustomMaskEdit`, it prevents users from entering alpha-characters into a numeric field.

> **NOTE**
>
> Editing a table requires that you set both `TTable::ReadOnly` and `TDBEdit::ReadOnly` to `false`.

`TDBListBox` and `TDBComboBox` add data-aware capability to `TListBox` and `TComboBox`. Both controls automatically change their selection as the user navigates through records. Both controls can edit values from a database. Like `TDBEdit`, some string to number conversions must occur when the controls work with numerically based fields. One drawback of using `TDBListBox` and `TDBComboBox` is that you must provide the list of strings to display. It can be a pain trying to figure out the possible values for a field. C++Builder provides two additional data-aware controls called `TDBLookupListBox` and `TDBLookupComboBox` that can simplify this process. How-To 11.9 demonstrates the `TDBLookupComboBox` control.

Posting on Close

This How-To requires a little snippet of code (step 4) to overcome a slight deficiency in how data-aware controls update the underlying database. The designers of C++Builder had to decide when an entry from a data-aware control should be written, or posted, to the database file. A meeting was probably called, and several code-writing gurus probably discussed the topic for hours on end. The designers were faced with several issues, one of which was dealing with a canceled change.

The data-aware controls allow you to cancel changes that you begin to make. To test this theory, run the program again. Focus the Combo box and then change its value. Leave the focus on the Combo box and press ᴱˢᶜ. The Combo box should restore the original value. This highlights the dilemma that faced the programmers at Borland. They had to decide when to actually post new values to the database table. Once a value has been posted, there is no turning back. The programmers at Borland decided that the value should be written when a new control receives the focus. This provides a user-friendly undo mechanism as long as the user does not select a new control.

One downside of this process is that changes don't automatically get posted if the user edits a value and then immediately closes the program without focusing a new control. You must handle this case yourself. The code from step 4 checks to see whether the user is editing `Table1` when the program closes. The code checks `Table1->State` to see whether the table is in edit mode. If `dsEdit` is detected, the `OnClose` handler asks the user whether they want to save changes.

Comments

Notice that you did not have to write any code to make the data-aware controls display information from a database. With the exception of the `OnClose` handler, you didn't have to help them edit the database either. The VCL library simplifies your programming chores greatly by encapsulating these tasks within its classes. Writing this program without the power of visual database controls would have required tons of code.

COMPLEXITY
BEGINNING

11.4 How do I...
Use VCL components to navigate a database?

Problem

I would like to allow users to quickly move around in my database by using VCR-like control buttons. Does C++Builder provide a control that can make this easy?

Technique

C++Builder provides a **TDBNavigator** component that can do what you ask. This How-To demonstrates how to use the **TDBNavigator** control in conjunction with a **TTable** control.

> **NOTE**
>
> Navigating a **TQuery** is also possible, but you should realize that you navigate the resultant set and not the actual database table. Also remember that SQL datasets have no concept of a cursor. The BDE provides query navigation as a bonus, but most other database environments don't allow this.

Steps

Run **VCLNAVIGATE.EXE**. You will see a program that looks like Figure 11-4. The program displays information from the **COUNTRY.DB** database table included as a sample with C++Builder. The buttons located in the lower right corner of the program make up the **DBNavigator** control. Use the **DBNavigator** to scroll through the database entries. You can move forward or backward one record, or you can jump clear to the beginning or the end of the table. Notice that the **DBNavigator** disables the appropriate buttons when you are at the beginning or the end of the table.

1. Create a new project. Name the unit **MAINFORM.CPP**. Name the project **VCLNAVIGATE.MAK**.

2. Table 11-5 lists the controls you need for this How-To. Start by placing the **Table** and **DataSource** controls using the same steps you used in previous How-To's. Place the **Label** controls on the form, too. Position these using Figure 11-4 as a guideline.

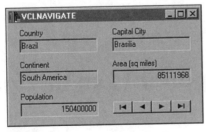

Figure 11-4 VCLNAVIGATE at runtime

Table 11-5 Components, properties, and settings for `Form1` in the `VCLNAVIGATE` project

COMPONENT	PROPERTY	SETTING
Form1	ClientHeight	150
	ClientWidth	295
Table1	DatabaseName	BCDEMOS
	ReadOnly	true
	TableName	COUNTRY.DB
	Active	true
DataSource1	DataSet	Table1
	AutoEdit	false
DBNavigator1	DataSource	DataSource1
	+VisibleButtons	
	−nbFirst	true
	−nbPrior	true
	−nbNext	true
	−nbLast	true
	−all others	false
DBEdit1	DataSource	DataSource1
	DataField	Name
	ReadOnly	true
	Color	clBtnFace
DBEdit2	DataSource	DataSource1
	DataField	Capital
	ReadOnly	true
	Color	clBtnFace
DBEdit3	DataSource	DataSource1
	DataField	Continent
	ReadOnly	true
	Color	clBtnFace
DBEdit4	DataSource	DataSource1
	DataField	Area
	ReadOnly	true
	Color	clBtnFace
DBEdit5	DataSource	DataSource1
	DataField	Population

continued on next page

continued from previous page

COMPONENT	PROPERTY	SETTING
	ReadOnly	true
	Color	clBtnFace
Label1	Caption	Country
Label2	Caption	Capital City
Label3	Caption	Continent
Label4	Caption	Area (sq miles)
Label5	Caption	Population

3. Now place the **DBEdit** and **DBNavigator** controls on the form and set properties to match Table 11-5. You can find both these controls on the Data Controls tab of the Component Palette. **TDBNavigator** contains a **DataSource** property that determines which table it will navigate. Set this property to **DataSource1**. Set the **DataSource** and **DataField** properties of the **DBEdit**'s using the same procedure from How-To 11.3.

4. Compile and test the program.

How It Works

The **TDBNavigator** control allows users to easily maneuver around in a database. **TDBNavigator** is a simple wrapper for the **Prior**, **Next**, **Last**, and **First** functions of **TDataSet**, the base class for **TTable**. **TDBNavigator** can also drive some of the other functions that delete and insert records and change the state of the table.

The **DataSource** property of **TDBNavigator** determines which dataset the navigator buttons will control. You configured this property in step 3 when you set **DataSource** to **Table1**. You should have also set the **VisibleButtons** property of **TDBNavigator** to limit the number of buttons displayed. The four visible buttons allow the user to move forward one record, back one record, or to jump to the first or last record in the table. The online help contains information about the other buttons and functions provided by **TDBNavigator**.

Comments

You may have noticed that **TDBNavigator** automatically enables and disables certain buttons. For example, the First and Prior buttons gray out when the navigator is at the first record in the table. In fact, the program starts with these two buttons disabled because the table opens with the cursor at the beginning of the table. Run the program again. Click the Next button and then click the Prior button. You should be back at the first record in the table. But notice that this time the buttons don't gray out. Why is this? Are you back at the first record?

The answer is simple. How can you be sure that you're back at the first record? Well, you can't. Another program could have inserted a record at the beginning of the table while the navigator was positioned on the second record. The BDE never equates cursor location with the beginning or end of a table. The BDE can only be sure that it's at the beginning or end of the table when the program starts, or when a request to move back or forward fails. You can test this notion by pressing the Prior button one more time. The request will fail which means `TTable` can be sure it's at the first record. Now the Prior and First buttons should gray out.

COMPLEXITY
BEGINNING

11.5 How do I...
Search a database?

Problem

Users often need to search a database interactively. How do I add searching capability to a C++Builder database program?

Technique

Believe it or not, this How-To actually requires you to write some code, albeit very little. `TTable` provides two methods, `SetKey` and `GotoKey`, that handle the task of searching a database table. Calling `SetKey` prepares the table for searching by changing `TTable::State` to `dsSetKey`. You perform the search by setting a field value and executing the `GotoKey` function.

> **NOTE**
>
> `SetKey` and `GotoKey` can only search the index fields of a table. Usually the index field is the left-most column of the table. The Database Explorer can show you which fields are the indexed fields of a table.

Steps

Run `SEARCH.EXE`. Figure 11-5 shows the program in action. Enter a four digit integer into the Edit box and click the Search button. The program searches the `CUSTOMER.DB` example table for a customer ID that matches the value you entered. The `DBGrid` highlights the search result if a match is found. The program pops up a message box if it cannot find a match.

1. Create a new project using File|New Application. Chose File|Save Project As and name the unit `MAINFORM.CPP` and name the project `SEARCH.MAK`.

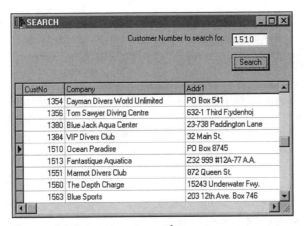

Figure 11-5 SEARCH at runtime

2. Table 11-6 lists the controls used in this How-To. Once again, you need to place a **Table**, **DataSource**, and **DBGrid** group of controls to the main form. Add the remaining controls after you establish the **Table/DataSource/DBGrid** connection.

Table 11-6 Components, properties, and settings for `Form1` in the SEARCH project

COMPONENT	PROPERTY	SETTING
Table1	DatabaseName	BCDEMOS
	TableName	CUSTOMER.DB
	Active	true
DataSource1	DataSet	Table1
DBGrid1	Align	alBottom
	Height	200
	DataSource	DataSource1
Label1	Caption	Customer Number to search for
Button1	Caption	&Search
MaskEdit1	EditMask	!9999;0;*
	+Font	
	−Name	Courier
	Text	"" (blank)

The `MaskEdit` control can be found on the Additional tab of the Component Palette. The `EditMask` property contains a button that launches the Input Mask Editor. You don't need the Input Mask Editor for this How-To, but you may want to launch it anyway to get acquainted with how it works.

3. Create an `OnClick` handler for `Button1` and type in code to perform the table search using `SetKey` and `GotoKey`.

```
void __fastcall TForm1::Button1Click(TObject *Sender)
{
  // Put the table into search mode.
  Table1->SetKey();

  // Set value into FieldValues property. Since we're in search mode,
  // the change is only temporary.
  Table1->FieldValues["CustNo"]=MaskEdit1->Text;

  // Execute GotoKey to locate a record whose customer number matches
  // the value placed in FieldValues. GotoKey returns false if no
  // matching record is found.
  if(!Table1->GotoKey())
  {
    AnsiString Str = "Could not find Customer Number " +
                     MaskEdit1->Text;
    Application->MessageBox(Str.c_str(),"Search Result",
                     MB_ICONINFORMATION|MB_OK);
  }
}
```

4. Compile and test the program.

How It Works

`TTable` contains several powerful methods that provide searching capability. This How-To utilizes the `SetKey` and `GotoKey` functions. Table 11-7 describes some of the other searching functions provided by `TTable`. Consult the online help for specific information on how to use each one.

The SQL language itself supports searching, so you won't find `SetKey` and `GotoKey` in the `TQuery` class. Instead, you could use

```
select * from Customer where CustNo = :value
```

where value is the number from the Edit box.

Table 11-7 The search methods of `TTable`

FUNCTION	PURPOSE
SetKey	Puts table into search mode for GotoKey and GotoNearest
GotoKey	Searches for matching fields starting from top of table
GotoNearest	Searches for closest match starting at the top of table
FindKey	Searches only indexed fields, starting at the top
FindNearest	Finds closest match in an indexed field, from the top
EditKey	Used for multiple searches
Locate	Fastest search method, uses filtering
Lookup	Fast, returns the record without moving table's cursor

Putting a `TTable` into Search Mode

You must set the **State** property of **TTable** to **dsSetKey** before you use the **GotoKey** function. The **SetKey** function performs this task for you. The **dsSetKey** state tells **TTable** that assignments made to **FieldValues** serve a searching purpose, and should not become part of the actual data. You entered the **SetKey** function with the rest of the code in step 3.

Executing `GotoKey` to Find the Record

TTable contains an array called **FieldValues** that allows you to access the data in a table. How-To 11.6 will demonstrate how you can use **FieldValues** to edit a database. In step 3 you assigned the number from the Edit box to the **FieldValues** array.

```
Table1->FieldValues["CustNo"]=MaskEdit1->Text;
```

This assignment becomes the search criterion because **SetKey** put **Table1** into search mode. **GotoKey** then searches for a record that matches the assignment made to **FieldValues**. **GotoKey** starts at the beginning of the table and returns **true** if it finds a match. It returns **false** if it reaches the end of the table without finding a match.

> **NOTE**
>
> Notice how a string was assigned to **FieldValues**, even though the **CustNo** field contains numbers. **FieldValues** is actually a variant property. This means it can automatically convert **MaskEdit->Text** into a number. Likewise, you could read numbers from **FieldValues** and store them directly into a string.

Comments

What if you wanted to search for records where the city name from the **CUSTOMER.DB** database matches a string you type in? You may be disappointed if you modify the

code from this How-To to work with **FieldValues["City"]**. **GotoKey** can only search for items located in the indexed fields of a table. **CustNo** is the primary index field in **CUSTOMER.DB** (you can verify this using the Database Explorer). Use the **Locate** function of **TTable** to search for records in nonindexed fields, or consider using the **TQuery** control.

COMPLEXITY
BEGINNING

11.6 How do I...
Edit a database without using data-aware controls?

Problem

For most situations, the data-aware controls can handle my database-editing chores. However, sometimes I need to edit a record directly. How do I manually change a record in code?

Technique

How-To 11.3 demonstrated how data-aware controls fetch input from a user and automatically place it in a database. There are many reasons why you may need to edit a table directly without using data-aware controls. Maybe you need to create a utility that updates the tax rate field of **CUSTOMER.DB** (or a similar database) whenever new tax laws are passed. Perhaps you need a database import utility that reads data from a text file and updates records in a database, or maybe you're creating a custom database control. This How-To shows how you can use the **FieldValues** property of **TTable** to manually access and change the data in a record.

Steps

Run **EDIT.EXE**. A simple form with a **DBGrid** will appear as depicted in Figure 11-6. **EDIT** contains a standard **TEdit** (not a **TDBEdit**) for entering a new company name. Select a record to edit, type in a new company name, and push the **Update** button to change the record. The **Company** field of the selected record will change to the string you typed in.

1. Make a new project. Save the project as **MAINFORM.CPP** and **EDIT.MAK**.

2. Table 11-8 lists the controls used in this How-To. Start by placing the database controls. Remember to set **Table1**'s **DatabaseName** property before setting **TableName**.

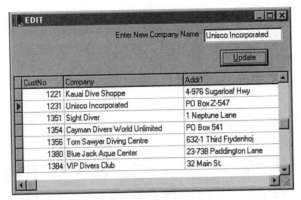

Figure 11-6 EDIT at runtime

Table 11-8 Components, properties, and settings for Form1 in the EDIT project

COMPONENT	PROPERTY	SETTING
Table1	DatabaseName	BCDEMOS
	TableName	CUSTOMER.DB
	Active	true
DataSource1	DataSet	Table1
DBGrid1	Align	alBottom
	Height	175
	DataSource	DataSource1
Label1	Caption	Enter New Company Name
Edit1	Text	""
Button1	Caption	&Update

3. Create an OnClick handler for Button1 and type this code:

```
void __fastcall TForm1::Button1Click(TObject *Sender)
{
  // Put the table into edit mode.
  Table1->Edit();

  // Set the data of the Company field to the value
  // from the Edit box.
  Table1->FieldValues["Company"] = Edit1->Text;

  // Write the changes to the database file. Post takes
  // table out of edit mode after saving the changes.
  Table1->Post();
}
```

4. Create an `OnClose` handler for `Form1` and insert this code to update the database when the program closes. This ensures that the latest changes from `DBGrid1` get saved. How-To 11.3 discussed the need to write final changes to a database when the program terminates. This code asks the users to save changes if they edit a record using `DBGrid1` and immediately try to close the program after making the change.

```
void __fastcall TForm1::FormClose(TObject *Sender, TCloseAction &Action)
{
  // Check to see if the table is in edit mode. If so, then an unfinished
  // grid entry exists. Ask the user if they want to save the changes or
  if(Table1->State == dsEdit)
  {
    if(Application->MessageBox("Your grid changes have not been saved.\n"
                               "Do you want to save them?", "Save⇐
                               changes?",
                               MB_YESNO|MB_ICONQUESTION) == ID_YES)
      Table1->Post();
  }
}
```

> **NOTE**
>
> This function has nothing to do with the code from step 3 and could be omitted if `Form1` did not contain `DBGrid1`.

5. Compile and test the program.

How It Works

Editing a record in a `Table1` requires three simple steps, all of which reside in the code from step 3. First, you must put `Table1` into edit mode by executing the `Edit` function. Calling `Edit` changes `Table1`'s `State` property to `dsEdit`. You can change a record once you put the table into edit mode. The `FieldValues` array allows you to set the data of any field in the current record. The array argument (`"CustNo"` in this How-To) determines which field gets changed. The final step is calling `Table1->Post` to write the changes to the database. `Post` saves your changes and then resets `State` to `dsBrowse`.

> **NOTE**
>
> The `Edit` and `Post` functions actually originate from the `TDataSet` class. `TTable` is a descendent of `TDataSet`.

Comments

You may remember that the `AutoEdit` property of `TDataSource` was discussed in How-To 11.1. The `AutoEdit` property allows data-aware controls to

automatically update a database when changes occur. For example, changes made in **DBGrid1** automatically get written to the database. When **AutoEdit** is **true**, the VCL automatically calls **Edit** when you click on a grid cell to change a record. The VCL calls **Post** when you finish the entry and select a different record. **AutoEdit** automates the same **Edit-Post** procedure you coded in step 3. This explains why the data-aware controls can be utilized without writing any code.

This How-To was pretty simple, but there is a catch. What happens when you try to edit a table whose **ReadOnly** property is set to **true**? What if the table isn't even open? Open the project back up and test what happens. Make **Table1->ReadOnly** equal **true** using the Object Inspector (you can't change **ReadOnly** if **Active** is **true**, so temporarily clear **Active** and then reset it to **true** after you change **ReadOnly**). Run the program. The grid will still display its data. Enter a new customer name, and then click Update. Whoa Nellie, you should see an exception trip!

TDataSet raises an exception if you try to place a **ReadOnly** table into edit mode. The same thing happens if the table has not been opened. You can check these two conditions before you call the **Edit** function. Alternatively, you could place the **Edit** call inside a **try-catch** block. The snippet of code below demonstrates one way of testing to see whether **Table1** can be edited.

```
if (Table1->Active == false)
  Table1->Open();  // Either open, ask to open, or return without editing

if(Table1->ReadOnly)
{
  Application->MessageBox("Your table is read only, unable to change⇐
                        record",
                        "Error", MB_OK);
  return;
}

Table1->Edit();
Table1->FieldValues["Company"] = Edit1->Text;
Table1->Post();
```

COMPLEXITY
BEGINNING

11.7 How do I...
Control the layout of database table displays at design time?

Problem

My database has too many fields to display in one grid. I want to cut down on the number of columns displayed in the grid to make it easier for users to locate critical information. How can I limit the number of fields displayed?

Technique

The `TTable` control contains a design-time helper dialog called the Fields Editor that can help you limit the number of fields that can be accessed from a table. This How-To utilizes the Fields Editor to control how many columns appear in a grid control. The Fields Editor settings take effect at design time.

> **NOTE**
>
> You can also limit the number of columns displayed by changing the `Columns` property of `TDBGrid`. The Fields Editor limits underlying access to a table, whereas the `Columns` property of `TDBGrid` just limits the number of columns displayed without tampering with the remaining fields in the table.

Steps

Run `FIELDS.EXE`. A form with a grid control should appear that looks like Figure 11-7. The grid displays information from the `CUSTOLY.DB` database provided with C++Builder. Notice that the form displays only four columns. Run the Database Explorer tool provided with C++Builder and verify that `CUSTOLY.DB` contains more than four fields.

1. Make a new project. Name the unit `MAINFORM.CPP` and name the project `FIELDS.MAK`.

2. Place controls on `Form1` using Table 11-9 as a guideline.

Table 11-9 Components, properties, and settings for `Form1` in the FIELDS project

COMPONENT	PROPERTY	SETTING
Table1	DatabaseName	BCDEMOS
	TableName	CUSTOLY.DB
	Active	true
DataSource1	DataSet	Table1
DBGrid1	Align	alClient
	DataSource	DataSource1

3. Double-click on `Table1` to launch the Fields Editor. Right-click anywhere on the Fields Editor, and select Add Fields from the popup menu. This brings up another dialog box titled Add Fields.

4. Select four fields from the Available Fields List box: `CustNo`, `Last_Name`, `First_Name`, and `EMail`. Figure 11-8 shows what you should see after

selecting these fields. You can use (CTRL) to select multiple items. Click OK when you finish selecting columns. The Fields Editor should now list the four fields you selected.

5. Close the Fields Editor; then compile and test the program.

How It Works

The Fields Editor provides a way to manipulate the fields available from the `TTable` and `TQuery` controls. By default, `TTable` will make all the fields in the database accessible by `TDataSource` and connecting visual controls. The Fields Editor allows you to cut down on the number of fields provided by `TTable`.

The Fields Editor works by adding `TField` pointers to the `TTable` control. You can see these pointers by inspecting the `TForm` class in `MAINFORM.H`. You should see something like this:

```
class TForm1 : public TForm
{
__published:  // IDE-managed Components
  TTable *Table1;
  TDataSource *DataSource1;
  TDBGrid *DBGrid1;
  TAutoIncField *Table1CustNo;
  TStringField *Table1Last_Name;
  TStringField *Table1First_Name;
  TStringField *Table1EMail;
```

The last four items coincide with the fields you selected using the Fields Editor. `TStringField` and `TAutoIncField` are both derived from `TField`. You should snoop around in the VCL Help file and locate some of the other `TField` descendants. These include `TIntegerField`, `TCurrencyField`, `TBooleanField`, `TDateTimeField`, `TBlobField`, `TMemoField`, and a handful of others. The Fields Editor knows which class to use for each field; all you have to do is select the fields you want to see. Only the fields entered into the Fields Editor will be available to the program when it runs.

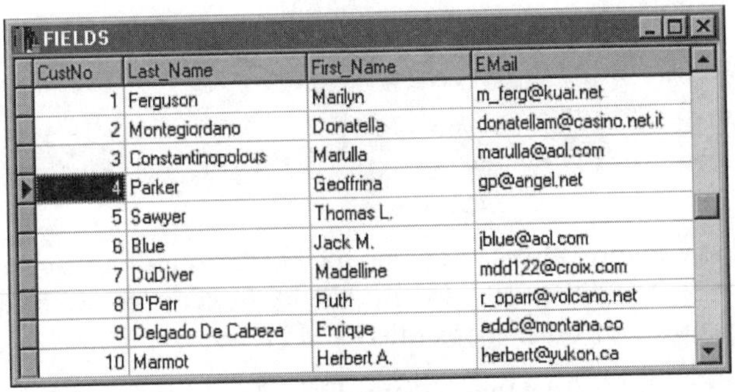

Figure 11-7 FIELDS at runtime

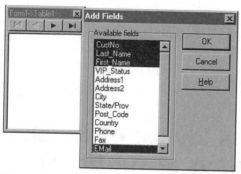

Figure 11-8 The Fields Editor and the Add Fields dialog

TIP

The added field objects can be inspected and modified using the Object Inspector. You can select a field into the Object Inspector by using the Combo box located at the top of the Object Inspector.

NOTE

TTable has a Fields property that contains an array of TField pointers. This array consists of the same pointers added to MAIN-FORM.H by the Fields Editor. The Fields array contains all the TField pointers for a table when you don't implement the Fields Editor in your project.

Comments

The Fields Editor contains many powerful features that were not utilized in this How-To. One of the coolest features is the ability to add calculated fields to a table. You can also add lookup fields and drag-and-drop fields.

You can add a calculated field to your project without exerting too much effort. Might as well give it a try now. Open the project back up so you can add a calculated field to your table. Double-click on **Table1** to launch the Fields Editor. Right-click on the Fields Editor and select New Field. Fill in the New Field dialog box so it matches Figure 11-9. Click OK when finished.

Create an **OnCalcFields** handler for **Table1** and insert this code. This handler calculates the values for the new field:

```
void __fastcall TForm1::Table1CalcFields(TDataSet *DataSet)
{
  Table1CombinedName->Value = Table1First_Name->Value + " " +
                              Table1Last_Name->Value;
}
```

Run the project; you should see a column with the first and last names combined into one field. You can easily extend this example to create columns that perform mathematical calculations.

COMPLEXITY
INTERMEDIATE

11.8 How do I...
Control the layout of database table displays at runtime?

Problem

Changing the grid control's appearance using the Fields Editor works great, but sometimes I need to reconfigure the grid layout at runtime. How can I duplicate the effects of the Fields Editor in my code at runtime?

Technique

Descendants of **TField** have a **Visible** property that determines whether the field can be displayed in a grid. Hiding or showing fields at runtime involves both design-time and runtime manipulation of **TTable** and its fields. First, you add all fields to the **TTable** control at design time using the Fields Editor. This step adds a series of field pointers to your **TForm** derived class. You interact with the **Visible** property of these pointers at runtime to hide or display a field.

Steps

Run **RUNTIME.EXE**. **RUNTIME** displays information from the **ORDERS.DB** table provided with C++Builder. Figure 11-10 shows the program during execution. Check

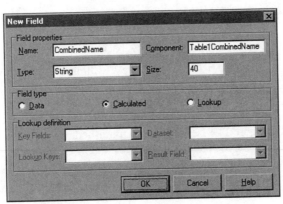

Figure 11-9 Creating a calculated field

or uncheck a menu selection under the **View** menu item. The program will add or remove columns depending on your selection.

1. Create a new project. Name the unit **MAINFORM.CPP** and name the project **RUNTIME.MAK**.

2. Table 11-10 lists the controls used by the program. Remember to set **Table1->DatabaseName** before setting **Table1->TableName** and **Table1->Active**.

Table 11-10 Components, properties, and settings for **Form1** in the RUNTIME project

COMPONENT	PROPERTY	SETTING
Table1	DatabaseName	BCDEMOS
	TableName	ORDERS.DB
	Active	true
DataSource1	DataSet	Table1
DBGrid1	Align	alClient
	DataSource	DataSource1
MainMenu1		

3. Now add every field of **Table1** to the Fields Editor. Double-click **Table1** to open the Fields Editor. Right-click on the Fields Editor, and choose Add Fields from the popup menu. Highlight all the fields in the Available Fields List box, and click the OK button. After clicking OK, each of the fields from **ORDERS.DB** should be listed in the Fields Editor.

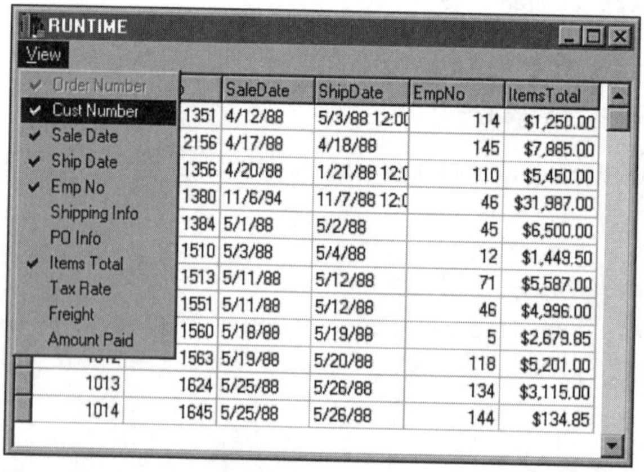

Figure 11-10 RUNTIME at runtime

NOTE

C++Builder automatically inserts a set of pointers in TForm1 when you add fields to the Fields Editor. You may want to open MAINFORM.H and verify that TForm1 contains a set of field pointers for ORDERS.DB.

4. MainMenu1 will control which fields the program displays. Double-click MainMenu1 to launch the Menu Designer. Add a View menu item and then add subitems using Figure 11-11 as a guideline. Don't forget to set the Checked properties using the Object Inspector.

TIP

The Order Number menu item should be disabled (Enabled = false) and checked. This How-To was designed to always display the OrderNo field. Using a disabled menu item tells the user that this column cannot be hidden.

5. Stay in the Menu Designer. The Menu Designer should still look like Figure 11-11. Click once on the Customer Number item. Press and hold SHIFT on the keyboard, and then click on the Amount Paid menu item. Each of the menu items, except the first one, should now be highlighted. Click on the Events tab of the Object Inspector, and type MenuChange into the OnClick block and press ENTER. This sets the OnClick handler for each highlighted menu item to the same function. Insert this code into the handler:

```
void __fastcall TForm1::MenuChange(TObject *Sender)
{
  // Use RTTI to convert Sender* to a TMenuItem*.
  TMenuItem *item = dynamic_cast<TMenuItem*>(Sender);

  // Toggle the check mark state of the item.
  item->Checked = !item->Checked;

  // Then re-synch the database table with the
  // menu-items.
  SynchTableWithMenu();
}
```

6. Open MAINFORM.H; add a function prototype to TForm1's private section. This function will set the field properties to match the state of the menu items.

```
private:  // User declarations
  void SynchTableWithMenu(void);
```

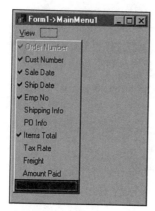

Figure 11-11 Adding
menu items to
`MainMenu1`

7. Go back to `MAINFORM.CPP` and type the function body for the
`SynchTableWithMenu` function.

```
void TForm1::SynchTableWithMenu(void)
{
  // Set each field's Visible property to match the state of the
  // corresponding menu item. The grid will automatically be updated.
  Table1CustNo  ->Visible = CustNumber1->Checked;
  Table1SaleDate->Visible = SaleDate1  ->Checked;
  Table1ShipDate->Visible = ShipDate1  ->Checked;
  Table1EmpNo   ->Visible = EmpNo1     ->Checked;

  // The Shipping menu-item controls all of the fields relating to
  // shipping information. Get the state of the menu-item and set
  // the shipping fields.
  bool ShipInfo = ShippingInfo1->Checked;
  Table1ShipToContact->Visible = ShipInfo;
  Table1ShipToAddr1  ->Visible = ShipInfo;
  Table1ShipToAddr2  ->Visible = ShipInfo;
  Table1ShipToCity   ->Visible = ShipInfo;
  Table1ShipToState  ->Visible = ShipInfo;
  Table1ShipToZip    ->Visible = ShipInfo;
  Table1ShipToCountry->Visible = ShipInfo;
  Table1ShipToPhone  ->Visible = ShipInfo;
  Table1ShipVIA      ->Visible = ShipInfo;

  // The PO menu item controls the 3 fields related to purchase
  // orders. Set these 3 fields to match the POInfo menu item.
  bool POInfo = POInfo1->Checked;
  Table1PO           ->Visible = POInfo;
  Table1Terms        ->Visible = POInfo;
  Table1PaymentMethod->Visible = POInfo;
```

continued on next page

continued from previous page

```
// Now set the remaining fields. Each field has a menu item
// all to itself.
Table1ItemsTotal->Visible = ItemsTotal1->Checked;
Table1TaxRate    ->Visible = TaxRate1    ->Checked;
Table1Freight    ->Visible = Freight1    ->Checked;
Table1AmountPaid->Visible = AmountPaid1->Checked;
}
```

8. Make an `OnCreate` handler for `Form1` that calls `SynchMenuItems`. This initializes the display to match how the menu items were checked at design time.

```
void __fastcall TForm1::FormCreate(TObject *Sender)
{
   SynchTableWithMenu();
}
```

9. Compile and test the program.

> **TIP**
>
> `SynchTableWithMenu` will cause compiler errors if the menu items you entered in step 4 don't match Figure 11-11 exactly. If you get errors, simply compare the `TMenuItem` pointer names in `MAINFORM.H` with the pointers in `SynchTableWithMenu`. Change the pointer names in `SynchTableWithMenu` if you find any discrepancies.

How It Works

C++Builder inserts field pointers in your form class when you add columns to the Fields Editor (step 3). These pointers can be found in `MAINFORM.H`.

```
__published:
...
   TFloatField *Table1OrderNo;
   TFloatField *Table1CustNo;
   TDateTimeField *Table1SaleDate;
   TDateTimeField *Table1ShipDate;
   TIntegerField *Table1EmpNo;
   TStringField *Table1ShipToContact;
...
...
   TCurrencyField *Table1AmountPaid;
```

Each pointer contains a `Visible` property that determines whether or not that field can viewed by a data aware control. Setting `Visible` to `false` hides a field and removes that column from the grid control.

`MainMenu1` controls which fields can be displayed. The `OnClick` handler of step 5 toggles a menu item each time the user selects that menu item. After toggling the

menu item, the `OnClick` handler calls the `SynchMenuItems` function. `SynchMenuItems` (step 7) sets the `Visible` property of each field to match the state of its corresponding menu item.

Comments

`TDataSet` contains a `Fields` property that contains an array of `TField` pointers. `Fields` contains the same pointers that were added to `TForm1` in step 3. You could have altered the `Visible` property of a particular field using code like this:

```
Table1->Fields[1] ->Visible = CustNumber1->Checked;
```

This statement would hide or show the `CustNo` field without requiring you to add fields to the Fields Editor. There is a catch though. `TDBGrid` allows users to rearrange the fields of a table by dragging on the column heading. The `Fields` array gets reshuffled when the user moves a column. This means that `Fields[1]` will point to the `OrderNo` field if the user moves the `CustNo` column one position to the left. The field pointers of `TForm1` don't suffer from this problem. Changing `Table1CustNo->Visible` will always hide or show the `CustNo` column, even if the user has rearranged the columns using the grid control.

COMPLEXITY
ADVANCED

11.9 How do I...
Use lookup controls in a relational database?

Problem

For many of my database programs, entries into a table should be confined to a list of valid responses. For example, I have a database program where the user enters a company name. I don't want the user to just type in a string. I would rather have him or her select from a list of valid company names. This would prevent mistakes and eliminate discrepancies due to case sensitivity or slight variations between two entries. How can I set up a lookup entry system using C++Builder?

Technique

C++Builder provides two cool lookup controls called `TDBLookupListBox` and `TDBLookupComboBox`. They reside on the Data Controls tab along with the other data-aware controls. In addition, the Win 3.1 tab contains two lookup controls provided for compatibility with Delphi 1.0. This How-To demonstrates the `TDBLookupComboBox` control, but the `TDBLookupListBox` control works in exactly the same way. These lookup controls fetch a list of valid entries from one database table that can be used as entries into a second table.

TIP
A lookup system is often referred to as a Master/Detail
relationship.

Steps

Run **LOOKUP.EXE**. Figure 11-12 shows what the program looks like. **LOOKUP** displays the **ORDERS.DB** table using a grid control. Notice that the grid control won't let you edit any records. Use the mouse to navigate around in the grid control, and observe how the Combo box changes as you move from record to record. Now use the Combo box to change the value of the **CustNo** field. Observe how the Combo box displays the company name as a string, but then changes the **CustNo** integer value.

1. Create a new project. Save the unit as **MAINFORM.CPP** and name the project **LOOKUP.MAK**.

2. Table 11-11 lists the controls used by the program. The grid control displays information from the **ORDERS.DB** database. Start by placing **OrdersTable**, **OrdersDataSource**, and **OrdersGrid** on the form and setting their properties.

Table 11-11 Components, properties, and settings for `Form1` in the
`LOOKUP` project

COMPONENT	PROPERTY	SETTING
Table	Name	OrdersTable
	DatabaseName	BCDEMOS
	TableName	ORDERS.DB
	Active	true
DataSource	Name	OrdersDataSource
	DataSet	OrdersTable
DBGrid	Name	OrdersGrid
	Align	alBottom
	Height	175
	DataSource	OrdersDataSource
	Options->dbEditing	false
	all others	leave unchanged
Table	Name	CustomersTable
	DatabaseName	BCDEMOS
	TableName	CUSTOMER.DB
	Active	true

COMPONENT	PROPERTY	SETTING
DataSource	Name	CustomersDataSource
	DataSet	CustomersTable
DBLookupComboBox	Name	DBLookupComboBox1
	DataSource	OrdersDataSource
	DataField	CustNo
	ListSource	CustomerDataSource
	ListField	Company
	KeyField	CustNo

3. The lookup Combo box uses the CUSTOMER.DB table as a source of valid entries for the CustNo field of ORDERS.DB. Place a Table and DataSource on Form1 that will provide access to CUSTOMER.DB. Table 11-11 lists these two controls as CustomersTable and CustomersDataSource.

4. All the necessary links are in place for the DBLookupComboBox control. Place a DBLookupComboBox on Form1. Set its properties to match Table 11-11.

5. Compile and test the program.

How It Works

TDBLookupComboBox performs a simple but amazingly useful purpose. In fact, it's hard to imagine designing a database system without using the services of TDBLookupComboBox or TDBLookupListBox. These controls handle situations where users must change a record by selecting from a list of possible entries.

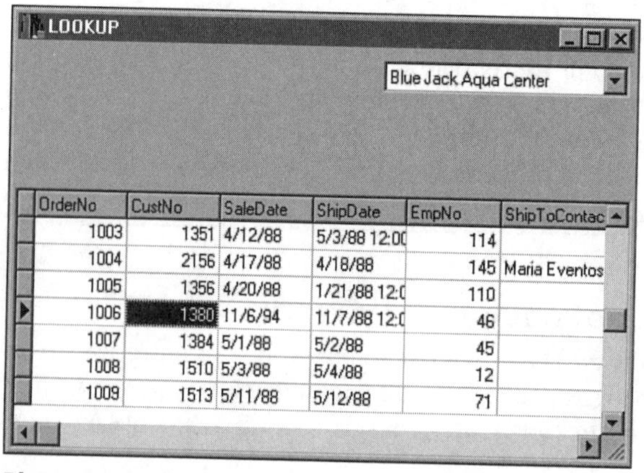

Figure 11-12 LOOKUP at runtime

Configuring TDBLookupComboBox

TDBLookupComboBox needs to interact with two different DataSource controls. One DataSource control tells TDBLookupComboBox where to retrieve a list of items that the user can choose from, while the other DataSource determines which table should be edited.

The ListSource property of TDBLookupComboBox points to the DataSource that will provide the list of possible values. ListField determines which field DBLookupComboBox will display values from. In step 4 you set ListSource to CustomerSource, the datasource for the CUSTOMER.DB database file. ListField was set to the Company field. Setting these two items causes the DBLookupComboBox to fill up with a list of company names provided by CUSTOMER.DB.

TIP

TDBLookupComboBox doesn't care which field you point the ListField property to. You could go back and set ListField to the Phone field. While this doesn't make much sense from the user's standpoint, DBLookupComboBox will oblige by displaying all the phone numbers from CUSTOMER.DB.

Now that DBLookupComboBox knows where to get items to display, it needs to know which table it should modify, or more precisely, which table it should provide the lookup service for. The DataSource property gives TDBLookupComboBox this information. You set DataSource to OrdersDataSource because you want the Combo box to modify and look up data for the ORDERS.DB database. The final step is to tell the DBLookupComboBox which field of ORDERS.DB it should modify. In step 4, you set DataField to CustNo, which tells DBLookupComboBox1 that it should modify the CustNo field of ORDERS.DB.

TIP

Take a minute to compare TDBLookupComboBox with TDBComboBox. Notice that both controls contain a DataSource and a DataField property. These properties mean the same thing to both controls. Think of TDBLookupComboBox as just a plain TDBComboBox with a souped up Items property. The lookup control replaces the conventional Items property with ListField and ListSource.

How TDBLookupComboBox Works

To understand how TDBLookupComboBox works, you first need to understand the relationship between CUSTOMER.DB and ORDERS.DB. These two files form a relational database. CUSTOMER.DB is considered the master table and ORDERS.DB is the

detail table. The `CustNo` field relates the two tables together. `CUSTOMER.DB` uses `CustNo` as its primary key, and as such, each record in `CUSTOMER.DB` contains a unique customer number. `ORDERS.DB` contains a list of orders placed by the companies in `CUSTOMER.DB`. Because one customer will probably place several orders, each `CustNo` value could appear in more than one record in `ORDERS.DB`. For example, `CustNo 1356` has nine orders located in the orders table.

`TDBLookupComboBox` provides a link between `ORDERS.DB` and its master, `CUSTOMER.DB`. When you select a record in `ORDERS.DB`, `DBLookupComboBox1` looks at the value of its `DataField` property, which points to the `CustNo` field. `DBLookupComboBox1` then takes that customer number and starts digging through the `CustNo` field of `CUSTOMER.DB` until it finds the single matching record. When it finds a match, `DBLookupComboBox1` retrieves the value from the field specified in `ListField` (company name) and displays that value on the screen.

When you click on `DBLookupComboBox1` to make a change, it begins by popping up all the company names in `CUSTOMER.DB`. Each company shows up only once because `CUSTOMER.DB` contains one unique record for each company. Clicking on a company name determines a new company for the current record in `ORDERS.DB`. `DBLookupComboBox1` looks up the `CustNo` for the company that was selected and enters this value into the current record of `ORDERS.DB`.

NOTE

The `DBLookupComboBox` provides a lookup function. In this How-To, the `DBLookupComboBox1` looks for `CustNo` values in `CUSTOMER.DB` that can be used in `ORDERS.DB`. Due to this lookup nature, the `DataField` property must be set to a field that is present in both datasources. Think of it this way: How could `DBLookupComboBox` look up `EmpNo` values if `CUSTOMER.DB` doesn't contain an `EmpNo` field?

Comments

The techniques of this How-To play a huge role in database design. By definition, a relational database revolves around relationships between two tables, much like the relationship between `CUSTOMER.DB` and `ORDERS.DB`. The lookup task is so prevalent that `TDBGrid` has been designed to provide an in-cell lookup Combo box. The `LOOKUP` example provided with C++Builder demonstrates how you can make `TDBGrid` provide lookup ability. You can find this example in the `\EXAMPLES\DBTASKS` subdirectory of C++Builder.

COMPLEXITY
ADVANCED

11.10 How do I...
Create a BDE alias at runtime?

Problem

I want to create an application that can read the database files located on the user's machine. I know that **InstallShield** can create BDE aliases for me when it installs my database applications, but I don't know what to do with the **DatabaseName** property of **TTable** and **TQuery** for database files that don't ship with my application. How can I create a BDE alias at runtime that can be used with **TTable** and **TQuery** controls later on?

Technique

Underneath the database controls of C++Builder lie the API functions of the BDE. The redistributable BDE DLLs provide the code for these functions. The data-access and data-aware controls of C++Builder merely encapsulate these BDE functions. You can use the BDE functions yourself to handle a wide assortment of tasks. This How-To utilizes the **DbiAddAlias** function to add an alias to the BDE. Other programs can use the alias once **DbiAddAlias** creates it.

Steps

Start the Database Explorer program provided with C++Builder. The Database Explorer shows a Tree view that lists the current BDE aliases. You should see **BCDEMOS**, the alias for the C++Builder examples, and maybe even **DBDEMOS** if you also have Delphi installed. Remember the list of aliases, and then close the Database Explorer. Now run **ALIAS.EXE**. Figure 11-13 shows the program in action. Type a new alias name into the Edit box. Select a directory for the new alias, and then click the Add Alias button. Wait for the program to churn through some code, and then run the Database Explorer, again. You will see the new alias among the other aliases that already existed.

1. Make a new project. Save the project as **MAINFORM.CPP** and **ALIAS.MAK**.

2. Add controls to **Form1** using Table 11-12 as a guideline. The **DirectoryListBox** control can be found on the System tab on the Component Palette.

Figure 11-13 ALIAS at runtime

Table 11-12 Components, properties, and settings for Form1 in the ALIAS project

COMPONENT	PROPERTY	SETTING
Label1	Caption	Alias Name
Label2	Caption	Alias Path
Edit1	Text	""
DirectoryListBox1	IntegralHeight	true
Button1	Caption	&Add Alias

3. Open **MAINFORM.CPP** and type in this #include statement for the BDE function prototypes:

```
#include <vcl\vcl.h>
#pragma hdrstop

#include <vcl\bde.hpp>
#include "MAINFORM.h"
```

4. Make an OnClick handler for Button1 and insert this code:

```
void __fastcall TForm1::Button1Click(TObject *Sender)
{
  // Make sure something was typed into the Edit box. If nothing typed,
  // return without doing anything.
  if(Edit1->Text.Length() ==0)
  {
    Application->MessageBox("Type an alias name first",
                            "Error",MB_ICONINFORMATION | MB_OK);
    return;
  }

  // Creating the alias could take a while; change the cursor
  // to an hourglass.
```

continued on next page

continued from previous page

```
Screen->Cursor = crHourGlass;

hDBISes Session;                        // Declare a BDE session handle.
DbiInit(NULL);                          // Initialize BDE.
DbiStartSession(NULL,Session,"");       // Start a temporaray BDE session.
AnsiString Path = "PATH:" +             // Formulate a path string.
                  DirectoryListBox1->Directory;
// Add the alias using the BDE function.
DbiAddAlias(0,Edit1->Text.c_str(),"PARADOX",Path.c_str(),true);
DbiCloseSession(Session);               // Close the session.
DbiExit();                              // Shut down the BDE.
Screen->Cursor = crDefault;             // Reset the cursor.
}
```

5. Compile and test the program.

How It Works

This How-To utilizes five BDE functions (step 4): `DbiInit`, `DbiStartSession`, `DbiAddALias`, `DbiCloseSession`, and `DbiExit`. `DbiInit` and `DbiExit` are opposites of each other. `DbiInit` initializes the BDE environment and must be called by every database program. `DbiExit` shuts down the BDE environment and frees up system resources consumed by the BDE. `DbiExit` should be the last BDE call made by a program.

TIP

If you have the VCL source code, you can see `TSession` calling `DbiInit` and `DbiExit` inside `\SOURCE\VCL\DB.PAS`. `TSession` does not play a role in this How-To.

`DbiStartSession`, as its name implies, begins a BDE session. The BDE help file (`BDE32.HLP`) describes the arguments to `DbiStartSession`. The `Session` handle is the most important argument to the function. `Session` contains a handle that must be saved. `DbiCloseSession` closes the session. The `DbiCloseSession` command uses the `Session` handle to determine which session should be closed. A program can start multiple sessions so this argument should not be ignored.

The `DbiAddALias` function plays the key role in this How-To. The other four functions exist in all BDE database programs, although the VCL usually calls them for you. `DbiAddALias` uses a path and a string to create an alias. Whatever you type into `Edit1` will become an alias that's on par with the `BCDEMOS` alias you have used throughout the chapter.

TIP

The BDE32.HLP file does not reside within the same directory as the rest of the C++Builder help files. You may need to use the Windows 95 Find program (F3) to track down the location of the file.

Comments

The BDE contains many useful functions that may come in handy in unique situations. Luckily, the VCL usually handles these calls for you, but nothing stands in your way from using these functions directly. You can always pop open the BDE32.HLP file to search for a unique function that suits your needs. When you find a useful function, you might want to search through the VCL source code to see whether it calls the function.

CHAPTER 12
THREADS

12

THREADS

How do I...

In the old Windows 3.1 days, one application could do only one thing at a time. If, for example, your database application was running a query that took ten minutes to complete, it would be unresponsive to user input for the entire time it took the query to execute. In fact, unless the application was well behaved, the entire system would become unresponsive while the query executed.

Things are different on Windows 95 and Windows NT. By default, applications still have only one thread of execution, but they can have many threads of execution if needed. Each thread is like a mini-program. The operating system automatically shares the CPU between threads to ensure that no single thread can lock up the system. Threads can be used to move time-consuming tasks into the background where they belong. Threads also make it easier to write applications that service multiple client connections, perform serial communications, or communicate over the network. In fact, threads help solve some very annoying programming problems in a very elegant, performance-efficient way.

Unfortunately, threads don't come for free. A Win32 program starts with one main thread but if you want additional threads, you have to start them yourself. Your application's threads need to be able to synchronize their efforts. They need to share data. They may have to share limited resources. Finally, when a thread's work is done, it has to be terminated.

This chapter will show you all the basic techniques. First, you'll learn about C++Builder™'s **TThread** object and how it can be used to build threads of execution. The basic techniques for sharing data and synchronizing efforts between threads will then be covered. Finally, the last How-To will show you the specifics of running database queries in a background thread.

12.1   Create a Separate Thread of Execution

This How-To demonstrates the basics of using the **TThread** object to create a separate thread of execution. Creating, starting, stopping, and destroying the thread are all covered.

12.2   Access the Screen from a Background Thread

By default, a C++Builder starts with a single main thread that I like to call the user-interface, or UI, thread because it is in charge of the main form. The UI thread is the only thread in an application that can reliably update the screen. Fortunately, **TThread**'s **Synchronize** method allows a thread to switch to the context of the UI thread temporarily so it can update the screen. This How-To shows you how to use the **Synchronize** method.

12.3   Safely Share Data Between Multiple Threads

Imagine what happens if two threads try to change and then use a shared piece of data at the same time. For example, what if two threads share an integer variable that is supposed to get filled with a random number and then is used to determine the outcome of something. If the first thread generated the random number, and the second thread changed it to a different random number before the first thread used the value, both threads would end up using the same random number, which would not be a good thing. This How-To shows you how to protect shared data so that conflicts can be avoided.

12.4   Safely Share Limited Resources Between Multiple Threads

What if an unknown number of threads are competing for access to the two serial ports on your computer? How does a single thread know when it is safe to use a serial port? How does the thread know which serial port is safe to use? This How-To shows you how to build applications that deal with those kinds of questions.

12.5   Make a Thread Wait for an Event to Occur

Sometimes an application needs to have a thread wait for an unspecified amount of time until something happens. For example, one thread might have to wait for some other thread to finish some setup work. This How-To shows you how to use

a Win32 Event object (not to be confused with a C++Builder event) to handle this sort of situation.

12.6 Start Threads with Different Priorities

Some threads need to be highly responsive. For example, the user interface thread needs to respond to user input fairly rapidly. On the other hand, some threads can be less responsive. For example, a thread that is printing in the background does not need as much priority as a user interface thread. This How-To shows you how to start threads at different priorities. It also demonstrates the **TThread** methods that allow an application to pause and resume a thread.

12.7 Run a Query in a Background Thread

If you work with databases in your application, you should be interested in this How-To. It is possible to move long queries into a background query but there are a couple of tricks. This How-To walks you through the process step by step.

COMPLEXITY
INTERMEDIATE

12.1 How do I...
Create a separate thread of execution?

Problem

I know that Windows 95 and Windows NT applications can have multiple threads of execution. How do I create a thread in C++Builder?

Technique

The **TThread** object encapsulates the concept of a thread in C++Builder. However, the **TThread** object is not complete. You must override the **Execute** method in a subclass to use a thread object in your application. This How-To shows you the basics.

Steps

Load **THREAD1.MAK** into C++Builder. Run it from the IDE. Select View|Threads from the C++Builder menu, and arrange the screen so both the thread window and **THREAD1** are visible. You will see the main UI thread displayed in the thread window. Press the Start Thread button. You will hear a beep every second from the background thread. The thread window will now show that two threads are running in the application as shown in Figure 12-1.

1. Create a new project. Save the default form as **THREAD1MAIN.CPP** and the project as **THREAD1.MAK**.

Figure 12-1 THREAD1 and
C++Builder's thread
window

2. Add the components and set their properties as shown in Table 12-1.

Table 12-1 Components, properties, and settings for THREAD1

COMPONENT	PROPERTY	SETTING
TForm	Caption	Simple Thread
TButton	Name	bStartThread
	Caption	Start Thread
TButton	Name	bStopThread
	Caption	Stop Thread
	Enabled	false

3. Switch to THREAD1MAIN.H. Add the class declaration for TMyThread above the declaration of the TForm1 class.

```
class TMyThread : public TThread
{
public:
  __fastcall TMyThread(void);

private:
  void __fastcall Execute(void);
};
//-----------------------------------------------------------------------
```

4. Declare a working variable in the private section of TForm1 to hold a pointer to a thread object.

```
private:// User declarations
  TMyThread *MyThread;
```

5. Double-click on the Start Thread button, and add the code that starts the beeping thread.

```
void __fastcall TForm1::bStartThreadClick(TObject *Sender)
{
  //Start the background thread
  MyThread = new TMyThread;
  //Enable the stop button
  bStopThread->Enabled = TRUE;
  //Disable the start button
  bStartThread->Enabled = FALSE;
}
```

6. Double-click on the Stop Thread button, and add the code that stops the beeping thread.

```
void __fastcall TForm1::bStopThreadClick(TObject *Sender)
{
  //Stop the background thread
  MyThread->Terminate();
  //Disable the stop button
  bStopThread->Enabled = FALSE;
  //Enable the start button
  bStartThread->Enabled = TRUE;
}
```

7. Open Form1's Object Inspector. Double-click the OnClose event, and add the code that cleans up just before the program ends.

```
void __fastcall TForm1::FormClose(TObject *Sender, TCloseAction &Action)
{
  //If the background thread is running
  if (MyThread)
    //Stop the background thread
    MyThread->Terminate();
}
```

8. Just beneath FormClose, add TMyThread's constructor.

```
__fastcall TMyThread::TMyThread(void) : TThread(TRUE)
{
  //Free the object after the thread is terminated
  FreeOnTerminate = TRUE;
  //Resume the thread
  Resume();
}
```

9. After the constructor, add TMyThread's main loop.

```
void __fastcall TMyThread::Execute(void)
{
  //As long as the thread is not supposed to be terminated
  while (!Terminated)
```

continued on next page

continued from previous page

```
{
    //Beep through the computer speaker
    MessageBeep(0xFFFFFFFF);
    //Go to sleep for 1000 milliseconds
    Sleep(1000);
  }
}
```

10. Compile and run the application.

How It Works

When the user presses the Start Thread button (step 5), the application creates a background thread by constructing a **TMyThread** object. It then disables the Start Thread button and enables the Stop Thread button. The **bStopThreadClick** function (step 6), which handles the **OnClick** event of the Stop Thread button, does the converse. The thread is ended by calling its **Terminate** method, the Start Thread button is enabled, and the Stop Thread button is disabled. The **FormClose** function (step 7) makes sure that if the thread is running, it is terminated before the application closes.

TMyThread's constructor (step 8) starts by calling **TThread**'s constructor, passing **true** to indicate that the thread should start in the suspended state. **FreeOnTerminate** is then set to **true** to force the object to free itself after the thread finishes executing. Calling **Resume** simply resumes execution of the thread.

The **Execute** method (step 9) is the thread's main loop. Because **Execute** is an abstract method, you may not directly use a **TThread** object in an application. Instead, you must create a **TThread** descendant that overrides the **Execute** method. For most threads, **Execute** should run until **Terminated** is **true**. **Terminated** is set to **true** when the thread's **Terminate** method is called.

In this How-To, the thread keeps running inside the **while** loop until **Terminated** becomes **true**. The **MessageBeep** Windows API function is passed 0xFFFFFFFF to make the PC speaker beep. The thread then goes to sleep for 1000 milliseconds and loops around again.

Comments

Creating a thread in C++Builder is pretty easy. Derive a new class from **TThread**, making sure to override the **Execute** method. Unless the thread has a finite job to perform, put the thread's code inside a **while** loop that ends when **Terminated** becomes **true**. Now that you know the basics, move on to the next How-To to learn how to safely update the screen from a background thread.

COMPLEXITY

INTERMEDIATE

12.2 How do I...
Access the screen from a background thread?

Problem

I followed the instructions in How-To 12.1 and added a background thread to an application I'm writing. I added some code to the thread to update the form display to keep the user informed about the background processing, but then weird things started to happen. Is there a trick to updating the screen from a background thread?

Technique

According to Borland, "Any methods that access a VCL component and update a form must only be called from within the main VCL thread." Does that mean a thread cannot update the screen? Of course not. This How-To shows you how to use `TThread`'s `Synchronize` method to allow a background thread to update the screen.

Steps

Load `THREAD2.MAK` into C++Builder. Open the thread viewer from C++Builder's View|Threads menu option. Type a message in the Thread Message Edit box, and press Start Thread. The Memo box will be updated repeatedly with the message you typed. Type a different message in the Edit box, and press Start Thread again. Notice that there are now three threads in the application. Press Stop Thread. Your screen will look like Figure 12-2. You should notice that the two messages are interspersed.

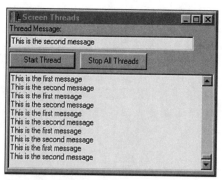

Figure 12-2 THREAD2 running inside the C++Builder IDE

1. Create a new project. Save the form as **THREAD2MAIN.CPP** and the project as **THREAD2.MAK**.

2. Add the components, and set their properties as shown in Table 12-2. Lay out the controls as shown in Figure 12-2.

Table 12-2 Components, properties, and settings of THREAD2

COMPONENT	PROPERTY	SETTING
TForm	Caption	Screen Threads
TLabel	Caption	Thread Message:
TEdit	Name	eThreadMessage
	Text	None
TButton	Name	bStartThread
	Caption	Start Thread
TButton	Name	bStopAllThreads
	Caption	Stop All Threads
TMemo	Name	mMessages
	Lines	None
	ReadOnly	true
	ScrollBars	ssVertical

3. Switch to **THREAD1MAIN.H**, and add the class declaration for the thread object above **TForm1**'s class declaration.

```
class TScreenThread : public TThread
{
public:
   __fastcall TScreenThread(String TheMessage);
private:
  String Message;

  void __fastcall Execute(void);
  void __fastcall UpdateScreen(void);
};
```

4. Add a **TList** pointer to **TForm1**'s private section that will be used to hold a list of running threads.

```
private:// User declarations
  TList *ScreenThreadList;
```

5. Switch back to **THREAD1MAIN.CPP**. Add **TScreenThread**'s constructor just beneath the constructor for **TForm1**.

```
//Thread constructor, calling TThread constructor with TRUE tells the
//thread to start in the suspended state
```

```
__fastcall TScreenThread::TScreenThread(String TheMessage) : TThread(True)
{
  //Thread object will be freed when the thread terminates
  FreeOnTerminate = TRUE;
  //Store the message in a private variable
  Message = TheMessage;
  //Start thread execution
  Resume();
}
```

6. Add TScreenThread's main loop just beneath its constructor.

```
void __fastcall TScreenThread::Execute(void)
{
  //Keep running until the thread is terminated
  while (!Terminated)
  {
    //Drop into the context of the UI thread to write the message to the⇐
    screen
    Synchronize(UpdateScreen);
  }
}
```

7. Add the TScreenThread method that updates the screen.

```
void __fastcall TScreenThread::UpdateScreen(void)
{
  //If there are too many lines in the memo box, clear it
  if (Form1->mMessages->Lines->Count > 200)
    Form1->mMessages->Lines->Clear();
  //Write the message to the screen
  Form1->mMessages->Lines->Add(Message);
}
```

8. Open Form1's Object Inspector. Double-click the OnCreate event, and add the code that initializes the thread list.

```
void __fastcall TForm1::FormCreate(TObject *Sender)
{
  //Create a TList object to hold threads
  ScreenThreadList = new TList;
}
```

9. Double-click the OnClose event, and add the code that cleans up just before the application ends.

```
void __fastcall TForm1::FormDestroy(TObject *Sender)
{
  int x;

  //Loop through all the threads
  for (x = 0; x < ScreenThreadList->Count; x++)
    //Terminate each one
    ((TScreenThread *)(ScreenThreadList->Items[x]))->Terminate();
```

continued on next page

continued from previous page

```
//Free the TList
ScreenThreadList->Free();
}
```

10. Double-click on the Start Thread button, and add the code that actually starts a thread.

```
void __fastcall TForm1::bStartThreadClick(TObject *Sender)
{
  TScreenThread *T;

  //Create a new thread to display the message in the edit box
  T = new TScreenThread(eThreadMessage->Text);
  //Clear the message area if this is the first thread
  if (ScreenThreadList->Count == 0)
  {
    mMessages->Lines->Clear();
  }
  //Add the thread object to the TList of threads
  ScreenThreadList->Add(T);
}
```

11. Double-click the Stop All Threads button, and add the code that terminates all the threads.

```
void __fastcall TForm1::bStopAllThreadsClick(TObject *Sender)
{
  //As long as there are threads in the TList
  while (ScreenThreadList->Count)
  {
    //Terminate the first thread in the list
    ((TScreenThread *)(ScreenThreadList->Items[0]))->Terminate();
    //Delete the thread just terminated from the list
    //The rest of the list items will move up (entry at index 1 will move⇐
    to 0 etc.)
    ScreenThreadList->Delete(0);
  }
}
```

12. Compile and run the application.

How It Works

The thread object's constructor (step 5) sets `FreeOnTerminate` to `true` to make the thread object free itself after the thread is terminated. The `Message` member, which is the string the thread will print to the Memo box, is assigned the string passed in the constructor. Finally, the thread is resumed.

The `Execute` method (step 6) is very simple. The `while` loop will make sure the thread continues to run until the `Terminated` member is set to `true` by a call to the thread's `Terminate` function. Each time through the loop, `UpdateScreen` is called through `TThread`'s `Synchronize` method to update the screen. The `Synchronize` method takes a single argument, the name of a member function that takes no parameters, and returns void. `Synchronize` switches to the thread context of the main user interface thread, makes the call to the function passed in its argument, and then switches back to the thread's own context. Therefore, the screen can be updated by the function passed to `Synchronize`. In this case, `UpdateScreen` writes `Message` to the next line of `Form1`'s `mMessages` Memo box.

Keeping Track of an Unknown Number of Threads

The rest of the code isinteresting, because it demonstrates how to keep track of an unknown number of threads using a `TList` object. The `TList` is initialized in the `FormCreate` function (step 8). The `FormDestroy` function (step 9) loops through the thread list and calls the `Terminate` method of each thread. Because `TList->Items` is an array of void pointers, the function must cast the `Items` element to a `TScreenThread` pointer before it can call the `Terminate` method. The `TList` object is freed at the end of `FormDestroy`.

The `bStartThreadClick` function (step 10) actually starts a thread. First, a new thread object is created with the current contents of the Edit box and assigned to a temporary variable. If this is the first thread in the list, the `Count` member of the `ScreenThreadList` will be zero, and the contents of the Memo box are cleared. A pointer to the `TScreenThread` object is then added to the list by calling its `Add` method.

The `bStopAllThreadsClick` function (step 11) is a little tricky. As long as there is a thread in the thread list, the first thread in the list is terminated, and its thread pointer is deleted from the list. The `while` loop works because when an item in a `TList` object is deleted, subsequent entries in the list move up to fill the empty space. For example, if element zero in a list with four elements is deleted, element four will become element three, element three will become element two, and so on.

Comments

It is very important to use the `Synchronize` method when updating the screen from a `TThread` object. If you fail to use `Synchronize`, your program may work during testing only to start acting weird at the worst possible moment. It may be a bit of extra work, but it is completely necessary. I know this from personal, painful experience!

12.3 How do I...
Safely share data between multiple threads?

Problem

I'm writing an application with two background threads that share some global data. I'm sure that there will be a problem if both threads try to access the data at the same time, because there is a good chance that the first thread will not be able to finish its work before the second thread starts changing the data. How can I make sure this does not happen?

Technique

The real challenge here is making sure that two threads do not simultaneously execute code that manipulates the shared data. The Win32 API includes functions that let you mark blocks of code as critical sections. The operating system then ensures that only one block of critical code can execute at a time. This How-To will show you the techniques you'll need.

Steps

Run **THREAD3.EXE**. Press the Start button, wait a few seconds, and then press the Stop button. The resulting screen should look something like Figure 12-3. The application is supposed to display the alphabet in either forward order or reverse order. Notice, however, that sometimes the alphabet is in forward order, sometimes it is in reverse order, and sometimes it is neither in forward nor reverse order. In fact, you are seeing the symptoms of two threads competing for the same shared data at the same time.

Figure 12-3 THREAD3 showing the results of threads competing for global data

Now, check the Use Critical Section Check box. Press Start, wait a few seconds, and then press Stop. This time the screen looks something like Figure 12-4. You should notice that the alphabet is either in forward order or reverse order. It is never jumbled like it was when you ran the threads without the critical section. It works because the critical section is making sure that the threads cannot try to access the shared data at the same time.

1. Create a new application. Save the form as **THREAD3MAIN.CPP** and the project as **THREAD3.MAK**.

2. Add the components, and set their properties as shown in Table 12-3. Lay out the components as shown in Figure 12-3.

Table 12-3 Components, properties, and settings for **THREAD3** project

COMPONENT	PROPERTY	SETTING
TForm	Caption	Critical Sections
TCheckBox	Name	cbUseCriticalSection
	Caption	Use critical section
TMemo	Name	mMessage
	Lines	None
	ScrollBars	ssVertical
TButton	Name	bStart
	Caption	Start
TButton	Name	bStop
	Caption	Stop
	Enabled	false

Figure 12-4 THREAD3 showing results of a run with a critical section

3. Switch to **THREAD3MAIN.H**. Add the class declarations for the thread object above **TForm1**'s declaration.

```
class TReversalThread : public TThread
{
public:
  __fastcall TReversalThread(void);
private:
  void __fastcall Execute(void);
};

class TDisplayThread : public TThread
{
public:
  __fastcall TDisplayThread(void);
private:
  void __fastcall Execute(void);
  void __fastcall UpdateDisplay(void);
};
```

4. Add two member variables to **TForm1**'s private section to hold pointers to the thread objects.

```
private:// User declarations
  TDisplayThread *DisplayThread;
  TReversalThread *ReversalThread;
```

5. Open **Form1**'s Object Inspector. Double-click the **OnCreate** event, and add the code that initializes some variables.

```
void __fastcall TForm1::FormCreate(TObject *Sender)
{
  char c;
  int x;

  //Initialize buffer to contain the alphabet in normal order
  c = 'A';
  for (x = 0; x < 26; x++)
  {
    Buffer[x] = c;
    c++;
  }
  //Initialize the critical section
  InitializeCriticalSection(&CriticalSection);
}
```

6. Double-click the **OnClose** event, and add the code that cleans up just before the application ends.

```
void __fastcall TForm1::FormDestroy(TObject *Sender)
{
  //If the reversal thread is running
  if (ReversalThread)
    //Terminate the reversal thread
    ReversalThread->Terminate();
```

```
  //If the display thread is running
  if (DisplayThread)
    //Terminate the display thread
    DisplayThread->Terminate();

  //Delete the critical section
  DeleteCriticalSection(&CriticalSection);
}
```

7. Double-click the Start button, and add the code that starts the threads.

```
void __fastcall TForm1::bStartClick(TObject *Sender)
{
  //Clear the display
  mMessage->Lines->Clear();
  //Start the reversal thread
  ReversalThread = new TReversalThread;
  //Start the display thread
  DisplayThread = new TDisplayThread;
  //Disable the start button
  bStart->Enabled = FALSE;
  //Enable the stop button
  bStop->Enabled = TRUE;
}
```

8. Double-click the Stop button, and add the code that stops the two worker threads.

```
void __fastcall TForm1::bStopClick(TObject *Sender)
{
  //Stop the reversal thread
  ReversalThread->Terminate();
  //Stop the display thread
  DisplayThread->Terminate();
  //Disable the stop button
  bStop->Enabled = FALSE;
  //Enable the start button
  bStart->Enabled = TRUE;
}
```

9. Add TReversalThread's constructor beneath bStartClick.

```
//Thread to reverse the alphabetical order of the array
//Calling TThread with TRUE makes the thread start in a suspended state
__fastcall TReversalThread::TReversalThread(void) : TThread(TRUE)
{
  //Tell the thread object to free itself when the thread is terminated
  FreeOnTerminate = TRUE;
  //Resume execution of the thread
  Resume();
}
```

10. Next, add TReversalThread's Execute function.

```
void __fastcall TReversalThread::Execute(void)
{
  int x;
  char c;
  bool UseCriticalSection;

  //As long as the thread is supposed to run
  while (!Terminated)
  {
    //Find out if we're supposed to use the critical section
    UseCriticalSection = Form1->cbUseCriticalSection->Checked;

    //If we're supposed to use the critical section
    if (UseCriticalSection)
      //This is the start of the critical section
      EnterCriticalSection(&CriticalSection);

    //Reverse the alphabetical order of the buffer
    if (Buffer[0] == 'Z')
    {
      c = 'A';
      for (x = 0; x < 26; x++)
      {
        Buffer[x] = c;
        c++;
      }
    }
    else
    {
      c = 'Z';
      for (x = 0; x < 26; x++)
      {
        Buffer[x] = c;
        c--;
      }
    }

    //If we're supposed to use the critical section
    if (UseCriticalSection)
      //This is the end of the critical section
      LeaveCriticalSection(&CriticalSection);

  }
}
```

11. Beneath TReversalThread's Execute function, add the constructor for TDisplayThread.

```
//Thread to display Buffer in memo box
//Calling TThread with TRUE makes the thread start suspended
__fastcall TDisplayThread::TDisplayThread(void) : TThread(TRUE)
```

```
{
  //Free the object when the thread terminates
  FreeOnTerminate = TRUE;
  //Resume execution of the thread
  Resume();
}
```

12. Next, add `TDisplayThread`'s main loop.

```
void __fastcall TDisplayThread::Execute(void)
{
  //As long as the thread is supposed to run
  while (!Terminated)
  {
    //Update the display in the context of the UI thread
    Synchronize(UpdateDisplay);
  }
}
```

13. After `TDisplayThread`'s `Execute` method, add the function that writes the current contents of the shared data array to a new line in the Memo box.

```
void __fastcall TDisplayThread::UpdateDisplay(void)
{
  bool UseCriticalSection;

  //If there are too many lines in the memo box, clear it
  if (Form1->mMessage->Lines->Count > 200)
    Form1->mMessage->Lines->Clear();

  //Find out if we're supposed to use the critical section
  UseCriticalSection = Form1->cbUseCriticalSection->Checked;

  //If we're supposed to use the critical section
  if (UseCriticalSection)
    //This is the start of the critical section
    EnterCriticalSection(&CriticalSection);

  //Update the display
  //If the critical section is not in use we might display the buffer
  //part-way through a reversal
  Form1->mMessage->Lines->Add(Buffer);

  //If the critical section is in use
  if (UseCriticalSection)
    //This is the end of the critical section
    LeaveCriticalSection(&CriticalSection);
}
```

14. Add the global variable declarations just above `TForm1`'s constructor.

```
char Buffer[26];
CRITICAL_SECTION CriticalSection;
```

continued on next page

continued from previous page
```
//----------------------------------------------------------------------
__fastcall TForm1::TForm1(TComponent* Owner) : TForm(Owner)
```

15. Compile and run the application.

How It Works

This example program is fairly simple. When the program starts, a global character array is initialized to contain the uppercase alphabet in forward order. When the user presses the start button, two threads start. The first thread, `TReversalThread`, looks at the first character of the global array. If it is an `A`, the thread replaces the array with the alphabet in reverse order. If the first character is a `Z`, it puts the array back in forward order. It repeats these steps over and over again as long as it is running. At the same time, `TDisplayThread` writes the current contents of the shared global character array to the Memo box. It updates the display over and over again as long as it is running.

If the critical section is not in use, `TDisplayThread` will often write the contents of the shared buffer to the screen while `TReversalThread` is in the middle of reversing the order of the buffer. The result is that forward and reversed runs of letters will be jumbled together. When the critical section is in use, it makes sure that only one thread at a time accesses the shared buffer.

Main Program

The `FormCreate` function (step 5) initializes the shared character array to contain the alphabet in forward order. It then initializes the critical section by calling the `InitializeCriticalSection` Windows API function. `InitializeCriticalSection` takes a pointer to a `CRITICAL_SECTION` structure that needs to be available to all the threads that will access the critical section. In this case, the critical section object is global to this module.

`FormDestroy` (step 6) cleans up things just before the program ends. If the threads are running, they are stopped by calling their `Terminate` methods. The critical section is then deleted from memory by calling the `DeleteCriticalSection` Windows API function passing the same `CRITICAL_SECTION` structure that had been passed to the `InitializeCriticalSection` function.

The functions that start and stop the threads are both very simple. The `bStartClick` function (step 7) clears the Memo box display, starts the two threads, enables the Stop button, and disables the Start button. The `bStopClick` function (step 8) stops the threads by calling their `Terminate` methods, enables the Start button, and disables the Stop button.

The `TReversalThread` Object

`TReversalThread`'s constructor (step 9) sets `FreeOnTerminate` to `true` to make the thread object free itself when the thread is terminated. The execution of the thread is then resumed because it was initially started in the suspended state by passing `true` to its parent's constructor.

TReversalThread's main loop (step 10) is enclosed in a **while** loop that makes the thread keep running until **Terminated** becomes **true**. As discussed in the other How-To's in this chapter, **Terminated** is set to **true** when the thread's **Terminate** function is called.

The main loop starts by determining whether the Use Critical Section Check box has been selected. **UseCriticalSection** is set to **true** if the Check box is checked and **false** if it is not checked. Next, if the critical section is in use, the **EnterCriticalSection** Windows API function is called to mark the beginning of the critical section. **EnterCriticalSection** takes a pointer to a **CRITICAL_SECTION** structure. Once **EnterCriticalSection** is called for a given **CRITICAL_SECTION** structure, that critical section is locked until the **LeaveCriticalSection** Windows API function is called for that critical section. If a thread calls **EnterCriticalSection** for a locked critical section, the thread will sleep until the critical section is unlocked by a call to **LeaveCriticalSection**. Therefore, only one thread at a time can enter the critical section.

Next, **TReversalThread** reverses the shared data buffer. The first character of the buffer is checked. If it is a **Z**, a **for** loop is used to fill it with the alphabet in forward order. Otherwise, the array is filled with the alphabet in reverse order.

Finally, if the critical section is in use, **LeaveCriticalSection** is called to unlock the critical section structure. When I first wrote this application, I did not use a working variable to store the state of the Check box. Instead, I directly tested the state of the Check box twice—once to see whether I needed to call **EnterCriticalSection** and again to see whether **LeaveCriticalSection** should be called. That was a big mistake because the user could change the state of the Check box in between the two times the Check box's state got tested. That made it possible to call **EnterCriticalSection** without calling **LeaveCriticalSection**. When that happened, one of the threads would hang. If you want to see this happen yourself, remove the call to **LeaveCriticalSection** and run the threads with the Use Critical Section Check box checked. Needless to say, you must be very careful when you use critical sections.

The TDisplayThread Object

Now that you understand how **TReversalThread** works, **TDisplayThread** should be very simple. Its constructor (step 11) works exactly like **TReversalThread's** constructor. **FreeOnTerminate** is set to **true** to make the thread free itself when it is terminated, and the **Resume** method is called to move the thread from a suspended state to a running state.

TDisplayThread's Execute function (step 12) calls the **UpdateDisplay** method through **Synchronize** to make the screen update work properly. The reasons for using the **Synchronize** method are discussed in How-To 12.2. **Execute** updates the screen over and over again until the **Terminated** flag is set to **true** by a call to the thread's **Terminate** function.

UpdateDisplay (step 13) writes the current contents of the shared character array to the next line in the Memo box. First, it sets the **UseCriticalSection** flag based on the **Checked** property of **Form1's cbUseCriticalSection** Check box. If the

critical section is in use, it calls `EnterCriticalSection` to lock the `CRITICAL_SECTION` structure. The screen is then updated, and, if the critical section is in use, `LeaveCriticalSection` is called to unlock the critical section.

Comments

There are a few important things to remember about critical sections. First, critical sections should be used to protect small blocks of code that cannot execute simultaneously. Second, you should never use a single critical section structure for more than one purpose. For example, if you needed to protect access to two unrelated pieces of global data, you should use two different critical section structures. At best, you'll end up blocking threads unnecessarily. At worst, you'll end up with one or more hung threads. Thirdly, you must be careful to avoid situations that can cause threads to hang because of critical sections. The most common problem is calling `EnterCriticalSection` but skipping a corresponding call to `LeaveCriticalSection`. Finally, you should use critical sections whenever you suspect that two or more threads will be competing over the same data. Finding and fixing problems that are a result of multiple threads fighting over the same data is very frustrating and time-consuming. Critical sections, if kept small, will not significantly impact the performance of your application.

COMPLEXITY
INTERMEDIATE

12.4 How do I...
Safely share limited resources between multiple threads?

Problem

I'm currently working on an application that services multiple user requests that come in over the network. I want to create one thread to service each user because that seems like the most natural solution. The problem is that, to service a request, the thread must send and receive some data through one of the two serial ports. I know that two threads should not be allowed to access one serial port at the same time, and so I need to know how I can make multiple threads share the two serial ports efficiently.

Technique

Win32 semaphores are designed to facilitate resource counting. They give a thread the capability to query the number of resources available. If a resource is available, the number of available resources is automatically reduced. If the resource is not available, the thread will wait until the resource becomes available. Note that a semaphore does not manage the resource for you. It simply counts resources.

This How-To will show you how a semaphore is used to control access to limited resources that must be shared among multiple threads. In addition, a critical section will be used to protect shared data elements as shown in How-To 12.3.

Steps

Run **THREAD4.EXE**. After a few seconds, the screen will look like Figure 12-5. You should notice that four threads are sharing three Memo boxes. Only one thread at a time is allowed to use a Memo box, so one thread is always waiting for a Memo box to become available.

1. Create a new project. Save the form as **THREAD4MAIN.CPP** and the project as **THREAD4.MAK**.

2. Add the components, and set their properties as shown in Table 12-4. Lay out the components as shown in Figure 12-5.

Table 12-4 Components, properties, and settings of **THREAD4**

COMPONENT	PROPERTY	SETTING
TForm	Caption	Limited Thread Resources
TLabel	Caption	Thread1:
TLabel	Caption	Thread2:
TLabel	Caption	Thread3:
TLabel	Caption	Thread4:
TLabel	Caption	Output:
TLabel	Name	lStatus1
	Caption	Not Running
TLabel	Name	lStatus2
	Caption	Not Running
TLabel	Name	lStatus3
	Caption	Not Running
TLabel	Name	lStatus4
	Caption	Not Running
TMemo	ReadOnly	true
TMemo	ReadOnly	true
TMemo	ReadOnly	true

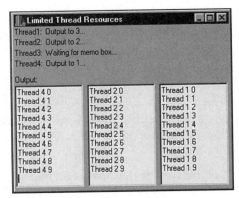

Figure 12-5 THREAD4 screen after running for a few seconds

3. Switch to THREAD3MAIN.H. Add TSemaphoreThread's declaration just above the declaration of TForm1.

```
class TSemaphoreThread : public TThread
{
public:
  __fastcall TSemaphoreThread(int TheThreadNum);

private:
  int ThreadNum, OutputMemo, OutputNum;
  String Status;

  void __fastcall Execute(void);
  void __fastcall ClearDisplay(void);
  void __fastcall UpdateDisplay(void);
  void __fastcall UpdateStatus(String s);
  void __fastcall UpdateDisplayStatus(void);
};
```

4. Add an array to hold pointers to the background threads to TForm1's private section.

```
private:// User declarations
  TSemaphoreThread *SemaphoreThreads[4];
```

5. Switch back to THREAD4MAIN.CPP. Add the following global variables above TForm1's constructor:

```
//Global variables
HANDLE Semaphore;
CRITICAL_SECTION CriticalSection;
bool MemoInUse[3];


//--------------------------------------------------------------------------
__fastcall TForm1::TForm1(TComponent* Owner) : TForm(Owner)
```

6. Open Form1's Object Inspector. Double-click the OnCreate event, and add the code that initializes some variables and then starts the four background threads.

```
void __fastcall TForm1::FormCreate(TObject *Sender)
{
  int x;

  //Create the semaphore with a maximum value of three
  //and a current value of three to indicate that all three
  //memo boxes are available
  Semaphore = CreateSemaphore(NULL, 3, 3, NULL);
  //Initialize the critical section
  InitializeCriticalSection(&CriticalSection);

  //Initialize the memo box availability array to indicate that all
  //three are available
  for (x = 0; x < 3; x++)
    MemoInUse[x] = FALSE;

  //Create the four worker threads
  for (x = 0; x < 4; x++)
    SemaphoreThreads[x] = new TSemaphoreThread(x + 1);
}
```

7. Double-click the OnClose event, and add the code that cleans up before the program ends.

```
void __fastcall TForm1::FormDestroy(TObject *Sender)
{
  int x;

  //Loop through the thread array
  for (x = 0; x < 4; x++)
    //If the thread is running
    if (SemaphoreThreads[x])
      //Terminate the thread
      SemaphoreThreads[x]->Terminate();

  //Delete the critical section
  DeleteCriticalSection(&CriticalSection);
  //Close the semaphore
  CloseHandle(Semaphore);
}
```

8. Add TSemaphoreThread's constructor just beneath FormDestroy.

```
//TSemaphoreThread constructor. Starts suspended because TThread is called
//with true
__fastcall TSemaphoreThread::TSemaphoreThread(int TheThreadNum) :
          TThread(TRUE)
{
```

continued on next page

continued from previous page

```
  //Assign the thread num variable
  ThreadNum = TheThreadNum;
  //Update the thread status
  UpdateStatus("Starting...");
  //Tell the object to free itself after it is terminated
  FreeOnTerminate = TRUE;
  //Start execution of the thread
  Resume();
}
```

9. Just beneath the constructor, add the function that is the thread's main loop.

```
void __fastcall TSemaphoreThread::Execute(void)
{
  int x;

  //Update the status
  UpdateStatus("Running...");

  //As long as the thread is not terminated
  while (!Terminated)
  {
    //Update the status
    UpdateStatus("Waiting for memo box...");
    //Wait for one of the three memo boxes to free up
    //When the wait returns the semaphore will decrement to indicate
    //that there is one fewer memo box available
    WaitForSingleObject(Semaphore, INFINITE);
    //Update the status
    UpdateStatus("Determining output destination...");
    //Enter the critical section that protects an array
    //that lets the thread determine which memo box to use
    EnterCriticalSection(&CriticalSection);
    //Initialize the selected memo box to -1 to indicate
    //that a memo box has not been selected yet
    OutputMemo = -1;
    //Loop through the memo box availability array
    for (x = 0; x < 3; x++)
    {
      //If this memo is not in use and a memo box has not been selected
      if ((!MemoInUse[x]) && (OutputMemo == -1))
      {
        //Indicate that this memo box is now in use
        MemoInUse[x] = TRUE;
        //Tell the thread that it should use this memo box
        OutputMemo = x;
      }
    }
    //End of critical section
    LeaveCriticalSection(&CriticalSection);

    //Update the status
    UpdateStatus("Output to " + IntToStr(OutputMemo + 1) + "...");
```

```
   //Clear the selected memo box
   Synchronize(ClearDisplay);
   //Output the numbers 1 to 10 to the selected memo box
   for (OutputNum = 0; OutputNum < 10; OutputNum++)
   {
      Synchronize(UpdateDisplay);
      Sleep(1000);
   }

   //Enter critical section that protects the memo box availability array
   EnterCriticalSection(&CriticalSection);
   //Thread is done with the memo box. Make it available to other threads
   MemoInUse[OutputMemo] = FALSE;
   //End of critical section
   LeaveCriticalSection(&CriticalSection);

   //Update the status
   UpdateStatus("Output completed");

   //Release the semaphore to indicate that there is one more memo box⇐
   available
   ReleaseSemaphore(Semaphore, 1, NULL);
 }
}
```

10. Next, add TSemaphoreThread's ClearDisplay method.

```
//Clear the memo box that is being used by this thread
void __fastcall TSemaphoreThread::ClearDisplay(void)
{
   switch (OutputMemo)
   {
      case 0:
        Form1->Memo1->Lines->Clear();
        break;
      case 1:
        Form1->Memo2->Lines->Clear();
        break;
      case 2:
        Form1->Memo3->Lines->Clear();
        break;
   }
}
```

11. After ClearDisplay, add the UpdateDisplay function.

```
//Put a line of text in the memo box that is being used by this thread
void __fastcall TSemaphoreThread::UpdateDisplay(void)
{
   String Output;

   Output = "Thread " + IntToStr(ThreadNum) + " " + IntToStr(OutputNum);
```

continued on next page

continued from previous page

```
switch (OutputMemo)
{
  case 0:
    Form1->Memo1->Lines->Add(Output);
    break;
  case 1:
    Form1->Memo2->Lines->Add(Output);
    break;
  case 2:
    Form1->Memo3->Lines->Add(Output);
    break;
}
}
```

12. Next, add the code for the UpdateStatus function that sets the Status member variable, and UpdateDisplayStatus that, actually, updates the thread's status on the screen.

```
//Assign the Status member variable and call UpdateDisplayStatus
//in the context of the UI thread to update the thread status display
void __fastcall TSemaphoreThread::UpdateStatus(String s)
{
  Status = s;
  Synchronize(UpdateDisplayStatus);
}
//--------------------------------------------------------------------
//Update the thread status display with the value contained
//in the private variable Status
void __fastcall TSemaphoreThread::UpdateDisplayStatus(void)
{
  switch (ThreadNum)
  {
    case 1:
      Form1->lStatus1->Caption = Status;
      break;
    case 2:
      Form1->lStatus2->Caption = Status;
      break;
    case 3:
      Form1->lStatus3->Caption = Status;
      break;
    case 4:
      Form1->lStatus4->Caption = Status;
      break;
  }
}
```

13. Compile and run the application.

How It Works

The `FormCreate` function (step 6) starts by creating a semaphore by calling the `CreateSemaphore` Windows API function. The first parameter is a security descriptor, the second is the maximum value of the semaphore, the third is the current value of the semaphore, and the last is the name of the semaphore. In this example, the semaphore has no associated security, has a maximum value of three because there are three Memo boxes, has a current value of three to indicate that all the Memo boxes are available, and is not named. `CreateSemaphore` returns a `HANDLE` value that refers to the semaphore object.

Semaphores are very useful for counting resources, but they have one funny quirk. When a thread gets access to a semaphore, it is impossible to determine which of the counted resources is available by looking at the semaphore. For example, a semaphore is used to manage three Memo boxes in this application. When one of the four threads gets access to the semaphore, it cannot look at the semaphore and determine which of the three Memo boxes is available. Instead, it must look in a separate boolean array that tells it which Memo box is available. Because the boolean array is shared among all the threads, it is protected by a critical section initialized in `FormCreate`.

Next, the `MemoInUse` array, used to indicate which Memo boxes are available, is initialized to indicate that all the Memo boxes are available. Once all the initialization work is done, four background threads are started, and pointers to the thread objects are stored in the `SemaphoreThreads` array for future reference. `TSemaphoreThread`'s constructor is passed a thread number which the thread uses to identify itself on the screen.

The `FormDestroy` function (step 7) takes care of clean up chores before the application ends. First, it loops through the thread pointer array and terminates each thread. Just to be safe, it makes sure that each thread object pointer is non-null before attempting to call the thread's `Terminate` function. `DeleteCriticalSection` is then called to delete the critical section object. Finally, the `CloseHandle` Windows API function is used to close the semaphore.

The Thread

`TSemaphoreThread`'s constructor (step 8) starts by assigning the thread number passed to it from `FormCreate` to a private member variable for later use. `ThreadNum`, a number between one and four, tells the thread which status label to use, and gets appended to text displayed in a Memo box. Next, the `UpdateStatus` is called to update the proper status label on the screen, `FreeOnTerminate` is set to `true` to tell the thread object to free itself when the thread is terminated, and `Resume` is called to start execution of the thread.

The `Execute` method (step 9) updates the screen status line before entering a `while` loop that will keep the thread running until the `Terminate` method is called. `UpdateStatus` is called again to update the status line. The `WaitForSingleObject` Windows API function is then called to make the thread wait until one of the three Memo boxes becomes available.

Semaphores are one of several kernel objects used to synchronize thread activities. Kernel objects have two states—signaled and non-signaled. A semaphore is signaled when the current value of the semaphore is greater than zero and not signaled otherwise. Threads call **WaitForSingleObject** to wait for a kernel object to become signaled. In this case, the call to **WaitForSingleObject** tells the thread to wait forever until the semaphore's count is greater than zero. Once **WaitForSingleObject** returns, the count of the semaphore is automatically reduced by one by the operating system. It should be clear that the semaphore in this application will become nonsignalled once all three Memo boxes are in use, making the fourth thread wait.

After updating the status line again, the thread determines which Memo box is available by examining the **MemoInUse** array. A critical section is used to protect the array because, if multiple threads accessed it at the same time, it would be possible for two threads to grab the same Memo box. (If you want to see what this problem looks like, remove the calls to **EnterCriticalSection** and **LeaveCriticalSection**.) Once it finds a **MemoInUse** entry that is **false**, it puts the Memo box number it will use in **OutputMemo** and sets the **MemoInUse** entry to **true** to indicate that it is using that Memo box.

Next, **Execute** prints ten messages to the Memo box at one second intervals. The function that actually updates the screen, **UpdateDisplay**, is called through the **Synchronize** method as discussed in How-To 12.2. Once printing is done, the thread sets the **MemoInUse** entry back to **false**. Again, to avoid conflicts with other threads, **MemoInUse** is accessed within a critical section. After updating the status line again, the **ReleaseSemaphore** Windows API function is called to indicate that one more Memo box is available. The count of the semaphore is updated by the amount passed in the second parameter of **ReleaseSemaphore**. Generally, you'll pass one in the second parameter just like this application does. The third parameter is an optional pointer to a long integer, which **ReleaseSemaphore** fills with the semaphore's count before adding the second parameter back to it. I have yet to run into a situation where I actually used the third parameter.

Now you should have the complete picture. **CreateSemaphore** creates a semaphore with a maximum count and a current count. When **WaitForSingleObject** is used with a semaphore object, it will wait until the semaphore's count is greater than zero as long as the second parameter to **WaitForSingleObject** is **INFINITE**. Once **WaitForSingleObject** returns, the semaphore's count will be reduced by one. When a thread has finished using the resource, it calls **ReleaseSemaphore** to increase the semaphore's count which, in turn, will release threads that are waiting on the semaphore. When the application is done with the semaphore, it should pass the semaphore object handle to **CloseHandle**.

The rest of the thread's code is involved in printing information to the screen. **ClearDisplay** (step 10), which must be called through **Synchronize**, uses the **OutputMemo** variable to determine which memo box to clear. **UpdateDisplay** (step 11), which also must be called through **Synchronize**, writes information to the Memo box identified by the **OutputMemo** variable. Finally, **UpdateStatus** and **UpdateDisplayStatus** (step 12) work together to update the proper screen

status line. **UpdateStatus**'s only purpose is to make it easier to call **UpdateDisplayStatus** because the status line is updated so often.

Comments

Imagine what the code would be like if there were no such thing as a semaphore. Each thread would have to poll a variable in a loop that looks something like the following:

```
while (!MemoBoxAvailable);
```

It would work, but it would eat a huge amount of processing time along the way. Kernel objects let a thread wait for something to happen without wasting computer resources. In the next How-To you'll learn about the most general kernel object—the event.

COMPLEXITY
INTERMEDIATE

12.5 How do I...
Make a thread wait for an event to occur?

Problem

I'm writing an application that has two background threads. One does some setup work, and then the other needs to take over. I've got it working, but, because the second thread is polling a variable while it waits, it is using up CPU time and making the application run slowly. Is there any way to make a thread wait for an event to occur without wasting processor cycles?

Technique

This How-To shows you how to use the event kernel object to make a thread wait quietly for something to happen. Not a single CPU cycle will be wasted in this example!

Steps

Run **THREAD5.EXE**. After a few seconds the screen will look like Figure 12-6. The count up and count down messages, produced by two separate threads, alternate because event objects are used to make the threads take turns.

1. Create a new project. Save the form as **THREAD5MAIN.CPP**, and the project as **THREAD5.MAK**.

2. Add the components, and set their properties as shown in Table 12-5. Arrange the components as shown in Figure 12-6.

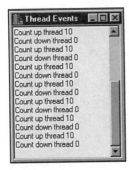

Figure 12-6
THREAD5.EXE after
running for a few
seconds

Table 12-5 Components, properties, and settings for THREAD5

COMPONENT	PROPERTY	SETTING
TForm	Caption	Thread Events
TMemo	Name	mMessage
	Align	alClient
	Lines	None
	ReadOnly	true
	ScrollBars	ssVertical

3. Switch to THREAD5MAIN.H, and add the class declaration for
TCounterThread above the definition of TForm1.

```
class TCounterThread : public TThread
{
public:
  __fastcall TCounterThread(bool TheCountUp);
private:
  bool CountUp;

  void __fastcall Execute(void);
  void __fastcall UpdateDisplay(void);
};
```

4. Add two private variables to TForm1's class declaration.

```
private:// User declarations
  TCounterThread *UpThread, *DownThread;
```

5. Switch back to **THREAD5MAIN.CPP,** and add the global variable declarations before **TForm1**'s constructor.

```
int Count;
HANDLE hCountUp, hCountDown;

//----------------------------------------------------------------
__fastcall TForm1::TForm1(TComponent* Owner) : TForm(Owner)
```

6. Open the Object Inspector for **Form1**. Double-click the **OnCreate** event, and add the code that initializes some things and then starts the worker threads.

```
void __fastcall TForm1::FormCreate(TObject *Sender)
{
  //Clear the memo box
  mMessage->Lines->Clear();
  //Set count to zero
  Count = 0;
  //Create the count up event as auto-reset and signalled
  hCountUp = CreateEvent(NULL, FALSE, TRUE, NULL);
  //Create the count down event as auto-reset and un-signalled
  hCountDown = CreateEvent(NULL, FALSE, FALSE, NULL);
  //Create the thread to count up
  UpThread = new TCounterThread(TRUE);
  //Create the thread to count down
  DownThread = new TCounterThread(FALSE);
}
```

7. Double-click the **OnDestroy** event, and add the code that cleans up just before the program ends.

```
void __fastcall TForm1::FormDestroy(TObject *Sender)
{
  //Terminate the count up thread
  UpThread->Terminate();
  //Terminate the count down thread
  DownThread->Terminate();
  //Close the count up event
  CloseHandle(hCountUp);
  //Close the count down event
  CloseHandle(hCountDown);
}
```

8. Just beneath the **FormDestroy** function, add **TCounterThread**'s constructor.

```
__fastcall TCounterThread::TCounterThread(bool TheCountUp) : TThread(TRUE)
{
  //Tell the object to free itself once it is terminated
  FreeOnTerminate = TRUE;
  //Remember whether we are counting up or down
  CountUp = TheCountUp;
```

continued on next page

continued from previous page

```
  //Resume execution of the thread
  Resume();
}
```

9. Next, add TCounterThread's main loop, the Execute method.

```
void __fastcall TCounterThread::Execute(void)
{
  //As long as the thread is not terminated
  while (!Terminated)
  {
    //If this is the count up thread
    if (CountUp)
      //Wait for the count up event to be raised
      WaitForSingleObject(hCountUp, INFINITE);
    //Otherwise, this is the count down thread
    else
      //Wait for the count down event to be raised
      WaitForSingleObject(hCountDown, INFINITE);

    //If this is the count up thread
    if (CountUp)
    {
      //Add 10 to count
      Count += 10;
      //Wait 1000 milliseconds
      Sleep(1000);
      //Update the screen
      Synchronize(UpdateDisplay);
      //Raise the count down event
      SetEvent(hCountDown);
    }
    //Otherwise, this is the count down thread
    else
    {
      //Subtract 10 from count
      Count -= 10;
      //Wait 1000 milliseconds
      Sleep(1000);
      //Update the display
      Synchronize(UpdateDisplay);
      //Raise the count up event
      SetEvent(hCountUp);
    }
  }
}
```

10. After Execute, add the code that displays the Thread's information on the screen.

```
void __fastcall TCounterThread::UpdateDisplay(void)
{
  //If there are too many memo lines, clear it
```

```
if (Form1->mMessage->Lines->Count > 200)
  Form1->mMessage->Lines->Clear();

//Write the appropriate message depending on which thread this is
if (CountUp)
  Form1->mMessage->Lines->Add("Count up thread " + IntToStr(Count));
else
  Form1->mMessage->Lines->Add("Count down thread " + IntToStr(Count));
}
```

11. Compile and run the application.

How It Works

When the program begins, the **FormCreate** function (step 6) executes. First, it clears the Memo box and sets the global **Count** variable to zero. It then creates two kernel event objects, one for the thread that counts up and one for the thread that counts down, by calling the **CreateEvent** Windows API function. **CreateEvent** takes a security descriptor, a flag that indicates whether or not the event will have to be manually reset to the nonsignaled state after a call to **WaitForSingleObject** succeeds, a flag that describes whether or not the event is born in the signaled state, and an optional name. For this application, both events are auto-reset, do not have a security descriptor, and do not have a name. The count up event starts in the signaled state, while the count down event starts life nonsignaled. The reason for this will become clear when **TCounterThread's Execute** function is described. After the events are created, two instances of **TCounterThread** are started—one to count up and one to count down.

The **FormDestroy** method (step 7) stops the threads and cleans up memory. The threads are stopped by calling their **Terminate** methods. The program also must close the kernel object handles by calling the **CloseHandle** Windows API function.

The Counter Threads

TCounterThread's constructor (step 8) should look pretty familiar if you've been reading the other How-To's in this chapter. **FreeOnTerminate** is set to **true** to make the thread object free itself after the thread is terminated, **CountUp** is set to the value passed into the constructor, and the thread is resumed.

The **Execute** function (step 9) stays in the **while** loop until the **Terminated** member is set to **true** by a call to the **Terminate** function. The thread immediately calls **WaitForSingleObject** to wait for the appropriate event to be signaled. When the threads first start, the count up event is signaled, and the count up thread's **WaitForSingleObject** call will return immediately. As soon as **WaitForSingleObject** returns, the event will reset to the nonsignaled state because the event was created as an auto-reset event.

After the `WaitForSingleObject` call returns, the thread either adds or subtracts from the counter, waits 1000 milliseconds to make the display update slowly enough to watch, calls `UpdateDisplay` through the `Synchronize` method to write a line into the Memo box, and then raises the event that will make the other thread's `WaitForSingleObject` call return. In essence, the two threads hand control to each other as they finish their work. The application simply ensures that one of the events is raised when the threads begin.

Comments

As you can see, the event object is very simple to use. Semaphores (How-To 12.4) and events are just two of a whole family of kernel objects that can be used to synchronize threads in a process, or even threads in different processes. Now that you have the basics, you should be ready to tackle the rest on your own.

COMPLEXITY
INTERMEDIATE

12.6 How do I...
Start threads with different priorities?

Problem

An application I'm writing needs two background threads. One prints documents in the background and should get less priority than the other which is involved in the user interface. How can I start threads with different priorities?

Technique

This How-To will modify the example program from How-To 12.2 to demonstrate how to set a thread object's `Priority` property. This will let you experiment with different thread priorities and how they affect thread performance.

Steps

Run **THREAD6.EXE**. Type a message in the Edit box and press the Start Thread button. Type another message in the Edit box, select Higher priority in the priority Combo box and press Start Thread again. Now, press the Resume All Threads button, wait a few seconds, and press the Suspend All Threads button. Your screen should look something like Figure 12-7. Notice that the higher priority thread's message is displayed twice as often as that of the normal priority thread. Experiment with the program to learn more about how relative thread priorities affect thread performance.

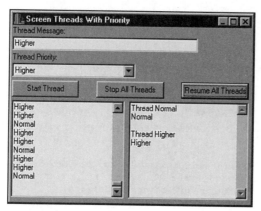

Figure 12-7 THREAD6 after running two threads at different priorities

1. Open THREAD2.MAK. Save the project as THREAD6.MAK and the form as THREAD6MAIN.CPP.

2. Add the new components, and set their properties as shown in Table 12-6. Components from THREAD2 are not included in the table. Lay out the components as shown in Figure 12-7. The new Memo box should go on the right, and the form's caption should be changed to Screen Threads With Priority.

Table 12-6 Components, properties, and settings for THREAD6

COMPONENT	PROPERTY	SETTING
TLabel	Caption	Thread Priority:
TComboBox	Name	cbPriority
	Style	csDropDownList
	Items	Idle, Lowest,
		Lower, Normal, Higher
TButton	Name	bSuspendResume
	Caption	Resume All Threads
	Enabled	false
TMemo	Name	mThreadInfo
	Lines	None
	ReadOnly	true
	ScrollBars	ssVertical

3. Switch to **THREAD6MAIN.H**. Replace the definition of **TScreenThread**'s constructor with the version shown here.

```
public:
    __fastcall TScreenThread(String TheMessage, TThreadPriority⇐
StartPriority);
```

4. Switch back to **THREAD6MAIN.CPP**. Add the following lines of code to **TScreenThread**'s constructor that assigns the priority passed into the constructor to the **Priority** property of the thread object:

```
//Thread constructor, calling TThread constructor with TRUE tells the
//thread to start in the suspended state
__fastcall TScreenThread::TScreenThread(String TheMessage,

TThreadPriority StartPriority)
                                        :TThread(True)
{
    //Thread object will be freed when the thread terminates
    FreeOnTerminate = TRUE;
    //Store the message in a private variable
    Message = TheMessage;
    //Assign the thread priority
    Priority = StartPriority;
}
```

5. Make the following changes to the **FormCreate** function that initializes the selection in the Combo box:

```
void __fastcall TForm1::FormCreate(TObject *Sender)
{
    //Create a TList object to hold threads
    ScreenThreadList = new TList;
    //Make the default combo box selection normal priority
    cbPriority->ItemIndex = 3;
}
```

6. Make the following changes to the **bStartThreadClick** function:

```
void __fastcall TForm1::bStartThreadClick(TObject *Sender)
{
    TScreenThread *T;

    //Create a new thread to display the message in the edit box
    T = new TScreenThread(eThreadMessage->Text, cbPriority->ItemIndex);
    //If this is first thread, clear the two memo boxes
    if (ScreenThreadList->Count == 0)
    {
        mThreadInfo->Lines->Clear();
        mMessages->Lines->Clear();
```

```
    }
    //Add the thread object to the TList of threads
    ScreenThreadList->Add(T);
    //If this is not the first line of the memo box
    if (mThreadInfo->Lines->Count != 0)
      //Add a blank line to the memo box
      //to separate this threads info from the last
      mThreadInfo->Lines->Add("");

    //Add information about this thread to the memo box
    mThreadInfo->Lines->Add("Thread " + eThreadMessage->Text);
    mThreadInfo->Lines->Add(cbPriority->Items->Strings[cbPriority⇐
    ->ItemIndex]);
    //Enable the button to suspend/resume threads
    bSuspendResume->Enabled = TRUE;
}
```

7. Make the following changes to the `bStopAllThreadsClick` function:

```
void __fastcall TForm1::bStopAllThreadsClick(TObject *Sender)
{
  //Disable the button to suspend/resume threads
  bSuspendResume->Enabled = FALSE;
  //As long as there are threads in the TList
  while (ScreenThreadList->Count)
  {
    ((TScreenThread *)(ScreenThreadList->Items[0]))->Resume();
    //Terminate the first thread in the list
    ((TScreenThread *)(ScreenThreadList->Items[0]))->Terminate();
    //Delete the thread just terminated from the list
    //The rest of the list items will move up (entry at index 1 will move⇐
    to 0 etc.)
    ScreenThreadList->Delete(0);
  }
}
```

8. Double-click the Suspend All Threads button, and add the code that suspends or resumes threads as appropriate.

```
void __fastcall TForm1::bSuspendResumeClick(TObject *Sender)
{
  int x;

  //If the button is currently for suspending
  if (bSuspendResume->Caption == "Suspend All Threads")
  {
    //Loop through the thread list
    for (x = 0; x < ScreenThreadList->Count; x++)
      //Suspend this thread
      ((TScreenThread *)(ScreenThreadList->Items[x]))->Suspend();

    //Change the button to a resume button
    bSuspendResume->Caption = "Resume All Threads";
```

continued on next page

continued from previous page

```
   }
   //Otherwise, this is a  resume button
   else
   {
     //Loop through the thread list
     for (x = 0; x < ScreenThreadList->Count; x++)
       //Resume this thread
       ((TScreenThread *)(ScreenThreadList->Items[x]))->Resume();

     //Change the button to a suspend button
     bSuspendResume->Caption = "Suspend All Threads";
   }
}
```

9. Compile and run the application.

How It Works

Setting the priority of a thread is as simple as setting the `Priority` property of the thread object. Available priorities range from zero or idle, which gives the thread no time unless the system is completely idle, to six or time critical, which gives the thread priority over everything else on the computer. Because the user interface thread runs at normal priority three, priorities above four (called Higher) will cause the user interface to become nonresponsive. To avoid problems, this example does not let the user set a thread priority above four.

The only moderately tricky function in this How-To is `bSuspendResumeClick` (step 8). It toggles the Suspend All Threads button's caption, and its function, from suspending the threads when they are running to resuming the threads when they are suspended. First, `bSuspendResumeClick` checks the button's caption to determine whether it is "Suspend All Threads." If it is, all the threads are suspended by looping through the thread list and calling the `Suspend` method for each thread object. The caption of the button is then changed to "Resume All Threads." If, on the other hand, the button's caption was not "Suspend All Threads," the threads are resumed by looping through the thread list and calling the `Resume` method for each thread object. The caption is then changed to "Suspend All Threads."

Comments

This How-To completes your introduction to basic thread operations. If you read through this chapter from the beginning, you know how to create a thread, make it update the screen, safely share data between threads, safely share limited resources between threads, make a thread wait quietly for an event to occur, and how to start threads at different priorities. Threads can be a very powerful addition to almost any application. Don't be afraid to use them.

12.7 How do I...
Run a query in a background thread?

Problem

One of the database applications that I've written needs to run a query that can take a couple of minutes to execute. I'd like to move it to a background thread so the user can continue to do other things while it executes. How do I do this in C++Builder?

Technique

The BDE is multithread safe, so it is possible to run a query in a background thread. The secret is that you have to create a separate **TSession** object for each thread. This How-To shows you how this is accomplished.

Steps

Run **BACKQUERY.EXE**. Start typing in the upper Memo box. After about ten seconds you'll notice a long pause in the display of characters you're typing. Database output then starts appearing in the lower Memo box. Now check the Run Query In Background Check box. Start typing in the upper Memo box. Before too long you'll notice that database output appears in the lower Memo box without interrupting your typing. Your screen will look something like Figure 12-8.

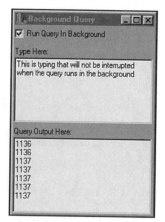

Figure 12-8
BACKQUERY.EXE after running a query in the background

1. Create a new project. Save the form as **BACKQUERYMAIN.CPP** and the project as **BACKQUERY.MAK**.

2. Add the components, and set their properties as shown in Table 12-7.

Table 12-7 Components, properties, and settings for BACKQUERY

COMPONENT	PROPERTY	SETTING
TForm	Caption	Background Query
TLabel	Caption	Type Here:
TLabel	Caption	Query Output Here:
TMemo (upper memo)	Lines	None
TMemo	Name	mOutput
	Lines	None
	ReadOnly	true
TCheckBox	Name	cbBackground
	Caption	Run Query In Background
Query1	DatabaseName	BCDEMOS
Timer1	Interval	10000

3. Switch to **BACKQUERYMAIN.H**. Just before **TForm1**, add the class definition of **TBackgroundQuery**.

```
class TBackgroundQuery : public TThread
{
public:
  __fastcall TBackgroundQuery(void);
  __fastcall ~TBackgroundQuery(void);

private:
  TSession *Session;
  TQuery *Query;

  void __fastcall Execute(void);
  void __fastcall UpdateDisplay(void);
};
```

4. Switch back to **BACKQUERYMAIN.CPP**. Add **TbackgroundQuery**'s constructor just beneath **TForm1**'s constructor.

```
//Thread starts suspended
__fastcall TBackgroundQuery::TBackgroundQuery(void) : TThread(TRUE)
{
  //Free thread memory when terminated
  FreeOnTerminate = TRUE;
  //Create a new BDE session
  Session = new TSession(Form1);
  //Create a new Query
```

```
  Query = new TQuery(Form1);
  //Session name is thread + unique thread id
  Session->SessionName = "Thread" + IntToStr(ThreadID);
  //Use the BCDEMOS alias
  Query->DatabaseName = "BCDEMOS";
  //Use newly created session
  Query->SessionName = Session->SessionName;
  //Run the thread at a slightly lower priority than the main thread
  //which is running at normal  priority
  Priority = tpLower;
  //Resume execution of the thread
  Resume();
}
```

5. Next, add the thread's destructor.

```
__fastcall TBackgroundQuery::~TBackgroundQuery(void)
{
  //Free the query
  Query->Free();
  //Free the session
  Session->Free();
}
```

6. After the destructor, add `TBackgroundQuery`'s main loop.

```
void __fastcall TBackgroundQuery::Execute(void)
{
  //Add the first query to the SQL property
  Query->SQL->Add("select * from customer order by company");
  //run it
  Query->Open();
  //As long as we haven't reached the end of the result set
  while (!Query->Eof)
  {
    //Write the first field to the memo box
    Synchronize(UpdateDisplay);
    //Go to the next record
    Query->Next();
  }
  //Close the query
  Query->Close();
  //Erase the old query
  Query->SQL->Clear();
  //Second query (works as above)
  //Using 2 queries to make it take long enough to
  //notice on fast computers
  Query->SQL->Add("select * from items");
  Query->Open();
  while (!Query->Eof)
  {
    Synchronize(UpdateDisplay);
    Query->Next();
  }
  Query->Close();
}
```

7. Add the thread's `UpdateDisplay` method after the `Execute` function.

```
void __fastcall TBackgroundQuery::UpdateDisplay(void)
{
  //Update the memo box display with the first field of the current result
set
  Form1->mOutput->Lines->Add(Query->Fields[0]->AsString);
}
```

8. Double-click the timer object, and add the code that triggers a query roughly every ten seconds.

```
void __fastcall TForm1::Timer1Timer(TObject *Sender)
{
  //Shut off the timer
  Timer1->Enabled = FALSE;
  //Clear the display memo box
  mOutput->Lines->Clear();
  //If the query is supposed to run in the foreground
  if (!cbBackground->Checked)
  {
    //Run the query in the UI thread
    //Methodology is like that in the Execute method of the thread
    //above
    Query1->SQL->Clear();
    Query1->SQL->Add("select * from customer order by company");
    Query1->Open();
    while (!Query1->Eof)
    {
      mOutput->Lines->Add(Query1->Fields[0]->AsString);
      Query1->Next();
    }
    Query1->Close();
    Query1->SQL->Clear();
    Query1->SQL->Add("select * from items");
    Query1->Open();
    while (!Query1->Eof)
    {
      mOutput->Lines->Add(Query1->Fields[0]->AsString);
      Query1->Next();
    }
    Query1->Close();
  }
  //Otherwise, the user has checked option to run the query in the⇐
  background
  else
  {
    //Create a background query thread
    //Don't have to save pointer because memory will be freed
    //when thread terminates
    TBackgroundQuery *t = new TBackgroundQuery;
  }
```

```
//Enable the timer
Timer1->Enabled = TRUE;
```

}

9. Compile and run the application.

How It Works

The secret to running a query in a background thread is all in the thread object's constructor (step 4). After setting `FreeOnTerminate` to `true` to make the thread object free itself after the thread terminates, a new `TSession` object is created. The session object's name is set to a unique value by appending the thread id onto the end of the word "Thread". A new query object is then constructed, its database name is set to "BCDEMOS" and the query's `Session` property is set to the name of the `TSession` object just created. This is all necessary because each thread that is going to interact with the BDE must have its own `TSession` object, and the default session normally used by data-aware components is part of the main thread. The constructor then sets the thread's priority to be slightly lower than that of the main thread to make sure the user interface stays very responsive while the query runs in the background. Finally, the execution of the thread is started by calling the `Resume` method.

The rest of the thread's code is straightforward. The destructor (step 5) frees the query object and the session object created in the constructor. The background thread's main loop (step 6) runs two queries and displays their results in the memo box by calling the `UpdateDisplay` function through the `Synchronize` method.

The `Timer1Timer` function (step 8) is the `OnTimer` event handler for the `Timer1` control. A `TTimer` triggers its `OnTimer` event every `Interval` milliseconds as long as it is enabled. In this How-To, the timer's `Interval` property is set to 10,000, so `Timer1Timer` is executed roughly every ten seconds. `Timer1Timer` starts by disabling the `Timer` control so another event cannot occur before the function completes. The Memo box is cleared, and, if the Run Query In Background Check box is not checked, the query is run in the main thread. If, on the other hand, the Check box is checked, a `TBackgroundQuery` thread is created to process the query in the background. Because `TBackgroundQuery`'s `FreeOnTerminate` property is `true`, and `TBackgroundQuery` automatically terminates when the query is completed, the thread object pointer does not have to be saved in a member variable. Finally, `Timer1Timer` re-enables the `Timer` control so that this function will be called in another ten seconds.

Comments

Running a query in a low priority background thread is an easy way to improve the apparent performance of a database application. As long as you remember to create a unique session for each thread, there is really nothing to it.

CHAPTER 13
OLE

13

OLE

How do I...

Object Linking and Embedding, OLE, started out with one simple idea—let applications produce compound documents that leverage the power of a number of applications. Do you need to create a report? Write the bulk of the document with Microsoft Word and glue a couple of spreadsheets right into it. Want to edit the spreadsheet you dropped into the middle of your document? No problem. Just double-click the spreadsheet and Windows will fire up Excel so you can edit it.

Over the years, though, OLE has become a whole lot more powerful. OLE 2.0 added the ability for OLE objects to activate in place within the containing application. Drop a spreadsheet object into Word, double-click the object, and like magic the Excel toolbars and menus take over the Word window. OLE Automation was added to give applications the ability to expose a reliable programming interface that other programming tools and macro languages could access. Need to create form letters from your C++Builder™ application? Open up the Word OLE Automation interface and you can control Word from your application and do just about anything you want.

This chapter shows you how C++Builder makes it easy to leverage OLE to enrich your application. After you work through this chapter, you won't quite be able to build your own version of Microsoft Word, but you will know how to use drag-and-drop to enrich an application's user interface, how to open OLE objects, and how to use OLE Automation as a client and as a server.

13.1 Use Drag-and-Drop in My Application

Drag-and-drop is a very powerful user interface tool that is very friendly to the user. What could be easier and more natural than picking something up and moving it to where you want it to go? This How-To will show you how to use the capabilities built into components inherited from TControl to add drag-and-drop to your application.

13.2 Use OLE Objects in My Application

Compound documents are still at the root of OLE. This How-To will show you how to use the TOleContainer object to handle OLE document objects in your application. Everything from creating new OLE objects to saving OLE objects in a file will be covered.

13.3 Create an Application That Can Be Controlled by Another Through OLE Automation

An application that exposes OLE Automation interfaces, which can be called from another application, is called an OLE Automation server. This How-To will take advantage of the capabilities built into C++Builder to build a simple OLE Automation server. It will also delve a little deeper to show you some of the details of OLE Automation server registration that are hidden by C++Builder.

13.4 Control Another Application Through OLE Automation

If you've been around Windows programming for a while, you have probably tried at one time or another to control either Microsoft Excel or Word through DDE. If you never had the pleasure of wrestling with DDE, let me tell you that, although it worked, it just wasn't easy and it was never reliable. For me, the day I first used OLE Automation felt like the first day the thermometer rises to sixty after a long, cold Midwest winter. It worked, it worked pretty fast, and it didn't fail randomly.

This How-To will demonstrate how to build an application that controls another application through OLE Automation. In this How-To, Microsoft Word is used to perform a mail merge with data from a TTable control. However, the techniques demonstrated can be used to control any OLE Automation server, including the one developed in How-To 13.3.

13.1 How do I...
Use drag-and-drop in my application?

Problem

I have a couple of dual list forms in my application that I created from the dual list form included in the C++Builder Object Repository. It would be really cool if users could drag-and-drop items between the two lists as an alternative to using the buttons. How can I do this?

Technique

All controls inherited from **TControl**, including the **TListBox** control, have drag-and-drop capabilities built in. This How-To will show you the properties to set and the events to handle in order to add drag-and-drop support to the dual list form. In addition, you'll see how drag-and-drop can even be used to move data across forms.

Steps

Run **DRAGDROP.EXE**. Three windows will appear as shown in Figure 13-1. Try moving items between the List boxes in the lower left window by selecting items and pressing the buttons. Now try dragging an item from the left List box to the right one. Continue to experiment with drag-and-drop. What happens when you drop an item onto the first item in a list? What about when you drop something onto the last? Try moving items from a List box in the lower left window to a List box in the lower right window. Try selecting multiple items in the List box before you do the drag-and-drop. Finally, make sure to see what happens when you drag the last item of a list over the first item of the same list. By the way, don't try pressing the buttons on the dual list dialogs because they don't do anything!

1. Create a new application. Save the form as **DRAGDROPMAIN.CPP** and the project as **DRAGDROP.MAK**.

2. Add the components, and set their properties as shown in Table 13-1. Lay out the components as shown in Figure 13-1.

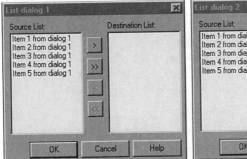

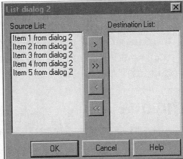

Figure 13-1 DRAGDROP's three windows when the application starts

Table 13-1 Components, properties, and settings of DRAGDROP's main form

COMPONENT	PROPERTY	SETTING
TForm	Caption	Drag & Drop
TListBox	Align	alClient
	Items	Main 1
		Main 2
		Main 3
		Main 4
		Main 5

3. Open the Object Repository by selecting File|New… from the C++Builder menu. Switch to the Forms tab (see Figure 13-2), and double-click on the dual list dialog icon to create a new form.

4. Change the component properties of the new form as shown in Table 13-2. If you are working on a 640×480 display, you will want to make the dual list form smaller. The form on the CD-ROM is sized appropriately for a 640×480 display.

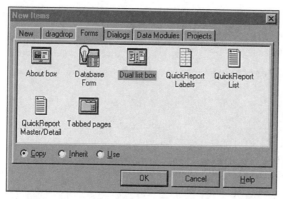

Figure 13-2 The Forms tab of the
C++Builder Object Repository

Table 13-2 Component properties of a new form that must be changed

COMPONENT	PROPERTY	SETTING
DualListDialog	Name	DualListDlgWithDragDrop
SrcList	DragMode	dmAutomatic
DstList	DragMode	dmAutomatic

5. Open the project options dialog by selecting Options|Project from the C++Builder menu. Switch to the Forms tab, and move the `DualListDlgWithDragDrop` form from the auto-create Forms list to the available Forms list. This will keep C++Builder from automatically creating a `DualListDlgWithDragDrop` form when the application starts.

6. Save the new form as `DRAGDROPDLG.CPP`.

7. Switch to `DRAGDROPMAIN.H`. Add the `#include` statement that makes `DRAGDROPMAIN` aware of the `DRAGDROPDLG` unit just beneath the other `#include` statements.

```
#include <vcl\Forms.hpp>
#include "dragdropdlg.h"
//-----------------------------------------------------------------------
```

8. Add a pointer array to the private section of `Tform1`. This array will hold pointers to the two dual list forms that will be created by this application.

```
private:// User declarations
  TDualListDlgWithDragDrop *Dialog[2];
```

9. Open the Object Inspector for **Form1**. Double-click the **OnCreate** method. Add the code that creates the two dual list forms and sets up the items in their List boxes.

```
void __fastcall TForm1::FormCreate(TObject *Sender)
{
  int x, y;

  //Loop from 0 to 1
  for (x = 0; x < 2; x++)
  {
    //Create a new dual list dialog that supports drag & drop
    Dialog[x] = new TDualListDlgWithDragDrop(this);
    //Set its caption
    Dialog[x]->Caption = "List dialog " + IntToStr(x + 1);
    //Clear the source list
    Dialog[x]->SrcList->Items->Clear();
    for (y = 0; y < 5; y++)
      //Create new source list items with a descriptive name.
      Dialog[x]->SrcList->Items->Add("Item " + IntToStr(y + 1) + " from⇐
      dialog " +
        IntToStr(x + 1));
  }
}
```

10. Double-click the **OnShow** event and add the code that adjusts the position of the various windows so that they fit better on the screen.

```
void __fastcall TForm1::FormShow(TObject *Sender)
{
  int x;

  //Place the main form at the upper left
  Left = 1;
  Top = 1;
  //Loop through the two list dialogs
  for (x = 0; x < 2; x++)
  {
    //Show the dialog
    Dialog[x]->Show();
    //Place the top of the dialog just below that of the main form.
    Dialog[x]->Top = Top + Height + 10;
    //Place the first dialog's edge at the far left.
    //Place the second dialog's edge just to the right of the first⇐
    dialog's
    //right edge.
    //Term in parentheses is equal to zero for the first dialog.
    Dialog[x]->Left = 1 + ((Dialog[0]->Width + 10) * x);
  }
}
```

11. Switch to DARGDROPDLG.CPP. Define CROSS_WINDOW_DRAG_DROP at the top of the file to enable drag-and-drop operations across forms. You can remove this **define** later to see how the application can disallow drag-and-drop operations between forms.

```
#include "dragdropdlg.h"
//Comment the following line to disable cross-window drag and drop.
#define CROSS_WINDOW_DRAG_DROP
//-------------------------------------------------------------------
```

12. Switch to DRAGDROPDLG.CPP. Open the Object Inspector for the SrcList (left) List box. Type ListStartDrag in the OnStartDrag event of SrcList and press ENTER. Do not double-click on the event. Add the code that executes when the OnStartDrag event occurs for either List box.

```
//Drag & drop operation has started
void __fastcall TDualListDlgWithDragDrop::ListStartDrag(TObject *Sender,
  TDragObject *&DragObject)
{
  TListBox *t;

  //Cast sender to a TListBox and save it to simplify the rest of the code.
  t = (TListBox *)Sender;
  //If there are no selected items in the list box
  if (t->SelCount == 0)
    //Use the drag cursor that represents no entries.
    t->DragCursor = crNoDrop;
  //If there are multiple selections in the list box
  else if (t->SelCount > 1)
    //Use the drag cursor that represents multiple entries
    t->DragCursor = crMultiDrag;
  else
    //Use the drag cursor that represents a single entry
    t->DragCursor = crDrag;
}
```

13. Type ListDragOver in the OnDragOver event and press ENTER. Add the code that determines whether the control that the object is being dragged over can accept a drop. This function will serve both List boxes.

```
//A drag operation has moved over the Sender control
void __fastcall TDualListDlgWithDragDrop::ListDragOver(TObject *Sender,
TObject *Source,
  int X, int Y, TDragState State, bool &Accept)
{
  String SourceClassName;

  //Get the class name of the drag&drop source control
  SourceClassName = Source->ClassName();
  //If it is a TListBox
  if (SourceClassName == "TListBox")
    //If cross window drag and drop is not allowed
```

continued on next page

continued from previous page

```
    #ifndef CROSS_WINDOW_DRAG_DROP
      //If the list boxes are not on the same form
      if (((TListBox *)Sender)->Owner != ((TListBox *)Source)->Owner)
        //Cannot accept the drop
        Accept = FALSE;
      //Otherwise
      else
        //The user is allowed to drop the data on this control
        Accept = TRUE;
    #else
      //The user is allowed to drop the data on this control
      Accept = TRUE;
    #endif
  //Source control is not a TListBox
  else
    //User is not allowed to drop here
    Accept = FALSE;
}
```

14. Type `ListDragDrop` in the `OnDragDrop` event handler and press ENTER. Add the code to handle a data drop. This function will serve both List boxes.

```
//A drag drop operation is ending
//Sender is the target of the drop
//Source is the source of the drop
//If this function is called we know that the source is, in fact, a
list box
//because otherwise ListDragOver would have rejected the attempt
void __fastcall ListDragDrop(TObject *Sender, TObject *Source,
  int X, int Y)
{
  int i, DestinationItemIndex;
  TListBox *t1, *t2;
  TStringList *Hold;

  //Create a couple working vars that cast Sender & Source to TListBox
objects
  t1 = (TListBox *)Sender;
  t2 = (TListBox *)Source;
  //Create a string list to hold entries to be moved
  Hold = new TStringList;

  //Iterate through the drag&drop source list box's items
  for (i = 0; i < t2->Items->Count; i++)
    //If the item is selected
    if (t2->Selected[i])
      //Add it to the string list
      Hold->AddObject(t2->Items->Strings[i], t2->Items->Objects[i]);
```

```
//Iterate through the drag&drop source list box's items
//From back to front. Otherwise, deleting items
//would create problems because when an item is deleted
//subsequent items move to fill the empty space in the list
for (i = t2->Items->Count - 1; i >= 0; i--)
  //If the item is selected
  if (t2->Selected[i])
    //Delete it
    t2->Items->Delete(i);

//Find the item index where the mouse button was released
DestinationItemIndex = t1->ItemAtPos(Point(X, Y), FALSE);

//Loop through the items to be dropped
for (i = 0; i < Hold->Count; i++)
{
  //Insert the item in the destination list at DestinationItemIndex
  t1->Items->InsertObject(DestinationItemIndex, Hold->Strings[i],
                          Hold->Objects[i]);
  //Increment the insertion point
  DestinationItemIndex++;
}

//Call the function that adjusts the buttons
SetButtons();
}
```

15. Type **ListEndDrag** in the **OnEndDrag** event and press ENTER. Add the code that updates the buttons on the form of the List box that was the source of the drag-and-drop operation. This function will serve both List boxes.

```
//Executes when drag operation ends for the source control
void __fastcall TDualListDlgWithDragDrop::ListEndDrag(TObject *Sender,
TObject *Target, int X, int Y)
{
  //Drag is over, update the buttons (this is the source of the drag &⇐
  drop)
  SetButtons();
}
```

16. Open the Object Inspector for **DstList**. Set the event handlers as shown in Table 13-3.

Table 13-3 Event handlers for `DstList`

EVENT	EVENT HANDLER
OnStartDrag	ListStartDrag
OnDragOver	ListDragOver
OnDragDrop	ListDragDrop
OnEndDrag	ListEndDrag

17. Compile and run the application.

How It Works

The application starts in the **FormCreate** method of **Form1** (step 9). Two dual list forms are created and manipulated in a **for** loop. First, the new **TDualListDlgWithDragDrop** form objects are created as children of the main form by passing the object pointer to the constructor. This ensures that the dual list forms will be destroyed automatically when the application ends. After a dual list form is created, its caption is set to include a sequential number. The first list form is captioned **List Dialog 1** and the second is captioned **List Dialog 2**.

Next, **FormCreate** puts some test items in each of the source List boxes. The **Clear** method of **SrcList**'s **Items** property is called to clear the List box. Five new items are then added by calling the **Items'** **Add** method. Note that each item is identified as belonging to one of the List boxes. For example, the first item in the first form is **Item 1 from dialog 1** and the second item in the second form is **Item 2 from dialog 2**. This makes the results of cross-form drag-and-drop operations clearer.

The **FormShow** method (step 10) is called just before the main form (upper window) is displayed. Its job is to position the various windows so they are visible. First, the main form is placed in the upper left corner of the screen. In a **for** loop, each of the List box forms is positioned to start just below the bottom of the main form. The first list dialog will be at the left side of the screen, while the second will be positioned just to the right of the first.

Adding Drag-and-Drop to the Dual List Form

C++Builder includes a set of events and properties that make it very easy to add drag-and-drop capabilities to a control derived from **TControl**. The first step is deciding whether to use automatic drag-and-drop or manual drag-and-drop.

This application uses automatic drag-and-drop by setting the **DragMode** property of the List box controls to **dmAutomatic**. When **DragMode** is **dmAutomatic**, the control will take care of the details of starting the drag-and-drop operation. In manual mode, you have to add a **MouseDown** event handler that calls the **StartDrag** method of the control when it is appropriate to start the drag operation. In most cases, automatic mode works well. However, if you need the extra control, it is good to know that manual mode is available.

Now let's review a little terminology. The place the user is dragging from is called the *source* control. The place the user is dragging to is called the *destination* control. The control that triggers an event handler is called the *sender*. For some events, the source is the sender; for others, the destination object is the sender. Source, destination, and sender objects are going to be popping up throughout the rest of this section so make sure you have them straight.

The first event associated with drag-and-drop is `OnStartDrag`. It is triggered by the source control when the operation begins. `ListStartDrag` (step 12), this application's `OnStartDrag` event handler, sets the `DragCursor` property of the source control to give the user visual feedback on the drag-and-drop operation. It starts by casting the Sender parameter to a `TListBox` pointer and then assigning the resulting `TListBox` pointer to a temporary variable. This is necessary because Sender is a `TObject` pointer and cannot access the member variables and functions of `TListBox` unless it is cast to a `TListBox` pointer. By assigning the cast result to a working `TListBox` pointer variable, the rest of the code is simplified, because it doesn't have to be littered with ugly cast operators. If no items are selected in the source List box, the List box's `SelCount` property will be zero, and `ListStartDrag` sets the `DragCursor` property to `crNoDrop`, which makes the drag icon a little circle with a line through it. This indicates that nothing will be dropped. If the `SelCount` property is greater than one, then `DragCursor` is set to `crMultiDrag` so that the drag icon will indicate that multiple list items will be dropped. Finally, if exactly one item is selected, `DragCursor` is set to `crDrag` to indicate that a single item will be dropped.

When an item is dragged over a potential destination object, the destination object triggers its `OnDragOver` event. Its job is to tell the system whether or not this control can accept the data being dragged. `ListDragOver` (step 13), the `OnDragOver` event handler for this application, calls the source control's `ClassName` method to get the actual class name of the source control. If the source control is a List box, and the program was compiled to allow cross-form drag-and-drop, `ListDragOver` tells the system that it can accept the data by setting the `Accept` parameter of the function to `True`. If the program was compiled without the ability to do cross-form drag-and-drop, an additional check is made to make sure the source control and the destination control are on the same form. If the source control is not a List box, `Accept` is set to `False`, which indicates that the data cannot be accepted.

When the `OnDragOver` event handler sets `Accept`, it does two things. First, it determines whether or not the control will accept the data. If the user drops data on a control that sets the `Accept` property to `False` in the `OnDragOver` event, the drag-and-drop operation will simply end. C++Builder will not trigger the destination control event that handles dropped data. Secondly, it provides visual feedback to the user by changing the drag cursor shown when the mouse pointer is over the control. If `Accept` is set to `False`, the cursor will be a little circle with a line through it to indicate that a drop will not work on the control. On the other hand, if `Accept` is set to `True`, the source control's `DragCursor` property will be used to determine what the mouse cursor looks like. In such cases, the mouse cursor will indicate that a drop is allowed as long as the source control had some list items selected.

When data is dropped on a control that indicated that it could receive the data, the **OnDragDrop** event is triggered. **ListDragDrop** (step 14), which handles **OnDragDrop** events, starts by casting the sender object, which is synonymous with the destination object in this case, and the source object to **TListBox** objects and storing them in working variables to simplify the rest of the code. A string list object, called **Hold**, is created to hold the dragged items from the source control. Next, the items selected in the source List box are copied into **Hold**. Notice that **Hold**'s **AddObject** method is used to make sure that, if there are objects associated with the list's items, they get copied in addition to the descriptive strings.

Once the selected items are copied, they are deleted from the source list. Notice that the list is traversed from back to front because when an item is deleted, subsequent items move back to fill the empty space. If you traverse a list from front to back and perform deletions, you will skip some items.

After deleting the items, **ListDragDrop** determines where in the destination list to insert the copied items based on where the data was dropped. The destination List box's **ItemAtPos** function is passed the point where the mouse was when the data was dropped. If the second parameter to **ItemAtPos** is **False**, as it is in this call, **ItemAtPos** will return the item index of the item over which the mouse cursor was located. If the mouse was not located over a list item, **ItemAtPos** will return the number of items in the list. If the second parameter to **ItemAtPos** had been **True**, and the mouse was not located over a list item, **−1** would be returned. This application passed **False** because if the mouse was not over a list item, the insertion point is, in fact, equal to the number of items in the list. This way, the dropped items will be added to the end of the list.

The last **for** loop traverses the **Hold TStringList** and adds its entries to the destination List box starting at either the location the data was dropped or at the end of the list if the mouse pointer was not over a list element. **InsertObject** is used to make sure that, if there is associated object data, it is added to the destination list. Each time through the loop, the **DestinationIndex** is incremented to allow the dropped items to be inserted in order. Finally, the form's **SetButtons** method is called to adjust the state of the dual list dialog's button.

When data is dropped on a control, the source control triggers the **OnEndDrag** event. **ListEndDrag** (step 15), which handles this event, is very simple. All it does is call the **SetButtons** method to adjust the state of the buttons on the source control's form. This is necessary to account for cases when data is being dragged from a different form.

Comments

Once you understand how the drag-and-drop events work, it is pretty easy to add drag-and-drop to your applications. The hardest part, if you use drag-and-drop extensively, is making sure that a control will not accept data it cannot handle.

COMPLEXITY
ADVANCED

13.2 How do I...
Use OLE objects in my application?

Problem

Sometimes I want to build applications that incorporate OLE objects to take advantage of available functionality. I've tried to plow through a couple of OLE programming books, and the whole thing looks very, very complicated. Is there an easier way in C++Builder?

Technique

The `TOleContainer` provides all the basic tools needed to build applications that contain OLE objects. This How-To will show you the many capabilities of the OLE container object.

Steps

Run `OLEAPP.EXE`. Click on the Insert|Object menu item. Select a word processor object type. For example, on my computer I selected Microsoft Word Document. Double-click on OLE Windows. If the OLE object you selected supports in-place activation, as Microsoft Word does, your display will look something like Figure 13-3. Experiment with the other menu entries, and other OLE object types, to see the rest of the capabilities of `TOleContainer`.

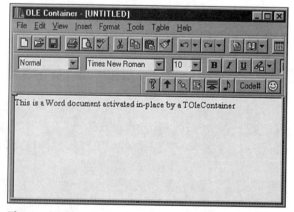

Figure 13-3 `OLEAPP` showing Microsoft Word activated in place

1. Open a new project. Save the form as `OLEAPPMAIN.CPP` and the project as `OLEAPP.MAK`.

2. Add the components, and set their properties as shown in Table 13-4. Lay out the components as shown in Figure 13-3.

Table 13-4 Components, properties, and settings for `OLEAPP`

COMPONENT	PROPERTY	SETTING
TForm1	Caption	OLE Container
TPanel	Align	alClient
	Caption	
TOleContainer	Align	alClient
	SizeMode	smAutoSize
TOpenDialog	Filter	OLE Files|*.OLE
TSaveDialog	DefaultExt	OLE
	FileEditStyle	fsEdit
	Filter	OLE Files|*.OLE
	Options	[ofHideReadOnly]
TMainMenu		

3. Add the menu items to the main menu, and set their properties as shown in Table 13-5.

Table 13-5 Menu items for `OLEAPP`

MENU	MENU ITEM	PROPERTY	SETTING
File		GroupIndex	0
	&New		
	&Open...		
	&Save		
	Save &As		
	-		
	Activate OLE Object	Enabled	false
	Deactivate OLE Object	Enabled	false
	-		
	E&xit		

MENU	MENU ITEM	PROPERTY	SETTING
Edit		GroupIndex	9
	&Paste		
	Paste Special...		
View		GroupIndex	9
	OLE Object As Icon	Enabled	false
Insert		GroupIndex	9
	Object...		
Options		GroupIndex	9
	Activate In Place	Checked	true

4. Switch to `OLEAPPMAIN.H`. Add the following declarations to the private section of `TForm1`:

```
private:// User declarations
  String CurrentFileName;
  String BaseCaption;

  void __fastcall OpenFile(String FileName, bool SaveAs = FALSE);
  void __fastcall SetMenuStates(void);
```

5. Open the Object Inspector for `TForm1`. Double-click the `OnCreate` function and add the application's initialization code.

```
void __fastcall TForm1::FormCreate(TObject *Sender)
{
  //Save the form caption
  BaseCaption = Caption;
  //Open a new file
  OpenFile("");
}
```

6. After `FormCreate`, add the function that adjusts the enabled state of various menu items.

```
void __fastcall TForm1::SetMenuStates(void)
{
  //If the current file is not a new file,
  if (CurrentFileName != "")
    //Enable save menu item
    Save1->Enabled = TRUE;
  //Otherwise, this is a new file
  else
    //Disable save menu item
    Save1->Enabled = FALSE;
```

continued on next page

continued from previous page

```
  //If an object is loaded in the container,
  if (OleContainer1->State != osEmpty)
  {
    //Enable save as menu item
    SaveAs1->Enabled = TRUE;
    //Enable Activate OLE Object menu item
    ActivateOLEObject1->Enabled = TRUE;
    //Enable OLE Object as Icon menu item
    OLEObjectAsIcon1->Enabled = TRUE;
  }
  //Container is empty
  else
  {
    //Disable save as menu item
    SaveAs1->Enabled = FALSE;
    //Disable Activate OLE Object menu item
    ActivateOLEObject1->Enabled = FALSE;
    //Disable OLE Object as Icon menu item
    OLEObjectAsIcon1->Enabled = FALSE;
  }
}
```

7. Next, add the OpenFile function.

```
void __fastcall TForm1::OpenFile(String FileName, bool SaveAs)
{
  //Try, if an error occurs jump to catch
  try
  {
    //If this is not a new file
    if (FileName != "")
    {
      //If this is not the save as function
      if (!SaveAs)
        //Load the file
        OleContainer1->LoadFromFile(FileName);

      //Append current file name to caption
      Caption = BaseCaption + " - " + FileName;
    }
    //This is a new file
    else
    {
      //Delete the OLE object
      OleContainer1->DestroyObject();
      //Append [UNTITLED] to caption
      Caption = BaseCaption + " - [UNTITLED]";
    }
    //Current file name is new name passed here
    CurrentFileName = FileName;
    //Set menu item states
    SetMenuStates();
  }
  //Catch VCL exceptions
```

```
  catch (Exception &E)
  {
    //Show the message
    ShowMessage(E.Message);
    //Quit
    return;
  }
}
```

8. Click on the File|New menu option, and add the code that creates a new file.

```
void __fastcall TForm1::New1Click(TObject *Sender)
{
  //Open a new file
  OpenFile("");
}
```

9. Click the File|Open menu item. Add the code that brings up an open file dialog and, if the user presses OK, calls the `OpenFile` function.

```
void __fastcall TForm1::Open1Click(TObject *Sender)
{
  //If the user presses OK on the file open dialog,
  if (OpenDialog1->Execute())
    //try to open the file.
    OpenFile(OpenDialog1->FileName);
}
```

10. Click the File|Save menu item, and add the code that saves the current OLE file.

```
void __fastcall TForm1::Save1Click(TObject *Sender)
{
  //Save the file
  OleContainer1->SaveToFile(CurrentFileName);
}
```

11. Click the File|Save As menu item, and add the code that saves the current file under a different name.

```
void __fastcall TForm1::SaveAs1Click(TObject *Sender)
{
  //If the user presses OK on the save as dialog,
  if (SaveDialog1->Execute())
  {
    //save the file.
    OleContainer1->SaveToFile(SaveDialog1->FileName);
    //Call OpenFile to change the caption and current file.
    //Passing TRUE in optional param tells OpenFile NOT to actually
    //open the file.
    OpenFile(SaveDialog1->FileName, TRUE);
  }
}
```

12. Because the File|Activate OLE Object menu item is disabled, open the Menu Editor by double-clicking the main menu control. Double-click the File|Activate OLE Object menu item, and add the code that activates the current OLE object.

```
void __fastcall TForm1::ActivateOLEObject1Click(TObject *Sender)
{
  //This causes the OLE object to activate
  OleContainer1->DoVerb(ovPrimary);
}
```

13. Double-click the File|Deactivate OLE Object menu item in the Menu Editor, and add the code that deactivates and activates the OLE object.

```
void __fastcall TForm1::DeactivateOLEObject1Click(TObject *Sender)
{
  //De-activate the OLE object
  OleContainer1->Close();
}
```

14. Click the File|Exit menu item, and add the code that closes the application.

```
void __fastcall TForm1::exit1Click(TObject *Sender)
{
  //Close the application
  Close();
}
```

15. Click the Edit|Paste menu item. Add the code, if any exists, that pastes data from the clipboard.

```
void __fastcall TForm1::Paste1Click(TObject *Sender)
{
  TClipboard *Clip;

  //Create a clipboard object
  Clip = new TClipboard;
  //Open the clipboard
  Clip->Open();
  //If there is data on the clipboard,
  if (Clip->FormatCount > 0)
    //paste it.
    OleContainer1->Paste();

  //Close the clipboard
  Clip->Close();
  //Free the object
  Clip->Free();
  //Set the menu states
  SetMenuStates();
}
```

16. Near the top of the file, add an **include** statement that lets the application use the **TClipboard** object.

```
#include <vcl\vcl.h>
#include <vcl\clipbrd.hpp>
#pragma hdrstop
```

17. Click on the Edit|Paste Special menu item, and add the code that brings up the Paste Special dialog box.

```
void __fastcall TForm1::PasteSpecial1Click(TObject *Sender)
{
  //Open the paste special dialog and paste the data if the user presses OK
  OleContainer1->PasteSpecialDialog();
  //Set the menu states
  SetMenuStates();
}
```

18. Double-click on the View|Object As Icon menu item in the Menu Editor, and add the code that changes the **Iconic** property of the OLE container object.

```
void __fastcall TForm1::OLEObjectAsIcon1Click(TObject *Sender)
{
  //Flip the checked status of the menu item
  OLEObjectAsIcon1->Checked = !OLEObjectAsIcon1->Checked;
  //If the menu option is checked set the container to display,
  //the OLE object's icon instead of its data.
  OleContainer1->Iconic = OLEObjectAsIcon1->Checked;
}
```

19. Click on the Insert|Object menu item. Add the code that brings up the Insert Object dialog box.

```
void __fastcall TForm1::Object1Click(TObject *Sender)
{
  //Open the insert object dialog, and insert an object if the user⇐
  presses OK
  OleContainer1->InsertObjectDialog();
  //Set the menu item states
  SetMenuStates();
}
```

20. Click on the Options|Activate In Place menu item, and add the code that toggles the **AllowInPlace** property of the OLE container object.

```
void __fastcall TForm1::ActivateInPlace1Click(TObject *Sender)
{
```

continued on next page

continued from previous page

```
//Flip the checked status of the menu item
ActivateInPlace1->Checked = !ActivateInPlace1->Checked;
//If the menu item is checked, allow in place activation
//Otherwise, activation will always be outside the app window.
OleContainer1->AllowInPlace = ActivateInPlace1->Checked;
}
```

21. Open the Object Inspector for `OleContainer1`. Double-click the `OnActivate` event, and add the code that is executed when the OLE object in the container is activated in place.

```
//When the container is double clicked and activated in place
void __fastcall TForm1::OleContainer1Activate(TObject *Sender)
{
  //Enable the deactivation menu item
  DeactivateOLEObject1->Enabled = TRUE;
  //Disable the activation menu item
  ActivateOLEObject1->Enabled = FALSE;
}
```

22. Double-click the `OnDeactivate` event, and add the code that is executed when an in-place, activated OLE object is deactivated.

```
//When an in-place activated OLE object is deactivated
void __fastcall TForm1::OleContainer1Deactivate(TObject *Sender)
{
  //Disable the deactivation item
  DeactivateOLEObject1->Enabled = FALSE;
  //Enable the activation item
  ActivateOLEObject1->Enabled = TRUE;
}
```

23. Compile and run the application.

How It Works

If you look at the sheer number of routines in this application, you might think that the `TOleContainer` is very hard to use. That just is not true. Most of the code in this application has next to nothing to do with OLE objects. In fact, most of the code is just the infrastructure required to build an SDI application framework around a `TOleContainer`. Therefore, instead of going line by line through the code, this How It Works section will concentrate on the ins and outs of using a `TOleContainer` control.

In-Place Activation

First, it is important to understand in-place activation, which was one of the most visible improvements made to OLE in version 2.0. In the old days, when an OLE object activated, another window popped up to edit the document. For example,

when you double-clicked an Excel spreadsheet in Word, Excel would fire up with the spreadsheet ready to edit. Although it worked, it fell far short of being transparent. In-place editing is much slicker. When you double-click on an OLE object that is capable of in-place editing, the application window literally becomes the other application—menus merge, new toolbars appear, and no extra windows pop up on the screen.

If you have played with **OLEAPP** at all, you have probably noticed that it supports in-place activation as shown in Figure 13-3. The **AllowInPlace** property of the OLE container controls whether or not an OLE object that supports in-place activation will actually be allowed to activate in place. If **AllowInPlace** is **False**, an OLE object will always activate in a separate window.

The other issue with in-place activation revolves around what happens to the application's menu. When an OLE object is activated in place, menu merging is performed based on the **GroupIndex** properties of the various top-level menu items. Main menu items with group index values of zero, two, and four remain untouched while those with other group index values are replaced. This allows you to decide which of your menus will remain when an OLE object is activated in place. In the sample application, the only menu that remains is the File menu with its **GroupIndex** property set to zero. The rest of the top-level menu items have their **GroupIndex** properties set to nine so that they will disappear when the object is activated in place.

TOleContainer **Dialogs**

TOleContainer supports two special dialogs that make it easier to work with OLE objects. The **InsertObjectDialog** method brings up the standard dialog used to create a new OLE object of a specific type either empty or initialized with the contents of a file in the proper format. A sample of the dialog is shown in Figure 13-4. **InsertObjectDialog** returns **True** if the user presses OK. If the user presses OK, the OLE container object automatically inserts the object, overwriting the contents of the control.

The **PasteSpecialDialog** method brings up the standard Paste Special dialog as shown in Figure 13-5. Just like the **InsertObjectDialog** function, it returns **True** if the user presses OK. If the user presses OK, the OLE container object pastes the data from the clipboard into the control, replacing its former contents, if any.

OLE Object Verbs

OLE objects support verbs that take action on an object. If the **AutoVerbMenu** of the container is **True**, the **TOleContainer** will automatically create a right-click menu containing the OLE object's verbs. To see a verb menu for yourself, load an OLE object into **OLEAPP** and right-click in the OLE container. The list of verbs supported by the currently loaded OLE object can be found in the **ObjectVerbs TStringList** property of the OLE container. The **PrimaryVerb** property of **TOleContainer** is the index of the default verb in the **ObjectVerbs** list.

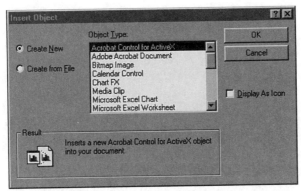

Figure 13-4 The Insert Object dialog box

Figure 13-5 The Paste Special dialog box

You can run any OLE object verb by calling the `DoVerb` method of the OLE container control. `DoVerb` takes as its single parameter the name of the verb. The special value, `ovPrimary`, represents the object's primary verb, which almost always is used to activate the object. The sample application uses a call to `DoVerb(ovPrimary)` to implement the Activate OLE Object menu item click function as shown in step 12.

Other Issues

The OLE container would not be complete without the ability to save and load files that contain an OLE object. `SaveToFile` and `LoadFromFile` do just what you would expect. However, the format used by these functions has absolutely nothing to do with the OLE object contained in the control. Despite my wildest wishes, saving a Word OLE object using `SaveToFile` does not create a Word format file! In fact, the file format is specific to C++Builder. You should also note that most applications, including Word and Excel, do not have a "save" verb for use with the `DoVerb` method.

The `Close` method deactivates an activated OLE object whether it is in place or not. `Close` takes no parameters. To actually delete an OLE object from a container, you call `DestroyObject` which also takes no parameters.

Comments

The `TOleContainer` is a very effective tool for adding limited OLE capabilities to an application. Imagine a database application that lets you store OLE documents in a field, and `TOleContainer` will help you deliver it. However, it is not a very good tool to use as the basis of a word processing program or something similar. For that, you'll have to read those OLE programming books.

13.3 How do I...

Create an application that can be controlled by another through OLE Automation?

Problem

I have a C++Builder application that does some specialized calculations that involve a database. Now, the folks in sales want a way to access some of the data from Microsoft Excel version 7.0. How do I add this capability to my C++Builder application?

Technique

You can turn any Windows application into an OLE Automation server. This allows functions and data elements that you specify to be accessed from other programs that support OLE Automation. This How-To will show you how a simple OLE Automation server is built with the help of C++Builder. You'll also learn a little bit about what goes on behind the scenes of C++Builder's OLE Automation server support.

Steps

Run `OLEAUTOSERVER.EXE` and then close it. The OLE automation server is now registered. If you have Excel version 7.0 or higher, load `TESTOLEAUTOMATION.XLS`. Select Tools|Macro from Excel's menu, select MyFunction from the dialog that appears, and press the Run button. After a few seconds, you'll notice that the OLE Automation Server from this How-To is running. The Excel icon on the Start bar will then start

blinking. Click it to see the first message box, and press OK when you are done. When it starts to flash again, click it a second time. This time a different message is displayed as shown in Figure 13-6. The messages are company names from the **CUSTOMER.DB** table included with C++Builder. After you press OK again, the OLE Automation Server program will stop.

1. Create a new application. Change the form's caption to "OLE Automation Server." Save the form as **OLEAUTOSERVERMAIN.CPP** and the project as **OLEAUTOSERVER.MAK**.

2. Drop a **TTable** control on the form. Set its **DatabaseName** property to **BCDEMOS** and its **TableName** property to **CUSTOMER.DB**.

3. Select File|New from the C++Builder menu. Double-click on the Automation Object icon in the dialog that pops up. Fill out the Automation Object Wizard dialog as shown in Figure 13-7. When you are done, press OK.

4. Save the new unit as **OLEAUTOSERVEROBJECT.CPP**.

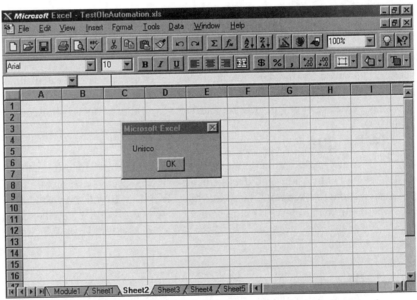

Figure 13-6 Excel displaying a message box with the results of an OLE Automation call to OLEAUTOSERVER

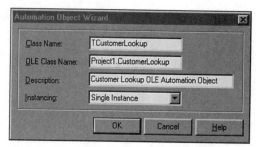

Figure 13-7 Filled-out Automation
Object Wizard dialog

5. Switch to OLEAUTOSERVEROBJECT.H. Declare the LookupCustomer function in the __automated section of the TCustomerLookup object to make
it available to OLE Automation clients.

```
__automated:
  __fastcall String LookupCustomer(String CustomerName);
```

6. Switch back to OLEAUTOSERVEROBJECT.CPP. Add the implementation of
LookupCustomer at the bottom of the file.

```
#pragma startup RegisterTCustomerLookup
//--------------------------------------------------------------------
String __fastcall TCustomerLookup::LookupCustomer(String CustomerName)
{
  String Result;

  Form1->Query1->Params->Items[0]->AsString = CustomerName;
  Form1->Query1->Open();

  if (Form1->Query1->Eof)
    Result = "I don't know";
  else
    Result = Form1->Query1->Fields[0]->AsString;

  Form1->Query1->Close();
  return Result;
}
```

7. Start Microsoft Excel. Make the Visual Basic for Applications toolbar visible
by checking it in the dialog that appears when you select View|Toolbars
from the menu.

8. Create a new VBA module in the Excel workbook by clicking on the Insert
Module button found in the upper left corner of the Visual Basic toolbar, as
shown in Figure 13-8.

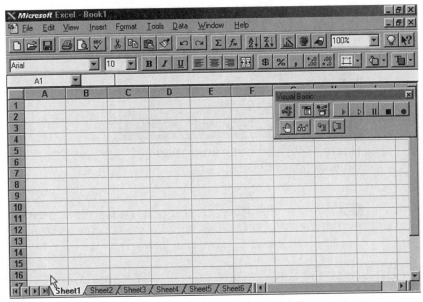

Figure 13-8 Excel displaying the Visual Basic toolbar

9. Type the following Visual Basic code into the new module that starts the OLE Automation server and calls the `LookupCustomer` function twice:

```
Sub MyFunction()
  Dim MyObject As Object

  Set MyObject = CreateObject("Project1.CustomerLookup")
  MsgBox MyObject.LookupCustomer("OK")
  MsgBox MyObject.LookupCustomer("Unisco")
End Sub
```

10. Compile and run the application to register the server. You are now ready to run the Excel program to test the automation server.

How It Works

I don't think Borland could have made creating automation servers any easier unless they designed a wizard that could read your mind and decide what functions and properties you wanted to expose through OLE automation. Any function, property, or variable that you place in the **__automated** section of the automation object is available to any other application through OLE Automation. The one limitation is that only certain variable and parameter types are allowed in the **__automated** section.

The real secret to an OLE Automation server in C++Builder is found in the object registration function generated automatically by the Automation Wizard and is run

automatically at program start up because of the **pragma startup** directive found just below it. The registration function is shown below.

```
void __fastcall RegisterTCustomerLookup()
{
   TAutoClassInfo AutoClassInfo;

   AutoClassInfo.AutoClass = __classid(TCustomerLookup);
   AutoClassInfo.ProgID = "Project1.CustomerLookup";
   AutoClassInfo.ClassID = "{39AEB6A1-A3AF-11D0-864D-00A02488FC53}";
   AutoClassInfo.Description = "Looks up customer in CUSTOMER.DB";
   AutoClassInfo.Instancing = acSingleInstance;

   Automation->RegisterClass(AutoClassInfo);
}
//---------------------------------------------------------------------
-
#pragma startup RegisterTCustomerLookup
```

ProgID is the name other programs will use to access this automation server. I left the default name provided by C++Builder, but in real-world applications you should change the name to something that makes more sense. Each automation server registered on a machine must have a unique name. Most vendors follow a naming convention like this:

```
<company name>.<application name>.<object name>
```

The long number assigned to the **ClassID** is the globally unique identifier, or GUID, of this automation object. This number is generated by a call to **CoCreateGuid** and is guaranteed to be absolutely unique. No other call to **CoCreateGuid** by any program at any time should return the same GUID. For Microsoft's sake, I hope the GUID in the automation object created on your computer is not the same as the one shown here.

The **Instancing** member determines what happens when multiple clients attempt to access the server. Most applications that expose OLE Automation objects should use **acSingleInstance** so that a separate copy of the application is started to serve each client. If **acMultipleInstance** is used instead, multiple clients will access a single instance of the OLE Automation server.

When this function is executed, several registry entries are created that let other programs open the automation server by program ID (**Project1.CustomerLookup**) or by the GUID. You can find the registry entries in your system registry editor under the keys shown in Table 13-6.

Table 13-6 Registry keys for an OLE Automation server

REGISTRY KEY
\\HKEY_CLASSES_ROOT\CLSID\<Program ID>
\\HKEY_CLASSES_ROOT\CLSID\<GUID>

Comments

An application, like this one, that includes an OLE Automation server is called an out-of-process server, because the client and server sides of the connection run in separate processes. If, instead, you package an OLE Automation server inside a DLL, it is called an in-process server, because it will run inside the process of the client application. In general, the techniques shown here will work for building in-process servers as well.

COMPLEXITY
INTERMEDIATE

13.4 How do I...
Control another application through OLE Automation?

Problem

I want to add a function to my application that allows a user to send some data to Microsoft Word to perform a mail merge. How can I do this with C++Builder?

Technique

Once again, OLE Automation comes to the rescue. This time, though, the C++Builder application will call the OLE Automation server built into Microsoft Word to get the job done.

Steps

Run **MAILMERGE.EXE**. Press the Create Letters button. Microsoft Word will load and perform a mail merge. The resulting document will look like Figure 13-9.

1. Create a new project. Save the form as **MAILMERGEMAIN.CPP** and the project as **MAILMERGE.MAK**.

2. Add the components and set their properties as shown in Table 13-7.

Table 13-7 Components, properties, and settings of **MAILMERGE**

COMPONENT	PROPERTY	SETTING
TForm	Caption	Word Mail Merge
TButton	Name	bMerge
	Caption	Create Letters
TTable	Active	true
	DatabaseName	BCDEMOS
	TableName	CUSTOMER.DB

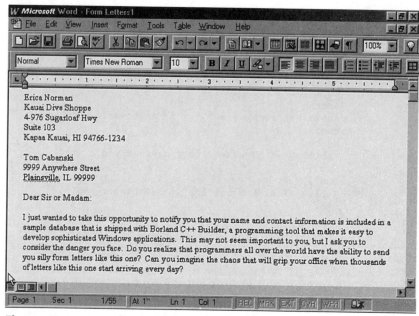

Figure 13-9 Microsoft Word displaying the results of the mail merge

3. Double-click the Create Letters button, and add the code that actually utilizes Word to perform the mail merge.

```
void __fastcall TForm1::bMergeClick(TObject *Sender)
{
  FILE *f;
  char Quote = '"';
  Variant MSWord;
  char CurrentDirectory[MAX_PATH + 1];

  bMerge->Enabled = FALSE;

  GetCurrentDirectory(MAX_PATH, CurrentDirectory);
  Table1->First();
  f = fopen("data.txt", "w");
  while (!Table1->Eof)
  {
    fprintf(f, "%c%s%c,%c%s%c,%c%s%c,%c%s%c,%c%s%c,%c%s%c,%c%s%c\n",
            Quote,
            Table1->FieldByName("Contact")->AsString.c_str(),
            Quote,
            Quote,
            Table1->FieldByName("Company")->AsString.c_str(),
            Quote,
```

continued on next page

continued from previous page

```
                Quote,
                Table1->FieldByName("Addr1")->AsString.c_str(),
                Quote,
                Quote,
                Table1->FieldByName("Addr2")->AsString.c_str(),
                Quote,
                Quote,
                Table1->FieldByName("City")->AsString.c_str(),
                Quote,
                Quote,
                Table1->FieldByName("State")->AsString.c_str(),
                Quote,
                Quote,
                Table1->FieldByName("Zip")->AsString.c_str(),
                Quote);
      Table1->Next();
   }
   fclose(f);

   try
   {
      MSWord = Variant::CreateObject("Word.Basic");
      MSWord.OleProcedure("AppMaximize");
      MSWord.OleProcedure("ChDir", CurrentDirectory);
      MSWord.OleProcedure("FileOpen", "Maildoc.doc");
      MSWord.OleProcedure("MailMergeOpenHeaderSource", "MailHeader.doc");
      MSWord.OleProcedure("MailMergeOpenDataSource", "data.txt");
      MSWord.OleProcedure("MailMergeToDoc");
   }
   catch (Exception &E)
   {
      ShowMessage("Mail merge error " + E.Message);
   }

   bMerge->Enabled = TRUE;
}
```

4. Compile and run the application.

How It Works

Because this How-To's purpose is to show you how to interface with an OLE Automation server from a C++Builder application, not how to perform mail merge with Microsoft Word, a header document that describes the merge fields and a document template that will be merged with the data from the application are supplied on the CD-ROM that accompanies the book. This application relies on the existence of those two files, **MAILHEADER.DOC** and **MAILDOC.DOC**, in the same directory as the executable, and the application will display an error message if they do not exist.

The **bMergeClick** function starts by disabling the Mail Merge button. Next, the **GetCurrentDirectory** Windows API function is called to put the current directory path, which should be the directory that contains the executable and the required Word files, in **CurrentDirectory**. The first parameter passed to **GetCurrentDirectory** is the length of the buffer.

After the current directory is determined, a comma-delimited ASCII file containing the data fields from the **CUSTOMER.DB** table is created. **Table1**'s **First** method is called to position the table at the first record. **DATA.TXT** is then opened for writing by calling **fopen**. In the **while** loop, the data elements are formatted and written to the file by **fprintf**, and **Table1**'s **Next** method is called to move to the next data record. When the table runs out of records, the **Eof** property of **Table1** will be **True**, and the **while** loop will end. After all the records have been written, **fclose** is called to close the file.

Accessing the Word OLE Automation Server

Before an application can access the functions, procedures, and properties of an OLE Automation server, it must open the server. This is accomplished by calling the **CreateObject** function, which is a static member of the **Variant** class. **CreateObject**'s parameter is the program ID of the automation server to open. In this case, the application wants to open the Word Basic automation server.

Once the automation object is open, you can use one of four member functions to access the automation server. **OleProcedure** is used to call functions of the automation server that do not return a value, **OleFunction** is used to call functions that do return a value, **OlePropertySet** is used to set the value of one of the server's properties, and **OlePropertyGet** is used to retrieve the value of a server property. **OleProcedure** and **OleFunction** are somewhat limited in that they do not support passing parameters by name. For example, in some languages you can call an OLE Automation function something like this:

```
OleObject.MyFunction ParmName1="Value", ParmName3="Value",⇐
ParamName2="Value"
```

This is especially handy when you want to skip some parameters. Unfortunately, C++Builder's OLE calling functions only support passing parameters by position. If a function supports six parameters, and you only need to set the first and the third, you must pass the first three. Notice that C++Builder is flexible enough to allow you to send only the first three parameters to the function.

This application uses **OleProcedure** to call several server functions. The first parameter is always the name of the function. Parameters to the function are passed, starting with the second parameter, to **OleProcedure**. Table 13-8 explains the calls made in this How-To.

Table 13-8 Word functions called by MAILMERGE

FUNCTION NAME	DESCRIPTION
AppMaximize	Maximizes Word
ChDir	Changes the current directory to the passed parameter
FileOpen	Opens the file in the first parameter
MailmergeOpenHeaderSource	Opens the mail merge header in the first parameter
MailMergeOpenDataSource	Opens the merge data file in the first parameter
MailMergeToDoc	Performs the mail merge to a new document

One of the limitations of OLE Automation is that there is no compile time checking of OLE object names, function names, procedure names, or parameters passed to OLE functions and procedures. As a result, you should always wrap OLE automation code inside a **try** block as this program does. If an error occurs, control will be transferred to the **catch** block where it can be handled in a reasonable fashion.

Comments

There are plenty of excellent OLE Automation servers ready and waiting for you to use. Examples include Microsoft Word, Microsoft Excel, Microsoft Project, Corel WordPerfect, and Lotus 1-2-3. The applications you can build to take advantage of OLE Automation servers like those listed above are only limited by your imagination.

CHAPTER 14
EXCEPTIONS

14

EXCEPTIONS

How do I...

An *exception* is an event that interrupts the normal flow of execution of a process. Unlike *interrupts*, which are created in response to external events, exceptions are always generated by actions made by the instruction stream. Exceptions can originate in the system hardware or they can be generated by the application. Generally, but not always, exceptions are thrown to signal an error condition. The term `raise` usually refers to the creation of an exception but C++ uses the term `throw` instead.

14.1 Display a Custom Message When an Exception Occurs

The `TApplication` class in the VCL library displays a standard message box when an exception occurs. You can define your own processing to take place when an exception occurs in your application.

14.2 Create a Custom Exception

In C++, an exception is an object. You can create your own exception classes to signal events that are unique to your application.

14.3 Trap an Exception

Within your code, you set up you own exception handlers to catch and process exceptions. Robust applications use exception handlers to protect resources that they allocate to insure they don't get deallocated.

14.4 Handle Hardware Exceptions

The operating system creates structured exceptions to notify an application when a hardware exception occurs. The procedure for trapping a hardware exception is slightly different from trapping a standard exception.

COMPLEXITY
BEGINNING

14.1 How do I...
Display a custom message when an exception occurs?

Problem

When a user enters an invalid value into a Mask Edit control, VCL displays a standard message box. How can I display a custom error message with more application-specific information when an exception occurs?

Technique

To display a custom error message when an exception occurs, you create a handler for the **OnException** event. Within the event handler, you display your custom form to display the message.

Steps

Run the program **APPLICATIONHANDLER.EXE**. The application's main form has a Mask Edit control set up for entering a telephone number. Click on the Done button without completely filling in the Mask Edit control. You should see a message like the one in Figure 14-1. Compare this to the default **TApplication** message shown in Figure 14-2.

1. Select File|New Application from the main menu to create a new blank project. Select File|Save Project As and save the project as **ApplicationHandler**.

2. Add the properties and settings as shown in Table 14-1.

Figure 14-1 The
`ApplicationHandler`
program displaying an
error message

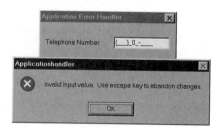

Figure 14-2 How the
`ApplicationHandler` would look
with the standard error message

Table 14-1 Components, properties, and settings for
`ApplicationHandler`

COMPONENT	PROPERTY	SETTING
Form1	BorderStyle	bsDialog
	Caption	Application Error Handler
	Height	160
	Position	poScreenCenter
	Width	300

continued on next page

continued from previous page

COMPONENT	PROPERTY	SETTING
MaskEdit1	EditMask	!\(999\)000-0000;1;_
	Left	160
	Height	24
	MaxLength	13
	Top	30
	Width	120
Button1	Caption	&Done
	Height	25
	Left	200
	Top	90
	Width	75
Label1	Caption	Telephone Number
	Left	10
	Top	30

3. Select File|Open from the C++Builder™ main menu and open the file
UNIT1.H. Add this declaration of the **HandleError** member function to
the definition of **TForm1** in the Code Editor:

```
class TForm1 : public TForm
{
__published: // IDE-managed Components
  TMaskEdit *MaskEdit1;
  TButton *Button1;
  TLabel *Label1;
private: // User declarations
  void __fastcall HandleError (TObject *Sender, Exception *EE) ;
public: // User declarations
  __fastcall TForm1(TComponent* Owner);
};
```

4. Select File|New Form from the C++Builder main menu. Use File|Save As
and save the form as UNIT2.CPP.

5. Add the properties and settings to the new form as shown in Table 14-2.

Table 14-2 Components, properties, and settings for `Form2`

COMPONENT	PROPERTY	SETTING
Form2	BorderStyle	bsDialog
	Caption	Severe User Error
	Height	350
	Position	poScreenCenter
	Width	230
Label1	Left	20
	Top	10
	Width	185
	WordWrap	True
Memo1	Height	180
	Left	20
	Lines	You are not using the product correctly and obviously need training. Please contact: Ripp Meoff Software at (704)555-4000 to sign up for a training course now!
	ReadOnly	True
	TabStop	False
	Top	90
	Width	185
Button1	Caption	&Terminate
	Default	True
	Height	25
	Left	75
	Top	280
	Width	75

6. Double-click on Terminate to create a handler for the `OnClick` event. Add the following code to `UNIT1.CPP` in the Code Editor:

```
void __fastcall TForm2::Button1Click(TObject *Sender)
{
  Application->Terminate () ;
}
```

7. Switch to file **UNIT1.CPP** in the Code Editor and add the **include** directive for **UNIT2.h**.

```
#include <vcl\vcl.h>
#pragma hdrstop

#include "Unit1.h"
#include "Unit2.h"
```

8. Add the definition of **HandleError** to the end of **UNIT1.CPP**.

```
void __fastcall TForm1::HandleError (TObject *Sender, Exception *EE)
{
   Form2->Label1->Caption = EE->Message ;
   Form2->ShowModal () ;
}
```

9. Double-click on the application's main form to create a handler for the **OnCreate** event. Add the following code to the event handler in the Code Editor:

```
void __fastcall TForm1::FormCreate(TObject *Sender)
{
   Application->OnException = HandleError ;
}
```

10. Use the mouse to select the application's main form; then press F11 to display the Object Inspector. Go to the Events page and double-click on the **OnDestroy** event to create a handler for it. Add the following code to the event handler in the Code Editor:

```
void __fastcall TForm1::FormDestroy(TObject *Sender)
{
   Application->OnException = NULL ;
}
```

11. Compile and test the project. When running the application in the IDE, the debugger will halt the application when the exception is raised. Press F9 to continue the application and display the error message. You can select Options|Environment from the C++Builder main menu and disable the Break on exception option to change this behavior within the IDE.

How It Works

The VCL library catches exceptions that occur while messages are being processed. If the application does not catch and handle an exception, the VCL exception handlers call the **Application** object's **HandleException** member function. If an event handler has been set up for the **Application**'s **OnException** event, **HandleException**

calls the event handler to process the exception. If the `OnException` handler does not exist, `HandleException` displays a message box describing the exception.

The member function `HandleError` is the event handler for the `OnException` event. Because properties and events cannot be assigned to the `Application` object at design time, the form's `OnCreate` event handler assigns `HandleError` to the `Application`'s `OnException` event. When the application throws an unhandled exception, the `Application` object calls `HandleError`, which displays a custom form to display the error message.

Comments

The `OnException` event is a good place to put global error handling. Besides displaying a custom message box, this is a good place to put error logging. Though the `OnException` event is a good place for reporting and logging errors, it is not suitable for handling errors and fixing them. See How-To 14.4 for more information on how to handle exceptions.

Although not absolutely necessary in this application, the `OnException` event handler is set to `NULL` in the form's `OnDestroy` event. It is a good idea to undo in the `OnDestroy` event what you do in the `OnCreate` event. If you had an application that dynamically created forms, you would not want the `Application` object's `OnException` event to point to a member function of an object that had been deleted.

COMPLEXITY
INTERMEDIATE

14.2 How do I...
Create a custom exception?

Problem

I have created a mathematical function library. There are cases where certain parameter values are invalid for some functions. Because these functions need to be able to be used in expressions, I cannot use a function return value to indicate an error. Because errors in these functions are relatively rare, I would like to use an exception. How can I generate a descriptive exception to signal that an error has occurred?

Technique

Inversion is an operation frequently used in matrix algebra. When a matrix is multiplied by its inverse, the result is the identity matrix consisting of all zeroes except for ones along the diagonal. If the rows of a matrix are not orthogonal, then it is a singular matrix which has no inverse. This application uses a function to invert a 2×2 matrix. The inversion function uses the C++ `throw` statement to create an exception when the matrix is singular.

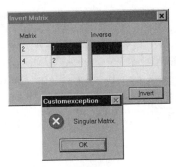

Figure 14-3 The
CustomException
application

Steps

Run the program CUSTOMEXCEPTION.EXE. The application's main form contains two 2×2 grids. Fill in the four cells of the first grid with numeric values; then click on the Invert button to display the inverse matrix in the second grid. Try entering a matrix where the values of one row are a multiple of the values of the other. You should get a message like the one in Figure 14-3.

1. Select File|New Application from the main menu to create a new blank project. Select File|Save Project As and save the project as CustomException.

2. Add the properties and settings as shown in Table 14-3.

Table 14-3 Components, properties, and settings for CustomException

COMPONENT	PROPERTY	SETTING
Form1	BorderStyle	bsDialog
	Height	200
	Position	poScreenCenter
	Width	350
Label1	Caption	Matrix
	Left	25
	Top	15
Label2	Caption	Inverse
	Left	175
	Top	15

COMPONENT	PROPERTY	SETTING
StringGrid1	ColCount	2
	FixedCols	0
	FixedRows	0
	Height	80
	Left	25
	+Options	
	−goEditing	True
	RowCount	2
	Top	40
	Width	145
StringGrid2	ColCount	2
	FixedCols	0
	FixedRows	0
	Height	80
	Left	175
	RowCount	2
	Top	40
	Width	145
Button1	Caption	&Invert
	Left	240
	Top	135
	Width	75
	Height	25

3. Select File|New Unit from the C++Builder main menu. This creates a file called **UNIT2.CPP**. Select File|Save As from the main menu and save the file as **MATRIX.CPP**. Go to **MATRIX.CPP** in the Code Editor and click on **MATRIX.H** in the **include** directive; then type CTRL-ENTER to edit **MATRIX.H**. Add the following code to **MATRIX.H**:

```
#ifndef matrixH
#define matrixH
//-------------------------------------------------------------------

// 2x2 Matrix class
class MATRIX
{
public:
  double values [2][2] ;
```

continued on next page

continued from previous page

```
} ;

// Exception Class.
class ESingularMatrix : public Exception
{
public:
  ESingularMatrix () ;
} ;

inline ESingularMatrix::ESingularMatrix () : Exception ("Singular Matrix")
{
}

MATRIX InvertMatrix (MATRIX input) ;
#endif
```

> **4.** Switch to the file **MATRIX.CPP** in the Code Editor. Add these function definitions to the end of the file:

```
static void ExchangeRows (MATRIX matrix)
{
  // Exchange two rows in the matrix.
  double tmp ;
  tmp = matrix.values [0][0] ;
  matrix.values [0][0] = matrix.values [0][1] ;
  matrix.values [0][1] = tmp ;

  tmp = matrix.values [1][0] ;
  matrix.values [1][0] = matrix.values [1][1] ;
  matrix.values [1][1] = tmp ;
}

MATRIX InvertMatrix (MATRIX matrix)
{
  // Matrix inverse function.
  MATRIX inverse ;

  inverse.values [0][0] = 1 ;
  inverse.values [1][1] = 1 ;
  inverse.values [0][1] = 0 ;
  inverse.values [1][0] = 0 ;

  if (matrix.values [0][0] == 0)
  {
    ExchangeRows (matrix) ;
    ExchangeRows (inverse) ;
  }
  if (matrix.values [0][0] == 0)
    throw ESingularMatrix () ;

  matrix.values [1][0] /= matrix.values [0][0] ;
  inverse.values [0][0] /= matrix.values [0][0] ;
  inverse.values [1][0] /= matrix.values [0][0] ;
```

```
    matrix.values [1][1] -= matrix.values [0][1] * matrix.values [1][0] ;
    inverse.values [0][1] -= matrix.values [0][1] * inverse.values [0][0] ;
    inverse.values [1][1] -= matrix.values [0][1] * inverse.values [1][0] ;

    if (matrix.values [1][1] == 0.0)
      throw ESingularMatrix () ;

    inverse.values [0][1] /= matrix.values [1][1] ;
    inverse.values [1][1] /= matrix.values [1][1] ;

    inverse.values [0][0] -= matrix.values [1][0] * inverse.values [0][1] ;
    inverse.values [1][0] -= matrix.values [1][0] * inverse.values [1][1] ;

    return inverse ;
}
```

5. Go the application's main form and create a handler for the Invert button's OnClick event by double-clicking on the button. Add the following code to the event handler in the Code Editor:

```
void __fastcall TForm1::Button1Click(TObject *Sender)
{
    MATRIX matrix, inverse ;
    // Load the matrix from the grid.
    matrix.values [0][0] = StringGrid1->Cells [0][0].ToDouble () ;
    matrix.values [1][0] = StringGrid1->Cells [1][0].ToDouble () ;
    matrix.values [0][1] = StringGrid1->Cells [0][1].ToDouble () ;
    matrix.values [1][1] = StringGrid1->Cells [1][1].ToDouble () ;
    inverse = InvertMatrix (matrix) ;
    // Store the inverse in the other grid.
    StringGrid2->Cells [0][0] = String (inverse.values [0][0]) ;
    StringGrid2->Cells [1][0] = String (inverse.values [1][0]) ;
    StringGrid2->Cells [0][1] = String (inverse.values [0][1]) ;
    StringGrid2->Cells [1][1] = String (inverse.values [1][1]) ;
}
```

6. Move to the top of the file **UNIT1.CPP** and include matrix.h.

```
#include <vcl\vcl.h>
#pragma hdrstop

#include "Unit1.h"
#include "matrix.h"
//-----------------------------------------------------------------
#pragma link "Grids"
#pragma resource "*.dfm"
TForm1 *Form1;
```

7. Compile and test this project.

How It Works

Exceptions are objects. In the header file **MATRIX.H**, the exception class **ESingularMatrix** is defined as a direct descendant of the VCL exception class. The constructor for the **ESingularMatrix** class calls the Exception constructor supplying "Singular Matrix" as the error message. Within the **InvertMatrix** function the line:

```
throw ESingularMatrix () ;
```

throws, or creates, an exception using an **ESingularMatrix** object. You can use any type of object in a **throw** expression. A statement such as

```
throw 42 ;
```

is perfectly legal but throwing an **int** object is not very descriptive of a error. **Exception** is used as the base class because it is convenient and provides a descriptive message to the user.

Once an exception has been thrown, the C++ run-time library will search the call stack for the first exception handler established for the class used to create the exception. If no exception handler is found, the application terminates. When processing messages, the VCL library catches exceptions and displays an error message before continuing the program with the next message.

It is not absolutely necessary for you to create your own exception class. You could have used

```
throw Exception ("Singular Matrix") ;
```

to throw the exception and produced pretty much the same effect in this application. However, by defining your own exception class, even one as trivial as **ESingularMatrix**, you allow applications that use your library to catch the **ESignularMatrix** exception and treat it as an event distinct from a generic exception.

Comments

Overuse of exceptions is a common mistake. There is a lot of overhead involved in processing exceptions, so exceptions should be thrown only in exceptional circumstances. An example of a situation where using an exception would not be appropriate would be for determining when a function for reading a file has reached the end. When you read sequentially from a file, eventually you hit the end. This is normal and expected, so, in this case, using a function return value is a better choice than an exception.

It also is possible to raise a silent exception. A silent exception can be used to halt an operation without generating a message for the user. A typical case where you may want to do this would be in the **BeforePost** event of a data set to prevent an update. To create a silent exception, derive the exception class from the **EAbort** class. If you do not need a specialized silent exception class, a simple way to abort an operation is to call the **Abort** function (with a capital **A**, not the **abort** function in the standard C++ library).

COMPLEXITY
INTERMEDIATE

14.3 How do I...
Trap an exception?

Problem

The default error handling built into VCL allows my application to continue when an exception occurs, but I have member functions that allocate memory and other system resources. How can I trap an exception so the application can always free what it allocates?

Technique

The C++ language includes the **try/catch** construct that can be used to trap and handle exceptions. Within the exception handler, the application can perform any required cleanup tasks.

Steps

Run the program **HandleException.EXE**. The main form of this application is for a hypothetical order entry system. It has text boxes for entering a part number and the number of items ordered. The application expects the number of items value to be an integer. If you enter a noninteger value in this field, it will throw an exception when you click on the OK button, producing a message like the one shown in Figure 14-4 when the application tries to convert the string to an integer. This message is not the default error message displayed by the **Application** object. The application traps the conversion exception and displays its own message. When you enter an invalid integer into the quantity field, the application clears the edit control and then gives it input focus.

1. Select File|New Application from the main menu to create a new blank project. Select File|Save Project As and save the project as **HandleException**.

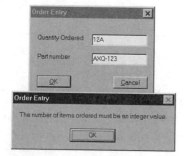

Figure 14-4 The
HandleException application

2. Add the properties and settings as shown in Table 14-4.

Table 14-4 Components, properties, and settings for HandleException

COMPONENT	PROPERTY	SETTING
Form1	BorderStyle	bsDialog
	Caption	Order Entry
	Height	190
	Position	poScreenCenter
	Width	280
Label1	Caption	Quantity Ordered
	Left	15
	Top	30
Label2	Caption	Part number
	Left	15
	Top	70
Button1	Caption	&OK
	Default	True
	Height	25
	Left	15
	Top	120
	Width	75
Button2	Cancel	True
	Caption	&Cancel
	Height	25
	Left	180
	Top	120
	Width	75
Edit1	Height	24
	Left	135
	Text	
	Top	30
	Width	120
Edit2	Height	24
	Left	135
	Text	
	Top	70
	Width	120

3. Select File|Open from the C++Builder main menu and open the file
UNIT1.H. Using the Code Editor, add the definition of the Order struct
and CreateOrder member function to the file UNIT1.H.

```
struct Order
{
  int Quantity ;
  String Part ;
} ;

class TForm1 : public TForm
{
__published: // IDE-managed Components
  TLabel *Label1;
  TLabel *Label2;
  TButton *Button1;
  TButton *Button2;
  TEdit *Edit1;
  TEdit *Edit2;
private: // User declarations
  void CreateOrder (Order *) ;
public: // User declarations
  __fastcall TForm1(TComponent* Owner);
};
```

4. Switch to the file UNIT1.CPP in the Code Editor and add the definition of
the CreateOrder member function to the end of the file.

```
void TForm1::CreateOrder (Order *order)
{
  // This function could save the order to a database. Right now it is a⇐
dummy.
  delete order ;
} ;
```

5. Double-click on the OK button to create a handler for the OnClick event.
Add the following code to the event handler using the Code Editor:

```
void __fastcall TForm1::Button1Click(TObject *Sender)
{
  // Allocate a structure to hold the order.
  Order *order = new Order ;
  try
  {
    // Exceptions that occur with this block will be caught.

    // The conversion from string to integer could generate an exception.
    order->Quantity = Edit1->Text.ToInt () ;
    order->Part = Edit2->Text ;
    CreateOrder (order) ;
    Close () ;
  }
  catch (EConvertError &error)
  {
    // This block catches and handles conversion exceptions.
```

continued on next page

continued from previous page

```
  Application->MessageBox (
          "The number of items ordered must be an integer value.",
          "Order Entry",
          MB_OK) ;
  Edit1->Text = "" ;
  Edit1->SetFocus () ;
  // We did not use the order so delete it.
  delete order ;
}
catch (...)
{
  // This block catches every exception.

  // We did not use the order so delete it.
  delete order ;
  Application->MessageBox ("An unexpected error occured",
                          "Order Entry",
                          MB_OK) ;
  // This block did not handle the exception so throw the exception⇐
again.
  throw ;
}
}
```

6. Double-click on the Cancel button to create a handler for its OnClick event. Modify the OnClick handler in the Code Editor so that it looks like this:

```
void __fastcall TForm1::Button2Click(TObject *Sender)
{
  Close () ;
}
```

7. Compile and test this project.

How It Works

Exception handlers are created using a C++ **try/catch** construct. Code that is to be protected against exceptions is contained in a block preceded with the keyword **try**. The **try** block is immediately followed by any number of **catch** blocks containing exception handlers. When an exception is thrown in a C++ application, the run-time library searches the call stack to find a **catch** block whose class argument matches the type thrown in the exception. The **catch** blocks following the **try** block are searched in sequence until a match is found. If no match is found, the search continues with the calling function. To create a **catch** block that matches any exception, use **...** as its argument.

The **OnClick** handler for the OK button allocates an **Order** structure, fills it in with the values entered on the form, and passes it to the **CreateOrder** function for processing. The problem is that, when an exception occurs, the **OnClick** event procedure will exit without the Order structure being deleted. This chews up system

resources each time an exception occurs. The `catch` blocks free the allocated resources.

This OK button's `OnClick` event has two `catch` blocks. Because we can anticipate the user's entering a nonnumerical value into the quantity field, the first one:

```
catch (EConvertError &error)
```

specifically catches integer conversion errors. The ampersand is required because VCL exceptions (those derived from the class `Exception`) must be caught by reference. The second `catch` block:

```
catch (...)
```

catches all other exceptions.

There is a fundamental difference in the processing between the two `catch` blocks. The first `catch` block not only catches the exception but handles it as well. After displaying an error message, it clears the erroneous value from the edit control and sets focus back to it. This block not only catches the error but completely recovers from it as well.

The other `catch` block catches the exception but does not handle it. In fact, it does not even know or care what the exception is. All it does is cleanup from any unanticipated exceptions. The last statement in this block is a `throw` with no arguments. This causes the exception to be rethrown so any exception handlers in the calling functions can try to handle it.

Comments

If your `catch` block does not cause the application to completely recover from the exception, it should have a `throw` statement at the end of the block. Using `catch(...)` indiscriminately without fixing or rethrowing is, unfortunately, a common programming technique that makes programs unreliable. If your exception handler does not repair the problem, then let another one get a chance to do it.

COMPLEXITY
ADVANCED

14.4 How do I...
Handle hardware exceptions?

Problem

I have an application that does a lot of numerical calculations. I have set up `try/catch` constructs to catch exceptions but I cannot seem to catch things like division by zero and floating point overflow. How do I handle these exceptions in C++Builder?

Technique

The problem is that the operating system uses a nonstandard mechanism known as Structured Exception Handling when it generates exceptions. Because it is the operating system that generates hardware exceptions, you need to use structured exception handling to catch them.

Steps

Run the program **TRAPEXCEPTION.EXE** shown in Figure 14-5. This program calculates the factorial function for an integer. The factorial function is used in probability and becomes very large for relatively small numbers. Try entering an integer in the Mask Edit control. Then click on the Calculate button. Notice that a relatively small value (**>34**) will result in a floating point overflow exception being thrown.

1. Select File|New Application from the main menu to create a new blank project. Select File|Save Project As and save the project as `TrapException`.

2. Add the properties and settings as shown in Table 14-5.

Table 14-5 Components, properties, and settings for `TrapException`

COMPONENT	PROPERTY	SETTING
Form1	BorderStyle	bsDialog
	Caption	Factorial Computation
	Height	135
	Position	poScreenCenter
	Width	260
Label1	Caption	
	Left	15
	Top	45
Button1	Caption	&Calculate
	Height	25
	Left	170
	Top	70
	Width	75
MaskEdit1	EditMask	999999999;_
	Height	24
	Left	15
	MaxLength	9
	Text	
	Top	15
	Width	90

3. Double-click on the Calculate button to create the `OnClick` event handler. Add the following code to the event handler in the Code Editor:

```cpp
void __fastcall TForm1::Button1Click(TObject *Sender)
{
  float value = 1.0 ;
  // Catch C++ Exceptions
  try
  {
    // Catch Microsoft Structured Exceptions
    try
    {
      int limit = MaskEdit1->Text.Trim ().ToInt() ;
      for (unsigned int ii = limit ; ii > 1 ; -- ii)
        value *= (float ) ii ;
      Label1->Caption = String (value) ;
    }
    __except (GetExceptionCode () == EXCEPTION_FLT_OVERFLOW)
    {
      Label1->Caption = "Too Large" ;
      // Clear out the floating point unit.
      _fpreset () ;
    }
  }
  catch (EConvertError &error)
  {
    Label1->Caption = error.Message ;
    MaskEdit1->Text = "" ;
    MaskEdit1->SetFocus () ;
  }
  return ;
}
```

4. Move to the top of UNIT1.CPP and add the following `#include` files:

```cpp
#include <vcl\vcl.h>
#include <math.h>
#include <float.h>
#pragma hdrstop
```

Figure 14-5 Two instances of the TrapException application showing a successful calculation and an error

5. Compile and test this project.

How It Works

In our situation we know that even when using a Mask Edit control to input a number, it is possible to get conversion errors and, possibly, a floating point overflow, when doing the factorial function. The `OnClick` event handler for the button uses two `try` blocks to catch both types of exception. The first block is a `try/catch` construct to catch C++ exceptions and the other is a `try/__except` block to catch structured exceptions thrown by the operating system. The argument to the `__except` statement is an integer value called the filter expression which can be one of the values shown in Table 14-6.

Table 14-6 `__except` arguments

VALUE	SYMBOL	MEANING
0	EXCEPTION_CONTINUE_SEARCH	Do not execute the handler.
1	EXCEPTION_EXECUTE_HANDLER	Execute the handler.
−1	EXCEPTION_CONTINUE_SEARCH	Restart at the point of the error.

Generally, symbolic values are not used in the filter expression. Instead, you usually compare a symbolic exception code to the value returned by the `GetExceptionCode` function and take advantage of the fact that comparison operators return `1` when `True` and `0` when `False`. Using a filter value of `−1` is generally not a good idea because it is difficult to repair an exception so that the application can be restarted at the point that caused it.

In the `__except` filter expression, we check to see whether the exception code is `EXCEPTION_FLT_OVERFLOW` (floating point overflow). When the function gets an overflow, it displays an error message; then, rather than rethrowing the exception, it calls the `_fpreset` to repair the error. The `_fpreset` function clears the state of the floating point unit in the CPU.

Try commenting out the call to `_fpreset`; then try to calculate the factorial for a large integer. Without `_fpreset`, the application will behave in an unpredictable manner after an overflow exception occurs. If you do not repair the situation after an exception, be sure to rethrow it. The VCL library will not handle a hardware exception. If a hardware exception is not handled by the application, the program will be terminated.

Comments

It is unfortunate that two separate mechanisms are required to handle all types of exception. The Borland documentation is somewhat nebulous when it comes to handling structured exceptions. If you need to handle structured exceptions generated by the operating system, you should take a close look at the file `EXCPT.H`. This is where the structured exception handling definitions are located.

CUSTOM COMPONENTS

15

CUSTOM COMPONENTS

How do I...

15.1 Create a custom component from an existing VCL class?

15.2 Use a custom component at design time?

15.3 Create a custom component from scratch?

C++Builder™'s VCL library comes with a wide variety of powerful, ready-to-use components. Sometimes an existing component does almost everything you want, but you need one little feature added. Other times you may need a control that is nothing like any existing control. One of the most powerful features of C++Builder is that you can build upon what already exists in the library to create new controls.

15.1 Create a Custom Component from an Existing VCL Class

Many of the How-To's in this book deal with how to add features to existing components in the VCL library. Instead of changing a control each time you use it, you create a new component that you can reuse over and over.

15.2 Use a Custom Component at Design Time

Once you have created a new component, you will want to be able to use it in design mode in the IDE with its own icon on the Component Palette.

15.3   Create a Custom Component from Scratch

If you need a component unlike anything that already exists, then you still do not need to start completely from scratch. Building a brand new component in C++Builder is not all that difficult.

COMPLEXITY
ADVANCED

15.1   How do I...
Create a custom component from an existing VCL class?

Problem

I have seen how I can add features to a component using the Win32 API. If I have to modify many components within a form's definition, the code gets messy. I would rather create my own component by taking an existing component and adding the features I need. How can I do this in C++Builder?

Technique

In this How-To we will take another look at the problem addressed in How-To 2.7. The standard VCL Scroll Bar control does not allow the size of the scroll box to be changed. How-To 2.7 showed how to add this functionality to a Scroll Bar control. In this How-To you will create a new scroll bar component with a page size property added. This application uses the new Scroll Bar control to scroll a line of text across a form. It adjusts the page size of the scroll bar so the user can visualize how much text is not visible.

Steps

Run the program **COMPONENT.EXE**, shown in Figure 15-1. The scroll bar at the bottom of the application's main form is a custom control. Use the scroll bar to view all the text on the form. Try resizing the form and notice how the size of the scroll box on the scroll bar changes.

Figure 15-1 The Component program with its scrolling text

1. Create a new project by selecting File|New Application from the C++Builder main menu. Choose File|Save Project As and save the project as `Component`.

2. Select Component|New from the main menu to display the Component Wizard. Enter the values shown in Figure 15-2 into the Component Wizard and click on OK.

3. The Component Wizard creates a file called **UNIT2.CPP**. Select File|Save As from the C++Builder main menu and save the file as **SCROLLBAR.CPP** in your project's directory.

4. Select File|Open from the C++Builder main menu and open the file **SCROLLBAR.H**. Go to the Code Editor and look at the class definition the Component Wizard has created for **THowToScrollBar**. Modify the definition of **THowToScrollBar** so that it looks like this:

```
class THowToScrollBar : public TScrollBar
{
private:
  unsigned int pagesize ;
  void DoSetPageSize () ;
  unsigned int __fastcall GetPageSize () ;
  void __fastcall SetPageSize (unsigned int size) ;
protected:
  virtual void __fastcall CreateWnd () ;
public:
  virtual __fastcall THowToScrollBar(TComponent* Owner) ;
__published:
  __property unsigned int PageSize = {
                            read=GetPageSize,
                            write = SetPageSize,
                            default = 0 } ;
};
```

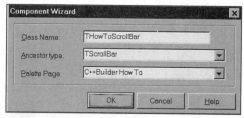

Figure 15-2 Value to enter when creating the new component

5. Switch to the file **SCROLLBAR.CPP** in the Code Editor and add this code to the **THowToScrollBar** constructor:

```
__fastcall THowToScrollBar::THowToScrollBar(TComponent* Owner)
  : TScrollBar(Owner)
{
  // Initialize properties to their default values.
  pagesize = 0 ;
}
```

6. Add the definitions of **DoSetPageSize**, **GetPageSize**, **SetPageSize**, and **CreateWnd** to **SCROLLBAR.CPP**:

```
void THowToScrollBar::DoSetPageSize ()
{

  // This function sets the scroll bar's page size to
  // match the value in the pagesize member variable.
  SCROLLINFO scrollinfo ;
  memset (&scrollinfo, 0, sizeof (scrollinfo)) ;
  scrollinfo.cbSize = sizeof (scrollinfo) ;
  scrollinfo.fMask = SIF_PAGE ;
  scrollinfo.nPage = pagesize ;
  SetScrollInfo (Handle, SB_CTL, &scrollinfo, true) ;
}

unsigned __fastcall int THowToScrollBar::GetPageSize ()
{
  // This function retrieves the PageSize property value.
  // If the scroll bar has been created, the value comes from the
  // control. Otherwise, the value comes from the pagesize member.
  if (HandleAllocated ())
  {
    SCROLLINFO scrollinfo ;
    memset (&scrollinfo, 0, sizeof (scrollinfo)) ;
    scrollinfo.cbSize = sizeof (scrollinfo) ;
    scrollinfo.fMask = SIF_PAGE ;
    GetScrollInfo (Handle, SB_CTL, &scrollinfo) ;
    pagesize = scrollinfo.nPage ;
  }
  return pagesize ;
}

void __fastcall THowToScrollBar::SetPageSize (unsigned int size)
{
  // This function sets the PageSize property value.
  pagesize = size ;
    // We only update the scroll bar control if it has actually
  // been created.
  if (HandleAllocated ())
    DoSetPageSize () ;
}
```

```
void __fastcall THowToScrollBar::CreateWnd ()
{

  // This virtual function gets called to create the control's
  // window. First call the ancestor's CreateWnd function to
  // create the window. Then update the scroll bar's page size
  // to match the value the PageSize property has been set to.
  TScrollBar::CreateWnd () ;
  if (pagesize != 0)
    DoSetPageSize () ;
}
```

7. Add components to the application's main form and set their properties as shown in Table 15-1.

Table 15-1 Components, properties, and settings for `ScrollBarPage`

COMPONENT	PROPERTY	SETTING
Form1	Caption	Custom Scroll Bar
	Position	poDefault

8. Select File|Open from the C++Builder main menu and open the file UNIT1.H. Edit UNIT1.H to include the file SCROLLBAR.H and to add scrollbar and ScrollChange to the definition of TForm1.

```
#include "scrollbar.h"
//---------------------------------------------------------------
class TForm1 : public TForm
{
__published: // IDE-managed Components
private: // User declarations
  THowToScrollBar *scrollbar ;
  void __fastcall ScrollChange (TObject *Sender) ;
public: // User declarations
  __fastcall TForm1(TComponent* Owner);
};
```

9. Switch to the file UNIT1.CPP. Add this message definition before the form's constructor:

```
#pragma resource "*.dfm"
TForm1 *Form1;

static const String message =
"
"Since we, long ago, my generous friends, resolved never to "
"be servants to the Romans, nor to any other than to God "
"himself, who alone is the true and just "
"Lord of mankind, the time is now come that obliges us "
"to make that resolution true in practice." ;
```

continued on next page

continued from previous page

```
//---------------------------------------------------------------------------
__fastcall TForm1::TForm1(TComponent* Owner)
: TForm(Owner)
{
}
```

10. Move to the end of the file **UNIT1.CPP** and add this definition for
ScrollChange:

```
void __fastcall TForm1::ScrollChange (TObject *Sender)
{
  Repaint () ;
}
```

11. Double-click on the application's main form to create a handler for the
OnCreate event. Edit the event handler in **UNIT1.CPP** using the Code
Editor so that it looks like this:

```
void __fastcall TForm1::FormCreate(TObject *Sender)
{
  // Create the scroll bar and place it at the bottom of the form.
  scrollbar = new THowToScrollBar (this) ;
  scrollbar->Parent = this ;
  scrollbar->OnChange = ScrollChange ;
  scrollbar->TabStop = false ;
}
```

12. Select the application's main form; then press F11 to display the Object
Inspector. Go to the events page and double-click on the value for the
OnResize event to create a handler for it. Using the Code Editor, modify
the OnResize handler to look like this:

```
void __fastcall TForm1::FormResize(TObject *Sender)
{
  // Set up the font before doing any measurements.
  Canvas->Font->Size = 12 ;
  Canvas->Font->Color = clRed ;
  Canvas->Font->Name = "Arial" ;

  // Position the scroll bar at the bottom of the form.
  scrollbar->Width = ClientWidth ;
  scrollbar->Top = ClientHeight - scrollbar->Height ;
  scrollbar->Min = 0 ;
  // See if the text fits without scrolling.
  if (Canvas->TextWidth (message) > ClientWidth)
  {
    // Adjust the page size and related values.
    scrollbar->PageSize = ClientWidth/2 ;
    scrollbar->Max = Canvas->TextWidth (message)
```

```
                        - ClientWidth
                        + scrollbar->PageSize ;
    scrollbar->LargeChange = scrollbar->PageSize ;
  }
  else
  { // All the text fits without scrolling
    scrollbar->Position = 0 ;
    scrollbar->Max = 0 ;
  }
}
```

13. Select the application's main form; then go to the Events page of the Object Inspector. Double-click on the value of the **OnPaint** event and then add the following code to the event handler:

```
void __fastcall TForm1::FormPaint(TObject *Sender)
{
  Canvas->Brush->Style = bsClear ;
  Canvas->TextOut (- scrollbar->Position, 10, message) ;
}
```

14. Compile and test the project.

How It Works

The first step in designing a custom control is to determine the requirements for the control. For this control, the requirements were quite straightforward. We wanted a control that behaved exactly like the **TScrollBar** class with the addition of the capability to set and examine the scroll bar's page size.

A component class must inherit from some other class. It is impossible to create a component that has no ancestor, so the next step is to determine what class the component should inherit from. For this component, the choice of **TScrollBar** as a parent class is obvious. In many cases, selecting the best parent class requires a bit of searching through the VCL source code.

Once you have determined what your component's parent class will be, you can design the interface for the component. A component may have two distinct interfaces: a public interface for general use and a protected interface for other component writers. The public interface consists of the component's public methods, published events, and public and published properties. For the scroll bar, the only new feature is the capability to change the page size. This could be implemented by having public **get** and **set** methods, but a property is a better choice because it presents a cleaner interface to the user and can be set at design time and stored with the form definition.

The last step in designing this class is to devise an implementation for the new **PageSize** property. A property can either directly access a member variable or go through member functions. As you saw in How-To 2.7, updating the page size in the scroll bar requires a call to the **SetScrollInfo** API function. Because you want the page size of the scroll bar to change when the **PageSize** property value changes, you are forced to use a function to update the property value. It might be possible to read the **PageSize** property directly from a member variable, but this would not be very reliable. Suppose some part of the application had changed the page size using the **SetScrollInfo** function directly. The page size value stored in the member variable could be different from the actual value of the page size for the scroll bar. The most reliable method is to use a member function that calls **GetScrollInfo** to read the property value.

The problem with using the **GetScrollInfo** and **SetScrollInfo** functions to get and set the page size is that they require a window handle to identify the control, and a handle does not exist until the scroll bar's window is created. There are several situations where a control with a window handle property (with **TWinControl** as an ancestor, for instance) can exist and its associated window does not. When VCL loads a form containing windowed controls, it calls the class constructor to allocate the object, initializes it, and then reads the object's property values from the form file to determine the initial state of the object. Once it has read the property values for all the controls on the form, the VCL library can create the window for the control. During the execution of the component's constructor and loading of property values, the control has no window or window handle.

The solution to this problem is to use a member variable to store the page size value whenever the control does not have a window. The **HandleAllocated** member function defined by the **TWinControl** class returns a **boolean** value that tells whether the control's window exists. The **THowToScrollBar** class uses this function to determine whether it should use the member variable or the control to determine the page size.

After the scroll bar's window is created, the **THowToScrollBar** needs to update the scroll bar's page size with the value stored in the member variable. Otherwise, the **PageSize** value stored in the form file will never get loaded into the scroll bar. The **TWinControl** class uses a virtual function called **CreateWnd** to create the window for a control. By overriding this function, the **THowToScrollBar** class is notified when its window is created. When you override **CreateWnd**, you must remember to call the parent class's **CreateWnd** function or else the window will never is created.

The **PageSize** property is defined as

```
__property unsigned int PageSize = {
                    read=GetPageSize,
                    write = SetPageSize,
                    default = 0 } ;
```

This definition specifies the property's data type (**unsigned int**), name (**PageSize**), and attributes. The **read** attribute specifies how the property's value is to be retrieved. The attribute value can be either one of the class's member variables or

a function having the same type as the property. The **write** specifies how the value of the property is updated. The value can be either one of the class's member variables or a void member function. To create a property that is read-only, you omit the **write** attribute in the property definition. You can use the **default** attribute to specify the most common value for the property. If the property is the same as the default, then it is not written to the form file.

The **PageSize** property uses a member function for both reading and writing the property value. If you refer to step 6, you can see that the **GetPageSize** and **SetPageSize** functions read and update the page sizes as described previously. When the scroll bar has a window handle, it reads from or updates the page size directly from the control, and when the control has no handle, it uses a member variable to read or update the page size. Though it might appear that one could eliminate the **GetPageSize** function altogether by defining **PageSize** as

```
__property unsigned int PageSize = {
                    read=pagesize,
                    write = SetPageSize,
                    default = 0 } ;
```

this mechanism is not completely reliable. If the **PageSize** property were defined like this, and somewhere in an application **SetScrollInfo** was called directly to update the control's page size (just as in How-To 2.7), then the value returned by the **PageSize** property would be incorrect. When you create a component, you have to expect that programmers will use your component in ways you do not intend.

The **DoSetPageSize** function shown in step 6 uses the **SetScrollInfo** API function to update the Scroll Bar control with the value of the **pagesize** member variable. When updating the **PageSize** property value, **SetPageSize** calls **DoSetPageSize** if the component has a window handle. The **CreateWnd** virtual member function also calls **DoSetPageSize** immediately after the window handle is created.

NOTE

One final thing to keep in mind when writing components is that all property **read** and **write** functions, as well as any virtual functions you want to override, must be declared with the __fastcall modifier. The C++Builder IDE relies on the property functions using the fastcall calling convention. All VCL virtual functions are declared with the __fastcall modifier, so you must include the directive to override the functions in descendent classes.

Comments

To cover all there is to know about writing components would take at least two books. The biggest difference between writing applications in C++Builder and writing components is that application development does not require any knowledge of object-oriented programming techniques, while OOP is the core of component

writing. Most Windows class libraries require that inheritance be used by application developers, but VCL's use of event handlers eliminates this requirement. For the component writer, on the other hand, knowledge of inheritance and polymorphism is essential. In many places in the VCL library, there are events and virtual functions with the same basic function (such as the `OnKeyDown` event and the `KeyDown` function). Rarely can a component writer use events like the application writer does; he is almost always forced to used virtual functions to extend a class.

It is a convention in VCL to begin all class names with a capital *T*. While you do not have to follow this convention with all of your classes, you should always do so with components.

One great advantage of C++Builder over almost every other visual development tool is that you can write controls using the same tool you use to write your applications, and you can debug them along with your application. Modifying an existing control in C++Builder is a relatively simple task for someone with a thorough knowledge of C++. The ability to set break points in your control's source code while you are running an application is one of the biggest time savers when debugging a control. Anyone who has debugged an OCX (now ActiveX) or VBX control knows what a nightmare it is. Component creation in C++Builder is a routine task rather than an elaborate chore.

NOTE

In this application you created your `THowToScrollBar` using the `new` operator rather than placing the control on the form using the Form Designer. When you are developing controls, this is typically how you perform the first phase of testing. If you have made an error in the control's interface, it may not function in the IDE properly. Creating the control in the `OnCreate` event allows you to fix your control's basic problems before tackling the IDE interface. The next How-To demonstrates how to use your control in the IDE.

COMPLEXITY

INTERMEDIATE

15.2 How do I...
Use a custom component at design time?

Problem

Now that I have created a custom component, I would like to be able to use it in design mode rather than have to use **new** at runtime. What is the procedure for making a component available at design time?

Technique

Though C++Builder will supply a default icon if you do not supply one, it is a good practice to create an icon for each of your components so you can identify the component on the Component Palette. If you used the Component Wizard to create your component, once you have your icon and component source, all you need to do is install it in the component library.

Steps

1. Create a new directory for a project.

2. Copy the files **SCROLLBAR.CPP** and **SCROLLBAR.H** that you created in How-To 15.1 to the new project directory.

3. Select File|New Application from the C++Builder main menu. Use File|Save Project As to save the project in the directory created in step 1.

4. Select Tools|Image Editor from the C++Builder main menu to start the Image Editor program.

5. From the Image Editor main menu select File|New|Component Resource File. This creates a window for a component resource file called **UNTITLED.DCR**.

6. In the new window select the line labeled *Contents*; then go to the main menu and select Resource|New|Bitmap. Create a 24×24 pixel 256-color bitmap, as shown in Figure 15-3.

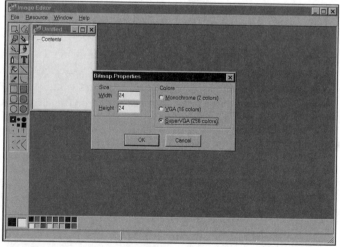

Figure 15-3 Creating the new bitmap

7. In the window for **UNTITLE1.DCR**, you will see a bitmap named **Bitmap1**. Click with the right mouse button over **Bitmap1** and select **Rename** from the context menu. Change the name of the bitmap to **THowToScrollBar**. This name is not case-sensitive, but it must match the name of the component class you created in How-To 15.1.

8. Select File|Save As and save the new file as **SCROLLBAR.DCR** in the directory you created in step 1. The filename must match the name of the file that contains your component. At this point, you have a component resource file with a blank bitmap for the component.

9. Choose File|Open and open **STDREG.DCR** in the C++Builder **LIB/OBJ** subdirectory. This file contains the Component Palette bitmap for the VCL **TScrollBar** class.

10. Expand the Bitmap node in the window for **STDREG.DCR**. Locate the **TScrollBar** bitmap and double-click on it.

11. Select the window containing the **TScrollBar** bitmap; then choose Edit|Select All, followed by Edit|Copy, from the menu.

12. Go to the **SCROLLBAR.DCR** window and double-click on the **THowToScrollBar** node to open the bitmap; then select Edit|Paste from the menu. The **THowToScrollBar** Component Palette bitmap is now a copy of the **TScrollBar** bitmap.

13. Close the window for the **STDREG.DCR** file, but do not save any changes to the file.

14. Go to the **THowToScrollBar** window. Use the drawing tools to modify the bitmap any way you like.

15. Save the file **SCROLLBAR.DCR** and exit the Image Editor program.

16. Select Component|Install from the C++Builder main menu. On the Install Components window, click on the Add button to display the Add Module window. Click on the Browse button and select the file **SCROLLBAR.CPP**. When you return to the Install Components window, click on the OK button to add your component.

17. When the VCL library finishes rebuilding, there will be a new C++Builder How To Tab page on the Component Palette with a button for the control, as shown in Figure 15-4. Place a **THowToScrollBar** on the project's main form and adjust the **PageSize** property in the Object Inspector.

18. Compile and test the project.

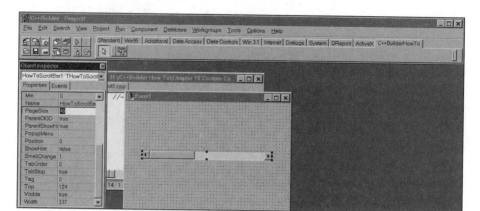

Figure 15-4 THowToScrollBar **installed on the Component Palette**

How It Works

The magic that installs your control in the C++Builder IDE was created for you in the file **SCROLLBAR.CPP** when you used the Component Wizard to create the component in How-To 15.1.

```
namespace Scrollbar
{
  void __fastcall Register()
  {
    TComponentClass classes[1] = {__classid(THowToScrollBar)};
    RegisterComponents("C++Builder How To", classes, 0);
  }
}
```

When C++Builder starts, it calls the **Register** function for each unit that has been added to the IDE. The **Register** function is used to perform all the steps needed to make any components defined in the unit (as well as any property editors and component editors) known to the IDE. Because each component unit requires a **Register** function, a **namespace** is used to make them all unique. The **namespace** name for the unit must be the name of the source file with all characters, except the first, in lowercase.

The **RegisterComponents** function, as its name suggests, registers components with the IDE. Its parameters specify the component page to place the controls on, the component classes to register, and the highest index in the component class array. It is possible to register any number of components in a single unit. Either you can make multiple calls to **RegisterComponents** or you can register more than one component in a single call like this:

```
TComponentClass classes[2] = {__classid(THowToScrollBar), classid⇐
(TSomeOtherControl};
RegisterComponents("C++Builder How To", classes, 2);
```

This call to `RegisterComponents` would register the `THowToScrollBar` class and the `TSomeOtherControl` class.

When the VCL library is rebuilt, C++Builder looks for a component's bitmap in the resource file with a `.DCR` extension and the same name as the source file where the component is registered. The bitmap for the component must have the same name as the component's class name.

Comments

Code reuse has been the Holy Grail of software engineering. Out of many who tried, only Bors, Percival, and Galahad were successful in the Grail quest. Software reuse has been just as elusive. Well-designed custom components are an excellent way to give your code a second or even third chance.

COMPLEXITY
ADVANCED

15.3 How do I...
Create a custom component from scratch?

Problem

I am writing a flight simulator and I need to create components that represent the instruments on an airplane. These look nothing like any of the existing VCL components, so I have no idea where to begin. How do I go about creating a brand new control using C++Builder?

Technique

For this How-To you are going to create a custom control that represents a VOR (VHF Omnidirectional Range) indicator. VORs are the primary instrument system used for navigation in aircraft. VOR ground transmitters are used to mark airways. The VOR station on the ground transmits two signals. One signal is a beam that rotates at 1,800RPM and transmits a pulse in one direction like a lighthouse beacon. The other signal travels in all directions. The two signals are in phase when the rotating signal is oriented to the North. By measuring the interval between the two signals, a receiver can determine the compass bearing from the transmitter to the receiver. The VOR ground station creates, in effect, an infinite number of paths that radiate outward. These *radials* are used to define the airways that aircraft use. Airways use one degree as the smallest increment so, for the purposes of course selection, the number of radials is finite. A radial selected for a course will be in the range 001 through 360 with 360 being North and 180 South.

The VOR indicator in an aircraft has a dial called an OBS (Omnibearing Selector) used to select the desired course. To select a course, the user turns the OBS knob,

rotating a card with heading markings, until the desired course is at the top. In the center of the VOR, a vertical needle indicates how far the aircraft is from the desired course. When the needle is centered, the aircraft is on course. The indicator has dots for every two degrees of course deviation. To stay on course, the aircraft is steered towards the needle.

After reviewing the FAA's *Instrument Flying Handbook*, we determined the requirements for the VOR control should be

✔ To look as closely as possible like an actual VOR indicator.

✔ To support navigation to and from a VOR transmitter.

✔ To enable the user to select a course by using the keyboard.

✔ To notify the application when the user changes the course selection.

✔ To allow the application to enter a course and radials through properties. Courses should be in increments of one degree and radials in increments of 1/10 of a degree.

The next step in the design phase is to determine what the parent class for the control will be. When creating a component from scratch, the three most likely starting points are **TGraphicControl**, **TWinControl**, or **TCustomControl**. **TGraphicControl** is out of the question because the requirements say that the control needs keyboard input. Though **TWinControl** could work, it is generally used only as a base class for controls based on an existing windows control. **TCustomControl** is the best starting point in this case. The class ancestry for the new control will be

```
TObject
  TPersistent
    TComponent
      TControl
        TWinControl
          TCustomControl
            TVOR
```

The requirements for this control directly specify two properties: the course and radial, or bearing, from the VOR transmitter. Because the user can use the keyboard with this control, having a **TabStop** property is implied from the requirements. The only event specified is to notify the application when the user changes the course setting with the keyboard.

Steps

Run the program **VORTEST.EXE**. Use the track bar to change the VOR radial. Select the VOR control with the mouse and use ⊞ and ⊟ or CTRL-⊞ and CTRL-⊟ to change the course selection. Figure 15-5 shows the VOR component with the aircraft 5 degrees to the right of course 360 (North), traveling away from the VOR ground station.

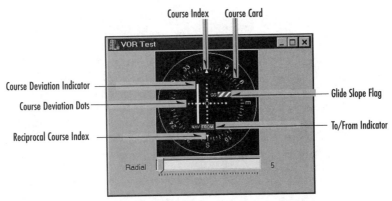

Figure 15-5 The TVOR component

1. Select File|New Application from the C++Builder main menu to create a new project. Save the project as **VORtest**.

2. Select Component|New from the C++Builder main menu. Enter **TVOR** as the Class Name, **TCustomControl** as the Ancestor Type, and **"C++Builder How To"** for the Palette Page. Click on the OK button to create a shell for the control.

3. Switch to the Code Editor and view the file **UNIT2.CPP** created in the previous step. Select File|Save As from the C++Builder main menu and save the file as **VOR.CPP**.

4. Select File|Open from the C++Builder main menu and open the file **VOR.H**. Add the following declarations to the definition of the **TVOR** class:

```
class TVOR : public TCustomControl
{
private:
  void SetCoordinateSystem (TCanvas &canvas) ;
  void DrawDot (TCanvas &canvas, int x, int y) ;
  void DrawIndicator (TCanvas &canvas) ;
  void DrawCourseDeviation (TCanvas &canvas) ;
  void DrawCourseWheel (TCanvas &canvas) ;
  void DrawCourseIndex (TCanvas &canvas) ;
  void DrawReciprocalCourseIndex (TCanvas &canvas) ;
  void DrawToFrom (TCanvas &canvas) ;
  void DrawGlideSlope (TCanvas &canvas) ;
  void DrawHash (TCanvas &canvas, int X, int y) ;

  Graphics::TBitmap *bitmap ;

  // Property Functions
  void __fastcall SetCourse (int newcourse) ;
  void __fastcall SetRadial (int newradial) ;

  // Property Values
```

```
   int course ;
   int radial ;
   // Event Property Values
   TNotifyEvent oncoursechanged ;

protected:
  // Message Procedures
  virtual void __fastcall WMEraseBkgnd (TWMEraseBkgnd &) ;
  // Overridden Procedures.
  virtual void __fastcall KeyDown(Word &Key,  TShiftState Shift) ;
  virtual void __fastcall MouseDown (TMouseButton button,
                                     TShiftState shift,
                                     int x, int y) ;

  virtual void __fastcall Paint () ;

BEGIN_MESSAGE_MAP
MESSAGE_HANDLER(WM_ERASEBKGND,TWMEraseBkgnd,WMEraseBkgnd)
END_MESSAGE_MAP (TCustomControl) ;

public:
  virtual __fastcall TVOR(TComponent* Owner);
  virtual __fastcall ~TVOR() ;

__published:
  __property int Course = { read=course, write=SetCourse } ;
  __property int Radial = { read=radial, write=SetRadial } ;
  __property TabStop ;
  __property TNotifyEvent OnCourseChanged = { read=oncoursechanged,
                                              write=oncoursechanged} ;
};
```

5. Switch to the file **VOR.CPP** in the Code Editor. Add the following definitions to the top of the file:

```
#include <vcl\vcl.h>
#include <math.h>
#pragma hdrstop

#include "VOR.h"

const int DotInterval = 100 ;              // Interval between course⇐
deviation dots.
const int DotRadius = DotInterval / 4 ; // Radius of a deviation dot.
// Inner and Outer radii of the course selection wheel
const int CourseOuterRadius = 1325 ;
const int CourseInnerRadius = 900 ;
// Logical window width and height.
const int WindowExtX = 2800 ; // 2600 ;
const int WindowExtY = - 2800 ; // -2600 ;
// Logical window origin.
const int WindowOrgX = -WindowExtX/2 ;
const int WindowOrgY = -WindowExtY/2 ;
// Length of the course indicator lines.
```

continued on next page

continued from previous page

```
const int LargeLineLength = 100 ;
const int ShortLineLength = 50 ;
// Coordinates for the To/From indicator
const int HashHeight = 150 ;
const int HashWidth = HashHeight * 5 / 2 ;
const int ToFromX = -HashWidth / 2 ;
const int ToFromY = -550 ;

inline int DeviceX (TCanvas &canvas, int x)
{
  // Conversion from logical to device coordinates.
  SIZE size ;
  GetViewportExtEx (canvas.Handle, &size) ;
  return (x - WindowOrgX) * size.cx / WindowExtX   ;
}

inline int DeviceY (TCanvas &canvas, int y)
{
  // Conversion from logical to device coordinates.
  SIZE size ;
  GetViewportExtEx (canvas.Handle, &size) ;
  return (y - WindowOrgY) * size.cy / WindowExtY   ;
}
```

6. Add the following code to the TVOR constructor:

```
__fastcall TVOR::TVOR(TComponent* Owner)
  : TCustomControl (Owner)
{
  TControlStyle style = ControlStyle ;
  ControlStyle = style ;
  Width = 150 ;
  Height = 150 ;
  course = 0 ;
  radial = 0 ;
  bitmap = new Graphics::TBitmap ;
}
```

7. Add the TVOR destructor to VOR.CPP.

```
__fastcall TVOR::~TVOR()
{
  delete bitmap ;
  return ;
}
```

8. Add the overridden virtual functions Paint, MouseDown, and KeyDown to
VOR.CPP.

```
void __fastcall TVOR::Paint ()
{
  // Set the bitmap to the correct size.
  bitmap->Height = Height ;
```

```cpp
  bitmap->Width = Width ;
  // Draw the VOR on the bitmap.
  SetCoordinateSystem (*bitmap->Canvas) ;
  DrawIndicator (*bitmap->Canvas) ;
  DrawToFrom (*bitmap->Canvas) ;
  DrawGlideSlope (*bitmap->Canvas) ;
  DrawCourseDeviation (*bitmap->Canvas) ;
  // Copy from the bitmap to the window.
  // The TCanvas/TBitmap methods for drawing do not work well when
  // the coordinate system has been changed.
  StretchBlt(Canvas->Handle, 0, 0, Width, Height,
             bitmap->Canvas->Handle,
             WindowOrgX, WindowOrgY,
             WindowExtX, WindowExtY, SRCCOPY) ;
}


void __fastcall TVOR::KeyDown(Word &Key,  TShiftState Shift)
{
// We use the +/- keys to change the course. CTRL-+/- changes
  // course by 10 degress.
  TCustomControl::KeyDown (Key, Shift) ;
  if (Key == 187) // +/= Key
  {
    if (Shift.Contains (ssCtrl))
      SetCourse (course + 10) ;
    else
      SetCourse (course + 1) ;

    if (oncoursechanged != NULL)
      oncoursechanged (this) ;
  }
  else if (Key == 189)  // _/- Key
  {
    if (Shift.Contains (ssCtrl))
      SetCourse (course - 10) ;
    else
      SetCourse (course - 1) ;

    if (oncoursechanged != NULL)
      oncoursechanged (this) ;
  }
}


void __fastcall TVOR::MouseDown (TMouseButton Button, TShiftState Shift,⇐
int X, int Y)
{
  // When the user clicks on the mouse, we want to shift input
  // focus to the VOR so that the user can use the +/- keys to
  // change the course.
  TCustomControl::MouseDown (Button, Shift,X, Y) ;
  if (TabStop)
    SetFocus () ;
}
```

9. Add the handler for the `WM_ERASEBKGND` message to `VOR.CPP`.

```
void __fastcall TVOR::WMEraseBkgnd (TWMEraseBkgnd &msg)
{
  // Ignoring the WM_ERASEBKGND messages eliminates flicker.
  msg.Result = 1 ;
  return ;
}
```

10. Add the `write` functions for the `Course` and `Radial` properties to `VOR.CPP`.

```
void __fastcall TVOR::SetCourse (int newcourse)
{
  // This function sets the value of the Course property.

  // Normalize within the range 1-360
  course = (newcourse + 359) % 360 + 1 ;
  if (course < 0)
    course += 360 ;
  Invalidate () ;
}

void __fastcall TVOR::SetRadial (int newradial)
{
  // This function sets the value of the Radial property.

  // Normalize the value to the range 0-3599
  radial = newradial % 3600 ;
  if (radial < 0)
    radial += 3600 ;

  Invalidate () ; // Force a control repaint.
}
```

11. Add the functions to draw the control to `VOR.CPP`.

```
void TVOR::SetCoordinateSystem (TCanvas &canvas)
{
  // This function sets the coordinate system up so that the
  // origin is at the center of the VOR and so that values
  // increase from bottom to top and left to right.

  // This sets the map mode so that the axes are scaled the
  // same amount.
  SetMapMode (canvas.Handle, MM_ISOTROPIC) ;
  // This sets the logical extent of the axes.
  SetWindowExtEx (canvas.Handle, WindowExtX, WindowExtY, NULL) ;
  // This sets the physical extent of the axes.
  SetViewportExtEx (canvas.Handle, Width, Height, NULL) ;
  // This should be the default. Place the physical origin at the
  // top left.
  SetViewportOrgEx (canvas.Handle, 0, 0, NULL) ;
  // More the logical origin to the center of the VOR.
```

```cpp
  SetWindowOrgEx (canvas.Handle, WindowOrgX, WindowOrgY, NULL) ;
}

void TVOR::DrawIndicator (TCanvas &canvas)
{
  // This function draws the VOR.

  // Fill in the background.
  canvas.Brush->Style = bsSolid ;
  canvas.Brush->Color = clBlack ;
  canvas.Rectangle (-WindowExtX/2, WindowExtY/2,
                     WindowExtX/2, -WindowExtY/2) ;

  // Draw the "On Course" circle
  canvas.Pen->Style = psSolid ;
  canvas.Pen->Color = clWhite ;
  canvas.Brush->Style = bsClear ;
  canvas.Ellipse (- DotInterval / 2, - DotInterval / 2,
                  DotInterval / 2, DotInterval / 2) ;

  // Draw the course deviation dots
  for (int ii = -5 ; ii <= -1 ; ++ ii)
    DrawDot (canvas, DotInterval * ii, 0) ;

  for (int ii = 1 ; ii <= 5 ; ++ ii)
    DrawDot (canvas, DotInterval * ii, 0) ;

  for (int ii = -5 ; ii <= -1 ; ++ ii)
    DrawDot (canvas, 0, DotInterval * ii) ;

  for (int ii = 1 ; ii <= 5 ; ++ ii)
    DrawDot (canvas, 0, DotInterval * ii) ;

  // Draw the circle around the indicator.
  canvas.Pen->Style = psSolid ;
  canvas.Pen->Color = clWhite ;
  canvas.Brush->Style = bsClear ;
  canvas.Ellipse (- CourseOuterRadius, - CourseOuterRadius,
                  CourseOuterRadius, CourseOuterRadius) ;
  // Draw the two course indicator triangles.
  DrawCourseIndex (canvas) ;
  DrawReciprocalCourseIndex (canvas) ;
  // Draw the numbers around the course wheel.
  DrawCourseWheel (canvas) ;
}

void TVOR::DrawDot (TCanvas &canvas, int x, int y)
{
  // This function draws a single course deviation dot.
  canvas.Pen->Style = psSolid ;
  canvas.Pen->Color = clWhite ;
  canvas.Brush->Style = bsSolid ;
  canvas.Brush->Color = clWhite ;
  canvas.Ellipse (x - DotRadius, y - DotRadius, x + DotRadius, y +⇐
  DotRadius) ;
}
```

continued on next page

continued from previous page

```cpp
void TVOR::DrawCourseDeviation (TCanvas &canvas)
{
  // This function draws the vertical line that indicates the course⇐
  deviation.

  int deviation ;

  int difference = (3600 + (10 * course - radial)) % 3600   ;
  if (difference > 1800)
    difference = difference - 3600 ;
  if (difference < -900 || difference > 900)
  { // Inbound tracking
    deviation = (3600 - difference ) % 3600 - 1800   ;
  }
  else
  { // Outbound tracking
    deviation = difference ;
  }

  canvas.Brush->Style = bsSolid ;
  canvas.Brush->Color = clWhite ;
  canvas.Pen->Style = psSolid ;
  canvas.Pen->Color = clWhite ;


  // The course deviation indicator should appear from beneath
  // the course wheel. Use a clip region to keep from going over
  // the wheel. The trick here is that clip regions use device
  // coordinates rather than logical coordinates.
  HRGN region = CreateEllipticRgn (
                  DeviceX(canvas, - CourseInnerRadius) + 2,
                  DeviceY(canvas, CourseInnerRadius) + 2,
                  DeviceX(canvas, CourseInnerRadius) - 1,
                  DeviceY(canvas, -CourseInnerRadius) - 1) ;
  try
  {
    SelectClipRgn (canvas.Handle, region) ;
    canvas.Rectangle (10 * deviation/2 - DotRadius, 525,
                      10 * deviation/2 + DotRadius, -525) ;
  }
  catch (...)
  {
    SelectClipRgn (canvas.Handle, 0) ;
    DeleteObject (region) ;
    throw ;
  }
  SelectClipRgn (canvas.Handle, 0) ;
  DeleteObject (region) ;
}

void TVOR::DrawCourseWheel (TCanvas &canvas)
{
```

```
// This function draws the course selection wheel. Large ticks are placed
// every 10 degrees and small ticks are placed every 5 degrees. A label
// is placed every 30 degrees. The text on the label must be rotated so
// that the bottom of the label faces the center of the VOR.

// Labels for the 10 degree marks.
static const String headings [] = {
                    "N", "", "",  "3", "", "",  "6", "", "",
                    "E", "", "", "12", "", "", "15", "", "",
                    "S", "", "", "21", "", "", "24", "", "",
                    "W", "", "", "30", "", "", "33", "", "",
                            } ;
// Draw the 10 degree marks
for (int ii = 0 ; ii < 360 ; ii += 10)
{
   int angle = (90 - ii + course) ;
   double x = cos (2.0 * M_PI * angle / 360.0) ;
   double y = sin (2.0 * M_PI * angle / 360.0) ;

   // Create some "smudges" so that wheel does not look
   // too perfect.
   if ((ii + 4) % 7 == 0)
     canvas.Pen->Color = clGray ;
   else
     canvas.Pen->Color = clWhite ;
   canvas.Pen->Style = psSolid ;

   canvas.MoveTo (CourseInnerRadius * x, CourseInnerRadius * y) ;
   canvas.LineTo ((CourseInnerRadius + LargeLineLength) * x,
                  (CourseInnerRadius + LargeLineLength) * y) ;

   // Not all the headings have labels.
   if (headings [ii/10] != "")
   {
     // Create a font that is rotated to fit the wheel.
     LOGFONT lf ;
     memset (&lf, 0, sizeof (lf)) ;
     strcpy(lf.lfFaceName, "Arial") ;
     lf.lfHeight = 200 ;
     lf.lfWeight = FW_NORMAL ;
     lf.lfEscapement = ii * 10 - course  * 10 ;
     canvas.Font->Handle = CreateFontIndirect (&lf) ;
     canvas.Font->Color = clWhite ;

     // Position and draw the text on the wheel.
     int textwidth = canvas.TextWidth (headings [ii/10]) ;
     int textheight = canvas.TextHeight (headings [ii/10]) ;
     canvas.Brush->Style = bsClear ;
     canvas.TextOut ((CourseInnerRadius + LargeLineLength) * x
                    - y * textwidth/2 + x * textheight,
                    (CourseInnerRadius + LargeLineLength) * y
                    + y * textheight + x * textwidth/2,
                    headings [ii/10]) ;
   }
}
```

continued on next page

continued from previous page

```
  // Draw the 5 degree marks
  for (int ii = 5 ; ii < 360 ; ii += 10)
  {
    int angle = (90 - ii + course) ;
    double x = cos (2 * M_PI * angle / 360) ;
    double y = sin (2 * M_PI * angle / 360) ;
    canvas.Pen->Style = psSolid ;
    canvas.Pen->Color = clWhite ;
    canvas.MoveTo (CourseInnerRadius * x, CourseInnerRadius * y) ;
    canvas.LineTo ((CourseInnerRadius + ShortLineLength) * x,
                   (CourseInnerRadius + ShortLineLength) * y) ;
  }
  return ;
}

void TVOR::DrawCourseIndex (TCanvas &canvas)
{

  // This function draws the course index on the VOR. This is
  // a triangle that points to the selected course on the wheel.
  const int pointcount = 4 ;
  TPoint points [pointcount] = {
                                  {0, CourseInnerRadius},
                                  {50, CourseInnerRadius - 100},
                                  {-50, CourseInnerRadius - 100},
                                  {0, CourseInnerRadius}
                               } ;
  canvas.Pen->Style = psSolid ;
  canvas.Pen->Color = clWhite ;
  canvas.Brush->Style = bsSolid ;
  canvas.Brush->Color = clWhite ;
  BeginPath (canvas.Handle) ;
  canvas.Polyline (points, pointcount - 1) ;
  EndPath (canvas.Handle) ;
  FillPath (canvas.Handle) ;
  return ;
}

void TVOR::DrawReciprocalCourseIndex (TCanvas &canvas)
{

  // This function draws the reciprocal course indicator on
  // the VOR.  This is a triangle at the bottom pointing to
  // the course wheel.
  const int pointcount = 4 ;
  TPoint points [pointcount] = { {0, -CourseInnerRadius},
                                 {40, -CourseInnerRadius + 80},
                                 {-40, -CourseInnerRadius + 80},
                                 {0, -CourseInnerRadius}} ;
  canvas.Pen->Style = psSolid ;
  canvas.Pen->Color = clWhite ;
  canvas.Brush->Style = bsSolid ;
  canvas.Brush->Color = clWhite ;
```

```
    BeginPath (canvas.Handle) ;
    canvas.Polyline (points, pointcount - 1) ;
    EndPath (canvas.Handle) ;
    FillPath (canvas.Handle) ;
    return ;
}

void TVOR::DrawHash (TCanvas &canvas, int X, int Y)
{

    // This function draws the red and white has marks when the an
    // indicator is not receiving a clear signal.

    canvas.Brush->Color = clRed ;
    canvas.Pen->Color = clRed ;

    // Each of these blocks draws the outline of a diagonal red hash
    // mark, then fills it in.
    BeginPath (canvas.Handle) ;
    canvas.MoveTo (X, Y - HashHeight/2) ;
    canvas.LineTo (X, Y - HashHeight) ;
    canvas.LineTo (X + HashHeight, Y) ;
    canvas.LineTo (X + HashHeight/2, Y) ;
    canvas.LineTo (X, Y - HashHeight/2) ;
    EndPath (canvas.Handle) ;
    FillPath (canvas.Handle) ;

    BeginPath (canvas.Handle) ;
    canvas.MoveTo (X + HashHeight/2, Y - HashHeight) ;
    canvas.LineTo (X + HashHeight, Y - HashHeight) ;
    canvas.LineTo (X + 2 * HashHeight, Y) ;
    canvas.LineTo (X + 3 * HashHeight/2, Y) ;
    canvas.LineTo (X + HashHeight/2, Y - HashHeight) ;
    EndPath (canvas.Handle) ;
    FillPath (canvas.Handle) ;

    BeginPath (canvas.Handle) ;
    canvas.MoveTo (X + 3 * HashHeight/2, Y - HashHeight) ;
    canvas.LineTo (X + 2 * HashHeight, Y - HashHeight) ;
    canvas.LineTo (X + 5 * HashHeight/2, Y - HashHeight/2) ;
    canvas.LineTo (X + 5 * HashHeight/2, Y) ;
    canvas.LineTo (X + 3 * HashHeight/2, Y - HashHeight) ;
    EndPath (canvas.Handle) ;
    FillPath (canvas.Handle) ;

    return ;
}

void TVOR::DrawToFrom (TCanvas &canvas)
{
    // This function draws the To/From indicator on the VOR.

    canvas.Font->Height = HashHeight ;
    canvas.Font->Name = "Arial" ;
```

continued on next page

continued from previous page

```
canvas.Brush->Style = bsClear ;
canvas.Font->Color = clWhite ;

// Position and draw the text on the wheel.
static const String label = "NAV" ;

canvas.TextOut (ToFromX - canvas.TextWidth (label + " "),
                ToFromY,
                label) ;

// Create a "window" for the To/From indicator to appear from.

HRGN region = CreateRectRgn (DeviceX(canvas, ToFromX),
                             DeviceY(canvas, ToFromY),
                             DeviceX(canvas, ToFromX +
                               HashWidth),
                             DeviceY(canvas, ToFromY-
                               HashHeight)) ;
try
{

   // To clearly see how the To/From indicator is implemented, try
   // commenting out the following SelectClipRgn call.
   SelectClipRgn (canvas.Handle, region) ;

   int difference = (3600 + (10 * course - radial)) % 3600  ;
   if (difference > 1800)
     difference = difference - 3600 ;
   if (difference < 0)
     difference = -difference ;


   // Initially set the top to the location of the "From"
   // indicator.
   int top = ToFromY ;
   const int delta = 200 ;
   if (difference > 900 + delta )
   {

      // We are clearly on the "TO" side of the VOR so display
      // "TO".
      top = top + 2 * HashHeight ;
   }
   else if (difference > 900 - delta)
   {

      // We are in the area where the TO/FROM indictor is in
      // between. Scale to the approximate position.
      top += (double) HashHeight *(difference - 900 + 2 * delta) /
                           (double) (2 * delta)  ;
   }
```

```
      static const String FROM = "FROM" ;
      canvas.Brush->Color = clRed ;
      canvas.Rectangle (-HashWidth / 2, top,
                        HashWidth / 2, top - HashHeight) ;
      canvas.TextOut (- canvas.TextWidth (FROM)/2, top, FROM) ;

      canvas.Brush->Color = clWhite ;

      canvas.Rectangle (-HashWidth / 2, top - HashHeight,
                        HashWidth / 2, top - 2 * HashHeight) ;
      DrawHash (canvas, -HashWidth / 2, top - HashHeight) ;

      canvas.Brush->Color = clBlack ;
      canvas.Pen->Color = clBlack ;
      static const String TO = "TO" ;
      canvas.Rectangle (-HashWidth / 2, top - 2 * HashHeight,
                        HashWidth / 2, top - 3 * HashHeight) ;

      canvas.TextOut (- canvas.TextWidth (TO)/2,
                      top - 2 * HashHeight, TO) ;
   }
   catch (...)
   {
     SelectClipRgn (canvas.Handle, 0) ;
     DeleteObject (region) ;
     throw ;
   }
   // Clean up.
   SelectClipRgn (canvas.Handle, 0) ;
   DeleteObject (region) ;

   // Draw a light outline for the To/From indicator.
   canvas.Pen->Color = clGray ;
   canvas.Brush->Style = bsClear ;
   canvas.Rectangle (ToFromX, ToFromY, ToFromX + HashWidth,
                     ToFromY - HashHeight) ;

}


void TVOR::DrawGlideSlope (TCanvas &canvas)
{

   // Glideslop deviation has not been implemented (It would
   // make no sense without implementing localizer deviation as
   // well.) Draw a glideslope active indicator but always show
   // the hashmarks to indicate that a glideslope signal is not
   // being received.
   canvas.Font->Height = HashHeight ;
   canvas.Font->Name = "Arial" ;
   canvas.Brush->Style = bsClear ;
   canvas.Font->Color = clWhite ;
   static const int labelx = DotInterval ;
```

continued on next page

continued from previous page

```
static const String GS = "GS" ;
static const int labely = DotInterval * 3 ;
canvas.TextOut (labelx, labely, GS) ;
canvas.Brush->Color = clWhite ;
int textspace = canvas.TextWidth (GS + " ") ;
int hashtop = labely
                - (canvas.TextHeight (GS) - HashHeight) / 2 ;

canvas.Rectangle (labelx + textspace, hashtop,
                  labelx + HashWidth + textspace,
                  hashtop - HashHeight) ;
DrawHash (canvas, labelx + textspace, hashtop) ;
}
```

12. Add components to the application's main form and set their properties as shown in Table 15-2.

Table 15-2 Components, properties, and settings for VORtest

COMPONENT	PROPERTY	SETTING
Form1	Caption	VOR Test
	Height	300
	Position	poScreenCenter
	Width	400
TrackBar1	Frequency	100
	Left	80
	Max	3600
	Top	200
	Width	220
Label1	Caption	Radial
	Left	30
	Top	210
Label2	Caption	0
	Left	310
	Top	210

13. Select File|Open from the C++Builder main menu and open the file UNIT1.H. Go to the Code Editor and include VOR.H in this file and add the definition of the vor member variable.

```
#include "vor.h"
//------------------------------------------------------------------
class TForm1 : public TForm
{
```

```
__published: // IDE-managed Components
   TTrackBar *TrackBar1;
   TLabel *Label1;
   TLabel *Label2;
private: // User declarations
   TVOR *vor ;
public: // User declarations
   __fastcall TForm1(TComponent* Owner);
};
```

14. Go to the application's main form and double-click on it to create the form's **OnCreate** handler. Add the following code to **UNIT1.CPP** in the Code Editor:

```
void __fastcall TForm1::FormCreate(TObject *Sender)
{
   vor = new TVOR (this) ;
   vor->Parent = this ;
   vor->Left = 90 ;
   vor->Height = 200 ;
   vor->Width = 200 ;
   vor->TabStop = true ;
}
```

15. Return to the application's main form and create the **OnClick** event handler for the track bar by double-clicking on the control. Add this code to the **OnClick** handler in **UNIT1.CPP**:

```
void __fastcall TForm1::TrackBar1Change(TObject *Sender)
{
   vor->Radial = TrackBar1->Position ;
   Label2->Caption = String ((double) TrackBar1->Position / 10.0) ;
}
```

16. Compile and test this project.

How It Works

Although this control is quite a bit more elaborate than the one in How-To 15.1, the interface structure of the two controls is similar. There are, however, some new techniques here. In step 4 notice that the **TabStop** property declaration contains the property name and nothing else. The **TabStop** property is defined in the **TWinControl** class as a protected property, and this declaration makes the property published so that it can be modified using the Object Inspector. You can make an ancestor's property more visible, but you cannot make it less visible. Many standard properties and events are created as protected so that ancestor classes can select which ones to make available.

Unlike the Scroll Bar control you created in How-To 15.1, this control defines a new event called `OnCourseChanged`. From the component writer's perspective, an event is a property whose data type is a special kind of pointer called a `closure`, which stores not only the address of the member function but the address of the object as well. By convention, event names start with `On`, and the first parameter to the event procedure is the address of the component for whom the event is being called. Notice how the `OnCourseChanged` event is called in the `KeyDown` member function. Because events are defined as closures, they are not called using the `.*` or `->*` operators. The type of `OnCourseChanged` property is `TNotifyEvent`, which is defined in the file `CLASSES.HPP`. If you need an event with additional parameters, you can define your own event type using the definition of `TNotifyEvent` as a guide.

Virtual Functions and Message Handlers

The `TVOR` class defines a message map and a message handler for the `WM_ERASEBKGND` message. A message map was used for dragging and dropping files in How-To 6.12. Message maps for a component are created exactly the same way. The default behavior for the `WM_ERASEBKGND` message is to clear the control's contents by drawing a rectangle over the control. In the VOR control, this causes an unwanted flicker, so the control defines a do-nothing handler for this message.

The `TVOR` class handles key down, mouse down, and paint messages by overriding the `KeyDown`, `MouseDown`, and `Paint` virtual functions shown in step 8. Unless you want to completely bypass the default processing of a message, you are always better off overriding an existing virtual function than creating a message handler. Before calling the `Paint` function, the default handler for the `WM_PAINT` message sets up the control's canvas by allocating a device context. If you were to use a message map to intercept the `WM_PAINT` message, you would have to do this processing yourself. There is no virtual function for handling the `WM_ERASEBKGND` message, which is why it is included in the message map.

Drawing the Control

Most of the code for this control is involved with painting it. There are several interesting techniques used in drawing this control. The VOR control is drawn with a large number of individual elements, many of which rotate. When elements are rotated, the background needs to be erased, which results in flickering. To eliminate the flicker, the control is drawn to a bitmap; then the bitmap is copied to the control, so everything is updated at once. Try changing the `Paint` member function to

```
void __fastcall TVOR::Paint ()
{
  SetCoordinateSystem (*Canvas) ;
  DrawIndicator (*Canvas) ;
  DrawToFrom (*Canvas) ;
  DrawGlideSlope (*Canvas) ;
  DrawCourseDeviation (*Canvas) ;
}
```

and you will see the flickering.

Two problems complicate drawing the VOR. First of all, the control's **Height** and **Width** properties could be set to any value, so the individual graphics that make up the control need to be scaled. In addition, drawing the graphical elements around a circle is more complicated when the origin of the drawing coordinates is not at the center of the circle. The **SetCoordinateSystem** function uses the techniques demonstrated in How-To 5.9 to solve both of these problems. Rather than scaling each item individually, this function sets the map mode to isotropic, meaning both axes are scaled the same, and uses the **SetWindowExtEx** function to establish a fixed logical size for the window and to change the direction of the Y axis to go from bottom to top. The **SetWindowOrgEx** function moves the origin of the logical window to the center of the VOR.

In the **DrawCourseWheel** member function, the **CreateFontIndirect** API function creates the rotated fonts used to draw the headings around the rotating course selection wheel of the VOR. The **lfEscapement** field of the **LOGFONT** structure specifies, in tenths of a degree, the angle of rotation of the font. Once the font is created, the **SelectObject** API function is used to make the new font the one used by the canvas.

In a real VOR indicator, the deviation needle appears from behind the course selection wheel. The **TVOR** control uses a clipping region to keep the deviation needle behind the course selection wheel. The **DrawCourseDeviation** member function calls the **CreateEllipticRgn** API function to create a circular region within the course selection wheel. The trick here is that **CreateEllipticRgn** uses absolute coordinates rather than logical coordinates. The **SelectClipRgn** function keeps the canvas from drawing outside this circular region. Clipping regions are also used to draw the To/From indicator. Take a look at the function **DrawToFrom** in step 11. If you comment out this call to **SelectClipRgn**

```
// To clearly see how the To/From indicator is implemented, try⇐
commenting
// out the following SelectClipRgn call.
SelectClipRgn (canvas.Handle, region) ;
```

and then recompile and run the application, you will be able to see clearly how clipping regions work.

Comments

The title of this How-To is a bit deceptive because you never write a control completely from scratch. The VCL classes that are ancestors of the **TVOR** class handle many functions, notably the interface to the IDE and the ability to save properties to a file.

If you are writing a flight simulator and need a control like this, you will have to add some more features. The most obvious feature to add is a horizontal glide slope deviation bar. From the system side, you may need more standard properties and events in addition to the **TabStop** property. This VOR control also calculates the deviation from the **Course** setting and **Radial** properties. For a full-featured VOR display

you would probably need to have the application calculate the deviation. This is because VOR indicators are used to display information from navigation sources other than just VOR transmitters. Different navigation systems use different methods for displaying the course deviation. For example, when displaying the deviation from a `localizer` course used for landing, each dot represents a deviation of half a degree rather than two. Once you have made your improvements, you can create a bitmap for your component and install it in the Component Palette just as in How-To 15.2.

CHAPTER 16
THE POLISHED APPLICATION

16

THE POLISHED APPLICATION

How do I...

Sometimes, usually after my wife has been driving my car, I marvel at the intelligent design of the power seat controls on my current car. There is this little lever on the left of the driver's seat. If I want the seat to go forward, I push the lever towards the front of the car. If I want the seat to go back, I push the lever toward the back. Moving the seat up and down is equally natural. Whenever I think about it, which is not often, I offer silent thanks to the Chrysler engineer who took the time to improve a very small, seemingly insignificant thing.

By now you're probably wondering what power seat controls have to do with C++Builder™. Well, this chapter is about the small touches that add polish to an application. Just like the power seat control of a car is not something you notice every day, the How-To's in this chapter will never be central to the functionality of your application. They might make it more flexible, they might make it more compliant with Windows standards, but the application's user will almost never notice them. Even so, they are important.

16.1 Make a Professional-Style About Box

An application with a clean, well-designed About box just seems a little more professional. It is also a great place for the development team to brag about who they are. However, it does not look very professional to plaster developer names on the About box. Instead, most development teams build special features into their About box to display credits only after the user performs some specific set of actions that are never documented. This How-To will show you how to add such an About box to your applications.

16.2 Create and Display Separate Balloon and Status Bar Hints

Most applications include balloon help and status bar help displayed when the mouse cursor moves over certain controls. Balloon help is displayed in a small window that pops up near the control when the mouse cursor is left in place for more than a couple of seconds. Because balloon help pops up over the application, it usually contains a very brief description of what the control does. Status bar help, on the other hand, usually can be a little longer because there is more room in the status bar, and the help message doesn't cover up anything. C++Builder makes its balloon help support very obvious, but it does not advertise the fact that it also supports status bar help. This How-To will show you this nearly hidden feature of C++Builder.

16.3 Make a Form That Can Be Translated into Other Languages

What if you want to translate the English form captions, labels, and other text elements in your program into Spanish? Can you imagine changing each label, caption, and text element individually? What happens if you need to maintain the code for ten languages? Of course, there is a better way. This How-To will show you how you can move the various text elements used by your program into a resource file. This way, translation does not require poring over thousands of lines of C++ code.

16.4 Use the Registry to Store Application Configuration Information

In the old days of Windows 3.1 programming, application configuration information was stored in INI files. There were a variety of problems with INI files. First of all, it was far too tempting for an application to store its configuration data in the main WIN.INI file. The result was that this main INI file threatened to reach

encyclopedic length. Of course, applications could (and did) have their very own INI files instead. Such an INI file could be just about anywhere, and, after a while, there would be hundreds scattered around the file system of a computer. It was far too easy for the user to delete them, edit them, and generally mess them up in ways that could break an application.

These days, most applications store their configuration data in the system registry. Although it is still possible to use INI files, professional, well-behaved applications stick to the registry. This How-To will show you how easy it is to use the registry from C++Builder.

16.5 Give the User the Ability to Customize Screen Labels

Sometimes, especially in database applications, users would like to customize screen labels. For example, one customer might like to call a particular field "Order Number" while another customer might want to call the same field "Requisition Number." This How-To will show you a slick way to add this capability to your C++Builder program with a minimal amount of effort.

COMPLEXITY
INTERMEDIATE

16.1 How do I...
Make a professional-style About box?

Problem

I want to add an About box to my application. Obviously it has to have all the basic stuff, but I really want it to have an Easter Egg in it. You know, hidden credits that appear only if the user double-clicks a certain spot twice within five seconds or something like that. How can I do this in C++Builder?

Technique

Besides showing you how to lay out a professional-looking About box, this How-To demonstrates how a Timer control can be used to add special effects to a form. In this case, the special effect is a rolling credits display.

Steps

Run **ABOUT.EXE**. Select Help|About from the menu and a standard-looking About box appears as shown in Figure 16-1. Double-click on the big picture once, and then again within five seconds. Credits will start popping up in the lower section of the About box as shown in Figure 16-2.

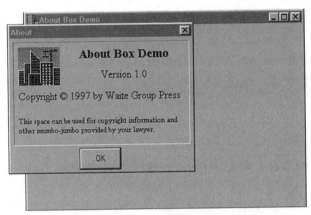

Figure 16-1 Basic About box display of ABOUT.EXE

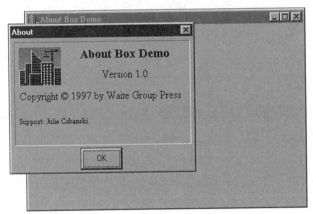

Figure 16-2 ABOUT displaying the credits

1. Create a new application. Save the form as **ABOUTMAIN** and the project as **ABOUT.MAK**.

2. Add the components, and set their properties as shown in Table 16-1.

Table 16-1 Components, properties, and settings of ABOUTMAIN form

COMPONENT	PROPERTY	SETTING
TForm	Caption	About Box Demo
TMainMenu		

3. Add a Help menu to the main menu component. Under Help, add a menu item labeled "About…".

4. Add a new form to the application. Save the unit as **ABOUTBOX.CPP**.

5. Add the components, and set their properties as shown in Table 16-2. Lay out the components as shown in Figure 16-1.

Table 16-2 Components, properties, and settings of the About box form

COMPONENT	PROPERTY	SETTING
TForm	Name	fAbout
	BorderIcons	[biSystemMenu]
	BorderStyle	bsDialog
	Caption	About
TPanel	BevelOuter	bvLowered
	Caption	None
	Position	poScreenCenter
TImage (On TPanel)	Image	Pick a reasonable image
	Stretch	True
TLabel (On TPanel)	Alignment	taCenter
	AutoSize	False
	Caption	About Box Demo
	Font	Times New Roman 14 Bold
TLabel (On TPanel)	Alignment	taCenter
	AutoSize	False
	Caption	Version 1.0
	Font	Times New Roman 12
TLabel (On TPanel)	Caption	Copyright © 1997 by Waite Group Press
	Font	Times New Roman 12
TLabel (On TPanel)	Name	lCredits
	AutoSize	False
	Caption	As shown in Figure 16-1
	Font	Times New Roman 8
	WordWrap	True
TButton	Name	bOK
	Caption	OK
	Default	True
TTimer	Enabled	False
	Interval	5000

6. Switch to **ABOUTMAIN.CPP**. Near the top of the file, add the **#include** statement that lets the main form access the About box form.

```
#include "aboutmain.h"
#include "aboutbox.h"
```

7. Click on the Help|About menu option, and add the code that modally displays the About box.

```
void __fastcall TForm1::About1Click(TObject *Sender)
{
  //Display About box in a modal fashion (does not return until about is⇐
closed)
  fAbout->ShowModal();
}
```

8. Switch to **ABOUTBOX.H**. Add the following private declarations to TfAbout:

```
private:// User declarations
  bool RollCredits;
  TStringList *Credits;
  String HoldCaption;
  int NextCreditString;

  void __fastcall DisplayCredits(void);
```

9. Open the Object Inspector for **fAbout1**. Double-click the **OnCreate** event, and add the code that initializes the About box's hidden credits feature.

```
void __fastcall TfAbout::FormCreate(TObject *Sender)
{
  //Create a string list and fill it with credits
  Credits = new TStringList;
  Credits->Add("The hard-working team behind the product");
  Credits->Add("Programming: Tom Cabanski");
  Credits->Add("Support: Julie Cabanski");
  Credits->Add("Editing: Stephanie Wall");
  Credits->Add("More credits here!!!!");
  //Copy the text that normally appears in the label
  //into a working variable
  HoldCaption = lCredits->Caption;
}
```

10. Double-click the **OnClose** event. Add the code that cleans up the credit's TStringList just before the application ends.

```
void __fastcall TfAbout::FormDestroy(TObject *Sender)
{
  //Destroy the credits string list
  Credits->Free();
}
```

11. Double-click the OnShow event, and add the code that executes each time the About box is displayed from the main application.

```
//About box is being popped up
void __fastcall TfAbout::FormShow(TObject *Sender)
{
  //Don't roll the credits
  RollCredits = FALSE;
  //Label should contain lawyer stuff
  lCredits->Caption = HoldCaption;
}
```

12. Double-click the OnHide event, and add the code that shuts off the rolling credits display before the About box is closed.

```
//Form is being hidden
void __fastcall TfAbout::FormHide(TObject *Sender)
{
  //Shut off the timer
  Timer1->Enabled = FALSE;
}
```

13. Open the Object Inspector for the image control, Image1. Double-click the OnDblClick event, and add the code that starts and stops the credits display.

```
//User double-clicked on picture
void __fastcall TfAbout::Image1DblClick(TObject *Sender)
{
  //If the timer is not running this is the first double-click
  if (!Timer1->Enabled)
  {
    //Start the timer
    Timer1->Enabled = TRUE;
    //exit this function
    return;
  }
  //Otherwise, timer is running
  else
  {
    //If credits are rolling shut them off
    //If credits are not rolling the user has just double-clicked twice
    //within five seconds so prepare to start them
    RollCredits = !RollCredits;
  }

  //If credits are supposed to roll
  if (RollCredits)
  {
    //Start at the first line of credits
    NextCreditString = 0;
    //Display line of credits
    DisplayCredits();
```

continued on next page

continued from previous page

```
  }
  //Otherwise, credits are not supposed to roll
  else
  {
    //Reset the label caption to the legalese
    lCredits->Caption = HoldCaption;
    //Shut off the timer
    Timer1->Enabled = FALSE;
  }
}
```

14. Double-click the timer control, and add the code that executes every five seconds when the timer is enabled.

```
//Timer has counted down its interval (5 seconds as originally built)
void __fastcall TfAbout::Timer1Timer(TObject *Sender)
{
  //If the credits are not rolling
  if (!RollCredits)
    //Shut off the timer. The user did not double-click in time
    Timer1->Enabled = FALSE;
  //Otherwise
  else
    //Display the next line of credits
    DisplayCredits();
}
```

15. At the bottom of the file, add the function that actually displays the next credits line in the About box.

```
void __fastcall TfAbout::DisplayCredits(void)
{
  //Display the next line of credits
  lCredits->Caption = Credits->Strings[NextCreditString];
  //Increment the line number
  NextCreditString++;
  //If it's past the last item in the list (TStringList is zero based!)
  if (NextCreditString == Credits->Count)
    //Wrap around to the beginning
    NextCreditString = 0;
}
```

16. Double-click the OK button. Add the code that closes the About box form and returns control to the main form.

```
void __fastcall TfAbout::bOKClick(TObject *Sender)
{
  //Close the dialog box
  Close();
}
```

17. Compile and run the application.

How It Works

The credit lines are stored in a **TStringList** created in the **FormCreate** function you added in step 9. After the string list is created, the credit lines are added to the list by calling **TStringList**'s **Add** method. The legalese in the label control that will be used to display the credits is then copied to **HoldCaption** so it can be restored after the credits are stopped. **FormDestroy** (step 10) only exists to destroy the **TStringList** just before the About box is destroyed.

The **FormShow** method (step 11) is executed each time the About box form is displayed by the main application. Because the About form is not destroyed after each time it is displayed, **FormShow** has to make sure that if the credits were being displayed the last time, the About box is returned to its default state. This is accomplished by setting **RollCredits** to **false**, and putting the legalese back into the **Caption** property of **LCredits**. The **FormHide** function (step 12) is the flip side of **FormShow**. It makes sure to shut off the timer so the About box doesn't waste time monitoring or updating the screen when it is not visible.

Image1DblClick (step 12) performs three functions. When the About box is first displayed, it waits for the user to double-click on the picture. When the user does so, it starts the Timer control. If the user double-clicks again within five seconds, the Timer control will still be running, and **Image1DblClick** will start the credits. Once the credits are running, a double-click on the picture box will make **Image1DblClick** shut off the credits.

Image1DblClick starts by checking the **Enabled** property of the Timer control. If **Enabled** is **false**, the timer is not running, so the timer is started and the function returns. If the timer is running, the state of **RollCredits** is reversed—if credits are rolling, **RollCredits** is changed to **false**, and if credits are not rolling, **RollCredits** is changed to **true**. If **RollCredits** is **true**, **NextCreditString** is set to zero so the credits display will start with the first line, and **DisplayCredits** is called to display the first line of credits. At this point, the Timer control takes over the responsibility of updating the credits display every five seconds. If, on the other hand, **RollCredits** is **false**, the legalese is put back in the label and the timer is stopped.

The **Timer1Timer** function (step 14) also has multiple jobs. If credits are not rolling, it is used by **Image1DblClick** to test whether the user double-clicks twice within five seconds. It does this by disabling the Timer control each time it is triggered when **RollCredits** is **false**. Once credits are rolling, it calls **DisplayCredits** every five seconds to change the credits display.

DisplayCredits (step 15) moves the **TStringList** item located at position **NextCreditString** to the caption of the Credits label. It then increments **NextCreditString**. If the resulting **NextCreditString** index is equal to the count of items in the **TStringList**, it is rolled back to zero so it refers to the first item in the list again. This makes sense, because the **Strings** array property of **TStringList** is zero-based, the first list item's index is zero, and the last item's index is **Count - 1**.

Comments

I must admit that the credits display in this How-To is pretty boring. Nevertheless, the techniques shown here can easily be used to add something fancier and a lot more exciting to your applications. Just be careful. If you work for a big corporation, the biggest challenge may be making sure that no one discovers your Easter Egg before the application is in production!

COMPLEXITY
BEGINNING

16.2 How do I...
Create and display separate balloon and status bar hints?

Problem

I've been using C++Builder for a little while, and I already know how to use the `Hint` property of controls to create balloon help. However, I've noticed that many applications also use the status bar to display a longer help message when the mouse cursor moves over a control. How can I add this feature to my C++Builder application?

Technique

Believe it or not, C++Builder includes support for adding a long hint to the status line. However, the event handlers and properties used to implement status bar hints are not immediately apparent. This How-To will show you the trick.

Steps

Run `HINT.EXE`. Move the mouse cursor over any of the controls and leave it there. You will see a balloon hint and a longer status bar hint as shown in Figure 16-3.

1. Create a new project. Save the form as `HINTMAIN.CPP` and the project as `HINT.MAK`.

2. Add the components, and set their properties as shown in Table 16-3. Lay out the controls as shown in Figure 16-3.

Table 16-3 Components, properties, and settings for the `Hint` project

COMPONENT	PROPERTY	SETTING
TForm	Caption	Hint
TStatusBar	SimplePanel	True
TLabel	Alignment	taRightJustify

COMPONENT	PROPERTY	SETTING
	Caption	Invoice:
TEdit	Hint	Invoice Number|Make sure you do not use the PO number!
	ShowHint	True
	Text	None
TLabel	Alignment	taRightJustify
	Caption	Inv Date:
TEdit	Hint	Date of Invoice|Their invoice date (not date received)
	ShowHint	True
	Text	None
TLabel	Alignment	taRightJustify
	Caption	Pay Date:
TEdit	Hint	Date to pay|Use due date unless there is a discount
	ShowHint	True
	Text	None
TLabel	Alignment	taRightJustify
	Caption	Amount:
TEdit	Hint	Invoice amount|Amount of Invoice
	ShowHint	True
	Text	None

3. Switch to HINTMAIN.H. Add the following public declarations to TForm1:

```
public:// User declarations
   __fastcall TForm1(TComponent* Owner);
 void __fastcall DoHint(TObject *Sender);
```

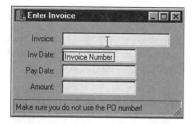

Figure 16-3 HINT.EXE showing
a balloon hint and a status
bar hint

4. Open the Object Inspector for **Form1**. Double-click on the **OnCreate** event, and add the code that assigns the event handling function that will update the status bar.

```
void __fastcall TForm1::FormCreate(TObject *Sender)
{
  //Set the event handler
  Application->OnHint = DoHint;
}
```

5. At the bottom of the file, add the function that actually updates the status bar.

```
//Application wants to display hint
void __fastcall TForm1::DoHint(TObject *Sender)
{
  //Put the current long hint in the status bar
  StatusBar1->SimpleText = Application->Hint;
}
```

6. Compile and run the application.

How It Works

The first part of the secret is that you can enter two help hint strings into the **Hint** property of any control by separating them with a | character. The first string is the one that appears in balloon help if the **ShowHint** property of the control, or its owner, is set to **true**. The second string is the status bar hint that will get assigned to the application's **Hint** property when the mouse moves over a control. The application's **Hint** property will be set regardless of how **ShowHint** is set, and, if no second string is specified in the **Hint** property, the first string will be used instead. Next, you have to point the application's **OnHint** event handler to a standard event-handling function like this How-To's **DoHint** function. From there on, everything is automatic.

Comments

Balloon help and status bar help are great additions to almost any application. C++Builder makes the programming so simple that the hardest part is dreaming up the hint messages for the various controls in the first place.

COMPLEXITY

INTERMEDIATE

16.3 How do I...
Make a form that can be translated into other languages?

Problem

I work for a company that has a distribution center in Mexico as well as several in the United States and Canada. I'm building an application right now that will be used in every distribution center. How can I make it easy to translate the application into Spanish?

Technique

This How-To will show you how to store the various text elements used by a form in a string resource. When it comes time to translate the application to another language, you simply translate the strings in the resource file and recompile the application.

Steps

Run **STRINGRESOURCE.EXE**, and you will see a screen display like that shown in Figure 16-4. Notice that the display of the form looks different than it does in the Form Designer. This is because the form and label captions were loaded from a string list stored in a resource file. The resource file included with this How-To has the strings in English, but it just as easily could contain strings in Spanish.

1. Create a new project. Save the form as **STRINGRESOURCEMAIN.CPP** and the project as **STRINGRESOURCE.MAK**.

2. Add the components and set their properties as shown in Table 16-4. Lay out the components as shown in Figure 16-4. The Label controls on your form, and the form itself, will have different captions than those shown in Figure 16-4.

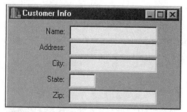

Figure 16-4 Screen display of
STRINGRESOURCE.EXE

Table 16-4 Components, properties, and settings for the
STRINGRESOURCE project

COMPONENT	PROPERTY	SETTING
TLabel	Align	taLeftJustify
	Caption	Label1
TEdit	Text	None
TLabel	Align	taLeftJustify
	Caption	Label2
TEdit	Text	None
TLabel	Align	taLeftJustify
	Caption	Label3
TEdit	Text	None
TLabel	Align	taLeftJustify
	Caption	Label4
TEdit	Text	None
TLabel	Align	taLeftJustify
	Caption	Label5
TEdit	Text	None

3. Select File|New from the C++Builder menu. In the New tab of the resulting dialog box, double-click on the text file icon. Type the following into the new document window:

```
STRINGTABLE
{
  1, "Customer Info"
  2, "Name:"
  3, "Address:"
  4, "City:"
  5, "State:"
  6, "Zip:"
}
```

4. Save the file as STRINGS.RC.

5. Open a DOS Window. Change to the directory that contains STRINGS.RC. Type the command to compile the resource script into a resource file. This example assumes that Borland's resource compiler, BRCC32.EXE (found in C++Builder's BIN directory), is in the path.

```
BRCC32.EXE STRINGS.RC
```

6. Close the resource script file. Near the top of STRINGRESOURCEMAIN, add the command that tells C++Builder to link the compiled string resource to the application.

```
#pragma resource "*.dfm"
#pragma resource "strings.res"
TForm1 *Form1;
```

7. Open the Object Inspector for **Form1**. Double-click on the **OnCreate** event, and add the code that loads the strings from the string resource into the various controls on the form.

```
void __fastcall TForm1::FormCreate(TObject *Sender)
{
  char Buffer[80];
  int BufferLen = 80;

  //Load a string from the resource file
  LoadString((void *)HInstance, 1, Buffer, BufferLen);
  //Assign it to the caption property of the control (form in this case)
  Form1->Caption = Buffer;
  //And so on...
  LoadString((void *)HInstance, 2, Buffer, BufferLen);
  Label1->Caption = Buffer;
  LoadString((void *)HInstance, 3, Buffer, BufferLen);
  Label2->Caption = Buffer;
  LoadString((void *)HInstance, 4, Buffer, BufferLen);
  Label3->Caption = Buffer;
  LoadString((void *)HInstance, 5, Buffer, BufferLen);
  Label4->Caption = Buffer;
  LoadString((void *)HInstance, 6, Buffer, BufferLen);
  Label5->Caption = Buffer;
}
```

8. Compile and run the application.

How It Works

The resource script you created in step 3 contains a typical string resource. As you can see, a string resource is simply a list of strings identified by number. In a real-world application that uses more than a handful of strings, you would use an application header file that looks something like the following to assign meaningful names to the numeric string resource identifiers.

```
#define FORM_CAPTION 1
#define NAME_LABEL 2

#define ZIP_LABEL 6
```

The **FormCreate** function (step 7) loads the strings from the resource file that was linked to the application because of the pragma resource statement you added in step 6. The **LoadString** Windows API function is passed the instance handle of the application, which C++Builder stores in the **HInstance** variable, the ID number of the desired string, a buffer to store the string in, and the length of the buffer. The buffer is then assigned to the appropriate control.

Comments

Building applications that can be translated quickly into other languages is not particularly difficult. For example, to translate the form from this How-To into Spanish you would translate the strings in the **STRING.RC** file, recompile the resource file with **BRCC32.EXE**, and rebuild the project by selecting Build All from the Project menu.

COMPLEXITY
BEGINNING

16.4 How do I...
Use the registry to store application configuration information?

Problem

I've written a single form application. Every time the application runs, the user sizes it and positions it on the screen. I know it would be fairly easy to save the position and size to an INI file so that, when the application is started again, it will remember the user's preferences, but I'd really like to be Windows 95 friendly and write the preferences to the registry instead. How do I do this in C++Builder?

Technique

This How-To shows you how to use the **TRegistry** class to make storing and retrieving preferences from the registry a snap. You'll also learn about the right place to put your application's registry data.

Steps

Run **REMEMBER.EXE**. Change the size and location of the window, and close the application. When you run it again, it will go back to the size and position it was when you closed it last.

1. Create a new application. Save the form as **REMEMBERMAIN.CPP** and the project as **REMEMBER.MAK**.

2. Change the caption of the form to "Remember...".

3. Switch to **REMEMBERMAIN.H**. Add the following header so the application can use the **TRegistry** object:

```
#include <vcl\Forms.hpp>
#include <vcl\Registry.hpp>
//-------------------------------------------------------------------
```

4. Add the following declaration to the private section of `TForm1`:

```
private:// User declarations
  TRegistry *Registry;
```

5. Open the Object Inspector for `Form1`. Double-click the `OnShow` event, and add the code that reads the form's size and position from the registry.

```
void __fastcall TForm1::FormShow(TObject *Sender)
{
  int iLeft, iTop, iHeight, iWidth;

  //Create a new registry object
  Registry = new TRegistry;
  //Root key is HKEY_LOCAL_MACHINE
  Registry->RootKey = HKEY_LOCAL_MACHINE;
  //Open the registry key (create it if it does not exist)
  Registry->OpenKey("SOFTWARE\\MyCompany\\Remember", TRUE);
  //Try block, if anything goes wrong, control will be transferred
  //to the catch(...)
  try
  {
    //Get the registry entries
    iLeft = Registry->ReadInteger("Left");
    iTop = Registry->ReadInteger("Top");
    iHeight = Registry->ReadInteger("Height");
    iWidth = Registry->ReadInteger("Width");

    //Execution gets this far only if the registry keys exist
    //Position and size the for
    Left = iLeft;
    Top = iTop;
    Height = iHeight;
    Width = iWidth;
  }
  //Catch errors and ignore them
  //usual case is that the registry did not exist on first run
  catch (...)
  {
  }
}
```

6. Double-click the `OnClose` event, and add the code that saves the form's size and position to the registry.

```
void __fastcall TForm1::FormClose(TObject *Sender, TCloseAction &Action)
{
  //Write the current form position and size to the registry
  Registry->WriteInteger("Left", Left);
  Registry->WriteInteger("Top", Top);
  Registry->WriteInteger("Height", Height);
  Registry->WriteInteger("Width", Width);
  //Free the registry object
  Registry->Free();
}
```

7. Compile and run the application. If the application is run for the first time from within the C++Builder environment, the debugger will stop on the exception caused when the application cannot find anything in the registry. If this happens, click on the OK button, and, then, press F9 to continue running the program. Note that the error message will not appear if the program is run outside the C++Builder environment.

How It Works

Before getting into the details of what this program does, it is important to understand how the registry looks. Start by running your system registry editor. On Windows 95, it is called **REGEDIT.EXE**. On Windows NT, it is called **REGEDT32.EXE**. Figure 16-5 shows the Windows 95 registry editor.

As you can see, the system registry is composed of several trees. There are some significant differences between Windows 95 and Windows NT, but the tree we're interested in, **HKEY_LOCAL_MACHINE**, is the same on both operating systems.

Double-click on **HKEY_LOCAL_MACHINE** in your registry editor. This registry tree holds information that applies to the machine, regardless of who is logged on. The key this application is interested in, called **SOFTWARE**, holds configuration information about the applications on the computer. Go ahead and open the **SOFTWARE** key by double-clicking on it. You should notice that there's an entry for **MyCompany**.

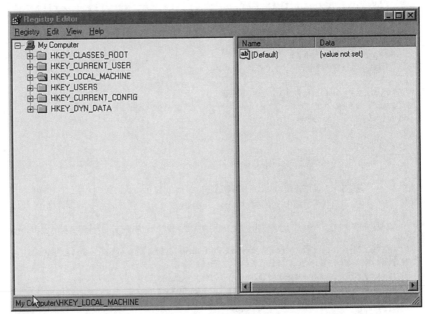

Figure 16-5 Windows 95 Registry Editor

Open it and then open the `Remember` key underneath it. You should now see the configuration items that `REMEMBER.EXE` put there (see Figure 16-6).

The Code

`FormShow` (step 5) attempts to read the configuration information from the registry. If the attempt is successful, it changes the `Left`, `Top`, `Height`, and `Width` properties of the form to match the values retrieved from the registry. To do this, it first constructs a `TRegistry` object, and sets the `RootKey` property to `HKEY_LOCAL_MACHINE`. It then opens the actual registry key that holds this application's information by passing the registry key name to `TRegistry`'s `OpenKey` method. `true` is passed in the second parameter of `OpenKey` to tell the object that it should create the registry key if it does not exist.

The rest of `FormShow`'s registry operations are enclosed in a `try` block. If an error occurs inside the `try`, control is transferred to an empty `catch` block which means that the error is ignored. The reason for this is simple. If this is the first run of `MEMORY.EXE` on this computer, the configuration information will not exist, and the registry calls will fail. There's no need to report these errors to the user because they are completely normal.

`FormClose` (step 6) does the opposite of `FormShow`. It writes the form's `Left`, `Top`, `Height`, and `Width` properties to the registry. The next time the application runs, the configuration will be in the registry, and `FormShow` will be able to position and size the form properly.

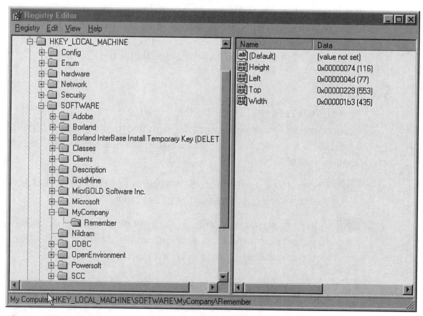

Figure 16-6 Registry entries for `REMEMBER.EXE`

Comments

You may wonder why the application reads the registry information in the `OnShow` event handler instead of the `OnCreate` event handler. Actually, there is a very good reason. If you assign the `Left`, `Top`, `Width`, and `Height` properties of a form in its `OnCreate` event handler, they will be overridden by the default values from C++Builder. By moving the registry code to the `OnShow` event handler, it is possible to read the registry and adjust the form in the same function.

COMPLEXITY
INTERMEDIATE

16.5 How do I...
Give the user the ability to customize screen labels?

I'm currently working on an order processing application that will be sold to a variety of customers. In talking to user groups, I've discovered that people would really like the ability to customize the application's screen labels to match the terminology in their office. How can I add this capability to my C++Builder application?

Technique

By now, you're probably pretty familiar with C++Builder Edit boxes. What you may not know is that, by setting a few properties, an Edit control can be made to look exactly like a Label control. Add a few event handlers, some registry code, and you've got an application that lets users customize the labels right on the screen by just double-clicking on the label and making their changes.

Steps

Run `CUSTOMIZELABEL.EXE`. Double-click the first label, and it will change into an Edit control as shown in Figure 16-7. Change the label and press ENTER. Close the application and start it again. You'll notice that the label you changed has the new caption you provided.

1. Create a new application. Save the form as `CUSTOMIZELABELMAIN.CPP` and the project as `CUSTOMIZELABEL.MAK`.

2. Add the components, and set their properties as shown in Table 16-5. Arrange the components as shown in Figure 16-7. It doesn't matter where you put the `eLabelEdit` edit box because it is invisible.

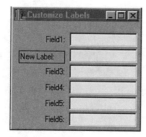

Figure 16-7
CUSTOMIZELABEL with
a label selected for
editing

Table 16-5 Components, properties, and settings for CUSTOMIZELABEL
project

COMPONENT	PROPERTY	SETTING
TForm	Caption	Customize Labels
TLabel	Alignment	taRightJustify
	AutoSize	False
	Caption	Field1:
TLabel	Alignment	taRightJustify
	AutoSize	False
	Caption	Field2:
TLabel	Alignment	taRightJustify
	AutoSize	False
	Caption	Field3:
TLabel	Alignment	taRightJustify
	AutoSize	False
	Caption	Field4:
TLabel	Alignment	taRightJustify
	AutoSize	False
	Caption	Field5:
TLabel	Alignment	taRightJustify
	AutoSize	False
	Caption	Field6:
TEdit (Create 6)	Text	None

continued on next page

continued from previous page

COMPONENT	PROPERTY	SETTING
TEdit	Name	eLabelEdit
	TabStop	False
	Ctl3D	False
	ParentColor	True
	TabOrder	0
	Visible	False

3. Switch to CUSTOMIZELABELMAIN.H. Add the header file that lets this application use the TRegistry object.

```
#include <vcl\Menus.hpp>
#include <vcl\registry.hpp>
//----------------------------------------------------------------------
```

4. Add the following declarations to the private section of TForm1:

```
private:// User declarations
  TLabel *lEditing;
  TRegistry *Registry;
```

5. Open the Object Inspector for Form1. Double-click the OnCreate event, and add the code that initializes the screen display.

```
void __fastcall TForm1::FormCreate(TObject *Sender)
{
  String ClassName, LabelCaption;
  int x;
  TLabel *Label;

  //Loop through the components on the form
  for (x = 0; x < ComponentCount; x++)
  {
    //Get the class name
    ClassName = Components[x]->ClassName();
    //If the class is TLabel
    if (ClassName == "TLabel")
      //Assign the double-click method
      ((TLabel *)(Components[x]))->OnDblClick = LabelDblClick;
  }

  //Create a new registry object
  Registry = new TRegistry;
  //Set the root key to HKEY_LOCAL_MACHINE
  Registry->RootKey = HKEY_LOCAL_MACHINE;
  //Open the registry key (create it if it does not exist)
  Registry->OpenKey("SOFTWARE\\MyCompany\\CustomizeLabels", TRUE);
  //Ignore errors
  try
```

```
  {
    //Loop through the components
    for (x = 0; x < ComponentCount; x++)
    {
      //Get the class name
      ClassName = Components[x]->ClassName();
      //If the class name is TLabel
      if (ClassName == "TLabel")
      {
        //Assign the pointer to a TLabel * for code clarity
        Label = (TLabel *)Components[x];
        //Attempt to get the label's caption from the registry
        //Registry variable name is label's name
        LabelCaption = Registry->ReadString(Label->Name);
        //Work around bug
        //ReadString does not throw error when string variable does not⇐
exist
        if (LabelCaption != "")
          Label->Caption = LabelCaption;
      }
    }
  }
  //Ignore errors
  catch (...)
  {
  }
}
```

6. Double click the OnClose event. Add the code that saves the label captions to the registry.

```
void __fastcall TForm1::FormClose(TObject *Sender, TCloseAction &Action)
{
  String ClassName;
  int x;
  TLabel *Label;

  //Read through the components
  for (x = 0; x < ComponentCount; x++)
  {
    //Get the class name
    ClassName = Components[x]->ClassName();
    //If the class name is TLabel
    if (ClassName == "TLabel")
    {
      //Put the pointer in a TLabel * to clarify rest of code
      Label = (TLabel *)Components[x];
      //Write the label's caption to the registry
      Registry->WriteString(Label->Name, Label->Caption);
    }
  }

  //Free the registry object
  Registry->Free();
}
```

7. Open the Object Inspector for the first label control. In the OnDblClick event handler type, do not double-click, "LabelDblClick" and press ENTER. Add the code that starts the label editor.

```
//User wants to edit a label
void __fastcall TForm1::LabelDblClick(TObject *Sender)
{
  //if the lEditing control is assigned
  if (lEditing)
    //Make it visible again in case it was editing
    //This is to account for fact that the label edit control
    //does not see an OnExit event when the user
    //double-clicks on a label
    lEditing->Visible = TRUE;

  //Assign the label control that raised this event to lEditing
  lEditing = (TLabel *)Sender;

  //Move the edit control over the label
  eLabelEdit->Left = lEditing->Left;
  eLabelEdit->Top = lEditing->Top;
  eLabelEdit->Width = lEditing->Width;
  eLabelEdit->Height = lEditing->Height;
  //Match the font of the label
  eLabelEdit->Font = lEditing->Font;
  //Put the label's caption in the edit control
  eLabelEdit->Text = lEditing->Caption;
  //Make the edit control visible
  eLabelEdit->Visible = TRUE;
  //Move focus to the edit control
  eLabelEdit->SetFocus();
  //Select the edit control's text
  eLabelEdit->SelectAll();
  //Make the label invisible
  lEditing->Visible = FALSE;
}
```

8. Open the Object Inspector for the eLabelEdit control. Double-click the OnExit event, and add the code that cancels the edit.

```
//User moved off edit control
//Cancel the edit
void __fastcall TForm1::eLabelEditExit(TObject *Sender)
{
  //Make the label visible
  lEditing->Visible = TRUE;
  //Make the edit control invisible
  eLabelEdit->Visible = FALSE;
}
```

9. Double-click the OnKeyPress event, and add the code that saves the results of the edit if the user presses ENTER.

```
//User pressed a key in the edit control
void __fastcall TForm1::eLabelEditKeyPress(TObject *Sender, char &Key)
{
  //If user pressed ENTER (wants to save the new label)
  if (Key == 13)
  {
    //If the edit box text is blank, return because we don't want blank⇐
labels
    if (eLabelEdit->Text == "")
      return;

    //Change the label's caption to the new version from the edit box
    lEditing->Caption = eLabelEdit->Text;
    //Make the edit box invisible
    eLabelEdit->Visible = FALSE;
    //Make the label visible
    lEditing->Visible = TRUE;
  }
}
```

10. Compile and run the application.

How It Works

The **FormCreate** function (step 5) starts by looping through all the components on the form and making the **LabelDblClick** function the **OnDblClick** event handler for all the labels on the form. The registry is then opened, and the application attempts to read the label captions from the registry. Just as in How-To 16.4, the registry code is enclosed inside a **try** block because **ReadString** is supposed to throw an exception when the data does not exist, which will definitely be the case the first time this program runs. Unfortunately, the version of C++Builder I have does not throw an exception. Therefore, just to be safe, **FormCreate** tests the string returned from the registry, and, if it is an empty string, it does not assign it to the label's caption.

FormClose (step 6) is responsible for writing the label's captions to the registry so they can be restored the next time the program runs. Once again, the application loops through the form's components array looking for **TLabel** controls. For each label, the **WriteString** method of **TRegistry** is called to write the string to the registry. Finally, when all the data is saved in the registry, the registry object is freed and the program ends.

The Label Editor

Conceptually, the label editor is very simple. When the user double-clicks on a label control, the invisible **eLabelEdit** control is moved over the label to be edited. The size and font attributes of the label are also copied to the Edit control. The label is then hidden and the Edit box is made visible so the user can perform an edit. If the user presses ENTER, the label's caption is changed, the Edit control is hidden, and the Label control is made visible again. If the user leaves the Edit box without press-

ing (ENTER),the edit is canceled by hiding the Edit control and showing the Label control without updating the label's caption.

In practice, the label editor is just a little tricky. When the user double-clicks on a label, **LabelDblClick** is called (step 7). First, it checks the **lEditing** member variable to see whether some other label may be in the process of editing. If so, the Label control referred to by **lEditing** is made visible. This is necessary because double-clicking on a label does not trigger the **OnExit** event of the Edit box which is used to cancel an ongoing edit.

Once any ongoing edit is canceled, **LabelDblClick** gets down to business. First, the Label box the user double-clicked on is assigned to **lEditing**. As you've seen in previous How-To's, the object pointer is cast to a **TLabel** pointer so the additional properties and methods of **TLabel** will be accessible. Next, various properties of the label are copied to the Edit box. After the properties are copied, the Edit control is made visible, focus is shifted to the Edit control, the Edit box text is selected, and the Label control is made invisible. At this point, the user is ready to start making changes.

The **eLabelExit** function (step 8) is the **OnExit** event handler for the label Edit box. Its job is to cancel the edit when the user tabs or clicks the mouse outside the Edit box. It does this by simply making the Edit control invisible and the Label control visible. This works because the label's caption is never changed until the user presses (ENTER).

The **eLabelKeyPress** function (step 9) actually changes the label's caption. It checks the **Key** parameter and takes no action until the (ENTER), decimal ASCII code 13, is pressed. When (ENTER) is pressed, it first checks to see whether the Edit box text is a blank string. If the text is blank, the function immediately returns, effectively rejecting the (ENTER) keystroke. If there is a string in the Edit box, it is assigned to the label's caption property, the Edit control is hidden, and the Label control is made visible. The edit is now complete, and the user can see the new label.

Comments

Never underestimate the power of terminology. If a particular office likes to call order numbers requisition numbers, they are going to find reasons not to like an application that forces them to constantly remember, when it says order number, they should think requisition number. Obviously, if all the people who use your application use the same terminology, you just have to make sure to set up the forms properly in the first place. However, if different users use different terminology, the techniques shown in this How-To will help you make all your users very happy.

CHAPTER 17
TIPS AND TRICKS

17

TIPS AND TRICKS

How do I...

As you use C++Builder™, you will come across various tricks that make development easier. The first four How-To's demonstrate techniques you probably won't find in any manual or help file and the last two show how to use documented features of C++Builder.

17.1 Evaluate a Numerical Expression

There are many free tools available through the Internet that generate C or C++ code which can be used with C++Builder. This How-To is a brief introduction to FLEX and BISON, tools that generate code for parsing text.

17.2 Create a Control Array like in Visual Basic

C++Builder does not have a design time control array like Visual Basic does. This How-To demonstrates how to implement the functionality of a control array in C++Builder.

17.3 Edit a Control as Text

In some situations it is easier to edit controls in a text format rather than using the Object Inspector. In this How-To you will learn how to use the clipboard to edit controls using a text editor.

17.4 View the Contents of a .DFM File

If something unexpected makes your form file unusable within the C++Builder IDE, all hope is not lost. This How-To shows you how to use the CONVERT utility to create a text version of the form file so that you can correct the problem.

17.5 Create a DLL

C++Builder allows you to create DLLs so that your code can be shared among several executables even if they are written with another development tool.

17.6 Use Modules Written in Delphi

If you have already been using Delphi, you probably will want to preserve your Delphi code and forms and even continue to do development with Delphi. A huge array of VCL controls written in Delphi are available as well. C++Builder allows you to use existing Delphi code in C++Builder projects. No conversion is necessary.

COMPLEXITY
ADVANCED

17.1 How do I...
Evaluate a numerical expression?

Problem

In my application the user needs to be able to enter a complex numerical expression. The application needs to evaluate the expression according to the standard rules of operator precedence. How can I do this using C++Builder?

Technique

One of the easiest ways to implement the parsing of text is to use the UNIX tools LEX and YACC. Many variants of these tools exist and have been ported to the PC. This example uses FLEX and BISON, which are LEX and YACC clones from the Free Software Foundation. These tools are included on the CD-ROM that comes with this book.

Steps

Run the program **EXPRESSION.EXE** shown in Figure 17-1. Enter a numerical expression into the memo control on the application's main form. The expression can contain floating point values using scientific notation, the +, -, *, and / operators, and parentheses to override the traditional precedence of operators. White space

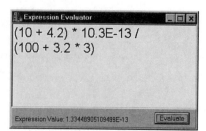

Figure 17-1 Evaluating a numerical expression

in the expression is ignored. Click on the Evaluate button to evaluate the expression. Try comparing the results to the value returned using a calculator.

1. Create a directory (`C:\BISON`) for installing the BISON program on the accompanying CD-ROM. Copy all the BISON files from the CD-ROM to the directory you created.

2. Create another directory (`C:\FLEX`) for installing the FLEX program on the accompanying CD-ROM. Copy all the FLEX files from the CD-ROM to the directory you created.

3. Using a plain text editor, such as Notepad or Edit, edit your `AUTOEXEC.BAT` file to add the directories you created in steps 1 and 2 to your PATH by adding a line like the following to the end of the file:

```
SET PATH="C:\BISON;C:\FLEX;%PATH%"
```

4. Reboot your computer.

5. Start C++Builder and select File|New Application from the main menu to create a new project. Select File|Save Project As and save the project as `Expression`.

6. Add the properties and settings as shown in Table 17-1.

Table 17-1 Components, properties, and settings for `Expression`

COMPONENT	PROPERTY	SETTING
Form1	Caption	Expression Evaluator
	Position	poDefault
Panel1	Align	alBottom
	Caption	
	Height	40

continued on next page

continued from previous page

COMPONENT	PROPERTY	SETTING
Label1 (On Panel1)	Caption	Expression Value:
	Left	8
	Top	12
Panel2	Align	alRight
	BevelOuter	vbNone
	Caption	
	Width	95
Button1 (On Panel2)	Caption	Evaluate
	Height	75
	Left	10
	Top	8
	Width	25
Memo1	Align	alClient
	+Font	
	−Name	Arial
	−Size	16
	Lines	

7. Go to the Code Editor and select the file UNIT1.CPP. Add the function and variable declarations as well as the function yy_input to UNIT.CPP.

```
#pragma resource "*.dfm"
TForm1 *Form1;

extern int yyparse () ; // Parsing Function
extern int yylex () ;    // Lexical Analyzer
static int numberread ; // Number of characters read
extern double yylval ;  // Parser Lexical Value

void yy_input (char *buffer, int &count, int max)
{
   int textlength = Form1->Memo1->Text.Length () ;
   if (numberread < 0)
   {
      // We set number read to -1 when there is no more text. Returning a
      // count of zero tells the lexical analyzer that we have hit the
      // "End-Of-File".
      count = 0 ;
   }
   else if (textlength - numberread > max)
   {
```

```
   // After this call to yy_input returns there will still be characters
   // remaining.
   memcpy (buffer,
           Form1->Memo1->Text.SubString (numberread, max).c_str (),
           max) ;
   numberread += max ;
   count = max ;
}
else
{
   // This call to yy_input consumes all the remaining characters in the
   // memo control
   count = textlength - numberread ;
   memcpy (buffer,
           Form1->Memo1->Text.SubString (numberread, count).c_str(),
           count) ;
   numberread = -1 ;
}
}
```

8. Go to the application's main form and double-click on the Evaluate button to create an `OnClick` event handler. Return to the Code Editor and add the following code to the `OnClick` event handler:

```
void __fastcall TForm1::Button1Click(TObject *Sender)
{
   numberread = 0 ;
   // Call the parser.
   if (yyparse () == 0)
   { // Successful Completion
     Label1->Caption = String ("Expression Value: ") + String (yylval) ;
   }
   else
   {
     // Error occurred.
     Label1->Caption = String ("Error In Expression") ;
     // Clear out the buffer so that things will be set up for the next⇐
call.
     numberread = -1 ;
     while (yylex () != 0)
       ;
   }
   return ;
}
```

9. Using any plain text editor, such as Notepad or the MS-DOS Edit program, create a file called **LEXER.L** in your project's directory and add the following text to it:

```
%{
/* Declarations copied literally to the start of the output file. */
```

continued on next page

continued from previous page

```
// Define the input function.
extern void yy_input (char *, int &count, int max) ;
#define YY_INPUT(buffer,count,max) yy_input (buffer, count, max)

// Define a do nothing yywrap function.
#define YY_SKIP_YYWRAP
static inline int yywrap () { return 1 ; }

// Include token definitions.
#include "parser_t.h"
%}

/* This section contains definitions used in rules. */

/* Basic pattern matching rules
 *   * => match zero or more of the preceding expression
 *   + => Match one or more
 *   ? => Match zero or one
 *   [] => match one member of the set of characters
 *   "string" => match the literal string.
 */

/* Matches a space character, tab or newline. */
spaces   [ \t\n]
/* Matches any of the characters 0, 1, .., 9 */
digit    [0-9]

%%
"+" { return '+' ; }
"-" { return '-' ; }
"*" { return '*' ; }
"/" { return '/' ; }
"(" { return '(' ; }
")" { return ')' ; }

{digit}+(\.{digit}+)?([Ee][+\-]?{digit}+)?  { return NUMBER ; }

{spaces}+

%%
/* No user functions for this file. Anything after %% would get copied */
/* to the output file. */
```

10. Using a plain text editor, create a file called PARSER.Y in your project's directory and add the following text to it:

```
%{
/* Declarations copied literally to the output file. */

#include <math.h>
```

```
// Define the data type for the stack. The $$, $1, $2, ..$n
// symbols are of this type.

#define YYSTYPE double

// Text for the current token maintained by FLEX.
extern char *yytext ;

// We need to define an error reporting function.
// We do not do any sophisticated error reporting.

inline void yyerror (const char *msg)
{
  yytext [0] = 0 ;
  return ;
}


// Declaration of the lexical analyzer.
int yylex () ;

%}
/* Token Declarations are in this section. */


/* Declare operator precendence and associativity. */
%left '+' '-'
%left '*' '/'
%right UMINUS
%token NUMBER

%%
/* Grammar rules go in this section. */

result : expression { yylval = $1 ; }
       ;

expression : NUMBER { $$ = atof (yytext) ; }
           | '(' expression ')' { $$ = $2 ; }
           | '-' expression %prec UMINUS { $$ = - $2 ; }
           | expression '+' expression { $$ = $1 + $3 ; }
           | expression '-' expression { $$ = $1 - $3 ; }
           | expression '*' expression { $$ = $1 * $3 ; }
           | expression '/' expression { $$ = $1 / $3 ; }
           ;

%%
// User-define functions could go in this section. They
// would get copied to the output file. There are none in this
// case.
```

11. Open a DOS window and go to the source directory for your project. Enter the following command to create a lexical analyzer from your FLEX description file:

```
FLEX -oLEXYY.CPP LEXER.L
```

12. Type the following commands to create a parser from your BISON description file:

```
BISON -d -oPARSER.CPP PARSER.Y
BISON -d PARSER.Y
```

13. Select Options|Project from the C++Builder main menu. On the Project Options window, go to the Directories/Conditionals Tab page. In the Conditional Defines window, add the string **"MSDOS"**.

14. Select View|Project Manager from the C++Builder main menu to display the Project Manager window. Click on the + button and add **PARSER.CPP** and **LEXYY.CPP** to your project.

15. Compile and test the project.

How It Works

When the user clicks on the Evaluate button, the text in the Memo control is processed in what is conceptually a two-phase process. The first phase is known as lexical analysis. In this process the input stream, which in this case is the Memo control, is broken down into a sequence of tokens. The second phase is known as parsing. During parsing, the tokens from the lexical analyzer are checked for correct syntax and are arranged into a tree structure to evaluate the expression.

If the user enters the string:

```
10 + 9 * 8
```

the lexical analyzer breaks this down into a stream of tokens that looks something like this:

```
NUMBER 10
+
NUMBER 9
*
NUMBER 8

END-OF-STREAM
```

Breaking the input stream into tokens is relatively simple. Assigning meaning to the token stream is the hard part. If the application processed the previous stream sequentially, the expression would be interpreted as **(10+9)*8**, which is not how expressions are normally interpreted. It is the job of the parser to transform the token stream from the lexical analyzer into this tree structure:

which unambiguously calls for the multiplication to be evaluated before the addition.

Lexical Analysis

The FLEX program creates a lexical analyzer function called `yylex` from a description file. The description file contains expressions that define at a high level how the input stream is to be broken into tokens. FLEX converts this file into a C source file that handles all the low-level details of matching patterns.

The general format of a FLEX file is

```
%{
--C Declarations --
%}
-- Definitions --
%%
-- Rules --
%%
-- User Functions in C --
```

The file **LEXER.L** created in step 9 contains this application's specification for a lexical analyzer. The definitions section contains three items that are declared as sets of characters.

```
spaces    [ \t\n]  -- Set containing the space, tab and newline characters
digit     [0-9]  - Set containing the characters '0', '1', '2',    '9'
exponent [eE]  - Set of 'e' and 'E'
```

These definitions are used in the rules section that defines the tokens, which are returned by the lexical analyzer.

The rules section defines patterns of characters for the lexical analyzer to match. A rule must fit on one line and contain a pattern to be matched, followed by the code to be executed, enclosed in braces, when the pattern is matched.

The first six rules are straightforward. They specify that when the lexical analyzer encounters an operator or parentheses in the input stream, it is to return the ASCII value for the character.

```
"+" { return '+' ; }
"-" { return '-' ; }
"*" { return '*' ; }
"/" { return '/' ; }
"(" { return '(' ; }
")" { return ')' ; }
```

The last two rules are a little more complicated. The + operator in FLEX means to match one or more characters. The line

```
{spaces}+
```

matches one or more spaces. Notice that this rule has no code following it. This causes spaces to be ignored. The big rule is the one that defines a number.

```
{digit}+(\.{digit}+)?([Ee][+\-]?{digit}+)?  { return NUMBER ; }
```

The **?** operator matches zero or one occurrence of the preceding expression. The result is that this pattern matches a string of numbers that can be followed by an optional fraction and an optional exponent.

This FLEX file does not contain any user functions. FLEX uses a macro called **YY_INPUT** to define the function used to retrieve input characters. The C declarations at the top define this macro to use the function defined in **UNIT1.CPP**. The definition of the function **yywrap** is a FLEX quirk and the file **PARSER.H** is included to bring in the token definition of **NUMBER** from the parser.

Parsing

The BISON program creates a parsing function called **yyparse** and an LALR parse table from a description of a grammar that defines how the stream of input tokens is to be parsed. The parse table consists of a number of states containing the action to be performed for each possible token when the parser is in the state.

The BISON parser uses the LR algorithm to parse the input stream. The parser maintains two stacks. One stack holds references to states in the parse table and the other holds values the application creates as values rules in the grammar are matched. When the parser receives a token, it goes to the state at the top of the state stack and finds the operation to be performed. The action can either be to push a new state on to the stack or, when a rule has been matched, to reduce the stack by popping items off the stack.

The general format for a BISON file is

```
%{
-- C Declarations --
%}
-- Token Definitions
%%
-- Grammar Rules
%%
-- User Written Functions
```

The heart of the application is found in the following lines in **PARSER.Y** from step 10:

```
expression : NUMBER { $$ = atof (yytext) ; }
           | '(' expression ')' { $$ = $2 ; }
           | '-' expression %prec UMINUS { $$ = - $2 ; }
           | expression '+' expression { $$ = $1 + $3 ; }
           | expression '-' expression { $$ = $1 - $3 ; }
           | expression '*' expression { $$ = $1 * $3 ; }
           | expression '/' expression { $$ = $1 / $3 ; }
           ;
```

This part of the grammar defines the rules for matching an expression. The definition of an expression is recursive. Each alternative is followed by a block of code to be executed when the corresponding rule is matched.

The items with dollar signs represent positions in the value stack. **$1** represents the value of the first matching part of the rule and **$2** represents the second and so

on. When a rule is matched, the matching items on the stack are popped and replaced with a single item represented by **$$**. For example, when this rule is matched:

```
| expression '+' expression { $$ = $1 + $3 ; }
```

three items are popped off the stack and replaced by a single value. The first expression (**$1**) is added to the second expression (**$3 - The symbol $2 represents the plus sign**) to produce the new value for the stack.

There is a problem in this grammar in that it is ambiguous. The grammar does not specify whether 2-2*2 should be (2-2)*2 or 2-(2*2) or whether 2-2-2 should be (2-2)-2 or 2-(2-2). Although it would be possible to rewrite the grammar to eliminate the ambiguity, it would make the grammar much more complicated. Instead, an order of precedence and associativity is defined for the operators.

```
%left '+' '-'
%left '*' '/'
%right UMINUS
%token NUMBER
```

The operators are listed in increasing order of precedence. **%left** and **%right** specify whether the operator associates from left to right or right to left. The token for **UMINUS** is a dummy that represents a unary minus operator's precedence. This is to differentiate the precedence of the minus sign in

```
10 - 5
```

from

```
- 10 * 5
```

In the grammar definition, **%prec UMINUS** on the line:

```
| '-' expression %prec UMINUS { $$ = - $2 ; }
```

instructs the parser generator to assign the precedence of **UMINUS** to this rule rather than the precedence of the subtraction operator.

Comments

This How-To just gives a quick peek at what you can do with LEX and YACC. Almost any type of program that needs to parse an input stream, such as scripting languages and SQL parsers, can be written using these tools. Even real C++ compilers have been written based on LEX and YACC. To learn more about LEX and YACC, you should look in a book on compiler writing. Several of these are listed in the references at the end of this book.

When you work with tools such as FLEX and BISON, keep in mind that they were designed to run on many types of operating systems and that their primary focus is UNIX. Consequently these tools rarely work right out of the box. You usually have to do some tweaking to get them to compile or you may have to use a command-line option or a special define to make things work right. You have to be patient.

There are many versions of LEX and YACC available besides BISON and FLEX. There are several other freely distributed versions as well as commercial ones. The

various LEX and YACC clones tend to have many incompatibilities. When switching from one program to another, your source files generally require some changes.

COMPLEXITY
INTERMEDIATE

17.2 How do I...
Create a control array like in Visual Basic?

Problem

In Visual Basic I can create an array of controls at design time that are grouped together. How can I create a control array in C++Builder?

Technique

Although VCL has no direct equivalent of Visual Basic's control arrays, you can implement all their functionality using other techniques. In this application a set of buttons are grouped using a **TList** container object.

Steps

Run the program **CONTROLARRAYS.EXE** shown in Figure 17-2. Click on the Add button and add a new button to the scroll box at the left of the main form. Click on a button in the scroll bar to select it; then click on the Delete button. Notice that when the button is deleted, the other buttons slide up to fill in the blank spot.

1. Select File|New Application from the main menu to create a new project. Select File|Save Project As and save the project as **ControlArrays**.

2. Add the properties and settings as shown in Table 17-2.

Figure 17-2 ControlArrays application

Table 17-2 Components, properties, and settings for `ControlArrays`

COMPONENT	PROPERTY	SETTING
Form1	BorderStyle	bsDialog
	Caption	Roman Emperors
	Height	320
	Position	poDefaultPosOnly
	Width	300
ScrollBox1	Height	260
	Left	8
	Top	8
	Width	100
Button1 (On ScrollBox1)	Caption	Augustus
	Height	25
	Left	0
	Top	0
	Width	75
Button2	Caption	&Add
	Height	25
	Left	210
	Top	8
	Width	75
Button3	Caption	&Delete
	Enabled	false
	Height	25
	Left	210
	Top	40
	Width	75
Panel1	Caption	
	Height	40
	Left	120
	Top	225
	Width	160

3. Select File|New from the main menu. Go to the Dialogs tab and double-click on the Standard Dialog icon showing buttons at the right.

4. Use the mouse to select the dialog form created in the previous step. Select File|Save As from the C++Builder main menu and save the form as UNIT2.CPP.

5. Add the properties and settings to the dialog form as shown in Table 17-3.

Table 17-3 Components, properties, and settings for the `Add` dialog

COMPONENT	PROPERTY	SETTING
OKRightDlg	Caption	Add Emperor
Label1	Caption	Emperor Name
	Left	20
	Top	20
Edit1	Left	20
	Height	24
	TabOrder	0
	Text	
	Top	40
	Width	260

6. Select File|Open from the C++Builder main menu and open the file `UNIT1.H`. Add the following declarations to the definition of `TForm1` in the Code Editor:

```
class TForm1 : public TForm
{
__published: // IDE-managed Components
  TScrollBox *ScrollBox1;
  TButton *Button1;
  TButton *Button2;
  TButton *Button3;
  TPanel *Panel1;
private: // User declarations
  TList *buttons ;
  TButton *selectedbutton ;
  void AddButton (const String &name) ;
public: // User declarations
  __fastcall TForm1(TComponent* Owner);
  virtual __fastcall ~TForm1() ;
};
```

7. Switch to the file `UNIT1.CPP` in the Code Editor. Include the file `UNIT2.H`.

```
#include <vcl\vcl.h>
#pragma hdrstop

#include "Unit1.h"
#include "Unit2.h"
```

8. Modify the TForm1 constructor to allocate a TList object.

```
__fastcall TForm1::TForm1(TComponent* Owner) : TForm(Owner)
{
  buttons = new TList ;
}
```

9. In the Code Editor, add the TForm1 destructor and the AddButton member function to the file UNIT1.CPP.

```
__fastcall TForm1::~TForm1()
{
  delete buttons ;
}

void TForm1::AddButton (const String &name)
{
  TButton *button = new TButton (this) ;
  button->Parent = ScrollBox1 ;
  button->Caption = name ;
  button->OnClick = Button1Click ;

  button->Width = ScrollBox1->Width - GetSystemMetrics (SM_CXVSCROLL) - 4 ;
  buttons->Add (button) ;
  if (buttons->Count > 1)
  {
    TButton *oneabove =(TButton *)(buttons->Items[buttons->Count - 2]) ;
    button->Top = oneabove->Top + oneabove->Height ;
  }
  else
  {
    button->Top = 0 ;
  }
  return ;
}
```

10. Double-click on the application's main form to create a handler for the OnCreate event. Add the following code to the OnCreate handler in the Code Editor:

```
void __fastcall TForm1::FormCreate(TObject *Sender)
{
  buttons->Add (Button1) ;
  Button1->Width = ScrollBox1->Width - GetSystemMetrics (SM_CXVSCROLL) - 4⇐
;
  static const String emperors [] = { "Tiberius", "Caius", "Claudius",⇐
"Nero",
                                      "Galba", "Otho", "Vitellus", "Vespasian",
                                      "Titus", "Domitian", "Nerva", "Traian",
                                      "Hadrian", "" } ;
  for (int ii = 0 ; emperors [ii].Length () != 0 ; ++ ii)
    AddButton (emperors [ii]) ;
}
```

11. Create an `OnClick` for the button labeled Augustus by double-clicking on it. Add the following code to the `OnClick` event handler in the Code Editor:

```
void __fastcall TForm1::Button1Click(TObject *Sender)
{
  TButton *button = dynamic_cast <TButton *>(Sender) ;
  // Make the index one based rather than zero
  int index = buttons->IndexOf (button) + 1 ;
  Panel1->Caption = "Button #" + String (index) + ": "
                    + button->Caption + " Selected" ;
  selectedbutton = button ;
  Button3->Enabled = true ;
}
```

12. Return to the application's main form and double-click on the Add button. Add the following code to the `OnClick` event handler that was created for the button:

```
void __fastcall TForm1::Button2Click(TObject *Sender)
{
  OKRightDlg->Edit1->Text = "" ;
  if (OKRightDlg->ShowModal () != mrCancel)
  {
    AddButton (OKRightDlg->Edit1->Text) ;
  }
```

13. Create an `OnClick` handler for the Delete button and modify it to look like this:

```
void __fastcall TForm1::Button3Click(TObject *Sender)
{
  int index = buttons->Remove (selectedbutton) ;
  // Slide the buttons above the deleted one down.
  for (int ii = index ; ii < buttons->Count ; ++ ii)
  {
    TButton *button = (TButton *) buttons->Items [ii] ;
    button->Top -= selectedbutton->Height ;
  }
  delete selectedbutton ;
  Button3->Enabled = false ;
  selectedbutton = NULL ;
}
```

14. Compile and test this project.

How It Works

A control array in Visual Basic does the following things:

✔ Allows multiple controls to share the same event handler

✔ Provides the only mechanism to add a control at runtime

✔ Provides a convenient grouping of controls

The first two items are not even an issue with C++Builder. You have already seen several examples, such as How-To 3.2, where more than one control shared the same event handler. C++Builder has the added advantage that controls of different types can use the same event handler. It makes a lot of sense for similar controls, such as mask edit controls and edit controls, to be able to share the same event code. As for dynamic allocation of controls, C++Builder does not have the restrictions that Visual Basic does. A C++Builder application can dynamically create any number and type of control. In fact, with C++Builder, you are not even required to build any of your forms at design time.

Grouping of controls at design time is the only feature of control arrays that Visual Basic has and C++Builder does not. This application uses a **TList** object to group the set of buttons. **TList** is a container class that allows objects to be accessed using an index like an array. Another alternative would have been to use an array of object pointers. Using the **TList** class eliminates the need for managing the allocation of the array. Its main drawback is that you have to cast the list items to an object pointer before you can use them. Although there is a fair amount of code in this application, very little of it, other than the first six lines of **AddButton** in step 9, is devoted to implementing the "control array." Most of the code handles the positioning of the controls.

Comments

The lack of a control array in VCL is a frequent complaint of people who are switching from Visual Basic. For using groups of controls, C++Builder's use of shared event handlers is more flexible but a little more complicated than a control array. Visual Basic control arrays can have their own difficulties, such as discontinuities in array subscripts. When you are switching from Visual Basic, bear in mind that things are just done a little differently in C++Builder.

COMPLEXITY
INTERMEDIATE

17.3 How do I...
Edit a control as text?

Problem

I need to create a form that has a lot of repeated groups of controls. Is there any way to edit a bunch of similar objects in a text editor?

Technique

There are several ways to edit a form as text. One way is to click on a form with the left mouse button and select View As Text from the context menu. This allows you to edit an entire form at once. If you only want to edit a few controls, you can use Cut and Paste to the clipboard and a text editor.

Steps

Run the program **CONTROLASTEXT.EXE** shown in Figure 17-3. This application's main form has several nearly identical button/label pairs except for their location and the label's caption.

1. Select File|New Application from the main menu to create a new project. Select File|Save Project As and save the project as **ControlAsText**.

2. Add the properties and settings as shown in Table 17-4.

Table 17-4 Components, properties, and settings for **ControlAsText**

COMPONENT	PROPERTY	SETTING
Form1	BorderStyle	bsDialog
	Caption	White House Phone System
	Position	poDefaultPosOnly
SpeedButton1	Left	8
	Top	8
Label1	Caption	Office of the President
	Left	40
	Top	12

3. Use the mouse to select the speed button. Press SHIFT and click on the label so that both controls are selected. Go to the C++Builder main menu and select Edit|Copy.

4. Start the Notepad program. Select Edit|Paste from the Notepad main menu. Your edit window should look like Figure 17-4.

5. Press CTRL-V four times to create a total of five copies of the control pairs in the window.

6. Using Notepad, change the names of the controls so that you have **SpeedButton1/Label1** through **SpeedButton5/Label5**.

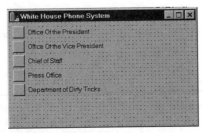

Figure 17-3 The **ControlAsText** ProgramExpression

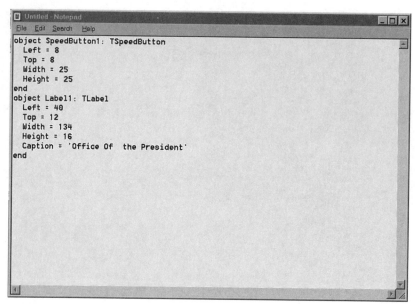

Figure 17-4 SpeedButton and Label pasted to Notepad

7. Change the Captions of Label2 through Label4 to

> Office Of the Vice President
> Chief of Staff
> Press Office
> Lincoln Bedroom Reservations

8. Add 30 to the value of SpeedButton2's and Label2's Top property. Do the same for SpeedButton3/Label3, except add 60. Add 90 for SpeedButton4/Label4 and 120 for SpeedButton5/Label5. Your Notepad window should look like Figure 17-5.

9. Use the mouse to select all the text in the Notepad except for the definition of SpeedButton1 and Label1; then select Edit|Copy from the main menu.

10. Return to C++Builder and select the application's main form. Choose Edit|Paste from the C++Builder main menu. If the Paste menu item is not enabled, you probably have a syntax error in the Notepad. Edit the text and try again. Adjust the widths of the labels so that the form looks like the one in Figure 17-6.

```
Untitled - Notepad
File  Edit  Search  Help
  Height = 16
  Caption = 'Office Of the President'
end
object SpeedButton2: TSpeedButton
  Left = 8
  Top = 38
  Width = 25
  Height = 25
end
object Label2: TLabel
  Left = 40
  Top = 42
  Width = 200
  Height = 16
  Caption = 'Office Of the Vice President'
end
object SpeedButton3: TSpeedButton
  Left = 8
  Top = 68
  Width = 25
  Height = 25
end
object Label3: TLabel
  Left = 40
  Top = 72
  Width = 131
```

Figure 17-5 Controls edited for placement on the form

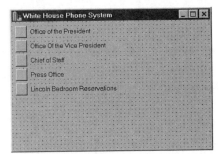

Figure 17-6 Controls pasted on
the form

11. Compile and run the application.

How It Works

When you copy a control to the clipboard, C++Builder stores a textual representation of the control. When C++Builder pastes a control from the clipboard, it uses that same textual representation of the control. You can use any application to create a control and copy it to the clipboard. As long as you follow the correct format, C++Builder does not care how it was created.

Comments

In most cases, it is simplest to add controls using the C++Builder Form Designer. However, there are certain situations, such as when adding many repeated groups of controls, where editing a form as text is easier. Using a separate program, such as Notepad, makes it easier to recover than if you edit a form using "View As Form." The only drawback is that you cannot cut and paste the form and its properties using this technique.

COMPLEXITY
INTERMEDIATE

17.4 How do I...
View the contents of a .DFM file?

Problem

A programmer who left our company modified a complicated form to use a control that he got from some site on the Internet. Unfortunately, we cannot find this control anywhere. When we load the form in C++Builder, we get an error that this control cannot be found. When we click on the Ignore All button, the form is displayed with nothing on it. How can we view and edit the contents of the .DFM file?

Technique

The **CONVERT** program that comes with C++Builder converts a .DFM file to a textual representation of its contents and text files to .DFM files.

Steps

1. Copy the project **DFMfile** from the accompanying CD-ROM to your hard disk; then open up the project. You will get an error telling you that the class **TSuperContainer** cannot be found. Click on the Ignore All button and you will see the form come up without anything on it. Close the project but do not save anything.

2. Open a DOS window and go to the directory containing the project.

3. Copy the file **MAIN.DFM** to **MAINSAVE.DFM**. Always make a backup copy before editing a form as text.

4. In the DOS window, type **CONVERT MAIN.DFM** to create the file **MAIN.TXT**. If you get an error that **CONVERT** is a bad command or filename, then the C++Builder **BIN** directory is not in your path. Either add this directory to your path and reboot or try again with the full path to **CONVERT.EXE**.

5. Use the DOS Edit program to edit `MAIN.TXT`. Delete lines from `Object SuperContainer1 : TSuperContainer` to `Height = 245` as shown in Figure 17-7.

6. Move to the end of the file `MAIN.TXT`. Delete any one of the lines that contains the word **end** by itself.

7. Exit the DOS edit program and save the updated `MAIN.TXT`.

8. At the DOS program, type `CONVERT MAIN.TXT`. This creates a new `MAIN.DFM` file. If something gets messed up, copy `MAINSAVE.DFM` to `MAIN.DFM` and start over.

9. Return to C++Builder and open the project `DFMText`. The project should open with no errors. Instead of being blank, the application's main form should have several controls and look like the one shown in Figure 17-8.

How It Works

The C++Builder .DFM files are Windows resource files that contain form definitions for the project. The `CONVERT` program creates a text file containing the textual representation of the contents of the .DFM file. The output from `CONVERT` is the same as you get when you select View As Text from a form's context menu. The text format of the form can be edited and you can use the `CONVERT` program to create a .DFM file from the text file.

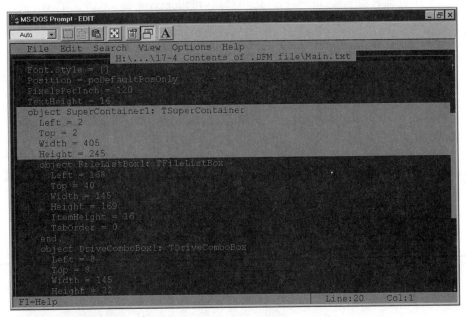

Figure 17-7 Deleting the `TSuperContainer ObjectForm`

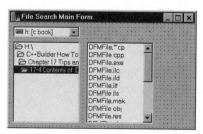

Figure 17-8 The recovered project

The **MAIN.DFM** file for this project contains a reference to a control class that does not exist. This causes an error when you try to open the form. All the other controls on this form were placed on top of the missing control, so they get deleted even if you click on the Ignore button when you get the error message. By editing the text file created by **CONVERT.EXE**, you can manually delete the missing control so that the form can be loaded with all the remaining controls.

Comments

Problems like this are rare but they happen from time to time. The most frequent cause of corruption in a .DFM is a control that does not save itself properly in a .DFM file. Not all the controls that you may find on the Internet are as well tested as the ones that come with C++Builder.

Another time to use the **CONVERT** program is when you are using a source control system like SCCS or RCS. These systems store a base file in their archives as well as the changes made with each revision. This type of program tends to handle binary files very poorly. Converting the .DFM to text before saving the file in an archive will make these programs work much better.

COMPLEXITY
INTERMEDIATE

17.5 How do I...
Create a DLL?

Problem

Often I create functions that I would like to share with applications written with other tools such as Visual Basic. I know that the way to do this is to create a DLL, but how do I do this with C++Builder?

Technique

A Dynamic Link Library or DLL is similar to an executable file except that a DLL cannot be run by itself. DLLs are used to share code among multiple executable files and a DLL can be used from many interpreted programming tools. A DLL can export functions that can be called from outside of the DLL.

The first step in creating a DLL is to determine the functions you want to export. In this How-To, you will create a DLL with one exported function that solves the wind triangle problem used for planning airplane flights. The function will take the aircraft's airspeed, desired course, and the wind speed and direction. The function will determine the heading needed to follow the course and what the ground speed will be.

Steps

Run the program **FLIGHTPLANNING.EXE**. Adjust the Track bars and observe how the heading and ground speed change in the Status bar and how the triangle showing the effect of the wind changes. A sample view is shown in Figure 17-9. The desired course is 360 (North) and the wind is coming from 150 (Southeasterly) at 30 knots. This is a tail wind from the right, so the ground speed is faster than the airspeed and the aircraft needs to be steered slightly to the right (009) to remain on the desired course. The solid red line shows the desired course, the blue line shows how the wind will push the aircraft, and the green line shows the heading to take to follow the desired course.

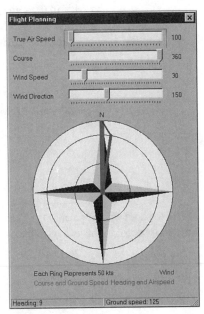

Figure 17-9 The FlightPlanning application

1. Select File|New from the main menu. On the New tab double-click on the DLL icon.

2. Select File|Save Project As from the main menu and save the project as `WindCalculations`.

3. Select File|New from the main menu. Double-click the Text icon to create a new source file. Add the following code to the blank file in the Code Editor:

```
#ifndef __WINDCALCULATIONS_H
#define __WINDCALCULATIONS_H



extern "C" void __export __pascal WindCalculation (
                    unsigned int tas,
                    unsigned int course,
                    unsigned int windspeed,
                    unsigned int winddirection,
                    int *groundspeed,
                    int *heading) ;
                    #endif
```

4. Select File|Save As from the main menu and save the file you created in the previous step as `WINDCALCULATIONS.H`.

5. Select the tab for `WINDCALCULATIONS.CPP` in the Code Editor and include `MATH.H` and `WINDCALCULATIONS.H` at the top of the file.

```
#include <vcl\vcl.h>
#include <math.h>
#pragma hdrstop
#include "windcalculations.h"
```

6. Move to the bottom of the file and add the definition of the function `WindCalculation`.

```
extern "C" void __export __pascal WindCalculation (unsigned int tas,
                    unsigned int course,
                    unsigned int windspeed,
                    unsigned int winddirection,
                    int *groundspeed,
                    int *heading)
{
  double wcangle = ((double) (winddirection + 180) - course) * M_PI
                   / 180.0 ;
  double sinvalue = (double)windspeed * sin (wcangle) / (double) tas ;
  if (fabs (sinvalue) <= 1.0)
  {
```

continued on next page

continued from previous page

```
      double hcangle = asin (sinvalue) ;
      double awangle = 2.0 * M_PI - wcangle - hcangle ;
      *groundspeed = (int) (sqrt (windspeed * windspeed
                                  + tas * tas
                                  + 2 * windspeed * tas * cos (awangle))
                                  + .5) ;
if (*groundspeed > 0)
    {
      double sinangle =  (double) windspeed * sin (awangle) /
                          (double) *groundspeed ;
      if (fabs (sinangle) <= 1.0)
      {
        double hangle = asin (sinangle) ;
        *heading = ((int) ((180 * hangle / M_PI) + .5) + course + 359) %
                      360 + 1 ;
      }
      else
      {
        // The aircraft is being blown backwards.
        *groundspeed = -1 ;
        *heading = -1 ;
      }
    }
    else
    {
      // The aircraft is being blown backwards.
      *heading = -1 ;
    }
  }
  else
  {
    // The aircraft is being blown backwards.
    *groundspeed = -1 ;
    *heading = -1 ;
  }
  return ;
}
```

7. Select Project|Build All from the C++Builder main menu to compile and link the DLL.

8. Open a DOS window and go to the directory where you created the DLL. Enter the following command at the DOS prompt:

```
IMPLIB WINDCALCULATIONS WINDCALCULATIONS.DLL
```

9. To test the DLL, return to C++Builder and Select File|New Application from the main menu. Select File|Save Project As from the main menu and save the project as `FlightPlanning` in the same directory where you created the .DLL.

10. Add the properties and settings as shown in Table 17-5.

Table 17-5 Components, properties, and settings for `FlightPlanning`

COMPONENT	PROPERTY	SETTING
Form1	BorderStyle	bsDialog
	Caption	Flight Planning
	Height	620
	Position	poDefaultPosOnly
	Width	410
Label1	Caption	True Air Speed
	Left	10
	Top	20
Label2	Caption	Course
	Left	10
	Top	60
Label3	Caption	Wind Speed
	Left	10
	Top	100
Label4	Caption	Wind Direction
	Left	10
	Top	140
Label5	Left	350
	Top	20
Label6	Left	350
	Top	60
Label7	Left	350
	Top	100
Label8	Left	350
	Top	140
Label9	Caption	N
	Left	195
	Top	180
Label10	Caption	Each Ring Represents 50 kts
	Left	50
	Top	510

continued on next page

continued from previous page

COMPONENT	PROPERTY	SETTING
Label11	Caption	Course and Ground Speed
	+Font	
	−Color	Red
	Left	50
	Top	530
Label12	Caption	Wind
	+Font	
	−Color	Blue
	Left	320
	Top	510
Label13	Caption	Heading and Airspeed
	+Font	
	−Color	Green
	Left	215
	Top	530
TrackBar1	Frequency	10
	Height	45
	Left	120
	Max	400
	Min	100
	Top	10
	Width	220
TrackBar2	Frequency	10
	Height	45
	Left	120
	LineSize	5
	Max	360
	Min	1
	Top	50
	Width	220
TrackBar3	Frequency	5
	Height	45
	Left	120
	Max	200
	Top	90
	Width	220

COMPONENT	PROPERTY	SETTING
TrackBar4	Height	45
	Left	120
	LineSize	10
	Max	36
	Min	1
	Top	130
	Width	220
PaintBox1	Color	clWhite
	Height	300
	Left	50
	Top	200
	Width	300
StatusBar1		

11. Go the application's main form and select the Status bar. Press F11 to display the Object Inspector. Double-click on the **Panels** property to display the Statusbar Panels Editor. Click on the New button twice to create two new panels. Select the first panel from the list and enter 200 for the width; then click on the OK button.

12. Select File|Open from the C++Builder main menu and open the file **UNIT1.H**. Add the declaration of **Calculate** and the private member variables to the **TForm1** class definition in the Code Editor.

```
class TForm1 : public TForm
{
__published: // IDE-managed Components
  TLabel *Label1;
  TLabel *Label2;
  TLabel *Label3;
  TLabel *Label4;
  TLabel *Label5;
  TLabel *Label6;
  TLabel *Label7;
  TLabel *Label8;
  TLabel *Label9;
  TLabel *Label10;
  TLabel *Label11;
  TLabel *Label12;
  TLabel *Label13;
  TTrackBar *TrackBar1;
  TTrackBar *TrackBar2;
  TTrackBar *TrackBar3;
  TTrackBar *TrackBar4;
  TPaintBox *PaintBox1;
```

continued on next page

continued from previous page

```
   TStatusBar *StatusBar1;
private: // User declarations
   void Calculate () ;
   unsigned int airspeed ;
   unsigned int course ;
   unsigned int windspeed ;
   unsigned int winddirection ;
   int groundspeed ;
   int heading ;
public: // User declarations
   __fastcall TForm1(TComponent* Owner);
};
```

13. Select the UNIT1.CPP page on the Code Editor. Include the files MATH.H and WINDCALCULATIONS.H in UNIT1.CPP.

```
#include <vcl\vcl.h>
#include <math.h>
#pragma hdrstop

#include "Unit1.h"
#include "windcalculations.h"
```

14. Go to the bottom of UNIT1.CPP and add this definition of Calculate:

```
void TForm1::Calculate ()
{
   airspeed = TrackBar1->Position ;
   course = TrackBar2->Position ;
   windspeed = TrackBar3->Position ;
   winddirection = 10 * TrackBar4->Position ;
   Label5->Caption = String ((int)airspeed) ;
   Label6->Caption = String ((int)course) ;
   Label7->Caption = String ((int)windspeed) ;
   Label8->Caption = String ((int)winddirection) ;

   WindCalculation (airspeed, course,
            windspeed, winddirection,
            &groundspeed, &heading) ;
   StatusBar1->Panels->Items [0]->Text = String ("Heading: ")
                        + String ((int) heading) ;
   StatusBar1->Panels->Items [1]->Text = String ("Ground speed: ")
                        + String ((int) groundspeed) ;
}
```

15. Double-click on the application's main form to create a handler for the OnCreate event. Add the following code to the event handler:

```
void __fastcall TForm1::FormCreate(TObject *Sender)
{
   Calculate () ;
}
```

16. Double-click on the first Track Bar control on the application's main form. This will create an event handler for the **OnChange** event. Modify the event handler in the Code Editor to look like this:

```
void __fastcall TForm1::TrackBar1Change(TObject *Sender)
{
  Calculate () ;
  PaintBox1->Repaint () ;
}
```

17. Go to the application's main form and select the second Track bar with the mouse. Press the [F11] key to display the Object Inspector. Go to the events page and select, but do not double-click, the **OnChange** event. Select **TrackBar1Change** from the drop-down list. Repeat this process for the two remaining Track bars.

18. Go to the application's main form and select the Paint box. Press the [F11] key to display the Object Inspector. Go to the Events page and double-click on the value for the **OnPaint** event. Add the following code to the event handler that was created:

```
void __fastcall TForm1::PaintBox1Paint(TObject *Sender)
{
  // Draw the compass outline.
  PaintBox1->Canvas->Brush->Style = bsSolid ;
  PaintBox1->Canvas->Pen->Style = psSolid ;
  PaintBox1->Canvas->Pen->Color = clBlack ;
  PaintBox1->Canvas->Pen->Width = 1 ;
  PaintBox1->Canvas->Ellipse (0,
                0,
                PaintBox1->Width,
                PaintBox1->Height) ;

  // Draw a compass rose.
  const int pointcount = 4 ;
  const int delta = 20 ;

  TPoint points [8][pointcount] =
  {
    { // Downward Arm
      {PaintBox1->Width/2, PaintBox1->Height/2},
      {PaintBox1->Width/2 + delta, PaintBox1->Height/2 + delta},
      {PaintBox1->Width/2, PaintBox1->Height},
      {PaintBox1->Width/2, PaintBox1->Height/2}
    },
    {
      {PaintBox1->Width/2, PaintBox1->Height/2},
      {PaintBox1->Width/2 - delta, PaintBox1->Height/2 + delta},
      {PaintBox1->Width/2, PaintBox1->Height},
      {PaintBox1->Width/2, PaintBox1->Height/2}
    },
```

continued on next page

continued from previous page

```
  { // Leftward Arm
    {PaintBox1->Width/2, PaintBox1->Height/2},
    {PaintBox1->Width/2 - delta, PaintBox1->Height/2 + delta},
    {0, PaintBox1->Height/2},
    {PaintBox1->Width/2, PaintBox1->Height/2}
  },
  {
    {PaintBox1->Width/2, PaintBox1->Height/2},
    {PaintBox1->Width/2 - delta, PaintBox1->Height/2 - delta},
    {0, PaintBox1->Height/2},
    {PaintBox1->Width/2, PaintBox1->Height/2}
  },
  { // Upward Arm
    {PaintBox1->Width/2, PaintBox1->Height/2},
    {PaintBox1->Width/2 - delta, PaintBox1->Height/2 - delta},
    {PaintBox1->Width/2, 0},
    {PaintBox1->Width/2, PaintBox1->Height/2}
  },
  {
    {PaintBox1->Width/2, PaintBox1->Height/2},
    {PaintBox1->Width/2 + delta, PaintBox1->Height/2 - delta},
    {PaintBox1->Width/2, 0},
    {PaintBox1->Width/2, PaintBox1->Height/2}
  },
  { // Rightward Arm
    {PaintBox1->Width/2, PaintBox1->Height/2},
    {PaintBox1->Width/2 + delta, PaintBox1->Height/2 - delta},
    {PaintBox1->Width, PaintBox1->Height/2},
    {PaintBox1->Width/2, PaintBox1->Height/2}
  },
  {
    {PaintBox1->Width/2, PaintBox1->Height/2},
    {PaintBox1->Width/2 + delta, PaintBox1->Height/2 + delta},
    {PaintBox1->Width, PaintBox1->Height/2},
    {PaintBox1->Width/2, PaintBox1->Height/2}
  }
} ;

for (int ii = 0 ; ii < 8 ; ii += 2)
{
  PaintBox1->Canvas->Brush->Color = cl3DLight ;
  BeginPath (PaintBox1->Canvas->Handle) ;
  PaintBox1->Canvas->Polyline (points [ii], pointcount - 1) ;
  EndPath (PaintBox1->Canvas->Handle) ;
  FillPath (PaintBox1->Canvas->Handle) ;

  PaintBox1->Canvas->Brush->Color = cl3DDkShadow ;
  BeginPath (PaintBox1->Canvas->Handle) ;
  PaintBox1->Canvas->Polyline (points [ii + 1], pointcount - 1) ;
  EndPath (PaintBox1->Canvas->Handle) ;
  FillPath (PaintBox1->Canvas->Handle) ;
}
```

```
    if (groundspeed < 0)
      return ;

    double angle ;
    double x ;
    double y ;

    // Determine the scaling factor to use for the diagram to make sure that
    // it all fits on the compass.
    double scale ;
    if (groundspeed > airspeed)
      scale = (double) PaintBox1->Width / groundspeed / 2.0 ;
    else
      scale = (double) PaintBox1->Width / airspeed / 2.0 ;

    // Draw 50 knot scale circles.
    PaintBox1->Canvas->Pen->Style = psSolid ;
    PaintBox1->Canvas->Pen->Color = clBlack ;
    PaintBox1->Canvas->Brush->Style = bsClear ;
    for (int ii = 50 ; ii * scale < PaintBox1->Height/2 ; ii += 50)
    {
      PaintBox1->Canvas->Ellipse (PaintBox1->Width/2 - ii * scale,
                    PaintBox1->Height/2 - ii * scale,
                    PaintBox1->Width/2 + ii * scale,
                    PaintBox1->Height/2 + ii * scale) ;
    }

    PaintBox1->Canvas->MoveTo (PaintBox1->Width/2, PaintBox1->Height/2) ;
    // Draw the course/groundspeed vector.
    angle = (2.0 * M_PI * (course + 270)) / 360 ;
    x = cos (angle) * scale * groundspeed + PaintBox1->Width/2 + 0.5 ;
    y = sin (angle) * scale * groundspeed + PaintBox1->Height/2 + 0.5 ;
    PaintBox1->Canvas->Pen->Color = clRed ;
    PaintBox1->Canvas->Pen->Width = 10 ;
    PaintBox1->Canvas->LineTo ((int) x,
                    (int) y) ;
    // Draw the heading/airspeed vector
    angle = (2.0 * M_PI * (heading + 270)) / 360 ;
    x = cos (angle) * scale * airspeed + PaintBox1->Width/2 + 0.5 ;
    y = sin (angle) * scale * airspeed + PaintBox1->Height/2 + 0.5 ;
    PaintBox1->Canvas->Pen->Color = clBlue ;
    PaintBox1->Canvas->Pen->Width = 2 ;
    PaintBox1->Canvas->LineTo ((int) x,
                    (int) y) ;
    PaintBox1->Canvas->Pen->Color = clGreen ;
    PaintBox1->Canvas->Pen->Width = 6 ;
    // Draw the wind vector.
    PaintBox1->Canvas->LineTo (PaintBox1->Width/2, PaintBox1->Height/2) ;
}
```

19. Select Project|Add To Project from the C++Builder main menu and add the file **WINDCALCULATIONS.LIB** to the project.

20. Compile and test this project.

How It Works

In this How-To you created two projects: the DLL and a program to test the DLL. The **WindCalculation()** function uses basic trigonometry to solve a wind problem. The course/ground speed vector is the sum of the air speed/heading and wind/wind speed vectors. The function uses the Law of Sines and the Law of Cosines to calculate the ground speed and heading. Because it is the interface to the function, rather than the function itself, that is the main concern, but we will skip the mathematical details here.

The most import part of the DLL source code is the declaration of the function **WindCalculation** in step 3. The **__export** directive instructs the compiler and linker to make the function available to users of the DLL. Omit the **__export** directive when you have internal functions that you do not want to make public in the DLL.

In order to support function overloading, C++ compilers create internal mangled names for functions using the function name given by the programmer and the arguments to the function. If the DLL contained a mangled name for the function, the function could only be called from programs written using the same compiler. In the problem statement, we said we wanted to create a DLL that could be used by other tools. This is why **extern "C"** is included in the function definition. This standard C++ directive tells the compiler to generate a function using the interface used by the C programming language. This tells the compiler not to mangle the name of the function in the DLL, but it also limits overloading the same name.

Although having **extern "C"** in the declaration will allow programming tools to locate the function using the name **WindCalculation**, there could still be problems calling the function. Different programming languages use different methods of calling functions. Parameters can be passed on the stack or in registers, the parameter order can vary, and there are different methods used for cleaning up the stack when the function returns. C++Builder can generate and use functions using any standard calling conventions. This is not the case with all programming tools. The Pascal calling convention is the closest thing to a universal calling convention and is the function call method used by all the Win32 API functions. Because the Pascal calling convention does not support some C++ language features, such as a function having a variable number of parameters, the Pascal calling convention is not the default method used by C++ compilers. The **__pascal** directive instructs the compiler to use the Pascal calling method for the function.

When you are creating functions for a DLL that you want to be used by different development tools, you should restrict the arguments to basic types (`int`, `char`, `char *`, and `double`). If you need to use a structure for a parameter, make the argument the address of the structure. The return value for the function should be void, an integer, or a pointer. If your function has any parameters that are classes, then it can only be used by C++ programs.

After you have compiled the DLL, use the `IMPLIB` program to create a library file that describes the contents of the DLL to a linker. When you need to use a DLL in a C++Builder project, you include the DLL's import library in the project, not the DLL itself.

Comments

If you want your DLL to be used only by C++Builder applications, many of the restrictions described above do not apply. The functions in the DLL can use any type of parameter and you can even export classes. Most of the problems in a DLL show up when you try to use it from some other tool. If you are having a problem using your DLL from outside C++Builder, check for the following:

✔ Missing extern `C` and `__pascal` directives.

✔ `double` or `struct` function return values.

✔ Structures passed by value.

✔ Classes or structures containing classes in the argument list.

✔ `AnsiString` arguments rather than `char *`.

✔ The caller has the correct number and type of arguments.

✔ Arguments are being correctly passed by value or reference.

 COMPLEXITY
BEGINNING

17.6 How do I...
Use modules written in Delphi?

Problem

We started to use C++Builder to write code for multiple operating systems. Over the past few years, however, we have developed a lot of code and forms written in Delphi. Because a user interface written for Windows is not portable, no matter what we do, not only do we not want to throw out our Delphi forms and code but we also want to continue development using Delphi. A lot of custom controls are written in Delphi. How can we use existing Delphi code with C++Builder?

Technique

C++Builder can compile Delphi units as well as C++ files. C++Builder automatically creates a C++ header file for a Delphi unit when you build the project.

Steps

Run the program **ADVERTISMENT.EXE** shown in Figure 17-10. The main form is written in C++Builder. The Marquee control is an existing control that was written in Delphi. This control scrolls a message across itself. Try resizing the control to see how the message adjusts to the form size.

1. Select File|New Application from the main menu to create a new project. Select File|Save Project As and save the project as **Advertisement**.

2. Copy the files **MARQUEE.PAS** from the accompanying CD-ROM to the directory containing the project you created in the previous step.

3. Add the properties and settings as shown in Table 17-6.

Table 17-6 Components, properties, and settings for **Advertisement**

COMPONENT	PROPERTY	SETTING
Form1	Caption	A C++Builder Message
	Position	poDefault

4. Select Project|Add To Project from the C++Builder main menu and add **MARQUEE.PAS** to the project.

Figure 17-10 The C++Builder advertisement

5. Select File|Open from the main menu and open the file **UNIT1.H**. Go to the Code Editor and add the `include` directive for the file **MARQUEE.HPP**. Add the marquee member variable to the **TForm1** class definition.

```
#include <vcl\Classes.hpp>
#include <vcl\Controls.hpp>
#include <vcl\StdCtrls.hpp>
#include <vcl\Forms.hpp>

#include "marquee.hpp"
//-------------------------------------------------------------------
class TForm1 : public TForm
{
__published: // IDE-managed Components
  void __fastcall FormCreate(TObject *Sender);
private: // User declarations
  TMarquee *marquee ;
public: // User declarations
  __fastcall TForm1(TComponent* Owner);
};
```

6. Double-click on the application's main form to create a handler for the `OnCreate` event. Add the following code to the event handler:

```
void __fastcall TForm1::FormCreate(TObject *Sender)
{
  marquee = new TMarquee (this) ;
  marquee->Parent = this ;
  marquee->Text =
    "C++Builder is the best Windows development tool ever! " ;
}
```

7. Compile and test this project.

How It Works

C++Builder compiles Delphi's Object Pascal in addition to C++. You can include Delphi Pascal units in your application as well as forms created in Delphi. You can even add components written in Delphi to the Component Palette as you did in How-To 15.2.

When C++Builder compiles a Delphi unit, it creates a C++-compatible include file with an .HPP extension. This include file contains all the Pascal declarations translated to C++.

Comments

The most difficult task when you develop applications using more than one programming tool is to create the interface definition and maintain it through the life of the project. C++Builder does this for you. When you add a Delphi unit to a project, create an .HPP file for the unit to find out how to use the unit from C++.

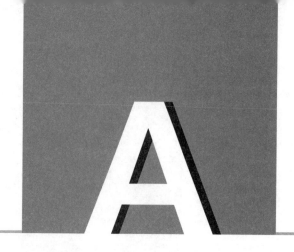

A

BIBLIOGRAPHY

lex & yacc
by John R. Levine, Tony Mason, and Doug Brown
O'Reilly & Associates, Inc., 1992
Sebastopol, California

The Theory and Practice of Compiler Writing
by Jean-Paul Tremblay and Paul G. Sorenson
McGraw-Hill, 1985
New York, New York

Compilers Principles, Techniques, and Tools
by Alfred V. Aho, Ravi Sethi, and Jeffrey D. Ullman
Addison-Wesley, 1986
Reading, Massachusetts

Windows 95 Win32 Programming API Bible, Books 1 and 2
by Richard Simon, Michael Gouker, and Brian Barnes
Waite Group Press, 1996
Corte Madera, California

Programmer's Guide to Microsoft Windows 95
Microsoft Corporation
Microsoft Press
Redmond, Washington

Instrument Flying Handbook
Federal Aviation Administration
United States Government Printing Office, 1980
Washington D.C.

B

GNU GPL AND LGPL

GNU General Public License Version 2, June 1991

Preamble

The licenses for most software are designed to take away your freedom to share and change it. By contrast, the GNU General Public License is intended to guarantee your freedom to share and change free software – to make sure the software is free for all its users. This General Public License applies to most of the Free Software Foundation's software and to any other program whose authors commit to using it. (Some other Free Software Foundation software is covered by the GNU Library General Public License instead.) You can apply it to your programs, too.

When we speak of free software, we are referring to freedom, not price. Our General Public Licenses are designed to make sure that you have the freedom to distribute copies of free software (and charge for this service if you wish), that you receive source code or can get it if you want it, that you can change the software or use pieces of it in new free programs, and that you know you can do these things.

To protect your rights, we need to make restrictions that forbid anyone to deny you these rights or to ask you to surrender the rights. These restrictions translate to certain responsibilities for you if you distribute copies of the software or if you modify it.

For example, if you distribute copies of such a program, whether gratis or for a fee, you must give the recipients all the rights that you have. You must make sure

that they, too, receive or can get the source code. And you must show them these terms so they know their rights.

We protect your rights with two steps: (1) copyright the software, and (2) offer you this license which gives you legal permission to copy, distribute, and/or modify the software.

Also, for each author's protection and ours, we want to make certain that everyone understands that there is no warranty for this free software. If the software is modified by someone else and passed on, we want its recipients to know that what they have is not the original, so that any problems introduced by others will not reflect on the original authors' reputations.

Finally, any free program is threatened constantly by software patents. We wish to avoid the danger that redistributors of a free program will individually obtain patent licenses, in effect making the program proprietary. To prevent this, we have made it clear that any patent must be licensed for everyone's free use or not licensed at all.

The precise terms and conditions for copying, distribution and modification follow.

Terms and Conditions for Copying, Distribution, and Modification

1. This License applies to any program or other work which contains a notice placed by the copyright holder saying it may be distributed under the terms of this General Public License. The "Program", below, refers to any such program or work, and a "work based on the Program" means either the Program or any derivative work under copyright law: that is to say, a work containing the Program or a portion of it, either verbatim or with modifications and/or translated into another language. (Hereinafter, translation is included without limitation in the term "modification".) Each licensee is addressed as "you". Activities other than copying, distribution and modification are not covered by this License; they are outside its scope. The act of running the Program is not restricted, and the output from the Program is covered only if its contents constitute a work based on the Program (independent of having been made by running the Program). Whether that is true depends on what the Program does.

2. You may copy and distribute verbatim copies of the Program's source code as you receive it, in any medium, provided that you conspicuously and appropriately publish on each copy an appropriate copyright notice and disclaimer of warranty; keep intact all the notices that refer to this License and to the absence of any warranty; and give any other recipients of the Program a copy of this License along with the Program. You may charge a fee for the physical act of transferring a copy, and you may at your option offer warranty protection in exchange for a fee.

3. You may modify your copy or copies of the Program or any portion of it, thus forming a work based on the Program, and copy and distribute such

modifications or work under the terms of Section 1 above, provided that you also meet all of these conditions:

1. You must cause the modified files to carry prominent notices stating that you changed the files and the date of any change.

2. You must cause any work that you distribute or publish, that in whole or in part contains or is derived from the Program or any part thereof, to be licensed as a whole at no charge to all third parties under the terms of this License.

3. If the modified program normally reads commands interactively when run, you must cause it, when started running for such interactive use in the most ordinary way, to print or display an announcement including an appropriate copyright notice and a notice that there is no warranty (or else, saying that you provide a warranty) and that users may redistribute the program under these conditions, and telling the user how to view a copy of this License. (Exception: if the Program itself is interactive but does not normally print such an announcement, your work based on the Program is not required to print an announcement.)

These requirements apply to the modified work as a whole. If identifiable sections of that work are not derived from the Program, and can be reasonably considered independent and separate works in themselves, then this License, and its terms, do not apply to those sections when you distribute them as separate works. But when you distribute the same sections as part of a whole which is a work based on the Program, the distribution of the whole must be on the terms of this License, whose permissions for other licensees extend to the entire whole, and thus to each and every part regardless of who wrote it. Thus, it is not the intent of this section to claim rights or contest your rights to work written entirely by you; rather, the intent is to exercise the right to control the distribution of derivative or collective works based on the Program. In addition, mere aggregation of another work not based on the Program with the Program (or with a work based on the Program) on a volume of a storage or distribution medium does not bring the other work under the scope of this License.

4. You may copy and distribute the Program (or a work based on it, under Section 2) in object code or executable form under the terms of Sections 1 and 2 above provided that you also do one of the following:

1. Accompany it with the complete corresponding machine-readable source code, which must be distributed under the terms of Sections 1 and 2 above on a medium customarily used for software interchange; or,

2. Accompany it with a written offer, valid for at least three years, to give any third party, for a charge no more than your cost of physically performing source distribution, a complete machine-readable copy of the corresponding source code, to be distributed under the terms of

Sections 1 and 2 above on a medium customarily used for software interchange; or,

3. Accompany it with the information you received as to the offer to distribute corresponding source code. (This alternative is allowed only for noncommercial distribution and only if you received the program in object code or executable form with such an offer, in accord with Subsection 2 above.)

The source code for a work means the preferred form of the work for making modifications to it. For an executable work, complete source code means all the source code for all modules it contains, plus any associated interface definition files, plus the scripts used to control compilation and installation of the executable. However, as a special exception, the source code distributed need not include anything that is normally distributed (in either source or binary form) with the major components (compiler, kernel, and so on) of the operating system on which the executable runs, unless that component itself accompanies the executable. If distribution of executable or object code is made by offering access to copy from a designated place, then offering equivalent access to copy the source code from the same place counts as distribution of the source code, even though third parties are not compelled to copy the source along with the object code.

5. You may not copy, modify, sublicense, or distribute the Program except as expressly provided under this License. Any attempt otherwise to copy, modify, sublicense or distribute the Program is void, and will automatically terminate your rights under this License. However, parties who have received copies, or rights, from you under this License will not have their licenses terminated so long as such parties remain in full compliance.

6. You are not required to accept this License, since you have not signed it. However, nothing else grants you permission to modify or distribute the Program or its derivative works. These actions are prohibited by law if you do not accept this License. Therefore, by modifying or distributing the Program (or any work based on the Program), you indicate your acceptance of this License to do so, and all its terms and conditions for copying, distributing, or modifying the Program or works based on it.

7. Each time you redistribute the Program (or any work based on the Program), the recipient automatically receives a license from the original licensor to copy, distribute, or modify the Program subject to these terms and conditions. You may not impose any further restrictions on the recipients' exercise of the rights granted herein. You are not responsible for enforcing compliance by third parties to this License.

8. If, as a consequence of a court judgment or allegation of patent infringement or for any other reason (not limited to patent issues), conditions are imposed on you (whether by court order, agreement, or otherwise) that

contradict the conditions of this License, they do not excuse you from the conditions of this License. If you cannot distribute so as to satisfy simultaneously your obligations under this License and any other pertinent obligations, then as a consequence you may not distribute the Program at all. For example, if a patent license would not permit royalty-free redistribution of the Program by all those who receive copies directly or indirectly through you, then the only way you could satisfy both it and this License would be to refrain entirely from distribution of the Program. If any portion of this section is held invalid or unenforceable under any particular circumstance, the balance of the section is intended to apply and the section as a whole is intended to apply in other circumstances. It is not the purpose of this section to induce you to infringe any patents or other property right claims or to contest validity of any such claims; this section has the sole purpose of protecting the integrity of the free software distribution system, which is implemented by public license practices. Many people have made generous contributions to the wide range of software distributed through that system in reliance on consistent application of that system; it is up to the author/donor to decide if he or she is willing to distribute software through any other system and a licensee cannot impose that choice. This section is intended to make thoroughly clear what is believed to be a consequence of the rest of this License.

9. If the distribution and/or use of the Program is restricted in certain countries either by patents or by copyrighted interfaces, the original copyright holder who places the Program under this License may add an explicit geographical distribution limitation excluding those countries, so that distribution is permitted only in or among countries not thus excluded. In such case, this License incorporates the limitation as if written in the body of this License.

10. The Free Software Foundation may publish revised and/or new versions of the General Public License from time to time. Such new versions will be similar in spirit to the present version, but may differ in detail to address new problems or concerns. Each version is given a distinguishing version number. If the Program specifies a version number of this License which applies to it and "any later version", you have the option of following the terms and conditions either of that version or of any later version published by the Free Software Foundation. If the Program does not specify a version number of this License, you may choose any version ever published by the Free Software Foundation.

11. If you wish to incorporate parts of the Program into other free programs whose distribution conditions are different, write to the author to ask for permission. For software which is copyrighted by the Free Software Foundation, write to the Free Software Foundation; we sometimes make exceptions for this. Our decision will be guided by the two goals of preserving the free status

of all derivatives of our free software and of promoting the sharing and reuse of software generally.

No Warranty

12. BECAUSE THE PROGRAM IS LICENSED FREE OF CHARGE, THERE IS NO WARRANTY FOR THE PROGRAM, TO THE EXTENT PERMITTED BY APPLICABLE LAW. EXCEPT WHEN OTHERWISE STATED IN WRITING THE COPYRIGHT HOLDERS AND/OR OTHER PARTIES PROVIDE THE PROGRAM "AS IS" WITHOUT WARRANTY OF ANY KIND, EITHER EXPRESSED OR IMPLIED, INCLUDING, BUT NOT LIMITED TO, THE IMPLIED WARRANTIES OF MERCHANTABILITY AND FITNESS FOR A PARTICULAR PURPOSE. THE ENTIRE RISK AS TO THE QUALITY AND PERFORMANCE OF THE PROGRAM IS WITH YOU. SHOULD THE PROGRAM PROVE DEFECTIVE, YOU ASSUME THE COST OF ALL NECESSARY SERVICING, REPAIR OR CORRECTION.

13. IN NO EVENT UNLESS REQUIRED BY APPLICABLE LAW OR AGREED TO IN WRITING WILL ANY COPYRIGHT HOLDER, OR ANY OTHER PARTY WHO MAY MODIFY AND/OR REDISTRIBUTE THE PROGRAM AS PERMITTED ABOVE, BE LIABLE TO YOU FOR DAMAGES, INCLUDING ANY GENERAL, SPECIAL, INCIDENTAL, OR CONSEQUENTIAL DAMAGES ARISING OUT OF THE USE OR INABILITY TO USE THE PROGRAM (INCLUDING BUT NOT LIMITED TO LOSS OF DATA OR DATA BEING RENDERED INACCURATE OR LOSSES SUSTAINED BY YOU OR THIRD PARTIES OR A FAILURE OF THE PROGRAM TO OPERATE WITH ANY OTHER PROGRAMS), EVEN IF SUCH HOLDER OR OTHER PARTY HAS BEEN ADVISED OF THE POSSIBILITY OF SUCH DAMAGES.

END OF TERMS AND CONDITIONS

How to Apply These Terms to Your New Programs

If you develop a new program, and you want it to be of the greatest possible use to the public, the best way to achieve this is to make it free software that everyone can redistribute and change under these terms.

To do so, attach the following notices to the program. It is safest to attach them to the start of each source file to most effectively convey the exclusion of warranty, and each file should have at least the "copyright" line and a pointer to where the full notice is found.

```
one line to give the program's name and an idea of what it does.
Copyright (C) 19yy   name of author

This program is free software; you can redistribute it and/or modify it
under the terms of the GNU General Public License as published by the Free
Software Foundation; either version 2 of the License, or (at your option)
any later version.
```

This program is distributed in the hope that it will be useful, but WITHOUT ANY WARRANTY; without even the implied warranty of MERCHANTABILITY or FITNESS FOR A PARTICULAR PURPOSE. See the GNU General Public License for more details.

You should have received a copy of the GNU General Public License along with this program; if not, write to the Free Software Foundation, Inc., 675 Mass Ave, Cambridge, MA 02139, USA.

Also, add information on how to contact you by electronic and paper mail.

If the program is interactive, make it output a short notice like this when it starts in an interactive mode:

Gnomovision version 69, Copyright (C) 19yy **name of author**
Gnomovision comes with ABSOLUTELY NO WARRANTY; for details type 'show w'.
This is free software, and you are welcome to redistribute it under certain conditions; type 'show c' for details.

The hypothetical commands 'show w' and 'show c' should show the appropriate parts of the General Public License. Of course, the commands you use may be called something other than 'show w' and 'show c'; they could even be mouse-clicks or menu items—whatever suits your program.

You should also get your employer (if you work as a programmer) or your school, if any, to sign a "copyright disclaimer" for the program, if necessary. Here is a sample; alter the names:

Yoyodyne, Inc., hereby disclaims all copyright interest in the program 'Gnomovision' (which makes passes at compilers) written by James Hacker.

signature of Ty Coon, 1 April 1989
Ty Coon, President of Vice

This General Public License does not permit incorporating your program into proprietary programs. If your program is a subroutine library, you may consider it more useful to permit linking proprietary applications with the library. If this is what you want to do, use the GNU Library General Public License instead of this License.

GNU Library General Public License Version 2, June 1991

Copyright (C) 1991 Free Software Foundation, Inc.
675 Mass Ave, Cambridge, MA 02139, USA

Everyone is permitted to copy and distribute verbatim copies of this license document, but changing it is not allowed.

[This is the first released version of the library GPL. It is numbered 2 because it goes with version 2 of the ordinary GPL.]

Preamble

The licenses for most software are designed to take away your freedom to share and change it. By contrast, the GNU General Public Licenses are intended to guarantee your freedom to share and change free software – to make sure the software is free for all its users.

This license, the Library General Public License, applies to some specially designated Free Software Foundation software, and to any other libraries whose authors decide to use it. You can use it for your libraries, too.

When we speak of free software, we are referring to freedom, not price. Our General Public Licenses are designed to make sure that you have the freedom to distribute copies of free software (and charge for this service if you wish), that you receive source code or can get it if you want it, that you can change the software or use pieces of it in new free programs; and that you know you can do these things.

To protect your rights, we need to make restrictions that forbid anyone to deny you these rights or to ask you to surrender the rights. These restrictions translate to certain responsibilities for you if you distribute copies of the library, or if you modify it.

For example, if you distribute copies of the library, whether gratis or for a fee, you must give the recipients all the rights that we gave you. You must make sure that they, too, receive or can get the source code. If you link a program with the library, you must provide complete object files to the recipients so that they can relink them with the library, after making changes to the library and recompiling it. And you must show them these terms so they know their rights.

Our method of protecting your rights has two steps: (1) copyright the library, and (2) offer you this license which gives you legal permission to copy, distribute, and/or modify the library.

Also, for each distributor's protection, we want to make certain that everyone understands that there is no warranty for this free library. If the library is modified by someone else and passed on, we want its recipients to know that what they have is not the original version, so that any problems introduced by others will not reflect on the original authors' reputations.

Finally, any free program is threatened constantly by software patents. We wish to avoid the danger that companies distributing free software will individually obtain patent licenses, thus in effect transforming the program into proprietary software. To prevent this, we have made it clear that any patent must be licensed for everyone's free use or not licensed at all.

Most GNU software, including some libraries, is covered by the ordinary GNU General Public License, which was designed for utility programs. This license, the GNU Library General Public License, applies to certain designated libraries. This license is quite different from the ordinary one; be sure to read it in full, and don't assume that anything in it is the same as in the ordinary license.

The reason we have a separate public license for some libraries is that they blur the distinction we usually make between modifying or adding to a program and simply using it. Linking a program with a library, without changing the library, is in some sense simply using the library, and is analogous to running a utility program or application program. However, in a textual and legal sense, the linked executable is a combined work, a derivative of the original library, and the ordinary General Public License treats it as such.

Because of this blurred distinction, using the ordinary General Public License for libraries did not effectively promote software sharing, because most developers did not use the libraries. We concluded that weaker conditions might promote sharing better.

However, unrestricted linking of non-free programs would deprive the users of those programs of all benefit from the free status of the libraries themselves. This Library General Public License is intended to permit developers of non-free programs to use free libraries, while preserving your freedom as a user of such programs to change the free libraries that are incorporated in them. (We have not seen how to achieve this as regards changes in header files, but we have achieved it as regards changes in the actual functions of the Library.) The hope is that this will lead to faster development of free libraries.

The precise terms and conditions for copying, distribution and modification follow. Pay close attention to the difference between a "work based on the library" and a "work that uses the library". The former contains code derived from the library, while the latter only works together with the library.

Note that it is possible for a library to be covered by the ordinary General Public License rather than by this special one.

Terms and Conditions for Copying, Distribution and Modification

1. This License Agreement applies to any software library which contains a notice placed by the copyright holder or other authorized party saying it may be distributed under the terms of this Library General Public License (also called "this License"). Each licensee is addressed as "you". A "library" means a collection of software functions and/or data prepared so as to be conveniently linked with application programs (which use some of those functions and data) to form executables. The "Library", below, refers to any such software library or work which has been distributed under these terms. A "work based on the Library" means either the Library or any derivative work under copyright law: that is to say, a work containing the Library or a portion of it, either verbatim or with modifications and/or translated straightforwardly into another language. (Hereinafter, translation is included without limitation in the term "modification".) "Source code" for a work means the preferred form of the work for making modifications to it. For a library, complete source code means all the source code for all

modules it contains, plus any associated interface definition files, plus the scripts used to control compilation and installation of the library. Activities other than copying, distribution, and modification are not covered by this License; they are outside its scope. The act of running a program using the Library is not restricted, and output from such a program is covered only if its contents constitute a work based on the Library (independent of the use of the Library in a tool for writing it). Whether that is true depends on what the Library does and what the program that uses the Library does.

2. You may copy and distribute verbatim copies of the Library's complete source code as you receive it, in any medium, provided that you conspicuously and appropriately publish on each copy an appropriate copyright notice and disclaimer of warranty; keep intact all the notices that refer to this License and to the absence of any warranty; and distribute a copy of this License along with the Library. You may charge a fee for the physical act of transferring a copy, and you may at your option offer warranty protection in exchange for a fee.

3. You may modify your copy or copies of the Library or any portion of it, thus forming a work based on the Library, and copy and distribute such modifications or work under the terms of Section 1 above, provided that you also meet all of these conditions:

1. The modified work must itself be a software library.

2. You must cause the files modified to carry prominent notices stating that you changed the files and the date of any change.

3. You must cause the whole of the work to be licensed at no charge to all third parties under the terms of this License.

4. If a facility in the modified Library refers to a function or a table of data to be supplied by an application program that uses the facility, other than as an argument passed when the facility is invoked, then you must make a good faith effort to ensure that, in the event an application does not supply such function or table, the facility still operates, and performs whatever part of its purpose remains meaningful. (For example, a function in a library to compute square roots has a purpose that is entirely well-defined independent of the application. Therefore, Subsection 2d requires that any application-supplied function or table used by this function must be optional: if the application does not supply it, the square root function must still compute square roots.)

These requirements apply to the modified work as a whole. If identifiable sections of that work are not derived from the Library, and can be reasonably considered independent and separate works in themselves, then this License, and its terms, do not apply to those sections when you distribute them as separate works. But when you distribute the same sections as part of a whole which is a work based on the Library,

the distribution of the whole must be on the terms of this License, whose permissions for other licensees extend to the entire whole, and thus to each and every part regardless of who wrote it. Thus, it is not the intent of this section to claim rights or contest your rights to work written entirely by you; rather, the intent is to exercise the right to control the distribution of derivative or collective works based on the Library. In addition, mere aggregation of another work not based on the Library with the Library (or with a work based on the Library) on a volume of a storage or distribution medium does not bring the other work under the scope of this License.

4. You may opt to apply the terms of the ordinary GNU General Public License instead of this License to a given copy of the Library. To do this, you must alter all the notices that refer to this License, so that they refer to the ordinary GNU General Public License, version 2, instead of to this License. (If a newer version than version 2 of the ordinary GNU General Public License has appeared, then you can specify that version instead if you wish.) Do not make any other change in these notices. Once this change is made in a given copy, it is irreversible for that copy, so the ordinary GNU General Public License applies to all subsequent copies and derivative works made from that copy. This option is useful when you wish to copy part of the code of the Library into a program that is not a library.

5. You may copy and distribute the Library (or a portion or derivative of it, under Section 2) in object code or executable form under the terms of Sections 1 and 2 above provided that you accompany it with the complete corresponding machine-readable source code, which must be distributed under the terms of Sections 1 and 2 above on a medium customarily used for software interchange. If distribution of object code is made by offering access to copy from a designated place, then offering equivalent access to copy the source code from the same place satisfies the requirement to distribute the source code, even though third parties are not compelled to copy the source along with the object code.

6. A program that contains no derivative of any portion of the Library, but is designed to work with the Library by being compiled or linked with it, is called a "work that uses the Library". Such a work, in isolation, is not a derivative work of the Library, and therefore falls outside the scope of this License. However, linking a "work that uses the Library" with the Library creates an executable that is a derivative of the Library (because it contains portions of the Library), rather than a "work that uses the library". The executable is therefore covered by this License. Section 6 states terms for distribution of such executables. When a "work that uses the Library" uses material from a header file that is part of the Library, the object code for the work may be a derivative work of the Library even though the source code is not. Whether this is true is especially significant if the work can be linked without the Library, or if the work is itself a library. The threshold for this to be true is not precisely defined by law. If such an object file uses only

numerical parameters, data structure layouts and accessors, and small macros and small inline functions (ten lines or less in length), then the use of the object file is unrestricted, regardless of whether it is legally a derivative work. (Executables containing this object code plus portions of the Library will still fall under Section 6.) Otherwise, if the work is a derivative of the Library, you may distribute the object code for the work under the terms of Section 6. Any executables containing that work also fall under Section 6, whether or not they are linked directly with the Library itself.

7. As an exception to the Sections above, you may also compile or link a "work that uses the Library" with the Library to produce a work containing portions of the Library, and distribute that work under terms of your choice, provided that the terms permit modification of the work for the customer's own use and reverse engineering for debugging such modifications. You must give prominent notice with each copy of the work that the Library is used in it and that the Library and its use are covered by this License. You must supply a copy of this License. If the work during execution displays copyright notices, you must include the copyright notice for the Library among them, as well as a reference directing the user to the copy of this License. Also, you must do one of these things:

1. Accompany the work with the complete corresponding machine-readable source code for the Library including whatever changes were used in the work (which must be distributed under Sections 1 and 2 above); and, if the work is an executable linked with the Library, with the complete machine-readable "work that uses the Library", as object code and/or source code, so that the user can modify the Library and then relink to produce a modified executable containing the modified Library. (It is understood that the user who changes the contents of definitions files in the Library will not necessarily be able to recompile the application to use the modified definitions.)

2. Accompany the work with a written offer, valid for at least three years, to give the same user the materials specified in Subsection 6a, above, for a charge no more than the cost of performing this distribution.

3. If distribution of the work is made by offering access to copy from a designated place, offer equivalent access to copy the above specified materials from the same place.

4. Verify that the user has already received a copy of these materials or that you have already sent this user a copy.

For an executable, the required form of the "work that uses the Library" must include any data and utility programs needed for reproducing the executable from it. However, as a special exception, the source code distributed need not include anything that is normally distributed (in either source or binary form) with the major

components (compiler, kernel, and so on) of the operating system on which the executable runs, unless that component itself accompanies the executable. It may happen that this requirement contradicts the license restrictions of other proprietary libraries that do not normally accompany the operating system. Such a contradiction means you cannot use both them and the Library together in an executable that you distribute.

8. You may place library facilities that are a work based on the Library side-by-side in a single library together with other library facilities not covered by this License, and distribute such a combined library, provided that the separate distribution of the work based on the Library and of the other library facilities is otherwise permitted, and provided that you do these two things:

  1. Accompany the combined library with a copy of the same work based on the Library, uncombined with any other library facilities. This must be distributed under the terms of the Sections above.

  2. Give prominent notice with the combined library of the fact that part of it is a work based on the Library, and explaining where to find the accompanying uncombined form of the same work.

9. You may not copy, modify, sublicense, link with, or distribute the Library except as expressly provided under this License. Any attempt otherwise to copy, modify, sublicense, link with, or distribute the Library is void, and will automatically terminate your rights under this License. However, parties who have received copies, or rights, from you under this License will not have their licenses terminated so long as such parties remain in full compliance.

10. You are not required to accept this License, since you have not signed it. However, nothing else grants you permission to modify or distribute the Library or its derivative works. These actions are prohibited by law if you do not accept this License. Therefore, by modifying or distributing the Library (or any work based on the Library), you indicate your acceptance of this License to do so, and all its terms and conditions for copying, distributing or modifying the Library or works based on it.

11. Each time you redistribute the Library (or any work based on the Library), the recipient automatically receives a license from the original licensor to copy, distribute, link with or modify the Library subject to these terms and conditions. You may not impose any further restrictions on the recipients' exercise of the rights granted herein. You are not responsible for enforcing compliance by third parties to this License.

12. If, as a consequence of a court judgment or allegation of patent infringement or for any other reason (not limited to patent issues), conditions are imposed on you (whether by court order, agreement or otherwise) that contradict the conditions of this License, they do not excuse you from the conditions of this License. If you cannot distribute so as to satisfy simultaneously your obligations under this License and any other pertinent obligations, then as a consequence you may not distribute the Library at all. For example, if a patent license would not permit royalty-free redistribution of the Library by all those who receive copies directly or indirectly through you, then the only way you could satisfy both it and this License would be to refrain entirely from distribution of the Library. If any portion of this section is held invalid or unenforceable under any particular circumstance, the balance of the section is intended to apply, and the section as a whole is intended to apply in other circumstances. It is not the purpose of this section to induce you to infringe any patents or other property right claims or to contest validity of any such claims; this section has the sole purpose of protecting the integrity of the free software distribution system which is implemented by public license practices. Many people have made generous contributions to the wide range of software distributed through that system in reliance on consistent application of that system; it is up to the author/donor to decide if he or she is willing to distribute software through any other system and a licensee cannot impose that choice. This section is intended to make thoroughly clear what is believed to be a consequence of the rest of this License.

13. If the distribution and/or use of the Library is restricted in certain countries either by patents or by copyrighted interfaces, the original copyright holder who places the Library under this License may add an explicit geographical distribution limitation excluding those countries, so that distribution is permitted only in or among countries not thus excluded. In such case, this License incorporates the limitation as if written in the body of this License.

14. The Free Software Foundation may publish revised and/or new versions of the Library General Public License from time to time. Such new versions will be similar in spirit to the present version, but may differ in detail to address new problems or concerns. Each version is given a distinguishing version number. If the Library specifies a version number of this License which applies to it and "any later version", you have the option of following the terms and conditions either of that version or of any later version published by the Free Software Foundation. If the Library does not specify a license version number, you may choose any version ever published by the Free Software Foundation.

15. If you wish to incorporate parts of the Library into other free programs whose distribution conditions are incompatible with these, write to the author to ask for permission. For software which is copyrighted by the Free

Software Foundation, write to the Free Software Foundation; we sometimes make exceptions for this. Our decision will be guided by the two goals of preserving the free status of all derivatives of our free software and of promoting the sharing and reuse of software generally.

No Warranty

16. BECAUSE THE LIBRARY IS LICENSED FREE OF CHARGE, THERE IS NO WARRANTY FOR THE LIBRARY, TO THE EXTENT PERMITTED BY APPLICABLE LAW. EXCEPT WHEN OTHERWISE STATED IN WRITING THE COPYRIGHT HOLDERS AND/OR OTHER PARTIES PROVIDE THE LIBRARY "AS IS" WITHOUT WARRANTY OF ANY KIND, EITHER EXPRESSED OR IMPLIED, INCLUDING, BUT NOT LIMITED TO, THE IMPLIED WARRANTIES OF MERCHANTABILITY AND FITNESS FOR A PARTICULAR PURPOSE. THE ENTIRE RISK AS TO THE QUALITY AND PERFORMANCE OF THE LIBRARY IS WITH YOU. SHOULD THE LIBRARY PROVE DEFECTIVE, YOU ASSUME THE COST OF ALL NECESSARY SERVICING, REPAIR OR CORRECTION.

17. IN NO EVENT UNLESS REQUIRED BY APPLICABLE LAW OR AGREED TO IN WRITING WILL ANY COPYRIGHT HOLDER, OR ANY OTHER PARTY WHO MAY MODIFY AND/OR REDISTRIBUTE THE LIBRARY AS PERMITTED ABOVE, BE LIABLE TO YOU FOR DAMAGES, INCLUDING ANY GENERAL, SPECIAL, INCIDENTAL OR CONSEQUENTIAL DAMAGES ARISING OUT OF THE USE OR INABILITY TO USE THE LIBRARY (INCLUDING BUT NOT LIMITED TO LOSS OF DATA OR DATA BEING RENDERED INACCURATE OR LOSSES SUSTAINED BY YOU OR THIRD PARTIES OR A FAILURE OF THE LIBRARY TO OPERATE WITH ANY OTHER SOFTWARE), EVEN IF SUCH HOLDER OR OTHER PARTY HAS BEEN ADVISED OF THE POSSIBILITY OF SUCH DAMAGES.

END OF TERMS AND CONDITIONS

How to Apply These Terms to Your New Libraries

If you develop a new library, and you want it to be of the greatest possible use to the public, we recommend making it free software that everyone can redistribute and change. You can do so by permitting redistribution under these terms (or, alternatively, under the terms of the ordinary General Public License).

To apply these terms, attach the following notices to the library. It is safest to attach them to the start of each source file to most effectively convey the exclusion of warranty; and each file should have at least the "copyright" line and a pointer to where the full notice is found.

```
one line to give the library's name and an idea of what it does.
Copyright (C) year   name of author
```

This library is free software; you can redistribute it and/or modify it under the terms of the GNU Library General Public License as published by the Free Software Foundation; either version 2 of the License, or (at your option) any later version.

This library is distributed in the hope that it will be useful, but WITHOUT ANY WARRANTY; without even the implied warranty of MERCHANTABILITY or FITNESS FOR A PARTICULAR PURPOSE. See the GNU Library General Public License for more details.

You should have received a copy of the GNU Library General Public License along with this library; if not, write to the Free Software Foundation, Inc., 675 Mass Ave, Cambridge, MA 02139, USA.

Also, add information on how to contact you by electronic and paper mail.

You should also get your employer (if you work as a programmer) or your school, if any, to sign a "copyright disclaimer" for the library, if necessary. Here is a sample; alter the names:

Yoyodyne, Inc., hereby disclaims all copyright interest in the library 'Frob' (a library for tweaking knobs) written by James Random Hacker.

signature of Ty Coon, 1 April 1990
Ty Coon, President of Vice

That's all there is to it!

INDEX

Message from the
Publisher

WELCOME TO OUR NERVOUS SYSTEM

Some people say that the World Wide Web is a graphical extension of the information superhighway, just a network of humans and machines sending each other long lists of the equivalent of digital junk mail.

I think it is much more than that. To me, the Web is nothing less than the nervous system of the entire planet—not just a collection of computer brains connected together, but more like a billion silicon neurons entangled and recirculating electro-chemical signals of information and data, each contributing to the birth of another CPU and another Web site.

Think of each person's hard disk connected at once to every other hard disk on earth, driven by human navigators searching like Columbus for the New World. Seen this way the Web is more of a super entity, a growing, living thing, controlled by the universal human will to expand, to be more. Yet, unlike a purposeful business plan with rigid rules, the Web expands in a nonlinear, unpredictable, creative way that echoes natural evolution.

We created our Web site not just to extend the reach of our computer book products but to be part of this synaptic neural network, to experience, like a nerve in the body, the flow of ideas and then to pass those ideas up the food chain of the mind. Your mind. Even more, we wanted to pump some of our own creative juices into this rich wine of technology.

TASTE OUR DIGITAL WINE

And so we ask you to taste our wine by visiting the body of our business. Begin by understanding the metaphor we have created for our Web site—a universal learning center, situated in outer space in the form of a space station. A place where you can journey to study any topic from the convenience of your own screen. Right now we are focusing on computer topics, but the stars are the limit on the Web.

If you are interested in discussing this Web site or finding out more about the Waite Group, please send me email with your comments, and I will be happy to respond. Being a programmer myself, I love to talk about technology and find out what our readers are looking for.

Sincerely,

Mitchell Waite

Mitchell Waite, C.E.O. and Publisher

200 Tamal Plaza
Corte Madera, CA 94925
415-924-2575
415-924-2576 fax

Website:
http://www.waite.com/waite

CREATING THE HIGHEST QUALITY COMPUTER BOOKS IN THE INDUSTRY

Waite Group Press

Come Visit

WAITE.COM
Waite Group Press
World Wide Web Site

Now find all the latest information on Waite Group books at our new Web site, **http://www.waite.com/waite.** You'll find an online catalog where you can examine and order any title, review upcoming books, and send email to our authors and editors. Our FTP site has all you need to update your book: the latest program listings, errata sheets, most recent versions of Fractint, POV Ray, Polyray, DMorph, and all the programs featured in our books. So download, talk to us, ask questions, on **http://www.waite.com/waite.**

The New Arrivals Room has all our new books listed by month. Just click for a description, Index, Table of Contents, and links to authors.

The Backlist Room has all our books listed alphabetically.

The People Room is where you'll interact with Waite Group employees.

Links to Cyberspace get you in touch with other computer book publishers and other interesting Web sites.

The FTP site contains all program listings, errata sheets, etc.

The Order Room is where you can order any of our books online.

The Subject Room contains typical book pages that show description, Index, Table of Contents, and links to authors.

This is a legal agreement between you, the end user and purchaser, and The Waite Group®, Inc., and the authors of the programs contained in the disc. By opening the sealed disc package, you are agreeing to be bound by the terms of this Agreement. If you do not agree with the terms of this Agreement, promptly return the unopened disc package and the accompanying items (including the related book and other written material) to the place you obtained them for a refund.

SOFTWARE LICENSE

1. The Waite Group, Inc., grants you the right to use one copy of the enclosed software programs (the programs) on a single computer system (whether a single CPU, part of a licensed network, or a terminal connected to a single CPU). Each concurrent user of the program must have exclusive use of the related Waite Group, Inc., written materials.

2. The program, including the copyrights in each program, is owned by the respective author and the copyright in the entire work is owned by The Waite Group, Inc., and they are therefore protected under the copyright laws of the United States and other nations, under international treaties. You may make only one copy of the disc containing the programs exclusively for backup or archival purposes, or you may transfer the programs to one hard disk drive, using the original for backup or archival purposes. You may make no other copies of the programs, and you may make no copies of all or any part of the related Waite Group, Inc., written materials.

3. You may not rent or lease the programs, but you may transfer ownership of the programs and related written materials (including any and all updates and earlier versions) if you keep no copies of either, and if you make sure the transferee agrees to the terms of this license.

4. You may not decompile, reverse engineer, disassemble, copy, create a derivative work, or otherwise use the programs except as stated in this Agreement.

GOVERNING LAW

This Agreement is governed by the laws of the State of California.

LIMITED WARRANTY

The following warranties shall be effective for 90 days from the date of purchase: (i) The Waite Group, Inc., warrants the enclosed disc to be free of defects in materials and workmanship under normal use; and (ii) The Waite Group, Inc., warrants that the programs, unless modified by the purchaser, will substantially perform the functions described in the documentation provided by The Waite Group, Inc., when operated on the designated hardware and operating system. The Waite Group, Inc., does not warrant that the programs will meet purchaser's requirements or that operation of a program will be uninterrupted or error-free. The program warranty does not cover any program that has been altered or changed in any way by anyone other than The Waite Group, Inc. The Waite Group, Inc., is not responsible for problems caused by changes in the operating characteristics of computer hardware or computer operating systems that are made after the release of the programs, nor for problems in the interaction of the programs with each other or other software.

THESE WARRANTIES ARE EXCLUSIVE AND IN LIEU OF ALL OTHER WARRANTIES OF MERCHANTABILITY OR FITNESS FOR A PARTICULAR PURPOSE OR OF ANY OTHER WARRANTY, WHETHER EXPRESSED OR IMPLIED.

EXCLUSIVE REMEDY

The Waite Group, Inc., will replace any defective disk without charge if the defective disc is returned to The Waite Group, Inc., within 90 days from date of purchase.

This is Purchaser's sole and exclusive remedy for any breach of warranty or claim for contract, tort, or damages.

LIMITATION OF LIABILITY

THE WAITE GROUP, INC., AND THE AUTHORS OF THE PROGRAMS SHALL NOT IN ANY CASE BE LIABLE FOR SPECIAL, INCIDENTAL, CONSEQUENTIAL, INDIRECT, OR OTHER SIMILAR DAMAGES ARISING FROM ANY BREACH OF THESE WARRANTIES EVEN IF THE WAITE GROUP, INC., OR ITS AGENT HAS BEEN ADVISED OF THE POSSIBILITY OF SUCH DAMAGES.

THE LIABILITY FOR DAMAGES OF THE WAITE GROUP, INC., AND THE AUTHORS OF THE PROGRAMS UNDER THIS AGREEMENT SHALL IN NO EVENT EXCEED THE PURCHASE PRICE PAID.

COMPLETE AGREEMENT

This Agreement constitutes the complete agreement between The Waite Group, Inc., and the authors of the programs, and you, the purchaser.

Some states do not allow the exclusion or limitation of implied warranties or liability for incidental or consequential damages, so the above exclusions or limitations may not apply to you. This limited warranty gives you specific legal rights; you may have others, which vary from state to state.

MACMILLAN COMPUTER PUBLISHING USA

A VIACOM COMPANY

Technical ----┐
             └---- **Support:**

If you cannot get the CD/Disk to install properly, or you need assistance with a particular situation in the book, please feel free to check out the Knowledge Base on our Web site at **http://www.superlibrary.com/general/support**. We have answers to our most Frequently Asked Questions listed there. If you do not find your specific question answered, please contact Macmillan Technical Support at **(317) 581-3833**. We can also be reached by email at **support@mcp.com**.

SATISFACTION REPORT CARD

Please fill out this card if you wish to know of future updates to
***Borland C++Builder How-To,* or to receive our catalog.**

First Name: _____ **Last Name:** _____

Street Address: _____

City: _____ **State:** _____ **Zip:** _____

Email Address: _____

Daytime Telephone: (_____)

Date product was acquired: Month _____ **Day** _____ **Year** _____ **Your Occupation:** _____

Overall, how would you rate *Borland C++Builder How-To*?
☐ Excellent   ☐ Very Good   ☐ Good
☐ Fair   ☐ Below Average   ☐ Poor

What did you like MOST about this book? _____
_____
_____

What did you like LEAST about this book? _____
_____
_____

Please describe any problems you may have encountered with installing or using the disc: _____
_____

How did you use this book (problem-solver, tutorial, reference...)?
_____

What is your level of computer expertise?
☐ New   ☐ Dabbler   ☐ Hacker
☐ Power User   ☐ Programmer   ☐ Experienced Professional

What computer languages are you familiar with? _____
_____
_____

Please describe your computer hardware:
Computer _____   Hard disk _____
5.25" disk drives _____ 3.5" disk drives _____
Video card _____   Monitor _____
Printer _____   Peripherals _____
Sound Board _____   CD-ROM_____

Where did you buy this book?
☐ Bookstore (name): _____
☐ Discount store (name): _____
☐ Computer store (name): _____
☐ Catalog (name): _____
☐ Direct from WGP   ☐ Other _____

What price did you pay for this book? _____

What influenced your purchase of this book?
☐ Recommendation   ☐ Advertisement
☐ Magazine review   ☐ Store display
☐ Mailing   ☐ Book's format
☐ Reputation of Waite Group Press   ☐ Other

How many computer books do you buy each year? _____

How many other Waite Group books do you own? _____

What is your favorite Waite Group book? _____
_____

Is there any program or subject you would like to see Waite Group Press cover in a similar approach? _____
_____

Additional comments? _____
_____
_____

Please send to: Waite Group Press
200 Tamal Plaza
Corte Madera, CA 94925

☐ **Check here for a free Waite Group catalog**

STOP!

BEFORE YOU OPEN THE DISK OR CD-ROM PACKAGE ON THE FACING PAGE, CAREFULLY READ THE LICENSE AGREEMENT.

Opening this package indicates that you agree to abide by the license agreements found in the back of this book. If you do not agree with it, promptly return the unopened disk package (including the related book) to the place you obtained them for a refund.

Borland International TRIAL EDITION SOFTWARE License Statement